The Telegraph
HISTORY
OF THE
WORLD

The Telegraph

HISTORY

OF THE

WORLD

Edited by Gavin Fuller
With an Introduction by Max Davidson

Aurum
Press

CONTENTS

General Introduction

So much has changed in the one hundred and sixty years since *The Daily Telegraph* first hit the newsstands that it is quite hard to get inside the heads of readers who relied on the printed word for literally all national and international news, from county cricket scores to victories on the battlefield. The readers were not receiving confirmation of stories that had already been copiously covered in news bulletins the day before: they were getting the stories newly-minted from reporters on the spot. The *Telegraph* was their television and their iPhone and their car radio. They trusted it implicitly, which is why they bought it.

The Victorian Age marked a revolution in the newspaper industry, with the news being disseminated quicker than ever before. In this selection of pieces originally published in the *Telegraph*, dating back to the end of the Crimean War, we have tried to capture the raw excitement of those early years of the paper. We have also brought the story bang up to date, ending the anthology with our report of the corruption scandal that engulfed Fifa in the summer of 2015. Time has not stood still for an instant. There have been myriad changes in news reporting, both technological and cultural, and the *Telegraph* had to adapt to those changes or risk going under.

In the nature of an enterprise such as this, we have only been able to reproduce a minuscule fraction of the *Telegraph*'s news output. Earlier publications in this series, such as the *Telegraph Book of the First World*

War, have already covered some of the ground. But we hope there is enough here, not just to take readers on a pleasurable journey down the memory lane of history, but to show the evolution of a great newspaper. Readers will be able to see how the paper reported some of the most celebrated events of the period, from the Abdication to the first Moon landing, from Stanley's meeting with Livingstone in Africa to the explosion of the first atom bomb in Hiroshima. We have also showcased the paper's reporting of major advances in science and medicine.

If the subject matter is broad, and the geographical scope of the reports even broader, some journalistic values remain constant, and there are some strong threads running right through this book. A good story is a good story, and a journalist lucky enough to have a ringside view of great events is sitting on a gold mine. From the correspondent who found himself in St. Petersburg on 23 January 1905, and saw at first hand the shooting of unarmed demonstrators by Tsarist soldiers – a seminal event in European history – to the correspondents able to provide eyewitness accounts of the Soviet invasions of Hungary and Czechoslovakia, *Telegraph* reporters have been challenged, harassed, but seldom found wanting.

One or two of the bylines will be familiar, but the *Telegraph* has never relied on star names to produce top-quality journalism. What you will find here again and again, from a bewildering variety of settings, is good old-fashioned news reporting: rooted in hard facts, always expertly marshalled for the reader's benefit, but also tinged with human colour. The reporter's eye might occasionally stray from the main picture, but it strays to good purpose, alighting on a child, a dog, an odd item of clothing, and giving the article a real sense of immediacy. Pooled news dispatches, however authoritative, will never bear the imprimatur of personal experience.

The reporter's relish in being the bearer of news good and bad is palpable. After the Relief of Mafeking in 1900, a *Telegraph* man was dispatched down the Strand 'as fast as his horses' legs could carry him' to share the glorious tidings with all and sundry. It is like a scene from the pre-newspaper age, supplemented by printed reports that capture the excitement of the day in nerve-tingling detail. From the Treaty of Versailles to D-Day, from the sinking of the *Titanic* to 9/11, *Telegraph* reporters raced to get the best vantage point of the action, then used all their skill and craft to bring what they were witnessing to a wider audience. In the early days of the paper, they toiled in anonymity, as 'Our Own Correspondent' or 'Our Special Correspondent'; in many cases, their identities are completely lost to posterity. But anonymity does not equate with blandness. The *Telegraph* has never been a stuffy paper, and its reports, even of solemn or tragic events, are rarely dry or po-faced. The best of them have the conversational fluency of a man returning from abroad and regaling his friends with his adventures. These anonymous correspondents were not just good at their job: they had a lot of fun in the process, and they managed to convey that to their readers.

There is a famous old saying that today's newspaper is tomorrow's fish-and-chip wrapping. But as we hope this wide-ranging selection from the *Telegraph* archives demonstrates, the best newspaper reporting never really goes stale: it has the freshness, the urgency, the authenticity, of the day it was written.

MAX DAVIDSON

July 2015

1

The Victorian *Telegraph*:
Empire and Europe
1856–1901

1
Introduction

The past is a foreign country, as everyone knows, and it seems very foreign indeed in some of these excerpts from the Victorian *Telegraph*, which cover the period between the Treaty of Paris in 1856 and the death of Queen Victoria in 1901. It was a momentous period in European history, and its broad outlines will be familiar. But what is so striking in these reports is the wealth of detail, the kind of minutiae that catch the eye of a contemporary observer but never seem to make it into the history books.

At the opening of the Metropolitan Line, the world's first underground railway, in January 1863, for example, the lamps in the stations are 'polished like claret glasses at a dinner party', which will give today's grime-stained commuters a wry chuckle. Readers will also smile at the account of the official opening of the Eiffel Tower in 1889, which culminates in 'the presentation of several large bouquets of flowers to M. Eiffel – not, however, by members of the fair sex, but by some of his horny-handed workmen'. How very French! A faint suspicion of Johnny Foreigner, laced with sly humour, creeps into many of the dispatches from the Continent.

But if these contemporary news reports are period pieces, they also have a thrilling immediacy. It is sometimes assumed, erroneously, that old-style newspaper reporting was soberly factual, free from personal opinions and editorial bias. In fact, the very opposite seems to have been the case. The reports might be attributed to 'Our

Own Correspondent' or 'Our Special Correspondent', but you never lose sight of the human being behind the byline. 'Emperor Alexander has at last fallen a victim of the attempts of the cowardly assassins', writes the *Telegraph*'s correspondent in St. Petersburg in March 1881, after the assassination of Tsar Alexander II – a line that would surely receive the red-pencil treatment today. The *Telegraph*'s correspondent in Paris in December 1894 sees nothing wrong with prefacing his report of the sensational Dreyfus trial with an extended description of the Christmas goodies he had seen in the Paris shop windows on the morning of the trial. Had he just been out shopping with his wife?

For sustained reporting brio, it is hard to better the account by 'Our Adventurous Correspondent' of his attempts to get out of Paris in October 1870 when the city was under siege by the Prussian army. The tone is ironic, even Flashman-esque. ('I found a revolver in the most disagreeable proximity to my head.') But the accretion of comic detail, from derogatory references to 'Prooshens' to being made to sleep five to a bed, is splendid. The writing belongs more to a picaresque novel than a newspaper.

What is also striking about these glimpses of news reporting in the pre-television age is how quickly news seems to travel. You get a real sense of urgency: newspapers busting a gut to get the news out on the street before their competitors. The accounts of the assassination of President Lincoln in 1865 are little different in character from reports of the assassination of President Kennedy a century later, with confusion reigning, initial reports being contradicted by later ones and the piecemeal emergence of details about the assassin, John Wilkes Booth.

The undoubted highlight of this opening chapter is the account of the Relief of Mafeking on 19 May 1900, old-style newspaper reporting at its electrifying best. 'At last!' begins the *Telegraph*'s report, which could be a modern tabloid headline. The paper then goes on to report – pretty modestly, in the circumstances – that it 'had the felicity of being the first to convey the intelligence to the public by means of a placard in the front window of its office'. There is nothing like a good scoop to galvanise journalists into action. The news from Mafeking spreads like wildfire across the capital, thanks not least to 'a *Daily Telegraph* representative who sped as quickly as his horse's feet could carry him up the Strand'. As theatre performances are interrupted, so that audiences can be told the good news, and bands strike up God Save the Queen, the spontaneous joy of a nation united in celebration is captured in a way that makes Twitter seem sluggish.

The chapter ends on a sombre note, with the death of Queen Victoria on 23 January 1901. But again, the drama of the moment is beautifully captured. The scene outside Osborne House on the Isle of Wight, where the Queen passed away, is appropriately subdued. ('The words "slowly sinking" were passed sadly through the sad throng.') But as the news reaches London – passers-by in Piccadilly learn of it through yet another *Telegraph* placard, this one in the newspaper's branch office – the sense of grief swells ineluctably. 'There were few in the vastness of lingerers who were dry-eyed,' notes the *Telegraph* correspondent posted outside Marlborough House – just the latest in a long line of anonymous newspaper men who chronicled their times to the best of their considerable literary abilities.

If the excerpts help the reader re-visit great events in world history, from the Indian mutiny in 1857 to the Treaty of Berlin in 1878, they also invite a fresh perspective on some of those events, introducing a wealth of unexpected detail into familiar stories. One of the most intriguing nuggets in this chapter is the account of Stanley's famous meeting with Dr. Livingstone in Africa in July 1872. Yes, Stanley really did greet his countryman with the words, 'Dr Livingstone, I presume?' But contrary to popular mythology, the ultra-formal greeting was not the result of Victorian starchiness. According to eyewitness accounts, Stanley was 'about to rush forward and embrace Livingstone' when he remembered that he was in the presence of Arabs, who 'were accustomed to conceal their feelings', and held back out of deference to local etiquette. If the two men had been alone, there would have been a full-on man-hug, 2015-style.

The moral is clear. Always trust contemporary newspaper reports, not what you have read in history books produced years after the event. These reports have the same unvarnished authenticity as witness statements at a criminal trial. Their authors were lucky enough to be in the right place at the right time, and could say, with an authority that brooked no challenge: 'I was there.'

31 March 1856: The Treaty of Paris brings the Crimean War to a close
SIGNATURE OF THE PEACE TREATY
LATEST PARTICULARS
BY SUBMARINE AND BRITISH TELEGRAPH
PARIS, SUNDAY EVENING

At two o'clock this afternoon the cannon of the Invalides announced the signature of the treaty of Peace by a salvo of 101 guns. At three o'clock the following proclamation was posted on the walls of Paris:

> 'Peace was signed to-day, at one o'clock, at the Ministry of Foreign Affairs.
>
> 'The Plenipotentiaries of France, Austria, Great Britain, Prussia, Russia, Sardinia, and Turkey, have affixed their signatures to the Treaty, which puts an end to the existing war, and assures the repose of Europe on a solid and durable basis.
>
> (Signed) 'The Prefect of Police,
> 'Pietri.'

By the provisions of the Treaty the objects of the war are attained. The independence and integrity of the Ottoman Empire are fully assured. Russia yields her pretensions, and changes her course of policy; and for this change we have sufficient guarantees in the permanent extinction of her naval power in the Black Sea, and the establishment of a new order of things in the East, under the safeguard of Europe. The

Patrie says that the four Guarantees are applied in a broad sense, and that the fifth paragraph has been realised in a manner to give to Europe all the security that can be expected, without at the same time humiliating Russia.

It will not be possible to publish the text of the Treaty until it is ratified. The signatures of the plenipotentiaries of France, Austria, Great Britain, Prussia, Russia, Sardinia, and Turkey, were affixed to the Treaty; but Sovereigns always reserve the right of reviewing the act of their representatives, and till the former, by their own signature, accept and confirm the deed, the Treaty is not final nor binding. Three weeks must, therefore, elapse before it will be possible to receive the ratification of the Treaty by the autograph of the Emperor Alexander II. The *Patrie* affirms that the Allies will retain their positions in the Crimea until after the ratifications have been exchanged.

The Field-Marshal Commanding in Chief, Viscount Hardinge, G.C.B., after a protracted interview with Lord Panmure, Minister of War, attended at the Horse Guards late yesterday afternoon, when it was determined that the news of the signing of peace at Paris should be announced, both at St. James's Park and at the Tower, by the firing of a salute of 101 guns.

Instructions were not issued from the Horse Guards until after seven o'clock, and in order that Divine service might not be interrupted in the metropolitan churches, the hour appointed for the ceremony was ten o'clock. The fact rapidly gained publicity, and a very large concourse of persons collected in St. James's Park, within the space leading from the entrance by the Horse Guards to the Duke of York's column. Fifty-one guns were brought from the gun-house into the Park, and arranged, with the mouths facing the Enclosure, by Sergeant Rickard and the invalid corps under his command, assisted by a fatigue party of the Scots Fusilier Guards from the Wellington barracks. A party of the Grenadier Guards kept the ground, in order that no accident might occur to the spectators. A large body of police was also in attendance.

At ten o'clock precisely the firing commenced, in the presence of a large crowd, which was rapidly increased from the influx of people from every opening into the Park. The flashes of the guns upon the surrounding darkness, and the sharp reverberation of the successive reports, had a striking effect upon the spectators, who at frequent intervals gave expression to their enthusiasm by loud cheers. Among the spectators were many of our brave countrymen who had shared the dangers and fatigues of the war.

The military bands at St. George's and Wellington barracks at the same time played the National Anthem, and when the Park guns had ceased, the report of the guns at the Tower were distinctly heard booming in the distance. At the termination of the firing, the people rent the air with loud acclamations, and passed out of the Park in large bodies up Regent-street, and other principal thoroughfares, still cheering as they proceeded. The bells of the different metropolitan churches rang merry peals, until after midnight, in commemoration of the happy event. Numbers of people of all ranks flocked towards the Royal Exchange, while others congregated in front of the Mansion House, expecting to hear from the lips of the Lord Mayor an official proclamation of the joyful news. In this, however, they were disappointed.

As early as eight o'clock the bells of several of the metropolitan churches rang forth a merry peal. The citizens, too, were testifying their joy on the occasion by a display of the flags of England, France, Turkey, and Sardinia, at their windows. Immediately on receipt of the news in London, messages were despatched by telegraph to the different artillery officers commanding at the outposts, to fire a salute in celebration of the glorious consummation of peace.

Lord Palmerston will, no doubt, announce this evening to the House of Commons the happy termination of the war, and the conclusion of a peace which will be found to be in every respect satisfactory, and affording the best prospect for the security and repose of Europe.

29 June 1857: News emerges of mutiny in India
GREAT REVOLT OF MOHAMMEDAN SOLDIERY
MASSACRE OF ENGLISH AT DELHI
PROCLAMATION OF A MOGUL PRINCE

The steamer *America* arrived here yesterday, having made the passage in 121 hours from Alexandria. The India Mails left Alexandria on the twentieth, with dates from Calcutta, 19 May; Madras, 25; Ceylon, 30; Bombay, 27; and Hong Kong, 9.

From Calcutta to Lahore the troops of the Bengal presidency are in open or undisguised mutiny. At Ferozepore, the 57th and 45th Native Infantry have mutinied; the 10th Cavalry stood by the Europeans, and the native regiments were broken and dispersed. Part of the 57th were coming in and delivering their arms. Delhi is in possession of 3,000 rebel Sepoys. Lieutenant Willoughby, in charge of the powder magazine, fired it and escaped. Fifty lacs of rupees have been plundered from the Delhi Bank, and several of the Europeans have been murdered. The mutineers have proclaimed the son of the Emperor of Delhi King of India.

General Anson, with a European force, was on the march from the hills to attack the insurgents, and troops from other points have been despatched. The storm was allaying. A private despatch says that eleven officers have been killed at Delhi.

The following is another account of this fearful mutiny and massacre: 'The mutiny in the Bengal army had spread in a most alarming manner. At Meerut, the 11th and 20th Regiments of Native Infantry had united with the 3rd Light Cavalry in open revolt. After some bloodshed, they had been dispersed by European troops; but they had fled to Delhi, where they were joined by the 38th, 54th, and 74th Native Infantry. Delhi was in possession of the mutineers, who had massacred almost all the Europeans without regard to age or sex, plundered the bank, and proclaimed the son of the late Mogul Emperor as King. Disturbances had also broken out at Ferozepore, but had been suppressed. The Rajah of Gwalior had placed his troops at the disposal of the British Government. Government was taking active measures to suppress the revolt, concentrating troops around Delhi. The 34th Native Infantry was disbanded on 7th June.'

All quiet at Lucknow and Benares. His Highness the Nizam of the Deccan died on the 19th May.

At Bombay the money market was much higher, and the banks had raised their rates of interest.

Transactions in the import market were very limited.

Oude is tranquil.

The barque *Ocean*, Captain Dodd, was lost at Pooree, the crew all saved.

The prospects of the Ceylon coffee crops are good. The Governor's proclamations state that the railway agreement will be carried out immediately.

10 January 1863: The world's first underground railway opens in London, and the great and good have a meal to celebrate
OPENING OF THE METROPOLITAN RAILWAY

'New brooms sweep clean,' says the proverb; and if solid excellence of work, coupled with newness, can ensure efficiency and consequent success, the Metropolitan Company will sweep all before it. New, indeed, looks everything on the three and a half mile route from Paddington to Holborn-hill. The platforms at the neat, spick-and-span stations have the appearance of the well-scrubbed deal tables in a servants' hall; the paint asserts its freshness in a prevailing smell of turps; the lamps are polished like claret glasses for a dinner party; the line itself partakes the general aspect; and the metals, so smoothly laid on longitudinal instead of transverse sleepers, are undinted by the pressure and friction of continually passing trains; whilst the very policemen and ticket porters are in new clothes. In short everything yesterday contributed to the formation of a picture that would have gladdened the heart of a Dutch housewife, and might be fittingly perpetuated by the precise pencil of Mr. Maclise.

At one o'clock members of both houses of the Legislature and of the corporation of the City of London, distinguished engineers, and men of note in various capacities, assembled at the yet unfinished station in Bishop's-road, where the Metropolitan Railway takes its source from the terminus of the Great Western. Lord Harris, a former governor of Madras, was one of the first to arrive. Professor Owen and M. du Chaillu divided much notice; and among the crowd which gradually filled the platform were observable the Lord Mayor, M.P.; Mr. Wilkinson, Chairman of the Metropolitan Company; Mr. Parson, the Deputy Chairman; Mr. H. Lore, of the Great Eastern; Mr. Robert Lowe, M.P.; Mr. Harvey Lewis, M.P.; Mr. Western Wood, M.P.; Mr. Alderman Phillips; Mr. Saunders, the Secretary of the Great Western; Mr. Fenton, the manager, and Mr. T. Marr Johnson, the resident engineer of the metropolitan line; Mr. Alderman Challis; Mr. Sheriff Jones; Mr. Charles Gilpin, M.P.; Captain Bulkeley; Mr. Burchell; Sir Morton Peto, M.P.; Mr. Bunning, the City architect; Mr. Ayrton, M.P.; Mr. Malins, M.P.; Col. Sir J. Hamilton, Bart.; Mr. Scott Russell; Sir Rowland and Lady Hill; Mr. S. Beale, M.P.; Mr. Lane; Mr. Gooch; Mr. Fairbairn, and all or nearly all the council of the Institute of Engineers.

The assembly, numbering between six and seven hundred, and including many ladies, were on this occasion private guests of the Metropolitan Company, invited to a trip of inspection, and to a banquet at the temporary terminus in Farringdon-street. Two trains were in waiting to convey them thither, each being drawn by two engines, and consisting of five of the immense carriages which have been built to run on the broad gauge of this railway. Lofty as well as wide, the carriages of each class offer comfortable accommodation to all who may be disposed to travel by them. Their roof is a curve or arch, and they are lit from the top by gas, which is carried in a collapsing tank. Six persons of more than average dimensions may sit on either side of the second and third-class carriages, though the divisions in the first class apportion this liberal allowance of space among only five occupants in a row. The room thus distributed measures ten feet and a half, so that first-class passengers have about twenty-five inches, and, second and third-class twenty-one inches apiece. In omnibuses the law prescribes that they shall have sixteen inches, and they may consider themselves remarkably fortunate if they get it. The carriages on the Metropolitan Railway are each forty feet long, and on an average they will hold eighty people.

The locomotives attached to the first train yesterday were the *Locust* and the *Bey*, two engines of great power and improved construction. They gave off a good deal of steam in the course of their journey, but this will not be the case henceforth, an efficient condensing apparatus being fitted to every engine. The cause of the vapoury clouds yesterday was the long delay at the stations. The actual run occupied but twenty minutes, reckoned by the time that the trains were in motion; but the stoppages prolonged this period into an hour and a half. Besides condensing their steam, these locomotives are constructed on a plan which obviates the discomfort of smoke. In the common form of engine, the steam that has done its work in propelling the piston-rods which move the wheels, escapes into the chimney, where it assists the draft; whilst the meeting wind is a constant blower to the open fire. The locomotive for the Metropolitan Railway has a valve in the chimney, to be worked by the driver from his station in the rear of the engine, so that the steam can be instantly shut off from its escape. It passes, instead, into cold water that is carried in a tank under the boiler, and there it condensed, as in the common stationary condensing engine. The under blowing of the fire is intercepted by letting fall a flap to the latter. The two valves or flaps are, in the tunnel portion of the line, shut; but in the open cuttings, the ordinary steam-jet draught and air-blowing of the fire, and the non-condensation or escape of the steam, are, exactly as in ordinary engines on other railways, allowed to go on, for the better accomplishment of the distance in the tunnel, with the husbanded force or pressure of the steam made whilst the locomotive was at the terminus, or travelling with space overhead.

The arrangement for avoiding the nuisance of smoke is rendered complete by the substitution of coke for coal.

A start was made at about half past one from the Bishop's-road Station; and before the passengers by the first train had found time to discuss the sensations of passing through a railway tunnel, they were at Lisson-street, Edgware-road. This is the least striking of any of the seven stations; but a considerable space of time was occupied in examining it. Another short run brought the party to Baker-street Station, which is an exceedingly novel and curious erection, lit from without in a most ingenious way. The light is obtained by taking space from the gardens of the houses, and constructing the vault of the station with a line of openings to the space. These apertures, or eyes, are lined with white tiles, as are also the sides of the areas; while the areas are roofed with thick glass carried on light iron gratings – small apertures, however, being left for ventilation – the upper surface of the glass being flush with the street-footway level, and the space being enclosed by a dwarf railing. The areas and the apertures in the tunnel vault can be got at for cleaning, and every portion is provided with drainage. The results of this original plan of lighting are excellent. It may be said that, for the first time, daylight has been sunk underground, and even in the afternoon of an overcast January day, the quality of light thus lowered beneath the surface of the earth was clear, white, and abundantly sufficient for all purposes.

The contrivance has, however, rendered imperative a special construction of the vault, that is to say the necessary strength in the haunches where the thrust was now to be carried from piers rather than a continuous support and abutment. The thickness is so distributed as to leave recesses of six feet three inches and piers of three feet six inches on the face; and the opening of each light is four feet nine inches by a considerably greater dimension of height. Sufficient abutment beyond the backing of concrete, exists in the thickness itself, and the nearly equilibrated form of the arch. Where the rooms below the booking-office and the staircases occur, the partition walls of these are the abutments; whilst, as the face of the pier is of slight width, a casting is built into the latter, and the soffit of each arch is carried and formed by a further arrangement of casting. Thus these separate piers, with the arches, are all connected together.

The next station, at Portland-road, strikingly diversifies the method of lighting. Two domes, and a large glazed opening in the crown of the arch, admit the light of day; and in either dome is a large gas-burner termed a 'sun-light'. These domes have been so contrived with ventilating apertures that an engine might stop under them and let off steam. The line is here on a curve. One platform is 217 feet in length, and the other is 209 feet. Gower-street Station, again, is almost a repetition of Baker-street. The King's-cross Station, which comes next in our course, is a very extensive and handsome structure, lofty within, though presenting very much the appearance of a low-lying shed without. And here we may remark that, in describing the several stations on this railway, we have purposely confined our view to the interior. It must be owned, that the outside of these buildings has little merit, being nothing more than roof. The peculiarity of their dwarfed look, as they crop up at various points of the line, could not be avoided. Everybody who sees them must know that they belong to a work the body of which is sunk below the level of the street, and to demand that they should rise as high as all surrounding edifices would be to require an anomaly.

From King's-cross to Farringdon-street the journey is, in great part, open to sky. Where it is underground, the elliptical span of the arch is maintained by Mr. Jay, the contractor for this part of the line, the same as in the work of Messrs. Smith and Knight, who have constructed the half which extends between King's-cross and Paddington. Not only in the tunnelling, but in the iron roof of the stations, the elliptical form is everywhere apparent, having been chosen in preference to the semicircle. Before quitting the King's-cross Station the visitors witnessed the interesting ceremony of presenting four silver watches to the workmen. It appears that, after a visit of minute inspection, Prince Napoleon left a sum of money to be distributed among the workmen on the line; and this gratuity, being invested in the manner we have indicated, lots were drawn for possession of the watches. A little boy, aged about eight years, son of Mr. Fowler, the chief engineer, performed the ceremony of presentation.

Arrived at their journey's end, the guests of the company were received with music from the band of the metropolitan police force. They then entered a long pavilion, tastefully adorned with flags, and containing a vast perspective of well-filled tables. This extemporised banqueting hall, the length of which was some 250 feet, covered two platforms and an intermediate line of rails, which had been boarded over for the occasion. The repast, a very sumptuous one, was supplied by the Messrs. Staples.

Mr. Wilkinson, who presided, gave the usual loyal toasts, which were of course heartily responded to. He then proposed 'The House of Lords', coupling with it the name of Lord Harris. Lord Harris briefly acknowledged the compliment, for the body whom he had the honour to represent on that occasion as well as for himself. The Chairman next proposed 'The House of Commons', many of whose members were among them. Sir Morton Peto, M.P., returned thanks, and said he supposed it was more as a building contractor, having especial connection with railways, than as a metropolitan member – although for the borough in which they were met – that he was selected for this great honour. Having paid a high tribute to Mr. Fowler's enterprise and skill, Sir Morton concluded by expressing his gratitude for the manner in which the toast had been received.

Mr. Lowe, M.P., in proposing the principal toast – 'Success to the Metropolitan Company' – said that the traffic of London had long been a reproach to the age. Latterly its magnitude had grown so formidable that a check was positively necessary. Dr. Johnson had talked of Charing-cross as bounding the full tide of London humanity; but the limits which he assigned had been far exceeded. The railway system had hitherto, so far from relieving the burden, added its sum of more to that which was too much. It had rendered almost impossible what had become most difficult – the free passage of the streets. To amend the evil, the Metropolitan Railway had been projected, and its vast obstacles to realisation had been successfully encountered by Mr. Fowler, the St. George who had four times grappled with that modern dragon, the Fleet Ditch, and who had at length vanquished the monster. It might perhaps be considered that Mr. Fowler was the man for the post, now vacant, of Admiral of the Fleet. (A laugh.) This railway differed from all others in the fact that, instead of circumstances being influenced by the line, it was the line which was wholly controlled by the nature of things around it. They had to take their level from that of the street; they had to find space amid gas and water mains for tunnels and deep cuttings; they had to work in a soil impregnated with sewage and gas. These difficulties they had overcome in a manner entitling them to the highest honour. The toast, which was most enthusiastically received, was followed by the appropriate air of the 'Young Recruit', played by the band.

The Chairman, in reply, entered into some particulars in the history of the undertaking. It had been first proposed as long ago as 1852. At that time the notion was to form a line from Bayswater to Holborn-hill. This was the idea conceived by Mr. Charles Pearson, who, however, abandoned it in favour of the present scheme. In 1859, after some difficulty in raising the necessary capital, Mr. Burchell, their worthy solicitor, applied to the Corporation, who responded to the appeal by agreeing to take up £200,000 worth of shares. It was to Mr. Burchell, after Mr. Pearson, that the company owed its very existence. Mr. Pearson proposed the health of the Lord Mayor, who responded, taking occasion to remark that he had warmly supported the proposition that the City of London should take its risk in the commercial success of this great undertaking.

Lord Harris then proposed, in eloquent terms, the health of Mr. Fowler, the chief engineer. Mr. Fowler, C.E., who was seated at one of the tables below the dais, was loudly called upon to mount the platform, and, with some appearance of reluctance, obeyed the general desire. His appearance in full view of the company was hailed with repeated cheers. He said he was much gratified by the manner in which the toast of his health had been received, and he confessed some pride that the work with which he had been so intimately associated was brought to a completion. They had heard from Mr. Lowe a very interesting account of the progress of the undertaking; but he might be permitted to add a few remarks. In 1854, after several projects had been abandoned, it was resolved to make the Metropolitan Railway. In 1859 the financial difficulties already adverted to occurred; and in 1863 they saw the line open for traffic. After some references in detail to the constructive character of the line, Mr. Fowler said that, with regard to the locomotives, there was little difficulty in making them suitable for the tunnel passage only, but it was more difficult to adapt them to both that traffic and the open air. With the assistance he had obtained this had been satisfactorily accomplished; and he could not conclude without acknowledging the valuable help which had been given him by Mr. Johnson, the resident engineer.

Mr. C. Gilpin, M.P., proposed 'The health of the Solicitors of the Company', to whom the success of the undertaking, up to its present point, was in great part ascribable. Mr. Burchell returned thanks for the honour conferred on him and his son. The Chairman proposed Messrs. Smith and Knight, and Mr. Jay, the contractors; and Mr. Jay briefly responded. The Lord Mayor gave the concluding toast of the evening, the health of the Chairman, who replied in graceful terms, and the company then separated.

One of the great features of this railway is the small sum of money spent in its construction. It is affirmed that the whole cost of the Metropolitan Railway will come to less than £1,300,000; whilst a viaduct line intersecting building property would have cost four times as much. The length of the line, as it exists, and deducting the branches, is three miles and three-quarters. The branches, added together, would make half a mile. Its accomplishment, so far, is a great step towards the realisation of a perfect system of railway traffic through London, connecting the farthest parts of the country.

27 April 1865: Almost two weeks after the event,
readers discover Abraham Lincoln has been assassinated
ASSASSINATION OF PRESIDENT LINCOLN
ATTEMPTED ASSASSINATION OF MR. SEWARD AND HIS SONS
OFFICIAL REPORT

Yesterday the United States' Legation in London received the following telegram, per Nova Scotian, conveying the astounding news of the assassination of President Lincoln, and the attempted assassination of Mr. Seward and his two sons:

> Sir – It has become my distressing duty to announce to you that last night (14th inst.) his Excellency Abraham Lincoln, President of the United States, was assassinated, about the hour of half-past ten o'clock, in his private box at Ford's Theatre, in the city. The President, about eight o'clock, accompanied Mrs. Lincoln to the theatre. Another lady and gentleman were with them in the box. About half-past ten, during a pause in the performance, the assassin entered the box, the door of which was unguarded, hastily approached the President from behind, and discharged a pistol at his head. The bullet entered the back of his head, and penetrated nearly through. The assassin then leaped from the box upon the stage, brandishing a large knife or dagger, and exclaiming, '*Sic semper tyrannis*', and escaped in the rear of the theatre. Immediately upon the discharge the President fell to the floor insensible, and continued in that state until twenty minutes past seven o'clock this morning, when he breathed his last.
>
> About the same the murder was being committed at the theatre another assassin presented himself at the door of Mr. Seward's residence, gained admission by representing he had a prescription from Mr. Seward's physician, which he was directed to see administered, and hurried up to the third-storey

chamber, where Mr. Seward was lying. He here discovered Mr. Frederick Seward, struck him over the head, inflicting several wounds, and fracturing the skull in two places, inflicting, it is feared, mortal wounds. He then rushed into the room where Mr. Seward was in bed, attended by a young daughter and a male nurse. The male attendant was stabbed through the lungs, and it is believed will die. The assassin then struck Mr. Seward with a knife or dagger twice in the throat and twice in the face, inflicting terrible wounds. By this time Major Seward, eldest son of the Secretary, and another attendant reached the room, and rushed to the rescue of the Secretary; they were also wounded in the conflict, and the assassin escaped. No artery or important blood-vessel was severed by any of the wounds inflicted upon him, but he was for a long time insensible from the loss of blood. Some hope of his possible recovery is entertained.

Immediately upon the death of the President notice was given to Vice-President Johnson, who happened to be in the city, and upon whom the office of President now devolves. He will take the office and assume the functions of President today.

The murderer of the President has been discovered, and evidence obtained that these horrible crimes were committed in execution of a conspiracy deliberately planned and set on foot by rebels under pretence of avenging the South and aiding the rebel cause; but it is hoped that the immediate perpetrators will be caught.

The feeling occasioned by these atrocious crimes is so great, sudden, and overwhelming, that I cannot at present do more than communicate them to you.

At the earliest moment yesterday, the President called a Cabinet meeting, at which General Grant was present. He was more cheerful and happy than I had ever seen him, rejoiced at the near prospect of firm and durable peace at home and abroad, manifested in marked degree the kindness and humanity of his disposition, and the tender and forgiving spirit that so eminently distinguished him.

Public notice had been given that he and General Grant would be present at the theatre, and the opportunity of adding the Lieutenant-General to the number of victims to be murdered was no doubt seized for the fitting occasion of executing the plans that appear to have been in preparation for some weeks, but General Grant was compelled to be absent, and thus escaped the designs upon him.

It is needless for me to say anything in regard of the influence which this atrocious murder of the President may exercise upon the affairs of this country; but I will only add that, horrible as are the atrocities that have been resorted to be the enemies of the country, they are not likely in any degree to impair the public spirit or postpone the complete final overthrow of the rebellion.

In profound grief for the events which it has become my duty to communicate to you, I have the honour to be, very respectfully, your obedient servant,

Edwin M. Stanton

The following telegram, received by Mr. Reuter, appeared in our Second and Third Editions yesterday:

PER NOVA SCOTIAN, VIA GREENCASTLE
NEW YORK

4 APRIL (EVENING)

Grant has removed his headquarters to Washington. Lee has arrived at Richmond. The Confederates report that Lee's surrender was compelled by the wholesale desertions of his troops, the Virginians refusing to leave the State.

The correspondent of the Associated Press states that Lee

surrendered with 8,000 men. The *Tribune* states that Lee's army at the time of the surrender numbered 30,000 men. There was no formal surrender. Many troops left on hearing that Lee had capitulated. The *New York Times* says that Lee, after his surrender, announced that he would exert himself to bring about a complete cessation of hostilities. W. H. Fitzhugh Lee has not been killed, but was captured at Selma.

NEW YORK, 15 APRIL (10 A.M.)

At 1.30 this morning Mr. Stanton reported as follows:

'This evening, at 9.30, President Lincoln, while sitting in a private box at Ford's Theatre, with Mrs. Lincoln, Mrs. Harris, and Major Rathburn, was shot by an assassin, who suddenly entered the box and approached behind the President. The assassin then leaped upon the stage, brandishing a large knife, and escaped in the rear of the theatre. A pistol ball entered the back of the President's head, penetrating nearly through. The wound is mortal. The President has been insensible ever since the infliction of the wound, and is now dying.

'About the same hour an assassin, whether the same or not is as yet unknown, entered Mr. Seward's apartments under pretence of pressing business. He was shown into Mr. Seward's sick chamber, when the assassin immediately rushed to the bed, and inflicted two or three stabs on the throat and two on the face. It is hoped that the wounds may not prove mortal; it is apprehended, however, that they will. The nurse alarmed Frederick Seward, who was in the adjoining room, and he hastened to the door of his father's chamber, when he met the assassin, who inflicted upon him one or more dangerous wounds. Frederick Seward's recovery is doubtful. It is not probable that the President will live through the night.

'General Grant and his wife were advertised to be at the theatre this evening, but they had started for Burlington. At the meeting of the Cabinet, at which Grant was present, the subject of the state of the country and the prospect of a speedy peace was discussed. The President was very cheerful and hopeful, and spoke very kindly of

Lee and others of the Confederacy, and of the establishment of the Government in Virginia. All the members of the Cabinet, except Mr. Seward, are now in attendance on the President. I have seen Seward. He and Frederick were both unconscious.'

At four this morning Secretary Stanton further reported that President Lincoln continues insensible, and is sinking. Seward remains without change, and his son's skull is fractured in two places, besides a severe wound upon his head. The President is still alive, but in a hopeless condition. Major Seward's wound is not dangerous.

It is now ascertained with reasonable certainty that two assassins were engaged in the horrible crime, Wilkes Booth being the one who shot the President, the name of his companion being unknown. His description, however, is so clear, that he can hardly escape apprehension. From a letter found in Booth's trunk it appears that the murder was planned before 4 March, but fell through then because the accomplice backed out until Richmond could be heard from.

Booth and his accomplice were at livery stables at 6 p.m., and left their horses about 10 p.m., or shortly before that hour. It would seem they had for several days been seeking their opportunity, but, for some unknown reason, the deed was not carried out until last night. One of them has evidently made his way to Baltimore; the other has not yet been traced.

Stanton reports at 8 a.m. that President Lincoln died at 7.32 a.m.

Unofficial reports state that Booth, after committing the deed, exclaimed, '*Sic semper tyrannis!*' Both assassins escaped on horses which were in waiting; one of the horses was found on the road near Washington.

There is evidence that Stanton was also marked for assassination.

Vice-President Johnson is at the White House.

The assassination of Lincoln occurred so suddenly, and so little time has elapsed since the event, that it is impossible to judge of the effect upon the public mind or commercial affairs. A general feeling of horror pervades the community.

NEW YORK, 15 APRIL (NOON)

Wilkes Booth, the assassin of President Lincoln, is the brother of Edwin Booth, and is known as a rabid Secessionist. According to the latest reports he has been arrested, and Mr. Frederick Seward is dead.

General Sherman moved in three columns from Goldsboro' on the 9th inst. Johnson evacuated Raleigh and moved west of the town, leaving it in possession of Hampton's cavalry. Johnson is reported to have gone to Greensboro'.

Mobile papers of the 4th instant confirm the capture of Selma, Alabama, with twenty-three guns and large amount of property. The Federals opened a furious fire on the defences of Mobile on the fourth, exploding a magazine in Spanish Fort. The amount of damage done is unknown. The siege continues. Two ironclad gunboats have been destroyed by torpedoes.

Thomas, with a large force, is expected on the north side of Mobile.

Wilson's cavalry is overrunning Alabama, and is also moving towards Mobile.

It is rumoured that Mr. Adams will be recalled from London to take charge of the State Department.

President Davis issued a proclamation, dated Danville, 6 April, announcing his purpose to continue the war, and never submit to the abandonment of one State of the Confederacy. The proclamation was issued some days before Lee's surrender.

It is said that the Governor of North Carolina will shortly convoke the Legislature to repeal the Secession ordinance and restore the State to the Union.

Business is almost entirely suspended on account of Lincoln's assassination. The Stock and Gold Boards will not meet today.

It is considered reliable that Sherman was to remove on the 11th from Goldsboro', in light marching order.

It is reported that the Federal naval force will be immediately reduced.

The *Herald* states that the French Consul at Richmond has left for Washington to submit a claim to the Government for the tobacco burnt at the former place.

Mr. Adams has given notice to the British Government of the termination of the reciprocity treaty on 17 March. Its receipt was acknowledged.

NEW YORK, 15 APRIL (1 P.M.)

Andrew Johnson was sworn in as President by Chief Justice Chase, at eleven o'clock this morning. Secretary McCulloch, Attorney-General Speed, and others were present.

Johnson said: 'The duties are at present mine; I shall perform them. The consequences are with God. Gentlemen – I shall lean upon you; I feel I shall need your support. I am deeply impressed with the solemnity of the occasion, and the responsibility of the duties of the office I am assuming.' Johnson appeared remarkably well, and his manner created a very favourable impression.

The whole of New York is draped in black, and there is general mourning throughout the country.

5 September 1870: Napoleon III loses his throne as the French suffer defeat in the Franco-Prussian War
SURRENDER OF NAPOLEON AND THE FRENCH ARMY AT SEDAN

When, on Saturday morning, we said 'capitulation could be only a matter of time' for the French army hemmed in at Sedan, that capitulation had already been for many hours a matter of fact. On Friday, at 1.22 p.m., King William had telegraphed to Queen Augusta from the scene of conflict 'before Sedan' the news that MacMahon's army were prisoners of war, and that the Emperor had surrendered to the Prussian Monarch in person. MacMahon, who was wounded – Count Palikao says 'grievously' – had resigned the command into the hands of General Wimpffen, with whom the capitulation was concluded. At the same time, the King informed his consort that the Emperor surrendered to him as 'having no command, and having left everything to the Regency at Paris', so that Napoleon III technically stands outside the terms of the capitulation. The two Monarchs held an interview at a small château close to the western face of the defences of Sedan; the Emperor, though 'cast down, was dignified in his bearing, and resigned'; and the King placed at his disposal, as a residence, the Castle of Wilhelmshöhe, three miles from Cassel – 'the German Versailles', as it has been called. It used to be the summer palace of the Electors of Hesse Cassel before the annexations of 1866; and with its luxurious appointments, its splendid fountains, and costly waterworks, in the French taste, it is not unhappily chosen as the temporary abode of the French Emperor.

Napoleon III has passed through Liege on his way to Germany – the Belgian Government, after consulting the protecting Powers, having complied with the joint request of the two Sovereigns that a passage through Belgium should be permitted. Thus the Emperor disappears from the scene of hostilities; and his son, of whose whereabouts nothing is confidently known, will probably soon join his retirement at Wilhelmshöhe. Before the Battle of Sedan, the Prince Imperial was at Avesnes or Mézières; a rumour was current in Brussels on Sunday morning that he was the guest of Prince Chimay at his château; but a telegram dated at noon yesterday pronounces the rumour 'premature', and another despatch places him at Maubeuge.

So far as military affairs are concerned, the telegrams this morning do not give us much that is new, beyond the capitulation of the remnants of MacMahon's army. That event, however, had become a foregone conclusion after the battle of Thursday; and the suddenness with which it followed on the close of the struggle, of itself bears abundant testimony at once to the severity of the losses, the overwhelming superiority of the German armies, and the shattered and hopeless condition of the French army. Although it fought so close to the frontier, not more than 15,000 men have made their escape into Belgian territory; of whom about 12,000, with cannon, eagles, and 1,200 horses – about a full division – appear to have crossed in a single body. A number of reports regarding the battles of last week, principally false or misleading, have been telegraphed from Paris, but they may be summarily dismissed – even more peremptorily than usual, since the proof of their falsity has followed so swiftly and strikingly on their promulgation. The number of the French who have capitulated at Sedan is variously stated. A proclamation by the Ministry at Paris, published in the *Official Journal* yesterday, sets the figure of the French troops at 40,000, and that of the Prussians at 300,000. A telegram from our correspondent at Brussels, on the other hand, informs us that 30,000 men surrendered; and we are disposed rather to accept the larger estimate, not only because it was the obvious policy of the French Ministers to underrate their own troops and overrate the forces of the enemy, but because that reckoning best agrees with the known facts. When he quitted Rheims, MacMahon had the First, Fifth, Seventh, and Twelfth Corps – the first two commanded by Wimpffen and De Failly, though it is uncertain which of these Generals had succeeded MacMahon at the head of the troops that had escaped from Wörth; the others, by Douay and Lebrun respectively. At the complete war which we are assured that they had regained, those corps would have mustered between 150,000 and 160,000 men. But the First Corps had probably not made up full ranks; and if we take at 130,000 the original strength of the Army of Châlons, the calculation will probably not be too low. By straggling and by minor combats 10,000 men may have been taken from that strength during the marches through the Argonne; 7,000 prisoners were made at Beaumont; and the other losses of Tuesday on both sides of the Meuse may be set down at 6,000 or 7,000 more. Of Wednesday's losses we have no means of judging; but both Prussian and Belgian accounts report those of Thursday to be 'most dreadful'; and considering the desperate character of the fighting, they cannot certainly be taken at less than 12,000 or 15,000. We are told from Belgium that 15,000 more have been disarmed and interned; and this statement would leave between 70,000 and 80,000 men unwounded at Sedan when Thursday's battle was over. But, as all the preceding operations must be included under the one general title of the Battle of Sedan, so we can say with literal truth, that the result of last week's fatal three days has been simply to annihilate in a military sense the army of MacMahon. It would seem that the Thirteenth Corps, under General Vincy, which had set out from Paris to reinforce MacMahon, had not reached him when he was cut off, and is now falling back on Paris. It is said to number at least 30,000 good soldiers; and should it regain the capital, it will add no insignificant element to the defence.

The victors are giving Paris but little time to recover the shock of Friday's disasters. Avoiding Mézières, and marching westward by the Hirson road, they are reported at Brussels to have reached a point eighteen miles from St. Quentin, probably about Guise or Vervins. St. Quentin lies some seventy-five miles north-west of the capital, on the railway to Lille; and a few miles to the south is the important junction of Tergnier, at which most of the lines from the Belgian frontier and the northern Departments converge. Some days must elapse before the enemy appears before Paris; but his approach to St. Quentin and Teigmer is one of the first indications of that isolation of the gay city from the world which now seems to be inevitable. In the capital itself, the news of disaster has been received with unexpected dignity and soberness. The full truth has been at last stated to the Legislature: Bezaine shut up at Metz, unable to cut his way out; MacMahon's army made prisoners of war; and the Emperor in captivity. But the Ministers hastened to declare that this cruel reverse does not daunt their courage; that Paris is now ready for the enemy; that the military forces of the country are being organised; that within a few days a new army will be under the walls of Paris, and another is in formation on the banks of the Loire; that they shall arrest their efforts only when they shall have expelled every Prussian from French territory; and that they trust in the patriotism, concord, and energy of the nation to save France.

The 'new army' is evidently meant to be composed of the 200,000 men of the National Guard Mobile who, according to General Palikao's statement in the Corps Législatif, are about to be called to Paris; and in the Corps which were not with MacMahon they will find a nucleus of

60,000 or 70,000 trained troops, who will facilitate the work of making them into an army. There is nothing blatant, intemperate, or hysterical about these and other utterances of the moment; but confidence is lost in the men now in power, always excepting General Trochu; and the Montauban Cabinet and the Napoleon dynasty have fallen together. Under a Republic, or under a Monarchy, however, there can be no doubt that the capital and the country are determined to fight, and that the war is not so near its end as readers of this morning's momentous news from the frontier might at first blush imagine.

The Napoleons have ceased to reign in France. Until a late hour we were without authoritative indication as to the course which events in Paris would take. But it was evident that some radical political change would be the result of the tremendous disaster on the Meuse. The honourable close of the Emperor's campaigning might, indeed, as it seemed, have somewhat redeemed, in the eyes of the Parisians, the tremendous sin of failure; but for France that is a sin which seldom or never is forgiven, whatever acts of heroism or self-denial are done to expiate it. We have said elsewhere that M. Jules Favre's proposal to depose the dynasty was received by the Corps Législatif in solemn silence. That silence was at once dignified and ominous. A similar thought was evidently wavering in the thoughts of many other members; for the bold barrister – the unswerving critic and opponent of the Empire – it was reserved to pronounce with emphasis and effect the fatal word 'abdication'. When the Corps Législatif met at noon yesterday, the first symptom that the wavering thought had found a place in the minds even of Imperialists, was given by Count Palikao's proposal that a Council of Government and National Defence should be formed, composed of five members chosen from among the Deputies of the people. M. Favre, however, re-insisted on his proposal, which, now not heard in solemn silence, was remitted to the Bureaux of the Chamber, along with the Government proposal and with a resolution – brought forward by M. Thiers on behalf of many moderate members – which added to the motion of Count Palikao a rider to the effect that a Constituent Assembly would be formed as soon as circumstances permitted.

A few hours afterwards the sitting was resumed – and then the people were themselves heard. They had been sending deputations to General Trochu, asking him to become Dictator, and shouting 'Abdication!' Now they filled the galleries and floor of the House shouting for deposition and a Republic. The Deputies of the Right and of the more moderate shades abandoned the Legislative Hall to the people and the people's friends – the members of the Left. Amid indescribable excitement, and while loud cheers were raised for the Republic, the people, the National Guard, and the soldiers fraternised. The remaining Deputies then declared the Napoleon Dynasty to be deposed; and a Provisional Government, at the head of which is General Trochu, and which is entirely composed of names prominent for hostility to the Empire, was about to be formed and proclaimed. To this brief statement of yesterday's Draconic judgment upon the errors and failures of the present campaign, we can only say, that no reader of the disastrous news from the theatre of war will be much surprised by what has taken place in Paris. The very terms in which, according to the King of Prussia, the Emperor made his surrender – neither as a soldier in command of any part of his army, nor as a Sovereign with power to treat for peace or take any part in public affairs – almost seemed to invite, as certainly they facilitated, the establishment in France of a state of political affairs which should know the Napoleons no more.

12 October 1870: A *Telegraph* correspondent finds himself in the thick of the Franco-Prussian War trying to return home from Paris
A FLIGHT FROM PARIS
By An Adventurous Correspondent

When I first went to Paris, some weeks ago, I determined to see the siege out; but, after I discovered that the Prussians meant to reduce the city, not by assault, but by starvation, I began to adopt a different view of the prospects of those within the capital. There would be some danger to a person in Paris were an attempt made to take it by storm; there would, on the other hand, be some scenes, the sight of which would have amply compensated for a little risk. But Paris invested so as to be starved out – what a vista, of days of monotonous and unchanging gloom, of common-place misery, did such a prospect bring up to my mind! I determined to fly; but how was this to be accomplished? There was one of two courses open to me. I could get out by balloon; or, by boldly facing the Prussian lines and trying to pass through them. The first plan would leave me so utterly helpless, so much at the mercy of circumstances over which I could have no control, that I at once adopted the second. Three well-known residents in London determined to accompany me. We engaged a covered carriage and two old racehorses, and we were fortunate enough to procure the services of a quondam jockey as coachman. We laid in a six days' supply of provisions; and thus prepared, we, in the afternoon of the twenty-second, started from the Grand Hôtel. I need say that our departure was witnessed by almost all the occupants of that establishment? Whatever the reason, we appeared to them all a most appropriate butt for every kind of 'chaff'. The ostlers grinned, the chambermaids smirked, the waiters addressed to us the most amazing interrogations with maddening politeness; while some English gentlemen were kind enough to indulge the national passion for gambling by betting, some that we should be shot, others that we should return that night.

Before I go any further, let me say a few words about the state of Paris, which may possibly be of interest. Never did a city so change its aspect. Sternness and solemn earnestness have succeeded to frivolity and unbounded gaiety. The determination of the citizens to defend the place to the last moment is unmistakeable. In every quarter, from all sorts of persons, I have heard the same intention invariably expressed, that rather than give up Paris, they will endure almost any extremity of misery. The forts taken, they will defend the walls; dispossessed of the walls, they will fight behind barricades; they will dispute with the enemy every inch of the city, street by street. Rather let it all – temples, churches, boulevards, houses – be for ever destroyed than that it should fall into the hands of the Prussians. Boastful words, possibly, these may appear; but to me they were said in no swaggering tone, but with quiet, earnest determination. Nor did the Parisians make known their resolve merely through words. The attention they displayed to the military exercises was beyond all praise. At five o'clock in the morning you would see them walking to the parade ground, and then going through their exercises with docile patience, and with an evident anxiety to learn. The conduct of the Gardes Mobiles particularly impressed me; and that force is, I think, the real hope of France. They are, for the most part, young men from the country – fine, handsome fellows – enthusiastically fond of their country, and apparently glad, rather than sorry of the opportunity for fighting.

Nor are the women of Paris less active. Thousands of them have volunteered to nurse the wounded, and there is scarcely a hole or corner in the city in which you will not see them cutting or sewing linen and charpie for the service of those injured in battle. Nor do their exertions stop here. In every café and hotel you are accosted by ladies, accompanied by some National Guards, who ask your aid for the wounded with entreaties that cannot be repulsed. One feature in the conduct of the Mobiles that I noticed with peculiar pleasure was their regularity of attendance at church. These fine lads, fresh from the country, have not yet forgotten the teachings of their pious *curé*, nor will their good resolves be put to any severe tests in Paris at present. After ten o'clock the streets are silent and deserted; and that hour, which was formerly the signal for the commencement of noisy and riotous excess, now heralds the gloomy and stern stillness of the night.

On our way through Paris we found companies of soldiers drilling everywhere. The whole city was, in fact, one immense camp. Our strange equipage, bearing two flags, the one white, the other a Union Jack – which some of my companions seemed to think an impenetrable coat of mail against all bullets, Prussian or French – did not fail to excite attention, and, I must add, some ridicule. In fact, the assaults of chaff, which began at the Grand Hôtel, were continually kept up until we arrived at the Porte Maillot, through which we passed out of the city. We were then close by the spot where once stood the beautiful Bois de Boulogne. How changed everything here and all around appeared to me! Many of your readers are doubtless aware that the space between the forts and the walls of the city is, to a considerable extent, occupied by market gardens. From these all signs of vegetation have disappeared. Whatever produce they contained has been removed within the city. It was intended, I believe, to raze to the ground the numerous houses which stand on the roads leading into Paris; but this intention was subsequently abandoned. These houses, now deserted by all the inhabitants, and with all the furniture removed, have a most forlorn appearance. In fact, of all the country surrounding Paris, it may be fairly said that desolation has marked it for its own. But, although the Parisians have not removed the houses to which I have referred, the Prussians must not on that account expect the entrance to the city to be easier. Many of these buildings are occupied by soldiers, and every means has been taken to make them something like forts in miniature. They are loopholed, and felled trees and earthworks surround them. The roads to Paris are, in fact, very well prepared for receiving the enemy. Crossing over the Pont de Neuilly, we soon found ourselves at the advanced French outposts. Here we were challenged, and asked for our permits authorising us to pass. Having been led at the English Embassy to believe that no such documents would be necessary, we had neglected to provide ourselves with them. To our disgust we found that strict orders had been given to allow no one to leave Paris without a special permit from General Ducrot, who commanded the Northern Division. We reasoned, but in vain; we remonstrated, but the only answer to our remonstrances was the information that General Ducrot's headquarters were at the Porte Maillot, through which, we had just passed. Slowly and most unwillingly we retraced our steps, and, after having been stopped at least half a dozen times, we found out the General's headquarters. Whilst waiting to see him, a young officer asked what possible reason induced me to leave Paris. 'If,' he added considerately, 'you want to be shot, our General can do that for you much more expeditiously, and perhaps more agreeably, than the Prussians.'

All my entreaties to General Ducrot for a pass were ineffectual; he politely but firmly declined to give me one without a special authorisation from General Trochu. A gloomy prospect enough now lay before us. To return to Paris, to re-enter the Grand Hôtel under the eyes of the ostlers peeping from the stables, the chambermaids giggling from the windows, our fellow-country men staring on us from the steps – was ever a man asked to go through such an ordeal? There was no help for it, so we went back (one of us had in the meantime been arrested and released) to Paris, and through Mr. Wodehouse, the Chief Secretary of the Embassy – whose very great kindness we have great pleasure in acknowledging – obtained the necessary permits from General Trochu.

The next morning we again set out from the Grand Hôtel, this time also the subjects of the same pitiless sarcasms which had before accompanied our departure. Our number had been meanwhile increased from four to five; for we had agreed, at his earnest solicitation to allow an Italian gentleman to accompany us. Little did we anticipate how much of our subsequent trouble would result from this somewhat rash act of politeness. Arriving at the advanced outposts, we produced, with something of display, and I think of defiance, General Trochu's permit. But our pride was soon levelled with the dust, for we were told peremptorily that we should not be allowed to pass until her permits had been countersigned by General Ducrot. We had again to return to the Porte Maillot; and, having obtained the necessary signature, we returned, and were allowed to pass through the outposts. We now fairly out of Paris, and on the road to Nanterre, a suburban village, about 11 kilometres from the city. The road which we passed brought us rather to Fort Mont Valérien. We could see the mouths of the cannons, the glitter of the bayonets; in the terraces a number of men were being drilled, and altogether the place looked like one that could not be easily taken. Nothing could be more melancholy or depressing than the appearance of the country around us. Not only was it everywhere devastated, but it was a solitude, unbroken by the sight or sound of man or beast. The doors of all the houses were closed, the furniture removed, the inhabitants fled. Arrived at Nanterre, we found it as silent and as solitary as if it had been struck with the plague. Suddenly, as we turned a corner, a few peasants – old men, trembling with age and fear – came in haste. They rushed up to our carriage, and, in accents of the greatest alarm, told us that the Prussians were at Reuil, a village about a kilometre off, and that we could not go forward without the greatest danger. In Reuil we found the same silence – the same solitude – broken only, as before, by a few grey-headed countrymen. These were still more terrified than those we had first met. They begged us not to proceed. There were 'millions' of Prussians, they said, on before us; they fired at everybody and everything. To go forward was certain death. We managed to get rid of them, and continued our onward course. After we had proceeded about half a kilometre, and were close upon Bougival, our English driver called out in the most ludicrous manner, using epithets which I cannot reproduce: 'Here are the Prooshens, and lots of 'em too.' Looking out of the carriage, we saw, at about thirty to forty yards ahead of us, two sentinels, behind whom, at some distance, were about forty or fifty soldiers, ranged across the road. We descended, and proceeded towards the sentinels, who were kind enough to keep their guns levelled at us. We produced our papers, showed them the card of Mr. Wodehouse, and the address of Colonel Walker, the British military attaché to the headquarters of the Crown Prince. But to all our papers and speeches they had but one word for answer – 'Versailles'.

So we had to go back to Reuil, where we entered a lane which leads to Versailles. As we were laughing over our first check, I felt uncomfortable when, turning round my head, I found a revolver in most disagreeable proximity to my head. Looking closer, found it was held by a peasant, not unlike in appearance to a Whitechapel costermonger. Pale with excitement, he ordered the carriage to be immediately stopped. At the same moment we were surrounded by a large body of *Francs-tireurs*. The Captain, a rather intelligent fellow, demanded our papers, and, although urged to arrest us by some of his companions, professed himself satisfied with them. He begged us, however, not to go on; if we did, we should be between two fires. About three hundred *Francs-tireurs* were on our left, a large body of Prussian riflemen on our right, and a skirmish was about to commence immediately. We went back once more to the Porte Maillot, determined to try the road to St. Cloud which runs by the side of the river. This, however, we found barricaded, with deep trenches cut across it. Luckily the towing-path next the river was open. And along this we proceeded to St. Cloud until we came to Suresnes. Here we found the timbers of the suspension bridge that had been blown up on the previous night still smoking. Passing along the Seine, we saw on the other side a large number of *Francs-tireurs*, who, though they appeared to regard our carriage with considerable attention, did not molest us. We ascended the pleasant slope on which St. Cloud stands, and here also we saw nothing but a few peasants who, scowling at us as we passed, retreated into their houses and closed the doors. Finding one who appeared less sulky than the rest, we beckoned him to the carriage, and asked where the Prussians were to be found. '*Nous sommes tous Prussiens*' ('We are all Prussians'), he replied, trembling. On revealing to him our nationality, he became reassured, and informed us that the Prussians had not yet occupied the town, but were hourly expected there. He advised us to leave the streets at once, as the *Francs-tireurs* fired at every one they saw in them; and a couple of shots, which whistled by our heads in rather disagreeable proximity, added weight to the advice. We left St. Cloud as fast as we could, and took the road to Versailles.

We had not proceeded for twenty minutes when we caught sight of two sentinels, standing bolt upright like those we had met before, the road behind them being barricaded with earth and trees, at the rear of which we could see the heads and guns of about fifty riflemen. Having shown our passes to the sentry, he went in search of an officer; this officer being found, *he* went in search of two others; these having come up, all three started in search of the Commandant; and so our appearance was the signal for a great deal of disturbance, of earnest debate, and rushing to and fro. At last we were told to move on; but, as the road was barricaded, we had to go into a field. Suddenly we came upon a ditch; but this obstacle was soon removed by the Prussian soldiers, who covered it with a number of trees, surmounted by an old mattress. The postilion cracked his whip, spurred the horses, and we cleared the ditch in regular steeplechase style. Proceeding onwards, we entered a park, the ground in which the La Marche races take place, and all at once found ourselves in the midst of a Prussian encampment. The officers were seated at tables, smoking, drinking wine, playing cards, evidently in the best humour. Some of the men were lying down, and they had above their heads a most ingeniously contrived substitute for a tent. It consisted of a number of boughs, which were plaited together by straw, and laid on supports.

A sour-looking officer very gruffly demanded our business; but before we could answer a dragoon galloped into the camp, and with great glee communicated some intelligence to the commander, pointing at the same time in the direction of St. Cloud. In a moment all was commotion. The men sprang to their arms, the officers mounted, and soon nearly all the occupants of the camp had disappeared. We, meantime, were hustled into the courtyard of the hospital, immediately opposite the park; and, having met the doctor, he informed us that the enemy were supposed to be in front, that an engagement would soon take place, but that we need not fear – the Prussians were sure to get the best of it. The officer in charge of us spoke with similar contempt of the French soldiers, and seemed to think that in a few days he and his friends would be comfortably quartered in Paris. After some time an aide-de-camp came into the yard; in a few moments we were hustled into the carriage, and, without being allowed to say a word, were driven back in the very direction by which we had first come – into the field, over the ditch, back to the sentinels again. Here we were told that back to Paris we should immediately go; and, finding that a deaf ear was turned to all our entreaties, we had begun to resign ourselves to a return to the Grand Hôtel, and meeting ostlers, chambermaids, waiters, fellow-countrymen, when a general officer, with a large staff, came down the road. In reply to his questions, we exposed our situation, and he told us to go back into the field, saying that he would do his best for us.

A Bavarian officer, who spoke English perfectly, and has some friends in England, advised us to write to the Crown Prince. A sheet of notepaper immediately became the object of our anxious search. At last we found a small piece of not over-clean paper, and, writing with a lead pencil, the carriage-step being our desk, we indited an epistle to his Royal Highness, dating it from 'Within the Prussian lines'. An officer soon after returned, and, telling us that positive orders had been issued from the headquarters on the previous day to let no one pass the lines, said there was nothing for us but to return to Paris by way of Sèvres. We immediately produced the letter which we had written to the Crown Prince, and at this he appeared sorely puzzled. After much solicitation, we induced him to let us stay where we were for the night. We spent it in an open stable at the rear of a little cottage, where we heard the whole night long the booming of the cannon of Fort d'Issy, and the continuous crack of the rifles of the *Francs-tireurs*. Morning came, and with it a sergeant, who told us he had orders to bring us to Sèvres, there to await the answer to our letter to the Crown Prince. Sèvres we found occupied by artillery and cavalry, and, what was much more important to us, a detachment of twelve dragoons and two officers was in waiting to receive us. Thus escorted, we proceeded along the road to Versailles. We had not gone far when we were met and stopped by a commanding officer. By him one of the officers in charge of us appeared to be soundly rated; and before many minutes the postilion was ordered to turn the horses' heads back to Sèvres. Here a further escort of about twenty dragoons arrived; a dragoon mounted the box; and we were all blindfolded. Thus, in utter darkness, not knowing whither we were going, but suspecting and fearing that they intended to send us back towards Paris, we proceeded. Suddenly, when our minds, which exclusion from the contemplation of all outward objects made particularly active, had conjured up all the horrors of being left in the middle of the two hostile lines, the carriage stopped. An officer asked us for our letter to the Crown Prince, which, as may easily be imagined, we produced with the greatest readiness. On again, still blindfolded, until once more we halted. This time the bandages are removed, and, tired of the darkness, we look around, finding a luxury in the use of our eyes. But we soon perceived that the Prussians had very tangible reasons for the kindness. We found ourselves in a lane, between two high walls. Look where we would, we could see, nothing but wall and road, for there was in the latter a curve that effectually prevented us from seeing any distance beyond. Having halted in this uninviting locality for some time, we again proceeded. After going along some distance we were allowed to get out of the carriage and walk. Here again the recovered use of our eyes was to bring us, not the pleasure we anticipated, but emotions the most painful.

Immediately in rear, tied by ropes to each other and to the saddle of a dragoon, were four unfortunate Frenchmen. Three were dressed in the blouse of the peasant; but the fourth appeared to be of a somewhat better class of life. One of them had fired at the soldiers; the others had been found in the possession of a sword-stick or some other arms. They were all ghastly pale; and no wonder, for certain death stared some of them at least in the face. One of them asked the officer in charge of us what he thought would be done to him. 'You are going on the grand tour, Monsieur,' was the reply. Never shall I forget the dreadful sight. The peasant who had shot at the soldiers particularly attracted my attention. He was a fine young fellow, dignified and fearless in his bearing; and whenever he looked towards his captors there was in his eyes the expression of unextinguishable hate. Poor fellow! He will no more love or hate, for he was shot on the morning after the day I saw him. Sad and depressed for the first time during all our journey, we again entered the carriage, our eyes being once more bandaged. Soon our carriage began to jolt – the wheels to rattle as if we were going over the stones of a street. By this we knew that we had arrived in Versailles. As we went along we could hear a crowd gathering in the wake of our carriage. '*Les pauvres malheureux!*' '*Dieu les protége!*' cried those who followed us, speaking in accents of the deepest pity. We perceived at once that the townspeople supposed that we belonged to the same party as the unfortunate peasants who followed us. We were brought to the Mairie, and an artillery officer, coming up to us, said that we were prisoners of war, and that we should remain there during the continuance of hostilities. We were conducted to two rooms upstairs, which, we were informed, would be our quarters. A sentry was placed in each room. We were allowed neither pen, ink, or paper. We were not to be permitted to go out for any purpose, and we were asked to sign a written parole that we would not attempt to escape – a proceeding which, I ventured to remark, appeared wholly unnecessary as long as we were guarded so strictly.

Though thus uncomfortably situated, we could not, when left to ourselves and the sentries, help laughing heartily. Our amusement was increased on discovering that there was but one bed for the five of us. While thus chatting gaily, and trying to make the best of bad circumstances, we suddenly heard without an altercation, in which the unmistakable accents of our countrywomen were audible. Before we had time to recover from, our surprise, three young ladies burst into the room, followed closely behind by the sentinel, in whose features bashfulness, puzzlement, and despair were visible by turns. 'Well, I never!' 'This is the height of impertinence!' 'And they are English!' 'I wonder what these people will do next?' These were the expressions we suddenly heard whizzing around us. Now the ladies spoke to us, now to the sentinels; they darted looks of compassion towards their countrymen, of indignation towards the Prussians; until at last one of them impatiently stamped her foot, and, as a climax to all she and the others had said before, exclaimed: 'I'll go and tell pa!' We thought that, however powerful the influence of the gentleman thus indicated, Colonel Walker would be, on the whole, the best man for us to apply to. So we asked our kind countrywomen to acquaint him with our situation, which they readily promised to do.

Next morning brought Colonel Walker, looking very serious. We had a brief conversation – he blaming us for our 'grave indiscretion' in displaying a white flag, and in bringing along with us an Italian gentleman. We replied to the first remark, that we knew no other ensign which would become our condition; and to the second, that we had only shown to a stranger that hospitality on which Englishmen always pride themselves. The Colonel promised to lay our case before the Crown Prince; and on returning told us that he had been referred by his Royal Highness to General Blumenthal. He again blamed our conduct. He wondered, he said, we had not been shot, as strict orders had been given to fire on all parties coming from Paris who attempted to enter the Prussian lines. He again assured us of his intention to do everything in his power for us. Colonel Walker left. This was Sunday; and during the rest of the day we heard or saw nothing of General Blumenthal. On Monday morning the officer in charge of us brought us separately into one of the rooms. Then we were subjected to a very strict search by three police agents. The investigation gave us much amusement, and I was particularly tickled by the puzzled air with which the iron spring of my cravat was regarded. I did not care to explain the mystery; and at last it was returned to me with a smile. Even our boots were not allowed to pass unexamined. They narrowly scrutinised the soles, lest any papers should be inserted between the leather. At last, the process over, we were sent under escort to the headquarters of General Blumenthal.

Ushered into his presence, we found ourselves in the front of an elderly peaceable-looking gentleman, who spoke English perfectly. He also soundly rated us for carrying a white flag, which he said ought to

be used only by belligerents. We answered that this was the sole protection which we, as neutrals, could use; that we had nothing to do with
the quarrel between France and Prussia; that we were, in fact, running
away from it. What crime, then, had we committed that we should be
imprisoned? Besides, we added, we did not come within the Prussian
lines voluntarily. 'True,' replied the General, 'my officers committed
a great mistake; they ought to have sent you back to Paris.' He then
produced our letter to the Crown Prince. Why had we in that omitted
to mention that we were accompanied by an Italian gentleman? After
some further inquiries, the General told us he would permit us to go
home; but that we should proceed by way of Germany. We strongly
remonstrated; and begged to be permitted to go on to Mantes, as we
expected to find a railway somewhere between that place and Rouen.
But the refusal was firm, though polite. We had, the General said, seen
too much already. Perhaps our Italian friend was a delegate from the
Parisian to the Tours Government, who, once clear of the German
lines, would proceed on his mission. After much ado we obtained permission to proceed to the Belgian frontier via Rheims and Sedan. As
the road, he said, was not very safe, he would give us an escort, which
would be at our service when we were ready to start.

The General then turned the conversation on Paris; and asked
several questions, which we endeavoured to answer in such a way
as to be polite to him and faithful to our duty to France. First he
inquired what was the cause of the firing in the streets of Paris. When
we replied that no such thing had occurred, he looked astonished
and somewhat incredulous. 'What is the amount of the forces?' was
his next question. We answered, about 400,000 to 500,000. Again he
looked surprised. 'Do you mean soldiers?' he said. 'No,' we replied,
'armed men.' 'How,' he went on, 'can you account for the fact that the
French refuse to fight? This is something quite new. The French are
considered fighting soldiers *par excellence;* now they are running away.'
We replied that the army was, doubles, much demoralised; but that
the young men from the provinces, particularly the Gardes Mobiles,

who were all fine, enthusiastic young men, would make a good fight, and were only longing for the opportunity. 'I only wish,' he replied, 'they would come out and give us a chance.' He then went on to ask us about the supplies of the city. 'Did they begin to feel the want of water yet?' 'Certainly not,' said I, 'for the morning I left I had my usual bath in the Grand Hôtel.' Again the General appeared somewhat amazed. 'Was small-pox very prevalent in Paris now?' 'Not more than usual,' answered we, adding that the Tuileries, it was rumoured, was to be used as a fever hospital. They had been told, he said, that there were a great many cases of small-pox in the city, and he should not like to take his men there, if such was the case.

Returning to the subject more immediately concerning us, the General remarked that it would not do to let any more neutrals out of the city – by doing so the number of mouths to be fed would be decreased. After some more questions he bade us good day, and we took our departure. Entering our carriage, we proceeded towards Sceaux. Did I not fear to weary your readers by prolonging an account which has already gone beyond reasonable limits, I could give you several other incidents of my journey. How, one of our horses having broken down, we had to take refuge in a villa, which turned out to be that of M. Ohausson, the well-known Champagne manufacturer of Epernay; how, at Meaux, we vainly searched every part of the town for a single cigar; how at Sedan I visited the battle-field; at Bazeilles the ruins of the village, in which not a house was standing: all these things I must pass by with this one remark – that I was astonished to see the weakness of communication between the German forces along the route. In Rethel, for instance, we found but fifty to one hundred Prussians; and between Rheims and that place we did not come across more than half-a-dozen. In like manner the field telegraph could be destroyed by the hand of a child, and with considerable chances of not being observed. Yet neither the small Prussian detachments nor the feeble telegraph are touched – two facts which speak most eloquently to the utterly subjugated spirit of the country through which the Germans have passed. I arrived in London fourteen days after my departure from Paris, with feelings divided between thankfulness that the dangers and fatigue of my journey were over, and regret that the commonplace and unvaried scenes of ordinary life have succeeded to the exciting and ever-varying incidents of my flight from Paris.

23 January 1871: Wilhelm I of Prussia is proclaimed
Kaiser of an Imperial Germany
INAUGURATING THE NEW EMPIRE
From Our Special Correspondent

[The following account of the ceremony in the Hall of Mirrors at Versailles last Wednesday should have reached us, by special despatch and telegraph, in time for our impression of Saturday, but was unfortunately delayed in transmission.]

A conference was held yesterday, at which the King, the Crown Prince, Count Bismarck, and his Excellency M. Schleinitz, Minister of the Royal Household, were present. The council lasted from two till half-past four o'clock. At its conclusion the King paid a formal visit to his eldest brother, Prince Charles, who, through the King's acceptance of Imperial rank and of a new title, becomes the senior representative, or *doyen*, of the Prussian Royal House of Hohenzollorn-Brandenburg.

In the evening, the Staatswache, which is composed of picked soldiers from every infantry and cavalry regiment belonging to the German Confederation, was relieved from duty at the Royal residences by the Coblenzer Garde Grenadier regiment, and took possession of the whole Chateau, guarding every state-room, passage staircase, and issue. It served during the remainder of the morning as the representative of the whole German army, and as witness on behalf of that body of the transformation achieved in the Constitution of Germany.

Delegates had been summoned from every regiment of the Third

Army, with the colours of its battalion or squadron. The colours of the Bavarian regiments were also brought to Versailles yesterday, and lodged at the Crown Prince's Headquarters for the night. This morning they were conveyed to the Château under escort, a guard of honour for that purpose being furnished by the 59th Regiment. They were then, being borne by colour-sergeants, arranged semi-circularly with the colours of the Prussian regiments before Paris. The colours were placed in the order of battle the regiments to which they belonged held in the line of investment. The Garde-Landwehr colours occupied the centre, upon a raised platform, two steps high, which was covered with red tapestry, and was erected on the northern-side of the Gallerie des Glaces. In front of this platform, guarding the flags, were the Gardes du Corps, the officers standing with drawn sabres.

On the side of the gallery facing the park was placed an altar. This was surmounted by several chaplains of the Third Army. In the centre stood the divisional chaplain, Rügger, the King's favourite preacher, who, as Court Garrison Prediger of Potsdam, may be said to have represented the resting-place of the ashes of Frederick the Great. To the right of the altar were ranged military choristers and musicians, furnished by the 7th (King's Own Grenadiers), the 2nd (West Prussian), the 47th (which was raised from the 7th when the Prussian army was increased and organised), and the 58th Regiments. To the left of the altar surgeons were told off to escort the colours and delegates from the Third Army, the non-commissioned officers and men decorated with the Iron Cross. Opposite the altar an open space was left for Royal and princely personages.

At eleven o'clock the company invited began to assemble. On the stroke of noon the King arrived, preceded by Court Marshals Counts Puckler and Perponchen, and followed in order by the Crown Prince, the Princes Karl and Adalbert, the Grand Dukes of Weimar and Baden and their heirs apparent, the Bavarian Prince Luitpold and Saxon Prince, the Duke of Würtemberg, Prince Leopold of Hohenzollern,

Prince of Anhalt-Dessau, Count Bismarck — who,
moted today to the rank of Lieutenant-General, wore the
a Colonel of Landwehr — his Excellency M. de Schleinitz,
Moltke, Kirchbach, and other high State officials. As the King ei
he bowed profoundly to the altar. The choristers immediately struck
up 'Jauchzet dem Herrn'. Some prayers from the Liturgy were then
read. Rügger delivered a consecration sermon, in which he referred to
the history of the Hohenzollern family, to the traditions of Versailles,
&c. The King stood under the portrait of Louis XIV, on which was the
inscription, '*Le Roi gouverne de lui-même*'. This legend was expatiated
upon by Rügger, and furnished a moral to the preacher.

The King wore the uniform of the 1st Guards, in which regiment
he first earned field rank in 1814. To his right was the Royal Prince,
a little withdrawn; the rest of the Sovereign Princes occupied places
still further back. Behind them were the Ministers of State. The group
looked like a Chapter of the Order of the Black Eagle; for the King
and many of the Prussian Princes wore the grand *cordon* of that Order
— there was but one bearer of the *cordon* of the Red Eagle. The King
wore those orders only which were actually gained in the battle-field
— namely, the full insignia of the Garter and St. George, Russian;
the round stars of the high Prussian orders were conspicuous on his
breast. The Order of the Black Eagle will probably become that of the
German Eagle.

When the Litany concluded, the choir began to chant '*Nun danket
alle Gott*'. The King, followed by all the German Princes, advanced
to the flags, stepped upon the platform, and, having turned round,
addressed the assembly. His Majesty concluded by saying: 'I command
my Chancellor to read aloud my proclamation to the German people.'
Count Bismarck then read in a calm voice and with a collected manner
the proclamation. The Grand Duke of Baden then advanced and
exclaimed in a loud voice: '*Es lebe Seine Majestat der Deutsche Kaiser
Wilhelm, hoch!*' The cheer was taken up with wild energy; the band
played '*Heil Dir im Siegeskranz*' and 'God save the Queen'. The

Emperor and Crown Prince embraced thrice, and the German Princes paid homage to the former as '*Deutscher Kaiser*'. This concluded the ceremony. The different personages then defiled, the officers passing the Emperor at twelve paces, and bowing deeply. This evening a grand banquet was given at the residence of the Emperor; 120 covers were laid. All the German Princes were invited. Mr. Odo Russell was also one of the guests.

The bombardment is to come off tomorrow on a greater scale. Fort d'Issy will be finally crushed.

Yesterday General von Werder fought his third day's battle, and announced that he could hold his own until the arrival of Manteuffel. Zastrow will join him to-morrow. The Emperor has sent Von Werder the oaken wreath of *ordre pour la mérite*. No orders were conferred or higher classes bestowed today. A new order will probably be founded in connection with the Empire.

The Bavarian Generals von der Tann, Hartmann, and Bothmer were present at the ceremony. The weather is very much rain and a high wind.

A sortie has been expected the whole day, but none has come. The health of the army is excellent.

The losses of the Second Army before Le Mans, in killed, wounded, and prisoners, were 177 officers, 3,203 men. The French loss was 22,000 prisoners, two flags, nineteen guns, and more than 1,000 waggons loaded with ammunition. Their loss in small-arms and commissary stores was also very great.

Bourbaki has retreated with the *gros* of his army, leaving three divisions to hold Von Werder in check. These the German General has announced his intention of attacking.

3 July 1872: Henry Morton Stanley writes about how he found
Dr. David Livingstone
DR. LIVINGSTONE'S SAFETY
OUTLINE OF HIS DISCOVERIES
THE NILE SECRET SOLVED

We are indebted to the courtesy of the London representative of the *New York Herald* for the following summary of long despatches from Mr. Stanley, the Special Commissioner despatched by that journal in search of Dr. Livingstone. The despatches were sent from Kwihara, Unyanyembe, by a trusty and swift messenger, who would arrive at the sea coast about a month before the *Herald* expedition on its homeward journey; and they contain most interesting details, not only of Mr. Stanley's adventures, or rather misadventures, on his way to Ujiji on Lake Tanganyiki but also of Dr. Livingstone's protracted wanderings in the quest – finally crowned with success – to find the true source of the Nile:

On 23 June, 1871, Mr. Stanley, the Special Commissioner of the *New York Herald*, who had left Zanzibar at the head of a large caravan organised by himself, reached Unyanyembe, having lost by sickness on the way one of the white men who had started out with him, two of his armed escort, eight pagazis, two horses, and twenty-seven asses. Resting here for a few days, he prepared to carry out his determination of proceeding to Ujiji, when, to his annoyance, he found that Mirambo, the King of Ujowa, had, in some fit of alarm or other at the incursions which had been made into his territory, announced that in future no caravan should pass to Ujiji, through the land owned by him, unless it went over his dead body. The Arabs, incensed at this curtailment of their rights, had declared war against Mirambo; and as they appeared to be confident of victory, and determined to fight well, Mr. Stanley judged that the better course was for him to combine with them in attacking the King of Ujowa.

Accordingly he joined his forces; and the united strength advanced into the enemy's territory.

The first day was successful for the Arabs, who succeeded in surprising three of Mirambo's villages, and captured, killed, or drove the inhabitants away. On the second day of the warlike expedition Mr. Stanley caught a fever, and was reconveyed to Unyanyembe. The third day an Arab detachment incautiously attacked another of the Ujowa villages, and were at first victorious; but Mirambo, who was commanding his men in person, gradually drew the Arabs into an ambush, and then defeated them with great slaughter, killing seventeen of their chieftains, and also five of the armed men who belonged to Mr. Stanley's expedition. This mishap appears to have thoroughly disheartened the Arabs, for on the fourth day of hostilities they deserted in every direction, at the same time carrying panic among the men who formed Mr. Stanley's force, so effectually that they, too, made the best of their way for the coast, leaving the American traveller with only an Englishman named Shaw, an Arab boy called Selim, and six of the armed escort. News of the break-up of his enemies' forces soon reached Mirambo, and that potentate immediately made preparations for attacking Unyanyembe itself, whereupon Mr. Stanley, who had by this time somewhat recovered from his fever, collected all the fugitives he could find, and, having succeeded in organising about a hundred and fifty of them into a tolerably compact band, and obtaining five days' provisions for them, barricaded a number of houses, hoisted the American flag, and awaited Mirambo's approach. The King of Ujowa at first advanced, and was apparently about to make an attack; but, somewhat cowed by the defiant attitude of the defenders of Unyanyembe, he beat a retreat, and was seen no more.

It now occurred to Mr. Stanley that the better course to pursue would be to leave the Arabs to fight out their own battles, and attempt to reach Ujiii by a more northerly route – the more so because he saw no prospect of any speedy conclusion to the war which had begun between the Arabs and Mirambo. To this the Arabs offered serious objection, doubtless from selfish motives; and, failing to dissuade Mr. Stanley, they did their best to intimidate his followers by means of extraordinary tales. In this endeavour they were so far successful that Shaw, the Englishman, declined to go further; and it was with great difficulty that the American could obtain bearers for his baggage, or an escort. At last, however, he started, and, entering the desert, passed through several hundred miles of country scarcely known to the Arabs themselves. Several times he was so seriously threatened by the rapacious chiefs of hostile tribes that he had the greatest difficulty in proceeding; it was only by cajoling here, by threatening there, that he was able to escape their attempted extortions and delays. On 3 November, 1871, he came in sight of the outlying houses of Ujiji; and, anxious to enter the African town with as much *éclat* as possible, he disposed his little band in such a manner as to form a somewhat imposing procession. At the head was borne the American flag; next came the armed escort, who were directed to discharge their firearms with as much rapidity as possible; following these were the baggage men, the horses, and asses; and in the rear of all came Mr. Stanley himself. The din of the firing aroused the inhabitants of Ujiji to the fact that strangers were approaching, and they flocked out in great crowds, filling the air with deafening shouts, and beating violently on their rude musical instruments.

As the procession wended its way into the town, Mr. Stanley observed a group of Arabs on the right, in the centre of whom was a pale-looking, grey-bearded, white man, whose fair skin strongly contrasted with the sunburnt visages of those by whom he was surrounded. Passing from the rear of the procession to the front, the American traveller noticed that the white man was clad in a red woollen jacket and wore upon his head a naval cap with a faded gold band round it. In an instant he recognised the European as none other than Dr. Livingstone himself; and he was about to rush forward and embrace him, when the thought occurred that he was in the presence of Arabs, who, being accustomed to conceal their feelings, were very likely to found their estimate of a man upon the manner in which he conceals his own. A dignified Arab chieftain, moreover, stood by, and this confirmed Mr. Stanley in his resolution to show no symptom of rejoicing or excitement. Slowly advancing towards the great traveller, he bowed and said: 'Dr. Livingstone, I presume?' to which address the latter, who was fully equal to the occasion, simply smiled and replied: 'Yes.' It was not till some hours afterwards, when alone together, seated on a goatskin, that the two white men exchanged those congratulations which both were eager to express, and recounted their respective difficulties and adventures.

Mr. Stanley's statement is that Dr. Livingstone appeared to be in remarkably good health, stout and strong, quite undismayed by all that he had gone through, and eager only to finish the task he had imposed upon himself. The Doctor having been shut out from the civilised world for so many years, Mr. Stanley found himself acting as a kind of newspaper to him, and the details of what had occurred in Europe and America interested him exceedingly.

Dr. Livingstone's story of his adventures was to the following effect: In March 1866, he started from Zanzibar. The expedition which he led consisted of twelve Sepoys, nine Johanna men, seven liberated slaves, and two Zambesi men – in all thirty persons. At first Dr. Livingstone travelled along the left hank of the Rovuma River; but, as he pursued his way, his men began to grow disaffected and frightened, and, in spite of all his efforts to encourage and keep them together, most of them left him and returned to their homes, spreading everywhere the report of his death as a reason for their reappearance there. The Sepoys, although they did not desert, exhibited shortly afterwards a mutinous spirit, and the explorer was obliged to discharge them also. In August 1866, he arrived in the territory of Mponda, a chief who rules over a tribe living near the Nyassa Lake; and here Wikoteni, a protégé of the Doctor's, insisted upon being absolved from going any further. After resting for a short time in Mponda's ground, Dr. Livingstone proceeded to inspect the 'heel' of the Nyassa Lake; and it was while carrying out this enterprise that the Johanna men, who had till now remained faithful, deserted him, alleging as their excuse that a chief named Mazitu had suddenly taken to plundering, and was ill-using travellers who ventured into his neighbourhood. It is probable that the Doctor would not have lost the services of these men, had their leader been a man of more decided character; but Musa – for that was his name – appeared to be more frightened than his subordinates, and when he deserted they fled also. To account for their conduct, they also invented a story of Dr. Livingstone's death, and their mendacious tales were the foundation of the reports which – though fairly exploded some years ago – have circulated more or less ever since. In December 1866, having previously collected a number of natives, Dr. Livingstone decided upon advancing in a northerly direction; and in pursuance of this determination he traversed the countries of Babisa, Bobembena, and Barungo, as well as the region of Londa.

Approaching King Cazembe's territory, he crossed a thin stream called the Chambezi, and here he found himself in great difficulty, being for a long while unable to discover to what the river belonged. The confusion which he experienced was greatly increased by the fact that Portuguese travellers had previously reported the existence of such a stream, and had asserted that it was a tributary of the great Zambezi river, having no connection whatever with the Nile. These statements Dr. Livingstone was disinclined to believe; and, determined to satisfy himself as to the rise and falling of the Chambezi, he made up his mind to devote himself to the task at once. From the beginning of 1867 to the middle of March 1869, he traversed the banks of the mysterious stream, tracing it wherever it ran, correcting the errors of the Portuguese travellers, and proving conclusively that the Chambezi was not the head of the Zambezi river, as had been hitherto supposed. So constantly did he remain at this work, and so frequent were the inquiries which he made in every direction, that the natives, in astonishment at his persistence, supposed him to be insane; and their frequent remark was: 'The man is mad: he must have water on the brain.' Their ridicule had, however, no effect upon him, for he continued his work in spite of every opposition, and, as the result of his labours in this region, coupled with his further researches, he has established conclusively (first) that the Portuguese Zambezi and the Chambezi are totally distinct streams; and (second) that the Chambezi is the head waters of the Nile. He discovered that, starting from about latitude 11 degrees south, it rolled on until it attained the extraordinary length of 2,600 miles.

In the midst of his wanderings Livingstone came upon Lake Liemba, which he discovered to be fed by Lake Tanganyika. His map of the last-mentioned lake shows that the southern portion of it resembles in shape the lower part of the kingdom of Italy. He found that it rises in 8 degrees 42 seconds south, and is 323 miles in length, being, thus seventy-three miles longer than was supposed by Captain Burton and Captain Speke. Leaving Tanganyika, the doctor crossed Marungua, and came in sight of a small lake called Lake Muero, which he found to be six miles in length, and to be fed by the Chambezi. In this way he traced the Chambezi running through three degrees of latitude, and, having thus satisfied himself of its total independence of the Zambezi, he returned to King Cazembe's country, and then made his way to Ujiji, where, early in 1869, he wrote letters and despatched them by messengers. A short rest was made at Ujiji, and, having explored the head of the Tanganyika lake – and thus finding out that the river Rusizi flowed into the lake, and not out of it, as had been supposed – he made preparations for another, and, as he then hoped, a final journey of exploration.

Leaving Ujiji in June 1869, he pushed through the Uguhba country, and, after fifteen days' march, came to Manyema, which he found to be a virgin country, the interior of which seemed utterly unknown, to anybody. As he was about to proceed, however, he was seized with an illness which at one time almost threatened to put an end to his explorations. Ulcers formed on his feet, and for six weary months he was obliged to rest and wait. So soon as he had recovered he started off in a northerly direction, and came shortly afterwards to a broad lacustrine river called Lualaba, which flowed in a northerly, westerly, and southerly direction. Strongly suspecting that this river was but a continuation of the Chambezi, which enters the Banguereolo, Luapula, and Muero lakes, he retraced his steps to Lake Kamolendo, and thence worked his way to latitude 4 degrees south, and after a long and difficult journey he found the point where the Lualaba and Chambezi joined, and proved them to be both one and the same river. He followed the course of this latter river for several hundred miles, and had come within 180 miles of that part of the Nile which has already been traced, when the men he had with him mutinied, and deserted him. Having now neither stores nor followers, he was obliged to retire to Ujiji, weary and destitute. It was soon after this that Mr. Stanley found him. In fact, the English explorer arrived at Ujiji on 16 October 1871, and it was, as already stated, no later than 3 November when the American searcher made his entry into Ujiji.

On 20 November, Dr. Livingstone and Mr. Stanley left Ujiji in company, and explored the northern end of the Lake Tanganyika, confirming by a second inspection the observations which Dr. Livingstone had previously made; and after twenty-eight days thus pleasantly spent, they returned to Ujiji, and there passed Christmas-day together. On 26 December they left for Unyanyembe, and, arriving there, stayed together till 14 March when Mr. Stanley, entrusted with letters from Dr. Livingstone, started for the coast, leaving the explorer to continue his searches for some time longer.

Dr. Livingstone states that he considers he has yet two problems to solve in connection with the Nile: the first, the complete exploration of the remaining 180 miles which lie between the spot where he was compelled to turn back and the part already traced; the second, the investigation of the truth of a report which has several times reached him, respecting four fountains which, he has been told, supply a large volume of water to the Lualaba. To complete this task, Dr. Livingstone estimates that he will require sixteen or eighteen months; Mr. Stanley, however, is of opinion that the work will occupy at least two years.

21 May 1873: The *Telegraph* sponsors an archaeological expedition to Nineveh, but recalls the scholar behind it just as he finds something
THE DAILY TELEGRAPH ASSYRIAN EXPEDITION
COMPLETE SUCCESS OF EXCAVATIONS
THE MISSING PORTION OF THE DELUGE TABLET DISCOVERED

The following message has been received from Mr. George Smith: MOSUL, 19 May (6 p.m.)

I am excavating the site of the King's Library at Nineveh, which I found without much difficulty. Many fresh objects of high importance have rewarded my search. Since my last message I have come upon numerous valuable inscriptions and fragments of all classes, including very curious syllabaries and bilingual records. Among them is a remarkable table of the penalties for neglect or infraction of the laws. But my most fortunate discovery is that of a broken tablet containing the very portion of the text which was missing from the Deluge tablet.

Immense masses of earth and debris overlie whatever remains to be brought to light in this part of the great Mound. Much time and large sums of money would be required to lay it open. I therefore await instructions from you and the Museum as the season is closing.

It will be gathered from the supremely interesting telegram which we have received from the scene of Mr. George Smith's labours at Nineveh that a success, eclipsing all his other good fortune, has crowned the energy and ability of our indefatigable Commissioner. He has discovered the missing portions of the world-famous 'eleventh tablet', and this primeval legend of the Deluge will now be completed for the world's perusal. No one will differ from us in calling this a most remarkable reward of the faith in which the young scholar was sent upon his expedition. That he should be able to make his way in a strange land to the right spot, and that he could tell his Arabs where to dig with the certainty of coming upon the 'King's Library' marks sufficiently the sound and perfect knowledge of his task which long study had given him. Those who, like Mr. Layard and Sir Henry Rawlinson, have imperishably connected their names with Assyrian research, will be foremost among all to recognise the merit displayed in these particulars.

But Mr. Smith had made himself too familiar at home with the ancient sites to expect applause on this ground: he knew well enough where to look. The great question was, whether the best-informed searcher could hope to find the minute, yet precious tablets which probably lay hid in the dust of that deep-buried Library. The odds were heavily against any such good fortune, almost as heavily as though certain duodecimo volumes were lying *perdu* under the South Downs, and a few months had been allowed to a party of excavators for the purpose of hitting upon them. But not only has our Assyrian decipherer gone straight to the right spot, conquered all difficulties of a strange land and a wayward, jealous people, and laid open the treasure-house of ancient literature, he has actually put his hand upon the one relic of all others which was most longed for, and found the earthen pages which complete the story of the primeval Diluvium.

It is evident that, beside this wonderful and most welcome 'find', there must result great gain to historical science from many other fruits of his research. In the telegram which we publish today, he speaks of a table giving a list of penalties for the neglect or infraction of laws, and this can hardly fail to throw light upon the jurisprudence of the Assyrian people. He tells us also of fresh tablets – syllabuses and bilingual inscriptions – which, added to the extraordinary quantity of similar relics he has already collected must make up for him a noble *trouvaille* to bring home to his Museum. But the chief interest – at least for the present – centres, and must centre, upon that singular and happy fact – the discovery of fragments which complete the broken text of the Deluge tablet, thereby crowning the wishes of those who bid him speed with an almost unexampled and absolute success. As to ourselves, we are more than rewarded for our part in the enterprise by so singular an achievement; and we feel sure that all England will be proud of the young *savant* who has thus done credit at once to British pluck and British scholarship by journeying, at the call of Science, so far from home, and, amid all obstacles and difficulties, putting his hand on the very thing which all desired, though it lay buried under the debris of twenty-six centuries.

With this good news before us, it becomes extremely interesting to consult afresh the imperfect but absorbing narrative which Mr. Smith read on the third of last December, and to notice where those *lacunæ* occur that may now be filled up. All will remember the names of Prince Izdubar and Ishtar, his wife; how the Prince conquered and reigned in Belesu; how he fell sick, and, being troubled with the fear of death, set out to find and question the patriarch Sisit, who had been translated to immortality without dying. The first important omission from that primitive story was an account off the dream which Izdubar had: this was wanting in the tablets at the British Museum. A second *hiatus* 'much to be lamented' – as old commentators have it – occurred in the description of the Prince's wanderings before he fell in with Urhamsi, that 'ancient mariner'. At the moment when the Royal traveller and his companion found Sisit and approached him, the text, as we hitherto possessed it, again broke off, and it could not be known when, or under what circumstances, the 'immortal mortal' was discovered and questioned. There was 'a water which divided them', but no explanation existed of this mysterious stream or ocean; and the inquiry which Izdubar addressed to the deathless Sisit was also wanting from the Museum tablets, along with the first portion of the momentous answer.

We drew attention at the time to this tantalising interruption of the narrative; we compared it to the silence which in Holy Writ is the only and too eloquent reply to Pilate's query: 'What is truth?' Who, indeed, would not have wished to hear how the oldest of our race framed the great central question about life and death which haunts the hearts and minds of men nowadays, as it did five thousand years ago, professing all the pathos of an ignorance which neither Nature, Science, nor Revelation have ever enlightened? Every Sunday in our Churches the prayer still goes up, 'Lighten our darkness, we beseech'; and such a prayer, it was evident, had been breathed by Izdubar, though the words and framing of it were gone. If those words and the response to them have been found by our Assyrian scholar, we should not have, of course, any oracular or infallible answer to this perpetual demand of the human spirit; but we should, at least, know how the old dread was felt in a remote antiquity, and what solace Sisit could give for the scribes of Warka to preserve within the Royal volumes.

Even in the less imperfect eleventh tablet, which contained the story of the Deluge, there were many missing passages, obviously possessing the greatest interest. Fifteen lines describing the building of the Ark; four lines describing the ceremonies observed for the purification of Izdubar – and a second passage, relating also to purification from sin, were absent. There was a mysterious mention of someone 'taken to dwell with death', which could not be clearly deciphered; and the latter part of Sisit's teachings was sadly mutilated. Finally, twenty-six lines of the inscription, apparently telling the subsequent adventures and wanderings of the Prince and the Sailor, were almost entirely gone – and the ingenuity of more than one foreign cuneiformist has since been vainly exercised upon the indications of these many broken hints. They will now await with ardent interest the arrival of the 'Mage' himself, who, after deciphering the unsuspected treasures of these clay fragments, has been to the King's Bibliotbeca and fetched the duplicate volumes almost as easily as if it had merely been necessary to step into the Museum Library and take the missing text down from its shelf.

Mr. Smith's errand is thus obviously and successfully fulfilled, so far as regards the Deluge Tablets; and, in reply to his request for instructions, we have desired him to close his labours and to return home. The hot season is now impending, when even at Koyanjik and Nimroud work becomes impossible; and nothing could be safely done out of doors after the end of this month – especially by an unacclimatised explorer – until the autumn brings cooler weather in the Valley of the Tigris. Even Mr. Layard and his comrades were driven by the intense heats of the Mesopotamian summer into the

Kurdistan mountains; and the Arabs themselves cannot labour there except by night. Moreover, after excavating the King's library Mr. Smith had evidently before him a monstrous mass of soil to be moved – rich, no doubt, in relics, like all the rest of these wonderful mounds, but demanding a great space of time, unlimited funds, and large bodies of labourers. If the main object of our search lay undiscovered, then we should have encouraged Mr. Smith to wait for the proper time; and dig on; but he has cleared out the spot which he went to examine, and he has found the most valuable of all the memorials which he sought. It is right, therefore, that he should be allowed to bring his treasures back while his health is unaffected, and, as far as *The Daily Telegraph* is concerned, he will do so.

The question has been submitted to the Trustees of the British Museum by his own request, whether, in view of his great success, they desire to retain him on the site of these discoveries; but rich as the ground evidently is, and great as are the advantages which an expert possesses in such investigations, it will be felt that the difficulties as to labour and season are very serious, while Mr. Smith's services at home are too valuable not to be greatly missed. It is probable, therefore, that we shall have the successful explorer back in England before long, with a new store of ancient monuments to work upon in 'the cell of the Mage', and no doubt need be entertained that he will be welcomed among us as his courage and learning deserve.

15 July 1878: The Treaty of Berlin stabilises Europe
THE BERLIN CONGRESS
SIGNING OF THE TREATY
DEPARTURE OF THE ENVOYS
[BY SUBMARINE TELEGRAPH]
From Our Special Correspondent

The Congress is over. Several of the Plenipotentiaries have already left, and Berlin is plunged today into its normal state of oppressive dullness. A few words will suffice for yesterday's formal proceedings, which were a mere repetition of the opening ceremonial, deprived of the sentiments of apprehension and hope.

The private secretaries of the Plenipotentiaries met at one, to affix to the various copies of the Treaty the seals of their respective chiefs. In accordance with the custom of this Court, the secretaries were compelled to appear in full evening dress instead of diplomatic uniform which they wore at the dinner afterwards given at the Schloss.

The rule observed as to precedence of signatures was that in the copies of the Treaty intended for each Power that Power should appear first in order, the others following alphabetically, according to the names of each country. Thus, in her own copy, Germany is placed first, whereas she is second in all other copies, the word 'Allemagne' taking precedence in alphabetical arrangement. England appears as 'Grande Bretagne', that is, fourth on the list, except on her own copies, where she stands first. The Treaty is printed, one copy being on vellum for preservation, while six others are sent to each Power for exchange, after ratification with the other Powers.

The Plenipotentiaries assembled at the Radziwil Palace in full uniform, as on the first occasion, and the Turks were again as then conspicuous by their absence. This time there was a more serious reason for their not joining their *confrères*. At the last moment they received,

I am informed, telegraphic instructions from Constantinople not to sign until the unsatisfactory state of the negotiations with Austria as to Bosnia and Herzegovina was regulated. The delegates repaired to Count Andrassy, and thought to obtain from him an undertaking as to a joint occupation of Bosnia and Herzegovina. The Count replied that he could give no such undertaking, whereupon the Turks declared that they could not sign the Treaty. Time was getting close; Count Andrassy was appealed to not to break off the negotiations, and he at length sent to the Turks a guarantee that his Government would make amicable arrangements before entering the Principalities. On this the Turks repaired to the Congress, where sketches were taken by Werner for an historical picture of the event which he is to paint.

The speech of Count Andrassy, to which Prince Bismarck delivered a fitting reply, has no doubt already been transmitted to you, as also one made by the Crown Prince at the State dinner. The Earl of Beaconsfield left this morning for Cologne. His secretaries, Mr. Austin Lee and Mr. Algernon Turnor, took their departure last night. A special boat will be ready on Tuesday at Calais and a special train at Dover to convey the Premier and Lord Salisbury to London.

Count Andrassy returned to Vienna this afternoon. Tomorrow morning he will confer with Count Bylandt, Minister of War, and Baron Hofman, Minister of Finance, respecting the last measures to be taken prior to the occupation of Bosnia and the Herzegovina. Negotiations with the Porte are all but concluded and although the inhabitants of the two provinces still manifest hostile intentions, the Government will not wait for their consent, but proceed to carry out the so-called mandate of Europe as soon as all preliminary formalities are terminated. The scheme itself continues to be the object of severe criticism both in Austria and Hungary. It has no partisans; indeed it is not too much to say that a more thoroughly unpopular step was seldom taken by any Government.

The acquisition is a most unprofitable one for Austria. A portion of Bosnia may prove advantageous, if duly turned to account; but at least one-third of that province, as also the entire of the Herzegovinian lowlands, will be a dead loss. They are not only barren, but unhealthy, many parts being as bad as the Dobrudscha. The inhabitants themselves are, for the most part, opposed to Austrian occupation. The Catholic element alone pronounces itself in a contrary sense. The orthodox Christians loathe the very name of Austria, and were unanimously in favour of annexation to Servia. The Mussulmans belonging to the better classes are no less dissatisfied at the prospect of Austrian domination. The Begs and Agas show extreme reserve just now, which leads to the impression that they are already conspiring against their new masters. I do not believe, however, that resistance is, or need, to be apprehended, and most likely when the population of the occupied provinces find out with whom they have to deal, the present anti-Russian feeling will rapidly subside. There can be no question as to the immense gain for Bosnia and the Herzegovina in falling under the Austrian *régime*. What people doubt is that Austria herself derives any benefit thereby.

To compete successfully with Russia for predominating influence beyond the frontier of her actual possessions, Austria must come to some kind of an understanding with the Porte. It has been rumoured from different sources within the last few days that an Austro-Turkish agreement, having more or less in common with the Anglo-Turkish Treaty, was under consideration, and would establish the protectorate of Austria over Turkey in Europe. I cannot assert that such an arrangement was never mooted, but I am in a position to state that at present there is no question of it. If Austria had accepted Turkey as an ally she would have forfeited all claim to the loyalty of her present and future Slav subjects. And yet Count Andrassy cannot be suspected of contemplating an alliance with Russia, whose interests in the Balkan peninsula clash more directly with those of Austria than of any other Power. He returns from Berlin with a plan of his own, which is to enable Austria to dispense with the co-operation either of Russia or the Porte, and to consolidate her position as the Slav Power *par excellence*. Servia is to be gradually drawn under the dependence of Austria. This is not to be done by means of the new railway and commercial treaties between the two Governments, although they may be considered as the prelude to other and more effective measures, and will, at all events, tend to loosen Russia's hold over the Principality. The object in view will require some little time to achieve, and will not be possible of accomplishment before Austria has a firm footing in Bosnia and the Herzegovina. But even then – and supposing, too, that she obtains control over Servia – she will nevertheless have to reckon either with Russia or the Porte for the further development of her influence, as an Eastern State. Her only other alternative would be to remain stationary, which, with such neighbours as she will have, will be impossible.

Besides, when the present dispositions have been carried out, the whole condition of the Monarchy will be changed. The Slavs of Bohemia, Croatia, Slavonia, and Dalmatia, together with the populations of Bosnia, the Herzegovina, and eventually of Servia, will submerge the German, Hungarian, and Polish elements, and the political centre of gravity will no longer be in Vienna or even 'in Pesth'. The danger of such a stake of things is manifest, and could only be averted if Austria secured the goodwill of one of the neighbouring powers.

From this outline of what the occupation scheme really involves, it will be seen that Austria has assumed a far greater responsibility than is generally supposed, and although Europe may rejoice to see that in at least two provinces of Turkey in Europe there is to be good government, Austrians themselves have some reason to complain that it should be at their expense. The dignified and correct attitude of the Poles during the Eastern crisis, and the moderation shown in their appeal to the Congress, inspires one of their critics with the following reflections: 'The true signification of the Polish Memorandum must be looked for in circumstances independent of the document itself; the 30,000 signatures appended to it are all those of Austrian subjects.' In the letter annexed to it, it is stated that the national rights of the Poles are respected in Galicia, and that there only is a collective manifestation possible. This constitutes its most important feature.

An evening journal publishes the following telegram from St. Petersburg, dated 14 July:

In semi-official circles here people give themselves the air of being very contented with the Anglo-Turkish Treaty and with the occupation of Cyprus, since Russia always offered England a share in the spoils of Turkey. Some alarm, however, is felt, the more so as it is evident that Prince Bismarck, having fully paid his debt of gratitude to Russia at the Congress of Berlin, will be more and more exacting if recourse is had to his assistance. Germany has preserved Russia from a humiliation and perhaps from a catastrophe, but the state of feeling in Germany is such that any new encroachment of Russia would meet with a formal resistance. Alarming reports come from several of the Southern towns, and particularly from Kiev. The population there is terrorised by the Nihilists, who exact contributions from all the rich people, the authorities not daring to protect them for fear of occult reprisals.

14 March 1881: Alexander II of Russia is assassinated
ASSASSINATION OF THE EMPEROR OF RUSSIA
ARREST OF SUPPOSED ASSASSINS
SCENE OF THE CRIME
From Our Own Correspondent

The Emperor Alexander has at last fallen a victim to the attempts of the cowardly assassins, who have so often vowed to compass his death. Today his Majesty attended as usual at the Rasvod or military parade, which is held every Sunday in the Riding Room. As he was returning to the Palace, in a closed carriage, accompanied by the Grand Duke Michael, a bomb was thrown at the carriage. The vehicle was terribly shattered and broke down at once. Several of the Cossack escort were severely wounded, and one of them fatally. His Majesty, however, alighted unhurt, and, stepping off the road upon the pavement, he leaned against the parapet of a railing overhanging the Ekaterinen Canal, which runs parallel to the roadway.

While he was standing surveying for a moment the wreck around him, a second shell was hurled with such accuracy as to fall and explode literally between his feet. This time the Emperor fell, having sustained mortal injuries. His lower limbs were fearfully shattered, and the explosion had caused severe internal injuries. Although shockingly maimed and senseless, the Emperor still breathed, and he was conveyed in all haste to the Winter Palace. Surgeons were immediately in attendance, but it was a hopeless case, and at four o'clock in the afternoon, just two hours after the murderous attack was made upon him, the Emperor Alexander II breathed his last.

His son, the Tsarewitch, and all the Princes of the Imperial family in St. Petersburg were present at the deathbed. Lord Dufferin, the English Ambassador, and many of the representatives of foreign States, had already arrived at the Palace when the sad news was announced. As soon as the Emperor had expired, the Tsarewitch drove home to his own Palace at the Anitchkin Bridge, and was greatly cheered on his route by the crowds which thronged the Nevsky. One or two persons who were near the scene of the crime, and are believed to have been implicated in its perpetration, have been arrested.

I have just visited the scene of today's terrible crime. On one side of the road is the Ekaterinen Canal, and on the other the low wall of the garden of the Palace of the Grand Duchess Helena. No damage has been done to the wall or to the railings on the canal bank, but the houses on the far side of the canal, at a distance of one hundred yards, have had all their upper windows smashed. I have learnt that the Grand Duke Michael was in the carriage with the Emperor, and the first bomb was thrown from behind after the carriage had passed. It injured only the back of the vehicle.

The escort was as usual formed of the body guard or convoy. Several of these Cossacks were wounded, and the violence of the explosion naturally threw the mounted men into confusion. His Majesty's carriage has, however, latterly been always followed by a fast sleigh, conveying a superior officer of police, and this officer, witnessing the whole occurrence, sprang from his sledge, and immediately arrested the individual who threw the first shell. Whilst he was interrogating him, the Emperor, who had alighted, moved as if towards the police-officer and his prisoner. The latter, whose thoughts were evidently intent on one object only, immediately drew a revolver and presented it at the Tsar, but the police-officer was sufficiently quick to be able to dash it from his hand before he had time to draw the trigger. This danger was, however, no sooner averted than a second individual, who in the confusion had been unnoticed, approached the Emperor. The

Tsar had now stepped back on the pavement, and the assassin threw another shell, with fatal accuracy, between his feet.

Uttering a cry for help, the Emperor fell senseless to the earth. His escort, who had by this time recovered from their first surprise, promptly seized the second culprit, and the unconscious, though still breathing, body of the Emperor was rapidly conveyed to the Winter Palace in the open sledge of the police-officer.

As far as I can learn, there were five persons killed besides his Majesty. It would seem that two of the escort, two bystanders, and a child which was being carried in the arms of a passing woman, perished in the two explosions. Of course, the news of this awful catastrophe has spread like wildfire through the capital, and consternation and alarm are depicted on every countenance; at the same time perfect quiet prevails. The authorities have, I understand, taken every needful precaution. Externally there is nothing to attract public attention beyond the Imperial flags waving mournfully half-mast high, and the numerous Cossack patrols around the Winter Palace.

1 April 1889: The Eiffel Tower opens prior to the Paris Exhibition
PARIS DAY BY DAY
From Our Own Correspondent

Flags are now waving from the summit of the Eiffel Tower in token that it has at last attained its full height of three hundred metres, and this afternoon a salute of twenty-one shots was fired from the look-out on the top in honour of the event. The lift is expected to be installed and in working order by 20 April, so in the course of a few weeks from this date the public will be able to enjoy the marvellous view which is to be obtained from this modern Tower of Babel. M. Eiffel is certainly to be congratulated on the result of his plucky undertaking, for his Tower has risen foot by foot without the slightest hitch, completely demonstrating the correctness of his calculations. It is a wonderful piece of engineering, and now that it is finished the whole thing looks so simple that it seems surprising that such an attempt was never made before; yet the amount of study required in planning the construction of the loftiest monument ever erected by Man must have been enormous. As it is, M. Eiffel's enterprise has now won unstinted praise even from those who at the outset most severely criticised the scheme. The Tower will be the prominent feature – in more senses than one – of an Exhibition rich in countless marvels. This afternoon it was scanned with even more than usual interest by the crowds that were lounging in the Tuileries Gardens and in the Champs Elysées in this mild but showery weather, for thousands are eagerly awaiting its formal inauguration to enjoy a bird's-eye view of Paris, the surrounding country, and of districts stretching many leagues beyond it.

The ceremony of hoisting the tricoloured flag on the summit of Eiffel's Tower was performed by the constructor himself, who was accompanied to the top platform by M. Berger and several Municipal Councillors and engineers. The flag is of voluminous dimensions, but seen from *terra firma* it seems but a filmy and flickering speck. It is inscribed with large gold letters 'R. F.', and when it was run up a speech was made by M. Contamin, a Government engineer, who complimented M. Eiffel on his success. Then Champagne was brought out, and M. Berger pledged a bumper to the constructor of the Tower and his workmen. The President of the Municipal Council called for various *vivats* in honour of France, the Republic, and M. Eiffel, and the calls were responded to with alacrity. Then everybody went down to the Champ-de-Mars, where M. Tirard, President of the Council and Minister of Commerce, and other officials awaited them. Luncheon was served to everybody, including the workmen in their *blouses*, and when the creature comforts had been disposed of, M. Eiffel read a little discourse thanking everybody, and announcing that a tablet would be placed on the Tower and inscribed with the names of all who had helped in its construction from the beginning. The workmen here cried out '*Vive Eiffel!*' and '*Vive la République!*' M. Tirard congratulated the ingenious constructor on the completion of his work, which, he said, would soon be admired by all Frenchmen and by foreigners from every land. Finally, the Minister announced, amidst applause, that he would recommend M. Eiffel for the grade of Officer of the Legion of Honour. The ceremony was terminated by the presentation of several large bouquets of flowers to M. Eiffel – not, however, by members of the fair sex, but by some of his own horny-handed workmen; the honest fellows being overcome with emotion, partly caused by their copious libations of the 'rosy', and partly by heartfelt gratitude towards a considerate and popular chief.

Tonight the Boulevards were at their best and brightest – for the first time, it may be said, during the present season. The showers which fell intermittently in the morning had completely cleared away, and although the sky was a little murky, the dark vapours overhead did not mar the brilliancy of the terrestrial scene. The long *façade* of the Grand Hotel, which has been freshly whitened, fairly gleamed above the myriads of gas-jets and illuminated semi-circular signposts which pointed the way to the various places of pleasure. All the principal Theatres, with, the exception of the Opéra, all the Circuses and *Café concerts*, were open, but the absolute mildness of the night made many people remain out of doors to lounge about or to sit on the 'terraces', as they are called, of the glittering cafés, just as if we were in the height of the Canicular Season.

Final arrangements for the brilliant inauguration of the approaching Exhibition and of the Centenary of the Great Revolution in Paris and Versailles have now been made by the Municipal authorities. On 5 May, the date of the opening of the States-General, all the Senators, Deputies, and official personages of the Department of the Seine-et-Oise, will assemble in Versailles before the old Hotel des Menus Plaisirs – now a barrack – and a tablet will be placed on the *façade* of the building to commemorate the ceremony. President Carnot will drive into the old Royal borough through the Avenue de Versailles, and will proceed to the Hall of Mirrors in the palace of all the Glories, where speeches will be made. Luncheon will be served in the Battle-Gallery, after which the big fountains will be set in motion in the Park for the delectation of the President and the public. In the evening Versailles will be illuminated. The Exhibition *Féte* of Inauguration will begin on the evening of 6 May, when the vast iron constructions on the Champ-de-Mars, Eiffel's Tower, the Gardens and the outlying portions of the Exhibition will be illuminated by means of gas-jets and Bengal-lights. A boat Carnival will take place on the Seine between the Île Saint-Louis and Grenelle Eyot, the bridges and river banks being ornamented with long festoons of lamps and lanterns. Fireworks and Bengal-lights will be used to envelope the Towers of the Trocadéro, the cascades and the artificial fountains in brilliant luminosity. Especial preparations have been made for a big torchlight procession, in which it is expected that 15,000 men of the Paris garrison will take part. The procession, headed by or interspersed with brass and fife and drum bands, local *fanfares* and choral societies, will start from the Trocadéro cascade, cross the Iéna Bridge, and proceed round the great Machinery Hall on the Champ-de-Mars. The troops will then march into the École Militaire, where refreshments will be provided. Among the latest features of the Exhibition will be a Bell pavilion similar to that which figured at the Exhibition of 1867. The peals will be rung by some of the ablest *carillonneurs* from the North of France.

19 March 1890: Kaiser Wilhelm II 'drops the pilot' as Bismarck is forced from office
RESIGNATION OF PRINCE BISMARCK ACCEPTED
THE EMPEROR'S POLICY
From Our Berlin Correspondent

Prince Bismarck formally handed in his resignation as Chancellor of the Empire, President of the Prussian Ministry, and other posts to Kaiser Wilhelm this morning, and, as I learn from an authoritative source, his Majesty has accepted it. For the past few weeks readers of *The Daily Telegraph* will have been prepared for this momentous event, for although certain authorities have denied that the Prince would retire from his post as Chancellor, I have repeatedly told you that this was inevitable. What was regarded as imminent last night is today an accomplished fact.

The news created no slight sensation in the highest spheres of Society this morning, where it was thought that the frictions between Kaiser and Kanzler had been got rid of, and that a *modus vivendi* – for a certain period, at least – had been arrived at, but on the Bourse, although there was a little depression at first, a sense of security supervened, and there was neither a panic nor even a want of confidence in the future.

The main causes of the inevitable breach are, as I learn from a thoroughly well informed source, the following: 'Kaiser Wilhelm is determined to rule more in accordance with the wishes of his people. There is no longer the slightest ground for the belief in an alleged estrangement between his Majesty and the Empress Frederick, who has fully regained that influence which she was said to have quite lost. This, together with the fact that others who run counter to Prince Bismarck's views internal policy have gained his Majesty's ear, was in the highest degree disagreeable to Prince Bismarck. Further, the composition of the New Reichstag has made it impossible for the Prince to continue to govern. His efforts to effect an understanding with Dr. Windthorst proved abortive. Such attempts were really made, despite, the repeated contradictions.'

The reports that the whole Ministry had also tendered its resignation are, at the moment I am writing, considered groundless – in fact, there is, *à priori*, no reason why they should do so.

The distinction recently conferred on Herr von Bötticher was intended and accepted as a special mark of confidence. The letter that his Majesty wrote to his Minister was couched in the most cordial terms, and the Kaiser expressed his hope that he might long count upon the service of his faithful servant. Herr von Bötticher, in his reply, consented to do so, and there is no doubt that he will remain at his post and become President of the Ministry.

I learn, however, that Professor Händl – a Radical Deutsch-Freisinnige – and Herr Miquel, the National-Liberal leader, will most probably receive portfolios, thus replacing two of the present Ministers. The Kaiser's choice of the above-mentioned gentlemen is regarded as a proof of his desire to attend to the wishes of the people, and in so doing his Majesty cannot be too highly applauded for his Constitutional principles.

The reason of the placid attitude preserved by the Bourse today was the hope and belief that Count Herbert Bismarck would remain as Foreign Minister. It is true that his Excellency has been observed during the last few days to be unusually serious in his demeanour, and it has been supposed he would retire with his father; moreover, he actually hinted that he would do so a day or two ago; but it is nevertheless hoped he will remain in order that the country should not completely break with those who have so long held the threads of German foreign policy in their hands. Although, however, there is a great deal of excitement today in all the Government offices, it is admitted that nobody can prevent Prince Bismarck from retiring if he chooses to do so, since his reasons for withdrawing from public life must be such that he cannot resist them. His absence from the Chancellorship, however, as I am authoritatively informed by a German statesman who has close relations with the Prince, will lead to no change whatever in Germany's foreign policy.

The world of the *haute finance* in Berlin is not in the least anxious about the future. The leading bankers have great confidence in the statesmanlike qualities of Kaiser Wilhelm, and believe that he is accepting the inevitable – the loss of his valued servant – because the people are crying for another system of Government. It is curious to listen to the reasons why the Conservatives have abandoned the Great Chancellor. They accuse him of having brought about the 'dreadful state of things' now prevailing in Germany, because he permitted Universal Suffrage, the claim of the peasants to move from the soil on which they were born, and the unlimited right to hold public meetings. The two last reasons are almost too puerile. There is no country in Europe except Russia where the holding of public meetings is so restricted, and any attempt to interfere with the right of the peasants to migrate.to towns, which they have, indeed, not possessed so very many years, would inevitably provoke a Revolution – in fact, could the Conservatives have their own will in domestic politics they would simply upset the Monarchy.

As the Chancellor's resignation has not yet been gazetted in the *Reichsanzeiger*, the *North German Gazette* contents itself tonight with quoting extracts from the morning papers. Of the Liberal Press, the *Vossische Zeitung* writes that, in consideration of the exceptional position held by the mighty statesman who has just resigned, it will not be easy to accommodate oneself to the new state of affairs. The Liberal party had never worshipped Prince Bismarck; it was always in strife with him, but it will not refuse him the Crown of Glory. With Blood and Iron he cured moribund Germany; with a hand of iron he upset thrones – a good Revolutionist, having much in common with Cavour, but wanting in uniformity and permanence of a general view of things. He entertained Liberal opinions whilst hating Liberalism. He brought about National Unity, disregarding the divine right of Princes, but refused to give the people and their representatives the decisive influence they demanded. He returned in his old age to his old mode of thought – hence his loss of power. It is characteristic that he did not fall owing to Parliamentary Opposition, but owing to the resistance of the Crown, the Sovereign in this case figuring as the champion of popular claims.

Prince Bismarck was the greatest diplomatist of his age, but Prince Bismarck was also the diplomatist in home politics. He regarded his opponents as his enemies. He not only tried to persuade and convince them, but also to destroy them. This embittered Parliamentary struggles. He despised men; and did not believe in their virtue – hence his bitterness against former friends; hence his resentment of every attack in the Press; hence this distrust of certain personages who might obtain influence and his complaints of friction. Many a talented and distinguished statesman ceased to work with him only to reap the reproach of want of Patriotism. He clung to the repressive measures of the past; one day he advocated Free Trade, the next high tariffs; he tried the *Culturkampf,* and then an alliance with the Pope; and all his many changes ended in general discontent. It was he who originated modem social politics, and it is this policy which has brought about his fall. He began financial reform, and could not follow it up. He was the author of the Imperial Rescript which declared that Ministers only had to carry out the policy of the Sovereign, and now he retires because it is the Kaiser, and not the Minister, who is to decide. But where light is, shadows are also to be found. Prince Bismarck has deserved so much of the German Nation that their gratitude will not be found wanting, He has always maligned Liberalism, but liberals will express their warmest recognition of him. They admire not only his deeds, but his personal character. His name will always shine in history.

Of the Conservative Press I may mention that the *Kreuz Zeitung* attributes the Chancellor's fall not only to differences of opinion with the Kaiser on domestic policy, but to the existence of diametrically opposed views on Colonial matters in Africa. This is not unlikely, as it is known that the young Kaiser lays much value in the future of German power in the Dark Continent. The *National Zeitung* says: 'Germany and Prussia are on the eve of a new era. The grand period of our history, which after the preliminary period from 1862 to 1876 began with the last-named year, is closed. Another is beginning, and Germany and Prussia will enter upon it with that confidence which is rooted in the trust the nation places in itself and in the Kaiser. It would be the worst kind of gratitude to the great statesman who is about to retire into private life, after having accomplished so much, if Prince Bismarck's resignation were to be contemplated with faintheartedness. He would, indeed, have created little if he had only united the nation in such a way that it could not continue its work without him. No, the gratitude of the German nation towards the renovator of Germany – the gratitude which fills the hearts of millions and millions of Germans at this decisive hour – will be best displayed if Fürst Bismarck can witness – we will hope for many years – the flourishing prosperity of Germany. Other men will continue his work with other talents, other methods, but with the same aim. But Prince Bismarck's influence will continue for generations, so that his spirit will not cease to determine all our questions for many years to come; and, apart from this, Prince Bismarck, though resigning his offices, will remain amongst us, and his counsel will always be in the reach of the Kaiser, should the state of Europe render it necessary to act on it. Germany will still be in the future the guarantee of the peace of the world. Thus foreign countries may rest assured. If he was the representative of any sentiment of the German nation, the First German Chancellor was the incorporation of this.'

In the Prussian Diet it was stated confidently today that General von Caprivi, who recently came up to Berlin, was destined to be the successor of Prince Bismarck. Nothing, however, can be said with certainty on this point, and Minister von Bötticher is still spoken of as the Chancellor's provisional successor. Count Waldersee, whose name has also been mentioned, will scarcely be transferred from his post as Chief of the General Staff. The Count is about to proceed on leave to Italy for change of air, having recently had an attack of influenza. He will be absent about a month. Prince Bismarck, who will celebrate his seventy-fifth birthday on 1 April, visited the members of the Labour Conference during their luncheon pause, and appeared to be in the best of spirits.

24 December 1894: The conviction for espionage of Captain Alfred Dreyfus plays second fiddle to seasonal hopping for the *Telegraph*'s Paris Correspondent

PARIS DAY BY DAY
FRENCH OFFICER CONVICTED OF TREASON
From Our Own Correspondent

It was utterly useless to try to meander at a business pace along the main boulevards this afternoon. Those who were in a hurry frequently found themselves brought to a full stop by the thick throngs of humanity clustering around the toy booths. Nearly all these ephemeral constructions for the sale of New Year trifles were open today, and attracted a good deal of attention if not custom. Among comparatively original exhibits are miniature field-pieces, from which it is possible to fire plugs of wood at cardboard forts; gyroscopes warranted to give youth a notion of the rotatory motion of the globe, and age a comprehension of the mysteries of centrifugal force; pugilists engaged in the noble art; aerial ships; a magnetic apparatus recalling Franco-Russian sympathies; macaws moving on their perches; ingenious machines worked by spirits of wine; dolls called here after Miss Helyett, but known under another name in London just now; bull-baiters and *horloger des petits gourmets*, with chocolate pendulums. These toys proved to be the most interesting of the collections inspected today by the boulevards crowds, and other annual novelties will no doubt soon be on view. The weather was all that could be desired for the opening of the fair. The extraordinary mildness permitted people not only to linger long before the *baraques*, but also to sit outside the cafés. There was even some sunshine in the early part of the day, and not a drop of rain fell to mar the enjoyment of the external amusements offered to the eager crowds of citizens, who slowly sauntered by the booths, lining both sides of the great central thoroughfares of Paris.

Alfred Dreyfus, captain in the 14th Regiment of Artillery, on the staff of the War Office, has been found guilty of having supplied a foreign Power with a certain number of secret documents regarding the national defence, and has been sentenced to transportation to, and imprisonment for life in, a fortress, and also to military degradation. Such is the result of the trial by court-martial, which closed last evening, and although this erewhile brilliant and promising officer was widely believed to have turned traitor to his country this confirmation of the terrible suspicion has produced a great and painful sensation. The man's name is execrated today in every household in France, and the cry of disappointment that the death penalty for such a crime should have been abolished is general. Such a case of treason had never been known in this country since Bazaine betrayed it in the terrible year.

As the hour approached when the trial should terminate yesterday the Crowd in the Rue du Cherche-Midi assumed formidable proportions, and intense excitement was displayed. When the proceedings were resumed at one o'clock in the afternoon, Maître Demange delivered his address for the defence, which was continued, with a brief interval during which the sitting was suspended, until half-past five. What the learned lawyer said has not been suffered to transpire, but it may be assumed that he merely pleaded for mercy. Only ten minutes sufficed for the reply of Commandant Brisset, representing the Government, and the barrister was then allowed to make a few more remarks. Nothing, however, could be more significant than the extreme brevity of Commandant Brisset's observations on the case. Then, while the officers composing the military tribunal withdrew to consider their decision, the prisoner was removed from the court to the infirmary, running down the staircase and along the passage in the hope of escaping the crowd which had gathered there while awaiting admission to the hall, for now that the decision was to be proclaimed the public were to have access to the court, which had been denied them ever since the preliminary proceedings had been entered on. Presently the veto was withdrawn, and in a moment the hall was filled. The officers were still absent, but Maître Demange was seated in his place, apparently overwhelmed with fatigue and absorbed by painful thoughts. It was seven o'clock when the cry of 'Present arms' rang through the hall, and while the small guard saluted the members of the court-martial returned. Dreyfus had not been led back, there being an express regulation that the prisoner shall not be present while the decision is read out, so that any compromising display of irritation on his part may be avoided.

A solemn silence prevailed as all rose to their feet, and then the President read out the sentence, beginning with the words, 'In the name of the French people', at which he and the other six officers composing the tribunal raised their hands to their képis with the military salute. 'The first Court-Martial of the Military Government of Paris,' he continued, 'had met, and the President had put the following question: "Is M. Alfred Dreyfus, Captain in the 14th Regiment of Artillery, Staff Probationer attached to the Ministry of War, guilty of having in 1894 procured for a foreign Power a certain number of secret documents connected with the National Defence, and of having been engaged in intrigues or in communication with that Power or its agents to induce it to commit hostile acts, or to undertake war against France or to procure it the means of doing so". The votes having been taken separately, beginning with the lowest grade, and the Colonel presiding having given his opinion last, the answer has been "Yes" with a unanimity of votes, the accused is guilty.' Then a cry of '*Vive la Patrie*' was uttered by someone in the hall amid intense emotion, but the President took no notice of it, and went on with his reading: 'Therefore and unanimously the First Conseil de Guerre condemns *le nommé* Alfred Dreyfus to perpetual transportation in a fortress, and condemns him to military degradation.' Then followed the reading of the different clauses of the Penal Code on which the sentence was based, and in which it was set forth that in cases where the death penalty was abolished it should be replaced by transportation to a fortress 'designated by law outside the Continental territory of the Republic. The persons transported will enjoy there all the liberty compatible with the necessity of guarding them securely. This done, the President asked Commandant Brisset to see that the sentence was at once communicated to the prisoner, in the presence of the guard, and to inform him that he was legally allowed twenty-four hours to apply for a revision of the sentence. 'The sitting is at an end,' added Colonel Maurel, and he left the court with his colleagues, while the public followed their example.

A few minutes afterwards Dreyfus was in the court, hearing the reading of the sentence by the clerk. He betrayed no emotion. Outside the building, in the Rue du Cherche-Midi, a dense crowd, indignant and menacing, had gathered, and a strong force of police had been told off to clear the road. All wanted to have a glimpse of the prisoner. 'We shall cry "*Vive la France*" when he passes,' exclaimed a workman.

'No; he is not worth that – the villain!' replied a comrade. At last Dreyfus was perceived leaving the building on his way to the prison in his artillery uniform. He hurried along so fast that the two officers who led him could hardly keep pace with him. There was a rush in his direction, in spite of the police, and an explosion of fury would have been witnessed if the prison-door had not suddenly closed with a bang, leaving Dreyfus safely within the courtyard. As has been explained, the prisoner can appeal, but in these cases the sentence can only be cancelled if there is a flaw in the procedure. Dreyfus had a consultation with his counsel this afternoon. Transportation to a fortress means removal to the Ducos Peninsula, in New Caledonia, settled by law twenty-two years ago. If, as is taken for granted, the decision is confirmed by the Conseil de Revision, a Military Court of Cassation, Dreyfus will undergo the sentence of military degradation, probably, in the large quadrangle of the École Militaire, his sword being broken and the insignia of his rank wrenched off in presence of the assembled troops, and he will then be removed to the Ile de Ré, pending his departure for New Caledonia, where his wife and family can join him. He can apply for a grant of land, and if his conduct has been good for five years he may be sent to another place.

Now an outcry is being raised that such a crime should be punished thus, and not with death. It is defined by the law as 'political', and people contend that the law ought to be better provided for dealing with such cases. At a court-martial held in the Gironde yesterday, a soldier was sentenced to death for spitting in the direction of the President and for flinging his képi at the representative of the Government. This is bad enough, in all conscience, but people are arguing that high treason is even worse, and that there ought not to be two weights and two measures. The Military Council of Revision will meet on Tuesday to consider the appeal made by Dreyfus against the sentence passed on him.

7 October 1897: Winston Churchill reports anonymously from a campaign in the Indian North-West Frontier
THE WAR IN THE INDIAN HIGHLANDS
By A Young Officer
Khar, 6 September

The first turning to the right, after crossing the Malakand Pass, leads to Khar. The road winds round the sides of the hills – is sometimes embanked and at others scarped out of the steep slopes – until, by a gradual descent, the fertile plain of the Lower Swat River is reached. The distance is about four miles, but in spite of the shortness of the way, and of the cowed and humble attitude of the natives in this valley, the regulations as to traversing it are strict. Individuals must be accompanied by an escort. Whenever possible they will arrange to go in couples, and in every case arms must be carried. Isolated instances of fanaticism have to be guarded against, and it is only through the precautions observed that no accident has so far occurred.

Riding along this road with an officer who took part in the recent operations, I learned many details of the fight. Every rock, every hill, every nullah had its story. Here their 'snipers' lay for two days firing into the Guides' camp. There was the ravine up which, they crawled; here was 'where we charged and chased them right up to those hills over there'; and, again, 'there is where poor So-and-So was killed'. On the left a square mud fort, its walls partly destroyed, and pierced by several ragged round holes, marked the spot where the picket of the 31st were rushed, and nearly all killed or wounded. The tribesmen made the holes in the wall, and broke in. The soldiers ran first to one hole and then to another to repel the attack, but it was like caulking a sieve, and they were overwhelmed.

At length a turn of the road displayed the Swat Valley – a broad, level plain, terminated by the hills on which the fort of Chakdara stands. The camp of the 2nd Brigade filled the foreground. Rows and rows of tents and lines of horses marked the streets of the canvas town.

A few standards, captured from the enemy, and the smoke of many fires, lighted to cook the evening meal, showed that it was occupied by soldiers. A group of khaki-clad figures, playing desultory football, on one side, and the smooth grass of the polo ground on the other, attested the nationality of its occupants. As we progressed we caught up long lines of camels, five or six on a string returning ungracefully from being watered to their pickets for the night. They walked silently on their padded feet. Whatever may be the beauties of the wild camel of the desert, they are not shared by the transport variety of the species. The air of sad disgust, which their faces wear seems to show the 'oont' appreciates his ugliness.

Within the camp everything was clean and orderly. The pipeclay of peace was gone, but in its place was the practical and businesslike regularity of service – a regularity which sometimes admits of a judicious irregularity. We found our way to a mess, and, dismounting, accepted a glass – a pewter glass – of the beverage of the British officer – whisky and soda, alas! without the ice which in India can alone make life worth living and drinks worth drinking. As we sat and chatted, the day drew to a close. Gradually the sun sank below the mountains, and the valley became plunged in shadows. A grey mist rising at either end obscured and contracted the view. The rugged tops of the hills still caught the sunlight for a little, but minute by minute the shadows rose, and presently it was quite dark.

The early stage in this letter at which night has come on might favour the supposition that the arrival of darkness was unexpected and inadvertent. I hasten to correct so erroneous an impression. It is when the curtain of night has descended upon the scene and when the actors and properties are removed from view that the spectator may amuse himself by considering the morality, the objects, and performance of the drama. Let us, then, begin as we hope to end, with the enemy. In the examination of a people it is always best to take their virtues first. This clears the ground and leaves sufficient time for the investigation of their predominant characteristics. The Swatis, Bonerwals, Mohmands, and other frontier tribes with whom the Malakand Field Force is at present engaged are brave and warlike. Their courage has been abundantly displayed in the present campaign. They charge home, and nothing but a bullet stops their career. Their swordsmanship – neglecting guards – concerns itself only with cuts, and, careless of what injury they may receive, they devote themselves to the destruction of their opponents.

In the selection of positions they exhibit considerable military skill, and as skirmishers their use of cover and preservation of order entitle them to much praise. It is mournful to be compelled to close the catalogue of their virtues thus early, but the closest scrutiny of the facts which have been placed before me has resulted in no further discovery in this direction. From year to year their life is one of feud and strife. They plough with a sword at their sides. Every field has its protecting tower, to which the agriculturalist can hurry at the approach of a stranger. Successful murder – whether by open force or treachery – is the surest road to distinction among them. A recent writer has ascribed to these people those high family virtues which simple races so often possess. The consideration of one frequent fact compels me reluctantly to abandon even this hope. Their principal article of commerce is their women – wives and daughters – who are exchanged for rifles. This degradation of mind is unrelieved by a single elevated sentiment. Their religion is the most miserable fanaticism, in which cruelty, credulity, and immorality are equally represented. Their holy men – the Mullahs – prize as their chief privilege a sort of '*droit de seigneur*'. It is impossible to imagine a lower type of beings or a more dreadful state of barbarism.

I am aware of the powerful influence of climate upon character. But the hill men cannot even plead the excuse of a cold and barren land for their barbarism. The valleys they inhabit are fertile and often beautiful. Once the spots where their squalid huts now stand were occupied by thriving cities, and the stone 'sangars' from which they defy their foes, are built on the terraces which nourished the crops of a long forgotten civilisation. Everywhere are the relics of the old Buddhists on whom these fierce tribes, thrown out of that birthplace of nations, Central Asia, descended. Their roads, their temples, and their ruins have alone survived. All else has been destroyed in that darkness which surrounds those races whose type is hardly on the fringe of humanity. But it may be urged: 'However degraded and barbarous these people may be, they have a right to live unmolested on the soil that their fathers conquered.' 'They have attacked your posts,' says the Little Englander, carefully disassociating himself from anything British, 'but why did you ever put your posts there?' To answer this question it is necessary to consider the whole matter from a wider point of view than the Swat Valley affords.

Starting with the assumption that our Empire in India is worth holding, and admitting the possibility that others besides ourselves might wish to possess it, it obviously becomes our duty to adopt measures for its safety. It is a question of a line of defence. The Indus is now recognised by all strategists as being useless for this purpose. The most natural way of preventing an enemy from entering a house is to hold the doors and windows, and the general consensus of opinion is that to secure India it is necessary to hold the passes of the mountains. With this view small military posts have been built along the frontier. The tribes, whose territories adjoin, have not been interfered with. Their independence has been respected, and their degradation undisturbed. More than this, the influence of the flag that flies from the fort on the hill has stimulated the trade of the valley, and increased the wealth of its inhabitants. Were the latter amenable to logical reasoning, the improvement in their condition and the strength of their adversaries would have convinced them of the folly of an outbreak. But in a land of fanatics common sense does not exist.

The defeat of the Greeks sent an electric thrill through Islam. The Ameer – a negative conductor – is said to have communicated it to the 'Mullahs', and they generated the disturbance among the frontier tribes. The ensuing flash has kindled a widespread conflagration. This must now be dealt with courageously and intelligently. It is useless, and often dangerous, to argue with an Afghan. Not because he is degraded, not because we covet his valleys, but because his notions interfere with the safety of our Empire, he must be crushed. There are many in England, though they live amid the prosaic surroundings of a highly developed country, where economics and finance reign supreme, who yet regard, with pleasure and with pride, the wide dominions of which they are the trustees. These, when they read that savages have been killed for attacking British posts and menacing the security of our possessions, will not hesitate to say, with firmness and without reserve: 'So perish all who do the like again'.

19 May 1900: The *Telegraph* is one of the first with the news that Mafeking has been relieved, and London goes wild
RELIEF OF MAFEKING
OFFICIAL REPORT FROM PRETORIA
BRITISH COLUMN ARRIVES

At last! Mafeking has been relieved. Baden-Powell and his heroic garrison are safe; their long privations are at an end; and the Union Jack is still flying over the little frontier town. Lord Roberts has nobly kept his word, thanks to the dauntless and invincible courage of the troops composing the column of relief. He asked the garrison to hold out until 18 May. True to his promise, succour arrived on that very day, and the news reached London last night after a day of anxious waiting and eager hope deferred hour by hour. It was just seventeen minutes past nine o'clock when the message containing the glorious news began to come over the tape from Reuter's Agency, and *The Daily Telegraph* had the felicity of being the first to convey the intelligence to the public by means of a placard in the front window of this office. It was greeted with cries of joy from the passers-by. Cheers were raised, and a crowd instantly collected. People gave vet to their long pent-up enthusiasm for the defender of Mafeking, who has captured the heart of the nation and Empire. Strangers shook one another by the hand; staid folk forgot their staidness and shouted their loudest; the infection of the cheering spread like wildfire, and the news was carried through the streets of

London like a flash. The bitterest enemies of Mr. Kruger sincerely professed their abiding gratitude to him for allowing the news to go forth from Pretoria that the guns of the relief column had heavily shelled the Boer laagers, and that Commandant Snyman had abandoned the siege. The Boer President might have suppressed the tidings had he chosen, and kept the British nation in suspense for forty-eight hours, until word had got through by other channels, and for this welcome candour the London crowd gave him hearty thanks. Until late in the night the sound of tumultuous happiness was heard, in the West and East alike. Pall-mall and Piccadilly-circus were almost impassable for hours. Vast processions marched up and down the main thoroughfares. At nearly every theatre and music hall the performances were interrupted to convey to the audience the long-hoped-for news, which was greeted with torrents of cheering and the singing of the National Anthem. Flags appeared as if by magic, and a few clubs where illuminations had been get ready for the great event became instantly ablaze with light. It was a scene which none privileged to witness it will ever forget – the capital of the British Empire rejoicing that, after 218 days of siege, Mafeking and its heroes, military and civilians alike, were once more tasting the sweets of freedom.

As soon as the news was received in London it was at once communicated to the Queen at Windsor Castle – where the Prime Minister, whose son, Lord Edward Cecil, is in Mafeking, was dining with her Majesty – and to the Prince of Wales at Marlborough House. It will be seen that though the War Office authorities were still at a late hour without confirmation of the news from Lord Roberts, Mr. Frank Baden-Powell, a brother of the gallant Colonel, received a telegram from a Dutch friend in Pretoria conveying the tidings of the relief of the garrison. Amid all the demonstrations last night the London crowd, always animated by a more human instinct than any other crowd in the world, had a stirring and chivalrous thought. It found its way to the house of Mrs. Baden-Powell, the mother of the hero of Mafeking. The ovation in St. George's-place was one of the most moving features of a memorable night.

About twenty minutes past nine the news was received at the Mansion House and, a momentary scrutiny having shown that there could be no doubt as to its authenticity, the device which had been made for the happy occasion was at once displayed above the terrace and in front of the massive columns. There were already a good many people in the neighbourhood, who had either heard rumours or were merely waiting on the off-chance of the important announcement being made last night, and a loud and lusty cheer greeted the exhibition of the large portrait of Colonel Baden-Powell, beneath which were the words, in conspicuous letters, 'Mafeking is Relieved'. The impulse started at this point radiated with astonishing rapidity, and the Mansion House drew to itself wandering bands, scattered parties, and stray individuals, as a magnet collects filings. In the course of a few minutes, the square in front of the Lord Mayor's official residence was thronged by an eager and delighted multitude, and still fresh accessions of strength poured in, till the people were packed from wall to wall, almost like herrings in a barrel, and late arrivals had to be content with a position on the fringe of the gathering, which was more comfortable, though removed from the perfervid and contagious warmth of spirit that characterised the centre of the mass. A scene to be remembered – and remembered with a vividness of vision – for ever and ever.

Dealers in bunting seemed to spring from the ground, and their wares were fought for, or would have been, if every unit of the crowd had not been in too good a temper to grumble at anything, or to be cross with anyone. The Union Jacks spread among the host, and were waved aloft. One agile fellow climbed the tall post which supports an electric lamp opposite the Mansion House, and from this position of eminence slashed at the air with so much vigour that he might have been engaged in inflicting a flagellation upon Mr. Kruger, while the crowd looked up at him and roared – and roared again – with delight. Those who had not been able to obtain flags, or who felt that so great an event called for a more substantial sacrifice on their part, hurled their hats, regardless of the glossiest sheen, high into the air, or waved them above their heads so recklessly that collisions between them were the rule rather than the exception. Handshaking was commonplace, and many men flung their arms round one another in an abandonment of joy; while girls submitted to the good-natured embraces of those against whom they were casually hustled without a word of anger or remonstrance. All this while a dull roar rose and ebbed without over ceasing, like the drone of bagpipes, while out of it, from time to time, sprung the National Anthem and 'Rule Britannia', to be bawled with all the strength of thousands of healthy lungs.

Meantime the Lord Mayor had come out upon the terrace, and his appearance was the signal for still louder cheering, still more frantic waving of hats, flags, handkerchiefs, and everything which possessed the quality of being waveable. The sight which greeted his Lordship's vision as he stepped between the columns in response to loud calls for a speech was a vast sea of upturned faces – a sea in which there was surge, and billow, and ripple, as the crowd swayed and swung – a sea, too, that bellowed as the fiercest breakers that ever beat on a rock-bound coast. Flags tossed on the surface, and hats, supported on the muzzles of rifles – which had somehow found their way to the spot in considerable numbers – were projected aloft, like the swollen heads of mooring-posts. It was all very well for the people to cry 'Speech!', but where was the Stentor to make his voice heard above that din? In vain did his Lordship wave his hat deprecatingly downwards; in vain did he exploit all the resources of that sign language which came instinctively to him in his emergency. Those who saw him held back their swelling enthusiasm for a moment, but those who saw him not sent up redoubled shouts, that no one might think that the collective energies were flagging. At last, in what would elsewhere have been a Pandemonium, but here was a lull in the storm, his Lordship began a short speech, every phrase of which was punctuated by a tempest of cheering, and which was almost exactly bisected by the fervent singing of 'Rule Britannia'.

The Lord Mayor's words were as follows: 'I wish the music of your cheers could reach Mafeking. For seven long, weary months a handful has been opposed by a horde. We never doubted what the end would be. British pluck and valour, when used in the right cause, must triumph. The heart of everyone vibrates with intense loyalty and enthusiasm, and the conscience of every one of you asserts that we have fought a righteous and a just cause. We have fought for our most glorious traditions of equality and freedom – not for ourselves alone, but for all those nations which have clustered in South Africa, practically under the protection of the British flag.'

His Lordship, who had uttered these few words in a tone of voice which must have seriously imperilled his vocal organs, then called for 'Three cheers for Baden-Powell'. This demand was met by one prolonged and deafening note, and the same was the case when the Lord Mayor asked that a similar compliment might be paid to Lord Roberts. His valediction to the crowd was as follows: 'The people in Bloemfontein and Mafeking are now singing "God Save the Queen". Now, sing it for yourselves.' The National Anthem was rolled out like thunder, and the chief officer of the City stepped back from the edge of the terrace.

The people, who had so far been held in some kind of restraint by the presence of constituted authority in so august a form, were now left to ease their bursting bosoms according to their own devices. For some time longer, the Mansion House was faced by dense crowds, who never let many seconds elapse without raising the strains of some loyal or patriotic melody. Gradually small bands detached themselves, and marched in procession along Cheapside, Cannon-street, Fleet-street, the Strand, and all the main avenues of the City, cheering and singing as they tramped. As the night drew towards morning, and as dried-up throats had again and again to be relaxed with the beverage of each man's choice (which was not inevitably spiritless), the frenzy and turbulence of the rejoicings increased rather than diminished. Even the stern virtue of the constable unbent. In the bars and saloons of the City district perpetual choruses were kept up, and tumblers and globes were shivered into atoms by beaters of time, without proprietors seeming to be a bit disturbed; while many impromptu dances were to be seen in such places, and also along most of the principal side streets. In a word, the City gave itself up to an unrestrained revelry, which none could a few months ago have imagined our national spirit capable of, which no one in this generation had seen before Ladysmith Day, and which few of us are likely to witness again. At one o'clock this morning crowds, singing and shouting, still thronged Fleet-street, celebrating the great event.

Never were people more mad with joy than when the glad tidings for which the Empire had waited more than two hundred days spread from mouth to mouth, from east to west. After so many false rumours of relief it was only natural that the news should have been received with some scepticism at first. As 'busmen and cabmen threaded their ways towards the Strand, men leisurely walking in the streets, catching the distant sound of cheering round the newspaper offices, shouted to the drivers of every vehicle for confirmation of the tale which their hearts eagerly longed to read into the roar of hurrahs. At half-past nine, when the telegram was exhibited in the window of *The Daily Telegraph* office, the streets were almost deserted. Those who had no urgent business had betaken themselves to some place of entertainment, but within a few minutes every by-thoroughfare began to add its human stream to the main arteries of traffic, and men, old, and young, and women and children were seen eagerly running to gain confirmation of their hopes from the announcements in the newspaper offices. For once in a way the trend of everyone at the eastern end of the Strand turned instinctively towards the Press centre, and, consequently, the news did not reach the West-end as quickly as it would have done under ordinary circumstances, and, as the streets were only thinly thronged with casual foot passengers, there was for half-an-hour after the receipt of the telegram no outward indication that intelligence had been received of the end of one of the most gallant struggles in the world's history. A *Daily Telegraph* representative, who sped as quickly as horses' feet could carry him up the Strand, found that no whisper of the relief of the little town on the wide-sweeping African veldt had reached the Savoy Theatre; while at the Tivoli little groups were eagerly asking if the vague rumours shouted by cabmen and omnibus-drivers were true. At the latter house there was an inclination to regard the tidings as too good to be authentic. 'Is it true?' was asked on every hand. 'Yes, a fact.'

'Then you're my friend.' 'Hurrah for Baden-Powell!' 'Well done, Mafeking!' were ejaculations. As soon as it was known that the heroic garrison's perils and hardships were really at an end, the manager eagerly learnt from the representative all the details then available, and decided to stop the performance, that his crowded audience might share his satisfaction. He refused to brook any delay to enable the news to he announced on the screen or by any other device, but decided to trust to the power of his own lungs. The audience were in blissful ignorance of the great news, and had hardly finished applauding one of the turns when the manager stepped on to the stage. 'Ladies and Gentlemen – I think you will pardon an interruption in our programme – I have great news' – immediately cheers rang out, some persons instantly jumped to a right conclusion, while everyone craned forward. 'Mafeking has been relieved,' was then shouted above the noise. Fired by one impulse, the whole audience rose to its feet; hats, handkerchiefs, programmes, in fact anything that was at hand was waved with delirious delight, and cheer after cheer sprang from every throat. Even ladies, who are not prone to this method of exhibiting their feelings, added their voices to the wild chorus. As soon as there was a slight lull the audience became aware that the orchestra was attempting to make the strains of the National Anthem heard above the roar. Instantly every head was uncovered, and with heartfelt sincerity every man and woman joined in the patriotic song – a song of loyalty interpreted for the moment as a song of thanks-giving for countless dangers past and the victory achieved at last.

It is only a few minutes' ride from the Strand to the Alhambra, but although the representative of *The Daily Telegraph* had remained to witness the scenes at the Tivoli, he was again the bearer of the first authentic information to Mr. Slater, the manager of this house of entertainment, who had already heard the rumour. No sooner did he receive the news than he hastily prepared to have it thrown on the screen. After the eleventh turn, then in progress, as though nothing had happened, the card for the next item was exhibited, but suddenly the curtain rose displaying a white sheet, the house found itself in darkness, and then read the tidings of great joy. In an instant the crowded gathering rose, the white dresses of the ladies and the spotless shirtfronts of the men showing up spectral-like, and every throat gave forth hurrah after hurrah – wild, unrestrained, ecstatic. The scene in this great darkened house as cheers were roared forth like some great triumphal chorus is not one which those who were privileged to witness it will soon forget. At length it was noticed that the conductor was gesticulating with his arms to his musicians, and gradually the cheers gave place to the strains of the National Anthem, once more sung by deep-throated men as well as by women as it has seldom before been heard.

At the Empire Theatre a vague rumour was received shortly before ten o'clock, and men ran into the street, hatless, to ascertain if it had any more foundation than the hundred and one too hopeful stories of the past few days. As soon as all doubt had been set at rest the news spread like quicksilver. The stage failed to offer any attraction, and the audience rose, gradually, seeking to learn what the cheers outside portended. In a twinkling the truth was known, in all its simple, convincing brevity, and once more was witnessed a scene of unbridled enthusiasm, with cheers for the gallant defenders of Mafeking, renewed again and again. Even the human, voice, however, has its limits, when it is a matter of wild applause, and, at last, the National Anthem once more impressively transformed the shouts into an orderly song of thanksgiving and loyal devotion. Similar scenes were witnessed at other halls and theatres. Where plays were in progress it was in many cases deemed inadvisable to break in on the thread of the dramatic stories, but there was at least one notable exception. On receipt of the information that *The Daily Telegraph* had posted the news of the relief of Mafeking, Mr. Charles Hawtrey announced the welcome tidings to the audience of the Avenue Theatre in the interval between the first and second acts of *A Message from Mars*, and called for three cheers for Colonel Baden-Powell and the gallant defenders of the little town. The announcement gave rise to an extraordinary scene of enthusiasm, such as it seldom falls to the lot of any theatre-goer to witness. The effect on the audience was electrical. The house rose to its feet as one man, and cheered frantically, while the orchestra played the National Anthem and 'Rule Britannia', the company joining in and singing the words lustily. It was fully ten minutes before the excitement subsided sufficiently to enable the performance to be proceeded with.

It would be impossible to convey any adequate idea of the scenes which were witnessed in the chief thoroughfares of the West-end shortly after ten o'clock as men and boys wildly shouted the joyful news from one to the other. At first it was not credited, but even a rumour was worth hunting down, and thousands of foot-passengers and hundreds of cabs were soon concentrating in Pall-mall, all bent on learning if there were official confirmation. But the vast majority of men and women who flocked into the streets were soon satisfied that they might give credence to the news, and the whole West-end became vocal with shouts and the blasts of wind instruments, and flags began to appear above the hurrying masses. 'Busmen and cab-drivers, in many cases, were prepared, and in a few moments the light from the street lamps revealed vehicles gaily decorated with the Union Jack and pieces of bunting. One more than usually active fife-and-drum band was quickly out in Regent-street, leading a crowd, who lustily joined in the National Anthem and other patriotic songs. The Strand became throbbed, thicker than its thickest at the busiest hour of the day, and the sight was witnessed of four-wheeled cabs crowded within, and with three or four men on the top, proceeding Westward, shouting and flag-waving under the very eyes of the police, unrebuked.

It was impossible, walking along Piccadilly-circus last night, where the enthusiasm was at its highest, to forget Mr. Cecil Rhodes's homely assurance at a time when the siege of Kimberley had not been raised. 'The streets of Kimberley,' declared Mr. Rhodes then, 'are as safe as Piccadilly-circus.' As a matter of fact, the thoroughfares of the besieged town must, in one respect, have been considerably safer than was the heart of the West-end last night. Without incurring some personal risk it was a matter of physical impossibility to make one's way through the shouting, dancing, glad-hearted crowd, who seemed to converge upon the circus from all parts of the metropolis. Along the pavements the only course open to one was to remain stationary; in the roadways, hansoms, omnibuses, and all vehicles, found it a matter of difficulty even to crawl slowly along. For the exuberance of the people who assembled there caused them to pay no heed to policemen, vehicular traffic, or remonstrating civilians. Every one of the thousands who, for hour after hour, shouted themselves hoarse felt it his duty to do only one thing. This was to wave a flag, assure you that 'B.-P.'s safe', and sing the patriotic refrains of the music-hall, with the National Anthem now and then thrown in.

Vendors of flags and newsboys even were too patriotic to exploit this national exultation for sordid purposes. Miniature Union Jacks were disposed of at prices above the ordinary, it is true, but ridiculously cheap had the economic axiom of supply and demand been acted on. It was close upon half-past nine when the first copies of the evening papers containing the news reached Piccadilly-circus. No credence was given to the news till the papers had been scanned and it was learned that the welcome intelligence emanated from Boer sources. Ladies formed themselves into small groups in order to read the news, and gentlemen mounted 'bus-steps in order to proclaim it.

An entire transformation appeared then to come over the Circus. The lofty lights which shed their rays on the moving throng apparently assumed a deeper glow, or were increased with extra means of illumination. Flags were suddenly displayed from all the buildings, and hansoms and 'buses which rolled up from the Pall-mall and the Strand found they had been anticipated in the conveyance of the tidings. They found the Circus thronged with people yelling themselves hoarse in their joy at the news. With amazing promptitude the younger generation in the crowd hit upon the right step to take. They suddenly formed squares, and people imitated in almost every corner of the Circus. They marched forward and backward, they marched around the Circus, and they marched up and down Regent-street. Hats were instantaneously enveloped in flags, quantities of brown paper were transformed into khaki puttees, and the martial spirit caused grey-haired men to vie with the youngest in the singing of 'Rule, Britannia'. Two or three Volunteers who were in uniform ready for the front, found themselves the recipients of awkwardly fervid enthusiasm. They were carried shoulder-high around the square, and they submitted to the ordeal as cheerily as they could. They were the representatives of the splendid little force who have thrilled the world with their gallantry at Mafeking, and that was enough for London's populace last night. A glimpse of their uniform was enough for the glad and enthusiastic Briton, who freely gave vent to his feelings. Old and young, rich and poor, respectable or disreputable, all displayed their emotions without displaying a little of that shyness which is supposed to characterise our race.

Westward the many battalions of lusty vocalists wended their way until they were stopped by the scene around 8 St. George's-place. Strained as their lungs had previously been as they sang their way from Piccadilly-circus, it was interesting to observe their attitude when they learnt who was the usual occupant of the house. Their vocal resources were exhausted; their arms were tired with prolonged exertions in flag-waving. But their spirits rose higher as they realised whom the dwelling belonged to. 'Rule, Britannia' and 'Soldiers of the Queen' suddenly ceased, and the refrain that alone filled the air was 'For he's a jolly good fellow'.

An enthusiastic demonstration interrupted for some minutes the performance last night of *Cyrano de Bergerac* at Wyndham's Theatre. It was exactly ten o'clock, and Mr. Wyndham and Miss Mary Moore were playing in the balcony scene, when a shout was heard from outside, and in a moment the audience realised that the good news had arrived, and raised cheer upon cheer till Cyrano's passionate appeal for Roxana's kiss, which a second before had held the house, was lost in a wild outburst of enthusiasm. Then, for a moment, Mr. Wyndham was no longer the noble-souled Gascon braggart and duellist, but an elated Englishman, as he stepped forward, cap in hand, and announced: 'The news for which we have waited so long has arrived.' Half a dozen voices shouted: 'Thank God', and there was more cheering, and then silence, till the end of the act, when the audience rose and sang 'God Save the Queen'. The orchestra then played 'Rule, Britannia', and stalls as well as gallery shouted with sheer delight. Nor was the succeeding act inappropriate. The siege scene challenged comparison with Mafeking, and one thought of Baden-Powell and his cheery optimism as Cyrano led the thoughts of his beleaguered Gascons to their own fair province.

Scarcely had the curtain fallen upon the second act of *Lohengrin*, at Covent Garden, when the good news found its way into the opera-house. There was a sudden stir of excitement in the amphitheatre, and an evening journal was seen to fly from hand to hand along the rows of spectators. Then the first few who grasped the welcome fact raised a cheer, and a voice shouted in jubilant tones: 'Mafeking is relieved!' Instantly the whole audience rose to its feet and gazed expectantly upwards. But the gallery had no more particulars to communicate. Their throats were too full of cheers to admit of coherent speech, and so round after round rang through the great theatre and opened the lips even of the most sedate in stalls and boxes. So suddenly had the news fallen upon the gathering that there were some who doubted if such glad tidings could really be true. Upstairs, however, there were none who hesitated. Wagner and the new tenor were forgotten, and cheers for the gallant little garrison went on for some time, varied only by a hearty attempt to render the National Anthem without the assistance of Mr. Mottl and his orchestra, who, unfortunately, had left their places. When the curtain rose upon the last act of *Lohengrin* the audience was appreciably diminished in numbers, for, one after another, opera-goers were drawn away from Covent-garden into the streets by their anxiety to learn more of the news that had sent London mad with joy.

After the first act of *Magda*, Mrs. Patrick Campbell announced to the audience at the Royalty Theatre that Mafeking had been relieved. When the outburst of cheering had subsided the orchestra played 'Rule Britannia' and 'God Save the Queen', the audience joining in with the greatest enthusiasm. Unbounded enthusiasm prevailed at both the Duke of York's and Garrick Theatres when the great news was learnt. It was announced from the stage of each house, and after an outburst of cheering the audience, accompanied by the orchestra, sang 'God Save the Queen' and 'Rule Britannia'. The glorious news of the relief of Mafeking, announced from the stage of the London Hippodrome by Mr. Frank Parker, created a thrilling effect. After a scene of the greatest enthusiasm the National Anthem was played, and Miss Lilian Lea sang a special ballad, 'There's a Land', by Francis Allitsen, eulogising the gallant defence of Mafeking by Colonel Baden-Powell. The song was encored eight times. News of the relief of Mafeking was posted at the Crystal Palace at ten o'clock, amid intense enthusiasm, the band playing the National Anthem. A fireworks display is being arranged for tonight in honour of the great day.

23 January 1901: The end of an era as Queen Victoria dies
DEATH OF THE QUEEN

It is our painful duty to present this morning the sad historic messages in which the official intelligence of the immeasurable calamity that has fallen upon the Empire is conveyed. Her Majesty the Queen is no more. The reign of reigns is closed. With the first bulletin yesterday morning the last lingering hope was quenched, and the end came with the gathering of the night. At half-past six of the evening Victoria, the Great and Good, sank to eternal sleep, 'surrounded by her children and grandchildren', and the long peace and splendour of an incomparable epoch was merged in tender and immortal memory with all the ancient glory of this land by the most softly gentle, touching, beautiful death-scene of which our history holds record.

Of the last sad scene of all Sir Arthur Bigge has communicated some few intensely interesting details. Her Majesty enjoyed many intervals of consciousness during the day, when she lovingly recognised those members of her grief-stricken family who rendered her the gentle offices that she needed. All who were at Osborne were continuously within close call, and the German Emperor, who took a brief stroll in the grounds during the afternoon, was never more than two hundred yards from the house. About five o'clock it became evident that the beloved ruler's strength was fast diminishing, and in the bedchamber there were assembled the Prince of Wales, with his gracious and beautiful Consort; the Duke of York, with the Duchess, who arrived just in time to see the last hours of one to whom she was bound by double ties of blood and love; the Emperor William, representing also his noble mother, whose long illness was one of the last sorrows in that life which had known so many griefs; the Princess Christian, with her husband, and Princess Victoria of Schleswig-Holstein, so constantly the bright and loving companion of her august grandmother; the Duchess of Saxe-Coburg, to whom the scene must have been a piteous reminder of her own great sorrow when her beloved husband was called away last August; Princess Louise Duchess of Argyll, with the Duke of Argyll; the Duke of Connaught, who especially embodied to the Queen that Army of whom she was ever so proud, the Duchess, and their son and daughters; Princess Louis of Battenberg, daughter of her own well-beloved daughter; Princess Alice, with her husband; and lastly Princess Henry of Battenberg, the life-long companion of her mother.

The Queen was suffering no pain, and was in almost a sleep, so calm, so peaceful was she as the last gentle breaths were drawn.

Nearby stood the Bishop of Winchester, Chaplain of the Most Noble Order of the Garter, and though it is not actually mentioned that any audible prayers were recited, there was from him at least the commendation to the Divine Mercy of her who essentially in her life and conversation was the Defender of the Faith. At half-past six came the end of the magnificent life so dear to a world-wide Empire, and with the sorrowing mourners of her family, her people mingle their tears in the greatest grief that the nation has ever known.

Throughout the final day the nation was oppressed with the feeling that the end was near. The early morning bulletin spoke of diminishing strength and the increased seriousness of her Majesty's condition. Then at mid-day came the news that the Queen had recognised several members of the Royal family by her bedside, and was sleeping. Four hours later there arrived the message that her Majesty was slowly sinking, and the Prince of Wales, telegraphing to the Lord Mayor, announced that the life of the beloved Sovereign was in the greatest danger. At a quarter to seven his Royal Highness sent a further telegram to the Lord Mayor announcing the death of his beloved mother, and the Lord Mayor, in reply, spoke of the profound distress and grief with which he had received the news of the nation's great loss, and respectfully conveyed the earnest sympathy and condolence of the City of London with all the members of the Royal family.

It is thoroughly in keeping with the habitual thoughtfulness of the Prince of Wales that he should, even at the moment of his most grievous anxiety, have had the consideration to insist, as he did emphatically, upon Lord Salisbury being spared the mental anguish which so sad an errand as a journey to Osborne would have imposed upon the Premier, whose fervent personal attachment to her Majesty he knew better than anyone, and be saved the risk of the passage in wintry weather. His Royal Highness therefore expressed a wish, indistinguishable from a command, that Mr. Balfour should represent the Prime Minister on this most mournful occasion. Mr. Balfour, therefore, went down to Osborne by a special train, in which the Duchess of York and the three children of the Duke and Duchess of Connaught also travelled. Balfour stayed the night at Osborne. Prince Christian also reached Osborne during the day, while the Duke of Cambridge crossed to Dover from

Calais and came to London, hence he will proceed to the Isle of Wight.

There is a mournful appropriateness in the fact that the last public function performed by the Queen was the message of blessing she despatched to the people of Australia upon the inauguration of the Commonwealth; it was, as events proved, a dying message from the venerable Sovereign to the latest-born nation which reverenced her benign sway. General gloom prevailed throughout the metropolis yesterday, which was intensified tenfold when the sad news came that all was over. Every theatre and place of entertainment at once closed its doors, and the mournful theme was on everybody's lips. In the east as in the west of London the people spoke in hushed voices of the good Queen they had lost, whose like they would never see again.

And the grief which brooded over London, dulling the keen edge of business and hushing the voice of gaiety, hung heavily over the United Kingdom, and, indeed, over all the world-wide dominions which paid the Queen a willing reverence. From every city, town, and hamlet comes the same word of heartfelt sorrow, the same of sharp, personal loss. A muffled peal was rung at St. Paul's Cathedral to announce to the citizens of London the death of her Majesty, and the minute bells of many scores of churches took up the doleful tidings.

In all the capitals of Europe the news of the Queen's death was received with every manifestation of public sorrow. The Austrian Emperor at once sent messages of condolence to the King of England, the German Emperor and the Emperor of Russia, and ordered the Austrian Court to go into mourning for four weeks. M. Loubet, the President of the French Republic, who on Monday had forwarded to the Prince of Wales his sympathy at the Queen's illness, again telegraphed his condolences to the King of England. Mr. McKinley immediately sent a message to the King, expressing his profound sorrow and sincere sympathy at the loss England has sustained through the death of the venerable and illustrious Sovereign who had won the affections of the world. The American Senate passed a resolution of condolence, and the Secretary of State, Mr. Hay, despatched to Lord Lansdowne a similar telegram of regret. Throughout the United States there is universal sorrow. Of all the newspaper articles which have been published in the Continental Press on the Queen's reign, none is more striking than that contributed to the *Figaro* by Baron d'Estournelles de Constant. He speaks of her Majesty as 'having been, throughout her life, hospitable and peaceably inclined to so many Frenchmen and foreigners'.

The new King will come to London this morning, and will immediately preside at a meeting of the Privy Council, at which the various formalities, usual on such occasions, will be observed. His Majesty will then be formally proclaimed at St. James's Palace and other places in the metropolis and the United Kingdom. At such meetings of the Privy Council, all Councillors have the right of attending, though special summonses are addressed only to certain functionaries, such as the Lord Mayor. After the formal business of the Council is despatched all members except the Cabinet retire, in accordance with precedent, rather than rule, since the Cabinet as such is unknown to the Constitution. Similar formalities are observed on obtaining assent to the Speech from the Throne. It is not perhaps generally known that prior to the accession of the Queen the Royal Prerogative of mercy was exercised by the Sovereign person, on the advice and in the presence of the judicial members of the Council. The previous practice was abolished by Lord Melbourne and the exercise of the prerogative transferred to the Home Secretary, because, in his anxious consideration for her Majesty's tender youth, her first Prime Minister determined that she should be spared the recital of the gruesome details inseparable from a deliberate decision on exorcise of the prerogative. Parliament will assemble today to take the oath of allegiance to the new Monarch.

It is difficult to convey a sense of the wall of isolation by which Osborne is shut off from those without its boundaries. Thus it is almost impossible to learn anything further than what is officially communicated, and certain indiscretions as to statements that have appeared have not tended to make it any easier. The midnight bulletin raised hopes in the minds of late inquirers as confirming the more cheering news of the rally that had followed upon the arrival of the German Emperor, but the one issued this morning at half-past eight was regarded as very gloomy, and, indeed, all this morning the most pessimistic rumours have been afloat. An hour or two before the midday report endorsed too sadly some of these fears it was known on reliable authority that the Queen's own sons and daughters, the German Emperor, and the younger members of the Royal family were gathering in the Queen's bed-chamber, and that the venerated Mother and Queen had bestowed loving recognition upon all. The Bishop of Winchester was summoned from Whippingham Rectory, where he is staying.

Her Majesty's suite of bed and dressing rooms are situated in the centre of Osborne House, in what is known as the Queen's Pavilion. The apartment in which the illustrious sufferer is lying is not a large one, but it is beautifully sunny and bright, and commands a lovely view over the blue waters of the Solent. The Princess of Wales, Princess Christian, Princess Louise, and Princess Henry are unremitting in their loving care and attention, and are constantly with the Queen, who, it is some slight satisfaction to record, does not suffer actual pain.

The Earl of Clarendon (Lord Chamberlain) was an early arrival at Osborne House this afternoon, and later came the Duke of Argyll. Shortly before five o'clock the Admiralty tender *Fire Queen* brought to the Trinity Pier the Duchess of York, who was accompanied by Prince Arthur of Connaught and his two sisters, Princess Margaret and Princess Victoria Patricia. Travelling with them was Mr. Arthur Balfour, who followed the Royal party to Osborne in one of the Queen's carriages. The mournful tidings of the afternoon's brief bulletin were well known to all the quietly waiting spectators who had assembled near the wharf, and only silent and respectful greetings were accorded. Prince Louis of Battenberg and Princess Louis have also arrived, and are staying on board the *Osborne*.

This afternoon there has been the largest crowd that has yet assembled round the Prince of Wales Gate. A notable feature in it are the large numbers of special correspondents from the chief Continental newspapers, showing the universal participation in the sorrow that has fallen upon the Empire. Three Indian natives of Madras, who have been lecturing on their country in the North of England, drove up in brilliant turbans and silken coats to ask permission to offer through the Queen's Munshi the expression of their own humble sympathy, which was shared throughout the length and breadth of the Queen-Empress's Eastern dominion.

Hope sometimes flickered up as one or another came from the house trying to say 'No worse', but at four o'clock the words 'Slowly sinking' were passed sadly through the quiet throng. Now and again as messengers came down from the house, eager inquiry was made, but there was no word of hope to give. 'Sinking', 'Sinking', 'Sinking rapidly' came to be the answer, given with shaking voice and eyes that filled with tears. The twilight deepened into gloom, and a cloudy mist hung overhead, while every mind was overwhelmed by the solemn, all-pervading thought that the life of the Mother of an Empire and the greatest woman of her time was ebbing to close. The moments passed slowly in impending consciousness that the dreaded tidings could not long be delayed, and when it came the announcement was made to the world with a pathos that could hardly have been surpassed. No formal bulletin, no Court herald proclaimed the melancholy news. At exactly eight minutes after seven, Mr. Charles Fraser, for years past Chief Inspector of the Household Police, and himself one of his Royal mistress's most devoted and faithful servants, arrived at the lodge gates, and, with his head gravely bowed, and in accents that betrayed deep personal emotion, said, standing on the steps of the little stone-built house: 'Gentlemen – I grieve to say that the Queen passed away at half-past six.' The momentous announcement was made at the instruction of General Sir John McNeill, V.C., and was followed almost immediately by the bulletin, which, as usual, was written in large, bold script on white foolscap.

Osborne House, 22 Jan (6.45 p.m.).
Her Majesty the Queen breathed her last at 6.30 p.m.,
surrounded by her children and her grandchildren.
James Reid, M.D.
R. Douglas Powell, M.D.
Thomas Barlow, M.D.

The completest quiet was observed at Osborne House during the evening, and intrusive curiosity part in the sacred grief overshadowing all, even to the humblest of the household dependents. No arrangements whatever are yet made with regard to the Queen's funeral, but it is possible that some preliminary details may be announced the course of tomorrow. Although Mr. Balfour arrived before her Majesty expired, he did not visit the room in which she lay. Immediately after the last bulletin was issued the Bishop of Winchester left Osborne. The King of the Belgians is not expected here, although statements have been made to the contrary. In the course of tomorrow the Duchess of Albany will leave for Buckingham Palace.

The grievous news found its way across the river to West Cowes with lightning swiftness. Business in Cowes usually ceases at eight o'clock, but many shops were closed at once. Everywhere grief was written on the faces of the people, grief and a kind of puzzled wonder that was more pathetic than more effusive demonstration. The passengers who arrived by the last boat from Southampton, soon after seven o'clock, were unaware of the sad event until they landed.

A great crowd assembled in front of St. Paul's Cathedral, where the tolling of the State bell was listened to with melancholy interest. It was, indeed, by the tolling of this bell – which is only used on occasions of the death of a member of the Royal family, the Archbishop of Canterbury, the Lord Mayor of London, the Bishop of London, or the Dean of St. Paul's – that the sad tidings were first conveyed to the greater portion of London's millions. On the instructions of the Dean, the tolling was continued at intervals of a minute for the space of two hours. It happened that just at the commencement of this painful undertaking a small congregation were leaving the West door of the Cathedral, having attended a week-night service. The crowd, misunderstanding the position, concluded that the doors were being thrown open for a special service, suitable to the occasion, and began to press for admission. The officials checked this by displaying in a prominent position a notice intimating that the Cathedral was closed to visitors. Many gathered round the tablet at the foot of St. Paul's steps, which marks the spot where Queen Victoria returned thanks for the sixtieth anniversary of her accession in 1897, and it was but natural that that time of rejoicing should be contrasted with the present hour of death. During the time of the present Dean and Chapter there has, of course, been no such momentous event as the death of the Queen; but in other cases of less importance it has been the custom, on receipt of the news of death, to drape the Cathedral in black; and for memorial services to be held. In connection with the death of the Queen, it is probable that, after morning and evening prayers, short memorial services will be held on certain days, to be fixed. In consequence of the death of her Majesty the Queen the selection from Mendelssohn's *St. Paul* will not be sung on Friday, 25, at four p.m. service.

The passing bell of St. Paul's is the largest of the three on which the clock is struck. Londoners are accustomed, therefore, to hearing its calling the hours after the striking of the quarters by its companions. Thus it happened that its first stroke was not at once recognised as the commencement of its tolling for the death of the Sovereign whose hours it had so long numbered. When, a minute later, the second stroke resounded, hats were at once removed and the great crowd stood in solemn stillness. For all members of the Royal family the ringers toll the bell for an hour; for the Prince Consort, and again last night for Queen Victoria, the tolling lasted two hours. By nine o'clock a concourse numbering some thousands was gathered before the sombre, unlighted front of the Cathedral, and remained until the bell had ceased to toll.

As the evening advanced the crowd outside the Cathedral assumed larger dimensions, and on all hands the people voiced their grief at the loss the nation had sustained. Ere long the front of St. Paul's presented a sea of faces, and this in spite of the fact that many City men had wended their way homewards before the sorrowful news came to hand. This was officially communicated to the Dean of St. Paul's by the Lord Mayor.

The intelligence, though it came after days of anxious suspense, and when all hope had been abandoned, occasioned most intense mourning in the City. Throughout the morning and afternoon there was the most eager anxiety for news from the sick-room at Osborne. It is difficult to describe the lassitude that manifested itself in commercial circles, caused by the feeling of uncertainty and dread fear. There the same congregation of members at every separate centre of mart as usual, but proceedings were dull. Men's thoughts were elsewhere. Every notice-board on 'Change, in Capel-court, the Baltic, Lloyd's, and the produce markets easterly way, was eagerly scanned for the latest bulletins. Only one official announcement was issued during business hours – that sent from the Isle of Wight at noon – but it was continually being supplemented by scraps of news transmitted over the telegraphic tapes, the substance of which passed among the business throngs as quickly as it was received. The display of feeling was entirely personal. There was no thought of the possible effects on prices by the momentous change resting in the balance of fate – and, as a matter of fact, there was no effect other than the depression accruing from the dull attitude of the markets – but there was observable the ever-present thought that the country was menaced by the loss of a Sovereign loved throughout her reign, and never more revered than at the commencement of this new century.

Outside the Mansion House businessmen and clerks, hurrying to their offices, crowded round the notice-board at the corner of Walbrook to read the eight o'clock bulletin. Thereafter, all through the forenoon, the spot was thronged by assembly, quiet, orderly, and undemonstrative, but keenly anxious to learn the latest news from the Isle of Wight. From an early hour in the morning inquiries as to the condition of the Queen were very numerous at the Mansion House. Knowing that the news of any immediately alarming change in her Majesty's health would be at once notified to the Lord Mayor by the Home Secretary from Osborne, there were many callers at the official residence, and many more letters and telegrams demanding response. In consequence a busy day for the civic servants, who in many cases were compelled, in sheer inability to answer all demands, to refer the visitors to the bulletin boards outside. Shortly after four clock the Lord Mayor received the following telegram from the Prince of Wales at Osborne:

My painful duty obliges me to inform you that the life of the beloved Queen is in the greatest danger.
    Albert Edward.
    Osborne, four o'clock.

This significant intimation was at once exhibited on the notice-board in Walbrook-corner, and the Lord Mayor, in reply, telegraphed to the Prince of Wales as follows: 'I have received your sad intimation with profound grief, which is shared by the citizens of London, who still pray that, under Divine providence, the irreparable loss of her Majesty's devoted family and loyal subjects may still be averted.'

Only a few minutes remained before Bow Bells would chime the hour of seven, when came to the Mansion House the intelligence which last night girdled the world with a sentence, in sound of which, to British ears, eloquence is dumb – 'The Queen is dead.' Passengers on 'bus or afoot travelling eastwards from Fleet-street two minutes past the hour already knew the tidings. Great Paul of St. Paul's and other bells slowly knelled out the solemn message. No need for vendors of evening papers, each the centre of a group of eager purchasers, to display the headline of the bill; and it was to the credit of their respect for reverence and for patriotism that many of them allowed the news bill to tell its own story.

The anticipated, yet dreaded, news came to the Lord Mayor in the following telegram:

> My beloved mother, the Queen, has just passed away, surrounded
> by her children and grandchildren.
>   Albert Edward
>   Osborne, 6.45.

Instantly upon its receipt a mounted messenger was despatched to St. Paul's with instructions that the great bell should be tolled, and meanwhile the Lord Mayor, standing at the window of the Venetian Parlour of the Mansion House, announced to a great crowd standing below the news he had received. His lordship said: 'Fellow Citizens – It is with deep sorrow that I have to read to you a telegram which has just reached me from the Prince of Wales.'

Then followed the recital of the brief but pregnant message, which was received in silence, but with evident and profound emotion. In reply to the telegram from Osborne the Lord Mayor transmitted the following:

> To his Royal Highness the Prince of Wales,
> Your Royal Highness's telegram announcing the nation's great
> loss I have received with profound distress and grief, and have
> announced this most sad intimation to my fellow citizens. Her
> Majesty's name and memory will live for ever in the hearts of
> her people. May I respectfully convey to your Royal Highness
> and all the members of the Royal family the earnest sympathy
> and condolence of the citizens of London in your great sorrow?
>   Frank Green
>   Lord Mayor

While this was occurring came a telegram to the Lord Mayor from Mr. Arthur J. Balfour, as representing her Majesty's Government, saying briefly: 'The Queen died peacefully at 6.30.' Shortly thereafter was read the following formal message from the Home Secretary, customary on the demise of a Sovereign, directing that Great Paul be tolled:

> Home Office, Whitehall, 22 Jan.
> My Lord,
> It is my painful duty to inform your lordship of the death of our Most Gracious Sovereign Queen Victoria.
> This melancholy event took place at Osborne, at 6.30 p.m. this day.
> I have to request that your Lordship will give directions for the tolling of the great bell of St. Paul's Cathedral. I have the honour to be
> Your lordship's obedient servant,
> Charles T. Ritchie

The blinds of the Mansion House were at once drawn – an example followed by all the places of business – and the Lord Mayor wrote an official letter to the Dean of St. Paul's informing him of the death of the Sovereign. At the usual dinner of Hilary Term at Gray's Inn last night, there were only two Masters of the Bench present – Masters Beetham and H. C. Richards Q.C., M.P. At the conclusion of dinner the former said: 'Brethren of the Society of Gray's Inn – It is my sad duty to announce that our beloved Queen has passed away, and amid our great sorrow we must follow the practice of the Constitution, and recite "God Save the King".' The chapel bell was then tolled eighty-two times, and the health of the King was given for the first time since 1837.

It was a painful day in the extreme for Londoners of every rank and station. Never has London passed through such a period of sorrow and suspense, and never, surely, did such heartfelt and universal sympathy go out to a Royal family in their hour of tribulation. With the afternoon, which found Buckingham Palace and Marlborough House the chief centres of interest and concern, came such tidings as could only convince those who had still looked to possibility of the august sufferer recovering that they were simply hoping against hope. To the majority of her Majesty's devoted subjects, no doubt, the official announcement that the Queen was slowly sinking did not come with the full shock of a surprise. But, from the solemn and pained demeanour of one and all who read the ominous words, it was clear that their sorrow was as sincere and overwhelming as though the blow had been wholly unexpected. No less fraught with gloomy significance was the message which, in the course of the afternoon, the Prince of Wales despatched to the Lord Mayor at the Mansion House, and which found its way swiftly enough to the rooms of the West-end clubs and to the columns of the evening papers. Again was the moving spectacle witnessed of all sections of the community – men, women, and children – reading the disconcerting tidings with indications of as much concern as though the life of someone very near and dear to them were in imminent danger, and some cherished family tie about to be severed.

Members of Clubland were turning in to dress for dinner about the time when the fateful words 'The end has come', were being passed from lip to lip, and a great sorrow fell upon all hearts. So loth were many to believe, notwithstanding the ominous tidings of the afternoon, that the worst had befallen that they hastened away to verify the mournful news. 'Is it officially given out?' Such was the nervous interrogation heard upon all sides, when, a minute or two following the stroke of seven, the solemn news was being circulated. In Piccadilly the announcement was first seen in the windows of the branch office of *The Daily Telegraph*, and thence, as the intelligence quickly spread, wayfarers turned their steps in various directions to obtain further particulars. To Marlborough House they made their way in large numbers, but, arriving there, they found still posted on its walls a copy of the afternoon bulletin, which intimated that her Majesty was slowly sinking. A considerable crowd collected as time went on, and, again and again, in subdued tones, was heard the question, 'Is it really true?' The constables on duty at this point soon found themselves surrounded by persons breathlessly inquiring whether the melancholy news was authentic. But no confirmation was forthcoming from this source, all who sought for information being referred to the official bulletin board, to which the dire intelligence had not yet found its way.

Many waited on, but others who were there bent their steps towards Buckingham Palace, expecting there to learn the very latest tidings. In front of the Palace quadrangle, at a quarter past seven, a considerable body of silent, anxious people kept their eyes steadily fixed upon the railings, to which the notice-board, which from an early hour of the day had been continuously watched, was affixed. There followed a scene of painful tension and suspense. At the time stated the afternoon bulletin was still exposed to view, but within a few moments an official, dimly seen through the night darkness, stole across the quadrangle and quietly removed the last message received from Osborne House. The blinds of the Palace were now drawn. But this could not, remembering the hour, be held to bear any sinister significance. Lights there were in some of the apartments, and vague figures could be seen within moving to and fro. Still the minutes wore on, and no sign was there of any bearer of further news. Every moment brought with it accessions to the ranks of those who stood and waited and watched, silent, anxious, and sorrowful. Passing carriages and cabs halted, and those within – many in evening dress, who had manifestly not heard the dread report of the end having come – alighted quickly and made towards the railings upon which all eyes were intent.

Hither came not a few whose faces told plainly enough, even before their lips gave utterance to the words, that they knew that the time had passed when any lingering hope could still be cherished. But the crowd of silent men and women heeded neither looks nor whispers, and stood on as though rooted to the spot. At length, when it wanted some six minutes to the hour of eight, there came an end to waiting and suspense. Again, through the darkness, a figure was seen to cross the courtyard from the little archway to the left of the equerries' entrance. The onlookers, who had kept patient vigil, pressed closer one to another, yet another brief period of painful tension followed, and then, upon the little board towards which all turned their expectant gaze, there appeared the following: 'Board of Green Cloth – Buckingham Palace, S.W. – To the Lord Steward. Buckingham Palace – The Queen died peacefully at 6.30. – (Signed) Arthur Balfour, 22 Jan. 1901.' Not all were near enough to read the fateful message, but swiftly its import passed from lip to lip, and then, when all had seen or heard the solemn tidings, and the last lingering doubt had been removed from the minds of those who had hoped against hope, the crowds slowly and sorrowfully melted away.

Big Ben had scarcely chimed seven o'clock when the mournful tolling of the bell of St. Margaret's Church informed the inhabitants of the Royal borough of Westminster that her Majesty had passed away. The news was received in the various Government offices in Whitehall soon after seven o'clock, and, although expected, came as a great shock to the officials. Immediately the flags flying at the mastheads of the Foreign Office, Home Office, Local Government Board Office, Education Department, and Treasury, were lowered half-mast high, as were the national flags at both the Scotch and Irish offices. All the great shipping offices in Cockspur-street lowered their flags, which included those of many nations, half-mast high.

Dreary and dark, but certainly not deserted, were the streets of the West-end after the dissemination of the dismal news. When, early in the week, the theatrical managers realised that the illness of the Queen might have a fatal termination, several of the more prominent held an informal meeting, and decided on the course which they would follow if the worst fears of the nation were realised. Their decision was that if the news of the Queen's demise came during a performance the curtain would be rung down, and the audience dismissed, unless the last act of the piece was nearly over, in which case they thought that it would be more decorous to allow the performance to end before announcing the sad news. They further decided – and those who manage the great music-halls were of the same mind – that in the event of the death of the Sovereign the houses which they control should be closed until after the funeral. As the news came before the performance in the theatres and music-halls had commenced, the managers were relieved of the painful duty of abruptly turning the audience into the streets, as at all places of amusement a notice was at once exhibited announcing that no performance would take place. The terms of the intimation varied. In some cases those who presented themselves at the doors of a theatre were confronted with the bald intimation 'Closed'. At other houses the statement was that there would be no performance last night, but at most places of amusement the announcement on the placards was that they would be closed nightly until further notice was given. Very few persons presented themselves at the West-end theatres, as the melancholy news spread so quickly that it reached those who had booked seats while they were yet at home. But at the entrances to the unreserved seats of many theatres and music halls the usual crowds had collected, and when the announcement was made that there would be no performance, and the reason was stated to them, they went their way silent and sad-hearted. All did not turn homewards, for the streets, until a late hour, were thronged with men and women representing all classes of society, who aimlessly traversed the leading thoroughfares, restless in their grief, and eager for news of the final scene at Osborne.

At six o'clock the rumour of the decease of her Majesty caused a large crowd to assemble at Marlborough House, but on finding that the statement was incorrect numbers left with hope that the gloomy reports of the afternoon would be falsified. The more pessimistic inquirers waited on in sad expectancy for the message that was to cause such profound grief. Every moment brought fresh arrivals, until, at about a quarter to seven, there must have been a concourse of several hundred persons, eagerly scanning the board for the latest bulletins. No information of the sad event of an official nature was posted, and the first announcement of the Queen's demise was made by a newspaper boy. The papers were eagerly read, but with scepticism, and still the crowd waited on doubtingly. Pall-mall presented an unusual sight, being filled with carriages to such a degree that the police found a difficulty in regulating the traffic. The officials at Marlborough House were kept busy answering the numerous inquiries. At half-past seven, there having been no official notice posted, a movement was made to the clubs, and from those places the sad intelligence was confirmed. Not until eight o'clock was the Queen's death notified to the public at Marlborough House. From that time until very late at night people flowed up Pall-mall from the Strand, and after a glance at the telegram turned sorrowfully away. When the grievous tidings were found to be true beyond a doubt an old gentleman and lady could not repress their profound sorrow and burst into tears, and there were few in the vastness of lingerers who were dry-eyed.

2

Wars, Disasters and Tragedies, Natural and Man-Made, Along with the Early Days of New Forms of Transport 1902–45

2

Introduction

The first half of the twentieth century witnessed not only some of the most dramatic events in the history of planet, but a revolution in newspaper reporting. 'Further news is lacking tonight,' writes the *Daily Telegraph*'s glum-sounding correspondent in Paris in May 1902, desperate for information about the eruption of Mount Pelée in Martinique, which had led to catastrophic loss of life. There would have been film footage of the eruption within minutes today, but with all the cable offices on the tiny Caribbean island destroyed by fire, reliable information was impossible to come by. Contrast that with the *Telegraph*'s reporting of the Hindenburg disaster in May 1937, when a German passenger airship exploded on its arrival in New Jersey, with heavy loss of life. There was no *Telegraph* man on the spot, but the local commissioner of police was able to give the paper a comprehensive first-hand account of events via a transatlantic telephone.

By the time of the Second World War, reporters were operating in an environment that had been totally transformed by communication technologies. The reporters also knew that they could get from A to B at a speed which their Victorian predecessors would have found unimaginable. After the D-Day landings, *Telegraph* readers were treated to a masterly first-hand account from Cornelius Ryan, a special correspondent embedded with the US 9th Air Force, who had personally flown over the Allied beachheads and was able to bring the scene to vivid life with his bird's-eye vignettes.

There were other changes, too. After long years of anonymity, lurking behind 'special correspondent' bylines, the named reporter was starting to become a regular feature. Some of them were not just names, but household names, who would have graced any newspaper at any time. In the Great War, the *Telegraph* was able to enlist the likes of Rudyard Kipling to add gravitas to their coverage.

Different authorial voices also allowed more than one perspective on the same event. Following the infamous bombing of Guernica in April 1937, *Telegraph* readers could digest reports from both Christopher Martin, a special correspondent attached to the Basque forces, and Pembroke Stephens, with the Nationalist forces. If the printing of contrasting versions of events suggests that the *Telegraph* was determined to report the Spanish Civil War impartially, it was not always so scrupulous. In October 1908, the paper printed an exclusive interview with Kaiser Wilhelm II that, with the benefit of hindsight, makes for uneasy reading. The unnamed interviewer listens to the Kaiser's repeated protestations that he is a friend of England and, shamelessly eliding news and comment, concludes: 'I would urge my fellow countrymen to weigh what I have written and to revise, if necessary, their estimation of the Kaiser.' The publication of the interview significantly damaged Anglo-German relations and led to an increase in international tension.

Another *Telegraph* correspondent who did not exactly cover himself in glory was the one reporting the signing of the Treaty of Versailles in 1919. There is page after page of florid description of the Palace of Versailles, hardly a ceiling or pilaster un-admired, but not a sceptical word about the treaty itself, which is hyperbolically hailed as 'the greatest combined effort of human goodwill and justice ever made to set right the affairs of this distracted earth'.

For the *Telegraph*, as for any newspaper, having a reporter on the spot was critical. Local stringers were all very well, and it is fascinating to see the proliferation of the paper's network of special correspondents as the century advanced. News of the death of Bonnie and Clyde in May 1934 was relayed to readers by a correspondent in Shreveport, Louisiana, news of a truce in the war between Bolivia and Paraguay in 1935 by a correspondent based in Buenos Aires. But there was no substitute for a having a heavyweight reporter in place at moments when events took a dramatic turn and history was being rewritten. After Bloody Sunday in St. Petersburg in 1905, when Tsarist troops fired on unarmed demonstrators, the *Telegraph*'s special correspondent was in the very thick of the action, one minute riding on a sleigh with a wounded student, who was cradling a dead colleague, the next attending an emergency meeting of writers and intellectuals, including Maxim Gorky. The prose may be old-fashioned to the point of parody. ('My watch pointed to half-past eleven as this deed of blood was done.') But the unfolding events are related with a sense of urgency that leaves an indelible impression.

Another *Telegraph* correspondent to enjoy a ringside seat was the paper's correspondent in Warsaw in August 1939, who was able to offer detailed corroboration of the imminent German invasion. Epoch-making events are described objectively and without histrionics. New York, then as now, was clearly a prized posting for a British newspaper man. The *Telegraph*'s reporting of the sinking of the Titanic is rendered extraordinarily poignant by the first-hand descriptions of the scenes of shock and confusion outside the White Star offices in New York, as news of the disaster filtered through.

In a quite different vein, there is a hilarious account of the arrest of Enrico Caruso in 1906, after an incident in the monkey-house at the New York Zoological Gardens. 'It was alleged that the singer had approached a lady in an offensive way,' reports the *Telegraph*'s man on the spot, with admirable restraint. The story then escalates deliciously, with every detail, every comic minor character, faithfully recorded for posterity.

Charles Lindbergh's arrival in Paris in 1927, after completing the first solo flight across the Atlantic, is another classic piece of reportage, with the dramatic events allowed to speak for themselves. The moment when Lindbergh pops his head out of the cockpit after landing in

Paris, and says, 'Hullo, boys, I am here! I am Lindbergh. Where am I?' is laugh-out loud funny. As so often in these plums picked from the *Telegraph* archives, you get the sense of a reporter with a great story to tell, thrilled to be at the centre of events and determined not to blow his opportunity.

10 May 1902: Mont Pelée erupts in Martinique, with horrific consequences for the island's capital
VOLCANO DISASTER IN MARTINIQUE
AN AVALANCHE OF FLAME
BRITISH STEAMERS BURNT
From Our Own Correspondent

One of the most terrible disasters in the annals of the world has befallen the once prosperous town of St. Pierre, the commercial capital of the French island of Martinique, in the West Indies. At eight o'clock on Thursday morning the volcano Mont Pelée, which had been quiescent for over half a century, but had been showing considerable signs of activity for several weeks past, broke into furious eruption. St. Pierre was completely destroyed, and practically the whole population, numbering from 30,000 to 40,000 souls, perished in an avalanche of fire, lava, and ashes. The shipping in the harbour was all overwhelmed, with the exception of the British steamer *Roddam*, which got away after losing seventeen men of her crew and sustaining much damage. The Governor of the Windward Islands, a British possession, telegraphs to the Colonial Office that a serious volcanic eruption has occurred in St. Vincent, one of the group, but that no details are known, as the cables are broken.

News of the disaster in the French colony of Martinique, in the West Indies, caused intense excitement and deep emotion in Paris today. Last evening a telegram to the Colonial Office stated that the volcanic eruption in the island was subsiding, and it was added that only twenty-three persons, who were probably living around the base of Mount Pelée, had disappeared. This morning the information came from London and New York of the destruction of the town of St.

Pierre by the eruption, and the news was confirmed at the Ministry of Marine this afternoon in a telegram from Fort de France, sent by the officer in command of the cruiser *Suchet*. The despatch is dated 8 May, 5.50 p.m., and runs as follows: 'Have returned from St. Pierre. Town was completely destroyed by a mass of fire at eight o'clock in the morning. Suppose that all the inhabitants have been overwhelmed and destroyed. Have brought away about thirty survivors. All the ships in the roads were burned and lost. I am starting for Guadeloupe, there to procure provisions. The eruption of the volcano continues.'

The publication today of this official telegram caused a tremendous rush to the Ministry of Marine of people who had relatives in Martinique or who were interested in the colony, either commercially or otherwise. The population of St. Pierre numbered over 20,000 persons, and out of these many had relatives in Paris and in other French towns. Hence the anguish and anxiety caused by the telegram from the commander of the *Suchet* to the Minister of Marine.

During the latter part of the afternoon further information come out. It was stated, for instance, that a steamer called the *Roraima* had been destroyed, and that another vessel, which carried the news of the disaster to the British island of Santa Lucia, had a narrow escape from destruction. Seventeen of the crew were drowned, and the captain was severely injured. M. Triard, a legal official at Martinique, who was among those rescued by the officers and men of the *Suchet*, has sent a despatch to Paris announcing that he and his family are all right.

This evening it was believed at the Colonial Office that M. Mouttet, Governor of Martinique, who was yesterday reported to be safe, is among the victims of the disaster. He telegraphed to the Colonial Office on the seventh to say that he was going to St. Pierre. M. Décrais, the Minister of the Colonies, was at Bordeaux when he received the bad news, and started immediately for Paris. The two offices of the Colonies and the Marine have despatched telegrams to the commander of the *Suchet* asking him for further and more complete information. The cables to Martinique are, however, destroyed, and it is thought that no news can be obtained until the *Suchet* returns from Guadeloupe with provisions. The vessel will take twenty-four hours on the passage. M. Bougenot, who has sugar plantations in Martinique, has received a despatch from a French agent, who says that he was unable to approach St. Pierre, as the whole coast was covered with lava and ashes and the town was filled with smoke and dust. Madame Knight, wife of the Senator for Martinique, is one of those connected with the colony living in Paris who will need much sympathy. Her husband is out at Martinique, where he owns large plantations, and he had been engaged in general election work in the island for the past month. His wife and children in Paris were in a state of grief today, as they could obtain no news of the absent head of the family, whom they begin to look upon as lost to them for ever.

It was on the night of Saturday, 3 May, that the volcano began to show signs of renewed activity. Great quantities of ashes were hurled into the neighbouring district, and the inhabitants had to take refuge at St. Pierre and other places. It was at first imagined that the eruption would not be of any special importance, but on Monday it was ascertained that the Guerin factories, situated at some distance from St. Pierre, had been destroyed, and that no less than 150 persons had disappeared. On the following day, the Governor informed the Minister of the Colonies that a torrent of burning mud was running down the valley of the River Blanche. It is this torrent of mud, which, changing into one of lava, has now overwhelmed the town.

Sir Edmund Monson called this afternoon at the Ministry of Foreign Affairs for the purpose of expressing condolence. A cablegram has been received at the Ministry of the Colonies from M. Lhuerre, Secretary-General of the Martinique Administration, which confirms the sad intelligence of the destruction of St. Pierre and its environs, as well as of the ships in the roadstead by 'a rain of fire'. M. Lhuerre fears that the inhabitants, with the exception of a few persons, have perished. He cannot give any information about M. Mouttet, the Governor, who had proceeded to St. Pierre.

*

Further news about the Martinique disaster is lacking tonight. M. Pecoul, junior, son of a planter, has been seen, and attributes the absence of supplementary information to the fact that the English and French telegraphic cables from the island have been destroyed. The English cable, he says, was first struck by the lava offshore, and the French cable was destroyed at seven miles distance out in the sea. M. Pecoul, junior, is inclined to believe that the reports of the disaster have been exaggerated. The Deputy in the last chamber for St. Pierre, namely, M. Denis Guibert, is not at present in Paris. In the destroyed town, of which M. Nicole was mayor, there were twenty-four lawyers of various grades, ten physicians, and four foreign Consuls. There were four financial establishments, including, it is stated, the Colonial Bank of London. Five newspapers were published in the town. Tonight the Minister of Marine cabled to Cayenne directing the commanders of two cruisers stationed there to proceed with their ships to Martinique, for the purpose of obtaining fuller information about the disaster, and of giving whatever assistance may be necessary.

23 January 1905: 'Bloody Sunday' in Russia, with the *Telegraph*'s correspondent in the thick of it
CARNAGE IN ST. PETERSBURG
HUNDREDS KILLED AND WOUNDED
BRUTALITY OF THE COSSACKS AND UHLANS
RISING SUPPRESSED
From Our Special Correspondent

As had been expected, the workmen's movement in St. Petersburg culminated yesterday in a terrible tragedy. The attempt of the unfortunate sufferers from the bureaucratic regime to make their grievances known to the Tzar by way of a great demonstration in front of the Winter Palace was frustrated by the huge force of soldiers and police employed by the authorities. The crowd, which included large numbers of women and children, appears to have behaved in a perfectly orderly manner, but was fired on and charged by the Cossacks and Uhlans, and was eventually dispersed, but not before many hundreds – some reports say thousands – of people had been killed or wounded by rifle bullets or the sabre.

Several distinct conflicts took place, at the Winter Palace Square, the Putiloff works, on the railway, and in the Vassili Ostroff district, all with the same result. The whole affair was under the superintendence of the Grand Duke Vladimir, uncle of the Tsar, and the Emperor failed to appear; indeed, his precise whereabouts was not known. Late last night the Vassili Ostroff district was the scene of great disorders, and the workmen were believed to be arming themselves in preparation for a renewal of the struggle today. The rumours that Father Gapon had been wounded and arrested are both incorrect. A priest named Sergius was killed in the Palace Square by the troops.

Among the revolutionary leaders, whether working men or members of the intelligent classes, nobody closed his eyes throughout the eventful night which inaugurated the revolution. Meetings were being held, speeches delivered, preparations made until seven o'clock, when the real work of the fateful day began. At first the streets were silent, and the workmen gathered indoors. Here and there a belated or early sleigh came gliding along, with its closely-wrapped, pale-faced fare. Artillery, too, rolled creakingly on wheels before the population was astir, and regiments of Cossacks, bodies of gendarme, squads of police kept scouring the broad, silent streets of the northern capital, and taking up commanding positions. Typical winter sunshine, a biting Arctic wind, and a temperature of 14 degrees constituted salient characteristics of the first day of the Russian revolution. At nine o'clock all the bridges were occupied by troops, the avenues to them shut off, and the people driven back, but two hours later isolated persons were allowed to pass. By 11 a.m. the whole of St. Petersburg presented the aspect of a conquered city. At every quarter of a mile troops were drawn up, arms were stacked, bonfires lighted, and even games inaugurated. The soldiers danced, wrestled, and skipped to keep themselves warm, or played hide and seek around the Red Cross vans, which were provided in abundance for the wounded, of whom an exceptionally large number was anticipated.

By noon the entire population was afoot, moving towards the Winter Palace. The Nevsky Prospekt was black with workmen in imitation astrakhan caps and dark coats, sometimes accompanied by their wives. There was no drunkenness, no disorder, no signs of disloyalty, or even of preconcerted action. Bells rang out merrily on the frosty air, but the churches were relatively deserted for the political pilgrimage to the Imperial Palace. The roofs of the low houses were in some streets crowded with youthful spectators, and thousands of residences had their windows wide open, with the inmates looking out, despite the terribly cold wind.

I repaired, together with Dr. Williams, to the Workmen's Club, in a distant district of the city, and we drove a quarter of the way through walls of soldiers or squadrons of Cossacks, only to find the club closed. Then we passed the residence of M. Witte, on Stone Island Prospekt, and there, too, faces were visible at the windows. A couple of hundred yards from there a multitude of men, with a sprinkling of girls, came marching very slowly towards Trinity Bridge, which leads to the quay, on the extremity of which the Winter Palace is situated. There were about six hundred persons all told, very orderly, very sedate, and very solemn. The first ten or fifteen ranks were composed of persons who were linked arm-in-arm. We stood up in our sleigh and watched them pass. They turned to us and other spectators, exhorting us to join them and share their fate. We drove round another street in order to be present when the crowd should reach the bridge.

When we arrived on the square formed by the Kronverk Prospekt, just where the bridge debouches on to several roads, near M. Witte's house, we met Cossacks on foot darting across the bridge at full speed. This was the more surprising in that all the avenues to the bridge were already occupied by gendarmes and mounted Cossacks. The

Cossacks on foot were heartily enjoying the fun, and in a few minutes they were at their posts laughing and chattering when the order was given to form in array and to fire. The merry bugle-sound thrilled the hearts of everyone, sending a police officer and some civilians who happened, like ourselves, to be in the centre of the square, scampering off, whereby the police-inspector fell on a snow-heap, and just as we got on the right side of the Cossacks they fired deliberately and calmly for several volleys on the advancing crowd. The black mass of men paused, wavered and drew back. Screams and shouts, subdued by the distance, struck our ears. Then came curses and prayers, and signs of the Cross, from the few fugitive spectators on the square. Lastly, there was a charge of mounted Cossacks against ourselves and the people in Dvoransky-street; and thereupon the incident seemed to vanish, together with the curling clouds of blue smoke which rose from the crackling bonfires and were scattered by the Polar gusts. The Cossacks grinned, cracked jokes, danced, and resumed their merry games, while the spectators, who were separated from the crowd of students and workmen by some forty yards, felt reassured by the light-hearted attitude of the troops, and exclaimed: 'Thank Heaven, it was only cartridge by way of warning.'

But meanwhile the Cossacks had made a dash on the crowd, driving them back, and then picked up the dead and wounded, who, unhappily, were not even the first victims of the revolution. My watch pointed to half-past eleven as this deed of blood was done. 'Where is the Emperor?' people asked, as they moved towards the Imperial residence between the masses of soldiery through the few streets open to traffic. Nobody was allowed to drive along the Neva banks by the Winter Palace, but only down Millionaya-street, and there merely for a short distance. The square in front of the palace had the appearance of a city before or after an attack by a foreign enemy. The groups of Cossack horses, the gatherings of corps' officers with shining medals and gleaming swords, and the red sparkling flames of the fires round which the troops were warming their hands and arousing themselves gave an unwonted aspect to the historic residence of the Russian Tsars. 'Will the Emperor come? Where is he now?' people asked as the Cossacks rode on the sidewalks, deliberately knocking down men and women with their horses or with their hands.

Few, however, knew that his Majesty's dwelling-place has been surrounded with unusual mystery since Thursday, when, after returning to the Winter Palace, official information was issued that the Emperor was starting for Tsarskoye Selo, whereas his Majesty really repaired in the evening to the Anitchkoff Palace on the Nevsky Prospekt, where the Dowager Empress resides, and spent the night there. On Friday morning he went to the Winter Palace, while official information is said to have been given out that he was at the Anitchkoff Palace, and on Saturday morning he was reported to have gone to Tsarskoye Selo, whereas he was really in the Winter Palace. Where his Majesty was today nobody appeared to know. 'Let the Tsar appear! Why does not he himself come to talk to the people?' were among the exclamations of the crowd.

From time to time the Cossacks made a charge against the throng, never using their whips, but only their hands, for the officers say that the order had been given to refrain from violence until the moment came to use rifles, and then to fire deliberately and thoroughly.

Dr. Williams and myself drove to the Imperial Library, where some Liberals had gathered together at two o'clock to compare notes. A speech was made in the public reading-room by the president of last night's committee to the haggard, nervous, and overstrung men and women who, like myself, had not gone to bed since Friday night. M. Annensky said the doleful news had come that blood had been shed, and he asked us all whether we could give particulars. A statement was then made public respecting the conduct of the troops, and several powerfully-built bearded men, like my friend Prugavin, burst into tears. Suddenly a messenger rushed into the hall, bloodless, panting, and trembling in every limb. 'I am sorry to have to announce that the troops are firing on the people, blood is being wantonly shed, the Government is treating Russians as enemies. I propose that we all march in a body to the Palace, and there share the fate of our comrades, even though it be a bloody death.' Indescribable excitement followed upon this short address. The hearers leaped to their feet, rushed down the spacious staircase, and marched in a body down the Nevsky Prospekt. It was then half-past two, and we drove towards the Palace, determined to penetrate as far as the farthest line of the crowd, but before we had traversed half the way Cossacks met us, turned us back, and charged the pedestrians, driving them pell-mell into the side streets. The crowd shouted 'Down with autocracy', and asked the troops why they had not fought like that against the Japanese.

The crowd had been driven further and further from the Winter Palace, and Dr. Williams and myself witnessed the repeated charges of mounted Cossacks, who seemed to enjoy the sport of knocking folks down or dealing them stunning blows on the ear and heads. The people who suffered especially were those collected in front of the Alexander Garden, which is opposite the Admiralty, and about a hundred and fifty yards from the Winter Palace. They clung tenaciously to the iron railings of the garden and refused to be dislodged, but their conduct was irreproachable. Having amused themselves for over an hour with this kind of sport, the Cossacks were quietly formed into martial line, and the order being given to fire, they blazed away at the front line of spectators, composed principally of students, with a zeal what would have worked: wonders in Manchuria. Execrations, screams, and moans arose on the frosty air; the panic-stricken crowd rushed away, and thirty odd men lay convulsed in the agonies of death on the crimson-dyed snow, while the Imperial flag floated proudly over the Winter Palace. To their credit be it said, the students did not flee, but picked up most of their comrades, put them in sleighs, and drove away. I accompanied one sleigh in which two students, one of them wounded, sat holding a dead comrade, whose open mouth, glazed eyes, waxen face, and protruding brains aroused a feeling of unspeakable horror in the spectators. Crowds followed the sleigh, devoutly bare-headed, making the sign of the Cross, and uttering curses on the noble heads which but yesterday were mentioned with bated breath.

When we had reached the Anitchkoff Palace, where the Dowager-Empress, and possibly the Tsar, is living, a squadron of Cossacks, hearing the wail of the people, rode up to learn the cause. Catching sight of the white, upturned visage, red stains, and the brains lying on the sleigh cloth, they shook their heads at us, grinning, and cantered off good-humouredly. Over Trinity Bridge, which ends at the British Embassy, another body of unarmed men was moving slowly without any red flags or other symbols of disaffection, when a police officer called out that they must go back. They did not obey, probably could not do so, and they certainly had very little time. Thereupon the police superintendent rushed up to the officer in charge of the Petroffsky Guards, shouted something, and then the word of command was uttered, and a volley was fired, but the cartridges were blank. The people laughed, and cracked jokes with the soldiers, and then another set of rifles blared sharply. Four or five men fell, and little streamlets of blood worked red furrows in the white snow, and flowed into pools which were growing larger, when another volley, and yet another, rang out into the frosty air, and a number of men, who the moment before were brim full of life and energy, dropped lifeless to the earth. One young officer in spectacles moved up to another, and, rubbing his reddish nose, remarked: 'The men are not playing fair; they are firing over the heads of the people and down upon the ground. Oh, if it were not for that over a hundred would now be lying low.'

And this was, doubtless, true. It was owing to the reluctance of the troops to kill their brethren that the list of casualties is relatively so light. I asked a Court official why so little ceremony was made today about killing unarmed workmen and students. The answer was:

Because the civil law is suspended, and martial law obtains. You are surprised that people are unaware of this, and your wonder is, perhaps, natural, but in Russia we cannot see things the way you do in England. Last night his Majesty decided to suspend the power of civil authority and to confide the maintenance of public order to the solicitude of the Grand Duke Vladimir, who is well read in the history of the French Revolution, and will stand no silly nonsense. He will not make the blunder committed by so many officers of Louis XVI.; he will display no weakness. His infallible cure for the constitutional complaints of the people has always been to hang a hundred of the malcontents in the presence of their comrades; but heretofore he has received no hearing. Today, however, Monseigneur is supreme, and can experiment *in corpore vile* to his heart's content. The Grand Duchess, however, is in despair, and the womenfolk in all the Grand Ducal palaces are sending messages every hour or less to ascertain the number of wounded in the hospitals, and how best to alleviate their sufferings. But the Grand Duke Vladimir has a golden opportunity to manifest his statesmanlike and Napoleonic qualities, and he has no misgivings about the results. Whatever else may happen, he will quell the spirit of the mutinous throng, even though he may have to turn out all the troops at his disposal against the population. And people who now at night are learning that the Grand Duke is responsible for the bloodshed are acclaiming, 'Red is Vladimir's day, but our day is coming, and we will sport the Grand Ducal colours when it comes'.

In this way the revolution has been thwarted, the working men and students have been triumphantly defeated, and autocracy has won the day. Men of unshaken nerves and level heads are amazed at the Government's blunder. Never before had the Autocrat of All the Russias such a splendid opportunity to forge links of affection between himself and his people than today, They came full of confidence, they disclaimed all treasonable and unfriendly objects, they proclaimed that if the Tsar granted any one of their demands, even though it were only the abolition of the inspectorate of factories, they would have sworn to live and die for him. The secret may now be divulged that down to this morning the intelligent classes feared, and not without grounds, that the lower layers of the population would espouse the cause of the autocracy on the appearance of the Tsar, whom they expected today, and that a terrible blow would have been struck at the cause of constitutional agitation. A mediocre statesman or level-headed politician would have built his plan upon that groundwork, advised the Emperor to receive the public homage of his subjects, granted one point of the demands, and made common cause with the masses against the malcontent classes. The problem was not easy, but neither was it very difficult, yet nobody in the environment of the Emperor seems to have thought seriously of it. To thousands of intelligent malcontents millions of working men and peasants have now been added, and the sanguinary struggle between the autocracy on the one hand and the Russian nation on the other has been inaugurated by the inglorious successes scored by troops on 'Vladimir's Day'.

As day wore into night messages were received from various parts of St. Petersburg describing further deeds of the soldiery which deepen the dye that characterises 'Vladimir's day'. From one quarter comes the sad news of the death of Father George Gapon, who is said to have fallen on Trinity Bridge, opposite the British Embassy. From another come reports of a score of victims besides those whose deaths I have already described. As dusk enwrapped the loud-murmuring city, Cossacks, guards, and gendarmes advanced from the Palace driving the 'rabble' further from the Imperial residence. The ruffianly concierges were summoned about five o'clock from the Fontanka to help beat the crowd on the Nevsky Prospekt, and the principal bridges were then permanently occupied by the troops. In Gorokhvaya-street, which runs parallel with the Nevsky, squares of soldiers are stationed every third of a mile, and each side of the square looks in a different direction from the other. Cossacks sweep the streets in flying columns, policemen in scores marshal the fugitives, shout abuse at them, and drive them in various directions. The dvorniks or concierges fall foul of every one who appears to be a sympathiser with the popular cause, and the population, which arose hopeful this bright winter morning, expecting to receive words of comfort from the Little Father, the Tsar, is reeling homewards, not drunk, but enfeebled, beaten, and despairing.

By ten o'clock the defeated populace, famishing, shivering, and hungry, gradually abandoned the streets to the military, sought its holes and corners in a very chastened mood, and took to heart the first severe lesson administered by the autocracy on 'Vladimir's Day'. About seven o'clock a crowd attacked the shops, especially the Government alcohol houses, for the purpose of showing hatred of the measures by which the rulers extort money from the population.

I have just visited some acquaintances among the workmen who are dying or wounded. Many of them are in private houses. They are generally young men, wounded in the legs or abdomen. Twelve of those wounded on the Nevsky Prospeckt have just died. Forty others were seriously hurt, and many of them will lose limbs. Father Gapon was wounded during the fore-noon, but not dangerously. A number of the workmen, when threatened by the soldiers, lay down in the snow with their wives and children, challenging the troops to annihilate them instead of the Japanese. The soldiers backed out, and the workmen crossed the Neva.

A leading workman, who is now attending to the wounded, assures me that a resolution has been passed to come to St. Petersburg tomorrow and continue the revolution. At a mass meeting held at the Imperial Economic Society a resolution was passed to write a letter to the officers of those regiments which fired upon the people, reproaching them with lack of patriotism, and affirming that the workmen's movement differs in no wise from the general movement in Russia against the bureaucratic régime.

According to the latest accounts from only two hospitals, there were thirty-three dead bodies in the Obukhoffsky Hospital, besides fifteen grievously and twenty-five slightly wounded. In the Alafuzoffsky

Hospital were thirty dangerously and forty-three slightly wounded. But wounded are still being carried in from private houses to the hospitals.

A deputation from the Liberal Committee entered the Alexandrinsky Theatre here and addressed the public, asking them to honour the dead, who had died for liberty, by causing the amusements to cease. The audience warmly applauded and left the theatre in a body.

At a meeting of the Liberal Committee late tonight, Maxim Gorky read the following letter to the workmen from Father Gapon, who is not wounded:

> Comrades, Russian Working Men
>
> There is no Tsar. Between him and the Russian nation torrents of blood have flowed today. It is high time for Russian workmen to begin without him to carry on the struggle for national freedom. You have my blessing for that fight. Tomorrow I will be among you. Today am busy working for the cause.
>
> (Signed) Father George

Russia is in the throes of a revolution. The foreign enemy is clean forgotten, the course of the war awakens no further interest, for the administrative dam has suddenly given way, and the waves of democracy are rolling in and sweeping away the secular landmarks. The very police are become fascinated spectators, looking and listening with curiosity or sympathy at the seething crowds of workmen addressed by fiery demagogues in the language of treason, instead of dispersing, arresting, and maltreating them as before.

Messages and messengers are continually passing between Tsarskoye Selo and St. Petersburg, bringing orders and counter-orders, which make confusion worse confounded. High officials and Ministers shrug their shoulders and ejaculate: 'I told you so.' Ingenious schemes for quelling the troubles are framed, approved, embodied in instructions to military generals and police officers, and then countermanded. Gendarmes, Cossacks, and constables are being despatched hither and thither. Batteries which ought to have gone to the provinces after the blessing of the water on the Feast of the Epiphany are kept here to be turned against the people. But there is no thinking head, no central government, nothing but panic, hesitation, and chaos.

This morning the workmen of St. Petersburg arose from their slumbers to toil not for bread but for elementary rights and political freedom. For the first time in the history of this great city the newspapers ceased to appear, with the exception of two German journals, which contain merely Friday's despatches, and the *Government Messenger*. News of current events was carried by word of mouth, as in the Orient, assuming fantastic shapes on the way. Thus rumours were spread of an epoch-making manifesto from the Tsar to be published in a few hours, of a massacre being arranged by the police, of the appointment of a bloodthirsty despot to succeed Prince Sviatopolk-Mirsky, of the imprisonment of Father Gapon, of suicides and arrests of generals and officers without end.

Meanwhile the working-men strengthened their resolve by taking a solemn oath to proceed to the Winter Palace on Sunday with their petition, to wait there till the Tsar should come from his palace in Tsarskoye Selo, and then to request the abolition of the autocracy, and if that were refused to prefer other highly treasonable demands of a personal nature. While the men were being sworn in before the eyes of their trembling wives in one part of the city, cannons were being wheeled along the crisp, soft snow of the Nevsky Prospekt, over the frost-bound Neva in Basil Island on the other side, and placed in positions whence they could play effectively upon the rebels. On the Nevsky Prospekt itself the Lord Mayor of the city was at his hospitable board entertaining a number of private friends and officials. Suddenly his Majesty's health was pledged in Champagne, and certain of the guests refused to rise up or to drink. Then a loyal address was handed round congratulating his Majesty on his escape from the mishap on

Thursday. But some of the guests refused to sign it, and hurriedly left the house.

In Liberal circles petitions of right, proclamations to the people, and plans of campaign were being drawn up, and in Government circles bold suggestions were being made for proclaiming martial law in the capital, and were discussed amid initial misgivings and final indecision. Arms, too, were collected industriously for the workmen, mainly revolvers and rifles, which, compared with the volleys of the regular regiments and the destructive shells from quick-firing guns, are as helpful as cork soles in a shipwreck. But the workmen explained that they wanted arms, not for attack, but defence. They would march peacefully to the Winter Palace, and would not fire unless first attacked by the Emperor's servants, and then nothing would be sacred in their eyes.

Never before has the Russian Administration been called upon to take measures against such a mysterious phenomenon. Last week scarcely anybody had heard of the priest Gapon, nobody dreamed of a strike, and the working men had shown no interest in political questions. The entire movement was created overnight, and nobody knows how. Elemental forces appear to be at work which cannot be gauged or shaped, and even Father Gapon himself is unable to give any clear explanation of his movement, because it was only partly deliberate.

Tonight several political webs were industriously woven indoors, of which all, like Penelope's, are now being undone, excepting one, which will go down to future generations as the Gobelin of Russian history. Four meetings were held; to my knowledge, each of which was fraught with far-reaching consequences, and at the two most important I was actually present. One was convoked under the presidency of Prince Sviatopolk-Mirsky, the Minister of the Interior in spite of himself, who is forced to play a prominent part in the great national drama of Russia against his own will. He was in conference with the Minister of Finances, one of the principal supporters of the autocracy, and several directors of departments in the Ministries of the Interior and Finances, and the subject of the discussion was how to deal with the 200,000 or 300,000 men who would assemble before the Winter Palace tomorrow. How that conference ended I cannot say, for I was then present with Maxim Gorky, Professor Karevoff, and six others, who at half-past ten tonight called on Prince Mirsky to present their demands and interrupted those deliberations.

In another specious apartment, brilliantly lighted with artistic electroliers, sat M. Witte, presiding over twelve persons, mostly officials, discussing the reform of peasant legislation, and disagreeing wholly with each and every one of them. In another part of the city, in a long, dimly-lighted hall, some hundreds of workmen were foregathered, waiting for Father George Gapon, whose name is now a clarion to all Liberal Russia. Some members of the literary class called upon them and asked whether they would publish their petition in the form of a proclamation and distribute it to the world. They answered, 'No', because the workmen hate secret societies and underground printing presses, but would be delighted to have their petition published in the newspapers, and would gladly send 10,000 men to protect the printing office against the police and set up the petition in type. The literary men inquired whether Father Gapon would arrive. The workmen sent to inquire, and received an answer that he would appear at eight o'clock, but when the time came he was not there, and the general impression was that he was hiding from the police until Sunday morning.

Then the workmen opened their meeting without him by reading the petition to be presented to the Tsar and delivering speeches explaining or supporting it. One Socialist rose to address the meeting, but was shouted down, and the workmen cried: 'Tomorrow we ourselves may be Socialists, but today we are followers of Father Gapon, and will have no other leader but him', whereupon the Socialist orator disappeared. Suddenly two intelligent-looking men entered the hall, wearing overcoats, under which were military uniforms; and one of them having asked to be heard, said: 'Brothers, tomorrow you are going to the Winter Palace, and perhaps to death. Are you really going?' 'We are going at all hazards,' was the reply. 'Do you wish the soldiers to refuse to fire upon you?' 'That we do, most heartily.' 'Very well, brothers; they will refuse to fire. At this moment they are talking it over among themselves. They will not shed your blood, and, if ordered to fire, they will refuse. We have come to tell you this.' Then hearty shouts arose of 'Long live our brothers, the soldiers!'

The next act of the meeting was to add several clauses to the petition, including a demand for the separation of Church and State. It was also resolved unanimously that the workmen should march on Sunday as peaceful and loyal subjects of the Tsar, trusting in his desire to redress their grievances, and armed solely for the purposes of legitimate defence. They further declared that if they had any preliminary guarantee that the soldiers and police would make no arrests, except for a genuine breach of the peace, they would go unarmed. Finally, they resolved that if the Tsar would merely accept from their hands the petition and say that he would consider it they would return home satisfied and grateful, but that if he did not appear they would stay before the Palace until he did come.

Meanwhile a literary man of eminence, on the part of various social groups, had called on M. Witte and requested him to throw the weight of his authority into the scale on the side of the people. M. Witte listened, and asked what was expected of him. The representative of liberal Russia said: 'Tomorrow 300,000 men are going to the Winter Palace, in the hope that the Tsar, who is at Tsarskoye Selo, will come to town, and receive from their hands a petition. They are peaceful men, truly loyal, and desirous of doing things without bloodshed or violence. What we ask is that soldiers should not be called out against them, that no measures of repression should be employed. Perhaps your Excellency would generously disregard formulas at a time when much more than formulas are being swept away, and would place the matter before his Majesty, who surely desires only what is just and fair.'

M. Witte, who took a lively interest in what was said, and showed a genuine desire to help, expressed profound regret that the needful machinery was beyond his reach. The matter belonged to the Minister of the Interior, and he was merely the President of the Committee of Ministers. True, he was invested with the privilege of making a direct report to his Majesty, but only on subjects connected with the reforms mentioned in the Imperial ukase. But to appear before his Majesty with an unsolicited report and a request on subjects which belong to the department of the Minister of the Interior, and without definite and weighty facts, would constitute an irregularity which neither the gravity of the moment nor the probable results would justify. For those reasons, greatly to his regret, he must decline to take active steps, but he would be visible again at half-past eleven at night if his interlocutor desired to consult him further or to communicate fresh data. Thereupon the delegate withdrew.

In the meanwhile twelve operatives, acting upon the advice of Father Gapon, informed the Minister of the Interior of the intention of hundreds of thousands of men to march to the Palace on the morrow, and with this object had signed the following letter, which was composed by Father Gapon himself: 'High Excellency – The workmen and inhabitants of St. Petersburg belonging to various social classes will and must see the Emperor at two o'clock on Sunday, 22 Jan. on the Palace Square, in order to lay before him the needs of the entire Russian nation. The Tsar has nothing to fear, because I, as spokesman of the clubs of Russian factory hands of St. Petersburg, likewise my comrades and fellow-workers, and even the so-called revolutionary groups of various shades, guarantee the inviolability of his person. Let him appear, then, to his people as a genuine emperor with strong heart, and receive a petition at your hands. This is indispensable to his interests, to the welfare of the inhabitants of St. Petersburg, and to the weal of the Fatherland. Otherwise that moral bond may be severed which heretofore has linked the Russian Tsar with the Russian people. It is your duty, your primary moral duty, to the Emperor, and, indeed, to the whole Russian nation, immediately, this very day, to bring to the knowledge of his Imperial Majesty what we have already said, and likewise the petition which accompanies this letter. Tell the Tsar that I, the working men, and many thousands of people, have irrevocably resolved to repair to the Winter Palace, peacefully, and full of trust in him. Let him, in turn, display confidence in us, but let it be confidence in action, not in manifesto. A copy of this letter has been taken as a justificatory document of a moral kind, and will be brought to the cognisance of the whole Russian people.'

This communication is signed by George Gapon and twelve workmen. It was presented at the Ministry of the Interior at seven o'clock yesterday evening, and an official, speaking through the telephone, acknowledged its receipt by the Minister at eight. Father Gapon presented it in person, for later on last night Prince Sviatopolk-Mirsky admitted to M. Witte that Father Gapon had been to see him, and had been sent by him to the Metropolitan Archbishop.

The meeting at which I was present consisted of about a hundred prominent literary men of St. Petersburg, including Maxim Gorky, members of the municipality, and representatives of the army, navy, civil service, and university, besides one intimate friend of Father Gapon. The first proposal made was by a member of the municipality, asking that measures should be taken before it was too late to dissuade the workmen from marching to the Palace lest they be shot down by soldiers. But Father Gapon's friend rose and said: 'It is already too late, for we have sworn to go, and go we will – not, indeed, as rebels or malcontents, but as loyal subjects asking the Tsar to receive a list of our grievances. There is, therefore, no need of violence, and if it be done blood will have been shed wantonly, for we shall give no provocation. Therefore, any suasion to be exercised should be tried, not upon us, who are calm and peaceful, but upon those who can and may shoot.'

Thereupon a motion was made: to appeal to the officers of all the regiments stationed here not to fire upon the people on Sunday, but after some discussion concerning the difficulties in the way and the hopelessness of the task, the suggestion was negatived. Finally a member remarked that as a demonstration would take place in any case, and as it would prove bloodless or sanguinary according to the attitude assumed by the Government, a deputation ought to be sent immediately to the Minister of the Interior and to M. Witte to request them to make representations to the Tsar with a view to induce him to repair to the Winter Palace, which is a twenty minutes' railway ride from Tsarskoye Selo, and to receive a petition from the working men. 'In the interests of the nation they will surely comply with this request, and the Tsar will prove his love of peace and of his people.'

This suggestion was discussed, shelved, and then finally passed unanimously. The meeting elected the following persons members of the deputation: Maxim Gorky, Professor Kareyeff, Messrs. Myatokin, Annensky, Peshakhonoff, Arsenieff, and Hessen, who is editor of the journal *Provo*. It was now ten o'clock at night, and these seven gentlemen, accompanied by a workman representing Father Gapon, took sledges, and set out for Prince Sviatopolk-Mirsky's residence. Meanwhile the meeting resolved itself into a permanent committee.

The delegation started full of hope. I asked them why they fancied the Ministers would through the barriers of etiquette, tradition, and forms, and go to the Emperor with a message at night. They answered: 'Because we are now on the other side of tradition and etiquette; we are in revolution, and the Government's duty is to prevent bloodshed. Therefore, they will act differently from ordinary times. They published this morning a notice to the people to keep away from the crowds if they wanted to keep from getting killed or wounded. That warning was ill-advised. But there is yet time to take a more prudent attitude, and they will probably profit by it; but if they do not the people's blood will be upon their heads, and we shall have done our duty.'

At half-past ten last night the deputation, in four little sleighs, reached the Ministry of the Interior, and were received by supercilious servants, who, looking at them askance, asked their business.

'We have business with the Minister of the Interior.'

'His Excellency never receives at night.'

'We know when he receives and does not receive, but we are come on a special errand of high importance to the State.'

'His Excellency cannot possibly receive you.'

'Then we will wait here until he can.'

Come tomorrow or Monday.'

'That will be too late. We must see him tonight.'

'It is impossible; his Excellency is absent.'

'Then we will await his return.'

At this conjuncture an officer suggests that they should see the Assistant Minister Rydseffsky, who is head of the police. After a short consultation they agree. The servant goes to M. Rydseffsky, announces them, and an officer appears.

'What's your business with his Excellency?'

'A matter of the highest importance to the State.'

'His Excellency is alone and cannot see you.'

'His being alone is no impediment; we come on a peaceful errand.'

'Come on Monday.'

'No, we must see him tonight; otherwise we will wait here.'

After a time they wore asked for their visiting cards, and the Post Office Directory was consulted; then they were received. M. Rydzeffsky was standing up, half protected by a sort of screen and partly by an official who stood in front of him. He spoke coldly, officially, evasively, while the words of the delegates were cordial, suasive, impassioned. Once when one delegate remarked: 'Our sole motive is to hinder bloodshed, and, as we presume you are actuated by the same desire, we hope you will see that no instructions are given likely to lead to violence.'

M. Rydzeffsky replied: 'As your convictions are profound and your humanity intense, why don't you go and try their effects on workmen and persuade them to abandon their intention instead of coming here to get the authorities to swerve from the path marked out?' The delegates answered that the workmen's resolution was irrevocable, and now they could influence only the authorities, if any one. 'I will give no promise of any kind, and I don't see why you should expect any; indeed, you ought not to have come to me, who am only Assistant Minister. You should have gone to Prince Mirsky; he can help you; I cannot.' 'We went to Prince Mirsky, but were sent to you, and if you cannot act independently you can communicate to the Minister what we have said to you, and if that has no effect neither would our interview with Prince Mirsky himself.' Then M. Rydzeffsky, who was stiff, formal, and repellent throughout the conversation, informed the delegates that the Government was well informed of all the facts, and had taken measures which no representations would change, and for that reason he held out no hope that their request would be complied with.

The deputation then left, and drove back across the ice-bound Neva to a distant part of the city, where M. Witte resides. M. Hessen, editor of the *Pravo*, who is well acquainted with the ex-Minister, and had spoken with him in the afternoon, introduced the deputation. M. Witte received them affably, offered them tea, which they refused, and, sitting down in an armchair in front of his desk, asked them what he could do to help them. They narrated the object of their visit, and by way of adducing fresh facts informed him that the soldiers had promised not to fire upon the people. What they did not themselves know, then, was that the soldiers had also brought aims to the workmen for the purpose of defence. M. Witte was all attention while he listened, and full of sympathy when he spoke, but for practical assistance they looked to him in vain. He said: 'Whatever the authorities will do tomorrow has been decided upon already. The Ministers of Finances, the Interior, and others have been concerting measures this evening, but my views were not asked, and if volunteered, would not be taken. I am nothing in the Administration. My role is circumscribed by the reforms foreshadowed in the Ukase. On those questions I may report to his

Majesty, but not on events which fall within the sphere of the Minister of the Interior, who knows all the facts. Besides, I have no data for exceptional action, and in no case would exceptional action on my part lead to the desired results. How can you expect that the Emperor would listen to me and suddenly come to St. Petersburg to receive a petition from 100,000 persons? If his Majesty ever consented to enter into relations with the people it would only be after long deliberation, and then he would not come to a countless throng, but would perhaps consent to receive a deputation. If that would satisfy the people there must be no haste. The demonstration should be put off.'

The delegates regretted that the procession was resolved upon irrevocably, and whatever M. Witte could or would do must be done quickly. The ex-Minster again regretted he could do nothing. He was a private man, nothing more, except in dealing with the Ukase, but the Administration had its own plan of campaign, and would carry out that without reference to him. Why did they not put their request to Prince Mirsky? They replied that they had been at the Ministry, but that the Prince was absent. 'I will telephone to him now if you like, and perhaps you can see him,' said M. Witte. The delegates thanked him and said: 'We will leave the room so as not to embarrass you during the conversation.'

M. Witte then called up Prince Mirsky, learned he was at home, and spoke to him very energetically. It is a proof of the excellent relations between them that they called each other 'thou'. M. Witte besought the Prince to receive the delegates, but Prince Mirsky refused, on the ground that he knew all the facts, had also heard their message from M. Rydzeffsky, and that the authorities would reserve their action for a suitable moment. And from time to time M. Witte's bass voice was heard asking: 'And have you no fears for tomorrow?' Like the refrain in a song came that fateful question: 'Have you, then, no fear for tomorrow? Well, you know best', and, turning to the delegates, the ex-Minister remarked: 'Prince Minsky will not receive you tonight, though I have asked him now. Do you suppose that I should be more successful if I asked something still more difficult of attainment? If you like, he will see you at half-past twelve tomorrow.'

The delegates declined, and returned at half-past one o'clock this morning, and reported progress to the meeting, which thanked them for their zeal. It was then resolved unanimously that everything possible had been done to hinder bloodshed, and that if men were killed or wounded today all Russia would recognise the ease with which it could have been prevented.

20 April 1906: An earthquake causes devastation in San Francisco
SAN FRANCISCO IN FLAMES
TOTAL DESTRUCTION EXPECTED
FEARED LOSS OF 5,000 LIVES
TROOPS MAINTAIN ORDER WITH THE RIFLE
DESTITUTE POPULATION
From Our Special Correspondent

Far from being exaggerated, the earlier reports of the catastrophe which has overtaken San Francisco gave hardly any idea of the real state of affairs. Total destruction by fire appears to be the rapidly-approaching doom of the metropolis of the Pacific Coast, for the flames have got completely out of control, there is no water supply, and the available stores of explosives used in checking the progress of the conflagration have been exhausted. From the business quarters of the city, already devastated by the earthquake, the fire spread with appalling rapidity during the night and yesterday morning to the residential sections, involving in destruction practically all the more important buildings, such as theatres, post offices, banks, and newspaper and insurance offices. It is estimated that from 300,000 to 400,000 people are homeless, and their number is being constantly increased. The Government is taking prompt steps for the relief of the unfortunate sufferers, and is despatching supplies to General Funston, commanding the troops at San Francisco

Other cities have suffered severely from the earthquake, notably Santa Rosa and San José, but no details have yet been received.

Estimates of the killed at San Francisco vary greatly, but certainly the number amounts to hundreds, while the injured may be counted in thousands. As regards damage to property the amount is placed at as much as £50,000,000. Of course, the loss to the insurance companies will be enormous, and much of this will fall on English societies.

A telegram from New York received just as we were going to press this morning places the death-roll at 5,000, and the damage to property at £60,000,000.

Last night the city resembled one vast shambles, with the red glare of fire throwing weird shadows across the worn, panic-stricken faces of the homeless, who are wandering about the streets or sleeping on piles of mattresses and clothing in the parks and on the pavements in those districts not yet reached by the fire. Thousands fled the city, forgetting for the moment the terrible suffering, physical and financial, that trails in the wake of the disaster. The scene presented by the flames was one of unspeakable grandeur. Looking over the city from a high hill in the western suburbs, the flames could be seen rolling skyward for miles and miles, while in the midst of the spitting red tongues of fire can be seen the black skeletons, and falling towers of the doomed buildings. At regular intervals the booming of dynamite tells of the work of the brave men who are attempting to save the city from annihilation.

Through all the streets ambulances and express wagons are hurrying, carrying the dead and injured to the morgues and hospitals. At the morgue in the Hall of Justice fifty bodies lie, but the flames rapidly approached this building, and the work of removing the bodies to Jackson-square opposite has begun. The police were carrying the dead to what appeared safe places, when showers of bricks from a building that had been dynamited to check the flames injured many of the workmen, and sent the soldiers in the procession hurrying to the hospitals. The work of removing the bodies was stopped, and the remainder of the dead were left to possible cremation in the morgue.

The city is now under stringent martial law, and squads of cavalry and infantry are patrolling the streets and guarding the sections that have not yet been touched by the flames. Despite their efforts to keep the crowds from the sections now being dynamited many persons have slipped through the guards, and not a few have suffered for their temerity. From the Barbary Coast a horde of vicious and criminal characters who infest that quarter poured forth, and started early last evening to loot the stores and rob the dead. Fearing some such fiendish climax to this day of horrors the Mayor and the Chief of Police had issued orders for the soldiers to kill all who were engaged in such work.

The earthquake has worked astonishing havoc in San Francisco's famous Chinatown. The Chinese theatres and joss-houses are in ruins, and rookery after rookery has collapsed, covering alive hundreds of Chinese. Panic reigns among the thousands of Chinese residents, and they fill the streets, dragging along whatever they can save. The Japanese quarter also has been burned, and the people have fled in terror, packing on their backs what household effects they could tie together. Thousands of men, women, and children from the Latin Quarter quitted in a throng when darkness began to fall, and marched in an endless procession towards the hills, or to the water front, frantically eager to get away from the city, lest other earthquakes should follow, and the flames trap them before they could make their escape.

At midnight the fire still roared, and the fleeing inhabitants could be seen for miles around amid the pillars of fire towering skyward. The after-crash of the falling ruins and the muffled reports of the exploding dynamite reach the ear at regular intervals. This disaster, which staggers comprehension, and in point of terror and damage is unprecedented on the coast, has not yet reached its culmination. Despite the vigilance of the police and soldiers many places were pillaged in the wholesale business regions. The liquor stores were broken into, and vagabonds are lying about the streets drunk.

Day dawned on a scene of death and destruction. During the night the flames had consumed many of the city's finest structures, and skipped in a dozen directions to the residential portions. They had made their way over it into the North Beach section, and, springing anew to the south, they reached out towards Third and Townsend streets. Warehouses and residences and manufacturers' concerns fell in their path, and this completed the destruction of the entire district known as South of Market-street. How far the fire is reaching to the south across the channel cannot be told, as this part of the city is shut off. The reports received from the interior are most alarming. Santa Rosa, one of the prettiest cities of the State in the prosperous county of Sonoma, is a total wreck, and there are 10,000 homeless men, women, and children huddled together. The loss of life cannot be estimated, but it will probably reach the thousands.

As the last great seismic tremor spent its force in the earth the whole business portion of Santa Rosa tumbled into ruins. Main-street is piled many feet deep with the fallen buildings, and not one business edifice is left intact. This destruction includes all the county buildings. The four-storey court-house, with its huge dome, is merely a pile of broken masonry. Nothing is left, and identification is impossible. What was not destroyed by the earthquake has been swept by the fire. Until the flames started there was hope of saving the residential district, but it was soon apparent that any such idea that might have been entertained must be abandoned. This was appreciated by the citizens, and they prepared to desert their homes. Not even their household goods were taken, but they made for the fields and hills to watch the destruction of one of the most beautiful cities of the West.

Messengers bring the saddest tidings of the destruction of Healdsburg, Geyserville, Cloverdale, and Ukiah. This report takes in the country as far north as Mendocino and Lake Counties, and as far west as the Pacific Ocean. These are frontier counties, and have not such large towns as those farther south. In every case the loss of life and property is as shocking as it is here. All the San Francisco theatres, including the Majestic, the Columbia, the Orpheum, and the Grand Opera House, are masses of ruins. The earthquake demolished them, for all practical purposes, and fire completed the work of demolition. The handsome Rialto and Casserly Buildings were burned to the ground, as was everything in that district. The scene at the Mechanics' Pavilion during the early hours of this morning, and up to noon today, when all the injured and dead were removed because of the threatened destruction of the building by fire, was one of indescribable sadness. Sisters, brothers, wives, and sweethearts searched eagerly for some missing dear one. Thousands of persons hurriedly went through the building inspecting the cots on which the sufferers lay, in the hope that they would find some loved one that was missing. The dead were placed in one portion of the building, and the remainder was devoted to hospital purposes. After the fire had forced the nurses and physicians to desert the building, eager crowds followed them to the Presidio and Children's Hospital, where they renewed their search for missing relatives. Up to a late hour yesterday afternoon more than 750 persons who were seriously injured by the earthquake and the fire had been treated at the various hospitals throughout the city.

The magnitude of the disaster grows hourly. Flames are still raging in the section of the city wrecked yesterday morning, and later despatches tell of the spreading of the fire into districts which escaped the full havoc of the earthquake shocks. That the loss of property will reach upwards of £35,000,000 seems highly probable. No human agency seems able to cope with the flames, and even the destruction of hundreds of buildings by dynamite to stop the flight of the fire has been unavailing, for the flames leap over the gaps made by the explosions and spread with alarming rapidity. Estimates of the loss of life still vary. Five hundred people have almost certainly perished, and it may prove that thousands have met an awful death. No way near an exact list of the dead will probably ever be obtained, as many bodies are believed to have been cremated in the burned buildings. The entire city seems doomed, as the flames are spreading in a dozen directions in the residential section.

Last night hundreds of firemen and rescuers were prostrated by the strain of their continual fight since early morning. In the crowds at many points people fainted, and in some instances dropped dead of shock. At the Mechanics' Pavilion scenes of heroism, and later on of panic, were enacted. The great building was turned into a hospital, with a corps of fifty physicians and nurses who had volunteered, and a Red Cross ship from the Government yards at Mare Island contributed doctors and supplies. Late in the afternoon, while the ambulances and automobiles were unloading the wounded at the building, the march of the conflagration up Market-street gave warning that the injured would have to be removed at once. Every available vehicle was pressed into service to get the stricken folk into the hospital and private houses of the western quarter. A few minutes after the last of the wounded had been carried through the door, fire shot from the roof, and the structure burst into a whirlwind of flame.

Down on the harbour-front the earth seems to have sunk from six to eight inches, and great cracks appear in the streets. These cracks were twisted into all shapes, and the buildings before they were destroyed by fire were seen to be out of alignment. Flames shot in sheets across the streets, and the street cars and Southern Pacific rolling-stock were burned to the truck-wheels. The Governor has issued a proclamation declaring the day a public holiday, when everyone is exhorted to do his best to restore order, public peace, and confidence. For the next few days citizens are enjoined not to leave their homes after dark. Yesterday's earthquake experience has vindicated the efficiency of the modern steel building, not one having suffered, even those in course of erection.

The flames are steadily completing their work of wholesale destruction, and from the business quarters, which are reduced to a heap of ruins, the fire is working havoc amongst the palatial private dwellings. If the entire city goes nobody will be surprised, and many people have fled, anticipating the event. Those people who remain know that relief trams are bringing succour from all parts.

Now another black night of terror threatens the city. There is no electricity or gas, and the only light available is the dull glare at the burning buildings. Over all hangs a dense pall of black smoke. The stench from the broken gas-mains and the burning materials is sufficient to overpower even the most experienced firemen. The tangle of broken wires, pipes, and rubbish of all kinds makes all movement well-nigh impossible. The people who remain seem almost dumbfounded, hardly realising the full extent of the calamity and fearing that others may happen. The poor are being fed by the authorities, and wait outside the relief stations in long, weary lines, pictures of abject misery. Nearly 150,000 persons are believed to be homeless, and the survivors are in a great plight for lack of water.

Most unhappily the first accounts of the appalling disaster which has laid the business quarter of San Francisco in ruins, and entailed a sacrifice of an as yet uncounted number of lives, were by no means exaggerated. The details which I was able to cable to *The Daily Telegraph* yesterday are corroborated in every respect, and the telegrams received today emphasise the awful character of the disaster. As regards the number of fatalities it will be impossible to give any precise facts for some days, but it is hoped and, indeed, believed, at the time of cabling, that the total will be considerably below one thousand. It is true that some estimates go as high as two thousand, and even more, while others go to the opposite extreme. After most careful inquiry, however, and allowing for possible exaggerations, I put the total at any figure between five hundred and seven hundred. The details of the disaster which has reduced nearly half the Metropolis of the Pacific Coast to ruins may be summed up briefly.

The first shock was felt at thirteen minutes after five o'clock on Wednesday morning, and a second shock came three hours later. The business part of the city, covering eight square miles, and about two hundred squares of buildings were wrecked. The residential portion of the city was shaken, but not badly damaged. The citizens rushed into the streets in panic. As fire broke out at various points, the Fire Department discovered that the entire water system was ruined, and there was no means with which to fight the flames.

The offices of the *San Francisco Examiner*, the Western Union, the Telephone, the Rialto, and nearly every modern business building in the city were wrecked to a greater or less extent, and left in the path of the flames which were swept onward by a fierce west wind.

General Funston ordered the troops to parade, and martial law was declared. In the absence of water, recourse was had to dynamite to check the flames. The Fire Chief, Mr. Sullivan, was killed while directing his men and soldiers, and policemen were injured while using giant powder to blow up buildings. Mayor Schmitz has appointed a relief committee of fifty prominent citizens, and established his headquarters in the Hall of Justice, the City Hall, which cost £1,500,000, having collapsed. The ferry docks slipped into the water, and the panic-stricken inhabitants were forced to escape from the city in tugs furnished by the Union Pacific Railroad. A view from the top of Telegraph-hill showed twenty-five fires blazing in various parts of the city.

Such, in brief, is an outline of the disaster, which no words can exaggerate, and the details, as filled in today, make the complete picture still more appalling. It is one of the ironies of the situation that, although telegraphic communication was described as utterly broken down, every paper in America today has columns upon columns of descriptive accounts from special correspondents at San Francisco. The explanation is that the telegrams, although written by representatives at the Golden City, are really despatched from distant suburbs, and, in some cases, from towns miles away. These accounts naturally differ greatly, and in some cases are very fragmentary, but it is abundantly clear on reading them in mass that the greatest earthquake in the history of the United States has taken place, and the damage will undoubtedly amount to a tremendous sum. Several experts, after a cursory glance round the devastated city at eleven o'clock this morning, put the total at £30,000,000, but exact figures in the case of property, as of life, are impossible to get at the present time. Even now fires are still raging, and the insurance companies, which will not suffer by the earthquake, are beginning to get very restive.

In a sentence, one can say, what with the earthquake and the fire about, all the business quarter of this prosperous and enterprising city has gone. Although the whole city was shaken up the great damage by the earthquake was limited to the low and 'made' lands which lie between the hills of San Francisco, and which are occupied by business buildings and warehouses, and, in the southern part, by cheap tenements. Happening as it did at five o'clock in the morning, the earthquake caused practically no loss of life among the business houses, but the tenement dwellings and especially the cheap lodging-houses suffered severely. Directly afterwards fire started in seven or eight places, and was aided by the broken gas mains. The water system failed, and all through the day the fire was fought with dynamite.

The Palace and St. Francis Hotels, where most tourists stay, escaped the earthquake, although the Palace was destroyed afterwards by fire. Almost all the larger buildings in San Francisco are lost. These include the magnificent City Hall, the new post-office, the *Call* newspaper building, twenty stories high, the Parrott building, which houses the largest universal stores in the West, the Grand Opera House, and St. Ignatius's Cathedral. There are conflicting reports about the fate of the Mutual Life building, the Chronicle building, the new Merchants' Exchange, and some of the hotels. The city remains under dose martial law, the whole regular garrison of the city and a regiment of militia being on guard.

It is probable that most of the better-class residential district, situated on the hills, escaped, and that the loss of life fell almost entirely on the poor tenement quarter. About one-third of the area of the city, and that the most closely congested part, was ravaged by the earthquake, and swept by the fire.

19 November 1906: Famous singer Enrico Caruso gets into hot water in New York
TENOR'S ADVENTURE
SIGNOR CARUSO ARRESTED AT NEW YORK
EXTRAORDINARY CHARGES
COMPLAINANT MISSING

Signor Caruso, the world's greatest tenor, and star of grand opera, was arrested yesterday under conditions exceptionally humiliating and painful. While he was in the monkey-house at the New York Zoological Gardens, it is alleged that the singer, who was alone, approached a lady and placed his hand on her in an offensive way. The lady, who gave the name of Mrs. Graham, was accompanied by a little boy. She feared to remonstrate or to say anything, and edged away, pushing her little boy along. Signor Caruso, she declared, followed and repeated his offensive action. Convinced that his attentions were not accidental, she still hesitated to do anything that might make her conspicuous or draw attention to her. She was preparing to leave the place when the action, it is charged, was again repeated. This time her anger overcame her womanly reserve, and she spoke sharply to the singer, saying: 'You must not do that again.'

A moment before, a policeman named Kane, who had been carefully watching Signor Caruso ever since he first took up his position close to Mrs. Graham, had walked over to the railing next to her little boy, and, by leaning forward, had observed every motion of the tenor. He heard Mrs. Graham rebuke Signor Caruso, and said to her: 'Madame, did that man touch you?' Mrs. Graham was in a semi-hysterical condition by this time from fright and embarrassment. She said: 'Yes, he did.' That was enough for Kane. With no gentle hand he reached over and caught Signor Caruso by the shoulder. 'You're under arrest, mister, and you're got to come along with me to the station house,' he said. Signor Caruso drew back indignant, but the muscular arm of the policeman shoved the singer, who is a stout little man, towards the door. At the station Signor Caruso gave his age as thirty-three, and described himself as an opera singer and a married man. 'Some terrible mistake has been made,' Signor Caruso ejaculated. 'It is horrible, it is awful. I did not touch this lady.'

Kane is a plain clothes officer, and is stationed in the monkey-house for the express purpose of detecting pickpockets and the vile class who force their attentions upon unaccompanied women and girls. He repeated his statement, and Mrs. Graham, a strikingly handsome young matron, aged thirty, told her story. Technically, Signor Caruso is charged with disorderly conduct. From the station house Kane took his prisoner to another district, where cells are provided. At the last address the chief officer entered the charge and told Kane to 'lock him up'. All this time Signor Caruso seemed in a semi-dazed, half-comprehending state, but on hearing the words 'lock him up' the famous tenor, who is the idol of the American opera-going public, recovered himself. 'You shall not put me in a cell,' he shouted. 'This is an outrage. I shall not submit.' However, into the cell Signor Caruso was put, and there he remained for nearly a couple of hours, until Mr. Conried, director of the Metropolitan Opera here, appeared hurriedly, and in a state of the greatest excitement, to bail out his most important artist. The sum was fixed at £100.

On the same evening Signor Caruso saw the reporters at his hotel here, totally denying the truth of the woman's accusation. Speaking half in English and half in Italian, the excited tenor declared solemnly that he was guiltless, and his accuser an irresponsible woman. While talking to the reporter Signor Caruso suddenly missed his black pearl stud, for which he paid £160 in London recently. This last calamity made him still more distraught. He said he must have lost it while dining out after leaving the police-station. He immediately instructed a search to be made, and a reward offered.

Today Signor Caruso and Mrs. Graham should have appeared at the police-court. But when the case was called neither appeared. Counsel for the singer said his client was suffering from sciatica, due to exposure, and was too ill to appear. The police, who professed to have sought for

Mrs. Graham diligently, declared that she had given a fictitious address, and that they could not obtain a trace of her. The magistrate said he would postpone the case until Wednesday. Naturally, this affair has excited the greatest curiosity, and in the police-court many members of the choruses and opera-going public were present. This morning the papers published many columns regarding Signor Caruso's arrest, and likewise portraits of the singer in his most famous roles.

Policeman Kane was really the only one of the principals in court today. He declared that he witnessed the alleged indignities, adding Signor Caruso had annoyed five other women before he went near Mrs. Graham. Kane insisted that he was right in making the arrest, and he declared that a year ago he had ejected Signor Caruso from the monkey-house for conduct similar to that of which he is now accused. 'It is impossible,' replied Mr. Dittenhoeffer, Signor Caruso's counsel. 'Signor Caruso could not have done such a thing.' Mr. Dittenhoeffer added that it was untrue that, as Kane alleged, the defendant had a false pocket in his long overcoat, through which he could thrust his fingers and touch persons while he appeared to have his hands in his pockets. The policeman, however, went into many details, and declared he had himself witnessed the alleged improper conduct on the part of the singer, and that he had tried to induce other persons to make a complaint against the tenor. 'All this,' said Mr. Dittenhoeffer, 'is untrue. I don't question the honesty of the police, but frequently, in their anxiety to make cases, they greatly exaggerate things. Signor Caruso is innocent.'

The polios are now instituting a canvass to discover the whereabouts of Mrs. Graham, and in the meantime Signor Caruso is reported to be confined to his room in a state bordering on nervous prostration. The grand opera season should commence here next week, and on the day of his visit to the Zoo Signor Caruso had been rehearsing a new role.

28 October 1908: An interview with Kaiser Wilhelm II creates a diplomatic stir
THE GERMAN EMPEROR AND ENGLAND
PERSONAL INTERVIEW
FRANK STATEMENT OF WORLD POLICY
PROOFS OF FRIENDSHIP

We have received the following communication from a source of such unimpeachable authority that we can without hesitation commend the obvious message which it conveys to the attention of the public.

Discretion is the first and last quality requisite in a diplomatist, and should still be observed by those who, like myself, have long passed from public into private life. Yet moments sometimes occur in the history of nations when a calculated indiscretion prow of the highest public service, and it is for that reason that I have decided to make known the substance of a lengthy conversation which it was my recent privilege to have with his Majesty the German Emperor. I do so in the hope that it may help to remove that obstinate misconception of the character of the Kaiser's feelings towards England which, I fear, is deeply rooted in the ordinary Englishman's breast. It is the Emperor's sincere wish that it should be eradicated. He has given repeated proofs of his desire by word and deed. But, to speak frankly, his patience is sorely tried, now that he finds himself so continually misrepresented, and has so often experienced the mortification of finding that any momentary improvement of relations is followed by renewed outbursts of prejudice, and a prompt return to the old attitude of suspicion.

As I have said, his Majesty honoured me with a long conversation, and spoke with impulsive and unusual frankness. 'You English,' he said, 'are mad, mad, mad as March hares. What has come over yon that you are so completely given over to suspicions quite unworthy of a great nation? What more can I do than I have done? I declared with all the emphasis at my command, in my speech at Guildhall, that my heart is set upon peace, and that it is one of my dearest wishes to live on the best of terms with England. Have I ever been false to my word? Falsehood and prevarication are alien to my nature. My actions ought to speak for themselves, but you listen not to them, but to those who misinterpret and distort them. That is a personal insult which I feel and resent. To be for ever misjudged, to have my repeated offers of friendship weighed and scrutinised with jealous, mistrustful eyes, taxes my patience severely. I have said time after time that I am a friend of England, and your Press – or, at least, a considerable section of it – bids the people of England refuse my proffered hand, and insinuates that the other holds a dagger. How can I convince a nation against its will?

'I repeat,' continued his Majesty, 'that I am the friend of England, but you make things difficult for me. My task as not of the easiest. The prevailing sentiment among large sections of the middle and lower classes of my own people is not friendly to England. I am, therefore, so to speak, in a minority in my own land, but it is a minority of the best elements, just as it is in England with respect to Germany. That is another reason why I resent your refusal to accept my pledged word that I am the friend of England. I strive without ceasing to improve relations, and you retort that I am your arch-enemy. You make it very hard for me. Why is it?'

Thereupon I ventured to remind his Majesty that not England alone, but the whole of Europe had viewed with disapproval the recent action of Germany in allowing the German Consul to return from Tangier to Fez, and in anticipating the joint action of France and Spain by suggesting to the Powers that the time had come for Europe to recognise Muley Hafid as the new Sultan of Morocco. His Majesty made a gesture of impatience. 'Yes,' he said, 'that is an excellent example of the way in which German action is misrepresented. First, then, as regards the journey of Dr. Vassel. The German Government, in sending Dr. Yaesel back to his post at Fez, was only guided by the wish that he should look after the private interests of German subjects in that city, who cried for help and protection after the long absence of a Consular representative. And why not send him? Are those who charge Germany with having stolen a march on the other Powers aware that the French Consular representative had already been in Fez for several months when Dr. Vessel set out?

'Then, as to the recognition of Muley Hafid. The Press of Europe has complained with much acerbity that Germany ought not to have suggested his recognition until he had notified to Europe his full acceptance of the Act of Algeciras, as being binding upon him as Sultan of Morocco and. successor of his brother. My answer is that Muley Hafid notified the Powers to that effect weeks ago, before the decisive battle was fought. He sent, as far back as the middle of last July, an identical communication to the Governments of Germany, France, and Great Britain, containing an explicit acknowledgment that he was prepared to recognise all the obligations towards Europe which were incurred by Abdul Aziz during his Sultanate. The German Government interpreted that communication as a final and authoritative expression of Muley Hafid's intentions, and therefore they considered that there was no reason to wait until he had sent a second communication, before recognising him as the *de facto* Sultan of Morocco, who had succeeded to his brother's throne by right of victory in the field.'

I suggested to his Majesty that an important and influential section of the German Press had placed a very different interpretation upon the action of the German Government, and, in fact, had given it their effusive approbation precisely because they saw in it a strong act instead of mere words, and a decisive indication that Germany was once more about to intervene in the shaping of events in Morocco. 'There are mischief-makers,' replied the Emperor, 'in both countries. I will not attempt to weigh their relative capacity for misrepresentation. But the facts are as I have stated. There has been nothing in Germany's recent action with regard to Morocco which runs contrary to the explicit declaration of my love of peace, which I made both at Guildhall and in my latest speech at Strasburg.'

His Majesty then reverted to the subject uppermost in his mind – his proved friendship for England. 'I have referred,' he said, 'to the speeches in which I have done all that a Sovereign can to proclaim my goodwill. But, as actions speak louder than words, let me also refer to my acts. It is commonly believed in England that throughout the South African War Germany was hostile to her. German opinion undoubtedly was hostile – bitterly hostile. The Press was hostile; private opinion was hostile. But what of official Germany? Let my critics ask themselves what brought to a sudden stop, and, indeed, to absolute collapse, the European tour of the Boer delegates who were striving to obtain European intervention? They were fêted in Holland; France gave them a rapturous welcome. They wished to come to Berlin, where the German people would have crowned them with flowers. But when they asked me to receive them, I refused. The agitation immediately died away, and the delegation returned empty-handed. Was that, I ask, the action of a secret enemy?

'Again, when the struggle was at its height, the German Government was invited by the Governments of France and Russia to join with them in calling upon England to put an end to the war. The moment had come, they said, not only to save the Boer Republics, but also to humiliate England to the dust. What was my reply? I said that so far from Germany joining in any concerted European action to put pressure upon England and bring about her downfall, Germany would always keep aloof from politics that could bring her into complications with a Sea Power like England. Posterity will one day read the exact terms of the telegram – now in the archives of Windsor Castle – in which I informed the Sovereign of England of the answer I had returned to the Powers which then sought to compass her fall. Englishmen who now insult me by doubting my word should know what were my actions in the hour of their adversity.

'Nor was that all. Just at the time of your Black Week, in the December of 1899, when disasters followed one another in rapid succession, I received a letter from Queen Victoria, my revered grandmother, written in sorrow and affliction, and bearing manifest traces of the anxieties which were preying upon her mind and health.

I at once returned a sympathetic reply. Nay, I did more. I bade one of my officers procure for me as exact an account as he could obtain of the number of combatants in South Africa on both sides, and of the actual position of the opposing forces. With the figures before me, I worked out what I considered to be the best plan of campaign under the circumstances, and submitted it to my General Staff for their criticism. Then I despatched it to England, and that document, likewise, is among the State papers at Windsor Castle, awaiting the serenely impartial verdict of history. And, as a matter of curious coincidence, let me add that the plan which I formulated ran very much on the same lines as that which was actually adopted by Lord Roberts, and carried by him into successful operation. Was that, I repeat, the act of one who wished England ill? Let Englishmen be just and say!

'But, you will say, what of the German navy? Surely, that is a menace to England! Against whom but England are my squadrons being prepared? If England is not in the minds of those Germans who are bent on creating a powerful fleet, why is Germany asked to consent to such new and heavy burdens of taxation? My answer is clear. Germany is a young and growing Empire She has a world-wide commerce, which is rapidly expanding, and to which the legitimate ambition of patriotic Germans refuses to assign any bounds. Germany must have a powerful fleet to protect that commerce, and her manifold interests in even the most distant seas. She expects those interests to go on growing, and she must be able to champion them manfully in any quarter of the globe. Germany looks ahead. Her horizons stretch far away. She must be prepared for any eventualities in the Far East. Who can foresee what may take place in the Pacific in the days to come, days not so distant as some believe, but days, at any rate, for which all European Powers with Far Eastern interests ought steadily to prepare? Look at the accomplished rise of Japan; think of the possible national awakening of China; and then judge of the vast problems of the Pacific. Only those Powers which have great navies will be listened to with respect, when the future of the Pacific comes to be solved; and if for that reason only Germany must have a powerful fleet. It may even be that England herself will be glad that Germany has a fleet when they speak together on the same side in the great debates of the future.'

Such was the purport of the Emperor's conversation. He spoke with all that earnestness which marks his manner when speaking on deeply-pondered subjects. I would ask my fellow-countrymen who value the cause of peace to weigh what I have written, and to revise, if necessary, their estimate of the Kaiser and his friendship for England by his Majesty's own words. If they had enjoyed the privilege, which was mine, of hearing them spoken, they would doubt no longer either his Majesty's firm desire to live on the best of terms with England or his growing impatience at the persistent mistrust with which his offer of friendship is too often received.

14 November 1908: The Ford Model T makes its British debut with a technical summary by the *Telegraph*
MOTORS AT OLYMPIA
SEVENTH INTERNATIONAL EXHIBITION
A SPLENDID DISPLAY

Although there was no formal opening of the Motor Exhibition at Olympia yesterday, the standholders were all ready for the public when they entered the building at ten o'clock that morning. A magnificent spectacle met their eyes as the visitors passed the turnstiles. Thousands of tiny electric lamps illuminated the various stands, and were reflected again and again by the glittering steel and silvered fittings on the cars. Thornycroft had festoons of smilax, with pink flowers in hanging baskets, the B.S.A. relied on their two silver chassis reflecting their lights as a thousand mirrors, and the big B.S.A. limousine here blazed with reflected glory in its polished panels. Rover cars, with the heart-shaped silver radiators, made a picturesque feature, while the chrome-yellow body of the Zedel two-seated carriage formed a contrast to the magnificent basket-work and damasked leather upholstery of the Gobron Brillé limousines. The carriage work is especially fine in the present exhibition. The Austin wholly-enclosed landaulette should not fail to be seen; it is quite original in many of its features. Lorraine-Dietrich have a limousine with panels in cane basket work, while the Pack's automatic lever fixed on several of the cars allowed the machinery to be seen as well as the carriage work. The attendance of the public was moderate in the morning, but increased steadily all the afternoon until the evening, when the entire hall was crowded with people. Then every stand was invaded by the visitors, and the attendants kept busily engaged answering their queries.

Messrs. Perry, Thornton, and Schreiber (Ltd.) provided the wit and humour of last year's exhibition in this hall with their little book of verses, 'After Omar'. In their spare moments they disposed of a number of 15 h.p. Ford cars, to their own and the buyers' satisfaction. This year they have a new model to attract visitors to their stand.

But before examining it every visitor should get the latest catalogue of Ford cars, and read it. It is full of quaint sayings in its foreword, besides giving the necessary technical details and description of the Ford cars. It starts with the premise that 'without the past record of the manufacturer as a guide' the prospective buyer of a car at the show 'must put his trust in the left hind foot of a rabbit caught in the full of the moon – and the rabbit may be the private property of the manufacturer himself', it naively adds. Then, with praise to the rest of the automobile world, it modestly adds that 'no better features or material as is found in the various Ford models can be bought anywhere on earth at any price'.

Joking apart, the catalogue tells the motorist to see and have a run on the cars instead of taking any notice of literary statements. Ford cars are made in America, and in that country they have brought standardisation to as near perfection as possible. Last year the Ford Company sold 15,000 cars. This year they are going to manufacture 25,000 cars, and expect to sell them. The reduction in the cost of manufacture on this large scale is tremendous, consequently visitors to the exhibition must not think that the low price of the Ford cars means rubbish for the buyer. On the contrary, the 15 h.p. Ford two-seater, for £185, gave the purchaser value for his money. This year this model remains unchanged, but another low-priced motor-vehicle of 20 h.p. is the novelty of the stand.

This 20 h.p. car is to be purchased, including a four-seated double phaeton body, Dunlop or Continental tyres complete, for £225. So far, in wandering round the exhibition, this is the cheapest car to be found for its size. The engine has its four cylinders cast in one block, three and three-quarter inch bore and four inch stroke, with water-jacketed cylinder heads detachable, similar to the new Daimler engine. This feature in itself is a novelty, as well as a distinct improvement, as it gives the easiest access to the cylinder possible. Another noticeable feature of this car is its lubrication. This is effected by a special 'splash system', worked by the fly-wheel. The latter is enclosed with a chamber for oil under it, and the system is so arranged that any excess of oil in the crank chamber or elsewhere runs back into this chamber under the fly-wheel. This 20 h.p. model has the usual Ford epicyclic gears running in an oil bath and other general details, but differs by not having the pump or starting-up crank in the radiator, aa in the 15 h.p. type, while the commutator is in the front, and not behind, as in former patterns. The springing of the chassis, too, differs by the whole being suspended on only two springs, placed transversely one in front and one behind. The length of the chassis is eight feet four inches, with a wider wheel-track than most cars of this size. This 20 h.p. car should be very successful, as it is sufficiently more powerful than the 15 h.p. to carry four passengers comfortably and well over any sort of roads in all districts, hilly or otherwise.

17 April 1912: News emerges of the scale of the disaster befalling the *Titanic* on her maiden voyage
DISASTER TO THE *TITANIC*
868 SURVIVORS ON THE *CARPATHIA*
1,400 LIVES LOST
RECORD CATASTROPHE

Last night the following message was received by the White Star Line from King George at Sandringham:

> The Queen and I are horrified at the appalling disaster which has happened to the *Titanic*, and at the terrible loss of life.
>
> We deeply sympathise with the bereaved relations, and feel for them in sorrow with all our heart.
>
> (Signed) George R. & I.

The White Star management replied, as follows:

> 'We are deeply grateful to your Majesty and the Queen for the gracious message of sympathy. The calamity is indeed overwhelming in its magnitude, and in the sorrow it must bring to so many hearts. We are taking necessary steps to ensure that the knowledge of your Majesties' sympathy shall reach all for whom it is intended.
>
> (Signed) Ismay, Imrie, and Company
>
> Managers, White Star Line

Queen Alexandra last night wired the White Star Line as follows:

> It is with feelings of the deepest sorrow that I hear of the terrible disaster to the *Titanic*, and of the awful loss of life. My heart is full of grief and sympathy for the bereaved families of those who have perished.

The White Star Company replied as follows:

> Your Majesty's gracious message of sympathy is deeply appre-
> ciated by us, and will be cherished by all who have suffered
> bereavement by the sad loss of the *Titanic*.

Among those who have communicated their sympathy to the managers of the White Star Line are the German Emperor, Prince Henry of Prussia, the President of the Board of Trade, and the Postmaster-General.

There is now, unfortunately, no possible doubt that the maiden voyage of the White Star liner *Titanic*, the largest vessel in the world, has resulted in a catastrophe of unprecedented dimensions, even in the annals of ocean tragedy. Down to an early hour yesterday morning it was confidently believed that the great vessel's collision with the iceberg had not given rise to loss of life, and that there was a fair chance of her being able to make the port of Halifax in safety. The earlier telegrams all led to the belief that the whole of the passengers had been removed from her in safety to other liners.

Unhappily, these optimistic views have been completely belied by events. The latest official news received by the White Star Company indicates that only 868 of the passengers and crew were saved. This is the number which the Cunard liner *Carpathia* has on board, and is bringing to New York, where she is expected to arrive either tomorrow night or on Friday morning. It is not yet known exactly how many of these are passengers, and how many are members of the crew, but there seems reason to suppose that the staff saved number about two hundred, the remainder being passengers. In all the death-roll will certainly exceed 1,200, and may approach 1,400. Partial lists of the survivors have already been received, either direct by the White Star Line or through Reuter's Agency. These lists total about 360, leaving upwards of another three hundred survivors yet to be recorded. It is explained that interferences by amateur wireless telegraphists have impeded the work of despatching their names, with the result that many of them have been mutilated or put into forms in which they do not appear in the liner's passenger lists.

The earliest intelligence of the sinking of the *Titanic* and of the terrible loss of life thereby caused came in shortly before one o'clock this morning simultaneously from Reuter's Agency and the Central News. The news of the foundering of the great liner appeared in the first edition of *The Daily Telegraph* yesterday, and that of the death-roll in all the subsequent editions.

Among those definitely known to have been saved are Mr. Bruce Ismay, chairman and managing director of the White Star Line, the Countess of Rothes, Mrs. John Jacob Astor, Sir Cosmo and Lady Duff-Gordon, who were travelling under the names of Mr. and Mrs. Morgan, and Mrs. C.M. Hays, wife of the president of the Canadian Grand Trunk Railway. The fate of Mr. Hays was at first uncertain, but it is now stated that he was among those rescued. Colonel J.J. Astor, the millionaire, is believed to have been drowned, but this is by no means certain. The same remark also applied to Mr. W.T. Stead, whose name, however, does not appear among the list of the survivors, and who is probably drowned. The fact that a whole day has passed without news of the safety of Mr. W.T. Stead leaves little hope that he escaped from the ill-fated ship. The dead also seem to include Mr. B. Guggenheim, a member of the millionaire copper firm, and Mr. E. Widener, son of the art collector, Mr. P.A.B. Widener. Mrs. Widener is safe. The terrible calamity has created consternation, not only in this country and in the United States, but also on the Continent, and on all hands great sympathy is expressed for the bereaved.

In the early morning a message from St. John's (Newfoundland) gave rise to the hope that the Allan liner *Virginian* had some of the survivors on board, and another straw eagerly clutched at was a statement made by the operator at Sable Island on Monday night, who, when asked as to the possibility of delivering messages to the *Titanic's* passengers, replied that it would be difficult to do so, as the passengers were believed to be dispersed among several vessels. Later, however, the sad intelligence arrived from Montreal that the Allan Line had received a communication to the effect that they were in receipt of a Marconigram, via Cape Race, from Captain Gambell, of the *Virginian*, stating he had arrived on the scene of the disaster too late to be of service, and was proceeding on his voyage to Liverpool. No mention was made of the rescue of any of the *Titanic*'s passengers. Another message also indicated that the Allan liner *Parisian* had no passengers belonging to the *Titanic*.

According to an official statement which arrived from New York early last evening, the White Star Line announced that they had received positive news that the number of the survivors from the *Titanic* was 868. The despatch was transmitted by the *Olympic*. At the West-end branch of the White Star Line in London there were numerous callers throughout the day to make inquiries as to relatives and friends on the ill-fated vessel. The Allan Steamship Company has received a cablegram from their agents at Montreal stating that they have received a wireless message from the *Virginian* saying that she had no passengers on board from the *Titanic*, and is proceeding on her voyage to the British side. Lord Ashburton, who was reported to have been on board the *Titanic*, is, as a matter of fact, a passenger on the *Olympic*.

As some doubt exists as to the exact number of persons on board the ill-fated *Titanic*, the Exchange Telegraph Company is officially informed that the following is as near the correct compilation of those on board as for the moment:

Passengers (first-class)	316
Second-class	279
Steerage	698
Total passengers	1,293

In addition, the crew numbered between 800 and 900.

It now appears that the message stated to have been received on Monday night by Mr. and Mrs. Phillips, of Godalming, from their son, the wireless operator aboard the *Titanic*, did not come from him at all, but from a brother in London. On receiving the message, the father came to the conclusion that it was from his son on the *Titanic*, but yesterday morning he stated that he felt he was mistaken.

Unprecedented scenes marked the early morning hours in and around the White Star offices, and at dawn today the endless crowd of weeping, sobbing, distraught men and women increased. All yesterday friends and relatives of the passengers had been prisoners of hope. Many of those who had left the office during the day, encouraged by the optimistic reports given out by the company's officers, and smiling at the thought of the early arrival of dear ones, returned last night in tears. They remained patiently awaiting most of today, albeit the news received was only of a fragmentary character, and, such as it was, confirming the worst fears. The officers and clerks replied to thousands of inquiries during the day. Some of them had been at the offices since 4 a.m. yesterday. They believed at first that all was well with the passengers on the greatest steamship afloat; then came the staggering news that hundreds of souls had gone down in two miles of ocean depth. People hoped against hope that messages from the *Virginian* and *Parisian* would relieve the anxiety and diminish the list of fatalities, but when at last the brief, laconic messages came, reporting 'Nobody rescued', everyone was despairing.

Not since the *Slocum* was burned to the water's-edge almost within sight of this city, with the sacrifice of 959 lives, chiefly women and Sunday-school children, had New York been so inexpressibly shocked. All today long lines of motor-cars crawled along close to the kerb, and richly dressed men and women hurried in to the White Star Company's building and up to the offices on the second floor. Weeping women and staggering men returned to their machines and drove off to make way for others. The company could not give a ray of hope; it could only say that there was nothing to contradict the report that hundreds had gone down with the liner, and we must await the arrival of the Cunard's *Carpathia* late on Thursday or early on Friday for full details.

Among the first to reach the offices and ask for information was Mr. Vincent Astor, son of Colonel John Jacob Astor. He was accompanied by Mr. William Dobbyn, Colonel Astor's secretary. They were led to the private office of Mr. Franklin, vice-president of the International Mercantile Marine, and remained half an hour. Young Astor had heard a rumour that his father had gone down with the ship, but his stepmother was saved. When the party came out he was sobbing, supported by his father's secretary. Neither would say what information they had obtained. Twice today young Astor drove to the offices, and when told that no complete list of the survivors had been received, he again left weeping with his face in his hands. 'Have you heard anything of your father?' he was asked. 'Not a word,' he replied. 'I fear the worst.'

Applicants for information came in scores throughout the day. They had read the morning newspapers and seen the list of survivors, but still hoped that the name of some loved one has been only accidentally omitted. They came tremulous with hope and fear, and always left sobbing. Hardened reporters assembled all day in the lobby of the White Star offices refrained from questioning them. Among those who made inquiry during the night and again today were Mr. William Force, father of Mrs. John Jacob Astor; Mr. Bradley Martin, junior, who would not tell for whom he was anxious; Mr. Pierpont Morgan, junior, who denied that the Morgans on the passenger list were relatives; and former Senator Clark, of Montana.

A young man and a young woman who refused to tell their names rushed into the offices before breakfast-time. 'Is it true the *Titanic* is sunk?' asked the man. He was told it was. 'My God,' he exclaimed. 'Then we are ruined; they are all lost.' The young woman became hysterical as she was led to the street.

In all the leading hotels rooms had been reserved for the *Titanic's* wealthy passengers. At the Ritz-Carlton, Lord Rothes patiently waited all night for some tidings of Lady Rothes, who was on board the *Titanic*.

Others on the *Titanic* who booked here were Mr. George Widener and his son Harry, and Mr. Bruce Ismay, chairman of the White Star Line. The Hotel Gotham reported that just before the wreck they received a wireless message from a man from Stockholm, who signed his communication Björnström Steffansson.

When the later reports of the disaster circulated in the big hotels, scenes of excitement and anxiety were instantly enacted. At every large hotel there is a steamship man, who has a desk, at which he arranges Transatlantic passages. These places were besieged by anxious friends and relatives of the *Titanic*'s passengers. Little groups stood about and discussed tragedies in the lobbies, and when some guest arrived with fresh news they circled around and made hurried inquiries. 'I have had more than thirty reservations from people on the *Titanic*,' said Mr. George Boldt, proprietor of the Waldorf Hotel. 'It seems almost inconceivable that such a thing should have occurred with such a ship at this time of the year. One man was coming from Scotland. He is old and infirm. I am afraid he would never make the lifeboat. Some of my dearest friends – people who have been here ever since I opened my house – were aboard the sunken liner. It is too bad.' Mr. Boldt was so much affected that he gave up his work for the night and sat in his private office receiving bulletins.

At the Hotel Plaza, Mr. W.T. Graham, president of the American Tin Can Company, anxiously awaited reports of his wife and daughter Margaret, who were to meet him here when the ship got in. Many people arrived here from distant parts of the United States and Canada to meet the *Titanic* and celebrate her maiden trip by a banquet on board. Most people here believed that the *Titanic* was unsinkable. They had been so assured by scores of apparently competent authorities on both sides of the Atlantic; Mr. Franklin, vice-president of the White Star Line, so assured *The Daily Telegraph* representative when he was asking for information. Nothing could more emphatic than his assurance on the point, and everywhere where his words were circulated people grew calm and confident.

Today we learn that Captain Smith has gone down with his

unsinkable ship, and Mr. Franklin, greatly depressed, has only this to say: 'I must take upon myself the whole blame for that statement. I made it, and I believed it when I made it. The accident to the *Olympic*, when she collided with the cruiser *Hawke*, convinced me that these ships, the *Olympic* and *Titanic*, were built like battleships, able to resist almost any kind of accident, particularly a collision. I made the statement in good faith, and upon me must rest the error, since the fact has proved that it was not a correct description of the construction of the unfortunate *Titanic*.'

Americans are appalled by the magnitude of the sea tragedy, and overwhelmed by the failure of the *Titanic*'s safety devices. They are asking today: 'Is there such a thing as an unsinkable ship?'

Mr. Lewis Nixon, the well-known naval architect, of New York, who designed the battleship *Oregon* and her class, believes that the *Titanic* crumpled up like an accordion. He admits that no stronger ship than the *Titanic* was ever built, and the fate that has befallen her may attend any other vessel striking a big iceberg or a submerged wreck.

A crowd assembled outside the office of the White Star Line this evening just as large as at any time yesterday. The latest bulletin says that 202 out of 325 first-class passengers have been saved, and 114 out of 285 second-class. Many domestic tragedies are revealed as one reads the list of survivors. In several instances wives have been saved and husbands lost, or husbands and wives have been lost and a child and a nurse saved. It is estimated that nearly 10,000 wireless messages to the *Carpathia* await answer.

Newspapers from all over the world have demanded a personal narrative from Mr. W.T. Stead, inviting him to name his own price, but Mr. Stead's name is not on the list of the survivors. Such fragmentary Marconigrams as come to hand indicate clearly that this newest and most luxurious and safest of ships, this unsinkable *Titanic*, found her grave in water two miles deep. The spot was only thirty miles south of the place where she received her death-blow from the ice, but the *Titanic* had been four hours in covering that distance in a hopeless quest for succour from the onrushing ships to which she was sending her frantic wireless appeals for help. None of the many vessels that received the summons and sped out of their course to respond, however, reached the *Titanic* before she went down. The stories printed here yesterday to the effect that the *Virginian* was towing the *Titanic*, and that the prospects of reaching Halifax were 'decidedly good' belong to the same series of stories as 'describe' the 'stampede for the boats', and the 'rowing through fields of ice', and other wireless myths.

The *Carpathia*, of the Cunard Line, in command of Captain Rostron, was the first to arrive, and she found twenty boatloads of survivors, most of them women and children, floating about among the ice-floes. All these people were finally taken aboard the *Carpathia*, after many hours' manoeuvring, by that vessel, to carry out the rescue work in a twenty mile-wide ice-field, without meeting the same fate as that which had overtaken the *Titanic*. The other vessels that responded to the call found only wreckage and bodies, for the most part the bodies of men, because the law of chivalry of the sea had prevailed, and it was 'the women and children first' in the last horrible hour of the *Titanic*. So far as one can interpret the brief wireless messages, it seems certain that the women and children, irrespective of rank or cabin, really did go first into the boats; that discipline was maintained; that the captain went down, as he would desire, with his ship; and that only so many of the crew escaped as were required to man the boats. Such is about the only consolation, apparently, to be derived. There has been no suggestion of a repetition of the scenes of panic which marred the last hour of the French liner *Bourgogne*.

Accounts vary as to whether seventy men or one hundred were saved. They change with every fleeting hour, and indicate, apparently, either an excusable state of confusion in the White Star receiving office, where the clerks are working night and day, or possibly a partial collapse on the part of the hard-working wireless operator on the *Carpathia*. All the liners which were near the scene of the disaster are now widely scattered, and give little hope of bringing definite information. The

Californian, which was reported to be in the vicinity of the wreck, is westbound to Boston, and is due there today unless she is delayed by the events which have just occurred. The *Olympic* is eastbound, and will probably not be able to give much further information until she reaches your side. The *Baltic*, which was also near the wreck, was scheduled to arrive at Queenstown tomorrow, but will probably be delayed by the help she sought to give to the wrecked ship. Other chance steamers may have been near the wreck, but their presence has not been reported in New York. The cable steamship *Minia*, which left St. Pierre Miquelon yesterday afternoon, is supposed to be in the vicinity of the disaster, but little hope is entertained that she will find any of the *Titanic*'s people.

The weather signal station on the Gulf of St. Lawrence reported today that heavy fogs lay off Nova Scotia. A violent thunderstorm broke over that neighbourhood last night, and is travelling eastward. It said that such conditions left little hope for the rescue of any survivors of the *Titanic* that might still be adrift in rafts and boats. The captains in port here do not encourage the hope that any of the survivors are still alive in the boats.

All these sailors, British and foreign alike, have a brotherly feeling of sympathy for the *Titanic*'s captain. 'Poor Smith! Poor Smith!' is the phrase one hears all along the waterside. They point to the fact that the *Carpathia*'s course has been diverted from Halifax to New York because of the ice. At 7.50 a.m., New York time, Captain Rostron said that he was proceeding to New York with eight hundred of the rescued passengers. 'After having consulted Mr. Bruce Ismay, and, considering the circumstances with so much ice about, I believed that New York was the best, in view of the large number of icebergs, and the twenty-mile field of ice with so many bergs.'

Mr. Franklin, vice-president of the White Star Line, when questioned by reporters this afternoon, repeated that he did not know any passengers that could be considered as safe outside of the 868 aboard the *Carpathia*. Mr. Franklin was repeatedly urged to make public the full text of the wireless message received last night from Captain Haddock, of the *Olympic*. This he refused to do. His attention was called to the fact that he had so far given only his own version of the message announcing the sinking of the *Titanic*. 'I thought Captain Haddock's message so disquieting that I didn't believe it's good policy to give the entire context. It's a curious thing,' he added, 'that no one received more definite information concerning the sinking of the vessel.' 'Do you think it good policy to keep back the entire truth?' he was asked. 'Nothing has been kept back,' was the answer, given emphatically. 'So far as the White Star Line is concerned everything has been made public.'

The brief wireless despatches indicate that the passengers and crew passed through thrilling experiences from the very moment the *Titanic* crashed into the berg in the dead of night until the *Carpathia*, several hours later, reached the scene and rescued the survivors from the lifeboats floating helplessly in the sea. The ice collision occurred at a time when most of the passengers had retired, or were about to go to bed. The shock of the collision sent many to the decks, partly dressed.

A wireless despatch came through Camperdown, Nova Scotia, that the passengers were ordered to the lifeboats at once. This would indicate that the *Titanic*'s condition was such that no time could be spared to return to the cabins for additional clothes, and danger still confronted even those so fortunate as to be put aboard the lifeboats. Huge quantities of field-ice covered the ocean, and in the darkness the crews had to guide their boats with the greatest care to prevent them from being jammed and overturned. The ice was so heavy that the lifeboats could not force their way through it, and as a result the boats became widely separated. The air was bitingly cold, and the chill that rose from the ice-floes caused the half-dressed passengers the greatest suffering. All through the night the lifeboats bobbed helplessly between the shifting cakes of ice, while the survivors prayed for dawn to come.

Shortly after two o'clock the sinking *Titanic* made her great dive into the sea, carrying with her over 1,400 persons to their death. Wireless reports of disputed authenticity describe her sinking with the captain clasping the rail of the bridge, and the wireless 'still spluttering for help'. Daylight came, and with it arrived the Cunarder *Carpathia*, which found only a score of lifeboats, filled with members of the crew and passengers, floating helplessly about the vicinity where the *Titanic* had gone down in two miles of water, and not more than thirty miles south of where she had met her death-blow four hours before.

Captain Smith, the commander of the *Titanic*, probably went to his grave with the ill-fated vessel without once being able to communicate direct with the agents of his line. Aside from the 'S.O.S.' sent by his wireless operator, not one word from him was received up to the time the *Titanic* sank, bow foremost, into the ocean. The White Star officials here impute not the slightest blame to Captain Smith. Mr. Franklin, in the moment of greatest stress, with his face haggard by the all-night watch, declared today: 'He was a fine sailor, brave as a lion. If anybody stuck to his post of duty to the last moment, I guess it was Captain Smith.' Another hero of the *Titanic* is believed to be the wireless operator, but here again for authentic news we still wait for the *Carpathia*.

One result of the White Star Line's misfortune is the increased prosperity of the Cunard's New York office. All today people who had booked by the *Titanic* were flocking into the competing office, where a special force of clerks worked under great pressure all day.

29 June 1914: Archduke Franz Ferdinand, heir to the Austro-Hungarian throne, is assassinated, and a spark is lit that will send Europe to war
ASSASSINATION OF THE HEIR-PRESUMPTIVE TO THE AUSTRIAN THRONE
BOMB AND PISTOL ATTACK
SHOT IN A MOTOR-CAR
EMPEROR'S GRIEF
From Our Own Correspondent

Another ghastly chapter was added yesterday to the tragedy of the Royal house of Austria-Hungary. We deeply regret to announce that the Archduke Franz Ferdinand, heir-presumptive to the Imperial Crown, and his wife, the Duchess of Hohenberg, were assassinated at Sarajevo, the Bosnian capital. The Archducal pair had been attending the manoeuvres in Bosnia, which concluded on Saturday. Yesterday they paid a visit to the Town Hall in Sarajevo, and near the building a bomb was thrown at their automobile. The Archduke warded off the missile with his arm, and it exploded near the car following, in which two persons were injured. The thrower, a Serb, was arrested. The Archduke and his wife attended the reception in the Town Hall as arranged. They were continuing their progress through the town, when shots were fired at them by a man in the crowd armed with a magazine pistol. Both were fatally injured, and died soon afterwards. The second assassin, a Serb student of nineteen, was with difficulty saved from the fury of the crowd, and arrested. It was known that the Archduke's life was threatened by a conspiracy of Serb political desperadoes, who resent the annexation of Bosnia to the Empire as a blow to the cause of 'Greater Servia'. The Archduke was warned, but decided not to change his plans.

At noon the terrible news was conveyed to the aged Emperor at Ischl. The horror felt throughout Europe at the crime must be mingled with deep anxiety as to the effect of this last shock upon a monarch weighed down with years and broken by so many tragic sorrows. 'I am spared nothing,' he is said to have murmured when the news was broken to him. In any event the political consequences of the assassination are likely to be grave. The next in succession to the throne of the Dual Monarchy is the young Archduke Karl Franz Josef, a nephew of the deceased Archduke.

The King and Queen, who were informed of what had happened by a telegram from the British Embassy in Vienna, were deeply distressed at the news, and caused inquiries to be made at the Austrian Embassy in London, while a telegram expressing their deep sympathy was despatched to the Austrian capital. It was announced last night that the English Court goes into mourning for one week, dating from yesterday. Tonight's State Ball has been postponed.

An event which throws everything that has happened within this century into the shade in this country, so frequently and hardly tried, took place at Sarajevo this morning, when the Archduke Franz Ferdinand and his wife, the Duchess of Hohenberg, were assassinated by shots from a Browning pistol. The circumstances of the attempt leave no doubt that there was a well-prepared conspiracy of 'Big Servian' origin, while it is no less certain that resort was had to the firearm a quarter of an hour after an attempt to assassinate the Archducal couple with bombs had failed, and both assassins are Serbs who have played a leading part in anti-Austrian agitation. When it was known at the Servian Ministry here that the Archduke Franz Ferdinand and his wife intended to go to the manoeuvres in Bosnia, a warning was uttered advising his Imperial Highness not to undertake this journey, as certain Servian desperadoes were planning an attempt on his life. In spite of this the Archduke decided to go, and undertook the journey with his wife.

Last Wednesday the Archducal pair journeyed to Sarajevo, and resided at Ilizde, a watering place near the Bosnian capital. Great festivities were arranged in Sarajevo and Ilizde in honour of the visit of his Imperial Highness and the Duchess. While the Archduke attended the mountain manoeuvres for two day near Tarin, not far from Sarajevo, the Duchess of Hohenberg remained in the capital, where she was much fêted. Yesterday the mountain manoeuvres of the 15th and 16th Army Corps concluded, and the Archduke, who was very pleased with the troops, issued an army order expressing his great satisfaction.

Today the Archducal couple went to the Bosnian capital together, and visited numerous public buildings and institutions. Just after 10 a.m. the Archduke and his consort, accompanied by a large suite, drove to the Town Hall through a large crowd of Sarajevo's population, who ranged themselves on either side of the street. Near the Town Hall a bomb was flung at the automobile in which the Archduke and his wife were seated, but the Archduke warded it off with his arm. It fell on the ground and exploded, but meanwhile the motor-car had driven on beyond danger. Two gentlemen seated in the second automobile, Count Boos-Waldeck and First Lieutenant Merizzi, were both slightly injured. Six persons among the public were more or less severely injured. The bomb was thrown by a printer of Trebinje, named Cabrinovic. He was immediately arrested.

After the reception in the Sarajevo Town Hall, the Archduke and his wife continued their journey, when a Servian student named Prinzip, of Grahovo, fired several times in succession at the Archducal pair from a Browning pistol. The Archduke's face was struck by a bullet, while the Duchess was struck in the abdomen. The Archduke and the Duchess were carried into the Konak, where they succumbed to their injuries. The second assassin was arrested with great difficulty, as the crowd attempted to lynch him.

The horror felt throughout the Monarchy is universal, and almost indescribable. The aged Emperor only went to Ischl yesterday morning, to spend summer there, as usual. The population of Vienna took advantage of the occasion to turn out in large numbers to prepare an ovation for the revered Monarch, in order to show their joy at his restoration to health. The Emperor arrived at Ischl in the best of health, and today, at noon, he learnt the terrible news, which moved him very deeply. General Adjutant Count Paar took over the difficult task of breaking the news to his Majesty. The Emperor became deadly pale, then withdrew to his own apartments, and no one was permitted to enter.

The Archduke Franz Ferdinand, who was born in Gratz on 18 December 1863, was the eldest son of the Archduke Karl Ludwig and of his second wife, the Archduchess Maria Annunziata. He had a military education, and did not come before the public especially until the catastrophe of 30 January 1889, when the Crown Prince Rudolf committed suicide. The Archduke Frantz Ferdinand then became Heir-Presumptive to the Throne of Austria-Hungary, as he was the eldest son of the eldest brother of the Emperor.

His Imperial Highness then undertook long journeys, including a voyage round the world, when he visited Asia and Australia. On his return he continued his military activity. In the year 1897 the Emperor nominated the Archduke his representative on certain occasions, especially for military and naval functions. At this time the Archduke commenced military action on large lines, which not merely included his attendance at manoeuvres and at all the most important exercises of the troops, but he also turned his attention to the solution of those problems which then stood before the military authorities in Austria-Hungary. He attended the conferences held annually under the presidency of the Emperor, at which personal questions, as well as those of inner organisation and armament, were discussed, and the Heir-Presumptive obtained more and more influence in the decisions taken as time proceeded.

The Archduke married Sophie Duchess of Hohenberg, née Countess Chotek von Chotkova, on 1 July 1900, following in this matter the dictates of his heart. The public had only received the news of the intended marriage a few days before when the Archduke Franz Ferdinand took an oath of resignation of all rights to the Throne of Austria-Hungary for his possible descendants, and declared his marriage merely morganatic. The Archduke Franz Ferdinand had become acquainted with his future wife in the house of the Archduke Friedrich, where Countess Chotek was Lady-in-Waiting to the Archduchess Isabella.

Countess Chotek was born on 1 March 1868, in Stuttgart. After Archduke Franz Ferdinand had been introduced to her he was a frequent guest in the house of the Archduke Friedrich, and almost a year before the announcement of the marriage it was known that the Archduke had resolved to wed the young Countess. All the efforts made to prevent this alliance were in vain, as the Archduke invariably swept all difficulties out of the way with his indomitable will.

When the Archduke was appointed an admiral, in 1902, his interest in naval matters was manifested on many occasions. He made frequent visits to foreign Courts, and was in England very recently, visiting the King and the Duke of Portland. He also visited St. Petersburg and went to London to attend the Coronation. He repeatedly travelled to Berlin to visit the Emperor William, and the latter returned his visits on many occasions. The Kaiser was lately in Brioni, and still more recently in Konopischt. These are all examples of the many occasions upon which the Archduke took over representative duties for the Emperor of late years. His Imperial Highness took up a decided position when important matters were at stake. A little while ago, for instance, when General Conrad von Hoetzendorf had a conflict with the late Foreign Minister, Count Aehrenthal, he stood firm for the former. The Archduke was well known for his great taste in art.

The marriage of the Archduke with the Countess Chotek was blessed with three children – Princess Sophie Marie Franziska Alberta, born on 24 July 1901, at Konopischt; Prince Maximilian Karl Franz, born in Vienna on 29 September 1902; and Prince Ernst Alfons Karl Franz Josef, born at Konopischt on 27 May 1904.

The next heir to the throne is the Archduke Karl Franz Josef, eldest son of the Archduke Otto, who died in 1906. The Archduke Karl Franz Josef is the son of the Archduchess Maria Josefa, née Princess of Saxony. He was born on 17 August 1887, at Persenburg. He is a First Lieutenant in the Austrian Army. On 21 October 1911, he married Zita, Princess of Bourbon-Parma, who was then nineteen. The Princess stayed for one year immediately after her father's death in the convent of Benedictine nuns in the Isle of Wight, where one of her elder sisters, Princess Adelhied, had already entered the order as Sister Maria Benedicta. She met her future husband at Franzensbad in the summer of 1909. Soon after her marriage the Archduchess accompanied her young husband to Galicia, living at Stanislau. The Archduke's eldest son, Archduke Franz Josef Otto, was born 12 November 1912, and a daughter, the Archduchess Adelheid, was born in January last.

Further details of the attempt show that the assassin jumped to the footboard of the automobile as it drove slowly through the street, and fired directly into the face of the Archduke. A second shot was fired directly into the abdomen of the Duchess in the same manner.

News comes from Ischl that the Emperor will start for Vienna immediately. He will arrive here at 6 a.m. The first person who condoled with the Monarch was the Duke of Cumberland, who hastened from his castle in Gmunden to Ischl immediately on hearing the news. The children of the Archducal pair are at the Castle of Chlumec, in Bohemia. The Archduke's brother-in-law, Count Wuthenau, who married the sister of the Duchess of Hohenberg, has gone to break the news of the tragedy to her children.

During the examination the student Gavrilo Prinzip said that he intended to murder an Austrian from Nationalist motives, and decided yesterday on assassinating the Archduke. He had studied in Belgrade for a long time. He declared that he had got the bomb from an Anarchist in Belgrade. Cabninovic tried to escape after the murder and jumped into the Miljacka River, but was dragged out. Near the spot where the attempt was made a second bomb was found. It had evidently been thrown away by the intending assassin, who had seen that Prinzip's attempt had succeeded.

31 October 1916: Rudyard Kipling turns his writer's eye on the Senior Service's most major action of the Great War
OUR DESTROYERS IN THE BATTLE OF JUTLAND
'Carrying On'
By Rudyard Kipling

What mystery is there like the mystery of the other man's job – or what world so out off as that which he enters when he goes to it? The eminent surgeon is altogether such a one as ourselves, even till his hand falls on the knob of the theatre door. After that, in the silence, among the ether fumes, no man except his acolytes, and they won't tell, has ever seen his face. So with the unconsidered curate. Yet, before the war, he had more experience of the business and detail of death than any of the people who contemned him. His face also, as he stands his bedside-watches – that countenance with which he shall justify himself to his Maker – none have ever looked upon. Even the ditcher is a priest of mysteries at the high moment when he lays out in his mind his levels and the fall of the water that he alone can draw off clearly. But catch any of these men five minutes after they have left their altars, and you will find the doors are shut.

Chance sent me almost immediately after the Jutland fight a lieutenant of one of the destroyers engaged. Among other matters, I asked him if there was any particular noise. 'Well, I haven't been in the trenches, of course,' he replied, 'but I don't think there could have been much more noise than there was.' This bears out a report of a destroyer who could not be certain whether an enemy battleship had blown up or not, saying that in that particular corner it would have been impossible to identify anything less than the explosion of a whole magazine. 'It wasn't exactly noise,' he reflected. 'Noise is what you take in from outside. This was inside you. It seemed to lift you right out of everything.' 'And how did the light affect one?' I asked, trying to work out a theory that noise and light produced beyond known endurance form an unknown anæsthetic and stimulant, comparable to, but infinitely more potent than the soothing effect of the smoke-pall of ancient battles. 'The lights were rather curious,' was the answer. 'I don't know that one noticed searchlights particularly, unless they meant business; but when a lot of big guns loosed off together, the whole sea was lit up, and you could see our destroyers running about like cockroaches on a tin soup plate.'

'Then is black the best colour for our destroyers? Some commanders seem to think we ought to use grey.' 'Blessed if I know,' said young Dante. 'Everything shows black in that light. Then it all goes out again with a bang. Trying for the eyes if you are spotting.' 'And how did the dogs take it?' I pursued. There are several destroyers more or less owned by pet dogs, who start life as the chance-found property of a stoker, and end in supreme command of the bridge. 'Most of 'em didn't like it a bit. They went below one time, and wanted to be loved. They knew it wasn't ordinary practice.' 'What did Arabella do?' I had heard a good deal of Arabella. 'Oh, Arabella's quite different. Her job has always been to look after her master's pyjamas – folded up at the head of the bunk, you know. She found out pretty soon the bridge was no place for a lady, so she hopped downstairs and got in. You know how she makes three little, jumps to it – first on to the chair, then on the flap-table, and then up on the pillow. When the show was over there she was, as usual.' 'Was she glad to see her master?' 'Ra-ather. Arabella was the bold, gay lady-dog then!' Now Arabella is between nine and eleven and a half inches long. 'Does the Hun run to pets at all?' 'I shouldn't say so. He's an unsympathetic felon – the Hun. But he might cherish a dachshund or so. We never picked up any ships' pets off him, and I'm sure we should if there had been.'

That I believed as implicitly as the tale of a destroyer attack some months ago, the object of which was to flush Zepplins. It succeeded, for the flotilla was attacked by several. Right in the middle of the flurry a destroyer asked permission to stop and lower dinghy to pick up ship's dog, which had fallen overboard. Permission was granted, and the dog was duly rescued. 'Lord knows what the Hun made of it,' said my informant. 'He was rumbling round, dropping bombs, and the dinghy was digging out for all she was worth, and the Dog-Fiend was swimming for Dunkirk. It must have looked rather mad from above. But they saved the Dog-Fiend, and then everybody swore he was a German spy in disguise.'

'And – about this Jutland fight?' I hinted not for the first time. 'Oh, that was just a fight. There was more of it than any other fight, I suppose, but I expect all modern naval actions must be pretty much the same.' 'But what does one do – how does one feel? I insisted, though I knew it was hopeless. 'One does one's job. Things are happening all the time. A man may be right under your nose one minute – serving a gun or something, and the next minute he isn't there.' 'And one notices that at the time?' 'Yes. But there's no time to keep on noticing it. You've got to carry on somehow or other, or your show stops. I tell you what one does notice, though. If one goes below for anything, or has to pass through a flat somewhere, and one sees the old wardroom dock ticking, or a photograph pinned up, or anything of that sort, one notices that. Oh, yes, and there was another thing – the way a ship seemed to blow up if you were far off her. You'd see a glare, then a blaze, and then the smoke – miles high lifting quite slowly. Then you'd get the row and the jar of it – just like bumping over submarines. Then, a long while after, p'raps you run through a regular rain of bits of burnt paper coming down on, the decks – like showers of volcanic ash, you know.' The door of the operating-room seemed just about to open, but it shut again. 'And the Hun's gunnery?' 'That was various. Sometimes they began quite well, and went to pieces after they'd been strafed a little; but sometimes they picked up again. There was one Hun-boat that got no end of a hammering, and it seemed to do her gunnery good. She improved tremendously till we sank her. I expect we'd knocked out some scientific Hun in the controls, and he'd been succeeded by a man who knew how.' It used to be 'Fritz' last year when they spoke of the enemy. Now it is Hun, or, as I have heard, 'Yahun', being a superlative of Yahoo. In the Napoleonic wars we called the Frenchmen too many names for any one of them to endure; but this is the age of standardisation. 'And what about our Lower Deck?' I continued. 'They? Oh, they carried on as usual. It takes a lot to impress the Lower Deck when they're busy.' And he mentioned several little things that confirmed this. They had a great deal to do, and they did it serenely because they had been trained to carry on under all conditions without panicking. What they did in the way of running repairs was even more wonderful, if that be possible, than their normal routine. The Lower Deck nowadays is full of strange fish with unlooked for accomplishments, as in the recorded case of two simple seaman of a destroyer who, when need was sorest, came to the front as trained experts in first-aid.

'And now – what about the actual Hun losses at Jutland?' I ventured. 'You've seen the list haven't you?' Yes, but it occurred to me – that they might have been a shade underestimated, and I thought perhaps—' A perfectly plain asbestos fire-curtain descended in front of the already locked door. It was none of his business to dispute the drive. If there were any discrepancies between estimate and results, one might be sure that the enemy knew about them, which was the chief thing that matters.

It was, said he, Joss that the light was so bad at the hour of the last round-up when our main fleet had come down from the north and shovelled the Hun round on his tracks. Per contra, had it been any other kind of weather the odds were the Hun would not have ventured so far. As it was, the Hun's fleet had come out and gone back again, none the better for air and exercise. We must be thankful for what we had managed to pick up. But, talking of picking up, there was an instance of almost unparalleled Joss which had stuck in his memory. A soldier-man, related to one of the officers in one of our ships that was put down, had got five days' leave from the trenches, which he spent with his relative aboard, and thus dropped in for the whole performance. He had been employed in helping to spot and had lived up a mast till the ship sank when he stepped off into the water and swam about till he was fished out and put ashore. By that time, the tale goes, his engine-room-dried khaki had shrunk halfway up his legs and arms, in which costume he reported himself to the War Office and pleaded for one little day's extension of leave to make himself decent. 'Not a bit of it,' said the War Office. If you chose to spend your leave playing with sailormen and getting wet all over, that's your concern. You will return to duty by tonight's boat.' (This may be a libel on the W.O., but it sounds very like them.) 'And he had to,' said the boy, 'but I expect he spent the next week at Headquarters telling generals all about the fight.'

'And, of course, the Admiralty gave you all lots of leave?' 'Us? Yes, heaps. We had nothing to do except clean down and oil up and be ready to go to sea again in a few hours.' That little fact was brought out at the end of almost every destroyer's report. 'Having returned to base at such and such a time, I took in oil, &c., and reported ready for sea at – o'clock.' When you think of the amount of work a ship needs even after peace manœuvres, you can realise what has to be done on the heels of an action. And, as there is nothing like house-work for the troubled soul of a woman, so a general clean-up is good for sailors. I had this from a petty officer who had also passed through deep waters. 'If you've seen your best friend go from alongside you, and your own officer, and your own boat's crew with him, and things of that kind, a man's best comfort is small variegated jobs which he is damned for continuous.' Presently my friend of the destroyer went back to his stark, desolate life, where feelings do not count, and the fact of his being cold, wet, sea-sick, sleepless, or dog-tired had no bearing whatever on his business, which was to turn out at any hour in any weather, and do or endure, decently, according to ritual, what that hour and weather demanded. It is hard to reach the kernel of Navy minds. The unbribable seas and mechanisms they work on and through have given them the simplicity of elements and machines. The habit of dealing with swift accident; a life of closest and strictest association with their own caste as well as contact with all kinds of men all earth over have added an immense cunning to those qualities; and that they are from early youth cut out of all feelings that may come between them and their ends makes them more incomprehensible than Jesuits, even to their own people. What, then, must they be to the enemy?

Here is a service, which prowls forth, and achieves, at the lowest, something of a victory. How far-reaching a one only the war's end will reveal. It returns in gloomy silence, broken by occasional hoot of the long-shore loafer, after issuing a bulletin, which, though it may enlighten the professional mind, does not exhilarate the layman. Meantime, the enemy triumphs, wirelessly, far and wide. A few frigid and perfunctory seeming contradictions are put forward against his resounding claims; a naval expert or two is heard talking 'off'; the rest is silence. Anon, the enemy, after a prodigious amount of explanation, which not even the neutrals seem to take any interest in, revises his claims, and, very modestly, enlarges his losses. Still no sign. After weeks there appears a document giving our version of the affair, which is as colourless, detached, and scrupulously impartial as the findings of a prize-court. It opines that the list of enemy losses which it submits 'give the minimum in regard to numbers, though it is possibly not entirely accurate in regard to the particular class of vessels, especially those that were sunk during the night attacks.' Here the matter rests and remains – just like our blockade. There is an insolence about it all that makes one gasp.

Yet that insolence springs naturally and unconsciously as an oath out of the same spirit that caused the destroyer to pick up the dog. The reports themselves, and tenfold more the stories not in the reports, are charged with it, but no words by any outsider can reproduce just that professional tone and touch. A man writing home after the fight points out that the great consolation for not having cleaned up the enemy altogether was that 'anyhow those east coast devils' – a fellow-squadron, if you please, which up till Jutland had had most of the fighting – 'were not there. They missed that show. We were as cock-a-hoop as a girl who had been to a dance that her sister has missed.'

This was one of the figures in that dance: 'A little British destroyer, her midships rent by a great shell meant for a battle-cruiser, exuding steam from every pore, able to go ahead but not to steer, unable to get out of anybody's way, likely to be rammed by any one of a dozen ships, her siren whimpering, "Let me through! Make way!" her crew fallen in aft dressed in lifebelts ready for her final plunge, and cheering as wildly as it might have been an enthusiastic crowd when the King passes.'

Let us close on that note. We have been compassed about so long and so blindingly by wonders and miracles; so overwhelmed by revelations of the spirit or men in the basest and most high, that we have neither time to keep tally of these furious days, nor mind to discern upon which hour of them the world's fate turned.

> Not in the thick of the fight,
> Not in the press of the odds,
> Do the heroes come to their height
> Or we know the demi-gods.

That stands over till peace.
We can only perceive
Men returned from the seas,
Very grateful for leave.

They grant us sudden days,
Snatched from their business of war,
We are too close to appraise
What manner of men they are.

And whether their names go down
With age-kept victories,
Or whether they battle and drown
Unreckoned is hid from our eyes.

They are too near to be great,
But our children shall understand
When and how our fate
Was changed, and by whose hand.

Our children shall measure their worth.
We are content to be blind,
For we know that we walk on a new-born earth
With the saviours of mankind.

10 November 1917: The Russian Revolution has a muted reception
SOVIET CONFERENCE
A DRAMATIC COUP
BOLSHEVIK AUDACITY
From Our Special Correspondent

PETROGRAD, THURSDAY

The revolution has advanced another stage, perhaps the most definite one of all. The history of the last thirty-six hours is peculiarly tangled. As far as is at present ascertainable, the honours lie with the Military Revolutionary Committee, now exactly a week old. On Tuesday night the Petrograd Soviet held a meeting, when the political situation was discussed in the light of Mr. Kerenski's threats a few hours earlier at the Democratic Council. The Bolshevik leaders, were still hesitating over the wisdom of a demonstration. The minority parties apparently took it for granted that an armed demonstration was improbable.

At three o'clock on Wednesday morning unanimity was reached as the result of a series of reports from the garrison units expressing their readiness to accept orders from the Military Revolutionary Committee. It was decided to strike. The Provisional Government was forthwith declared non-existent. At 4.30 the first detachments left the Soviet headquarters and descended upon the Government Bank in accordance with a plan produced by the Military Revolutionaries. The whole success of the Bolshevik coup turns upon this plan of campaign. The promoters are naturally unwilling to divulge its details yet, but gossip at Smolny Institute, their headquarters, declares that its authors were three hitherto unheard-of youths, and dwells lovingly on the completeness of the details.

Petrograd awoke and went about its normal business, and only towards midday realised, except in the centre, that the old Government had been painlessly replaced. Some hundreds of young men, members of the Officers' Training Corps, and women and soldiers formed the sole defence of the Provisional Government. These encircled and garrisoned the Winter Palace, and were themselves surrounded by garrison troops. The cruiser *Aurora* arrived from Kronstadt, and took up a position in the Neva opposite the Winter Palace. In the afternoon the cruiser fired a blank shot as a warning to the Palace inmates. This started a slight panic, and a party of sailors, landing for a *pourparler*, were fired on, one being killed and one wounded. This apparently was the most serious case of bloodshed on Wednesday. In the afternoon the Nevsky was cleared of traffic, and machine guns and quick fires were placed at the principal crossings throughout the city. Perfect quiet was maintained.

I have been spending the night at the Smolny Institute. The great building, formerly a school for the girls of the Russian aristocracy, still preserves its slightly convent-like effects inside, forming an odd background to the crowds of soldiers filling it. The All-Russian Conference of Soviets was timed to open here at noon, but delay after delay was imposed on the patient and steadily-increasing crowd of delegates packing the large hall. In the afternoon various sectional meetings were held, the Bolsheviks being addressed by Lenin and Zinoviev. Apparently the secret of Lenin's successful disguise lies in the fact that he has shaved off his beard. At 9 p.m. a final postponement of one hour was announced. At 10.45 the Conference at last opened.

The proceedings, which lasted till 5.30 a.m., were threefold. At first there were the usual wranglings about procedure. Then came the adoption of the programme of the new Soviet Government. Finally, occasional bulletins were read from the Military Revolutionary Committee reporting progress. These last invariably recorded success for the Bolshevik operations. The entire Provisional Government, excepting Mr. Kerenski, was stated to be under arrest, principally at the Fortress of Peter and Paul, where a curious irony makes them fellow inmates of the ex-Ministers who provoked the March revolution. Commissaries had been appointed by the Military Revolutionary Committee at all important stations exhorting the soldiers moving on Petrograd not to obey the Provisional Government's orders. The entire garrison was now supporting the Soviet. Mr. Kerenski had disappeared. At 5 a.m. he had left Petrograd. At 10 a.m. he had exhorted a great meeting of soldiers at Gatchina to come to the rescue of the Provisional Government. The soldiers, principally Cossacks, communicated with the Soviet, and refused. Mr. Kerenski was now, apparently, at the front, seeking an army willing to march on the capital.

The programme adopted by the Conference declares that the Provisional Government is suppressed, and that the Conference has sovereign power. On the immediate fronts democratic peace terms are to be formulated, and if offered and refused by Germany the war is to continue. Privately-owned land is to become the property of the peasants' committees for redistribution by them. Working-men are to control the factories. The Soviets are to tackle the food problem. The soldiers at the front are exhorted to stay in the trenches until further notice and to keep cool.

The discussion showed that the Bolsheviks were complete masters of the Conference. The Mensheviks, Internationalists, Jewish Bundists, and a section of the .Social Revolutionaries in turn denounced the Bolshevik usurpation and refused their co-operation, but these sections formed a small minority of the Conference. We had been told that the Councils of Peasants' Delegates and the army organisations were opposed to the Conference, but the Bolsheviks produced a long array of peasants and soldiers, every one of whom declared in one-minute speeches that the peasants and soldiers generally were imbued with Bolshevik enthusiasm. In spite of the protests of the Mensheviks and others, an enormous majority of those present completely accepted the Bolshevik Government.

It should be noted that the moderate leaders, Mr. Chkheidze and Mr. Tsereteli, were absent, both being in the Caucasus recuperating from overwork. Mr. Chernov, a doubtful quantity, the leader of a fluctuating section of the Social Revolutionary Party and the Council of Peasants'

Delegates, was also absent. Just now, to be absent is to be forgotten. Today the new Government probably will be elected. It is said that the Bolsheviks will have no Premier, the members of the Cabinet taking turns to preside. Perfect order prevails in Petrograd. The Conference was particularly anxious to avoid all bloodshed. At two o'clock this morning the Winter Palace was entered at the bayonet-point. The defending troops surrendered, having practically no ammunition, but they killed six and wounded many of the attackers. The defending party sustained no losses. Only then the C.W.S.D. learned that twenty-four hours earlier Mr. Kishkin, by this time in jail, had been appointed Dictator.

30 June 1919: The Treaty of Versailles ends the war with Germany, but the *Telegraph*'s correspondent seems more interested in the surroundings
SIGNATURE OF THE PEACE TREATY AT VERSAILLES
GERMANY'S DAY OF FATE
From Perceval Landon

VERSAILLES, SATURDAY

The treaty is signed. After seven months of labour and anxiety unspeakable the great work of human regeneration which the Allies set before themselves in 1914 has been accomplished. Militarism, with all its disciplined brutality and unbridled lust of conquest, is at an end. At an end, too, is the German Empire. The world looks forward from today not only to a full generation of peace, but to the hope of rising, during that generation, to a higher plane, and, so far as human effort can attain that end, looks forward to the end of warfare itself. The signature of the terms of peace in the 'Hall of Mirrors' at Versailles today marks the close of an epoch as clearly and as certainly as did Wolsey's great puppet show of the Field of the Cloth of Gold. The Cardinal ended the Middle Ages only to inaugurate the hazardous regime of the balance of power in Europe. Today we have put that all behind us as a thing dead and out of date, and we look forward to a new dispensation – to a federation of the world.

And yet there was no sense of rejoicing today in the Galérie des Glaces; there was scarcely even a deep feeling of relief. Only the night before last the President of the United States had well said that whatever had been accomplished, there remained still more to do. The work still to be done is, indeed, greater than that which has been done, By that work which the three Great Powers have completed they have deliberately laid up for themselves unending and unrelenting work, watchfulness, and anxiety for the next fifteen years.

One felt that even as the German signature was being written the military party in Germany were venturing their all upon a '*coup d'état*', and that the machine-guns were even then rapping out death along the Polish frontier. Still, there this great Treaty is – signed, sealed, and delivered in due form on the fifth anniversary to the day of that double murder in Sarajevo which was the opportunity, if not the cause, for the letting loose of the long-threatened German menace. It stands for all that white civilisation hopes to achieve in this world, and whatever the immediate results, it will stand for ever as the greatest combined effort of human goodwill and justice ever made to set right the affairs of this distracted earth.

After a winter unparalleled for its wet and cold, after the latest spring that France has ever remembered, and after sixty days of sunshine unrelieved by even a centimetre of rain, the weather of the great day of the signature of peace was awaited with anxiety. The dawn broke cool and grey, with promise of sun later on. There was scarcely a breath of wind, and the half-million flags of Paris hung in splendid lines, and garlands and trophies along every boulevard and every street. The whole city was astir early, and, though the day had not been officially proclaimed, there were few shops open except those which provided for the refreshment and merry-making of the crowds. As early as ten o'clock the long serpents of beribboned schoolboys began to make circulation difficult in the greater thoroughfares. Yet there was a certain dignity and restraint about the Parisians that reminded of the Government's proclamation set out by the Mayor of Versailles – 'It desires that the ceremony shall preserve the character of austerity which it is fitting should attend the memory of the mournings and sufferings of France'. All this will be forgotten tonight in a blaze of enthusiasm, but there is noticeable, not among the people only, but in the newspapers as well, a certain thoughtfulness which tinges the note of jubilation. One newspaper boldly places in the place of honour a significant list of the things that the Conference has yet to agree upon and carry through. But a touch of sun, and the news that the Treaty is actually signed, will cure all that, and with the return of the thousands who go out to the Château of Châteaux today the rejoicings will begin in earnest.

The road from Paris to Versailles was crowded. From the earliest dawn the avenue of the Bois de Boulogne was filled with a never-ending concourse of pilgrims to the shrine of the Great Renunciation. Across the river the inhabitants of St. Cloud were out of doors to a man watching the unending caravan of motorcars and carriages that climbed its steep streets and whirled round its sharp corners. Except along the black, mirror-like road of tarmac that the Anglo-Saxon races presented to the French nation during the war to facilitate communications between the Military Council in Versailles and the Government in Paris, the dust rose everywhere in steady clouds, blanketing the little houses by the roadside and covering with dust the gardens gay with their June flowers. The forest of St. Cloud merged into the folds of woodland round 'Fausses Repose', where far and wide beneath the trees the stragglers of the great company of sightseers were taking rest before they descended across the railway into Versailles itself.

Here was the first sign of official preparation. The troops, which must have been concentrating upon the royal suburb since dawn, had taken up their positions upon the three great avenues that form the three members of the huge broad-arrow, the point of which transfixes the central court of the great château. It was a change indeed from the scene of the presentation of the terms. Then there was little excitement in the streets. Now all Versailles and no small part of Paris must have gathered in these broad boulevards, and above them, the house-fronts and balconies of Versailles rippled with the flags of the Allies. Except for the distinction which troops lend even to the greatest of courtyards there was little decoration of the château itself. On the other side of the long façade the gardens lay out, carefully tended and freshly trimmed, partly filled already with privileged guests, determined, if they could see nothing else, at least to watch the windows of the famous gallery while the momentous event was taking place within it. As yet the famous cascades and fountains were still.

Before I go on to describe the scene of the signature those of my readers who know their Versailles will forgive me if I try to make for those who are less fortunate some sort of picture of the surroundings in which this great ceremony has taken place. The Château of Versailles, lying as it does among gardens, grounds, and parks all laid out to add to its glory, is the crown, too, of the little town which the Kings of France designed to be its handmaid and attendant. The château is of gigantic size. It marks perhaps the zenith of human self-glorification in stone and marble, bronze and inlay, parquet, paint, and gold that has been attained since the day when the King of Babylon saw his palace and city fresh from the builders' hands. Exact in every detail, and practically complete within the space of fourteen years, there is a unity and harmony about the great façades that is denied to the only two palaces in Europe – Windsor and the Vatican – which can challenge Versailles on its own scale. A critic may find fault with it for its very harmony and monotonous perfection of design; to a modern eye the huge walls lack the rest and relief of sculpture – the alternation of light and shade. But criticism must needs be silent before the splendid ensemble of the palace wherein for 230 years the very heart of France has been housed so gorgeously. Were Louis XIV to return today he would find little changed in his lordly pleasure house. From the windows of the gorgeous bedroom in which he died he would see no great change in the lay-out of the little town below him; and on the other side, from the windows of the Hall of Mirrors, he would look down over a sylvan scene in which scarcely a terrace or a pool has been altered since Le Notre gazed critically over his work in the evening of his life and saw that it was very good.

Inside the building there has been even less alteration, so far, at least, as the great halls of ceremony are concerned; and in that long gallery, which by common consent is the heart of all its luxury and splendour, and in which the treaty was signed this afternoon, there is not a mark of the troubled history of two full centuries of crowded life. The Galérie des Glaces is in length two hundred and thirty-five feet, in width thirty-five, and a clear forty to the centre of the barrel vault. Human ingenuity could not have composed these faultless proportions more perfectly, and yet they are due to mere accident. The gallery was a later addition – built over a pillared verandah on the roof of which a 'hanging garden' had been arranged as a private pleasaunce for the King.

Even now as you look up from outside you will see in the clustered trophies on the roof that mark the limits of the old building, a proof that this great gallery was in fact an after-thought. But what an after-thought. If the reader will stand for a moment with me looking into it from the northern archway he will see before him on his left a long colonnade of seventeen arches divided by clustering pilasters of the richest marble and gilded bronze. The space between these marble piers is filled with the famous mirrors which give the gallery its name – and to which I shall return. Above these arches is a gilded architrave upborne by the golden capitals of Le Brun. Above it again one of the most magnificent cornices in the world juts forward and supports in turn the spring of the painted roof. It is a roof of which it is difficult to give a general impression, save that of a softened richness and strangely happy medley of colour. One knows that it is alive, and one feels that there are figures adorning it by hundreds, but one neither knows what its meaning is, nor greatly cares to know. The details are probably not worth deciphering; one is merely content that the gallery should have this splendid ceiling of rich and tempered colour. The supreme success of harmony is the chamber's great boast. It is not this or that within it; it is the gallery itself that is all in all. On the other side, to the right, are the great windows, looking out over the gardens, each of them framed with the snipe far-brought marbles and gilt bronze. Underfoot, until today, there was nothing but the polished oak parquet, over which two hundred years ago – so curious was the mingling of majesty and the masses in old days – the small boys of Paris had to be prevented from making slides. The effect of the room is one of rich unity of design, yet even this is not the first, as it is not the last, impression that is left upon the eye.

No one who has ever been inside the Galérie des Glaces has ever forgotten the curious atmosphere and faint aquamarine light that distinguishes it from every other Royal chamber or corridor on earth. For a moment one thinks that window-glass of some extreme thickness tints the air, but one soon realises that is the mirrors and nothing else which causes this strange fascination of pale verdancy – a fascination which is almost literally not of this earth. In truth it has the effect of some dream vision seen far down in tropical waters. Everything is caught and transfigured by this eerie and exquisite glaze of – of what? – of blue that is almost green – of green that is almost blue. Let us go and look at it. Imagine for a moment a wall of beryl-tinted crystal hanging like a screen between each opening of the arcade of marble and gold – and then straightway forget it as the whole thing turns before your eyes into the most gorgeous tapestry, billowing, strained and awry, that ever man set up. For reflected in it dimly and unevenly, with just that twist of warp and weft which makes one think that some ghostly wind had made it heave inwards here and there, you will see the gardens and trees of Versailles depicted with the charm and eccentricity which mark the work of the greatest Flemish masters of the weavers' art. There is no hard perspective amid its hundred vanishing points, for there is scarcely a square that gives back an untortured reflection. One is so delighted with the lovely vision that one hesitates for a moment to go closer and see why it is that there is no reflection in the world to rival it; then curiosity gets the better of sheer delight and one goes up to examine more closely this thing of unrivalled beauty.

Some years ago, after the oblivion of centuries, the secret of the life and charm of the nobler mosaic work of Byzantium and Italy was found to lie in the fact that the tesserae and quarrels were every one of them set at a different angle to the wall that held them. It was no secret to the artist-glaziers of Louis XIV. The life and play of the huge screen is due to this almost wanton counter-setting of the uneven panes of glass. But it is the colour that remains the fascination and the glory. Just as in Georgian days England delighted to set up in her palaces windows of a purple tint, so green was preferred in France, and through this green every reflection has, of course, to pass twice before it strikes the eye, mellowed, chilled, and tarnished by the million streaks and dots of rust or damp or mildew that break the silvered backs of these famous crystal panes. It has one curious effect. No woman looks her best in this gallery – but it was not built for women. Even florid Bismarck, at the famous gathering in January 1871, must have looked anaemic and bedraggled in the reflections of the pale winter day. Drowned in the same faint green this afternoon, the German Empire was wiped from the face of the earth. There is in the mere colour of this mirrored hall something which distinguishes from all other events in history those which take place within it: and in spite of the richness of the gallery – is there a richer chamber in the world? – in such an atmosphere as that which encircled the still sinking Lusitania, the great event that I have now to describe was immersed from its beginning to its end.

The arrangement and furnishing of the gallery deserves a special description. Underfoot is a magnificent carpet originally made for this very room by the orders of Louis XIV at the Savonnerie. A long table, shaped like a capital E (without the central serif or tongue), is placed opposite the windows. Here are, or will be, seated the delegates to the Conference, who are expected to number about eighty-three. Inside the 'E' are placed small tables for the secretaries and other officials attached to the delegations. Here, too, are placed the three tables on which the signatures of the delegates will be written. That which will support the copy of the Treaty itself has been taken from the treasures of the Louvre for the occasion, and is a fine piece of the best Louis XV period. The story is well known of Clemenceau's objection to the tortoise ink-stand which originally was intended for use there. Perhaps if he had stayed to remember that, according to the belief of the religion which numbers most adherents in the world, the earth is supported upon the back of a tortoise, he might have been willing to allow the unconscious symbolism to remain.

The representatives of the three Great Powers will soon take their places at the centre of the long table, with their backs to the mirrors, facing the windows and the gardens. A passing fancy reminds one that, by accident of its construction, Mr. Wilson is so placed that he looks straight out – as straight as man could have planned it – towards the spot in the Atlantic where the greatest of German naval crimes was committed, and the United States thereby drawn into the War. For the rest it need only be said that the tables are covered with golden-brown silk, and that the chairs add a note of crimson to the colour scheme. Such is the arrangement of the gallery so far as the central part is concerned, the whole of which is raised about a foot above the floor of the gallery. At each end there are about 350 seats reserved, for the Press to the north, and for distinguished visitors to the south. The reader has now some idea of the appearance of the gallery in which the great ceremony is to take place. But he must not think that the tables and chairs have been all this time without their human occupants.

Long before the appointed hour the delegates and guests began to assemble in the Galérie des Glaces, and from the first one noticed a different mood from that in which the presentations of the terms to Germany and Austria took place. There were indeed the same greetings, many of the delegates having returned specially from visits to London or elsewhere for this last scene, but a sense of the importance of the moment hushed the low murmuring of conversation. It seemed

almost impossible to believe that after these weary years of warfare
and weary months of Conference the end was not only in sight, but
was going to take place before them within an hour or so. Probably
there was no one there among all those present who was not impressed
by the most obvious thought of the occasion – the many scenes and
many great men who had been reflected in those glasses for an hour
or two, or a year or two, and then had passed out of existence to make
room for others as important, as splendid, and perhaps as transitory.

Among the first to arrive were the representatives of Oriental races
– echoes of the rare Eastern visitors to the Court of the Sun King. But
they were neither as numerous nor as distinguished by their raiment as
their predecessors of the seventeenth century. Little by little the greater
figures of the Conference moved to their places or talked together in
twos and threes. Many of them exchanged a few words with the guests,
or with the representatives of the Press, before going to their seats
at the great triple table whereon the usual paraphernalia of pens and
paper and portfolios were arranged.

It is scarcely necessary once more to sketch the well-known
figures that one by one added an ever-increasing sense of weight and
responsibility to the gathering, but among them, as men who had played
great parts in this great settlement, one could but notice the keen genial
personality of Venizelos – the saviour of his country if ever man was in
these latter days – and that of the patriarchal Pasitch, the most splendid
figure of all who have attended the Conference. Across the table was
the keen, hard-bitten, and resolute Australian Premier, of whom it has
been justly said that he has done more by his tense silence at Conference
and commission meetings than most others by their words. There again
was Massey, the tall and watchful guardian of the least interests of 'The
Long White Cloud'. The less familiar figures of Mr. Sifton and Mr.
Doherty, who were to lead the procession for the Dominions, fittingly
represented Sir Robert Borden, whose absence was seriously regretted
by his fellow-delegates. The sturdy, well-set-up figure of Botha, with
his companion-in-arms as well as colleague in council, Smuts, seemed

to remember less than anyone there the strange and significant past of both statesmen – that past of fair and honest hostility and fair and honest peace which, in a day of trial, bound South Africa closer to England than mere treaties could. When the history of the Conference comes to be written he will be a shrewd chronicler who is able to give even in a shadow the vast moral championship of English ways and English justice that the presence of the friendliest of our old foes constantly afforded on its councils. It should be noted here that General Smuts, who signed the Treaty in due form, issued this afternoon a protest, directed not so much against any particular clause in it, as against the general attitude taken up by the Allies in whose hands the salvation of the new world is placed. He says that in the Treaty 'we have not yet achieved the real peace to which the peoples are looking, and I feel that the real work of making peace will only begin after this Treaty has been signed'. His references to the possible remission of 'punishments foreshadowed' was considered by no small part of those who took part in today's ceremony as inopportune and untimely. What need is there to describe again what a Frenchman called the smile and tall sagacity of Mr. Balfour, the steady and concentrated attention of Lord Milner's grey eyes, the capable determination of Mr. Barnes, or the business-like and courteous personality of Mr. Bonar Law? On the right the new Italian delegation was placed, Sonnino, the Marchese Imperiali, and Crespi. The Conference could not help regretting the absence of Orlando, one of the most popular personalities of the Congress.

Another face that one missed was that of the President of Brazil, called home to take up his new duties. He has assured me himself of his disappointment at not being able to be present to see the completion of the work which owes more to him than the world in general recognises. In the absence of the Emir Faisal, Rustem Haidar was present as the plenipotentiary of the new Arabian kingdoms. Not far away the unmistakable vignette of Paderewski stood out like a cameo among his surroundings. From the picturesque one turned to the practical. The three leaders of the Conference sat in the same order as on previous occasions. Over the face of Clemenceau there was perhaps a shade of tired satisfaction. One felt that he will regard his life's work is done when he lays the pen down. There was not on the face of President Wilson any confession of weariness, though perhaps the strange light of the gallery added a touch of cynicism to the sculptured smile. And last of all there was David Lloyd George, representative of the British Empire, and in some degree the man on whom the heaviest burden has been laid of all the delegated. He seems less inclined to talk than usual, but there was the same quiet confidence in his eyes. Except Clemenceau, there was no man present who was able to take the great ceremony of peacemaking with such complete or such well-assumed indifference.

On the last occasion on which the Conference and the enemy had faced each other there was a long delay. Not so on this occasion. Only a few minutes elapsed before the head of the German delegation appeared in the doorway and halted a moment and bowed to the Allies. It was remarked at once that the Conference did not rise to its feet to receive the Germans. Herr Müller was the first to come in through the great southern door in the mirrored wall leading from the Hall of Peace. He, his companion, Johann Bell, and the interpreters and secretaries, were unfamiliar figures to the Peace Conference, and for that reason this first meeting with their enemies on such an occasion of high ceremonial was a severe trial to their steadiness. But, tired men as they were after their long night journey, with an ordeal before them that greater men than they had been afraid to face, they bowed gravely to the Allies and walked firmly to their seats. They took their places at the high table, sitting by themselves on the inside of the E – to the left of the President and at some distance from him. They had given their own and their country's word, and they were accorded places as equals once more among the representatives of the civilised world, or they were to be accorded this honour in a few moments. They had come in through the gardens not through the Court of Honour, and had been escorted up the wooden staircase in the southern arm of the château. They were to go out from the palace by the marble staircase with the either delegates.

We did not know certainly whether the President of the Conference was going to speak or not. When the subject was first mooted, he had expressed himself against the suggestion with his accustomed vigour, and it might well be that the events of the last few days had reinforced his determination. But we did not know whether, on the other hand, those events had convinced him that to speak on this solemn and final moment was his duty. We were not long left in doubt. The familiar figure rose almost at once with the words: '*La séance est ouverte.*' He then went on to say that the copy of the Treaty specially printed for the ceremony of the signature was identical with the two hundred copies printed and distributed to the previous German delegation. The signature would now take place, and would be regarded as a solemn undertaking on the part of each Power to fulfil its conditions loyally and faithfully.

Then the executive ceremony of the day began. M. William Marlin brought forward the special copy of the Treaty, printed with wide and rubricked margins on Japanese vellum – which is to remain in Paris as the authentic record of the great settlement – and laid it on the central table. The Germans at once rose and signed it, and the three subsidiary treaties. There was no delay, and it was remarked by many that the German delegation looked merely relieved when the ceremony was over. Then, in turn, the Americans, the British, and the French came round the table and signed the Treaty. It was interesting to note the way in which the Great Three went through the critical moment of the life of each. The President of the United States smiled and signed. M. Clemenceau signed his name with the pen presented to him by the 'Lost Provinces' of France, and for a second he closed his eyes. It was no unworthy 'Nunc Dimittis' that must have sung itself through his mind in that brief space. Mr. Lloyd George wrote his name without the ghost of an expression crossing his face. If there were any man present who knew his thought it was only Mr. Lloyd George himself. Two other volumes, containing the protocol and the Polish annex were similarly signed by the three chief delegates, each on one of the four tables placed for the purpose, beside which the long procession of signatories began and continued for twenty-five minutes. The Rhineland annex, which affects few of the Powers, was signed by them at the main table. There was not much of interest in this formal ceremony, though one after another of the great figures of the Conference rose in turn to pledge his country to the observance of the great peace. It was the crowning hour of the Conference, and one could not help remembering its long, slow course – long, but filled every moment with hard work and harder tasks of decision and conciliation – slow, but very sure. Whatever may happen in the course of the next few months or years, the future progress of the world must inevitably run in large measure along the course indicated in this Treaty – this enormous reconstitution of the earth, hammered out by the sense of justice and the hard business instincts of the greater races, and tempered by their ideals, humanity, and hope.

The ceremony did not take nearly so long as was expected. In fact, the friendly signing of names on interchanged agenda papers before the session opened took much more time. Among the nominal correspondents for the French Press were half a score of the best-known litterateurs in France, and on the seats reserved for distinguished visitors there was a summary of all France, and no bad representation of the rest of the Allies. The scene rapidly lost its orderly dignity, and conversation was general from one end of the gallery to the other. The aeroplane that had roared overhead while Clemenceau was speaking returned while the procession of signatories was still using the same gold pen and the indelible ink that the Chef du Protocol had provided.

To the surprise of everyone present, the last delegate had made his three signatures by a quarter to four, and the great work was over. M. Clemenceau then rose again and formally declared that peace had become an accomplished fact, and that the *séance* was closed. Instantly a salvo of guns, fired from the Swiss basin beyond the Orangerie, announced the achievement of peace to the scores and hundreds of thousands who were waiting all round the château and thronging the roadside half way back to Paris. The supreme moment was received in a burst of prolonged cheering that must have been heard for miles. The thin police cordons in the grounds were broken through in half a hundred places, and everyone embraced his neighbour for sheer joy. The great fountains of Versailles rumbled for a moment, choked, and then leapt upwards into the full silver glory that they had never shown for fifty-nine months of war. Looking down from the windows of the Galérie des Glaces, the crowd in the gardens was like a great black carpet streaked with blue, where soldiers had lost all dressing and control, and mingled happily with the delighted crowd. All were waiting to greet the protagonists of the great drama on the first and greatest act of which the curtain had just fallen.

The Germans left the château first. As they got into their motorcars and drove away there was no hostile demonstration, though much interest was shown in the personality of the two men who had come to make the great renunciation on behalf of the defeated enemy. But these were not those that the crowd wished and determined to honour. The cry that has rung in the streets of Paris for many months, a staccato 'Clemenceau!', with an ever-increasing accent on the last syllable, was now heard from the throats of the specially invited thousands of the population of Paris and Versailles. There was no affectation of misunderstanding the vociferous demand. The 'Tiger' came forward and stood facing the excited mass. He bowed his acknowledgment, and remained for a moment bareheaded in the afternoon light. It was such a moment as it had been given no Frenchman to live through for a hundred years. Perhaps never in all the known history of man has there been so crowded a minute of glorious life. But there was no loss of dignity or restraint in the deeply-cut face of the man who has saved not France only, but the hopes of man. From underneath his shaggy eyebrows he gazed down almost thoughtfully at the cheering multitude for a few moments, and then turned back into the gallery. But the crowd would not be denied. So Clemenceau led the way and descended to the ground floor, and walked out among his people followed closely by Mr. Wilson and Mr. Lloyd George. They did not know what they were in for. The three men linked arms, and it was as well they did for they at once became the centre of a seething maelstrom of humanity, screaming, cheering, shouting, and struggling at all cost to got within sight and within reach of the Great Three. If ever men were mobbed they were. Watching the heaving and staggering progress from above it seemed almost impossible that the trio should ever make their way in safety to where the automobiles of the Council were waiting. It was a snail's progress, but luckily those who were actually in touch with the three defended them as best as they could. It took ten minutes for the two hundred yards or so to be crossed, and even at the door of the motor there would have been more friendly danger if fifteen or twenty soldiers had not come to the rescue. All three got into the same car, but even that for a moment did not avail them much. At last the chauffeur in desperation crawled forward, and a lane was reluctantly left through which the big car, limpeted with seven or eight joy-riders, ambled off through the crowd. Once free it turned sharply to the right, and drove rapidly away from the scene of still roaring enthusiasm.

M. Clemenceau, Mr. Lloyd George, and President Wilson characteristically enough left this scene of frantic excitement to resume work then and there, in the annex to the Château where the election of the Presidents of the French Republic takes place. After an hour and a half's work they returned to Paris. It may here be noted that the Triple Alliance of the three countries they represented, which guarantees the performance by the Germans of the terms of peace, was signed in the morning.

The road back from Versailles to Paris was lined with sightseers and an almost unending string of motorcars. Flags waved from every window, and there was scarcely a child on the road that did not claim some fancied President or delegate in each car that bore the 'signature rosette'. The way must have been a long triumph for the Three, if indeed in the dusty and much-handled figures wearing top-hats that had almost ceased to bear any resemblance to their morning's selves the critical eye of the Frenchmen could believe that Clemenceau, Lloyd George, and Wilson were veritably disguised.

The guns were still booming and the bronze whirr of the aeroplanes was still vibrating in the sky when the rest of the Conference began to break up and follow their leaders back to the capital. It had been a day of success whatever the difficulties ahead might be, and though the actual ceremony itself was unmarked by pomp or circumstance of any kind whatever, it teemed with significance to those who had but a trace of imagination. A great foundation has been laid, a foundation of justice and of human co-operation for the future – and a success achieved which in some part must console the survivors for the terrible cost at which it has been purchased.

The Chinese delegates were not present at the signature. They were informed four days ago that it was not possible for any delegate to sign the treaty with reservations. They therefore abstained, and have issued a statement protesting against the articles in the Treaty which deal with the Shantung question. Their manifesto ends: 'The Peace Conference having denied China justice, and having in effect prevented the Chinese delegates from signing the Treaty without sacrificing their sense of right, justice, and patriotic duty, the latter submit their case to the impartial judgment of the world.'

23 May 1927: The first solo flight across the Atlantic is made
NEW YORK TO PARIS IN LESS THAN ONE AND A HALF DAYS
LINDBERGH'S TRIUMPH
ALL RECORDS BROKEN BY LONE ADVENTURER

At 10.22 on Saturday night Captain Charles Lindbergh, the lone American aviator, arrived at Le Bourget aerodrome, Paris, after a record-breaking journey of 3,600 miles from New York, which was performed in thirty-three and a half hours. He received a tremendous welcome from huge crowds, which broke through the military and police cordons, and literally stormed the landing ground.

Lindbergh appears to have carried out his flight with mathematical precision, and ahead of his schedule time. He had expected to reach the south coast of Ireland about 7 p.m., but by that hour he had passed South Devon, and was on his way over the Channel to the French coast. The following is an approximate time-table of his itinerary:

Friday, May 20

12.50 p.m. Left New York

2.40 p.m. Passed Halifax (Massachusetts)

6 p.m. Over Nova Scotian coast

7.50 p.m. Passed Strait of Canso

8 p.m. Passed southern extremity of Newfoundland

8.50 p.m. Passed over St. John's (Newfoundland) and turned
    eastward over the Atlantic

Saturday, May 21.

7 a.m. (about) Sighted by C.P.R. liner five hundred miles east of
    Newfoundland

1.10 p.m. Seen by S.S. *Hilversum* five hundred miles from Irish
    coast

5.20 p.m. Passed Smerwick (County Kerry)

7.40 p.m. Passed St. Germans, near Plymouth

7.45 p.m. Passed Prawle Point

8.30 p.m. Passed Cherbourg

10.22 p.m. Arrived at Le Bourget (Paris)

It is stated that the engine, of 250 h.p., built by the Wright firm founded by the two famous aviation pioneers, was still running perfectly when Lindbergh landed. He had sufficient petrol for another one thousand miles. Captain Lindbergh is to receive the Legion of Honour at the hands of President Doumergue tomorrow at Le Bourget. Today the airman will be presented by the Aero Club de France with its gold medal. Yesterday Sir Alan Cobham flew over from Croydon to congratulate him on behalf of British airmen, and to convey an invitation to him from the Royal Aero Club to visit London. This he is understood to have accepted in principle.

The Stars and Stripes and the Tricolour are flying together from hundreds of windows in Paris today in celebration of the success of Captain Charles Lindbergh, who reached Le Bourget last night at 10.22 on the conclusion of his record-breaking flight from New York. When the first report of his arrival reached the boulevards there was a period of hesitation, for Parisians have not yet forgotten the premature rejoicings over the attempt of Nungesser and Coli. But when the news was confirmed, citizens indulged in a spontaneous outburst of enthusiasm such as has not been witnessed for many years. In theatres and cafés the intelligence was greeted by the rendering of the 'Star-Spangled Banner' and the 'Marseillaise', while cheering crowds assembled in front of the newspaper offices and in the Place de l'Opéra so densely that traffic was partially held up.

But it was at Le Bourget that the excitement waxed most intense, for the Paris airport has never in its history witnessed such scenes as those of last night, when a crowd estimated at between 100,000 and 200,000 swept down the iron barriers and, despite the efforts of a force of five hundred troops and police, swarmed on to the landing-ground as soon as Lindbergh's machine was sighted. Shortly after ten o'clock there arose a murmur of long-suppressed excitement as the Ryan monoplane swung into the field of light created over the aerodrome by the searchlights and arc lamps. Twice the pilot made a circuit of the landing-ground, and then, having carefully chosen his point of descent, came down with a neatness and precision which astonished the observers, who declared it would have done credit to an air 'ace' who had only been out for an hour's flight. But after his thirty-three and a half hours' journey Lindbergh was still perfectly steady and alert, as he showed in making this fine landing, for as he remarked, the lay of the ground he noticed also the faces of the crowd straining at the barriers on the eastern side of the ground, and so took a sudden sweep to the western end, so as to land about four hundred yards away from the densely-packed mass that waited to welcome him. It was then that the barriers were broken down as the crowd swept in one great wave toward the monoplane. It was owing to the pilot's cool calculation that there are no serious incidents to deplore, for within a few seconds of the propeller having ceased to turn thousands were pressing and struggling round the machine.

'Hullo, boys, I'm here!' said Lindbergh as he thrust his head out of the cockpit, and then, as though he could not quite believe that he had succeeded, he said, 'I am Lindbergh. Where am I?' On being assured that he was in Paris, he simply replied, 'Good', and then proposed to restart his motor in order to taxi to the hangar, but, happily, was dissuaded from attempting this final manoeuvre, for the crowd was by this time clustered so thickly round his machine that the restarting of the propeller could only have resulted in wholesale decapitations. He was still cool and smiling as he called to one of those who had run to meet him, 'Come along, old fellow, and help me to leave my box.' While the field rang with cries of '*Vive Lindbergh!*' and '*Vive l'Amérique!*' Lindbergh was lifted out of his seat by two stalwart French airmen, but was immediately submerged in a sea of clutching arms. A moment later a helpless figure was being borne on the heads or shoulders of the crowd towards a hangar. But this was not Lindbergh. The aviator, still smiling and wearing a straw hat, was smuggled quietly into the background while the crowd surged round a mechanic who, despite his protests that he was not the hero and had nothing whatever to do with the flight, was borne in triumph off the field, while Lindbergh was led unnoticed, and finally disguised as a French aviator, to a waiting motorcar which, by a circuitous route, bore him to the headquarters of the aerodrome, where he was greeted by the American Ambassador, the Minister of Labour, representatives of the President of the Republic and the Minister of War, and a number of prominent French pilots.

While, he rested on a mattress stretched across three chairs he bravely protested that he was still not overcome by the need for sleep, but medical officers and the Ambassador prevented his rising to satisfy the demand of the crowd which had stormed the building, breaking doors and windows and clamouring for a sight of the Transatlantic hero. Meanwhile another section of the crowd had stormed the machine, and before this could be stowed in a hangar under a strong guard of troops it had suffered considerable damage at the hands of souvenir hunters, who had torn off large pieces of the wing covering, chipped off lumps of aluminium, and even broken stays in their eagerness to secure a relic of the record-breaking achievement. The monoplane is now carefully watched in its hangar at Le Bourget, whither thousands of people have gone today in hopes of catching a glimpse of it.

It was not until the crowd had thinned considerably that Lindbergh was smuggled out of the building by a back door, and driven off towards Paris. By way of throwing over-enthusiastic sightseers off the scent the car bearing the airman set out in the opposite direction from Paris, and then returned by devious ways to the American Embassy, where Lindbergh is the guest of Mr. Myron. T. Herrick. An incident which has profoundly touched French sentiment occurred en route, for Lindbergh, despite his fatigue, asked to be allowed to halt for a moment at the tomb of the Unknown Soldier, where, shortly after one o'clock this morning, he paid a silent tribute to the French heroes.

When Lindbergh arrived at Le Bourget last night he had during his thirty-three and a half hours' flight covered 6,000 kilometres. By beating the flight of 5,396 kilometres made by Costes and Rignot on the flight from Paris to Jask [in Persia] he has thus established a new record. At the United States Embassy in the Avenue Iena the first thing for which Lindbergh asked was a bath, after which he took a light meal of soup, eggs, and milk. While eating this he gave in lively fashion some account of his journey to the representative of a Press agency. Before he left New York he had been handed meteorological forecasts predicting excellent weather over the Atlantic; nevertheless, he had had to fly for over 1,000 miles through heavy rain.

'I rose and fell,' he said, 'in order to try to find better weather. At some moments I was ten feet above the water, at others 10,000 feet, but at no height did I find fine weather. I saw no vessel during the day and the lights of only one during the night. But this is easily explained, as there was a lot of fog and 1 had flown for many hours without seeing the sea at all. To tell the truth, I was horribly bored. I was not in the least sleepy, and I never made any use of the caffeine and other stimulants I had taken with me as a precautionary measure. I only drank water, but I don't mind telling you that when I arrived I had a most devilish thirst.'

Lindbergh first saw the lights of Le Bourget when he was about thirty miles away, and he had no difficulty in finding his way across France, thanks to the lights and to having carefully studied the map. Of luggage he had none, and it was, in pyjamas and a dressing-gown borrowed from the Ambassador that he gave his interview. The only regret that Lindbergh seemed to have last night was that he had not controlled his petrol consumption more exactly, as he found on arriving that he could have flown for another 1,000 miles, he said.

It must be realised that, once in his machine, Lindbergh, owing to the features of its construction, could never look out straight ahead directly, but only by means of a periscopic arrangement. To the left and to the right his view was uninterrupted through the windows. He carried no lights on board, but all the dials of his instruments were luminous. His steering – this is what surprises the experts – was done entirely by means of one small compass. His route was marked out on maps on a scale of 1-in-1,000,000, besides those for the British Isles and France on a very much bigger scale. Lindbergh wore for his flight breeches, thick woollen stockings and shoes, a moleskin waistcoat under his coat and over this an overcoat, for he was entirely enclosed. Behind him in the cockpit of this machine was a chronometer, and on one side a bag of provisions and a tin of water. But there was no parachute and no wireless apparatus. A large knife, a pair of pliers, and the sealed barograph completed the equipment.

France is celebrating the achievement of Captain Lindbergh in no niggardly fashion, and the impression gained in conversation with Frenchmen and from newspaper comment is that the feat of the young

American airman could not have been more generously applauded had he been one of their compatriots. Its very magnitude has raised it above simply national considerations. As soon as the President of the Republic received news of the arrival he addressed the following telegram to Mr. Coolidge: 'On the morrow of the attempt of our aviators whose misfortune was so keenly felt by the generous hearts of your countrymen Charles Lindbergh has achieved what Nungesser and Coli attempted, and, by a bold flight, has established an aerial link between the United States and France. All Frenchmen unreservedly admire his courage and rejoice in his success. I send you the hearty congratulations of the Government of the Republic and of the whole French people.' Mr. Coolidge replied: 'I thank you for your cordial message, which I share with the American people. I rejoice in the success of the young man who so courageously undertook his lonely flight, but neither myself nor the people of the United States forget to share in the mourning of France for the recent loss of your two brave aviators. Progress in aviation is due in large measure to French genius, which has contributed to our rapprochement and so increased our heritage of sympathy and good understanding.'

While Lindbergh still slept this morning at the American Embassy, the Ambassador received a number of distinguished visitors bearing official congratulations. Among those were M. Pierre Godin and M. de Castellane, the President and Vice-President of the Municipal Council, who brought the congratulations of the City of Paris; M. Bouju, Prefect of the Seine; M. Paul Claude, and M. Leroy, who, as representative of M. Briand, was charged to inform the American Ambassador that the flag of the United States had been hoisted over the Ministry of Foreign Affairs. The American flag also flies over the Ministry of Finance, which is the seat of the Presidency of the Council, and the importance of this compliment may be gathered from the fact that never has a foreign flag been hoisted at either place before, save in honour of a Chief of State. A telegram of congratulations has also been sent to the American Ambassador by M. Georges Leygues,

Minister of Marine. General Girod, leader of the aviation group in the Chamber of Deputies, has sent the congratulations of the group to Mr. Herrick, and at the same time has addressed the following letter to M. Briand: 'I have the honour to ask, knowing that I am realising your own thought, that the Legion of Honour be immediately awarded to Captain Lindbergh and solemnly presented to him by the President of the Republic when on Tuesday next he visits Le Bourget, on the spot where cross the lines of departure and of arrival of three heroes, named Nungesser, Coli, and Lindbergh, all three of whom are indissolubly united in our fervent homage.'

Another ceremony which will probably take place at Le Bourget shortly will be the affixing of a tablet to mark the spot on which Lindbergh arrived. Lindbergh took his first two hours' rest immediately after landing. The Ambassador has been asked to invite Captain Lindbergh to a reception to be given in his honour by the Chamber of Deputies on Wednesday.

25 October 1929: The Wall Street crash doesn't appear quite so calamitous in the pages of the *Telegraph*

AMAZING DAY ON WALL STREET

RECORD SLUMP AND RALLY

13,000,000 SHARES SOLD

BANKERS' HOPEFUL VIEW

From Our Own Correspondent

Yesterday was another day of frantic excitement on the New York Stock Exchange. It is described as the worst in the history of that institution. The stupendous total of 13,000,000 shares changed hands on the Exchange while the curb market dealt in 6,500,000. The ticker-tape was nearly three hours behind. On the announcement that leading bankers were meeting to deal with the situation, however, a remarkable rally occurred, and at the close the leading stocks were only two to ten points below their previous close, while many had actually advanced.

Wild excitement prevailed during the slump, and twelve brokers had to be taken to hospital in a state of collapse. The bankers took the view that the situation was technical rather than fundamental, and stated that no brokerage or banking houses were in difficulties. According to Washington despatches, Government officials did not consider the position dangerous. Hopes that the Federal bank rate would be reduced were not realised, but the decline in brokers' loans was welcomed. The slump affected exchanges in other American cities, where several were closed prematurely. There were also repercussions in Canada.

Wall Street's nerves were so badly shattered by three days of frantic selling that the stage was set today when the Stock Exchange opened amid tense excitement for the greatest slump in its history, with panic prevailing for virtually three hours. As the great wave of liquidation, unrivalled even in the early days of the Great War, hit the market, the bottom dropped out amid scenes of demoralisation never before witnessed.

All records for the volume of trading were broken, the total transactions on the Stock Exchange reaching 13,000,000 shares, while 6,500,000 shares were thrown into the Curb market. So great was the avalanche of selling, with prices dropping from five to ten points between sales, that Mr. Charles Mitchell, Mr. J P. Morgan, and other leading bankers hastily assembled at the Morgan offices to discuss plans for ending the panic, which had seemingly gripped the entire country. When news of the conference was flashed about Wall Street in the early afternoon the stock market commenced a rally which was almost as remarkable as the slump, and declines ranging from twenty to fifty points, representing many thousand million pounds, were restored. At the close of the market the leading stocks were only from two to ten points below their previous close, and many showed actual gains.

Feverish excitement prevailed in New York throughout the day, and great crowds assembled at the intersection of Broad and Wall Streets to witness the arrival of the financial leaders at the Morgan offices. So large did the mob become that police reserves and the riot squad were called out to disperse it and restore traffic. When the bankers left in their motorcars after an hour's conference, the crowd surged forward with cheers, as it was seen that the market had taken a turn upward, and the mounted police had all they could do to afford them protection. Later, Mr. Thomas Lamont, of Morgan's, announced that the bankers considered the situation technical rather than fundamental, and held out hope that the worst was over. Reports that the bankers had appealed to Mr. Andrew Mellon, Secretary of the Treasury, for advice could not be confirmed, but Washington despatches were quick to support Mr. Lamont's statement that the stock market was merely undergoing a technical readjustment and that Government officials did not consider the general situation in danger.

Wall Street's hopes that the New York Federal bank rate would be lowered from six per cent to five and a half, or even five, in order to instill some very much desired confidence into stocks were not realised. The retention of the six per cent rate, however, is interpreted tonight as evidence that high banking officials are not unduly worried by today's events, but are confident that the market will find its proper level without seriously injuring business. At the close of trading there was another item of cheer for the starved 'bulls' in the announcement that brokers' loans had decreased during the week by nearly £33,000,000. The sum is not large in view of the terrific amount of liquidation, but Wall Street had feared that owing to the tremendous issues of new securities loans might even show an increase. The decline in brokers' loans may be expected to help sentiment when the markets are called upon again tomorrow to meet another test. The net stock market declines today were probably smaller than in any of the recent breaks, but at the depth of the decline it was estimated that another £5,000,000,000 had been wiped off the slate.

The effects of the Stock Exchange crash in New York, which was predicted months ago by Mr. Roger Babson, America's foremost statistician and market 'meteorologist', extended to all parts of the country. In Chicago, Baltimore, and Philadelphia, where the frightened bulls scattered before the determined bears just as wildly as in New York, the exchanges were ordered to be summarily closed before the end of the day's session. It is understood that a similar project was discussed in New York, but conservative counsels prevailed.

Distinguished financiers protest that there is absolutely nothing in the general conditions to warrant pessimism, and that the deluge of selling today performed a great economic service in pumping tons of water from a great number of highly saturated securities. The unfortunate fact remains that good issues, as well as questionable, were almost equally affected by the series of crashes, which excite dismay and fears for the financial structure at a time when industry remains good and there is no immediate prospect of a big drop.

Bankers, interviewed this evening by the Correspondent of *The Daily Telegraph*, all agree that the chief cause of the panic conditions must be attributed to the technical inefficiency of the present methods of dealing with such a tremendous and unexampled amount of business. Scenes of great excitement were witnessed last evening in Throgmorton Street. Nervousness with regard to the condition of the American market caused hundreds of brokers to remain in Shorter's-court – the entrance to the 'House', where dealings in Anglo-American securities are transacted after the close of the 'House' – to watch events in the interests of their clients. Soon it became apparent that Wall Street was in the throes of another crash, the prices coming over the wires from New York recording tremendous falls. Prices fell away with such bewildering rapidity that it was only with the greatest difficulty that business could be conducted. Quotations were extremely erratic, with differences from one minute to the next so great as to be almost incredible. Notwithstanding the rain, the crowd of brokers and jobbers did not disperse until after seven o'clock.

24 May 1934: Bonnie and Clyde meet their end
GIRL GANGSTER SHOT DEAD
FORMER WAITRESS'S MAD CAREER
85 M.P.H. DRIVE INTO POLICE TRAP
From Our Own Correspondent

The mad career of Clyde Barrow, a notorious gangster and outlaw of twenty-three, and of 'Bonnie' Parker, his nineteen-year-old girl companion famed for cigar-smoking, ended today. For the past few months Barrow and his associates had terrorised the South-Western States with a series of murders and hold-ups. Today, after a sharp fight, detectives, led by a captain of the Texas Rangers, shot and killed him and the woman as they were returning to their secret and favourite rendez-vous in a small town in Louisiana. Barrow and Parker drove at 85 m.p.h. into a roadside trap which the police had prepared and kept ready every day for three weeks. Their bodies were riddled with shots from police machine-guns. The car was overturned and completely wrecked, and Barrow was found dead under the steering wheel, while the girl's body was doubled over a portable machine-gun in her lap. The car contained a miniature arsenal of shot-guns, revolvers and ammunition.

So bold and ruthless had been their crimes that the pair earned the sobriquet of 'the wild human rats'. Scores of police officers had been scouring the South-Western States for them for months past. Only a month ago Barrow and his associates were within an ace of capture when they gained their freedom behind a fusillade of machine-gun bullets, which killed one officer. A week earlier the gang had murdered two highway patrolmen in cold blood. 'Bonnie' had been a waitress in a cheap coffee house before she joined Barrow. Previously she had been married to a murderer who is now serving a life sentence for killing a sheriff.

2 July 1934: The Night of the Long Knives consolidates Hitler's hold in Germany
HITLER'S EXECUTION OF HOSTILE NAZIS
CAPTAIN RÖHM DECLINES SUICIDE AND IS SHOT
PURGE OF BROWN SHIRTS IN BERLIN AND MUNICH
MORE LEADERS REPORTED TO HAVE BEEN PUT TO DEATH
GUARD SET ON VON PAPEN'S HOUSE
From Our Special Correspondent

Captain Ernst Röhm, leader of the Nazi Storm Troopers, was executed in the Stadelheim Prison, Munich, this evening. This was the sequel to the most critical weekend for Herr Hitler since he assumed power seventeen months ago. Captain Röhm's execution followed the shooting of the former Chancellor, General von Schleicher, and the execution of a number of prominent Storm Troop leaders. The official statement issued tonight says that Röhm, after being deposed from his leadership, was given a revolver to shoot himself. Until late this afternoon he had not done so. Police, therefore, went into his prison cell and shot him dead.

The entire staff of the Nazi Storm Troopers' headquarters, the Brown House, in Munich, has been cleared out. The official reason given is that the staff has been sent away on a month's leave. Further executions of Nazi leaders are reported to have been carried out during today. Tonight, Dr. Goebbels, the German Minister of Propaganda, told the German nation that they owed a tremendous debt to Chancellor Hitler for his personal work in suppressing the attempted revolt by Röhm. He sternly warned other possible traitors that they would receive no mercy.

Germany is dazed and bewildered by the dramatic, and in many ways inexplicable, events of this amazing weekend. As the official communiqué of the Nazi party and the statements of General Göring to the Press explain, a 'second revolution', directed against Hitler and the Reichswehr, has been killed at birth. It has been killed by dramatic personal actions in the full limelight by Hitler in Munich and by Göring in Berlin.

What the alleged 'second revolution' was to have been, against whom and by whom, is still a complete mystery. Many people think the events of the weekend were a purging of the Nazi party's discreditable elements and political suspects. What there could have been in common between General Schleicher and Röhm, the two principal victims, it is difficult to imagine.

The following facts are certain:

1. No revolt actually took place and there has been no fighting.
2. On a pre-arranged signal Hitler in Munich and Göring in Berlin moved almost simultaneously against the undesirables in the early hours of yesterday morning.
3. The former Chancellor, General von Schleicher, and his wife were shot when the General resisted being arrested in his house and his wife tried to shield him.
4. Ernst Röhm, commander of the Storm Troops, having been deposed and arrested by Hitler personally, was executed this evening.
5. Seven other prominent Storm Troop leaders were arrested and shot out of hand. They are: Chief Group Leader August Schneidhuber, Munich; Chief Group Leader Edmund Heines, Silesia; Chief Group Leader Karl Ernst, Berlin; Group Leader Wilhelm Schmid, Munich; Group Leader Hans Hayn, Saxony; Group Leader Hans von Heydebreck, Pomerania; Detachment Leader Count von Spreti, Munich.

Herr von Bose, chief of the Prussian Press Department, was shot dead in von Papen's office. Vice-Chancellor von Papen's house has been surrounded by police and no one is allowed to pass. Whether he is merely being guarded for his own protection or is under house arrest the Government so far declines to state. Herr Klausar, the German head of Catholic Action, was, it is reported on good authority, shot dead yesterday for offering resistance when police officers came to search his house. Herr Klausar is the first non-political figure whose death is reported and the consequences may be serious for the Nazi régime.

During my flight across Germany this morning from Vienna to Berlin in a special aeroplane chartered by *The Daily Telegraph* I was able to see that the general appearance of the country is absolutely normal. Everywhere excursionists, on Elbe pleasure steamers, on foot and in motor-cars, were enjoying the usual German Sunday outing. No troops were in motion, and there were none of the guards on railway lines and bridges that one sees everywhere in Austria. At Dresden, where my plane was forced by the strong head wind to land for refuelling, several thousands of persons, including hundreds of uniformed Storm Troops, were watching a special exhibition of flying.

Behind the dramatic story of yesterday's events lies a tale of devotion and courage of a woman. She was Frau Elizabeth von Schleicher, wife of General von Schleicher, who fell trying to shield her husband. Her death in this manner is arousing more public feeling than the news of the crisis. The order for General von Schleicher's arrest was signed yesterday morning by General Göring. At 12 noon, four truckloads of black-uniformed men left the Nazi party police barracks in Berlin and headed for Potsdam. At the villa in Neubabelsberg, near Potsdam, where General von Schleicher and his family were in residence, no warning had been received. The General, his wife, and her twelve-year-old daughter by a former marriage, were sitting down to luncheon when the dramatic happenings were taking place in Berlin. The sudden crunch of brakes outside and the thump of heavily-booted feet on the polished floor were the first alarming signs to reach this family. The General left the table, but before he could reach the door the house was swarming with police. Before turning to face the intruders the General pushed his young stepdaughter out of the room.

Events then followed so quickly that no one has a clear picture yet of what actually happened. The General, when informed that he was under arrest, made a move to reach his revolver, whether to shoot himself or another will never be told. The police answered with a volley. Frau von Schleicher, who was standing near the door, suddenly sprang across the room and threw herself at the Storm Troop commander, beseeching him to cease firing. It was too late. She fell mortally wounded, with a bullet meant for her husband.

An addition to this eye-witness's story is supplied by a friend of the von Schleicher family. In 1931, shortly after the General's second marriage, he went to have his horoscope read. The reader told him that he had a long and active life ahead of him and that he would die at an advanced age.

Broadcasting tonight, Dr. Goebbels, Minister of Propaganda, described his experiences with Herr Hitler during the Munich arrests. He emphasised constantly how much of the work of suppression was carried out by the Leader personally and pointed out how great was the new debt owed him on this account. 'I still see the Leader standing on the terrace of the Godesberg Hotel,' he said. 'The Leader looks seriously into the dark sky. Nobody knows yet what threatens. The Leader is true to his own principles. The Leader is full of determination reading the reactionary rebels who have cast the nation into unlimited disturbance. Reports come to him from Berlin and Munich. After only a few minutes' conference the decision is made not to wait until the next morning. We start at two in the night. At four we are in Munich. On the aerodrome the Leader receives reports. Hitler interviews the rebels. He throws his anger into their pale faces and tears off their identification lapels. Then he decides to go into the lions' den.' A dozen times Dr. Goebbels punctuated his speech with the sternest warnings to possible traitors to the Leader, that they were playing with their heads and need expect no mercy.

General Göring today ordered the arrest of the staff of the Berlin and Brandenburg Storm Troops, together with the staff bodyguard. The force has meanwhile been put under the command of Police General Daluege. The arrested men will remain in custody until it can be established which of them were involved in the 'plot'. They were told that, even if innocent, they had only the traitors who formerly commanded them to thank for their imprisonment. The holiday for the entire body of Storm Troops is not disturbed. During this time no uniforms, and above all no 'dirks of honour', are to be worn. Berlin Storm Troop leaders are to be confined to their homes to await further orders. Anyone who calls a Storm Troop meeting, even if held in civil clothes and with the good intention of explaining the Leader's actions, will be called to account.

A further appeal has been issued by General von Blomberg to the army announcing the cessation of a state of emergency. He says: 'The Leader, with soldierly resolution and ideal courage, has himself attacked the traitors and mutineers and struck them down. The fighting forces, as the defenders of the people removed from the internal political struggle, will show their thanks through devotion and loyalty. The good relations with the new Storm Troops which the Leader demands will be furthered with pleasure by the fighting forces in consciousness of the common aim.'

Every criticism of the summary executions, announces General Göring, and any discussion of the measures undertaken by the Leader and his lieutenants, will be punished with the utmost severity.

Herr Hitler's final plans to crush the mutineers yesterday were laid during a visit to Essen and the factories of Westphalia in order to preserve the impression of absolute order and not alarm Röhm and his friends. Herr Lutze, district governor of Hanover, was secretly named Chief of Staff in place of Röhm and made privy to Herr Hitler's plans for a sudden action.

At 2 a.m. yesterday, at Godesberg, near Bonn, the Leader decided to go at once to Munich by air. 'The bearing of the Leader,' writes an eye-witness, 'was one of extraordinary resolution when he embarked on this night flight into the unknown.' With a few companions, Herr Hitler reached Munich at 4 a.m. There he learned that the Munich Storm Troops had been called out by their commanders with the cry: 'The Leader is against us, the army is against us. Storm Troopers, out on to the streets.'

But as he drove to the Ministry of the Interior only a few groups of dejected Storm Troopers were still to be seen. Acting with the speed which has characterised the movements of Herr Hitler's adherents, Herr Wagner, Bavarian Minister of the Interior, had deprived their leaders, Schneidhuber and Schmid, of their command and ordered the Brown Shirts to their homes. At the Ministry of the Interior Schneidhuber and Schmid were formally arrested in the presence of the Leader, who himself tore the emblems of their ranks from their uniforms. The two mutineers were taken to Stadelheim Jail and executed.

At 5.30 a.m., again with only a few companions, Herr Hitler went to Bad Wiessee, where Röhm was spending his sick leave. Heines, the troop commander of Silesia, was also passing the night there. Röhm was arrested in his bedroom by the Leader in person. He surrendered without a word and without resistance. Heines was in an adjoining room. Describing events there the eye-witness's story continues: 'A shameless sight presented itself to the eyes of those who entered. Heines lay in bed with a homosexual youth. The disgusting scene which took place on the arrest of Heines and his companion is not to be described. It throws a clear light on the state of affairs in the immediate environment of the former Chief of Staff.' With Röhm most of his staff were also arrested.

Herr Hitler then returned to Munich by car. On the way and at Munich railway station more guilty Storm Troop commanders were arrested. After a short conference with General von Epp, Governor of Bavaria, Herr Hitler addressed the meeting of Storm Troop commanders in the Brown House. His reception assured him that the majority of the commanders and their men were loyal.

Immediately afterwards, in Berlin, General Göring struck with the speed and efficiency of a practised revolutionary. Yesterday morning the peace of the Tiergarten was shattered by the arrival at the Storm Troop headquarters of several wagon-loads of green-clad police of the special 'Kommando Hermann Göring'. All had rifles and steel helmets. The building and house nearby were quickly surrounded and occupied, and sentry posts were thrown out into the park. Traffic was diverted from the Tiergarten Strasse.

A cordon was also thrown round the house of General Göring, and blue uniformed police guarded the doors of the Colombus building on the Potsdam Platz, a modern block of offices. American newspaper correspondents trying to enter their offices were turned back. The police were searching for a certain person who is believed to be the 'well-known obscure personality' in Berlin referred to in an official statement, who was acting as go-between, it is alleged, in the negotiations between Röhm and an unnamed foreign power. Telephones were closed for two hours yesterday afternoon until General Göring had explained to representatives of the foreign Press, hurriedly summoned to the Propaganda Ministry, that a small group of Storm Troop commanders had plotted a second revolution in an endeavour to establish their ridiculous Government. Röhm and others had hoped to put pressure on the Leader, but the Leader had decided that whoever resisted him should lose his head.

General Göring emphasised that he had acted against all those who believed themselves able to overthrow the State, whether they stood on the Right or the Left. Many plotters, he said, realising that their plans were known, had committed suicide. The ordinary Storm Trooper, he declared, knew nothing of the plans of the leaders. A ruthless scourge on the organisation and the policy would take place. 'Some journalists,' concluded General Göring with a twinkle in his eye, 'like to make a story (he used the English word) out of very little things. You need not make a story out of this; it is there all right.'

Herr Hitler returned to Berlin at ten o'clock last night. With him was Dr. Goebbels, Minister of Propaganda, who had been summoned to join him at Godesberg on the way to Munich, and had taken part in the arrest of Röhm and Heines. Dr. Goebbels had been on a visit to the Rhineland.

8 February 1935: The *Telegraph* is an early adopter of television
MAGIC ON THE SCREEN
By The *Daily Telegraph* television correspondent

What is the secret of television? It lies in a tiny spot of light of varying intensity which travels to and fro across the screen, writing its pictorial message line by line at the rate of thousands of feet per second. The accommodating eye sees the pictures as a whole and gives them move-ment. If the spot-light has to cover the whole area of the picture in only thirty lines, as in the present B.B.C. transmissions, the resulting images are crude. If it can be accelerated and the lines knitted closer together, as in the coming 240-line transmissions, the quality approaches that of a home-cinema. The dark streaks which disfigure the present trans-missions disappear; definition improves in a striking manner.

This week I have had the novel experience of receiving both the old and the new television. I picked up the B.B.C. 30-line transmission in *The Daily Telegraph* offices on an old type of mirror-drum receiver. In Victoria-street I tuned-in an experimental Baird 180-line transmission from the Crystal Palace on a new cathode-ray receiver. The experiences illustrated the mechanical versus the electrical method of reception. There are, I should mention, newer mechanical methods for high-definition reception.

On the mirror-drum receiver there was the motor speed to regulate and the 'framing handle' to manipulate. Furthermore I needed two sets, one to receive the sound, the other the vision. The cathode ray receiver gave me both sound and tuning, contrast, and brilliance. It had five controls, two for sound tuning and volume, and the others for vision. Tuning the mirror-drum receiver was an elusive art. I was agreeably surprised at the ease of handling the cathode ray model, considering that ultra short waves are used for the transmission. It was also most interesting to find that both sound and vision could be picked up with a special type of indoor aerial.

Those pioneer enthusiasts who possess television sets now will have noticed the steady progress in B.B.C. Studio technique, while the method of transmission has remained unchanged. I talked yesterday with the man who has struggled for two and a half years with the limitations of the old 30-line system and its crude images. He is Mr. Eustace Robb, the B.B.C.'s television producer, whose experience should prove invaluable to the new department. Consider that the present television transmitter can, in the studio, at most embrace a field about five or six feet wide and eleven feet high. A maximum number of four dancers can be shown as tiny figures shoulder to shoulder. Mr. Roth, by gradual stages, has worked up to the presentation of a ballet and a complete musical comedy. A special caption machine creates atmosphere by all the tricks of the film title trade. Mr. Robb is the first man to have written 'B.B.C.' on the air.

10 June 1935: A South American war comes to an end
TRUCE DECLARED IN GRAN CHACO WAR
THREE YEARS' CONFLICT WHICH COST 50,000
BUENOS AIRES PEACE PARLEY PREPARES TERMS
HOW 6,000 MEN REPULSED A GERMAN-TRAINED ARMY OF 80,000
From Our Own Correspondent

Today, with dramatic suddenness, a truce was declared in the three years' death struggle in the fever-ridden jungle of the Gran Chaco between Bolivia and Paraguay. The terms drawn up by a peace conference of various South American countries are: Fighting to cease at once; both armies to be reduced by 5,000 men; and an international Commission to define a Neutral Control Zone. It is provided that both countries will seek a final solution by direct negotiation. In the event of a breakdown the dispute shall go before The Hague Court. This news, was made known in Asuncion, the capital of Paraguay, by screaming sirens. In La Paz, the Bolivian capital, it was received in silence. It is estimated that 50,000 lives have been laid down in the futile struggle.

This desperate encounter really began because Bolivia, at the foothills of the Andes, with all the wealth of her mineral deposits and her oil, felt herself hemmed in and deprived of facilities for exporting her products. Her eyes turned to the River Paraguay, placidly bearing its steamship traffic to the open sea. Between Bolivia and this desirable exit stretched the empty forests of the Gran Chaco, uninhabited and uninhabitable except for a narrow fringe along the western bank of the River Paraguay. Moreover, the boundary had never been properly defined. The Gran Chaco was a no-man's land. For years Bolivia, with a population of 3,000,000, had claimed the right to occupy it.

In 1932, after years of controversy, Bolivia's army of 80,000, German-trained under a German general, equipped with all the latest armaments of European and North American factories, began silently to penetrate into the heart of the Chaco. The result seemed a foregone conclusion. Paraguay, economically poverty-stricken, had only 800.000 inhabitants, her standing army numbering only 6,000, untrained and unarmed except for a few obsolete rifles.

One thing had not been reckoned with – the grim determination of the Paraguayans. Young Paraguayans flocked from the universities of Argentina, Europe, and North America to the colours. The Government could not arm them. They seized any weapons – axes, knives – and marched to face the intruder. The Chaco itself fought on their side. Its tortuous mazes of forest hid them. The silence, the apparent emptiness, the sudden attack from an unseen foe bewildered the Bolivians. They had been trained to sight their rifles at a visible object a given distance away, and were soon driven back into the malaria belt.

Within a year the first Bolivian army had been annihilated, and the second was retreating in disorder. At this crucial state Paraguay, in reply to the League of Nations Commission which had visited both countries, offered a ten days' armistice. This was lengthened to sixteen, but the League Commission failed, and the Bolivians, working day and night, had consolidated their position so effectively that when war began anew in January last year it took the Paraguayans six months to break through. When they succeeded they advanced one hundred miles in three months. Now, at the end of nearly three years, with both countries reduced to economic ruin, comes news of a truce.

15 June 1935: The first colour film is screened
HISTORIC SCREEN EVENT
FIRST FULL-LENGTH COLOUR FILM
QUALIFIED U.S. APPROVAL
From Our Own Correspondent

NEW YORK, FRIDAY

The most important event in the history of films since the talking pictures were perfected – the making of the first full-length colour film – was celebrated in New York's largest cinema, Radio City Music-hall, last night. The occasion was the showing of the film *Becky Sharp*, based on Thackeray's novel. The fashionable midnight audience which saw the picture, hitherto jealously guarded from the eyes of critics, became excited about the possibilities of the technicolour process which it employs and which is based on the use of red, violet, green and their complementary colours. Praise, however, was in every instance qualified. It was only too obvious that, skilful though Mr. Rouben Mamoulian and his assistants had been in handling this strange new screen element, much has yet to be learned.

This, of course, was to be expected, and the outstanding impression was one of enchanting effects never before achieved, and of infinite new possibilities in the realm of entertainment and aesthetic satisfaction. The scene which particularly enforces this feeling is one that formed the highlight of the George Arliss film *The Iron Duke* – the ball at Brussels on the eve of the Battle of Waterloo. This is transformed into a glorious spectacle, which is also more than a mere blaze of colour. The colours, used with rare cunning, achieve an effect of rising emotion, for the pastel shades of the opening scenes deepen into more vivid splashes of blue, green, and scarlet as the climax approaches, until at last the bright martial uniforms completely take the place of ballroom gowns on the screen.

12 December 1936: King Edward VIII abdicates his throne
EDWARD VIII SAILS FROM ENGLAND
PORTSMOUTH EMBARKATION IN DESTROYER
FAREWELL BROADCAST TO THE EMPIRE
'IT MAY BE SOME TIME BEFORE I RETURN'
PROCLAMATION TODAY OF KING GEORGE VI

Edward VIII left England in the early hours of this morning in a destroyer with another destroyer as escort. It is believed that he is bound for Italy, where Lord Grimthorpe has offered him the use of his villa at Ravello, near the Bay of Naples. He left Fort Belvedere by car just before 11 p.m., after bidding farewell to his mother, Queen Mary, his sister, the Princess Royal, and his brothers, King George VI, the Duke of Gloucester and the Duke of Kent. Shortly after midnight his car drove into Portsmouth Dockyard, and in great secrecy he embarked in the destroyer, which sailed at 1.45 a.m.

An hour before leaving Fort Belvedere King Edward broadcast his farewell message to his former subjects throughout Britain and the Empire. He said: 'Now that I have been succeeded by my brother, the Duke of York, my first words must be to declare my allegiance to him. This I do with all my heart. You must believe me when I tell you that I have found it impossible to carry this heavy burden of responsibility and to discharge my duties as King as I would wish to do without the help and support of the woman I love. I now quit altogether public affairs and I lay down my burden. It may be some time before I return to my native land.'

He was introduced by Sir John Reith as 'His Royal Highness, Prince Edward'. It is understood, however, that this designation is unauthorised and that a new title will be bestowed upon him by King George VI after the Proclamation ceremonies have been concluded today. Before making his broadcast King Edward attended a farewell dinner party given by King George at Royal Lodge, Windsor. Other members of the Royal party were Queen Mary, the Duke of

Gloucester, the Duke of Kent, the Princess Royal, Princess Alice Countess of Athlone, and the Earl of Athlone. A few hours before this historic gathering – the only occasion in English history on which a reigning Sovereign and his predecessor have sat together at the same table – the Duke of York had formally ascended the Throne. At 1.52 p.m. a Royal Commission, appointed by King Edward as his last Royal act, signified, in the House of Lords, his assent to the Abdication Bill.

Queen Mary last night issued a moving message to 'The People of This Nation and Empire'. In the course of this she said: 'I need not speak to you of the distress which fills a Mother's heart when I think that my dear son has deemed it to be his duty to lay down his charge. I know that you will realise what it has cost him to come to this decision; and that, remembering the years in which he tried so eagerly to serve and help his Country and Empire, you will ever keep a grateful remembrance of him in your hearts. I commend to you his brother, summoned so unexpectedly, and in circumstances so painful, to take his place. I ask you to give to him the same full measure of generous loyalty which you gave to my beloved husband, and which you would willingly have continued to give to his brother.'

King George will take the Oath of Accession at a meeting of the Accession Council at St. James's Palace at eleven o'clock this morning. This afternoon he will be proclaimed, with ancient ceremonial, at four points in London:

3 p.m. – Friary Court, St. James's Palace
3.30 p.m. – Charing Cross
3.45 p.m. – Temple Bar
4 p.m. – Royal Exchange

The Proclamation will also be made in the principal cities of Britain and the Empire.

King Edward spent his last hours at Fort Belvedere today collecting a few mementos of his short reign. Small personal possessions which he will take with him on his future travels will include his favourite portrait of his father. At the moment when he ceased to be King he was lunching with his youngest brother, the Duke of Kent, Mr. Winston Churchill, and Mr. Waller Monckton, K.C.M. Attorney-General to the Duchy of Cornwall. Mr. Churchill visited Fort Belvedere today as a personal friend of King Edward.

During the day a small saloon car drove up to the main gates of the Fort. It contained four bearded Indians wearing turbans. They told me that they were students living in London and had visited Fort Belvedere in the hope of seeing King Edward. 'We come from the Punjab, and we wanted to catch a last glimpse of the King-Emperor. We have waited here for some time in the hope of seeing him, but we have realised that it is impossible.'

One Royal estate worker said today that certain personal servants have been offered the opportunity of remaining in King Edward's service. Police activity in the neighbourhood of Smith's Lawn, King Edward's private flying field, was renewed today. There were strong police guards inside and outside the Fort while the final preparations for the departure were completed. The bulk of King Edward's luggage has already left.

A farewell dinner party without parallel in British history was held at Windsor Royal Lodge tonight. It was given in honour of King Edward by King George VI. It was the first time that he had acted as host since the accession. The guests were seven members of the Royal family. In addition to King Edward, the others were: Queen Mary, the Duke of Gloucester, the Duke of Kent, the Princess Royal, Princess Alice Countess of Athlone and the Earl of Athlone. King George and the Duke of Gloucester drove from London to Royal Lodge during the evening. Almost immediately they drove over to Fort Belvedere through Windsor Great Park and returned to Royal Lodge with King Edward and the Duke of Kent, who had been with him most of the day. Shortly after 8 p.m. Queen Mary arrived by road, accompanied by the

Princess Royal, Princess Alice and the Earl of Athlone. Her car was about a quarter of an hour late, due to fog on the road from London.

Soon after 9.15 p.m. King Edward left the party to go to Windsor Castle to make his broadcast. He was driven to the Castle by a chauffeur. King Edward was seated in the back, with his hat drawn over his eyes. He was wearing a light coat and a light coloured muffler. He was driven up the Long Walk and entered by the Sovereign's Entrance at 9.40 p.m. The car entered the quadrangle of Windsor Castle, and within a minute of King Edward's arrival two lights were switched on in the suite he formerly occupied as Prince of Wales in the Augusta Tower. He was received by the Master of the Household and B.B.C. officials, and then went to the Augusta Tower.

There King Edward sat alone in a swivel chair in a barely furnished room. Before him was a plain oaken table drawn up before the fire. On it was the microphone. He had not used the room since he was Prince of Wales, when it was his favourite apartment at the Castle. After the broadcast he chatted and said farewell to a number of the Castle officials and old servants. He then left by the way he had come, the Sovereign's entrance, and on passing through the Cambridge Gate into the Park he was warmly cheered by a crowd of several hundred, which included many who were attending a dance close at hand. Instead of covering his face, as he had done on the journey to the Castle, King Edward leaned forward in his seat and doffed his hat in reply to the loud cheers he received. His face was lit up by the headlights of cars, which had stopped on the Windsor–Ascot road and the flashlights of photographers.

King Edward returned to Royal Lodge and remained there for a time with the King and Queen, Queen Mary, the Duke of Kent and the Duke of Gloucester, who had listened to the broadcast from there. Later he motored to Fort Belvedere before leaving for Portsmouth.

The rest of the Royal family then returned to London.

Under conditions of great secrecy King Edward left England early this morning in a destroyer which sailed from Portsmouth dockyard at 1.45 with another destroyer as escort. The two destroyers were

Wolfhound and *Fury*. The circumstances of the departure were as dramatic as any of the events which have marked the past ten days.

After his broadcast last night King Edward returned to Royal Lodge, Windsor, where he said farewell to King George VI, Queen Mary, the Princess Royal and the Duke of Gloucester. These four drove off from the Lodge in a car, and a few minutes later King Edward himself left by the Englefield Green entrance and returned to Fort Belvedere. King Edward left Fort Belvedere just before eleven o'clock, and his car covered the sixty-five miles to Portsmouth in about an hour and a half. It arrived at the Unicorn-street entrance to the dockyard at 12.20 a.m. The blinds were closely drawn and it was impossible to see who was inside, but it is understood that King Edward was accompanied by his equerry, the Honourable Piers Legh.

The Royal car was escorted by a police car and accompanied by two yellow shooting brakes filled with luggage. With its headlights on full it swept through the dockyard gates at about 30 m.p.h., but slowed down a second or two later as a sergeant of the dockyard police challenged it. There was a muffled word from the car and the sergeant sprang to attention. Two naval officers who had been pacing up and down saluted, and the royal car and its attendant vehicles proceeded towards the waterside. It then became apparent that the authorities were prepared for King Edward's arrival, though the fact had been kept a strict secret, and there were only a few dockyard workers about.

King Edward first proceeded to the residence of the Commander-in-Chief at Portsmouth, Admiral Sir William Fisher, and spoke with him for some time before embarking. The slight figure in a heavy ulster coat vanished in the shadows on the destroyer's deck, and shortly afterwards the vessel moved slowly from her berth. She passed through the narrow strip of water leading past the Southern Railway jetty and out towards Spithead, with the other destroyer in attendance.

The *Wolfhound*, which is a vessel of 1,100 tons, belonging to the First Anti-Submarine Flotilla, had left Portland at five o'clock last night under sealed orders. It was then strongly rumoured in Weymouth that the departure was connected with King Edward's projected journey to the Continent. The *Wolfhound* crept into Portsmouth under cover of darkness in the early part of the night and slipped alongside the quay where she waited with full steam up. All was bustle and activity on board her. But ashore there was no sign of anything unusual until King Edward arrived. The roads around the dockyards were silent and deserted. Only the usual number of police officers remained on duty at the gates, and even they had been kept in ignorance. The only circumstance which called for note was the fact that the Unicorn-street gates were not closed as usual at midnight. Once the Royal car was inside, however, they swung to. In the escorting police car was Chief Inspector David Storrier, who has been King Edward's personal detective throughout his reign. One member of his domestic staff also accompanied him.

28 April 1937: Guernica is bombed
MORE SPANISH TOWNS SET ON FIRE
MOLA BLASTING HIS WAY TO BILBAO
'PLANES ARRIVE TO HELP BASQUES
BID FOR AIR SUPREMACY
From Christopher Martin, *Daily Telegraph* Special Correspondent
with the Basque Forces

BILBAO, TUESDAY

Señor Prieto, the Spanish Air Minister, arrived here today from Valencia with thirty-two aeroplanes, which have been sent to the assistance of the Basque Government. The Basques hope thus to regain mastery of the air and defend themselves against the Nationalist forces advancing on Bilbao.

General Mola, the Nationalist commander, is blasting his way towards Bilbao by air bombardment. Yesterday Eibar was a mass of smoking ruins. Today Guernica, the holy city and ancient capital of the Basques, only eight miles from Bilbao, has also been bombed out of existence. The villages of Bolivar, Arbacegui and Guerricaiz have also been wiped off the map by aircraft bombs which leave craters twenty feet wide by forty feet deep. Earlier reports, from the Nationalist side, indicated that Eibar had been set on fire by the retreating Government forces. The Basque authorities, however, state that the town was destroyed by General Mola's incendiary bombs. The Nationalist aircraft rained bombs on their objectives three at a time – two explosive and one incendiary. The destruction which the explosive 300 lb bombs did not effect was completed by the incendiary bombs.

The defenders of Bilbao are emphatic that they will die fighting rather than surrender. If they maintain their determination to resist it is doubtful whether General Franco can take Bilbao except by destroying every building from the air. Bilbao today is fortified and sand-bagged. Famine no longer is feared since the arrival of the British food ships, and three more are waiting to sail from St. Jean de Luz. General Mola's troops are believed to have paid a heavy price for their successes on the Bilbao front. Some of their formations are stated to have lost eighty per cent in killed and wounded.

30 April 1937: More on Guernica
NATIONALISTS IN RUINED CITY
SCENE OF DESOLATION
From Pembroke Stephens, *Daily Telegraph* Special Correspondent
with the Nationalist Forces

GUERNICA, THURSDAY

The still smoking ruins of Guernica, the ancient Basque capital, were occupied by the Nationalist forces today. The Basque forces evacuated the town and withdrew in the direction of Bilbao an hour before the Nationalists entered the ruins. Guernica is fifteen miles north-east of Bilbao, just outside the second line of the city's defences. All the country behind Guernica – to the north and east of an estuary which joins Guernica to the sea – is being occupied by the Nationalists.

The importance of the advance along the coast is that it will enable

Nationalist artillery to dominate Bermeo, the port of Bilbao. This will strengthen the blockade. Ships will now find it more difficult to unload cargoes. I entered Guernica with the Nationalist vanguard one hour after the departure of the Basque forces. Guernica presents an appalling spectacle of desolation. The destruction is even greater, even more complete, than at Eibar. Here and there a solitary wall of a house rears its gaunt and blackened silhouette against the blue sky. There is little else except wrecked houses blocking practically every street.

A group of excited and distracted women wearing a queer medley of garments – men's socks and shoes, ill-fitting blouses and skirts and overcoats too big for them – told me that they had lost everything in the fire. Their homes were destroyed at night. They had to flee in their night-dresses, grabbing clothes as was they went from the wreckage of other houses that had not been destroyed by the flames. The women hid in these ill-assorted garments in the woods until the arrival of the Nationalists. They had had nothing to eat for three days. I gave them what tinned food I had brought with me.

General Franco's headquarters at Salamanca again strongly denied yesterday that Nationalist 'planes with incendiary bombs had destroyed Guernica. An official statement declared:

'The city was destroyed by petrol fires by the Red hordes in the service of the criminal Aguirre, President of the Basque Republic. We can prove at any time that the Nationalist aircraft did not fly on Tuesday over Guernica or elsewhere on the Basque front, owing to fog. Aguirre prepared the repulsive destruction of Guernica to evoke the indignation of the Basques, who are beaten and demoralised.'

On the other hand, the Reuter correspondent at Bilbao stated yesterday: 'General Franco's denial of the bombing of Guernica is adequately refuted by many thousands of survivors, including a number of priests.'

5 May 1937: The end of the airship age as the Hindenburg explodes on arrival in America
DISASTER TO GIANT AIRSHIP: FIFTY DEAD
HINDENBURG DESTROYED BY EXPLOSION
HELD UP BY STORM: CRASH IN FLAMES
SOME OFFICERS AND CREW JUMP TO SAFETY

Disaster befell the German airship Hindenburg when she arrived in America yesterday. An explosion occurred as she was mooring and the vessel was quickly enveloped in flames. There were approximately one hundred occupants on board, of whom about half perished. The American Air Lines Company reported that fifteen passengers and thirty-five members of the crew survived. Both the commander, Captain Max Prüss, and Captain Lehmann, who was acting in an advisory capacity, are among the survivors, although both are badly burned and in a critical condition.

A United States Navy report attributed the disaster to a hydrogen fire originating in the stern. This inflammable gas, and not helium, was used to inflate her. The explosion occurred as the Hindenburg was about to moor at Lakehurst, New Jersey, the landing ground for New York, from which it is fifty miles distant. For an hour the Zeppelin had cruised around, a thunderstorm making it impossible for her to land.

When the weather improved she approached the mooring mast. It was then that the explosion took place. The flames spread with great rapidity. The airship collapsed to the earth, and was soon a mass of twisted wreckage. Detachments of sailors were summoned to help in the rescue work. Roads near the airport were blocked with fire-engines, ambulances and. the cars of police and doctors. The ship cost £380,000 to build. Her insurance was largely covered in London.

'I am looking at the blazing wreck of the Hindenburg now. My impression is that many of the occupants have been trapped and burned to death. I can't tell you how many are dead. The airship crashed in a mass of flames, scattering hundreds of people near the mooring mast.'

Shouting at the top of his voice, Commissioner of Police Deering told to a representative of *The Daily Telegraph* on the Transatlantic 'phone from Lakehurst the story of the disaster. 'I was at the field when the giant came over. I was not there on business, but to meet a dear friend on board. Everything was O.K., and the wires were out for her at the mooring mast. Without warning there was a blast of fire, and the vast bulk just surged to the ground in a mass of flame.

'I don't know how many there were on board. As I speak to you I can see the rescue parties battling with the debris. In thirty years I have never seen such a sight . . . it is terrible. All I can say is that she just exploded and burned . . . just flopped to the ground.

'I can't stay here any longer, I have to get to the ground again. As I talk to you I can see the crowds surging on to the field. Police cars and ambulances are arriving amid a terrific roar of sirens and whistles. The flames leapt to a great height when she reached the ground, and then, in a terrific blast, myriads of sparks flew in the air, while the crowds fell back in a solid mass from the heat. There is nothing but a mass of twisted steel left.'

Communication Officer Watson, speaking from Lakehurst early this morning, said: 'The airship is a total loss. There are some survivors. They are terribly injured, and have been taken to hospital. Police officers are at their bedsides.

'It is a terrible scene. The news has spread, and there are thousands of people here. Just as she reached the mast and the wires were out there was a terrific explosion, and I can only compare the explosion with a set scene on the talkies. She just went in the air in bits and pieces. I doubt whether we shall be able to identify anyone on board; they were just blown to bits.'

The disaster to the Hindenburg occurred about 7.30 p.m., Eastern Standard Time – 12.30 p.m. British Summer Time – as she was about to land at the New York airport at Lakehurst, New Jersey. The airship was totally destroyed. At 11 p.m. the Chief of the Lakehurst Police said that about fifty of the thirty-nine passengers and sixty-one crew were dead. Thirty-four people were still unaccounted for. Some of these, however, may be alive. 'The survivors include twenty passengers and about half the crew,' he added. 'Nearly all of them are more or less seriously injured.'

The local police force had been reinforced by three hundred men from New York, 125 State troopers, and numbers of sailors from adjacent naval stations. So many spectators were arriving that they could not control the crowds.

Twenty-seven of the survivors were taken to the nearest big hospital, at Asbury Park, on the New Jersey shore. By 10 p.m. nineteen unidentified bodies had been removed from the wreckage. Detachments of sailors were extricating others as rapidly as the wreckage cooled sufficiently to enable them to approach. All the bodies were burned beyond recognition

The survivors included: Commander Prüss, a Zeppelin veteran, who was in command of the airship. He was critically injured; Captain Lehmann, the former commander. He leaped from the control cabin and is now in hospital with serious burns; Captain Samtt, third in command; Herr Speck, the radio operator; Herbert O'Laughlin, of Chicago, who jumped when the ship was ten feet from the ground; and Philip Mongole, of New York. He had severe burns on the arms and head.

Dense clouds of smoke hid the tangled wreckage from the horrified ground crew. Passengers were at the windows laughing and waving to those on the ground when the explosion occurred. Immediately afterwards a great cloud of flame and smoke burst out and the airship dropped to earth. Members of the ground crew ran for their lives to escape from the blazing wreckage. The spectators stood sobbing, many of them hysterical, as army trucks with screaming sirens sped to the blazing wreckage. The crash of the explosion shook the entire neighbourhood. The ship appeared to split in two before falling to the ground. The airship, which had been delayed for twelve hours by headwinds over Newfoundland and a heavy thunderstorm over the airfield, was preparing to land. She had dropped her landing lines and was about three hundred feet above the ground when the explosion occurred.

One American passenger named Spar saved his life by leaping from a cabin window. Two other men who leaped with him also survived. I found Mr. Spar staggering around the field, too dazed to give a coherent account of the disaster. He appeared more interested in finding his dog, which he had brought with him from Germany and which he feared had been killed in the explosion.

At 8.45 p.m. Commander Rosendahl, Commandant of the United States naval air base at Lakehurst, said to me: 'We are still fighting to get the flames under control. It is impossible yet to say how many have been killed or just what happened.' Emergency calls were broadcast as soon as the accident occurred for all available hospital units and fire-fighting apparatus. Within a short time dozens of engines were racing over the New Jersey roads towards the scene.

A few minutes later it was stated that the flames had been extinguished, but workers were still unable to approach the white-hot tangle of wires and framework. The firemen were forced to watch helplessly as the victims were burned to death. One member of the ground crew said: 'We got three bodies from the stern of the ship. All were burned beyond recognition, but one was still breathing, although his features were unrecognisable. The clothing on all three had been burned off. Even after the wreckage had dropped to the ground minor explosions continued. The screams of the victims could be plainly heard.'

Lightning was flickering around the ship as she came down, and observers believe that the explosion might have been caused by a flash. A witness of the crash, Mr. Robert Novins, a lawyer, told me that he saw several men and women leap from the airship just before she crashed. 'The Hindenburg was about three hundred feet up,' he added, 'when I saw a flash of flame. It was followed by a crash so violent that it shook the ground on which I was standing, some distance away. The flash was exceptionally brilliant, and its reflection lit up the sky for miles around. Lightning had been flashing around the ship all the time she was coming down, and some of my neighbours who were watching believe that a flash hit the ship and started the fire. I saw some of the passengers through the windows, rushing about panic-stricken but helplessly trapped.'

First news of the disaster reached Americans through the medium of a broadcasting company which had just broadcast a talk by Sir Josiah Stamp, speaking from London on the Coronation. The Hindenburg was due to sail for Europe tomorrow with seventy passengers, twenty of whom intended to fly by 'plane to London from Frankfurt for the Coronation. She left Frankfurt-on-Main at 8.15 p.m. on Monday. All her new 'outside' cabins had been booked. The airship was to have taken on her next trip to the United States films of the Coronation to be shown in American cinemas.

The Hindenburg was making her first flight of the season, under the command of Captain Max Prüss, who succeeded Captain Lehmann. Prüss was a veteran with the Zeppelin Company, with a quarter of a century's experience. He had flown more than 1,000,000 miles in airships. He was a protégé of Dr. Eckener and had already made several crossings as a junior officer.

1 October 1938: 'Peace for our time' claims Neville Chamberlain after he returns home with the Munich Agreement
PREMIER'S TUMULTUOUS WELCOME HOME
CHEERED FOR FIVE MINUTES ON PALACE BALCONY
REJOICING IN PARIS, ROME AND BERLIN
BRITISH TROOPS GOING TO CZECHOSLOVAKIA

The Prime Minister was given one of the greatest ovations ever accorded to a British statesman when he arrived in London last night from Munich. He was greeted by vast, cheering crowds at Heston aerodrome, where he broadcast the declaration renouncing war signed by Herr Hitler and himself yesterday morning. From there he drove to Buckingham Palace, where his appearance for five minutes on the balcony with the King and Queen and Mrs. Chamberlain was the occasion of a memorable demonstration. On arrival at Number 10, Downing-street Mr. Chamberlain made a short address to the great throng, in which he said that his mission to Germany had resulted in peace with honour. 'I believe it is peace for our time,' he added.

Similar welcomes were received yesterday by Monsieur Daladier, the French Premier, and Signor Mussolini when they returned to their capitals. A tremendous reception is being organised for Herr Hitler when he enters Berlin this morning as a peacemaker.

Britain is to send a brigade of infantry including, it is expected, battalions of Foot Guards to assist in maintaining order in Sudeten areas during the period of transition. German troops will enter a limited zone of the ceded Czechoslovak territory today. Last night it was reported from Warsaw that simultaneous occupation of Teschen-Silesia by Polish troops was contemplated. A further meeting in the near future, possibly at Rome, between Mr. Chamberlain, Signor Mussolini and Monsieur Daladier is hinted at in Italian political quarters. It is thought that such a conference might attempt to reach a settlement on Spain.

Scenes reminiscent of Armistice night in November 1918 marked Mr. Chamberlain's return to London from Munich last night. The enthusiasm of the huge crowds which greeted him everywhere reached its greatest pitch when Mr. Chamberlain, accompanied by his wife, appeared with the King and Queen on the balcony of Buckingham Palace. After five minutes of unbroken cheering, during which the Premier stood in the glare of a searchlight, waving to the huge throng, the crowd began spontaneously to sing the National Anthem. Again, when he returned to Downing-street there was a great demonstration, and the Prime Minister had to appear at a window and make a brief speech before the crowd could be persuaded to disperse.

Mr. Chamberlain had driven to Buckingham Palace from Heston airport, where he landed in the plane which brought him from Munich. Heavy rain failed to damp the enthusiasm of the thousands of people who had waited hours to greet him. Many had no protection from the downpour, yet so determined were they to be among the first to welcome the Prime Minister that all kept their places. At 5.30 the Prime Minister's plane was seen circling over the aerodrome. As soon as it touched the ground and began to taxi across to the tarmac a roar of cheers broke out. These were redoubled when it came to a stop and the Prime Minister was seen looking out of the window. He looked tired after his exertions, but he immediately gave a broad smile.

Viscount Halifax, the Foreign Secretary, was cheering loudly. Mr. Malcolm MacDonald, Colonial Secretary, waved his hat. Mr. Hore-Belisha, War Minister, Mr. Geoffrey Lloyd, Minister in charge of A.R.P., and Captain David Margesson, the Chief Whip, laughed and cheered together. Cheers came from Mr. Vincent Massey, Mr. S.M. Bruce, Mr. Te Water and Mr. Dulanty, the High Commissioners for Canada, Australia, South Africa and Eire. Count Grandi, the Italian Ambassador, clapping his hands, cried: 'Viva!'

As Mr. Chamberlain appeared on the steps of the plane, he hesitated momentarily and looked as though he were about to fall. He immediately recovered himself, and with a smile and wide wave of his hat, he stepped to the ground. The first man to meet him was the representative of the King, the Earl of Clarendon, Lord Chamberlain. He handed the Prime Minister a letter in the handwriting of the King. Mr. Chamberlain carefully placed this in his pocket to read at a quieter moment. Then, Lord Halifax stepped forward, grasped Mr. Chamberlain's hand in both of his and shook it with great warmth while he congratulated him. Monsieur Corbv, the French Ambassador, Count Grandi, and Dr. Kordt, the German *Chargé d'Affaires*, next shook hands.

Next it was the turn of the Lord Mayor of London, Sir Harry Twyford, to offer the gratitude of Londoners, and then the Prime Minister, looking a happy man, walked over to the microphone. Addressing the crowd, he said: 'There are only two things I want to say. First of all I received an immense number of letters during all these anxious times. So has my wife – letters of support and approval and gratitude, and I cannot tell you what an encouragement that has been to me. I want to thank the British people for what they have done, and next I want to say that the settlement of the Czechoslovakian problem, which has now been achieved, is in my view only a prelude to a larger settlement in which all Europe may find peace.'

Great cheers punctuated his remarks, but the most dramatic moment of all came when Mr. Chamberlain said: 'This morning I had another talk with the German Chancellor, and here' — he broke off, smiled at his hearers, handed his hat to Lord Halifax, groped tantalisingly in his pocket and suddenly produced a document — 'here is the paper which bears his name on it as well as mine.' At this there was a roar of approval. Mr. Chamberlain laughed delightedly, and waved the paper slowly backwards and forwards, so that the two signatures on it — his own and that of Herr Hitler — could be clearly seen by those standing near. Then he read the document, the terms of which had been announced in Munich earlier in the day.

When the Prime Minister had concluded his speech the crowd swept towards him cheering and shouting. Cabinet Ministers were pushed aside as men and women attempted to clap Mr. Chamberlain on the back. Women, unable to get near, threw flowers towards his car. Police struggled to clear a passage. Hats were flung in the air or rolled unheeded in the mud. The car was able to travel only a few yards towards the aerodrome exit when it was brought to an abrupt stop by wildly cheering people. The police cordon was tossed aside. Women knocked on the car windows. A few got their arms inside and patted his shoulder. Cheering men and boys stood on the running boards. Finally the police were able to press back the crowd and clear a narrow passage. At a walking pace the car began its journey to London.

When the Premier's car arrived outside Buckingham Palace at 6.50 it was again forced to stop while mounted police cleared a way through the huge throng. Lord Halifax was at the Premier's side. The Premier was shown to the King's private apartments. Here, Mrs. Chamberlain, who had arrived earlier, greeted her husband, and the King and Queen congratulated him on the success of his long efforts. Outside the Palace everyone was still cheering. Even stolid police inspectors raised their voices and waved their caps.

Then started the cry: 'We want Chamberlain!' It was instantly taken up by the crowd. It grew louder, measured and insistent. When the King's page was seen to come to the windows of the Palace balcony and open the window, the call rose higher. Then two footmen came out and laid down carpet. The beam of a searchlight, mounted on an Auxiliary Fire Brigade tender, was focused on the balcony. Into the pool of light stepped the King, followed by the Queen. Immediately after them came the Prime Minister and Mrs. Chamberlain. Mrs. Chamberlain appeared to want to stay in the background, but the King led her forward to stand between him and her husband. At once the crowd began to sing 'For he's a jolly good fellow', and again cheered itself hoarse. Mr. Chamberlain shaded his eyes with his hand. Then he bowed to the crowd, and waved. The Queen, talking to the Prime Minister, also waved. For a few seconds the Prime Minister and his wife stood on the balcony alone. Then they, too, turned and disappeared.

Once again Mr. Chamberlain was held up by the crowds as he left the Palace at 7.12 with Mrs. Chamberlain. Slowly the car made its way to Downing-street with people tapping at the windows and riding on the running-board. Whitehall had been packed with people since before 4.30 p.m. Thousands of office workers arrived later to swell the throng. Occasionally a section of the crowd struck up 'For he's a jolly good fellow'. It must have been sung a dozen times. Later came 'O God Our Help', sung with very deep fervour, 'Rule Britannia' and 'Land of Hope and Glory'. People stood on the roofs of cars to obtain a view and windows of Government offices were packed. As the Premier's car was seen approaching, cheering broke out and swelled to a crescendo.

On the steps of Number 10 Sir John Simon, as Chancellor of the Exchequer, Sir Thomas Inskip, Minister for Co-ordination of Defence, and other Ministers led the cheering. Mr. Malcolm MacDonald and Mr.

Geoffrey Lloyd jumped on to a window sill to see better what was happening. Mr. Chamberlain stepped out at the door of Number 10 and turned to meet the outstretched hands of his colleagues.

The cheering continued, minute by minute, before the closed door of the Prime Minister's house. The police were powerless to prevent a surge forward to the railings. All eyes were fixed on the lighted open window on the first floor. At last Mr. Chamberlain appeared. It was fully another minute before his gesture for silence was understood. Then suddenly the deafening uproar died away. In a clear and strong voice he said: 'My very good friends, this is the second time in our history that there has come back from Germany to Downing-street "peace with honour". I believe it is peace for our time. We thank you from the bottom of our hearts. And now I recommend you to go home and sleep quietly in your beds.'

As he spoke the last sentence he raised his head and looked towards the sand-bagged window of the Foreign Office, opposite his own. It was a gesture which was appreciated by everyone, and the last cheer surpassed all that had gone before. Mr. Chamberlain's remark regarding 'peace with honour' was a reference to the Earl of Beaconsfield's return from the Berlin Conference in 1878, which removed the threat of a conflict in the Near East.

London last night was more crowded than on any evening since the Coronation. Of the thousands who came from the suburbs to welcome Mr. Chamberlain, few returned straight home. Whitehall presented an extraordinary scene. Until late evening thousands of people were walking up and down apparently with no other object than to glance into deserted Downing-street. The majority seemed to be young people, women more numerous than men. All were cheerful, some laughing groups with linked arms stretched right across the pavement. But the crowds were not uproarious. Restaurants were full and theatres and music-halls did excellent business.

1 November 1938: Orson Welles's radio production of *The War of the Worlds* causes alarm in America
U.S. 'INVASION' PANIC: INQUIRY ORDERED
TERROR SPREAD BY RADIO PLAY
THOUSANDS FLEE FROM HOMES
PROTEST ISSUED BY MR. H.G. WELLS
From Our Own Correspondent

The Federal authorities today began an investigation of the most amazing episode in the history of broadcasting, the dramatisation of H.G. Wells's novel *The War of the Worlds*, which last night flung thousands into a state of panic, and convinced them that the United States was being invaded by a host of supermen from Mars. The names of American cities were substituted for the original place-names, and Mr. Wells today cabled his American representative, Mr. Jacques Chambrun, stating that 'totally unwarranted' liberties had been taken. He also expressed deep concern at the effect of the broadcast.

Mr. Chambrun has placed the matter in the hands of his lawyers. He said to me: 'At no time was it explained that this dramatisation would take liberties that amounted to complete rewriting of the novel, rendering it an entirely different story. Mr. Wells and I consider that in doing this the Columbia Broadcasting System and Mr. Orson Welles – the producer and principal actor in the play – far overstepped their rights. I believe that the Columbia Broadcasting System should make a full retractation.'

The play was presented as a series of news bulletins and commentaries. Monsters as tall as skyscrapers and armed with death rays were described by the announcer. 'One of the gigantic creatures,' he said, 'is straddling the Pulaski skyway [The road carried on a viaduct out of Jersey City]. We warn the people to evacuate New York City as the Martians approach.' Fantastic as it may seem, scores of reports from every part of the country bear witness to the fact that the wildest fear took hold of hundreds of households from Rhode Island to California.

Mr. Welles was stunned by the results of his efforts because, he said this afternoon, he hesitated to put the show on, thinking 'it might bore people'.

The Columbia Broadcasting System, no less perturbed, points out that the programme was interrupted four times with reminders to listeners that it was all just a play from the New York studio. The panic was caused by the fact that many persons who tuned in casually became convinced that they were listening to authentic news bulletins describing the wholesale destruction of cities in Eastern America. A wave of terror swept the nation from coast to coast and produced results without precedent. Thousands of people in New York and New Jersey fled into the streets. Scores were treated in the hospitals for shock, and many suffered heart attacks.

When the truth became known the victims of this mass hysteria were naturally highly indignant and typical expressions of opinion today were 'rotten', 'asinine', 'criminal', 'disgraceful', and 'a public outrage'. Never has an authentic news announcement brought such startling reaction. Some people ran about affirming that they had actually seen the invading Martians and heard terrific explosions. People who believed these strange events had come to pass had only one thought – to escape. They snatched a few belongings, packed their families into their cars, and started driving wildly towards the open spaces. Policemen on traffic duty were dumbfounded by the spectacle of cars rushing past well in excess of the speed limit.

Terror took hold of certain districts in Harlem in New York, where people either fled or crowded into the churches to pray. Residents of many Southern cities gathered in the streets to pray. At Indianapolis a woman ran screaming into a church where evening service was being held and shouted: 'New York has been destroyed. It's the end of the world. Go home and prepare to die.' One man arrived home to find his wife in the act of taking poison, and another man, who had gone to Reno for divorce proceedings, immediately took a 'plane for New York to give any help he could to his wife.

Police stations and newspaper offices were swamped by telephone calls. Philadelphia police received 3,000 calls in an hour, and the Philadelphia radio station, which relayed the programme, received 4,000. New York police received 2,000 calls in fifteen minutes. Unable to get the Columbia studios on the 'phone, New York police sent a motorcyclist to find out what was happening.

In New Jersey traffic jams were caused by the press of people, who rushed into the streets, and police cars searched for persons reported to be injured by the falling meteor in which the Martians were supposed to have landed. Some people believed that the destruction had actually been caused by the meteor, and two geology professors of Princeton University hunted for fragments. They had been told that 1,500 persons had been killed by the meteor at a point a few miles away. At Newark, New Jersey, all the occupants of blocks of flats left their homes with wet towels round their heads as improvised gas masks. Men of the National Guard of New Jersey started reporting for mobilisation, and a man at San Francisco telephoned the police, saying: 'Where can I volunteer? We've got to stop this awful thing.' Throughout the night all broadcasting stations made announcements intended to allay these astonishing fears, and the panic subsided as quickly as it spread.

Among the more lurid passages of *The War of the Worlds* broadcast, which were spoken to the accompaniment of stage explosions and other startling sounds were: 'Ladies and gentlemen, I have a grave announcement to make. Incredible as it may seem, strange beings who landed in New Jersey tonight are the vanguard of an invading army from the planet Mars. At this moment martial law prevails throughout New Jersey and Eastern Pennsylvania. We take you now to Washington for a special broadcast on the national emergency by the Secretary for the Interior.'

At this point the actor taking the part of the Secretary addressed the nation. Hair-raising descriptions of the futile efforts to repulse the Martians followed, culminating with this passage: 'There are Martian cylinders all over the country. There is one outside Buffalo and one in Chicago. I am speaking from the roof of the broadcasting building in New York. The bells you hear are warning the people to evacuate the city as the Martians approach. This may be the last broadcast. We will stay here until the end. People are now holding a service below us in St Patrick's Cathedral. This is the end. Black smoke is drifting over the city. People in the streets are running towards the East River. Thousands of them are dropping like rats. Now the smoke is spreading faster. It has reached Times-square. The people are trying to run away. It is no use. They are dropping like flies. The smoke is crossing Fifth-avenue. It is one hundred yards away. It is fifty feet.' There the actor's voice trailed off, in a well-simulated last gasp.

29 August 1939: The *Telegraph* breaks the news of the imminent German invasion of Poland
1,000 TANKS MASSED ON POLISH FRONTIER
TEN DIVISIONS REPORTED READY FOR SWIFT STROKE
From Our Own Correspondent

WARSAW, MONDAY

I learn on reliable authority that Germany has now concentrated ten mobile divisions, including nearly one thousand tanks, on the Polish frontier near Mährisch Ostrau. This force is apparently intended for a sudden stroke North-eastwards against Polish Upper Silesia and the important industrial area of which Katowice is the centre. Reports that a general mobilisation has been proclaimed in East Prussia are confirmed in official Polish quarters tonight. This is only one of many signs that the German military machine is now ready for instant action.

Today I crossed the frontier between Polish and German Upper Silesia, and spent several hours in Beuthen, Hindenburg and Gleiwitz. The frontier is still closed to all local traffic. Everywhere I saw signs of the most intense military activity. In the two miles between Hindenburg and Gleiwitz I was passed by sixty-five military despatch riders on motorcycles. The only cars to be seen were those belonging to the military. The three towns I visited are completely dead so far as the civil population is concerned. Streets, shops and cafés – all are deserted. In a chemist's shop, where I tried to buy some soap, I was told that they had had to send the entire stock to Berlin. The food shortage is very serious.

New fortifications which were not there a month ago have been erected all along the German side of the frontier. There are many tank traps and machine-gun nests and miles of electrified barbed wire. On the Polish side of the frontier everything is comparatively normal. While Poland prepares to meet a German attack, which is now expected almost hourly, the national minorities, which make up about thirty-five per cent of the population, are rallying round their adopted country in her hour of need. The National Democratic Ukrainian party has already issued a manifesto of loyalty to Poland, and this example has been followed by the Jewish Parliamentary party. Of the 750,000 members of the German minority about one-third are anti-Nazi and completely loyal to Poland. The Polish Government tonight issued a strong protest through the official Polish Telegraph Agency against Herr Hitler's allegation that the German minority in Poland is being brutally treated.

It is learned from Danzig that the 13,040-ton German training ship *Schleswig Holstein*, which has been on a visit to Danzig since Friday, shifted her moorings today so that her guns are trained on the Polish port of Gdynia. The *Schleswig Holstein* is an out-of-date warship, which could soon be put out of action by the Polish coastal batteries on the Hel Peninsula.

Traffic across the Polish province of Pomorze – the Corridor – between the Reich and East Prussia, is still proceeding normally, a curious commentary on the constant German complaints about the alleged difficulties placed by Poland in the way of this traffic. All railway traffic on the other main lines between Germany and Poland has been held up at the German frontier. The Danzig Senate today published a decree stopping all goods traffic by rail between Danzig and Poland. All goods trains travelling via Danzig to Gdynia from Poland are to be requisitioned by the Nazi authorities, and two trains were seized today at Hohenstein and Zoppot. M. Chodacki, the Polish Commissioner-General, has lodged a protest with the Danzig Senate. Sir Howard Kennard, the British Ambassador in Warsaw, saw Colonel Beck, the Polish Foreign Minister, again today.

4 September 1939: A Second World War as Britain, France, Australia and New Zealand declare war on Germany after it invades Poland
GREAT BRITAIN AT WAR
THE KING'S MESSAGE TO THE EMPIRE
MR. CHURCHILL FIRST LORD; POST FOR MR. EDEN
PREMIER SETS UP WAR CABINET
VISCOUNT GORT TO COMMAND FIELD FORCE

The Prime Minister announced yesterday in a message broadcast to the Empire, that as from eleven o'clock in the morning, Great Britain was at war with Germany. The Commonwealth of Australia proclaimed a state of war three hours later. New Zealand followed and France was at war from five o'clock in the afternoon. Canada has given an assurance of effective co-operation. The House of Commons met at noon to hear from Mr. Chamberlain the declaration that Britain was at war. In the Lords a similar announcement was made by Lord Halifax. M.P.s will meet again today at three o'clock.

At six o'clock in the evening the King broadcast a rallying call to the Empire. An hour later Mr. Chamberlain had an audience of his Majesty. It was later announced that the Prime Minister has established a War Cabinet, consisting of eight members in addition to himself. It includes Mr. Winston Churchill, who has joined the Government as First Lord of the Admiralty, the post he held at the outbreak of war in 1914. Mr. Eden returns to the Government as Dominions Secretary, without a seat in the War Cabinet, to which he will have special access.

It was also announced that the King has appointed: General Viscount

Gort, V.C., Chief of the Imperial General Staff, to be Commander-in-Chief of British Field Forces; General Sir Edmund Ironside to succeed as Chief of the Imperial General Staff; and General Sir Walter Kirke to be Commander-in-Chief of Home Forces.

Half an hour after Britain entered the War there was an air raid warning. It proved to be a false alarm, but it provided a test for the machinery. An Order in Council makes today a banking holiday and no savings bank business will be transacted. New regulations for motorists provide that the running boards and bumpers of cars must be painted white. Petrol to be rationed from 16 September. The Admiralty announced that all British merchant ships are liable to be examined for contraband. The Navy is at its war stations in full strength, supplemented by armed merchant ships as auxiliary cruisers. The naval convoy system has already been reintroduced.

Hitler is to take over supreme command of the German forces on the Eastern front. In a proclamation to the German people he found it necessary to state that whoever offended against national unity 'need expect nothing other than annihilation as an enemy of the nation'.

The following message was broadcast by the King from Buckingham Palace throughout the Empire at six o'clock last evening:

> In this grave hour, perhaps the most fateful in our history, I send to every household of my peoples, both at home and overseas, this message, spoken with the same depth of feeling for each one of you as if I were able to cross your threshold and speak to you myself.
>
> For the second time in the lives of most of us we are at war. Over and over again we have tried to find a peaceful way out of the differences between ourselves and those who are now our enemies. But it has been in vain.
>
> We have been forced into a conflict. For we are called, with our Allies, to meet the challenge of a principle which, if it were to prevail, would be fatal to any civilised order in the world.

It is the principle which permits a State, in the selfish pursuit of power, to disregard its treaties and its solemn pledges; which sanctions the use of force, or threat of force, against the Sovereignty and independence of other States.

Such a principle, stripped of all disguise, is surely the mere primitive doctrine that might is right; and if this principle were established throughout the world, the freedom of our own country and of the whole British Commonwealth of Nations would be in danger.

But far more than this – the peoples of the world would be kept in the bondage of fear, and all hopes of settled peace and of the security of justice and liberty among nations would be ended.

This is the ultimate issue which confronts us. For the sake of all that we ourselves hold dear, and of the world's order and peace, it is unthinkable that we should refuse to meet the challenge.

It is to this high purpose that I now call my people at home and my peoples across the Seas, who will make our cause their own. I ask them to stand calm, firm and united in this time of trial. The task will be hard. There may be dark days ahead, and war can no longer be confined to the battlefield. But we can only do the right as we see the right, and reverently commit our cause to God.

If one and all we keep resolutely faithful to it, ready for whatever service or sacrifice it may demand, then, with God's help, we shall prevail.

May He bless and keep us all.

The Germans occupied Rybnik, Teschen, Frvstat, and have reached the suburbs of Katowice. They are pouring in by the Moravian Gate to cut communications between Katowice and Crakow. Constant raids occurred at Crakow today. The civilian population has evacuated Katowice. From Crakow heavy rifle and artillery fire is heard from all along the frontier. The German minority indulged in sabotage and espionage in this area and cut all telephone lines from Katowice at noon today. Nazi bands took refuge in the coal mines at Siemianowice. They resisted machine-gun fire, but surrendered when heavy artillery was called in.

Preparations are far advanced for the formation of an independent Czech Legion on Polish soil to fight for Czech freedom. The Czechs are greatly encouraged by the declaration of solidarity with Poland issued by the Slovak Minister in Warsaw. A Polish company is defending the munitions depot at Westerplatte, Danzig, against a German division. They are offering desperate resistance in the face of bombardment by heavy artillery and the guns of the warship *Schleswig Holstein*. The total German losses are now given as thirty-seven 'planes.

News of the British War declaration caused a tremendous outburst of joy in Warsaw. A crowd, numbering tens of thousands, marched to the British Embassy in Nowv Swiat-street, shouting: 'Long live King George' and 'Long live England'. Colonel Beck appeared on the balcony of the Embassy with the Ambassador, Sir Howard Kennard. Raising a hand to hush the cheering, Colonel Beck said: 'We never doubted that England would fight with Poland.'

Still cheering, the crowds surged on to the French Embassy, stopping on the way to raise cries of 'Long live Jugoslavia' at the Jugoslav Legation. There were moving scenes outside the French Embassy. The crowd sang the patriotic song 'Never shall the German foe tread our soil', with two fingers of the right hand solemnly raised. A French military attaché who appeared was lifted into the air by students. The next objective of the crowd was the British Consulate, where the Consul, Mr. F. Savery, one of the most popular figures in Poland, appeared on the balcony, waving a huge Union Jack amid deafening cheers. A spokesman in the crowd, knowing English, cried: 'Long live Great Britain and King George; long live British democracy and twentieth-century civilisation.'

Warsaw had constant raid alarms after dawn today. I heard heavy firing on the outskirts, but no 'planes reached the city. In the neighbour-hood of Warsaw bombing appears to be confined to military objectives, like roads and railways. Friday's raid on Otwock was probably intended for a military establishment, but a bomb hit a Jewish children's home with terrible results. The population is now accustomed to scatter for shelter on hearing the siren warning. The A.R.P. organisation, work-ing at maximum efficiency, clears the streets instantly.

Ten were killed in Warsaw yesterday and twenty-five wounded. Explosive bombs to the number of 120 were dropped, chiefly in the suburbs of Siekierki, Grochów, Pruszków and Radość. Twelve people were killed at Warka, near Warsaw. Great indignation was caused by the bombing of the sacred city of Częstochowa – the Polish 'Lourdes' and the home of a famous Madonna image. The city is reported to be in flames.

Warsaw is now settling down to Wartime conditions. All windows are criss-crossed with strips of paper. At night there is complete darkness. Trams and 'buses, showing blue lights, rattle along at little more than a walking pace through the black streets. Night life is dead, cabarets being deserted. The present half-hearted German raids on Warsaw have given the population a chance to grow accustomed to the A.R.P. instructions. Admirable discipline is shown and no panic.

A communiqué issued on Saturday night states that the German Government proposed on Friday to Poland, through the Dutch Legation in Warsaw, that bombing be confined to military objectives. The Polish Government accepted. It is alleged that Germany bombed twenty-five open cities on Saturday, several, including Toruń, Radom, Bydgoszcz, Grudziądz and Mielec more than once. At Toruń children's playgrounds were bombed. The communiqué adds that elsewhere villages, farms, even individuals and farm carts, were bombed. The total casualties in the first two days' war are estimated to be 1,500 killed and wounded, including many women and children.

11 May 1940: Winston Churchill takes the helm in Britain
MR. CHURCHILL BECOMES PREMIER
OLD MINISTERS STAY TILL NEW GOVERNMENT FORMED
By Our Political Correspondent

Mr. Chamberlain last night tendered to the King his resignation, together with that of the whole Government. The King, on the advice of Mr. Chamberlain, entrusted Mr. Winston Churchill with the formation of a new Government. It was officially announced that the new Prime Minister desired all Ministers to remain at their posts while the necessary arrangements for the formation of a new Administration were made.

Mr. Chamberlain's decision to resign was announced to his Cabinet colleagues at a special meeting at 10 Downing-street early in the evening as soon as it was known that the National Executive of the Socialist party at a meeting in Bournemouth had agreed to participate at once in the Government only on condition that a new Prime Minister took over from Mr. Chamberlain. In view of that decision and because he recognised that the swift change in the War situation called for the immediate formation of a Coalition upon the broadest basis of national unity, Mr. Chamberlain had no hesitation in resigning.

Mr. Churchill's appointment and the resignation of Mr. Neville Chamberlain were announced from 10 Downing-street in a notice as follows: 'The Right Honourable Neville Chamberlain, M.P., resigned the Office of Prime Minister and First Lord of the Treasury this evening, and the Right Honourable Winston Churchill, C.H., M.P., accepted his Majesty's invitation to fill the position. The Prime Minister desires that all Ministers should remain at their posts and discharge their functions with full freedom and responsibility while the necessary arrangements for the formation of a new administration are made.'

Earlier in the day Sir Archibald Sinclair, the Liberal leader, had seen Mr. Chamberlain at 10 Downing-street. Although he declined to serve under Mr. Chamberlain, he expressed his willingness to see the formation of a new Government postponed for some days in view of the invasion of the Low Countries.

From early yesterday morning until late last night, Whitehall was the scene of intense and uninterrupted activity. The first full Cabinet meeting of the day was held at 8 a.m.; another followed at 11.30 a.m.; and a third late in the afternoon. The early meetings were attended by the Chiefs of Staff, who also had separate consultations during the day, and by Sir John Anderson, the Minister responsible for civil defence. That Parliament will be recalled well before the end of the recess which had been arranged, is now certain. The Speaker has power to summon the House at the shortest notice.

Yesterday afternoon, Mr. Amery presided over a private meeting of M.P.s who normally support the Government, but most of whom voted with the Opposition this week. It was stated later that on behalf of fifty members an appeal was being made for the immediate recall of the House.

1 June 1940: A miraculous escape at Dunkirk
DEFEAT TURNED TO VICTORY
SEVENTY-FIVE PER CENT OF B.E.F. ALREADY HOME
DAY AND NIGHT VOYAGES ACROSS CHANNEL

At an early hour this morning it was estimated that some seventy-five per cent of the British Expeditionary Force had been evacuated from Dunkirk. Some of the men who arrived home last night had been engaged in a rearguard action as late as yesterday morning. For days they had been fighting their way back to the coast without rest from near the Luxembourg border. While these troops were being taken off in one of the most hazardous, and brilliantly executed, evacuations of all time, other forces continued throughout yesterday to bar the way to the German hordes attempting to encircle them and reach the port. Gallant French soldiers, side by side with the British, fought like cats in defence of what has appropriately been termed the Corunna Line, recalling the historic exploit of Sir John Moore in Spain, in 1809.

Little remained of Dunkirk itself, which was subjected to terrific bombing. But the defences protecting the area remained intact, and it was authoritatively stated that there is no intention that they or Dunkirk shall be abandoned. Apart from a narrow corridor through which the Allied troops were withdrawing, the whole region to the north-east and south-west had been flooded to a depth of nearly two feet, making it impracticable for enemy infantry and mechanised units alike. This inundation, let loose by Allied engineers, released much-needed troops to defend the Line of the Flanders Hills, twenty-five miles to the south. Here a particularly fierce battle was raging as the Germans, foiled in their attack on Dunkirk by the rising flood waters, redoubled their efforts to cut off the French forces under General Prioux, who were hacking a way through to Dunkirk from the Lille region – a distance of seventy miles. Some of General Prioux's forces had already arrived at Dunkirk. Others had reached the line of the hills. The rest were stated to be not far behind, but their position was critical.

Reports from Paris last night indicated that the Germans had been everywhere held. British troops, supported by their defiantly-courageous French comrades-in-arms, were turning defeat into victory. At all points the Germans were thrown into the battle regardless of cost. Authentic documents in French hands show that German losses since the Low Countries were invaded three weeks ago total 500,000 men. Forty per cent. of the enemy's mechanised forces are said to have been lost. Returned members of the B.E.F. expressed the view that the German casualties were at least six or seven times as great as those of the Allies.

Major-General Sir Charles Gwynn, *The Daily Telegraph* Military Correspondent, states that not only can the invincibility of the German heavy tank be over-rated, but that there is an astonishing consensus of opinion among the men who have returned that the German soldier, when not covered by armour in tanks, is far inferior to the German infantry of the last war.

At Dunkirk the evacuation went on day and night. Troops, who were constantly shelled as hour after hour they waited uncomplaining on the beaches, were embarked packed like sardines, as rapidly as accommodation be provided. There was continual coming and going of an armada of vessels of every conceivable type. Ships which had crossed the Channel loaded with men returned at once with supplies of food, medical stores and ammunition for those still to be taken off and defending the withdrawal. Almost the whole of the material of the retreating Allied Army has been destroyed either in battle or deliberately before the withdrawal. Most of the motor transport had to be burned because it was impossible to get it past the columns of civilian refugees.

Meanwhile, sharp fighting is reported from the Somme front, where the French recaptured the western part of Abbeville, a triangular section bordered on the north and east by the river and on the west by the Somme Canal. The Germans suffered heavy losses in this action, including several entire motorised columns. At another point near the Somme Estuary, French troops crossed the river and gained a foothold on the north bank. The German High Command stated yesterday that divisions in Artois and Flanders were free for fresh tasks. It was clear that they were already attempting a test of strength of the new Allied front.

8 December 1941: Japan enters the war with an attack on Pearl Harbour
JAPAN DECLARES WAR ON BRITAIN AND U.S.
PEARL HARBOUR AND HONOLULU BOMBED
WHITE HOUSE REPORTS HEAVY DAMAGE: MANY DEAD
FOUR ENEMY SUBMARINES SUNK: *OKLAHOMA* ON FIRE

Imperial Headquarters in Tokyo announced last night that Japan had entered into a state of war with Britain and the United States in the Western Pacific as from dawn yesterday. Several hours before this announcement was made, news had been received that Japanese bombers had heavily attacked United States naval bases in the Pacific. The first raid was made at 8.10 a.m. (7.40 a.m. B.S.T.) on Pearl

Harbour, Oahu, the chief island of the Hawaii group. Much damage was done, and it was officially announced that casualties among army forces alone were 104 killed and three hundred injured. Honolulu city, also on Oahu island, was bombed.

According to a broadcast from the Honolulu representative of the Columbia Broadcasting Corporation, three United States worships in Pearl Harbour were hit by bombs and the battleship *Oklahoma* was set on fire. United States forces were said to have sunk one Japanese aircraft carrier and four submarines and to have shot down six 'planes. The broadcast report added that the United States fleet had steamed out of Pearl Harbour. At the same time it was announced from the White House, Washington, that the island of Guam, another American naval base in the Pacific, had been attacked by a squadron of 'unidentified' 'planes. Yet another United States base, Wake Island, between Hawaii and Guam, was said to have been occupied by the Japanese.

While the attacks on Hawaii and the Philippines were actually in progress, the Japanese Ambassador, Admiral Nomura, and the special envoy from Tokyo, Mr. Kurusu, were conferring with Mr. Cordell Hull, United States Secretary of State, in Washington. Mr. Hull told that the Japanese reply to his proposals was 'crowded with infamous falsehoods and distortions'.

The United States War Department has ordered the mobilisation of all military personnel throughout the country. 'Counter-measures' have already been applied. President Roosevelt, who immediately conferred with Service chiefs, called a special Cabinet meeting late last night. Congress has been summoned for today when Mr. Roosevelt is expected to ask for a declaration of war on Japan. The Netherlands East Indies, has declared war against Japan, according to a New York report of the National Broadcasting Corporation. Mr. Winant, the United States Ambassador, conferred with Mr. Churchill last night.

7 June 1944: Operation Overlord commences
ALLIED INVASION TROOPS SEVERAL MILES INTO FRANCE
FIGHTING IN CAEN: 10,000 TONS OF BOMBS BLASTED AWAY
PILOTS WATCH BATTLE, SAY 'BEACHES OURS'
MASSED FIGHTERS HUNT IN VAIN FOR LUFTWAFFE

Allied Armies began the liberation of Europe early yesterday morning
when the greatest invasion of all time was launched with landings from
sea and air at several points on the coast of Normandy. Late last night
fighting was going on in the streets of Caen, an important road junction ten miles inland at the base of the Cherbourg peninsula.

Communiqué number two, issued from General Eisenhower's
H.Q. just after midnight, stated that 'reports of operations so far show
that our forces succeeded in their initial landings. Fighting continues'.
Pilots returning from the front last night reported Allied troops moving
inland, with the 'beaches completely in our hands'. They said soldiers
could already be seen standing up on the beaches, where convoys were
already assembling, while Allied tanks were moving towards Caen.
Concentrations of German armour were seen moving towards the
battlefield from the back areas.

Mr. Churchill made two statements in the House of Commons yesterday. In his first announcement of the invasion he said there were
hopes that tactical surprise had been attained. In the second statement
later in the day he stated that operations were continuing in a 'thoroughly satisfactory manner', with effective landings on a wide front
and with penetrations in some cases several miles inland. Losses were
very much lighter than had been expected.

According to German accounts, the landings were made at about
twelve points along 135 miles of coast from west of Cherbourg to Le
Havre. Late reports from Berlin stated that the Allied beachhead was
thirteen miles long and several miles deep across the River Orne, about
midway between Cherbourg and Le Havre. Heavy fighting was raging
in the whole area, especially along the Cherbourg–Carentan–Caen

road, where Allied paratroops had gained a firm grip on both sides of the road. Paris radio reported heavy battles against new landings by airborne troops north of Rouen. Algiers radio quoted a German report which stated landings had taken place near Calais and Boulogne and that an airfield near Calais had been captured by paratroops.

First official news of the invasion came at 9.01 a.m. in Communiqué number one from Supreme Headquarters, Allied Expeditionary Force, which said: 'Under the command of General Eisenhower, Allied naval forces, supported by strong air forces, began landing Allied armies this morning on the northern coast of France.'

It was revealed last night that the invasion was postponed for twenty-four hours on the advice of the weather experts. The original date was the fourth anniversary of the last evacuation from Dunkirk. The landings, which involved the use of 4,000 ships, with several thousand smaller craft; were made under cover of the most gigantic air umbrella yet seen. Between midnight and dawn over 1,000 R.A.F. heavy bombers dropped 5,000 tons of bombs on ten coastal battery targets – the greatest single night bombing attack on record. They were followed at dawn by 1,300 American heavy bombers supported by hundreds of medium and fighter-bombers, which hammered coast defences, roads, railway bridges and attacked troop concentrations. R.A.F. Bostons laid smoke screens to conceal the movement of the transports and their escorts. More than 10,000 tons of bombs were dropped in 7,500 sorties, with no opposition from enemy fighters, in weather which compelled the pilots to fly low to locate their targets. Between midnight and 8 a.m. 31,000 Allied airmen were over France.

Opposition from the coast defences was not so serious as had been expected, it was learned at S.H.A.E.F. (Supreme Headquarters, Allied Expeditionary Force) last night. The invasion armadas were led by two hundred mine-sweepers which swept channels and marked them for miles against great difficulties. The air preparation was described as 'a magnificent job', which resulted in opposition from the coastal batteries being spasmodic. The bombing was supported by a bombardment from 640 naval guns, ranging from sixteen inches to four inches. Battleships, cruisers, monitors, destroyers and specially designed close-support vessels were engaged.

Naval losses were reported to be 'surprisingly small'. One battleship moved close to the shore to silence a group of fortifications. Admiral Sir Bertram Ramsay, the Allied Naval C.-in.-C., stated last night that the Allied Navies' task of landing the invasion troops had been 'in effect' one hundred per cent successful. 'We have broken the crust,' he added. A naval officer who returned from the beaches to S.H.A.E.F last night reported that all main points had been gained and that by 1 p.m. reinforcements were pouring across the Channel. The first landings were made during the night when airborne troops of both British and American formations flew in well over 1,000 troop-carrying aircraft and gliders to descend at many points said by the Germans to be from west of Cherbourg to Le Havre. They formed part of the Army Group commanded by General Montgomery which led the assault. The air armada went out with navigation lights ablaze and stretched across two hundred miles of sky. They landed their troops with great precision and suffered slight loss in the biggest airborne landing yet carried out.

A remarkable feature of the day's operations was the absence of effective opposition by the Luftwaffe despite Goering's special order which said the invasion must be stopped 'even if the Luftwaffe perishes in the attempt'. Up to about mid-morning German aircraft had been reported over the battle zone. Allied fighter squadrons swept seventy-five miles into France in their vain hunt for the Luftwaffe. It was stressed at S.H.A.E.F. that this did not mean that the Luftwaffe would not fight. There are between 1,500 and 2,000 fighters in Germany and the West, in addition to production and reserves. Goering is also believed to have about five hundred heavy bombers, some of them specially equipped for attacks on shipping.

Despite the weight of the air support of the invasion, the attacks on Germany itself will not be stopped, and it is obvious that Hitler must reinforce his air forces in the West at the expense of the air defences of the Reich itself.

The invading armies have successfully surmounted the first four or five hurdles of the operation, and it was felt at S.H.A.E.F. that there was 'definitely no cause for pessimism'.

It was stressed, however, that it was too early yet to assess the position in Normandy, but opposition so far had been much less severe than expected, both on the sea passage and to the actual landing operations. The Germans had not yet disclosed themselves in strength. There is as yet no official news from Allied sources as to the points at which the Allies have landed.

Zero hour for the seaborne forces was between six and eight o'clock yesterday morning. It varied at different points because of the different depth of the defences. The engineers and naval parties landed as far as possible at low tide to deal with the under-water obstacles dryshod instead of having to destroy them in deep water. The tidal rise is some twenty feet on parts of the coast.

Swiss radio reported last night that the German Overseas News Agency stated late yesterday afternoon about two hundred vessels had assembled off Étretat, north of Le Havre, and had been attempting to land troops.

FROM CORNELIUS RYAN, *DAILY TELEGRAPH* SPECIAL CORRESPONDENT AT A UNITED STATES 9TH AIR FORCE MARAUDER BASE, TUESDAY

I was the last correspondent to fly over the Allied beachhead this evening. We took off from this base to bomb gun emplacements on the French coast. The attack was led by the Commanding Officer of this base, Colonel Joe W. Kelly. It was my second attempt in eight hours to fly over the Allied beachhead. My first proved abortive because our plane had to return when we were about five miles off the French coast because of a mechanical failure.

After entering formation over the field here this evening we flew towards the English coast, and set our course for the Allied bridgehead. Unlike the earlier missions, we had excellent visibility and could see up and down the Channel for many miles. After we had left the coast I suddenly became aware of hundreds of aircraft which thundered over us, forming the area fighter cover. The whole sky as far as one could see in any direction was just one mass of aircraft of every type. Below us, their wings glinting in the sunlight, I could see fighters only a few feet from the water returning to England.

Down below, the Channel looked cold and choppy. Away to the west I saw a sight I shall never forget. Hundreds of craft of every kind were moving towards France. From our height they were only distinguishable by the white wash which churned from their sterns. They looked as if they were strung together by some invisible chain. Away on the horizon another fleet of vessels moved forward. They were all headed the same way – towards the Allied beachhead. After some time I could just make out in the distance the coast line between Le Havre and the tip of the Cherbourg Peninsula.

Suddenly below us I saw what appeared to be heavy cruisers. They followed each other in circles, and as each came abreast of the French coast it fired a broadside. It was a fascinating sight. As they fired their guns a black plume of smoke smudged with crimson flame rolled forward across the water for perhaps thirty to forty yards. No sooner had the smoke disappeared from one cruiser than another was firing. We saw them firing as we went in to bomb our target. They were still firing relentlessly when we came out. Then we saw what must have been thousands of landing craft and shipping of all types dotting the shores and lying on the beach. They stretched for miles from a point low down on the Cherbourg Peninsula.

In the distance I could just make out a small town. Two columns of black smoke drifted up. The whole area here was covered with white puffs of smoke like balls of cotton wool. A little past this area another great column of smoke rose to the sky. Our gunners were tense. We expected that by now the Germans would have thrown in heavy fighter forces – but we need not have worried. Throughout the whole of the mission and our subsequent return not one member of the formation reported having even seen a German plane. Neither were we bothered with heavy flak. All they could muster was twenty millimetre light ack-ack fire.

Our target lay just two miles past a town. It was situated between the beach and a coastal road. I could see the target clearly as we made our bombing run. This section of the beach was entirely deserted. As the plane levelled off I saw our bombs go pirouetting down to explode with a lurid flash of red flame followed by dense smoke. One by one the other formations, who by now had broken into flights of six, dropped their bombs. The target area sparkled with flame. Then we were in white cloud and the beach was temporarily obscured. When we came out of this cloud we were some miles from the French coast. Below us the cruisers were still firing. Above us the fighters still patrolled and away to our left streams of shipping continued to flow towards the Allied beachhead.

As far as I could see on the actual beachhead itself everything seemed calm, and but for the towering pillars of smoke it would be difficult to imagine that anything out of the ordinary was taking place. Our pilot, Lieutenant John Lytle, set course for England and once again we passed over innumerable convoys of shipping before we finally reached the English coast. We landed here shortly after 8.30 p.m.

8 May 1945: Victory in Europe
GERMANY CAPITULATES!
TODAY IS VE-DAY: 'COMPLETE AND CRUSHING VICTORY'
THE KING AND PREMIER TO BROADCAST
UNCONDITIONAL SURRENDER SIGNED AT GENERAL EISENHOWER'S H.Q.

2.40 A.M. CEREMONY IN RHEIMS SCHOOLHOUSE

This is VE-Day. The War in Europe is over. After five years and eight months 'complete and crushing victory' has, in the words of the

King, crowned Britain's unrelenting struggle against Nazi Germany. Germany has surrendered unconditionally to Great Britain, the United States and Russia. Resistance has ceased in all areas where the German Government is still in touch with its remaining forces.

The Ministry of Information last night issued the following statement: 'It is understood that in accordance with arrangements between the three Great Powers an official announcement will be broadcast by the Prime Minister at 3 p.m., 8 May. In view of this fact tomorrow, Tuesday, will be treated as Victory-in-Europe Day, and will be regarded as a holiday. The day following, Wednesday, 9 May, will also be a holiday. His Majesty the King will broadcast to the peoples of the British Empire and Commonwealth tomorrow at 9 p.m. D.B.S.T. Parliament will meet at the usual time tomorrow [2.15. p.m.]'

First news of the enemy surrender was given by the new German Foreign Minister, Count Von Schwerin von Krosigk, in a broadcast over Flensburg radio at 2.30 p.m. yesterday. Then, shortly before four o'clock, a Reuter message from Rheims stated that the surrender actually took place at 2.41 a.m. in the small red school-house there, where General Eisenhower, Allied Supreme Commander, has his headquarters. General Bedell Smith, General Eisenhower's Chief of Staff, signed for the Supreme Allied Command, General Ivan Suslaparov for Russia, and General François Sevez for France. Colonel-General Gustav Jodl, the new German Army Chief of Staff, signed for Germany. After signing General Jodl said: 'With this signature the German people and the German armed forces are, for better or worse, delivered into the victors' hands.'

A procession over a mile long, including students of London University carrying a large flag, marched up and down the Strand last night. It then went through the Admiralty Arch and down The Mall to Buckingham Palace. It was a cosmopolitan crowd with many representatives of the Allied Nations present. Flags, rattles and hooters were in abundance. There was singing and dancing outside the Palace. Several of the crowd shouted: 'We want the King.' People appeared at a window of the Palace and there was loud cheering. Eventually the light at the window went out and the students, with flags and hurricane lamps, left in the direction of Piccadilly. A crowd remained outside the Palace. During daylight the people sat on the steps of the Queen Victoria monument facing the Palace and around the water basins. The Royal Standard fluttered in the breeze from the Palace roof, indicating that the King was in residence.

In the evening flags appeared as if by magic all over London. Not only public buildings, but private-houses and blocks of flats throughout the metropolis were dressed with bunting. After nightfall hundreds of bonfires threw a lurid glow over the metropolis. It was reminiscent of the 'fire-raising' raids on London of 1940–41. Two of the biggest bonfires were in Haymarket and Coventry-street. Fuel for the Haymarket fire included advertising boards from outside the Gaumont Cinema. Orange boxes and anything the crowd could gather were used to keep it alight. Above the roar of cheering, singing and shouting was heard the hum of aircraft circling overhead. This awakened even more vivid memories of The Blitz days.

In Piccadilly Circus thousands of people formed into circles, waved flags, danced and sang 'There'll always be an England'. There were British Servicemen, Americans, civilians, repatriated prisoners of war, including slouch-hatted Australians and New Zealanders. For half an hour the crowd laughed uproariously as a 'bus slowly edged its way across the Circus. On its roof three British soldiers, two British sailors and four airmen executed a war dance.

Bonfires burned in the derelict basements of bombed buildings in Soho and Mayfair. With a background of skeleton walls the crowds danced up and down, waving flags and singing. Nearly all sported conical cardboard hats in red, white and blue. An R.A.F. man stood with his back to a cinema in Leicester-square chanting in Arabic. He continued to do so until one of the large gathering of spectators took the airman's hat and started to collect money. Public houses sold out of beer rapidly. In the immediate vicinity of Piccadilly Circus there were no houses open. Fireworks exploded every few seconds.

Until well past midnight Trafalgar-square was crowded. A banjo player seated himself at the foot of one of Nelson's lions and a score of men and girls danced to his accompaniment. Other groups formed impromptu community-singing parties. In a street nearby a harmonica player was the 'orchestra' for another group of dancers. Policemen stood by in small groups. They had an easy time, because the revellers kept their merriment within reasonable bounds.

A crowd of several thousands gathered in Whitehall early in the afternoon. An array of loudspeakers outside the Ministry of Health building, with a microphone in the centre of the balcony above the main entrance, indicated that something might happen. Many taxis, with occupants sitting on the hoods, swung by. An American Army car drove into the centre of the street with its wireless working. A small crowd gathered round and shouted out to the people on the pavement as the various news items were given out.

About six o'clock there was a stir, and the atmosphere became tense with expectation. But as the chimes of Big Ben died away and nothing happened, a wave of disappointment swept the people. Soon afterwards a police official passed on the news that no announcement might be expected for some time at least. The crowd broke up, leaving only a few watching the microphone on the balcony. Just after 8 p.m. Mr. Churchill left Downing-street in his car. He smiled at the crowd which surged around, lifted his hat and gave the V-sign.

Speaking from the balcony of the Mansion House after the six o'clock news, the Lord Mayor of London, Sir Frank Alexander, said: 'We have had the announcement of the cessation of hostilities in Europe through the papers, and we feel that this is, indeed, a joyous moment. But even when the War in Europe is brought to an end there is still a hard task for us to accomplish. It is important to us that patience and endurance should carry us through the coming years as they have fortified us in the past.'

Poplar wardens gathering for a farewell meeting last night heard ships' sirens celebrating the end of the War, and finished their meeting by singing 'Auld Lang Syne'. Large bonfires on bomb sites and in the middle of the streets were lit.

Bombed and blasted Battersea is rejoicing with the rest. Queenstown-road, in the centre of the borough, was transformed into a highway blazing with flags. As dusk fell, for the first time since September 1939, the tall chimneys of Battersea Power Station were floodlit against the sky.

Doors were pulled off and windows wrenched from their sockets to start a fire in Rayleigh-road, Hammersmith. The fire brigade was called, but when they arrived the firemen lit a fire on the side of the road and, with the young children, danced around the flames.

In Northolt-gardens, Edgware, flames from a gigantic bonfire in the street licked twenty to thirty feet into the sky. The bonfire was stoked by ex-Fireman C. Butler, a veteran of the 'Blitzes' on Coventry, London, Portsmouth and Southampton.

In Cambridge several thousand students, Service men and others held their own celebrations on the Market Square. Home-made fireworks exploded all round and there was a big blaze when a paper salvage dump was set on fire.

7 August 1945: The first news of the development of the atomic bomb comes with its dropping on Hiroshima
ALLIES INVENT ATOMIC BOMB: FIRST DROPPED ON JAPAN
2,000 TIMES THE BLAST-POWER OF R.A.F. 11-TONNER
ENEMY THREATENED WITH 'RAIN OF RUIN' FROM THE AIR

The Allies have made the greatest scientific discovery in history: the way to use atomic energy. The first atomic bomb has been dropped on Japan. It had more than 2,000 times the blast power of the largest bomb ever before used, which was the British 'Grand Slam', weighing about eleven tons, and more power than 20,000 tons of T.N.T. Yet the explosive charge is officially described as 'exceedingly small'. A spokesman at the Ministry of Aircraft Production said last night that the bomb was one-tenth the size of a 'blockbuster', yet its effect would be 'like that of a severe earthquake'.

The first atomic bomb, a single one, was dropped on Hiroshima, a town of twelve square miles, on the Japanese main island of Honshu. Tokyo radio said that the raid was at 8.20 a.m. yesterday, Japanese time, and that the extent of the damage was being investigated. The official announcement yesterday of the existence of the bomb was made sixteen hours after its first use. Late last night no report had been made on the damage done because it had been impossible to see the result through impenetrable clouds of dust and smoke.

Statements were yesterday issued by Mr. Churchill from Downing-street, by Mr. Truman from the White House, by Mr. Stimson, United States Secretary of War, giving an account of the research which led to the development of the new weapon; of the terrible fate awaiting Japan if she does not immediately yield; of the future use of atomic energy as a source of power and an instrument for keeping the world's peace.

In the Downing-street statement Mr. Churchill was quoted as saying: 'By God's mercy British and American science outpaced all German efforts. The possession of these powers by the Germans at any time might have altered the result of the War and profound anxiety was felt by those who were informed.' Mr. Stimson said the bomb would prove a tremendous aid in shortening the War against Japan. It had an explosive power that 'staggered the imagination'. President Truman described the results as the greatest achievement of organised science in history. The Allies had spent the sum of £500,000,000 on the 'greatest scientific gamble in history', and had won. If the Japanese did not now accept the Allies terms, he said, they might expect 'a rain of ruin from the air the like of which had never been seen on this earth'. The method of production would be kept secret, while processes were being worked out to protect the world from the danger of sudden destruction. Congress would be asked to investigate how atomic power might be used to maintain the future peace.

British, American and Canadian scientists collaborated in developing this tremendous new source of power. Mr. Stimson also disclosed that Dr. Niels Bohr, the Danish Nobel Prize winner, had been whisked from the grasp of the Nazis and had helped in the bomb's development. By agreement between Mr. Churchill and Mr. Roosevelt research was carried out in the United States and in Canada, safe from enemy attacks. Canada has undertaken to build a plant to investigate one method of making the necessary material. The Canadian Government had also taken over the Eldorado Mining and Refining Company, and was exploring for new sources of uranium ore. An important element in the manufacture of the bomb is the radio-active metal element uranium. It is obtained from pitchblende, which is found in Canada, the United States, Cornwall, Bohemia and the Belgian Congo. Much of the original research in the development of the new power was carried out at British universities.

The first test of the new atomic bomb took place at 5.38 a.m. on 16 July at the air base of Alamogordo, in a remote section of the New Mexico desert, the War Department disclosed today. When the test was over the explosion had completely vapourised the steel tower on which the weapon was mounted. Eye-witnesses said that where the tower once had stood there remained only a huge sloping crater. The explosion had such an impact that a blind girl near Albuquerque exclaimed, 'What was that?' when the flash of the test lighted the sky, even before the explosion was heard. The blast caused consternation throughout South-West New Mexico and Southern Arizona. Forest rangers over 150 miles away thought there had been an earthquake. Windows rattled 250 miles away in Gallup, New Mexico. An Army flier saw the flash from the explosion nearly 350 miles away in California. A fiery cloud rose 40,000 feet into the stratosphere in five minutes.

The final assembly of the bomb had begun four days earlier in an old ranch house. As the components arrived from distant points tension among the scientists mounted. They knew that a false move would destroy them and all their effort. There were grave moments when the assembly on one vital section of the bomb was delayed. But at length it was pieced together. On 14 July it was raised to the top of the steel tower. Rainy weather delayed the test for more than an hour. At the appointed time Major-General Groves, director of the project, posted himself and his aides about ten miles from the atomic bomb.

The nearest observer was 10,000 yards from the tower, at a point where the controls for the weapon were housed, in a timber and earth shelter. The actual detonation was in charge of Dr. Bainbridge, of the Massachusetts Institute of Technology. The robot mechanism took over forty-five seconds before the deadline. A soldier-scientist was stationed at a reserve switch to attempt to stop the explosion should the order be issued. When the bomb was set off, a burst of light brilliant beyond comparison illuminated the whole area more intensely than daylight, Dr. Groves said. About forty seconds later came a shock wave which knocked down two men outside the control area. Then there was a tremendous sustained roar. A massive cloud was formed, which surged and billowed upward with visible power, reaching a great height and being dispersed by winds as it rose.

Giving details of the preparations which led to this test, the War Department stated that in a 59,000-acre reservation in Tennessee, completely self-contained and isolated from the outside world, 78,000 workers built the first atom bomb factory. The men and women who went to live and work at this Government-owned and operated city, known as Oak Ridge, with the factory in its midst, faced unknown hazards. Some 10,000 houses, like the prefabricated dwellings the United States has shipped to Britain, dormitories for 13,000 single workers, more than 5,000 trailers and barracks for 16,000 more provided living accommodation. The first family moved in in July 1943. Soon after, 1,000 houses were built each month. This spring, 11,000 children attended Oak Ridge schools, living in secret barracks. Planes circled the area night and day, ready to shoot down intruding aircraft.

One of the closest security blackouts of the War covered their lives, on President Roosevelt's direct orders. They were in hourly danger of a force which even the United Nations' greatest scientists could not calculate. A second similar 'atom city' was set up in another isolated 430,000-acre reservation in the north-western State of Washington. There 17,000 workers and their families lived. Only a few of them knew the exact purpose of their work. There are other small plants at various points in the United States and Canada.

Until now, Oak Ridge has never been referred to by name. The few who had to know about it called it 'Manhattan Engineers' District'. One of the workers said: 'It had an air of unreality. We saw tons of material coming in and nothing going out. We worked night and day; apparently producing nothing that could be seen or touched.' Members of Congress were continually asked by their constituents to tell them what was going on at the vast plants, but the secret was kept. The organising brain behind the scheme was Dr. Robert Oppenheimer. He planned the scientific research in a desert laboratory in New Mexico.

31 January 1948: Mahatma Gandhi is assassinated
ASSASSINATION OF MR. GANDHI
HINDU'S THREE SHOTS AT POINT-BLANK RANGE
MOURNERS FILE PAST BEDSIDE ALL NIGHT
DELHI CREMATION TODAY: NATIONWIDE FAST
From Colin Reid, *Daily Telegraph* Special Correspondent

NEW DELHI, FRIDAY

Mr. Gandhi was assassinated this afternoon as he walked to his prayer meeting across the gardens of Birla House, New Delhi, the home of Mr. G.D. Birla, the Indian industrialist. He received three bullet wounds, two in the chest and one in the head, and died twenty-five minutes later. He was seventy-eight. The assassin, Nathuram Godse, thirty-one, a Hindu Brahmin of Poona, who fired the shots at point-blank range, was arrested. The police escorted him from the grounds of the house, where the crowd of about one thousand was about to lynch him. The body of Mr. Gandhi will be cremated in Delhi tomorrow. It will be a day of fast throughout the country, and mass memorial services will be held. Throughout the night crowds filed past the bed on which the body had been laid for a last look at their beloved leader.

Mr. Gandhi was still weak from his recent fast for Hindu-Moslem unity as he was helped this afternoon by his two granddaughters, Manu Gandhi and Ava Gandhi, on the fifty-yard walk from his room to the terrace where prayers were being said. He had just ascended the short flight of steps leading to the lawns and the dais on the terrace when the assassin, in the full view of the congregation, stepped from among the crowd and drew a revolver from his breast. It was then 5.15 (about noon G.M.T.). After firing three shots at Mr. Gandhi the gunman turned the revolver upon himself, but the fourth shot went into the air. As Mr. Gandhi sank dying to the ground, he raised his hands and folded them in front of his face in the customary Hindu greeting, as a gesture to the murderer. He was carried back to the house, and died at 5.40.

The assassin, who is said to have been known personally by Mr. Gandhi, and was greeted by the old man with a smile and a word, was seized by the crowd, but the police took him away under strong escort to Tughlak-road police station. He is stated to be a member of a political group. Of powerful build and wearing a bush shirt and grey flannels, he was practically uninjured.

Among the first to reach Birla House were Mr. Gandhi's son, Mr. Devdas Gandhi, Pandit Nehru, the Prime Minister, and Sardar Patel, Deputy Prime Minister. While they were taking part in the prayers at the low bedside other ministers arrived, with Earl Mountbatten, the Governor-General, and Lady Mountbatten. Mr. Gandhi's body, draped in a white cotton sheet with the face uncovered, was carried on to the terrace of Birla House tonight. Lights were switched off except for a spotlight focused on the body.

Tomorrow again will bring poignant and unforgettable scenes on the banks of the Jumna River, Delhi, where the body will be cremated. From Birla House the funeral procession will start at 11 a.m. for the Jumna River. The ritual and mourning will continue until it reaches its climax about 4 p.m. with the cremation on the burning 'ghat', or funeral pyre. An official state of mourning will be observed throughout India for thirteen days, the Prime Minister's office announced here tonight. Flags will be flown at half-mast and no public entertainments will be held during that period.

Within a few minutes of the assassination, the news was spreading to all.parts of the capital and the rest of India. From the grounds of Birla House, I watched processions on foot and thousands of cyclists and cars streaming towards the scene. Reinforced police and guards struggled to keep them outside the grounds. Meanwhile, Mr. Gandhi's body had been laid in the room which was the scene of his latest fast. Huddled round the body I saw his most faithful personal attendants, men and young women, in attitudes of grief and prayer. There they stayed as the darkness gathered and the vast crowds in the main avenue increased. Still uppermost in their demeanour, as in that of the jostling crowds, was the sense of shock. But in every mind in the capital tonight there was also a fear of the consequences which this wild deed may heap upon the leaders and the people of a nation which has already had so much of bloodshed and horror.   .

Urged to speak to the vast, impatient crowd outside the house, Pandit Nehru, under the stress of deep emotion, as Mr. Gandhi's life-long devotee, moved among them instead, telling them the tragic story and urging them to refrain from giving violent expression to their sense of loss. In a broadcast to the nation tonight he again urged all the people to refrain in this hour from violence and to keep calm. He said: 'I do not know what to tell you and how to say it. Our beloved leader is no more. We, who have seen him for these many years, cannot turn to him anymore for advice or seek solace from him, and that is a terrible blow not only to me, but also to the millions and millions of this country.'

Appealing for unity, Pandit Nehru added: 'We must hold together, and all our petty troubles, difficulties and conflicts must be ended in the face of this great disaster. Although the light has gone out of our lives and there is darkness everywhere, Mahatma Gandhi's light will be seen in a thousand years. The best prayer we can offer him and his memory is to dedicate ourselves to truth and to the cause for which this great countryman of ours lived, and for which he died.' He called the assassination 'the act of a madman'. 'There is bound to be anger as well as sorrow in the heart of the nation, but no one of us dare misbehave.'

Sardar Patel then gave a short broadcast. He said he had seen Mr. Gandhi at four o'clock in the afternoon, and talked to him for an hour. 'Mahatma Gandhi then took out his watch and said to me, "Now it is time for me to go to prayers". I saw him after he was shot, and there was the same calm, serene expression of forgiveness on his face. Gandhi recently undertook a fast because he was not satisfied with the prevailing state of affairs. How good it would have been if he had passed away during his fast rather than have this thing happen today.' Armed police guarded the doors and corridors of All-India Radio here while Pandit Nehru and Sardar Patel were broadcasting. All Delhi newspapers tonight produced special black-edged editions announcing the assassination.

It was the second attempt on Mr. Gandhi's life in eleven days. On Tuesday of last week a young Hindu was arrested after exploding a bomb at the prayer meeting. A hand grenade was found in his possession. The police are still trying to trace his accomplices, who disappeared in a green saloon car. The very fact of these outrages being planned against the life of Mr. Gandhi would be interpreted only as proof of the strong undercurrents of feeling against the magnanimity of his attitude towards the Moslems, save that the alleged assassin now in custody, and only slightly wounded after his attempt at suicide, is reputedly a follower of Mr. Gandhi. On the other hand, there is considered to be no doubt that Mr. Gandhi's death removes from the tragic Indian political scene the supreme bulwark against the extension of communal bitterness. Less than twenty-four hours before the assassination two 'suspicious-looking men' carrying hand grenades were arrested at a meeting which Pandit Nehru was addressing in Amritsar, in the Punjab. Pandit Nehru then warned communal organisations throughout India to desist from opposing the Government.

Looting, arson and stabbing broke out in Bombay two hours after the news of Mr. Gandhi's death. Police had to fire repeatedly at Hindu and Moslem rioters in the Null Bazaar, a notorious communal storm centre. Tonight, armoured cars moved through the deserted streets and troops were sent to action stations. It was officially stated that the situation was under control. An all-night curfew was imposed over an area of four square miles.

The clashes were attributed by the police to 'misapprehension regarding the identity of Mr. Gandhi's assassin'. Reports from hospitals late tonight put the casualties at fifteen dead and about fifty injured. The rioting brought all transport to a halt. All Moslem shops were closed after looting had begun in the central part of the city. Stone battles broke out and attacks were made on tramcars and buses.

3

Cold War, Decolonisation and Scientific Progress 1945–99

3

Introduction

If producing authoritative news reports during the Second World War would have tested any newspaper, the challenge was about to get even harder. The events covered by the *Telegraph* in the second half of the twentieth century stretched from Prague to Vietnam, from Ghana to Chernobyl, even to the Moon. There was no *Telegraph* representative waiting to interview Neil Armstrong after the first lunar landing in 1969, but it feels as if there should have been. The paper seemed to have reporters everywhere.

And its readers certainly got the benefit, with first-hand reports from trouble spots where, if others had had their way, there might have been a complete news black-out. Russia's invasion of Hungary in 1956 lives again here in Gordon Shepherd's fine eyewitness accounts, which had to be brought out of the country by an Austrian refugee, who carried it across the border for safe transmission to England. 'As this is being written, my hotel window is vibrating with the noise of tanks rumbling along the Danube embankment,' begins one particularly vivid report. In another dispatch, detailing the mowing down of women and children by Russian tanks, Shepherd's car is mobbed by desperate locals, shouting: 'For God's sake, tell the truth about these massacres.' And Shepherd, fearlessly, did just that. Seldom has the importance of journalists being prepared to put themselves in harm's way to serve a higher good been better illustrated.

When history repeated itself in 1968, with the Russian invasion of

Czechoslovakia, the *Telegraph* again had a reporter perfectly placed to convey the reality on the ground. David Floyd, the paper's Communist Affairs Correspondent – his very job title a sign of the times – made his way across the border to Bratislava, where he was able to observe angry locals daubing swastikas on Russian tanks. Other intrepid *Telegraph* reporters whose dispatches are reprinted here include Peter Gill, who chose to remain in Saigon after the dramatic denouement of the Vietnam War in 1975, and Graham Hutchings, who narrowly escaped a close encounter with a tank in an alley off Tiananmen Square in 1989.

Plucky individuals aside, news reporting was increasingly becoming a team effort, with major events reported from multiple perspectives. When the Berlin Wall crumbled in 1989, the unfolding drama was relayed to readers by Daniel Johnson in East Berlin, Clive Freeman in West Berlin, Ian Brodie in Washington and others. The byline at the top of *Telegraph*'s report of the death of Diana, Princess of Wales, in 1997 lists no fewer than five separate names. As the dramatic news came in from Paris, it was obviously all hands to the pump and a desperate scramble to meet deadlines.

Once or twice, it has to be said, the paper did take its eye off the ball, devoting comically little coverage to what feel, with hindsight, like major events. There is a single-paragraph dispatch from Peking on the Chinese Communist Party's introduction of its notorious 'one child' policy in 1980. The birth of the first test-tube baby in 1978 receives equally perfunctory treatment. And if Vincent Ryder and David Shears had realised the iconic significance of Martin Luther King's 'I have a dream' speech in Washington in 1963, their report would surely have had a mite more urgency – as it is, they sound underwhelmed by the whole occasion.

But, in general, the quality and depth of the coverage is remarkable. All kinds of familiar stories – from the Suez Crisis in 1956 to the fire at Windsor Castle in 1992 – are told with skill and authority. And it is that sense of authority which is the real key. One of the most noticeable features of this period is the way that, in an age of huge scientific advantages, specialist correspondents were becoming almost as important as old-style news reporters. Look out for a magisterial piece by Anthony Smith, the paper's science correspondent, in the wake of the announcement, in April 1961, that Russia's Yuri Gagarin had become the first man in space. Cock-a-hoop Russian scientists had put out a detailed timetable of Gagarin's journey for the world's consumption. But Smith was properly sceptical. 'The timetable does not make sense,' he complained. 'Major Gagarin could not have been in an orbit that followed that course.' His forensic examination of the information he had been spoon-fed in a press hand-out is in the highest journalistic tradition.

There is scepticism, too – Euro-scepticism in this case – in the *Telegraph*'s report of the signing of the Maastricht Treaty in 1992. The byline is familiar: Boris Johnson, no less, at that time the paper's correspondent in Brussels. And the tone is typically irreverent. What document was Douglas Hurd, Britain's foreign secretary, actually signing? Did he know? Did anybody know? Far from being invited to be solemn witnesses to great events, readers are being gently nudged to see the funny side of them.

If a novelist does not enjoy writing a novel, the chances are the readers will not enjoy reading it. The same is true of journalism. Bored reporters produce jaded copy – while ones with a joy in their vocation and, where appropriate, a sense of fun and irony, can hook their readers from the first paragraph. What fun *Telegraph* reporters Trevor Fishlock and Alec Russell must have had filing their gloriously tongue-in-cheek dispatch from Pretoria on the jamboree that followed the election of Nelson Mandela in 1994. Important dignitaries from overseas were entertained at an official banquet at the presidential palace, while lesser guests had to make do with an informal 'African lunch' on the lawn outside. Unfortunately, the Duke of Edinburgh, after problems with his transport, ended up at the latter function – eating springbok pate, smoked ostrich and crocodile. At such God-given moments, the life of a reporter ceases to be drudgery, and becomes one of the best jobs in the world.

15 August 1947: India and Pakistan gain independence
INDIA IS NOW TWO DOMINIONS
POWER TRANSFERRED AT MIDNIGHT
KING'S MESSAGE TO PAKISTAN
EARLDOM CONFERRED ON LORD MOUNTBATTEN

The Dominions of India [Hindustan] and Pakistan came into being at midnight Delhi time [7.30 B.S.T. last night] and British rule in the whole of India came to an end after 163 years. In a message to Pakistan yesterday the King said that the support of the British Commonwealth 'will not fail you in upholding democratic principles'. Mr. Attlee sent a message to the Prime Ministers of India and Pakistan conveying greetings from himself and the other members of the British Government. Every member of the Constituent Assembly in New Delhi took a pledge after the last stroke of midnight. It said: 'At this solemn moment . . . I dedicate myself in all humility to the service of India and her people . . .'

It was announced from 10 Downing-street last night that an Earldom is being conferred upon Viscount Mountbatten. With the creation of the two new Dominions the Viceroyalty ceases to exist, but Lord Mountbatten becomes Governor-General of the Dominion of India. He is forty-seven.

Shortly after midnight this morning Dr. Prasad, President of the Indian [Hindustani] Constituent Assembly, and Pandit Nehru, the first Prime Minister in the new Government, called on Lord Mountbatten at the Viceroy's House and requested him to accept the Governor-Generalship of the Dominion. Lord Mountbatten formally accepted. The Indian leaders went straight from a memorable meeting of the Assembly which had received Lord Mountbatten's nomination with approval without a single dissentient voice.

A packed session of 250 members, and the public overflowing into the streets, had burst into cheering as the Assembly chamber clock chimed midnight and India's new era of independence dawned. Springing to their feet, all the members first swore an oath of personal dedication in these words: 'At this solemn moment, when the people of India through suffering and sacrifice have secured freedom, I, a member of the Constituent Assembly of India, dedicate myself in all humility to the service of India and her people to the end that this ancient land shall attain her rightful place in the world and make her full and willing contribution to the promotion of world peace and the welfare of mankind.'

Led by Dr. Prasad and Pandit Nehru, successive speakers emphasised the historic significance of the hour. In an address that gripped the House, Pandit Nehru said:

'Long ago we made a tryst with destiny. Now the time comes when we shall redeem our pledge, not wholly or in full measure, but very substantially.' Members of the Assembly and the public stood in silence for two minutes in memory of members of Congress and others who had died in the cause of independence. There was, however, not a single adverse reference to the British part in India's destiny.

Having listened earlier in Karachi to the celebration of Pakistan's independence I found the underlying sentiment in this Congress-dominated House no whit less cordial to Britain.

Sir S. Radhakrishnan said: 'After midnight we can no longer blame the British. The very fact that we are appointing Lord Mounbatten Governor-General shows the spirit in which this transfer has been made. When we see what the Dutch are doing in Indonesia and the French in Indo-China we cannot but admire British sagacity.' Until an early hour the streets of New Delhi resounded with the national cry of 'Jai Hind' [Victory for India].

In the new Cabinet announced tonight Pandit Nehru remains Prime Minister and Foreign Minister, Sirdar Patel, has the Home Information and Indian States portfolio, and the Cabinet of fourteen is built substantially around that of the Congress bloc in the old Interim Government.

In a message to the Dominion of India issued to-day, Pandit Nehru said: 'The appointed day has come, the day appointed by destiny, and India stands forth again after a long slumber and struggle awake, vital, free and independent. To the peoples of the world we send greetings and pledge ourselves to co-operate with them in furthering peace, freedom and democracy.'

Mr. Nehru defined the charter of independent India thus:

To bring freedom and opportunity to the common man, peasants and workers of India;

To fight to the end poverty and ignorance and disease;

To build up a prosperous, democratic and progressive nation and to create social, economic and political institutions which will ensure justice and fullness of life to every man and woman.

In Karachi yesterday the most deeply impressive event in the ceremonial and pageantry that launched the Dominion of Pakistan was the reading in the Constituent Assembly the greetings and God-speed of the King. Delivered with feeling by Viscount Mountbatten on the last day of the King-Emperorship and the Viceroyalty in India, the King's moving message of congratulation, good wishes, sympathy and support was heard in a deep hush The message was as follows:

I send you my greeting and warmest wishes on this great occasion, when the new Dominion of Pakistan is about to take its place in the British Commonwealth of Nations. In thus achieving your independence by agreement you have set an example to the freedom-loving peoples throughout the world.

I know that I can speak for all sections of opinion within the British Commonwealth when I say that their support will not fail you in upholding democratic principles. I am confident that the statesmanship and the spirit of co-operation which have led to the historic developments you are now celebrating will be the best guarantee of your future happiness and prosperity. Great responsibilities lie ahead of you and your leaders.

May the blessings of the Almighty sustain you in all your

future tasks. Be assured always of my sympathy and support as I watch your continuing efforts to advance the cause of humanity.

Members of the Assembly, ministers designate, high-ranking officials of the new Government and Moslem women in the Purdah section and in the crowded public gallery had watched Lord Mountbatten, in white naval uniform, take his seat on the dais side by side with Mr. Jinnah, the Governor-General of Pakistan. Lord Mountbatten went on to pay tribute to Mr. Jinnah and to all who had helped to keep the machinery of Government running in India or worked night and day to solve the innumerable problems of partition. 'I am speaking to you today as your Viceroy,' he said. 'Tomorrow the Government of the new Dominion of Pakistan will rest in your hands and I shall be the constitutional head of your neighbour, the Dominion of India. The leaders of both Governments, however, have invited me to be the independent chairman of the Joint Defence Council. This is an honour which I shall strive to merit.

'Tomorrow two new sovereign States will take their place in the Commonwealth – not young nations, but the heirs of old and proud civilisations. The birth of Pakistan is an event in history. We who are part of history and are helping to make it are not well-placed, even if we wished to moralise on the event, to look back and survey the sequence of the past that led to it. History seems sometimes to move with the infinite slowness of a glacier and sometimes to rush forward in a torrent. Just now in this part of the world our united efforts have melted the ice and moved some impediments in the stream and we are carried onwards in the full flood. There is not time to look back. There is time only to look forward.'

In his tribute to Mr. Jinnah and others, Lord Mountbatten said: 'All this has been achieved with toil and sweat. I wish I could say also without tears and blood, but terrible crimes have been committed. It is justifiable to reflect, however, that far more terrible things might have happened if the majority had not proved worthy of the high endeavour of their leaders or had not listened to that great appeal which Mr. Jinnah and Mahatma Gandhi together made and which the respective future Governments reiterated in a statement made by the Partition Council.'

Lord Mountbatten recalled that by the terms of that statement the two Governments declared their intention to safeguard the legitimate interests, rights and freedoms of all citizens, irrespective of religion, caste or sex, and not to discriminate against those who may have been political opponents. 'The honouring of these words,' he said, 'will mean nothing less than a Charter of Liberty for a fifth of the human race.' He added: 'Some days ago I went to Lahore. From the reports I had received I expected to witness a scene of unparalleled devastation. Those of you who have not visited Lahore will be relieved to hear that the destruction is far less than I expected. It amounts to not more than eighteen houses per 1,000 of the whole municipal area. I do not say this in extenuation of the madness which caused even so much wanton damage. Rather I wish to pay my tribute, and ask you to do the same, to those who have saved Lahore from complete ruin – to the police and fire services, to the soldiers and the Civil Administration, and to all public-spirited citizens who resisted or prevented the powers of destruction.'

Concluding, Lord Mountbatten said: 'Now the time has come to bid you farewell – on behalf of his Majesty's Government, on behalf of my country, and on behalf of myself, also on behalf of my wife, whose thoughts and prayers will be so much with the women in Pakistan. This is a parting between friends who have learned to honour and respect one another even in disagreement. It is not an absolute parting, I rejoice to think, not an end of comradeship. "May Pakistan prosper always. May her citizens be blessed with health and happiness. May learning and the arts of peace flourish in her boundaries, and may she continue in friendship with her neighbours and with all nations of the world.'

In reply to Lord Mountbatten, Mr. Jinnah thanked the King, on behalf of the Pakistan Government, for his message. He said: 'We greatly appreciate his assurance of sympathy and support and I hope you will please communicate to his Majesty our assurance of good will and friendship for the British nation and to him as the Crowned Head of the British Government. I thank you and Lady Mountbatten for your kindness and good wishes. We are parting as friends and I sincerely hope we shall remain so.' He said that messages of good will and friendship had been received from other nations.

After the Assembly had adjourned, Lord Mountbatten and Mr. Jinnah drove side by side through the streets of Karachi, the new Capital city, followed by Lady Mountbatten and Miss Fatima Jinnah, sister of the new Governor-General. Karachi had become a blaze of Pakistan flags and festoons overnight. Popular enthusiasm reached a markedly high level compared with the previous days. Many hundreds of cars and horse-drawn vehicles, in places five abreast across the route, attempted amid the utmost confusion to follow the Viceroy's car. All normal traffic in the city was paralysed for hours. Lord and Lady Mountbatten then returned by air to New Delhi.

The King has approved that the title 'Royal', where previously used in the title of a service corps, regiment or battalion in the armed Forces of India, shall continue, the word Pakistan being substituted for Indian where applicable. In a message of greeting to General Sir Frank Messervy, Commander-in-Chief, Pakistan Army, General. Sir R. Lockhart, Commander-in-Chief, Army of India, has declared that the Indian Army will cherish the ties they have shared with their Pakistan colleagues in the past' Replying, General Messervy speaks of their common dead who lie honourably together and expresses the hope that the armies of India and Pakistan will continue in the same spirit of co-operation and in remembrance and friendship towards their old comrades in arms.

The Nizam of Hyderabad at a banquet to the retiring Resident. Mr. Herbert, yesterday said: 'It is still my desire and the desire of Hyderabad to remain within the family of nations known as the British Commonwealth, which looks to his Majesty the King as the living symbol of its unity. After all these years of friendship, I am confident that the ties which bind Hyderabad to Britain will not be severed. I greatly hope that some form of standing conference may soon be established with regular meetings which may assist the new Dominions and such States as may decide to remain autonomous to co-operate actively in all matters concerning their common welfare, as members of what may grow to be regarded as a united Indian Commonwealth.'

15 May 1948: Israel is established
ARABS MARCH ON PALESTINE
ACTION BY EGYPT AND TRANSJORDAN
JEWS SET UP STATE OF ISRAEL
UNITED STATES RECOGNISES TEL-AVIV GOVERNMENT
From Eric Downton, *Daily Telegraph* Special Correspondent

With the end of the British mandate in Palestine at midnight (11 o'clock B.S.T. last night), troops of the surrounding Arab countries were reported on the march. Nokrashy Pasha, Egyptian Prime Minister, declared in a midnight broadcast that orders had been given to the Egyptian forces to enter Palestine. Amman despatches said that the last Arab Legion units still in Transjordan had moved into Palestine. Martial law was enforced by Egypt, Irak, Syria and the Lebanon.

At 4 p.m. yesterday the Jewish State of Israel had been pro-claimed in Tel-Aviv by the Jewish National Council and a provisional Government formed under Mr. Ben-Gurion, the Jewish Agency leader. The proclamation gave no indication of the boundaries of the new State. President Truman announced immediately that the Jewish provisional Government was recognised *de facto* by the United States. General Sir Alan Cunningham, High Commissioner for Palestine since 1945, sailed from Haifa at midnight as Britain laid down the man-date after nearly twenty-five years.

To the sound of a lament, played by a piper, General Sir Alan

Cunningham, the High Commissioner, left Government House this morning for Haifa and Britain. An hour after his departure, the Union Jack was hauled down and the big square building on Hill South, Jerusalem, was occupied by the International Red Cross. The High Commissioner took leave of the Holy City with a minimum of ceremony. He inspected a guard of honour of the Highland Light Infantry drawn up in the courtyard and was obviously moved as he walked along the ranks. Then he stepped into a waiting car and was driven under heavy escort of armoured vehicles through the city and five miles north to Kalandia airfield. For the last time a British High Commissioner passed by the walls of the Old City.

Eleven hours before, Sir Alan had made his last effort to bring peace to Jerusalem and save the sacred places within those walls. His closing public act here was to broadcast a farewell message last night, appealing yet again for moderation and peace in the wake of the British withdrawal. During these final minutes in Jerusalem, as he drove rapidly through the guarded streets, his anxiety could not have lessened. Occasionally he heard the sharp crack of the shots. A Jewish reconnaissance plane came in sight – a reminder of the two battles being fought not far away, at Kfar Etzion and Bab-el-Wad. Sir Alan knew, too, that strict precautions were taken to protect him on the ride from Government House to the airfield. Armoured cars stood at strategic corners. Throughout the preceding night, armoured cars had patrolled the route. Armed troops commanded all road junctions. The Army believed it possible that the Stern Gang, or other extremists, Jewish or Arab, might make an attempt on his life.

At Kalandia, he inspected a guard of honour before entering the plane which flew him to Haifa. Behind him came another plane, carrying Lieutenant-General MacMillan, G.O.C. Palestine. A little later the last British officials in Jerusalem flew from the same airfield direct to Britain. The small party included the Chief Secretary, Sir Henry Gurney, and Sir William Fitzgerald, Chief Justice. Today, for the first time since Allenby's victorious entry, there is not one

British Government official in the capital of Palestine. More troops left Jerusalem today, some convoys going north to Haifa, others south to Egypt. By tomorrow most of the military will have gone. A small covering force, including Royal Marine commandos, is remaining for a few days.

Jerusalem spent a nervous night, and despite the cease-fire which is still in effect, there was sporadic shooting. Before dawn, Haganah troops began moving into the security zone in the centre of the city, around Princess Mary-avenue and Jaffa-road. They are standing by waiting to seize several key buildings immediately the British leave. Some clashes between Jews and the outnumbered Arabs in Jerusalem seem inevitable. Serious trouble may occur around the Jewish section of the Old City. Now the British Army is no longer available to take in food supplies to these isolated Jews through surrounding Arab quarters, Haganah must organise convoys. Unless the Arabs are willing to come to some agreement, perhaps negotiated by the Red Cross or the United Nations Truce Commission, there is the threat of a battle occurring in the Old City.

After a two-day assault, Arabs appear to have captured the main portion of the Kfar Etzion block of Jewish settlements south of Bethlehem. A battalion of the Transjordan Arab Legion carried the brunt of the attack, supported by hundreds of irregulars, according to Jewish reports. The International Red Cross has been summoned to tend the wounded. The Jewish Agency has asked the United Nations Truce Commission to supervise the surrender of Jews still holding out. Fighting continues in the Bab-el-Wad area where several thousand Arabs are attacking in an effort to cut the Tel-Aviv highway again. In Jerusalem there is now only enough Diesel fuel oil left to keep the City's electric supply going for eight days. Haganah formations entered Jaffa this morning and took over all the strategic points in the town. Haganah forces were also reported to be attacking Acre, the fortress in Northern Palestine.

The birth of the Jewish State of Israel was proclaimed in the hall of Tel-Aviv Museum this afternoon by Mr. David Ben-Gurion, head of the Jewish Agency executive. Later, it was announced that Mr. Ben-Gurion had been made Prime Minister and had appointed twelve Ministers of the Cabinet of a Provisional Government. Tension is mounting here and defence measures are being speeded up. Haganah today appealed to all Jewish populations to be ready for the possibility of air raids. It asked for a black-out in all Jewish cities and for shelters and trenches to be prepared.

The proclamation of the new State, made at an assembly of the Jewish National Council, said: 'We members of the National Council, representing the Jewish people in Palestine and the Zionist movement of the world, met together in solemn assembly on the day of the termination of the British mandate for Palestine, and by virtue of natural and historic right of the Jewish people, and by resolution of the General Assembly of the United Nations, hereto proclaim the establishment of a Jewish State in Palestine to be called "Israel". As from the termination of the mandate at midnight tonight, and until the setting up of duly elected bodies in accordance with the Constitution to be drawn up by the Constituent Assembly not later than 1 October 1948, the present National Council shall act as the Provisional Government of the State of Israel.'

The State would be open to all Jewish immigrants, would uphold social and political equality for all, and would guarantee full freedom of education and culture. An appeal was made to the United Nations to assist the Jewish people in building their State and admission into the United Nations was sought. Arab inhabitants of 'the State of Israel' were called upon to return to ways of peace and were promised full and equal citizenship and representation in the State bodies and institutions. Peace was also offered to neighbouring Arab peoples.

In the Provisional Government Mr. Ben-Gurion will hold the Defence portfolio in addition to the Premiership. Mr. Moshe Shertok is Foreign Minister and there are nine other portfolios and two Ministers Without Portfolio. The first official act of the Jewish Provisional Government was revoke the British White Paper of 1939 limiting immigration to Palestine and legislation limiting land sales. All other existing laws remain in force in the Jewish State.

Most vehicles are now sporting the new flag of Israel, which has a white ground with two narrow horizontal bars and the Shield of David in the centre in pale blue.

Mobilisation of Haganah, which is now formally the army of the new State, proceeds rapidly. A Haganah spokesman revealed that there are at present about 30,000 trained, well-equipped troops, including some women, under arms and that this number might be expected to reach 50,000 soon.

19 March 1949: NATO is formed
ATLANTIC PACT 'ROOF OVER OCEAN'
MR. BEVIN WELCOMES TWENTY-YEAR TREATY
EIGHT STATES PLEDGE MUTUAL ARMED AID
SAFEGUARD FOR OCCUPATION FORCES IN EUROPE
By Our Diplomatic Correspondent

The text of the twenty-year North Atlantic Treaty was issued yesterday. In a statement in the House of Commons Mr. Bevin described it as a 'roof stretching over the Atlantic Ocean'. It was, he said, one of the greatest steps towards world peace and security since the end of World War One. There were no secret clauses. The treaty was 'purely defensive' and no nation innocent of aggressive intentions need have the slightest fear.

Full agreement on the Treaty, which consists of a preamble and fourteen articles, has been reached between the Governments of Britain, the United States, Canada, France, Belgium, the Netherlands, Luxembourg and Norway. Representatives of these eight States will sign the Pact in Washington a fortnight on Monday. Invitations to join have also been sent to Denmark, Iceland, Italy and Portugal.

Under Article five it is agreed that an armed attack against one or more of the signatories will be considered an attack against all. Each will help the party attacked by taking immediately 'such action as it deems necessary, including the use of armed force'. The next article says that action would be taken in the event of armed attack on: Signatories' territory in Europe, North America or the French Departments of Algeria; Occupation forces in Europe (Western Germany, Austria and Trieste); Islands under signatories' jurisdiction; or Vessels and aircraft in the North Atlantic area north of the Tropic of Cancer.

Statements made yesterday on the Treaty included:

United States: Mr. Acheson, Secretary of State, said there could be only one answer to an all-out armed attack on any signatory – the United States would go to war. An attack on aircraft flying into Berlin over the Soviet zone would be regarded as an 'armed attack' under the terms of the Pact. Referring to Article four, which deals with the territorial integrity, political independence or security of any of the parties, Mr. Acheson said help could be given if a country felt that a minority, supported from outside, was attempting a coup.

France: M. Schuman, the Foreign Minister, stated that the Pact was justified by the 'notorious disequilibrium' between the forces of Western Europe, now disarmed, and the Eastern bloc.

Belgium: M. Spaak, the Prime Minister, declared that the Treaty would ensure peace. It was the first time the United States had assumed such commitments in Europe.

The Atlantic Treaty makes a simple and direct promise of allied intention to resist attack. The underlying reason is that the Washington negotiators felt that the people of Western Europe must be given the strongest possible assurance, short of automatic commitment to go to war, that the power of the United States was firmly allied to them in the event of aggression. Before the Atlantic Treaty comes into effect it must be ratified by a majority of the signatories, including the United States, Britain, Canada, France, Belgium, the Netherlands and Luxembourg. It will come into effect for other signatories when their ratifications are deposited.

It was pointed out officially in London yesterday that the Treaty can be regarded as a reinsurance against war. It should prove a stern and effective deterrent to potential aggression. The seven countries which took part throughout in the Washington negotiations have a total population of 250 million and a great proportion of the world's resources. When the Foreign Ministers meet in Washington at the beginning of next month they will discuss the establishment of the organisations required under the Treaty. It is likely that some at least of the Brussels Treaty machinery will be incorporated in some way with the Atlantic Treaty administration.

Article four is important. The signatories agree to consult together if their political independence, territorial integrity or security is threatened. The possibility of action is not however excluded. Thus, if Finland were invaded and Norway regarded this as a threat to her security, it would be open to the signatories to consider if they should take any action. The inclusion of the phrase 'as it deems necessary' in the crucial Article five dealing with action in the event of armed attack, should satisfy United States Senate critics who had feared that the American Government was signing away the exclusive power of Congress to declare war.

Article six brings Western Germany effectively within the protection of the Treaty, so long as she is occupied by troops of the Treaty's signatories. Article eight says that agreements, such as the Anglo-Russian Treaty of 1942, to which Britain is a party, do not conflict with the Atlantic Treaty. But the Soviet Government may take a different view. Article six of the Anglo-Russian Treaty stipulated that the signatories would 'not conclude any alliance or take part in any coalition directed against the other'. Russia has already made it clear that she regards the Atlantic Treaty as directed against her. This the Atlantic Treaty Powers categorically deny.

2 June 1953: Everest is finally conquered
EVEREST CLIMBED BY BRITISH EXPEDITION
NEW ZEALANDER AND SHERPA REACH THE SUMMIT
QUEEN TOLD OF CONQUEST
From Colin Reid, *Daily Telegraph* Special Correspondent

KATHMANDU, MONDAY

Everest has been conquered by the British expedition. The climbers to reach the summit of the 29,002-feet peak were E. P. Hillary, the New Zealander, and Tensing, the Sherpa. The news of the success was conveyed in a message from the leader of the expedition, Colonel Hunt. The feat was carried out on Friday.

News of the conquest of Everest was communicated to the Queen at Buckingham Palace last night. In America announcers broke into radio and television programmes to give the news.

Tensing, with Lambert, the Swiss guide, climbed to within 810 feet of the summit last year. Messages reaching Kathmandu from the Khumbu Glacier base camp stated that an unsuccessful assault on Everest was made by the expedition on 25 May. This attempt should have taken place on 23 May, but it was thrown off schedule by the delay in carving a traverse route to the South Col across the face of Lhotse, 27,890 feet. Camp seven was ultimately established above the windswept South Col above 26,000 feet on 22 May, these reports said. The first assault group was reported to have set out on 24 May from Camp six, and it had plans to establish Camp eight on the final ridge in case it failed to reach the summit the following day.

Planning for this year's attempt on Everest was carried out with scientific thoroughness. In this the expedition had the benefits of the accumulated experience of previous unsuccessful attempts during the last thirty-two years. It was recognised that the chief factor in the achievement of success would be the state of the weather. Given a calm interlude between the dying down of winter winds and the onset of the monsoon, Colonel Hunt felt that, with the great advantage of its latest improved equipment, the expedition was more likely to be successful than any previous party.

For months before the expedition started out, every item of the equipment to be used was given close consideration. Special equipment included new lightweight oxygen breathing apparatus for use particularly on the last stages of the long slow climb through rarefied air. Improved high-altitude clothing to defeat cold included nylon smocks and trouser and down suits. Lightweight boots, insulated and rubber-soled, were specially designed by scientists for the final 6,000 feet of the assault on the peak.

British expeditions to Mount Everest before the War were accustomed to tackling the northern side of the mountain, but since Tibet came under Communist control this has no longer been practicable. Later attempts have been made from the southern side, through Nepal. This approach was partly traced by Eric Shipton two years ago, and by the two Swiss expeditions last year. The Swiss expedition of last spring narrowly failed to reach the summit on 28 May, achieving the record height of about 28,200 feet. This great climb was made by Lambert and Tensing. Without sleeping bags or a stove to melt snow for drinking water they spent the night of the final climb on the open mountain at 27,500 feet. The second Swiss expedition, in the late summer of last year, made the only attempt that has been made to climb Everest after the monsoon.

Members of the British Everest Expedition, sponsored jointly by the Royal Geographical Society and the Alpine Club, sailed from Tilbury on 12 February with equipment for their attempt. Colonel Hunt left London by air a fortnight later. 15 May had originally been planned as D-day for the beginning of the final assault on the summit. By careful timing from the base camp, stage by stage up the mountain, the expedition calculated to have the assault party poised within striking distance of the summit at exactly the right moment.

Members of the British team, led by Colonel Hunt, included Major C.G. Wylie, thirty-three, second in command; Mr. W. Noyce, thirty-five; Mr. T.D. Bourdillon, twenty-nine; Mr. A. Gregory, forty; Mr. G.C. Band, twenty-four; Mr. R C. Evans, thirty-four; Mr. E.P. Hillary, thirty-four; Mr. G. Lowe, twenty-eight, a New Zealander; Mr. M. Westmacott, twenty-eight; Dr. M. Ward, twenty-eight; Dr. L.G.C. Pugh, forty-three, physiologist; and Mr. T. Stobart, thirty-five, photographer. Seven of the team, Ward, Bourdillon, Hillary, Evans, Lowe, Pugh and Gregory, were already experienced in Everest climbing.

7 May 1954: Athletics history as the four-minute mile mark is conquered
BANNISTER RUNS MILE IN UNDER FOUR MINUTES
FOUR-MINUTE MILE
Daily Telegraph Reporter

Roger Bannister, twenty-five, British one-mile record holder, yesterday became the first man to run a mile in under four minutes. On the Iffley Road ground, Oxford, he covered the distance in three minutes 59.4 seconds, a new world record which officials said last night was certain to be ratified by the international athletics federation. He made his successful attempt in a match between the Amateur Athletic Association and Oxford University in conditions which were not perfect. Blustery weather, which might have caused postponement of the attempt, eased about an hour before the race. There was a 15 m.p.h, cross-wind during the run.

The fastest time for the mile previously recorded was four minutes 1.4 seconds by Gundar Hägg, the Swede, in 1945. Bannister, tall and fair-haired, is a student at St. Mary's Hospital, London, and a former president of the Oxford University Athletic Club. In the race with Bannister were C.J. Chataway, of Oxford; C.W. Brasher, the Olympic steeplechaser; W.T. Hulatt, Northern Counties champion; and two Oxford runners, G.F. Dole and A.D. Gordon.

Lord Burghley, former Olympic hurdler and President of the International Amateur Athletic Federation, said last night: 'It is wonderful that one of our British runners should have been the first. It is the most outstanding achievement for years.' Lord Burghley said that he must not prejudge official confirmation of the time as a world record, which would have to wait for the meeting in August at Berne, Switzerland, of the Council and Congress of the International Federation. All record claims were scrutinised carefully. When full information from timekeepers, track measurers and other officials at Iffley Road were passed to the British Amateur Athletics Board they would be considered and, if accepted, sent to the International Federation for consideration. 'I and the secretary of the Federation have power to accept such records provisionally and make recommendations to the Council and Congress.'

Sydney Wooderson, who broke the world mile record in 1937 with a time of four minutes 6.4 seconds, said: 'I am very pleased that it was a British runner. I expected that Bannister would be the first to do it. I have always considered him a better runner than the others likely to do it.' Wooderson retired from the track in 1946.

Just over two hours after making the new record, Bannister was seen by television viewers in the B.B.C. programme *Sports View*. His first words, after he had been congratulated by commentator Peter Dimmock, were: 'Well, I feel rather bewildered, having been in Oxford so recently and now being in London.' Bannister said that the main problem was the weather. 'Like the cricketers, we have been pretty upset this week and we were worried about the very strong wind, which certainly was going to slow us down.' With a smile, he added that it had become urgent to 'have a shot' because both the Americans and the Australians have been trying to beat the record.

At the Oxford Union debate last night a member from the floor of the house proposed, amid cheers, that the debate should be adjourned for three minutes 59.4 seconds to mark Bannister's achievement. The president, Raghavan Iyer, said the motion could not be accepted 'because no notice has been given'.

27 October 1956: Russia invades Hungary to remove a liberalising Government
BUDAPEST'S BATTLE IS OUTRIGHT CIVIL WAR
HUNGARIAN ARMY AS SPEARHEAD OF REVOLT
RUSSIAN TANKS BLOCK DANUBE BRIDGES
UNARMED CIVILIANS WERE MOWN DOWN IN STREETS

The following eye-witness dispatch by Gordon Shepherd, *Daily Telegraph* Special Correspondent, from Hungary's isolated capital was brought out yesterday by an Austrian refugee who carried it across the frontier for safe transmission to London.

Russian T.34 tanks and 'loyal' Hungarian troops were still fighting in the streets of this shattered and sealed-off capital today to crush the great Budapest uprising. To judge from the fading scale of gunfire over the past eighteen hours since my arrival here, the last defiant flickers of organised resistance are now being extinguished. But the popular tumult in the capital is so intense that new slaughters can flare up in an instant out of the most harmless-looking street scene.

As this is being written, my hotel window is vibrating with the noise of tanks rumbling along the Danube embankment towards the southern end of the town. Heavy gunfire comes across the misty river from Csepel, where a pitched battle has been going on all night. This is no mere revolt of a disgruntled party junta. It is no mere demonstration which has got out of hand due to trigger-happy citizens. It is an outright civil war in which ninety per cent of Hungary's anti-Communists have struggled to express their hatred for the regime and its Russian protectors.

The number of dead and dying is impossible to estimate. One doctor assessed it for me at more than 3,000 killed and seriously wounded. But he was judging only from the state of the Budapest hospitals. Every ward of these, he said, has been crammed since Wednesday with injured, lying sometimes two in a bed and one on the floor space between.

I drove slowly through the centre of the city soon after dawn today.

It was like a front-line strongpoint in a major military campaign. Tanks blocked the main Danube bridges and covered all principal crossroads. Burnt-out lorries and cars lay on their sides in the street.

Broken glass glistened on the pavements and the smashed cable wires of the tram system trailed on the ground. From some blackened doors came that acrid war-time smell of debris mingled with spent gunfire and corpses. It was last in the air of Budapest in 1944. On that occasion the Russian troops came as 'liberators'. Now hatred against them has provided the mainspring of the uprising and the popular fury which has kept it going for more than seventy-two hours.

From what I have seen and been told already there is no doubt that the spearhead of the revolt was in units of the Hungarian Regular Amy itself. The Kossuth Academy, the Hungarian officers' training school, went over en bloc to the rebels. Other centres, like the Hadik barracks, were taken by force, but after half-hearted resistance. Several military commanders are said to have shown themselves 'benevolently neutral' by taking no part, but offering the rebels free pick of their arsenal. Three independent eye-witnesses told me how they had seen Hungarian officers distributing arms to the civilian demonstrators. The rebels had also been in possession of some Soviet-type tanks, whose number is put conservatively at about a dozen. One which roared down the Danube embankment with its turrets open was piled high with civilians throwing out patriotic leaflets.

But all accounts of tank incidents are blurred by the problem of identification. The entire armoured element of one Soviet mechanised division, numbering more than 150 tanks, is thought to have been called in with other Russian troops. In an attempt to disguise the detested Soviet presence, Hungarian flags have been hung on many of their tanks. In other cases Hungarian tanks are filled with Russian crews. The rebels seem to have only one clear way of identifying themselves. This is to fly Communist flags with the hammer and sickle slashed away to leave a ragged hole in the middle. Reports that some Russian troops fraternised with the rebels and taught them how to fire from Soviet tanks are probably wishful thinking, arising from this identification muddle. It seems fair to say that in some cases the Soviet troops appeared reluctant to carry out their unpleasant job. Yet in other cases their hastiness or wilful brutality have caused needless slaughter.

One of the worst massacres of the last three days happened when Russian tanks opened fire without reason on a crowd of passive and unarmed people in Parliament Square yesterday. The total dead here alone is put at over one hundred. Women and children were among the dozens mown down. Ambulances had removed the bodies when I drove by three hours later but some bloodstains were still on the pavement.

A few minutes later I witnessed a scene which showed well enough the part Hungarian units are playing in the uprising. It took place in the army printing press in the Bajesy Bilinski Street. This had been seized on Wednesday by the political police forces of the regime and had been recently retaken by military rebels. From the windows and balconies officers in uniform were hurling to cheering crowds below copies of a manifesto which had just been found inside. It spoke in the name of the 'Provisional Revolutionary Hungarian Government', and demanded the immediate end of martial law, the disarming of the political police, and Hungary's withdrawal from the Warsaw Pact under the terms of which Soviet troops are stationed in the country. Neither this rebel leaflet nor any other I have seen so far openly demands the end of any form of Communist rule in Hungary. This is probably because the word Communism has lost here any specific meaning. But the demand also printed on this sheet for 'genuine democratic government' told its own language. So did the roars of assent from the crowd as they read the smeared and crumpled leaflets under the headlamps of cars.

This is the most impossible thing to convey out of the tragic Budapest scene yet the most important, the chocking hate of the ordinary people against their present masters, and the Russians who protect them. For these three days and nights, under the cloak of a military revolt with which they were mostly unconnected, they have been able to give vent to this hate. The worst side of this hatred is a still unshaken joy and hope at seeing anything western. A dozen or more times driving around Budapest my car has been hemmed in by passers-by, shouting in English, German or Hungarian: 'For God's sake tell the truth about these massacres', and 'Do they know in the West what these Russians are doing?' One man, thrusting an old Hungarian blade through the car window, cried: 'This is our only weapon. When are you going to help us?'

My drive here from the Austrian frontier was across one hundred miles of Hungarian countryside, strangely deserted except for a few troops. Until I got to within fifty miles of the capital none of these units was much above patrol strength, and there were no convoy movements on the road. My document checks began only twelve miles inside Hungary, and continued at irregular intervals, sometimes by stray patrols, sometimes with regular road-blocks with barbed wire and machine-gun posts. Fortunately, no one could read my English passport. It was only by describing myself as anything but a journalist that I got through to the capital. The most effective description was 'delegate'. This worked where 'diplomat' failed. Two colleagues and I were the first and only foreign correspondents to get into Budapest by any route since the fighting began.

31 October 1956: The Suez Crisis commences
BRITISH AND FRENCH MOVING ON SUEZ
ACTION SPEEDED UP: 2.30 a.m. REPORT
CAIRO REJECTS TWELVE-HOUR ULTIMATUM
FLEET SAILS EAST: TROOPS FLY FROM CYPRUS AT DAWN

It was understood in London at 2.30 this morning that British and French forces were moving to take up key positions at Port Said, Ismailia and Suez following the warning given to Egypt and Israel yesterday afternoon. This called on them to withdraw their military forces to a distance ten miles from the Suez Canal. If the warning was disregarded or rejected these strategic points would be occupied. A twelve-hour time limit set for replies was due to expire at 4.30 a.m. But at 9.30 p.m.

Colonel Nasser announced that the warning was unacceptable in any circumstances. Israel accepted just before midnight, but only providing there was a positive reply from Egypt. British Ministers, after a midnight meeting, felt that in the light of these replies it was no longer necessary to wait for the time limit to expire. Action was sanctioned immediately so that the plan could be implemented as speedily as possible.

Yesterday a large British force, with an escort of warships, was sailing eastwards in the Mediterranean. At least four aircraft carriers were included in a combined force of British and French warships moving in the same direction. The Mediterranean Fleet cancelled its plans for exercises and also turned eastwards. Throughout the day tanks, guns and heavy lorries moved to embarkation ports in Malta. Landing craft assembled in Valletta harbour with Royal Marine Commandos and infantry. From Cyprus, at dawn, transport planes were flying British and French troops to an unknown southerly destination.

Sir Anthony Eden announced the despatch of the warning in the House of Commons in the afternoon after talks with M. Mollet, French Prime Minister, and M. Pineau, Foreign Minister, who made a hurried visit to London. He said the troops would act as a buffer between the belligerents and guarantee freedom of transport to ships. He was asked by Mr. Gaitskell, Leader of the Opposition, for an assurance that no action would be taken until the Security Council, which was discussing the matter last night, had pronounced an opinion. Sir Anthony would give no such assurance. In a debate which followed, the Socialists, acting on a decision taken at a meeting of their 'Shadow Cabinet', decided to divide the House because the assurance was not forthcoming. This resulted in a vote of 270 to 218 for the Government, a majority of fifty-two. At the request of the Opposition there will be another debate today.

Dr. Fawzi, Egypt's Foreign Minister, announced last night that he had sent a letter to the Security Council asking that the 'threat of force by the British and French Governments to occupy Egyptian territory' should be considered immediately. The Council agreed to this. A resolution introduced by the United States called on all United

Nations members to refrain from the use of force or threat of force and to refrain from giving aid to Israel as long as she refused to withdraw from Egyptian territory. Britain and France decided last night to veto this and also a Russian resolution calling for a cease-fire.

President Nasser summoned the British, American and Russian Ambassadors and the French Chargé d'Affaires to the Presidency tonight. They saw him separately for about twenty minutes each. Mr. Kisselev, the Russian Ambassador, saw the President first and discussed the Anglo- French ultimatum. On leaving, Mr. Kisselev said he would ask Moscow for instructions. The British Ambassador Sir Humphrey Trevelyan, then spoke with Colonel Nasser for half an hour. On leaving he declined to comment.

Cairo radio stated last night: 'President Gamal Abdel Nasser summoned at 10.30 p.m. tonight (20.30 G.M.T.) the British Ambassador and communicated to him that the ultimatum addressed by Britain in her and France's name to the Government of Egypt today is unacceptable to Egypt under any circumstances and that it constituted an attack on the rights and dignity of Egypt and a flagrant violation of the United Nations Charter. President Nasser said, "At a time when Egypt is defending herself within her territories against the Israeli aggression, Britain and France are making reservations about attacking the attacked".'

Cairo radio continued: 'The President warned that Egypt would not falter in the face of any attack that may occur against her to defend her rights and her honour. The President also summoned the Chargé d'Affaires at the French Embassy and communicated to him the same warning. Further the President summoned the American Ambassador, briefed him on the situation and sent a message on this subject to President Eisenhower. The President further summoned the Soviet Ambassador and sent a message to Marshal Bulganin, the Premier of the Soviet Union. Then the President summoned of Ambassador of Jugoslavia, and sent a message to Marshal Tito. The President also summoned the Chargé d'Affaires at the Indian Embassy and sent a message to Pandit Nehru.'

7 March 1957: The wind of change starts blowing through Africa as Ghana gains independence
DUCHESS OPENS GHANA'S FIRST PARLIAMENT
MESSAGE FROM QUEEN READ
From R.H.C. Steed, *Daily Telegraph* Commonwealth Affairs Correspondent

ACCRA, WEDNESDAY

The first Parliament of the new Commonwealth country of Ghana, which attained independence at midnight last night, was opened today by the Duchess of Kent, representing the Queen. She read the Speech from the Throne. Ceremonial observed at Westminster was followed in great detail. A bizarre contrast was provided by the exotic colour of the surroundings and the ebullience of the M.P.s on the Government side. Among the spectators were representatives of fifty-six countries at the independence celebrations, including Mr. Butler, Home Secretary, and Mr. Nixon, United States Vice-President. All 104 M.P.s were in brightly-coloured dress.

This afternoon 3,000 people attended a garden party given in the Duchess's honour by Ghana's first Governor-General, Sir Charles Arden-Clarke, and Lady Arden-Clarke, at the Residence, Christiansborg Castle. The Duchess wore a beige chiffon and lace dress, with an ostrich feather hat. Tonight the Duchess attended a ball given by Dr. Nkrumah, the Prime Minister, at the State House. Hundreds of thousands were out in the streets again today celebrating independence. Many young men and women wore smocks and blouses in the national, colours, with large heads of Dr. Nkrumah printed across the back and front.

In Parliament this morning the toga-like Kente garment predominated among the seventy-two M.P.s on the Government side. Among the Opposition rich gowns and headdress in the emir style from the remote Northern Territories were much in evidence. Two Opposition leaders who had shaved off their beards as a symbol of having gained a victory in the new Constitution were welcomed with chaffing and mild horseplay by Government back-benchers. Government supporters rose to their feet when Dr. Nkrumah entered. They waved their right arms in the salute of the Convention Peoples' party and chanted 'Freedom' with emphasis on the 'dom', followed by the new slogan: 'Serve Ghana now.'

The Royal Commission changing the status of Sir Charles from Governor to Governor-General was lead. Then Sir Charles took the oath of allegiance administered by Sir Arku Korsah, the Chief Justice. The entry of the Duchess was announced in traditional form by three knocks on the doors of the House. The Duchess was in a white lace dress, embroidered with rhinestones, and she had a diamond tiara and necklace.

In the Speech from the Throne, which the Duchess read, the Queen stated: 'My Government in the United Kingdom has ceased from this day to have any authority in Ghana.' This was greeted with smiles and loud murmurs of 'Hear, hear' from the Government M.P.s.

The Duchess read a personal message from the Queen, which stated:

> I have entrusted to my aunt the duty of opening on my behalf the first session of the Parliament of Ghana.
>
> My thoughts are with you on this great day as you take up the full responsibilities of independent nationhood and I rejoice to welcome another new member of our growing Commonwealth family of nations.
>
> The hopes of many, especially in Africa, hang on your endeavours. It is my earnest and confident belief that my people in Ghana will go forward in freedom and justice, in unity among themselves and in brotherhood with all the peoples of the Commonwealth. May God bless you all.

According to the Westminster procedure, Dr. Nkrumah moved that a humble address of thanks be sent to the Queen. He said that they parted from the former Imperial power with the warmest feelings of friendship and goodwill. Instead of that bitterness often born of colonial struggle they entered on their independence in association with Great Britain and with good relations unimpaired. They had maintained the ceremonies which had marked the opening of Parliament because they were common to the countries of the Commonwealth and emphasised a common approach to the problems of democracy. Success in the new task would demonstrate to the world that a former tropical African colonial territory was as capable of conducting its own affairs as any country in the world. 'If, on the other hand, we fail, if we show ourselves disunited, inefficient or corrupt, we shall have gravely harmed all those millions in Africa who put their trust in us.'

When Dr. Nkrumah mentioned 'corrupt' there was an outburst of ironical 'Hear, hears', from the Opposition. There was genuine applause from both sides when he said that the way the Government and Opposition had reached a compromise solution of the Constitution showed that Ghana had achieved political maturity. Dr. Busia, Leader of the Opposition, paid tribute to the enduring benefits Ghana had received under British rule.

One of the two R.A.F. Transport Command Comet aircraft flown here for the celebrations has been demonstrating jet travel to chiefs and schoolchildren. On Monday the Comet took six chiefs from the coastal areas on flights over their territory. Secondary schoolchildren have also taken part. When the invitation was made every boy and girl in the upper forms wanted to go so that the selection had to be by ballot.

26 March 1957: The EEC is established by the Treaty of Rome
WEST EUROPE UNITY PACTS SIGNED IN ROME
From Our Own Correspondent

Ministers of six Western European countries signed draft treaties here tonight for the setting up of a common market and an atomic energy pool. The participants are West Germany, France, Italy, Belgium, the Netherlands and Luxembourg. The Common Market, an economic community of countries with a total population of 160 million, will be developed in stages over fifteen years. Its basic aims are to allow the free movement of goods, manpower and money among the six member States, and to abolish Customs tariffs among them.

The treaties take the place of the abortive European Defence Community of three years ago. To become effective they must be ratified by the six Parliaments. Despite opposition from industries in some countries, and from agricultural interests in others, spokesmen of member States tonight expressed confidence that the treaties would be ratified before the end of the year This would enable the Common Market and Euratom to come into being on 1 January next.

The signing took place in the Palazzo Senatorio, seat of the Mayor and Municipal Council, on the Capitoline Hill. The signatories were Dr. Adenauer, West German Chancellor; M. Pineau, French Foreign Minister; M. Spaak, Belgian Foreign Minister; M. Beck, Luxembourg Foreign Minister; Mr. Luns, Netherlands Foreign Minister; and Signor Segni, Italian Prime Minister. Millions of viewers saw the ceremony in a Eurovision link-up. Bells rang out on the Capitoline Hill and seven million Italian school children were given a holiday to celebrate the signing.

Dr. Adenauer described the occasion as a 'historic moment'. He pointed out that not all details of the treaties had found unanimous agreement everywhere, but 'we must not fail to see the wood in looking for the trees. Only an ever closer union of our six States guarantees the survival of all of us, and safeguards our development in freedom and our social progress.'

Signor Martino, the Italian Foreign Minister, said the signing 'opens a new phase in our relations. We have chosen a way of survival, knowing the efforts in store for us in the future. We must look ahead and realise that what we have forged tonight is no more than a tool for the creation of the greater moral and political solidarity of Europe. In the world of today Europe can only survive if it unites.'

The ruling body of the Common Market will be a Council

of Ministers, which will have to reach all major decisions either unanimously giving the power of veto to every member, or by a majority of twelve votes. France, West Germany and Italy will have four votes each. Belgium and Holland will have two, and Luxembourg one. The Euratom Treaty will provide for the free exchange of atomic information and for the common development of the European economy to meet the vast power of Russia and the United States.

15 September 1960: OPEC is formed
OIL COUNTRIES GET TOGETHER
NEW ORGANISATION DISCUSSES PRICES
From Our Own Correspondent

BAGHDAD, WEDNESDAY

The sole tangible result when the five-day conference of oil-producing areas ended here today was the formation of an Organisation of Petroleum Exporting Countries to be known as OPEC. Founder members are the five participants in the conference, Iraq, Kuwait, Persia, Saudi Arabia and Venezuela. The new organisation was described by Iraq's acting oil minister, Dr. Al Shaibani, as one that will have an active effect on world oil policies. It will be open to other exporting countries on the approval of the founding five.

The conference resolved that producing countries could not stand by while oil companies revised prices, but must demand fixed prices and a return to the price level before recent cuts. The conference thought that price fluctuations obstructed economic development in producing and consuming countries. It adopted the principle of consultation between participating countries and oil companies in future developments, and also agreed to study matters that may stabilise prices and limit production in a manner to guarantee producing countries a stable regular income. The Secretariat of OPEC will be set up in Baghdad, and its next meeting will take place in Caracas, Venezuela, in January.

13 April 1961: Yuri Gagarin is the first man in space, but not everyone is impressed
RUSSIAN SPACE MAN SAFELY BACK
PIONEER EIGHTY-NINE-MINUTE ORBIT OF THE EARTH
SKY 'VERY, VERY DARK' AND WORLD 'BLUE'
ATTEMPT ON MOON FORECAST: MR. KENNEDY'S PRAISE

Major Yuri Alexeyevich Gagarin, twenty-seven, dubbed 'the Columbus of interplanetary space' by Moscow radio, yesterday won for Russia the race to make the first manned space flight. His four-and-a-half-ton space ship completed an orbit of the earth in 89.1 minutes, at a height of up to 190 miles, landing safely at the chosen place. The rocket carrying the space ship Vostok [East] was launched at 9.07 a.m. Moscow time (7.07 B.S.T.). Major Gagarin, wearing a space suit and strapped to a couch, could do nothing to control his flight, though he had a two-way wireless to operate and instruments to read.

Television enabled scientists to watch Major Gagarin during the flight, while instruments transmitted information about his physical reactions. Braking rockets to bring the ship back to earth were fired ninety minutes after the launching and at 8.55 a.m. B.S.T. the major was back on Russian soil.

He said on landing: 'I feel well. I have no bruises or injuries,' Jeremy Wolfenden, Special Correspondent of *The Daily Telegraph*, telephoned from Moscow last night. Mr. Khrushchev, holidaying by the Black Sea, at once telephoned his congratulations to the major. The major said to him: 'I could see seas, mountains, big cities, rivers and forests.'

Major Gagarin, who is married with two daughters, is now under-going a thorough medical examination. He is expected to make a public appearance in Moscow tomorrow. There were carnival scenes in the Russian capital until well after nightfall yesterday. Students marched with banners, loudspeakers played music and crowds surrounded passing Air Force officers to congratulate them. After the landing a radio correspondent said the major's first description of the scene he had witnessed from outer space was: 'The sky looks very, very dark and the earth bluish.'

Recordings of the major's messages sent to earth during the flight were also broadcast. They were:

'Carrying out observations of the earth. Visibility good.'
'Flight continues well. Can see everything.'
'Flight continues. Everything normal. Everything working well.'
'Feeling well and cheerful. Machine functioning normally.'

The space flight lasted a total of 108 minutes, including the climb of the rocket and the return to earth. An official timetable of the flight issued by the Russians has caused some confusion over the vessel's course. It is:

Launching	7.07 B.S.T.
Over South Africa	7.22
Over Africa	8.15
Start descent	8.25
Landing	8.55

Professor Leonid Sedov, head of Russia's space programme, who is visiting the United States, said in Boston that his country would send a man 'to the moon or some planet in the foreseeable future'. Mr. Macmillan and President Kennedy both praised the Russian achievement.

This morning Russia sent the first man into space. Major Yuri Alekseyevich Gagarin, of the Russian Air Force, flew nearly two hundred miles from the earth, stayed in orbit round it for an hour and three-quarters, and came safely back to land at the appointed place.

It was about 9 a.m. Moscow time that the rocket carrying Major

Gagarin's space ship, named *Vostok* (East) left the ground. Soon afterwards Radio Moscow broke off its programme for the solemn announcement that Major Gargarin was in space. It added that all the instruments of his ship were functioning perfectly. An hour later Moscow Radio broadcast a transmission from Major Gagarin, who was then over Latin America. He said that all was well, and that he was not too much troubled by the feeling of weightlessness. Shortly afterwards another transmission from Major Gagarin was also broadcast. He was now over Africa.

Then the braking rockets were fired to bring the 'Cosmonaut', as the Russians call him, down out of orbit. And before 11 a.m. Major Gagarin was back on Russian soil after a flight of one hour and forty-eight minutes. His first words were: 'I wish to report to the Party and Government and personally to Mr. Khrushchev that the landing was normal. I feel well. I have no bruises or injuries. The completion of a flight of man into space opens magnificent prospects for mankind's conquest of space.'

The space ship *Vostok* was described by Tass as weighing just over four and a half tons with Major Gagarin aboard. It took 89.1 minutes to make a full circuit of the earth. The rest of Major Gagarin's flight was occupied in taking off and landing. The orbit of the space ship reached a maximum distance of about 190 miles from the earth and a minimum distance of about 110 miles. The orbit was inclined at an angle of sixty-five degrees to the axis of the earth.

During the flight Major Gagarin was in constant two-way radio communication with Russian scientists on the ground through a number of different radio circuits. In addition, electrical measuring devices were attached to his body and transmitted his physical reactions to the medical experts. He was also watched throughout his flight by television cameras in the space ship. Though his part in the flight was essentially passive, one of its most important results has been to show that the human body can leave and re-enter the atmosphere without apparent ill-effects.

The flight came at the end of a week of increasing suspense and rumours. Two days before it took place Russian sources indicated that something was in the wind. Then the preparations appeared to have been called off. Last night there were again rumours that the flight had actually taken place. An announcement was expected saying that the pilot had returned but in no fit state to appear publicly. But there is every reason to believe that today's flight was made as and when the official announcement says.

Major Gagarin was born in March 1934, and brought up at Gzhatsk in the Smolensk district. He went to the Air Force School at Orenburg, and in 1957 entered the Russian Air Force. He met his wife, Valentina, twenty-six, when she was a medical student at Orenburg. They have two daughters, Yelena, two, and Gala, who was born recently.

Soon after the flight, photographs of Major Gagarin were shown on Moscow television. They showed him as a dark, heavily built young man, wearing a tight, dark space suit and a black helmet fitted tightly to his head. After his landing Major Gagarin received a telegram from Mr. Khrushchev, the Russian Prime Minister. Mr. Khrushchev congratulated him on 'an outstanding act of heroism', and said he hoped to meet him soon. The intensely patriotic Russians have burst into rejoicing. Students and young people have been happily demonstrating and cheering in the centre of Moscow. Similar scenes are reported from other large towns in Russia.

Tonight the Central Telegraph Office in Moscow reports that it has received over 100,000 telegrams. Many of them are addressed: 'Major Gagarin, c/o The Kremlin', for transmission by radio to him. Radio Moscow also reports that it has been flooded with telegrams and telephone calls carrying questions from listeners. The questions are not only about the engineering and electronics of the flight but also about Major Gagarin's personal life. A special panel of experts has been set up at the studios to broadcast answers to some of these questions. Moscow Radio has also burst into poetry, contributed by listeners, ranging from professional poets to schoolchildren.

The Russians have still not made it clear how their space traveller made his journey. But it is certain that he did only one revolution round the earth. As he took 108 minutes for the journey, and as he was fired into an orbit that was not very far above the earth's atmosphere, he must have landed in roughly the same latitude as the one from which he took off. The earth continued to revolve during his flight. He would therefore have ended up about twenty-five degrees west of the launching site. The Russians have announced that he was in an orbit which would have taken him round the earth in 89.1mins. It would take a few minutes after firing before he was accelerated to orbital speed.

At the other end of the journey a certain amount of time would be spent while the spaceship was slowed down by its retro-rockets. Taking starting and stopping time into account, it is likely that it would take 108 minutes to go once round an orbit that would normally take eighty-nine minutes. The Russians have confused everything by giving a timetable of the flight. This timetable, the only official one so far, does not make sense. Major Gagarin could not have been in an orbit which followed that course. He was fired, presumably from somewhere in Western Russia, where all the other sputniks have come from, at sixty-five degrees to the equator. He could not possibly have been over South America only fifteen minutes later.

Major Gagarin has said nothing about the discomforts of his journey. They must have been considerable. For the first few minutes he must have been subjected to five to ten times the force of gravity. This would be enough to cause a blackout and unconsciousness unless a man had been trained and adapted to such an excessive pull. Then, with the sudden cessation of the rocket's motors, after perhaps five to seven minutes of flight, the tremendous vibrating noise, and the gravity forces, would suddenly stop. The traveller would enter the silent, unreal world of weightlessness. The eighty minutes or so of weightlessness would be ended with a sudden jerk as the retro-rockets started showing the space ship from its orbiting speed of 17,000 m.p.h. Again the Major would suffer a pull many times that of gravity.

He would have had little directly to do with the control of his space ship. The calculations as to where and when he should begin his descent could be done only by a computer and that would almost certainly have been back on Russian soil. Major Gagarin could not have been expected to plot, or to assess accurately, his position above the earth. That would have been too much to expect of a buffeted, presumably frightened and weightless 'cosmonaut' peering out through a porthole. His retro-rockets and the manner of his descent must have been arranged for him by his Russian comrades who launched him. But he could have done a lot of useful work registering his impressions, seeing if he could observe instruments and their readings, describing the earth's appearance beneath him – 'it was light blue' – and transmitting his feelings back to Russia.

The odds in favour of Major Gagarin's safe return, taking the previous space ship firings into account, were not particularly good. The first satellite to carry an animal, and therefore a kind of space ship, was launched on 3 November 1957, with the unfortunate dog, Laika, on board. Russian technology in those days was not up to bringing satellites back. The first real space ship was launched just eleven months ago, on 15 May 1960. But the dummy man on board burnt up in the atmosphere. The second, carrying two dogs, was launched on 19 August. The dogs returned safely. The third space ship, launched on 1 December, was a failure and its two dogs died. The fourth, launched on 9 March this year was a success, and brought its menagerie of animals back to earth.

It is likely that the next man sent into space would make fifteen, or even thirty, circuits of the earth. This is because an orbiting satellite lies in a fixed plane while the earth revolves within it. As the satellite takes about one and a half hours to make each circuit, and as the earth spins on its axis once every twenty-four hours, the satellite would pass over an area twenty-five degrees west every time. If he travelled over Moscow on his first time round, the space man would pass over Berlin on the second, the extreme west of Ireland on the third, and well out into the Atlantic on the fourth. Assuming the Russians wanted to bring him down on their own territory, they would have to wait until the earth had revolved sufficiently to be passing overhead once again.

14 August 1961: The beginnings of the Berlin Wall
EAST GERMANS SEAL BERLIN BORDER
TEAR-GAS AND HOSES USED ON CROWDS
ALLIES IN 'URGENT' CONSULTATIONS

East German troops and police closed the border between East and West Berlin yesterday, blocking the route through which thousands of refugees have escaped from Communism. Barbed wire entanglements were set up and train services between the two sectors of the city were cut. Angry scenes developed last night. East German police used rubber truncheons, tear-gas and hoses on milling crowds near the border. At the Brandenburg Gate, 4,000 West Berliners jeered the Communist cordon, while at another point they trampled down the barbed wire, but fell back as the guards advanced with bayonets. Herr Brandt, Mayor of West Berlin, appealed to East Berliners and East Germans not to revolt despite the provocation. 'You cannot be held in slavery for ever,' he said in a broadcast.

A Foreign Office spokesman in London said the Communist restrictions were contrary to the four-Power status of Berlin. Britain was urgently considering these developments with her Allies. Mr. Rusk, American Secretary of State, denounced the 'flagrant violation' of East-West agreements and said there would be a vigorous protest to Russia. Dr. Adenauer, West German Chancellor, said 'appropriate counter-measures' would be taken in conjunction with the Allies. Calm and resolution were needed to face the challenge and nothing should be done to exacerbate the situation.

A crowd of about four thousand West Berliners at the Brandenburg Gate, the main crossing-point between the East and West sectors of the city, were late last night cat-calling the cordons of Communist troops and police on the other side. Some of them carried lighted torches.

Their most frequent cries, in chorus, were 'Hang old goat-beard', their nickname for Herr Ulbricht, the East German Communist leader, and 'Put your guns away'. Through the eighty-foot-high columns of the gate could be seen twelve armoured cars of the 'People's Army' and two scout cars. These scenes followed yesterday's closing of Berlin's East–West border by East German forces.

Early today I was in East Berlin. At midnight I travelled in a car with Danish markings through the Brandenburg Gate. All was quiet on the Western side. The car was stopped fifty yards inside East Berlin by Communist police. But a policeman, checking the driver's Danish passport and my own, saluted and wished us 'a good trip'. There were anti-Communist demonstrations in the Eastern sector yesterday. But early today I saw only small groups of people apparently going about their normal business. After another brief, polite check, we crossed into the French sector.

British troops in uniform estimated at 'several score' were among yesterday's crowds on the Western side. They were cheered by West Berliners. Photographers rushed to take pictures of them. West Berliners were saying to the British: 'It's grand to see you.' At one stage yesterday 400 West Berlin police were sent near the Brandenburg Gate. Russian sentries on duty guarding the Red Army War Memorial on the Western side of the Gate shook their fists and spat at crowds of West Berliners who were shouting: 'Dirty dogs, go home.' The guards had been reinforced during the day from the usual two to six. Later the memorial was cordoned off by West Berlin police. When I crossed the border at midnight these police were still standing by. A few hundred West Berliners were still gathered there. The Red Army memorial, in the British sector, dates from the days after the conquest of Berlin when the Russians occupied the entire city.

Eye-witnesses said that yesterday East German police threw teargas across the border into the American sector at a crowd of jeering West Berlin youths, then charged them, hauled one West Berliner across the line and took him away. It was the first report of a West

Berliner being arrested by the Communists. Scores of West Berliners trampled down a barbed-wire barricade fence at one point just across the border. They were faced by East German police with bayonets. West Berlin police succeeded in driving the crowd back to their own sector. Later thousands of people were held back behind rope barriers at the Brandenburg Gate. The Communist police turned their water hoses, mounted on lorries, on a Western crowd that shouted: 'Down with Ulbricht.'

A handful of East German refugees yesterday found 'secret ways' through ruins, gardens and backyards to break the blockade in East Berlin as heavily armed Communist forces broke up crowds along the sector boundary. A young couple with a three-year-old child, and two men, fled by swimming a canal this afternoon. The father tied the child to his back. One East Berliner, aged about twenty, in a car burst through the barbed wire at one section of the border and reached the French sector before the Communist police took any action. The car pulled some of the wire with it. Another East Berliner got through the Brandenburg Gate check-post last night by pretending to be an East German journalist. He ran in a zig-zag fashion while West Berliners cheered him on.

Tear-gas and smoke bombs, were used at least five different times to break up anti-Communist demonstrations in the Eastern sector. Steel-helmeted East German troops, armed with automatic weapons, assisted strengthened police cordons to enforce the border measures throughout yesterday. Barbed wire barriers and road blocks, of paving stones and tarmac torn from the streets, were set up. Long queues of West Berlin and foreign cars waiting to cross into the Eastern sector were allowed to do so. The Communists said the blockade would not hinder legitimate traffic from West Berlin to the Eastern sector.

The electric railway that serves all parts of Berlin is at a standstill. The underground railway now does not stop at those stations where East Germans could get off to get through to the Western sector.

There is a limited underground shuttle service still operating inside the Western sector. All main line trains from East Germany are being routed to the main station of Friedrichstrasse. Onward passage towards the West is allowed only to holders of police permits.

A problem that will present itself to West Berlin today will be the situation of the 50,000 Eastern sector 'border crossers' who normally work in West Berlin, and the 13,000 West Berliners who normally work in East Berlin. Under the new Communist measures the East Berliners will not be able to cross.

Herr Brandt, Mayor of West Berlin, appealed to the West Berlin population to remain calm and reasonable. 'Today the real test begins for our people,' he said. He said the Western Powers should insist that East Germany withdrew its measures. Not only protests should be made, he added. Herr Brandt also appealed to East Berliners and East Germans not to revolt. 'Do not be provoked despite the provocation,' he said in a broadcast. 'The barbed wire will not last for ever.'

The East German measures are based on a resolution of the Warsaw Pact States. The aim of the resolution is stated to be to 'restore order on the boundaries of West Berlin'. A Communist party decree stated that the new measures would remain in force 'until the conclusion of a German Peace Treaty'. The measures have the effect of turning the East–West sector boundary of Berlin into a Stale frontier, and of closing the last gap in the iron curtain.

29 October 1962: The world steps back from the brink as the Cuban missile crisis is resolved
RUSSIA TO SHIP HOME CUBA MISSILES
KHRUSHCHEV ACCEPTS U.N. SUPERVISION
STATESMANLIKE, SAYS MR. KENNEDY

Russian missiles in Cuba are to be dismantled, crated up and shipped back to the Soviet Union, Mr. Khrushchev announced yesterday. He agreed that this should be done under United Nations supervision. His message to President Kennedy, broadcast by Moscow Radio, did not repeat his demand that missile bases in Turkey should be removed as a condition of the Russian withdrawal. But it accused the United States of sending a 'spy-flight' plane over eastern Siberia yesterday.

Mr. Khruschev added that he was anxious to continue talks on general and complete disarmament, and on a nuclear test ban. Mr. Kuznetsov, Russian First Deputy Foreign Minister, had been sent to New York to assist U Thant, United Nations acting Secretary-General, in negotiations. U Thant plans to leave New York for Cuba tomorrow to arrange supervision of dismantling by about fifty officers.

Mr. Kennedy greeted Mr. Khrushchev's decision as 'statesmanlike' and an 'important and constructive contribution to peace'. He said he would approach U Thant about 'reciprocal measures' to assure peace in the Caribbean. In his formal reply to Mr. Khrushchev last night, the President apologised for the American flight over Siberia. Every precaution would be taken to prevent a recurrence. The State Department said last night that the blockade was still in effect. No Soviet ships were near.

American officials said Mr. Kennedy had made no 'deal' involving either Turkey or Berlin to persuade Mr. Khrushchev to withdraw the missiles. There had been several unpublished communications between Washington and Moscow. American military action was very close when Mr. Khrushchev made his withdrawal decision. The British Government welcomed Mr. Khrushchev's message warmly, and hailed Mr. Kennedy's diplomatic victory.

Dr. Castro, the Cuban Prime Minister, who was not consulted about the removal of the missiles, demanded in a broadcast yesterday that the United States should abandon its naval base at Guantanamo. Chou En-lai, Prime Minister of Communist China, said in a telegram to Dr. Castro that the Chinese people would always be 'the most reliable and loyal comrades-in-arms of Cuba'.

Mr. Khrushchev promised today to abandon his missile bases in Cuba. In a message to President Kennedy, he said he had given orders that 'the weapons which you call offensive' should be dismantled, crated up and returned to the Soviet Union. But at the same time he accused the Americans of having again violated Soviet airspace with a reconnaissance aircraft today. The message was broadcast by Moscow radio and repeated at intervals for more than an hour.

Mr. Khrushchev seems now to have met the condition set by President Kennedy which was that the bases should be removed under United Nations supervision before negotiations were started. He said he was prepared to take this step because Mr. Kennedy had given an assurance that Cuba would not be invaded. Thus the arms were no longer necessary. But he pointed out that Cuban exiles had fired on Havana from the sea and had attacked merchant ships, including a British cargo vessel. These exiles, he said, must have a base somewhere and the United States, with its ships patrolling the Caribbean, must be able to control them.

He also protested against reconnaissance flights by American aircraft over Cuba. 'The violation of Cuban air space by American aircraft could have serious consequences,' he said. He then went on to accuse the Americans of flying over Soviet territory as recently as today. 'A spy plane,' he said, had crossed Soviet territory in the Chukotka peninsula, the far eastern tip of Siberia. Mr. Khrushchev referred to former spy flights, and the influence they had had on international relations. But, he said, he was anxious to continue the exchange of views on relations between the NATO and Warsaw Pact blocs, on general and complete disarmament and on the ending of nuclear tests. 'We must not allow the situation to get any worse and we must see no other conflicts take place which might lead to a nuclear world war,' he declared. He added that he was sending Mr. Vasily Kuznetsov, Mr. Gromyko's chief deputy at the Russian Foreign Ministry, to New York for talks with U Thant, United Nations acting Secretary-General.

President Kennedy today welcomed as 'statesmanlike' Mr. Khrushchev's decision to withdraw Russian missiles from Cuba. He said: 'This is an important and constructive contribution to peace.' He would be in touch with U Thant, the United Nations acting

Secretary-General, 'with respect to reciprocal measures to assure peace in the Caribbean'. The President's special statement was issued while the official text of Mr. Khrushchev's message was still being translated. It was followed later in the day by a formal reply. There was no crowing over Mr. Khrushchev's decision, though it was evident that Mr. Kennedy had come out on top in a raw contest of power politics.

One week, almost to the hour, after Mr. Kennedy was presented with the conclusive intelligence report on the presence of the missiles the position was this:

1 – Russia had agreed to withdraw the missiles, perhaps only days before direct American military action would have been taken against them;

2 – Russia had an assurance that the United States would not invade Cuba as long as it was not an 'offensive' military base, a position Mr. Kennedy had adopted earlier and maintained throughout the crisis;

3 – The way was opened for negotiations, perhaps at the Summit, on the whole question of East–West relations.

Both sides showed readiness today to switch their attention to the main area of confrontation, Europe. Mr. Khrushchev said he was ready to exchange views on 'the regulation of relations between the NATO and the States of the Warsaw Pact'. In a letter sent off yesterday Mr. Kennedy said the United States was 'quite prepared' to discuss with her allies any Russian proposals for a detente in Europe. He returned to the theme in today's statement. 'It is my earnest hope that the Governments of the world can, with a solution of the Cuban crisis, turn their urgent attention to the compelling necessity for ending the arms race and reducing world tensions,' he said. 'This applies to the military confrontation between the Warsaw Pact and the NATO countries as well as to other situations in other parts of the world where tensions lead to the wasteful diversion of resources to weapons of war.'

Another round of East–West negotiations is in prospect on such major topics as Berlin, a German settlement, nuclear tests and other preliminary stages of disarmament. Final decisions on such matters are unlikely to be made at a lower level than the Summit. Some senior American officials believe Mr. Khrushchev was making a reckless 'power play' out of increasing frustration at lack of success of Russian policies in recent years. They point to his failure to frighten the West out of Berlin, the growing strength of Western Europe in contrast with Eastern Europe, Russia's failure to win a substantial following among the new countries and her troubles with Communist China. Neither side paid much attention to Dr. Castro. His demand today that America evacuate the naval base at Guantanamo as part of the agreement struck a jarring note in the middle of the Kennedy–Khrushchev exchanges.

Mr. Kennedy was not prepared to 'swap' the withdrawal of Russian missiles from Cuba for the withdrawal of American missiles from Turkey. But the Jupiter missiles in Turkey, nearing obsolescence, might be removed in the context of a disarmament agreement between NATO and the Warsaw Pact. American officials were surprised that Mr. Khrushchev raised the 'swap' idea yesterday after apparently taking a different line in a message on Friday night. He may have been playing for time. If so, the speed of the rejection must have suggested to him that Mr. Kennedy was very close to ordering direct military action against the missiles. Official hints on Friday had pointed to the same thing. Aerial reconnaissance over Cuba continued today. It was reported to be inconclusive on whether work on the missile sites had stopped.

9 August 1963: A famous robbery leads to one of the *Telegraph*'s dullest headlines
INQUIRY ORDERED ON MAIL SECURITY
OVER £1 MILLION HAUL BY RAIL RED SIGNAL GANG
LONDON NIGHT HUNT IN CAFES AND CLUBS
From Guy Rais

CHEDDINGTON, THURSDAY

A full-scale inquiry into security in Royal Mail trains was ordered last night by Mr. Bevins, Postmaster-General. This followed yesterday's mailbag robbery, with an estimated haul of well over £1 million, near Cheddington, Buckinghamshire. Mr. Bevins interrupted a holiday at his Liverpool home to return to London after an armed gang ambushed a 'travelling Post Office' train from Glasgow to Euston. He said that the possibility that it was an 'inside job' could not be ruled out. The Post Office offered a reward of £10,000 for information leading to the thieves. A City firm of loss adjusters, acting for the National Provincial and British Linen banks, offered £25,000.

The thieves, all masked, stopped the train by faking a signal to show red. They separated the first two coaches from the other ten and forced the driver, whom they coshed and handcuffed to his co-driver, to take the locomotive and the two vans along the line to a point where accomplices were waiting. They threw the mailbags over a bridge into a narrow road. There the bags were loaded into a lorry. The robbery, the biggest-ever in Britain, was all over in about twenty minutes. Last night police all over Britain were hunting the gang. In London Flying Squad men combed cafes and clubs.

A worn brown glove and four large torch batteries were all the equipment used by a gang who ambushed a G.P.O. mail train near here early today and carried out the biggest and most audacious train robbery in British history. Late last night Detective Superintendent Fewtrell, head of Buckinghamshire C.I.D., described the amount taken as 'clearly well over £1 million'.

The gang, armed and masked with balaclavas and scarves and

believed to number between eight and fifteen, operated with split-second timing. They tampered with a long-distance signal; set another automatic signal on the main line between Leighton Buzzard and Cheddington stations at red; stopped the train, known as the Travelling Post Office, split it in two and after coshing the driver and handcuffing him to the co-driver; escaped with about 120 mailbags containing over £1 million.

The G.P.O. described the loss as 'very heavy indeed' and said 'it may well run into seven figures'. Mr. Bevins, the Postmaster General, who interrupted a holiday at his home in Liverpool to fly to London to confer with senior officials, offered a reward of £10,000 for information. Hart & Co., loss adjusters, of Lawrence Lane, City, offered another reward of £25,000. This was on the instructions of the National Provincial Bank and the British Linen Bank, of Edinburgh.

The Great Train Robbery began at about 3.10 this morning as the Post Office train, which left Glasgow at 6.50 the previous night for London, had just passed Leighton Buzzard station.

Jack Mills, fifty-eight, of Newdigate Street, Crewe, the driver gently applied the brakes in the cab of his 2,000 h.p. diesel-electric locomotive Number D326, as he passed an amber signal. This was the first signal the gang tampered with. As the twelve-coach train approached lonely Sears Crossing, about two miles from Cheddington station, Mills saw the signal set at red against him. It was this signal which, two minutes before, had been changed from green to red by some of the gang. They climbed up to the gantry of the signals, which straddle the main line, and placed the glove over the bright green signal, completely blocking its light. Then they wired four torch batteries bound together with insulation tape, to the bulb of the red signal, lighting it up.

As the train stopped the gang swung into action. Some, armed with picks, who had been hiding beside the track came out of the darkness and began uncoupling the first two coaches. These contained the most valuable registered packages. Other members of the gang climbed into the diesel cab and coshed Mills. He was alone because a few seconds earlier David Whitby, twenty-six, his co-driver, also of Crewe, had stepped down on the track to investigate the danger signal. Whitby found the telephone wires along the track had been cut. Realising something was wrong, he ran back to warn Mills. As he did so, he saw a man who had been uncoupling the coaches peering out from between the second and third coaches. Whitby was grabbed by the shoulders by another man who threatened to kill him if he made a noise. He was forced back to the locomotive and put inside with Mills.

Then Mills, suffering from a head injury, was ordered to drive the diesel forward. He did so, leaving the remaining ten coaches, with seventy sorters still inside unaware of what was happening, stranded on the track. When the two coaches hauled by the diesel reached Sears Crossing, close to the Mentmore Park estate of the Earl of Rosebery, Mills was ordered to stop on Bridego Bridge. This takes the track over a narrow country road about 200 yards from the B488 Leighton Buzzard–Tring road. Other members of the gang who had been waiting by the bridge climbed up to the padlocked coaches. They had left a piece of white towelling on a stick at the side of the track to tell their confederates where to have the diesel stopped. Some had stolen railwaymen's caps from a hut.

The four G.P.O. men who were inside had realised that they had been ambushed and had barricaded themselves in. The gang, using crowbars, attempted to smash their way through the padlocked doors and the wooden parts of the coach. For a few minutes they were frustrated. Then they smashed a glass window in one of the coaches before forcing their way in through the end communicating door of the second. They told the G.P.O. men that they would use guns if they continued resisting. They overpowered them with a concerted rush. Then, watched by Mills and Whitby, who had been handcuffed together and made to sit on the track with a guard on them, the thieves threw nearly 120 mailbags down a fifteen-foot high embankment. A lorry was drawn up by the side of the bridge.

After they had finished and. the bags stacked inside the truck, the gang took Mills and Whitby into the coach. They told them to wait half an hour before doing anything, shut the doors and drove off. It is believed that they also used two cars when they left the scene at an estimated time of 3.45. Police were given the first information of the raid at 4.26, giving the raiders fifty-six minutes to make their getaway to a prearranged rendezvous.

Meanwhile the guard of the train, left high and dry, had got down on to the track to investigate the danger signal. He saw that the telephone wires had been cut and that the diesel was missing with the two coaches containing the most valuable load. In accordance with safety precautions he walked back about 400 yards along the track behind the train laying detonators on the rails. These would warn any oncoming trains of the danger in their path. When he returned to the train and told the G.P.O. sorters what had happened, two of them walked along the track until they came to a small railway bridge leading to Redborough Farm. They wakened the farmer, Mr. Cecil Rawding, and his wife. The farm has no telephone and Mr. Rawding lent one of the men a bicycle. He cycled to Linslade police house, about a mile and a half away, to raise the alarm.

About a mile from the station the diesel was discovered with the smashed coaches. Mills and Whitby, still handcuffed together, were in a coach with four G.P.O. men, who were unhurt. An ambulance took Whitby and Mills to the Royal Bucks Hospital, Aylesbury, where Mills was detained with head injuries. Firemen had to cut through the handcuffs.

Buckinghamshire police warned neighbouring forces and set up road blocks in the area. At dawn detectives visited houses and farms asking whether any strangers had been seen. Detectives heard from Mr. Rawding of a man who had filmed trains going by. He told me: 'During the past few weeks I have seen several cars and vans parked near the little bridge, which carries the railway line near my farm. Last week I saw a man taking a cine film of the trains and the stretch of line towards Cheddington. He had a car with him, but I took no special interest because there are always train spotters about here. My wife told me she had seen a grey van late at night close to the bridge. It was still there the following morning.'

Whitby, who joined the railway eleven years ago and has been a driver's mate since Easter, said: 'We were going down the line when we saw a signal at danger. We stopped and I got out to go to the telephone at the signal and found the wires had been cut. I went back to tell Mills and as I did so I saw a man looking out from between the second and third coaches. I said, "What's up, mate?" He crossed the line and said, "Come here". As I reached him he pushed me down the bank and another man grabbed me, put his hand over my mouth and said, "If you shout, I'll kill you". He marched me back to the engine and I found they had coshed Mills. They put one end of the handcuffs on my wrists and then they ordered Mills to take the diesel forward to Sears Crossing. When we stopped they handcuffed me to him, made us get out of the cab and get down beside the rail.

Detectives believe that some of the men in the gang had extensive knowledge of railway working. They knew how to change the signals so as not to arouse suspicion in the signal box, and they realised that a current of approximately twenty-four volts was needed to light up the red signal.

Superintendent G. McArthur, of Scotland Yard, is leading the hunt in which police all over Britain are helping. He conferred with senior Yard officers before leaving for Cheddington with Brigadier Cherry, Chief Constable of Buckinghamshire, and Detective Superintendent M. Fewtrell, head of the county C.I.D. In London every available Flying Squad man was called in to help police and detectives combing clubs and cafés used by thieves. They were sifting gossip which might give a lead to the raiders.

29 August 1963: Martin Luther King's dream escapes the *Telegraph*
'QUIET STROLL' CALL TO END COLOUR BAR
KENNEDY PLEDGE OF CONGRESS PRESSURE

The Great March on Washington yesterday turned out to be an orderly, good-humoured stroll around the Lincoln Memorial by the 200,000 Civil Rights demonstrators. Only two arrests were made. One was of a follower of George Rockwell, the United States Nazi leader. Police hustled him away when he tried to make a speech. President Kennedy stated after the march that it had advanced the cause of twenty million people. He promised continued pressure on Congress to pass the Civil Rights Bill and eliminate racial discrimination in engaging workers.

In Atlanta, Georgia, the Ku Klux Klan leader James Venable announced that a mass rally of the hooded klansmen from all over the United States was being planned there for next Saturday. It would be 'the white man's answer' to yesterday's Civil Rights march.

Before the 200,000-strong Civil Rights march in Washington today was half over, Mr. Bayard Rustin, deputy organiser and the real moving spirit, spoke of the next move. He said: 'Already one of our objectives has been met. We said we would awaken the conscience of the nation and we have done it.' The next move would be a 'counter-filibuster' if opponents in the Senate tried to talk the proposed Civil Rights Bill to death. On every day of this 'filibuster' 1,000 people would be brought into Washington to stage a demonstration.

Mr Walter Reuther, president of the United Auto Workers' Union, said: 'It is the responsibility of all Americans to share the impatience of the Black American.' The other leaders applauded. A great roar of approval met the warning by the Reverend Martin Luther King, the integrationist leader, that America was in for 'a rude awakening' if she thought she could go back to business as usual. 'Let us not seek to satisfy our thirst for freedom by drinking from the cup of hatred and bitterness,' said Mr. King. They would go on with the struggle until 'justice flows like water and righteousness like a stream'.

From a Louisiana prison, where he is awaiting trial for taking part in a Civil Rights demonstration, came a sober but strong message from Mr. James Farmer, national director of the Congress of Racial Equality. 'Act with valour and with dignity and without fear. Some of us may die but our war is for life, not for death. We will not stop our demand for "Freedom Now". We will not stop till the heavy weight of centuries of oppression is removed from our backs and like proud men everywhere we can all stand tall again.' The cheers rolled over the crowd, jammed in front of the Lincoln Memorial and along the shallow reflecting pool.

It was a day of quiet triumph, a mingling of fervent demands with a show of orderly, relaxed calm. Earlier fears of disorder seemed almost laughably out of place. Personalities in the march included Marlon Brando, Burt Lancaster, Lena Horne, Judy Garland, Sammy Davis, Sidney Poitier and Josephine Baker, who flew from Paris. Among white demonstrators was a sprinkling of young men with unkempt beards and straight-haired girls who would not look out of place in an Aldermaston march. One had a placard: 'I would rather marry a black.' People heckled him, saying: 'Do you really think that will help our cause?'

In one corner a disgruntled George Rockwell, leader of the tiny American Nazi party, commented: 'This thing will be like a Sunday School picnic.' He and fifty followers were allowed on the grounds as long as they did not display posters, hand out leaflets or try to interfere with the demonstrators. There were thirty-five police and National Guardsmen to see they did not. Just after noon one of his followers was arrested for trying to make a speech. Rockwell led the rest from the scene.

For two hours the marchers' numbers swelled around the monument, within sight of the White House and the Capitol, which houses Congress. They were entertained by singers and by brief speeches from their heroes, Jackie Robinson, the baseball player, and a man who roller-skated all the way from Chicago, and admitted his legs were tired. The organisers expected that this sort of distraction would be necessary to keep tempers under control. They need not have worried. The crowd seemed almost as determined to be respectable as to demand civil rights.

Black suits and dresses predominated. A group of poor people from Parksville, Mississippi, were in well-pressed overalls. There were clerical collars by the dozen. Clergymen of every denomination joined the demonstration. A group from Savannah, Georgia, made the great hall of Washington's railway station echo and re-echo with the words of 'Whose side are you on?' But they, too, had lapsed into cheerful chatter among themselves at the monument.

By then the Civil Rights demonstrators had started their march. It proved to be more of a stroll. They were to have formed up in two great columns behind some of the heroes of the movement and marched from the Washington Monument to the Lincoln Memorial, almost a mile away. Instead they started moving towards the memorial before the organisers realised what was happening. Strolling along with placards held high, occasionally singing, but mostly quiet, they formed two loosely-knit, unbustling processions.

The posters approved by the march organisers were explicit:

'We demand equal rights now.'
'We demand a fair employment law now.'
'No U.S. dough to help Jim Crow grow.'

The last was a demand for withholding Government funds from schemes where racial discrimination is practised. Everywhere the emphasis was on 'Now'.

Those who were to have led the march simply slipped into the procession and walked along with the rest. Mr. Philip Randolph, at seventy-four an elder statesman of the movement, and the man who first proposed the march, was to have walked alone at the head of the crowd. Instead, he was somewhere in the middle, a few paces behind a group wheeling a coffin with a Confederate flag on it, one of the rare shows of vehemence during the day. At least one in ten of the marchers was white. Not all marchers were from the South. James Baker, fifty-nine, and Jesse Gadson, thirty, steel workers, of Steubensville, Ohio, had their own troubles. Baker said his firm had only sixteen Black men among 400 unskilled workers. Restaurants there were desegregated, but 'beer joints' were not. The schools were integrated for pupils, but teachers had not yet been taken on the same basis.

The very respectability of today's demonstration may be a cause of trouble if the Civil Rights campaign in general does not bring new and dramatic successes. Angrier voices may say that tougher tactics are needed.

President Kennedy said tonight the Great March had advanced 'the cause of twenty million people'. After meeting for seventy-five minutes at the White House with the leaders of the demonstration he said: 'One cannot help but be impressed with the deep fervour and the quiet dignity of the demonstrators.' It showed their faith and confidence in democracy. 'This nation can properly be proud of the demonstration that has occurred here today.'

In a message for Labour Day next Monday but released today to coincide with the march, President Kennedy called on the American people to 'accelerate our effort to achieve equal rights for all our citizens'. He said: 'These recent months, one hundred years after the emancipation proclamation, have seen the decisive recognition by the major part of our society that all our citizens are entitled to full membership in the national community. The gains of 1963 will never be reversed.'

23 November 1963: The world reels to news of another assassinated American President

PRESIDENT KENNEDY IS ASSASSINATED
SHOT IN THE HEAD IN OPEN CAR ON TEXAS FESTIVAL DRIVE
FORMER DEFECTOR TO RUSSIA ARRESTED
LYNDON JOHNSON SWORN IN AS NEW PRESIDENT

From Stephen Barber, *Daily Telegraph* Special Correspondent

DALLAS, TEXAS, FRIDAY

John Fitzgerald Kennedy, forty-six, the thirty-fourth President of the United States, died this afternoon within half-an-hour of being shot in the head as he drove through Dallas in an open car. He was on his way to make a speech at a political festival. The shooting happened as the President's car drove through cheering crowds. Shots rang out and he slumped down in his seat. Mrs. Jacqueline Kennedy, who was also in the car, jumped up and cried: 'Oh, no!' She cradled her husband in her arms as the car sped to nearby Parkland Hospital. Police motorcyclists with sirens blaring cleared a path through the crowds, and the traffic. At the hospital President Kennedy was given an immediate blood transfusion and a Roman Catholic priest was called to his bedside to administer the last rites. The President died twenty-five minutes after being shot.

Vice-President Lyndon Johnson, fifty-five, who was sworn in later as the new President, was travelling in the car behind President Kennedy's but was unhurt. The Governor of Texas, Mr. John Connally, forty-six, who was in the President's car, was shot in the chest and head. Tonight his condition was described as 'serious'. Crowds waiting outside the hospital groaned as priests announced the President's death. Many people collapsed in tears.

Police tonight seized Lee H. Oswald, twenty-four, chairman of a pro-Castro 'Fair Play for Cuba' committee. Oswald, wearing a brown shirt, was taken screaming from a cinema. A shot was fired during the arrest. A Dallas policeman had earlier been shot and killed near the cinema. Oswald, of Fort Worth, Texas, a former Marine, defected to the Soviet Union in 1959, and said he had applied for Soviet citizenship. He returned to the United States last year with his Russian wife. Police said he was the prime suspect in the assassination, but had denied all knowledge of the crime. He was later charged with the murder of a policeman.

Eye-witnesses reported seeing a rifle being withdrawn from a window in a building overlooking the President's route. A TV reporter said: 'A policeman fell to the ground, pulled his pistol and yelled, "Get down".' It is not known whether Secret Servicemen in the President's bodyguard returned the assassin's fire. Police found an Italian-made rifle with telescopic sights in a building nearby. Three spent cartridges were found beside the rifle.

President Kennedy, who was worried by opposition in the Southern States to his Civil Rights Bill, had arrived in Dallas by air during a political tour of Texas. Thousands lined the streets as he drove to the town's Trade Market to speak at a lunch, and the President had the bullet-proof glass top of his car lowered so that he could wave to the crowds.

A woman witness, Mrs. Jean Hill, said in a radio interview that the President and Mrs. Kennedy were looking at a dog in the middle of the road, near an underpass, when the shots rang out. She said: 'There were three shots. He grabbed his chest and fell over his seat, and Jackie fell over him.'

The President was unconscious when he arrived at the hospital. Doctors found that the bullet had struck the President's neck, just below the Adam's apple. There was also a gaping wound in the back of his head. An emergency operation was performed on his throat, to enable him to breathe. In a corridor Mrs. Kennedy, her clothing stained with her husband's blood, sobbed quietly as doctors fought to save her husband's life. Before it was announced that he was dead, Mrs. Kennedy was led into a private room. She was later stated to be suffering from shock. About an hour after his death,

President Kennedy's body was placed in a bronze coffin to be flown to Washington. His body will lie in state and he will be given a state funeral.

The first that we of the Press knew that anything so terrible had occurred was when we saw the cars hurtle past the Trade Mart auditorium where we had been waiting to hear President Kennedy's speech. Sirens shrieking, the cars raced straight by to the Parkland Hospital, three miles away. When the President's car reached the hospital his limp body, his wife still clutching his arm, was gently lifted on to a trolley. On the floor of the car, spattered with blood, lay a bouquet of flowers presented to Mrs. Kennedy earlier.

The horror of it all was accentuated by the golden sunshine. As if in Kennedy's honour, a grey drizzle had cleared away upon his arrival at Dallas Airport. To the now understandable dismay of his bodyguard, he had walked across the tarmac to the railings of the public enclosure, Mrs. Kennedy in a gay pink suit and saucy pillbox hat beside him, to shake hands with children and their parents some of whom had driven hundreds of miles to get a glimpse of him.

Dallas, the second largest town in Texas, is stunned by what has happened. It is true that it is the home of some of the late President's bitterest critics. Only a few weeks ago Mr. Adlai Stevenson, America's Ambassador to the United Nations, was spat upon by Right-wing demonstrators in the town and hit by an offensive placard. Because of that incident, however, specially, stringent measures were taken for President Kennedy's trip, which was to have been the highlight of a three-day tour of Texas. Four hundred extra police and an undisclosed number of Secret Service men from Washington had been flown in to make sure that precisely what has happened would not.

A film cameraman on the spot recorded the shooting, sprinting towards the Presidential car with his camera running. The film shows a crazy jumble of upside-down buildings and running people. The final scene, in focus, showed the Presidential car speeding away to the hospital. This film of the procession of cars as it was before the shooting, and the mad moments immediately afterwards, will probably survive as one of the historic records of the assassination.

Police said that the policeman named Tippit was shot about five streets from the cinema in which Oswald was arrested. The cashier there had reported that a suspicious man had entered. Four policemen, including Tippit, went after him. After shooting Tippit, police said Oswald tried to shoot another policeman, but his revolver misfired. F.B.I. men questioned both Oswald and his brother, Robert. Oswald's Russian wife, who does not speak English, was questioned through interpreters.

The President's parents, who are staying at their holiday home at Hyannis Port, Cape Cod, were told by a workman of the assassination. The President's father, Mr. Joseph P. Kennedy, former U.S. Ambassador to London, is a semi-invalid as the result of a stroke he suffered several years ago. He was sleeping when the workman heard the report of the shooting and ran to the house with the news. The President had planned to spend the Thanksgiving holiday next week at Hyannis Port.

President Kennedy was the fourth American President to be killed in office. He had been President for two years ten months. The last shooting incident involving an American President was on 1 November 1950. Two men identified as members of a Puerto Rican Nationalist movement tried to shoot their way into Blair House, Washington, in an attempt to kill President Harry S. Truman. One was killed. The other was wounded but recovered, and was tried for the killing of a member of the President's bodyguard. He was sentenced to death. President Truman commuted this to life imprisonment.

Politically, the assassination will upset all previous calculations. While Mr. Kennedy's re-election next year was almost a foregone conclusion, Mr. Johnson's chances could fairly be described as marginal. They would depend, of course, on his showing in the Presidency during the coming year. But he has not been considered seriously for the highest office. Most political observers would feel that Mr. Kennedy's death must inevitably increase the Republicans' chances of winning next year. One person who might be able to make things difficult for them is the President's brother, Mr. Robert Kennedy, the Attorney-General. It has been reported that he was preparing to resign his office in order to help his brother with his re-election campaign in 1964. It can safely be predicted that the idea of nominating him as the candidate will be canvassed when the nation has got over the shock of the President's death.

President Kennedy was last in England for two days in June, during his European tour. British people saw little of him, for he spent the time at Birch Grove, the Sussex home of Mr. Macmillan. Their serious discussions on world affairs and Anglo–U.S. relations were preceded by the President's almost hilarious tour of Eire. This was a sentimental journey to the land of his peasant ancestors, with no great political issues involved. A previous attempt to assassinate President Kennedy was made in December 1960 by a man who parked his car loaded with seven sticks of dynamite in front of the Kennedy home in Palm Beach, Florida.

President Kennedy's body came home to Washington tonight in a short, sad ceremony. The Air Force Plane Number One, which carried him to so many places around the world, brought the coffin from Dallas. President Lyndon Johnson travelled with it. Mrs. Kennedy watched as the coffin was lowered with some difficulty into a Navy ambulance. Mr. Robert Kennedy, Attorney-General and the dead President's brother, jumped from the platform to help Mrs. Kennedy jump the two or three feet to the ground. A slight grimace was the only sign of strain as she got into the curtained ambulance. It drove to where a helicopter waited to carry her and her husband's body to the White House.

The first news of the shooting had struck Washington like a thunderbolt. Horrified citizens gathered in groups at street corners and in cafés to exchange reports and rumours. In one restaurant the proprietor shouted: 'Someone took a potshot at the President.'

Immediately customers gathered round a transistor radio broadcasting a non-stop report.

Senator Mansfield, the Senate Democratic majority leader, was called to the telephone by an American news agency and told of the shooting moments after it occurred. 'This is terrible,' he replied after a shocked silence. 'I can't find words.' Senator Dirksen, the Senate Republican leader, called to the telephone by Senator Mansfield, said: 'Oh God. This is the most distressing thing that could ever happen. I am shocked.' Both men rushed on to the floor of the Senate. The recess ensued on Senator Mansfield's motion.

It was immediately noted in Washington that Texas was the scene of the recent attack on Mr. Adlai Stevenson, American Ambassador to the United Nations. When he spoke at a Dallas meeting he was pushed and jostled by extremist anti-United Nations demonstrators.

Texas is also the home State of Major-General Edwin Walker, who played a leading role in the rioting against the admission of a Negro student to the University of Mississippi just over a year ago. Right-wing groups such as the John Birch Society have drawn much of their strength in recent years from Texas. But the 'Lone Star' State of Texas is also the home of President Johnson.

At the White House the telephone switchboard was swamped with calls. Even the Washington telephone service began to show signs of strain minutes after the shooting. Reporters hurried to the previously deserted White House Press room. White House employees were stunned by the news. Mr. Theodore Sorensen, Mr. Kennedy's chief speech-writer and an old friend for many years, stood silently in front of a telephone set in the office of Mr. Salinger, the Press secretary. Asked by a reporter if he had anything to say he shook his head and turned away to go.

President Kennedy, like any other President, was guarded at all times by the White House 'secret service'. This is a crack formation with its own *esprit de corps*. It is run directly by the American Treasury and quite distinct from the Federal Bureau of Investigation. Whenever the President drives in an open car procession he is surrounded by these highly-trained bodyguards. Usually a carload travels immediately behind or in front of the Presidential limousine. When the procession is at walking pace some 'secret servicemen' usually walk alongside.

Mr. Lyndon B. Johnson, was sworn in as the thirty-fifth President of the United States at 3.39 p.m. (8.39 p.m. G.M.T.) today within hours of President Kennedy's assassination. The new President will serve the remainder of Mr. Kennedy's term, until January 1965. The next Presidential election will be in November 1964. Mr. Johnson took the oath aboard the Presidential plane at Dallas's Love Airfield when he was preparing to fly to Washington to take over the American Government. He was sworn in by District Judge Sarah Hughes, the first woman judge in the Dallas Federal District. She was crying during the ceremony.

President Johnson promised on arrival in Washington tonight: 'I will do my best, that is all I can do. I ask for your help, and God's.' He spoke into a battery of microphones at Andrews Air Force base, where he alighted from the Presidential plane which brought Mr. Kennedy's body from Dallas. He began: 'This is a sad time for all people. We have suffered a loss that cannot be weighed. For me it is a deep personal tragedy. I know that the world shares the sorrow that Mrs. Kennedy and her family bear.'

The area was ringed by a cordon of soldiers and Air Force men. Thousands of people stood silently behind barriers. President Johnson and his wife left the plane after the coffin was borne down the stairs to the tarmac. He then walked grim-faced to a microphone to address the nation.

President Johnson did not meet the members of the Diplomatic Corps who, with the Press, were kept some distance away from the aircraft. When it became obvious that the scream of jet helicopters waiting nearby to take him and his party to the White House would make it impossible for him to be heard, orders were given for the engines to be switched off. Pale, drawn, and still showing traces of the shock he had undergone, Mr. Johnson delivered his brief address in a deep voice, speaking deliberately and in measured tones. It was announced that all United States Navy ships and shore stations throughout the world would fire salutes at half-hour intervals from 8 a.m. to sunset tomorrow in honour of the dead President.

12 November 1965: Rhodesia's unilateral
Declaration of Independence meets with a hostile response
SWIFT SANCTIONS ON REBEL RHODESIA
BRITAIN'S REPLY TO BREAKAWAY
SMITH PUTS COUNTRY ON WAR FOOTING

Britain yesterday outlawed the Rhodesian Government. This was Mr. Wilson's swift answer to Rhodesia's seizure of independence, announced in a broadcast by Mr. Ian Smith. Five hours before Mr. Smith made his proclamation, Mr. Wilson, who had been up almost all night, made a final effort by telephone to stop him going over the brink. The Prime Minister is reported to have said: 'I cannot understand why a man of your stature allows himself to be surrounded and kicked around by the bunch of thugs you have now.'

It became clear to Mr. Wilson that a breakaway was imminent when he learned that Sir Humphrey Gibbs, the Governor of Rhodesia, had been constrained to sign orders transferring some of his powers to members of Mr. Smith's Government. An Enabling Bill to be passed on Monday will empower the Government to revoke that part of the Constitution under which the Governor had to assign these powers. Mr. Wilson told a hushed Commons that the Rhodesian Government had been 'hell-bent on illegal and self-destroying action'. Sir Humphrey Gibbs had informed Mr. Smith and his Ministers that because of their rebellion against the Crown they had ceased to hold office. It was the duty of British subjects in Rhodesia to remain loyal to the Crown and to recognise the British Government's authority. Mr. Wilson said Britain would have no dealings with the rebel Government. The British High Commissioner in Salisbury was being withdrawn and the

Rhodesian High Commissioner in London was being asked to leave.

Parliament, which is to debate Rhodesia today, is to be asked on Monday to approve a Bill imposing the following sanctions:

1. Imports of Rhodesian tobacco and sugar to be banned;
2. Exports of arms and spare parts to cease;
3. Rhodesia to be removed from sterling area, to lose Commonwealth preference and to receive no more British aid;
4. Special exchange control restrictions to be applied, exports of British capital to Rhodesia to stop and Rhodesia to be barred from London capital market;
5. No further cover from Exports Credits Guarantee Department for exports to Rhodesia.

Mr. Smith's Government put Rhodesia on a war footing last night when the Government assumed wide emergency economic powers, including the power to impose rationing. Press and broadcasting censorship prevented people from learning of Britain's reprisals, but Mr. Wilson's broadcast last night reached those with short-wave radios. The new constitution states that if the Queen does not appoint a Governor-General, on the advice of the Rhodesian Government; within fourteen days, a 'regent' will be appointed. His role will be that of a constitutional president. In Zambia, Rhodesia's land-locked northern neighbour, President Kaunda announced last night that his Government is imposing emergency powers to combat any possible Rhodesian action.

Mr. Stewart, Foreign Secretary, flew to New York last night for a meeting of the United Nations Security Council today. The meeting was called by Britain, because, as Mr, Wilson explained to Conservative interrupters in the Commons, 'if we don't somebody else will'. The General Assembly, by 107 votes to two, called on Britain to take measures, including force, against Rhodesia. South Africa and Portugal voted against, France abstained, and Britain did not take part. President Johnson ordered the recall of his consul-general in Salisbury and announced that the United States would not recognise the 'rebel regime'.

4 May 1968: Martin Luther King is cut down in Memphis
MARTIN LUTHER KING SHOT DEAD
HUNT FOR WHITE MAN: TWO ARRESTS
By Ian Ball

NEW YORK, THURSDAY

Dr. Martin Luther King, thirty-nine, the 1964 Nobel Peace Prize winner, and America's most respected Civil Rights leader, was assassinated tonight as he stood on the balcony of his hotel in the centre of Memphis, Tennessee. A single shot, apparently fired from a passing car, struck him in the neck and chin. 'Martin Luther King is dead,' said a police official about an hour after the Civil Rights leader had been taken by ambulance to a Memphis hospital.

Riot-equipped police were rushed to the hotel and sealed off a large area of the Memphis business section. Two men were arrested several hundred yards from the hotel. Police would not say whether they were suspected of murdering Dr. King or whether they were implicated in the killing. Police broadcast a bulletin instructing all units to look for a young white man. He was seen running from the scene and police said he dropped a weapon.

'He didn't say a word. He didn't move,' said one of Dr. King's key assistants, the Reverend Andrew Young. He and leaders throughout America were grief-stricken at the murder of a well-loved public figure. There was horror and public grief as the news spread through New York's Harlem. Men and women stood with heads bowed as they listened to the news in the street and in restaurants and bars. Many wept openly. President Johnson, on the eve of his departure for talks in Honolulu on peace moves in Vietnam, was deeply moved by the news from Memphis. He announced he would delay his departure for Honolulu for a day. In Memphis police reported sporadic acts of violence as news of the shooting spread. A curfew was placed on Memphis tonight. The Governor of Tennessee, Dr. Burford Ellington, ordered four thousand National Guardsmen into the city to keep order.

Dr. King was with the Reverend Jesse Jackson and other members of his Southern Christian Leadership Conference in the hotel room preparing to eat dinner. Dr. King stepped out on to the balcony of the second floor room to get some evening air. 'He had just bent over,' said the Reverend Jesse Jackson. 'If he had been standing up he would not have been hit in the face.' A shot rang out, Mr. Jackson said he knocked Dr. King down to protect him from being hit a second time. 'When I turned around I saw police coming from everywhere. They said, "Where did it come from?", and I said, "Behind you".'

Others who were with Dr. King said that moments before they stepped out on to the balcony he had talked about a meeting in Memphis tonight. 'Be sure to sing "Blessed Lord" tonight and sing it well,' were his last words before he was shot. Dr. King's face was covered with a white towel as he was taken into the hospital's emergency room. 'We are in a state of emergency here,' said Memphis police director Frank Holloman. 'We don't know what happened as yet.' Memphis police were protecting the city without the aid of National Guard troops for the first day since Dr. King led a march last Thursday in support of the striking dustmen.

Mr. Andrew Young, executive president of the Southern Christian Leadership Conference of which Dr. King is president, said that Dr. King was standing on the balcony alone when the shot was fired. 'It sounded like a firecracker.' Within half an hour of the first report of the shooting, the Federal Bureau of Investigation was instructed to begin an investigation at the specific request of Mr. Ramsey Clark, Attorney General.

In 1964 Dr. King was awarded the Nobel Peace Prize. The citation read: 'He consistently goes in for the principle of non-violence. In 1955 he was appointed to lead the coloured people's boycott of the buses in Montgomery, Alabama, and he has since acted as leader in the fight for civil rights.' Dr. King had been the subject of repeated assassination threats over the past ten years. There were at least two serious attempts on his life. Two years ago a knife was hurled at him while he was speaking in Chicago's Marquette Park. In January 1957, a bomb placed on the porch at his home in Montgomery failed to explode. The fuse burned out just before reaching the explosive – twelve sticks of dynamite bundled together. In 1960, a court sitting at Decatur, Georgia, to hear Dr. King's appeal against a four-month sentence for a minor traffic offence, was interrupted several times by telephoned bomb threats. In June 1964, Sheriff L.O. Davis, of St. Augustine, Florida, said that he had received threats to lynch Dr. King while he was being held in jail there following a civil rights march. In January 1965, the leader was punched and kicked in the groin as he registered at a previously all-white hotel in Selma, Alabama.

22 August 1968: The Russians put down the 'Prague Spring' in Czechoslovakia
PRAGUE TELLS RUSSIANS 'GO HOME'
DUBCEK ARRESTED BY SOVIET TROOPS
PRESIDENT ON 'FREE RADIO': CIVILIANS RESISTING

Fires raged in Prague last night as the Russian invaders tried to stamp out pockets of Czechoslovak resistance. At least twenty-five people were killed and hundreds injured throughout the country as Czech civilians took to the streets, most to shout abuse and to plead with the invaders to leave, but some to fight back with stones and Molotov cocktails. Mr. Dubcek and several other liberal Communist leaders were arrested by Soviet troops yesterday. The tape-recorded voice of President Svoboda, also reported to have been arrested, was broadcast last night by clandestine radio stations set up after the Russians closed down official stations.

The President said: 'We are living through an exceptionally grave moment in the life of our nation.' Russian and Warsaw Pact forces had 'entered our territory without the consent of the constitutional authorities of our state'. The Prague Government 'must achieve the speedy withdrawal of the foreign forces'. He had done everything possible to negotiate a settlement and hoped agreement would be reached tomorrow. 'There is no way back,' he said, from freedom and democracy.

Mr. Dubcek, Mr. Smrkovský, President of the National Assembly, and two colleagues were arrested at 8 p.m. An eye-witness said they were led from the tank-ringed building of the Central Party committee, put in a Russian armoured troop carrier and 'taken to an unknown place'. Mr. Černík, the Premier, was arrested by Russian troops at 5 p.m., and Dr. Cisar, chairman of the central committee, by two men in raincoats.

The Russians, who crossed Czechoslovakia's borders with East Germany, Poland, Hungary and the Soviet Union at 11.30 on Tuesday night, were firmly in control militarily last night. Tanks stood at street corners in almost all major towns. But in spite of this the clandestine radios were still broadcasting and the legal Czechoslovak Government succeeded in issuing a ringing appeal for freedom. It called on the Russians to release party and Government officials already interned and to leave the country at once.

The occupation of Prague yesterday was almost complete by 8 a.m. But in places barricades blocked the Russians' way and a vast crowd ringed the Prague Radio building. Troops fired over their heads. During rioting outside the building an ammunition lorry exploded, setting fire to buildings, two Russian tanks and other vehicles. At least four were killed and thirty injured. At the same time other Russian troops were occupying the National Assembly building as deputies were in session and the offices of Ceteka, the Czech news agency, which had been giving the world details of the invasion.

President Johnson yesterday called on Russia and her allies to withdraw from Czechoslovakia. 'It is never too late for reason to prevail,' he declared. An emergency session of the United Nations Security Council was convened last night. The Russian Ambassador, Mr. A. Malik, immediately took the floor and declared the meeting was not necessary because the troops had been called in at the request of the Czech Government. Earlier, U Thant, United Nations Secretary-General, denounced the invasion as 'a blow to world order and East–West relations'.

Russia yesterday made a major effort to justify her conduct, Frank Taylor telephoned from Moscow. *Pravda* said Russian troops had invaded to forestall an attempt to restore capitalism by Czech liberals supported by 'Imperialists'. The news agency Tass said the troops were invited in by a mysterious 'group of members of the Czechoslovak Communist party, Government and National Assembly'. But Mr. Stewart, the British Foreign Secretary, said there was no evidence of a Czech invitation. Tass said the occupation forces would leave as soon as the danger of reactionary rebellion had passed. Reports that Mr. Kosygin, Russian Prime Minister, and Marshal Grechko, head of the armed forces, had resigned were denied. Last night Russia admitted that her troops in Czechoslovakia were meeting with civilian resistance. Tass said that in Prague and some other towns anti-Communist elements were carrying out acts of 'provocation in the streets' against the occupying forces. These 'hostile sallies' were accompanied by the distribution of 'slanderous leaflets' and 'incendiary statements' over the radio, television and in the Press.

The recall of both Houses of Parliament, which will probably sit to discuss the crisis for two days, Monday and Tuesday, was announced yesterday after Mr. Wilson and Mr. Stewart had cut short their holidays to fly to London. Mr. Wilson was informed of the invasion by Lord Chalfont, Minister of State, Foreign Office, after Mr. Smirnovsky, Russian Ambassador, had called at Lord Chalfont's Chelsea home at 1.30 a.m. to tell him of Russia's action. Just before 1 p.m. a 114-word statement was issued from 10 Downing Street denouncing the invasion as a flagrant violation of accepted standards of international behaviour. 'This is a tragedy not only for Czechoslovakia, but for Europe and the whole world.'

Mr. Stewart said later that Britain and others would take action in the United Nations Security Council. Britain proposed to continue recognising Mr. Dubcek's Government. 'We cannot recognise a Government simply because the Government of the Soviet Union says it is the Government of Czechoslovakia.' Mr. Stewart said that what had happened to Czechoslovakia put at risk the rights of every small country. 'No country within reach can feel entirely safe.'

The invasion was condemned by Mr. Dubcek's east European allies, Romania and Jugoslavia, as well as by west European Communists, ands Governments throughout the world. In a strongly-worded statement, Mr. Ceauşescu, the Romanian leader, pledged his country's 'full solidarity' with the Czechs. 'Nothing can justify this armed action.' Mr. Ceauşescu demanded immediate withdrawal by Russia, and announced that the Romanian National Assembly would meet in emergency session today. President Tito said the invasion was a 'heavy blow' for Communism. Its consequences would be 'far-reaching and very negative'. He called an immediate meeting of the Jugoslav Communist party central committee. The British, French and Italian Communist parties yesterday condemned the invasion. The Communist *Morning Star* says today that many friends of Russia will feel that 'a tragic mistake has been made'.

But an official East German statement praised the invasion as 'a brilliant example of Socialist internationalism'. In Bonn, Herr Brandt, West German Foreign Minister, said that it was 'especially depressing' that East German troops had taken part in the invasion.

Columns of Russian tanks this evening came rolling into this city, which has been occupied since early morning. It is clear that the Russians intend to establish complete control of the country for a long period. The Russian commander has set up his HQ on the south bank of the Danube facing the city. His camp is surrounded by artillery trained on the centre of the city across the water. In the city itself Russian tanks and armoured troop carriers are posted at all strategic points. There were twenty tanks on the main square when I last drove through it.

Russian soldiers and officers were exhausted by their long journey to Bratislava. They had been days without sleep or food.

The people of Bratislava stood around silently, staring at the unexpected and unwanted Russian occupying forces. Some argued and joked with the Russian soldiers. Children had chalked derisive words on the Russian tanks and trucks. These included: 'Go back to Moscow', 'Occupiers', 'Fools'. Several tanks had scrawled on them the Russian word 'Inturist' – the Russian State tourist organisation. Others bore the German swastika.

I visited the HQ of the Slovak Communist party and found they were not occupied by the Russians. Mr. Bilak, First Secretary of the Slovak Communist party, was said to be in Prague with the rest of the Presidium of the Czechoslovak party. Other members of the Presidium of the Slovak party were said to be meeting in the building. Officials told me they had lost all contact with Prague.

I found Russian soldiers posted inside the building of Bratislava radio, which Russian technicians had put off the air. The building was not occupied, but a Russian tank posted two hundred yards down the road had its guns trained on the entrance. At least fifty Russian tanks were in Bratislava by this evening, apart from many armoured troop carriers and communication vehicles. As darkness fell more tanks came sweeping into the city by the main roads.

The Russians occupied Bratislava in the early hours of this morning when tanks and motorised troops moved swiftly into the city from Hungary. Everyone was taken by surprise, and by the time the people of Bratislava awoke, their city was in Russian hands. I arrived in Bratislava in the mid-afternoon after driving across Slovakia from the Tatra Mountains. I first came across the Russian troops fifteen miles south of Banská Bystrica. Russian helicopters were hovering over the town of Zvolen and a column of armoured troop carriers was moving out of the town westwards. At one I point the head of the Russian column was only a few hundred yards behind me, moving at 40-50 m.p.h,

The Russians' 'blitz' occupation has paralysed Czechoslovak

com-munications, intimidated the population and thwarted any immediate possibility of resistance. The occupation has centred on the main cities, Prague and Bratislava, and the regional centres. The Russians have cut communications without yet taking over the radio or Press. Apart from the top leaders, no one appears to have been arrested.

If the Dubcek regime capitulates and agrees to changes in the leadership and in policies, then the 'soft' occupation may continue. If not, in the next stage the Russians will take over and operate all means of communication. This will involve widespread arrests of liberal-minded officials and intellectuals. Further Russian forces will be moved in, probably at airfields in Russian hands.

The timing of the Russian occupation of Czechoslovakia was dictated by the Communist party congresses due to take place in the near future. The Russians' apparent climbdown at Čierna and Bratislava and their acceptance of the Dubcek regime appear to have persuaded the leaders in Prague that the danger was over for the time being. Many leading officials went off on holiday. No special precautions appear to have been taken against a possible Russian coup. The Communist congresses due to take place in Slovakia next week, and in Prague at the beginning of September, would have removed the pro-Russian elements from the party leadership and reduced the possibility of a restoration of the old regime. The Russians had to move before the Slovak Congress. Large-scale military manoeuvres in surrounding countries were a cover for their preparations.

The Russians will find it more difficult today to enlist Quisling leaders than they would have done a year ago. Most top men have identified themselves with Dubcek liberalism. The whole Presidium of the party was behind him at Čierna. Those who were half-hearted have been pushed into support by public opinion. But in circumstances of foreign occupation some former supporters of the Russians may switch back. Mr. Bilak, Slovak party leader, is thought to be very close to the Russians. Mr. Jindra, one of the secretaries of the Czechoslovak

Communist party, is an opponent of Mr. Dubcek. Twenty or thirty members of the Central Committee who were due to lose their places at the forthcoming congresses, will now support the Russians. So will many old guard officials in the provinces for whom the liberal reforms meant the eventual loss of their jobs.

Long queues had formed at all the food shops in Slovak towns and villages which I passed through in the course of the day. Food shortages were already apparent in Bratislava by the evening. The Slovak Minister of Trade introduced rationing, which restricted purchases to a maximum of 4lb of flour, ½lb rice, 1lb sugar, 1lb meat and sausage meat, ¼lb butter, five eggs, one piece of soap to any one purchaser. Tourists from the Warsaw Pact countries which invaded Czechoslovakia today were quickly on the move this morning to return to their countries.

21 July 1969: Man lands on the moon
AMERICANS WALK ON THE MOON
LUNARNAUTS' PERFECT LANDING
'IT HAS A SOFT BEAUTY ALL ITS OWN'
By Dr. Anthony Michaelis and Adrian Berry, Science Staff,
at the Manned Spacecraft Centre, Houston

Neil Armstrong, the thirty-eight-year-old American commander of the Apollo 11 mission, became the first man to set foot on the moon at 3.56 a.m. B.S.T. today. As he stood on the moon, he said the surface was 'like a fine powder, a very fine grain surface' and it had 'a soft beauty all its own like some desert of the United States'. Armstrong climbed slowly down the nine rungs of the *Eagle*'s ladder and placed his left foot on the lunar surface first. Television pictures of excellent quality were sent back live from a camera on *Eagle*.

Waiting inside *Eagle* to join him was Colonel Edwin 'Buzz' Aldrin, thirty-nine, lunar module pilot, who sent a message back to earth asking for people to give thanks for the events of the past few hours. Aldrin stepped on the moon at 4.15 a.m. President Nixon, speaking to the astronauts from the White House at 4.48 a.m., told them: 'Because of what you have done the heavens have become part of man's world.'

'It's a very soft surface but here and there where I poke with the sample collector I run into a very hard surface,' Armstrong reported, even though 'it appears to be the same material. I'll try to get a rock here,' he said. Aldrin said: 'There's a slight tendency, I can see now, to topple backwards due to the soft, very soft texture' of the lunar soil. On reaching the surface, Aldrin did a three-foot jump. His first words were: 'Beautiful, beautiful.' Armstrong replied: 'Isn't it something?' The lunarnauts moved with a curious bouncing, floating motion, like someone walking under water. The Stars and Stripes was implanted at 4.41 a.m.

Earlier, as the lunar module made a perfect landing on the Sea of Tranquillity, Armstrong reported: 'The *Eagle* has landed. We are breathing again. Thanks a lot.' Almost immediately Mission Control began referring to *Eagle* with a new radio call-sign of 'Tranquillity Base'. Aldrin said he took over manual control before touchdown and landed four miles away because the target 'would have taken us right into a football pitch-sized crater with a large number of big boulders'. They said the surface was 'ashen grey'. Overhead, at a height of less than seventy miles, Colonel Michael Collins, thirty-eight, orbited the moon in the command module *Columbia*, to which Armstrong and Aldrin are due to return tonight.

Then Armstrong made a quick description of the touchdown scene, saying that *Eagle* was 'surrounded by a lot of rocks about ten feet high. We are in a relatively smooth plain with many craters five to fifty feet in size. We see some ridges. And there are literally thousands of little one and two feet craters. We see some angular blocks some feet in front of us, about two-to-three feet in size.' He could see a hill about 'half a mile away'. No description came until they had made sure *Eagle* was in a proper condition to stay.

At about midnight, they settled down to man's first meal on the moon. They had bacon squares, peaches, biscuits and fruit drink.

Armstrong said: 'There was no difficulty' in adapting to the lunar gravity, one-sixth that of earth. All was going so well that the lunarnauts, in collaboration with Mission Control, decided to advance by five hours the time of their moonwalk. Five and a half minutes before touchdown, *Eagle* had reported to Control:

'Got the moon right out our window ... even better than simulator.' When *Eagle* was at 40,000 feet, Mission Control said: 'Everything is looking good to us.' Aldrin replied: 'Looks real good.' Altitude 1,600 feet, then 1,400 feet: 'Still looking very good.' Controllers then called off height and speed measurements. Two hundred feet above the surface, *Eagle* reported: 'Picking up some dust.'

Final preparations for the moon landing began when Aldrin crawled through the tunnel linking *Columbia* to *Eagle* at the end of Apollo's tenth lunar orbit. Armstrong later joined Aldrin in the lunar module to prepare it for undocking from the command module. Separation took place behind the moon and out of contact with the earth. As the lunar module reappeared at 6.50 p.m. B.S.T., Armstrong confirmed the manoeuvre was correct with the words: 'The *Eagle* has wings.' Collins was then alone in *Columbia*. He has already been nicknamed the 'taxi driver', waiting patiently for his fare to return from their moon excursion. The first thing *Eagle* did was a yaw manoeuvre to the left by sixty degrees and a pitch-up manoeuvre by 110 degrees so that it would be in the right position for Collins to look it over. Aldrin spun the spidery *Eagle* slowly while Collins visually checked that the landing legs were fully extended and locked in position.

Both spacecraft flew in formation for about twenty-five minutes before *Columbia* fired its small engines for eight seconds to move away from the twenty-two feet by thirty-one feet *Eagle* and left it free to descend to the moon. As Collins moved two miles ahead of *Eagle*, he said: 'See you later,' later being thirty hours from then. Numerous exchanges preceded the crucial decision to undock and separate. Flight director Eugene Kranz had to be sure not only of radio and telemetry systems but also altitude, orbital velocity, correct navigation, maintenance of pressure and temperature in *Eagle*, fuel supplies in both craft and, above all, that *Eagle*'s landing systems were in good order. Had any of these systems been malfunctioning, undocking would have had to be delayed until they were corrected. If they seemed beyond repair, the moon landing would have had to be abandoned.

Armstrong and Aldrin had to stand upright in the cramped cabin, and they were unable to see the lunar surface as they descended. Aldrin reported rolling activity and asked ground control for an explanation. He was calm and the rolling did not appear to be severe. He said he may have accidentally knocked against a control switch, causing 'roll activity'. One essential and very complex check-out involved the computer to be used for the landing. One computer programme allows Aldrin to land automatically, and another demands that he does the job manually.

There were several alarms as the *Eagle* descended to the moon but none were serious.

One series of alarms came from the on-board computer. The alarms, called the 'Bail-Out Alarm', was a signal that the computer thought it was being overworked at the moment and rejected new data to concentrate on navigation. As long as it did not happen repeatedly, agency officials said, there was no problem. *Eagle* was guided down without the data the computer rejected. Another alarm was on the fuel consumption. When the alarm goes off there is 114 seconds of fuel left in normal consumption. Eagle used sixty-five seconds beyond the alarm point, or half of the remaining fuel in the descent stage. As the descent stage is left on the moon that would have no effect on the rest of the mission.

A few minutes after the moon landing a group of about twenty Negro demonstrators invaded the gardens of the Manned Spacecraft Centre and sat down singing: 'We shall not be moved.' Nobody tried to move them. Tourists milled around photographing them. The demonstrators sat in the sunshine with placards saying: 'NASA shoots for the moon, we want to shoot for cheap food.' And: 'Remember the hungry in America, too.'

Immediately *Eagle* had landed, Dr. Thomas Paine, chief of NASA, telephoned President Nixon at the White House and reported the lunarnauts were ready to start their exploration. Dr. Paine expressed thanks to the Soviet Academy of Science for what he called their 'unprecedented co-operative move' in telling American astronaut Frank Borman the orbital parameters of their unmanned satellite, Luna 15. He added he did not know where Luna 15 was when *Eagle* landed or what it was doing.

16 February 1971: Britain goes decimal
AN 'ALL CHANGE' DAY FULL OF GOODWILL
By Gerda Paul

It was as a nation of shopkeepers that Britain came into its own on D-Day yesterday. In the great majority of shops, large or small, there was nothing but helpfulness and goodwill. Selfridges was among the big stores which had it cut and dried, and with remarkable efficiency. The store accepted only decimal currency and had installed not only fifteen money-changing counters but also a strolling team of 'Miss Decimals' in white polo neck sweaters and midis over hot pants, to help with the facts. 'We have had queues, and questions – mostly from the elderly – but it has gone remarkably well,' a spokesman said. 'Most customers have told us that it is nice to see us going bang over to decimal without messing about.'

For most other shops it was really C-Day; 'C' for compromise. Debenhams used all-decimal pricing, but the counters still accepted the old currency. There were patient explanations, and gentle persuading of customers to part with a minimum of the equivalent of 2½p in old coins (6d). 'Everything going very smoothly,' was the report. The big MacFisheries supermarket in Kensington High Street priced all its goods in new pence. But there were understanding smiles for the woman who wanted a 'shilling-size kipper'. The assistant said: 'I know what you mean,' and weighed one up – price 5½p.

In the little shops, the will was there – even if the new cash registers were not. I found a tobacconist, who charged me 27p for a packet of cigarettes, and rung up 5s 3d on his till. 'There is a queue for new tills, and we will not get one for a fortnight,' he said. 'But I want to go along with things. I have written out all my price tickets in the new money, but I have to convert back again to put the money in the till.'

Everyone agreed that old people found the new money most difficult. An old lady in Woolworth's who had been choosing her own sweets could not believe that her huge bagful came to 18p. The manager was called and, after a long explanation, she went away still a little upset about having to convert at all, but reasonably convinced. The biggest row was, understandably, in the branches of Boots the chemists which are not yet 'converted'. I heard a woman arguing: 'I have been trying to get rid of all these pennies and 3d bits, and I do not see why I should get them all back from you.'

9 August 1974: The fall of 'Tricky Dicky' as the Watergate scandal claims its biggest scalp
NIXON TELLS AMERICA: 'I RESIGN'
BELEAGUERED PRESIDENT ENDS THE AGONY OF WATERGATE
SACRIFICE FOR COUNTRY, SAYS FORD WHO TAKES OVER TODAY
By Stephen Barber in Washington

Richard Milhous Nixon last night announced his resignation as President of the United States, brought low by the Watergate affair just one year, nine months and a day after being re-elected with a land-slide sixty-two per cent of the vote. He will be succeeded at noon today by Mr. Gerald Ford, the sixty-one-year-old Vice-President.

The official news that Mr. Nixon would become the first American President to give up office came in a nationwide television speech in which he said: 'I shall resign the Presidency effective at noon tomorrow.' Saying that he had never been a 'quitter' he said he decided to step down because America needed 'a full-time President and a full-time Congress'. His only acknowledgement of guilt in the Watergate affair was to say: 'If some of my judgments were wrong – and some were wrong – they were made in what I believed at the time to be in the best interest of the nation.'

It was a dignified address. Mr. Nixon looked astonishingly calm. There was none of that sweating that he has often in previous appearances shown because of the hot television lights.

He spoke from the Oval Office of the White House. He wore a dark grey suit and a black tie and sported an American flag in his lapel.

Immediately after Mr. Nixon had finished speaking, Mr. Ford emerged from his suburban home in Alexandria, Virginia, to say: 'This is one of the saddest incidents I have ever witnessed. I think the President has made one of the greatest sacrifices for the country and one of the greatest decisions for all of us by his decision to resign.' Mr. Ford announced that Dr. Kissinger, Secretary of State, had agreed to stay in office, and added: 'I pledge to you that I will work for what's good for America and what's good for the world.'

The initial reaction of Congressmen last night was subdued. There was some dismay that the departing President had strongly implied that his problems were due to a loss of support amongst them rather than to his involvement in the Watergate scandal. The die was cast for resignation at a midnight meeting at which Dr. Kissinger made up the President's mind for him even though Mr. Nixon's family had urged him to fight on. Soon Washington was awash with rumours of impending resignation. Speculation continued yesterday morning, but at 11 a.m. Mr. Ford met Mr. Nixon and was told that he would become America's thirty-eighth President. Mr. Nixon and his family will leave the White House today and fly in an Air Force plane to their home at San Clemente, California.

Of all the questions raised by the Watergate affair, the one which wounded President Nixon most grievously was put by a junior lawyer for the Senate Watergate Committee to a little-known former White House official on a sultry afternoon last year. It was Friday, 13 July when Mr. Alexander Butterfield was asked almost casually by Donald Sanders, deputy ministry counsel on the Watergate Committee, whether any of the President's conversations had been recorded. To the staff lawyer's astonishment, he said they were all recorded, routinely but in secret. Mr. Butterfield repeated his stunning disclosures at a public session of the committee three days later and President Nixon's fate was sealed.

The knowledge that tapes existed which could show exactly 'what did the President know and when did he know it' was sufficient eventually to turn what Mr. Nixon called 'the broadest but thinnest scandal in American history' into grounds for his impeachment by Congress. Disclosure of the President's secret taping system led to exposure of his involvement in the Watergate cover-up. It was, in many ways, a worse blow for him than the discovery a year earlier that his campaign workers had broken into Democratic Party headquarters at the Watergate building in Washington. It led to constitutional confrontations between the White House and the Senate Watergate Committee and the dismissal of Mr. Archibald Cox, the first Watergate Special Prosecutor, who pressed too hard for the tapes. The departure of Mr. Cox brought the resignations of Mr. Elliot Richardson, the Attorney-General, and his deputy and resulted directly in the House of Representatives Judiciary Committee's Impeachment inquiry.

After nine months of national anguish the President produced an edited transcript of some of his secret recordings last 30 April. He said on television that they gave a complete account of his Watergate role, but even former Nixon loyalists recoiled in disgust when they examined when had been delivered. 'Innocence is innocence and my father is innocent,' Mr. Nixon's elder daughter, Tricia, protested later. But the tapes revealed a foul-mouthed, vacillating President prepared to consider any dubious option which might 'keep the cap on the bottle'. He appeared to order the payment of hush money to one of the original Watergate conspirators and made no protest as his aides sat in his office discussing how to get the Mafia to help pay it. He spent hours with his advisers, Bob Haldeman and John Ehrlichman, trying to construct a 'scenario' which would throw the blame for Watergate on to John Mitchell, his former Attorney General and 1972 re-election campaign manager, and later John Dean, the turncoat White House counsel.

Senator Hugh Scott, the Senate Republican leader, said the transcripts showed a 'shabby, disgusting and immoral performance'. Even staunchly Republican newspapers turned against the President. Republicans in Congress volunteered to join delegations to ask for his resignation. It was not until ten weeks later, when the Judiciary Committee released its own transcripts of some of the tapes, that Americans realised they had still not heard the worst. The committee's transcripts, made with sophisticated audio equipment, contained words, phrases and sometimes whole sections of conversations which were not shown in the transcripts published by the President. According to the committee's written version of the tapes, Mr. Nixon talked explicitly of a 'cover-up plan' and told his assistants: 'I don't give a shit what happens. I want you all to stonewall it. Let them plead the Fifth Amendment, cover-up or anything else, if it'll save it – save the plan.' He instructed his staff that if they were questioned by a grand jury investigating Watergate, 'just be damned sure you say, "I don't remember".'

Tapes, tapes, tapes. The President was inextricably tangled in them, caught up by an off-the-cuff question by a junior investigator in a preliminary interview. Nothing he could do, nothing he or his family could say, was enough to cut him free. There was nowhere he could go to escape the evidence on the taping system he himself ordered to be installed. Even his trips to the Middle East and Russia failed to turn the inrushing impeachment tide.

Almost as accidental as the disclosure of the tapes' existence was the discovery of the burglary at the Watergate building on 17 June 1972. A nightwatchman noticed a strip of adhesive across the lock on a basement door. He removed it but later found it had been replaced. He called the police who caught a motley group of five intruders. They wore surgical gloves and carried burglary show tools, cameras, electronic bugging equipment and, most damaging of all, $6,500 in new notes, which were later found to have come from Nixon campaign funds.

Cynical Americans were growing to accept illegal wire-tapping as a way of political life and it looked as if the matter might end with the arrest of the five burglars. Then one of them was identified as James McCord, chief security officer for the Committee to Re-elect the President (CREEP). He was disavowed by Mitchell, the campaign manager, and dismissed. An address book carried by one of the four Cuban Americans arrested with McCord contained the name of Howard Hunt, a former C.I.A. agent working as a White House consultant. Hunt was later arrested with Gordon Liddy, a former F.B.I. agent working as a lawyer for CREEP.

Despite clear links between the break-in, the White House and the Nixon campaign teams, Mr. Ronald Ziegler, the President's spokesman, dismissed the affair as a 'third-rate burglary attempt'. The *Washington Post* refused to believe that and kept two young reporters on the Watergate trail. On 30 April 1973, the President was forced to dismiss John Dean, while Haldeman and Ehrlichman resigned. Mr. Nixon conceded for the first time that: 'There had been an effort to conceal the facts.'

About the same time it was revealed that in 1971 White House agents had broken into the office of the psychiatrist treating Dr. Daniel Ellsberg, who was acquitted in 1973 of stealing and leaking to the Press secret Pentagon papers on the Vietnam War. After publishing its transcripts of the Watergate tapes, the Judiciary Committee released more than 10,000 pages of evidence it had studied privately, covering the Watergate break-in, the White House cover-up, misuse of Government agencies to persecute political 'enemies', White House wiretapping and snooping, Mr. Nixon's personal finances and allegations that the International Telephone and Telegraph Corporation and dairy groups bought political favours from the White House. In a 'summary of information' presented to the committee as it approached the final stage of voting on Articles of Impeachment, Mr. John Doar, the committee's chief counsel, said the Watergate cover-up 'had the full-approval of the President' between the time of the break-in and the election which Mr. Nixon won overwhelmingly in November 1972.

Quoting from the tapes, the donnish Mr. Doar said that as early as 30 June 1972 Mr. Nixon told Haldeman and Mitchell that he wanted to 'cut the loss'. On 15 September 1972, he told Dean and Haldeman: 'So you just try to button it up as well as you can and hope for the best.' And on 21 March 1973, the President told Dean: 'You had the right plan, let me say, I have no doubts about the right plan before the election. And you handled it just right. You contained it. Now, after the election, we've got to have another plan, because we can't have, for four years, we can't have this thing.' After doing his best to 'contain' the Watergate scandal and limit the original F.B.I. investigations of the break-in, Dean briefed Mr. Nixon on the scope of the cover-up on 21 March 1973. He told the President that payments had been made to Watergate defendants, that the payments constituted an obstruction of justice and that, as well as himself, Haldeman, Ehrlichman and Mitchell were involved.

Mr. Doar told the committee: 'In response to this report the President did not condemn the payments or the involvement of his closest aides. He did not direct that the activity be stopped. The President did not express any surprise of shock. He did not report it to the proper investigatory agencies. He indicated familiarity with the payments scheme, and an awareness of some details – such as the use of a Cuban committee.' When Dean went on to convey a demand for $120,000 blackmail by Howard Hunt, one of the original Watergate conspirators, the President said: 'For Christ's sake get it', if only as a 'buy-time thing'.

Following the 21 March meeting, Mr. Doar told the committee the President told Haldeman and Ehrlichman to agree on a 'cover' story that payments to Watergate defendants were made not to obstruct justice but for legal fees and family support. On 15 April, according to

Dean's testimony, Mr. Nixon told Dean he had been joking when he said on 21 March that it would be easy to raise a million dollars to buy the defendants' silence. The White House claimed, many months later, that the 15 April conversation had accidentally never been recorded. Another key conversation, between the President and Mitchell was also said never to have been taped and an eighteen-and-a-half-minute gap was found on the tape of a conversation the President had with Haldeman a few days after the original break-in.

Mr. Doar told the committee that the taped evidence showed Mr. Nixon misled the public when he said he had never offered anyone executive clemency. He also alleged that the President also misled Americans when he said he had ordered and even personally under-taken investigations which showed no White House involvement in Watergate. The true purpose of the reports he ordered, Mr. Doar said, was 'to mislead investigators and insulate the President from charges of concealment'. Asking Dean for one such report, Mr. Nixon was recorded as saying: 'Make it very incomplete.'

The President found out what he could about the Watergate investigation from Mr. Richard Kleindienst then Attorney-General, and Mr. Henry Petersen, the Assistant Attorney-General. He persuaded Petersen to pass on secret grand jury testimony in confidence and minutes after Petersen had left his office relayed it to the White House aides who were being investigated. The transcripts show that in April 1973, when the cover-up was falling apart and Dean and Jeb Magruder, deputy manager of the Nixon re-election campaign, were beginning to talk to the prosecutors, Mr. Nixon spoke frequently to Petersen still striving for 'containment' while portraying himself as tenaciously seeking the full truth. As he told Haldeman: 'I've got to appear to co-operate.' He privately ordered Petersen not to investigate 'the Presidency' and urged him not to let Dean testify under a promise of immunity from prosecution. Mr. Nixon told his aides he had Petersen 'on a short leash'.

In May 1973, the Senate Watergate Committee began hearings

with Senator Sam Ervin as chairman and Mr. Cox was named special Watergate Prosecutor. Senator Ervin was determined to ferret out all illegal, unethical and improper conduct during the 1972 Presidential campaign. James McCord, who had broken the Watergate case open with a letter to Judge Sirica at his trial saying higher-ups were involved, was joined by Magruder in implicating senior White House officials. Then Dean gave a week of sensational testimony aimed directly against the President. 'The President was involved,' said Dean in a husky baritone. 'I hope the President is forgiven.'

As the Ervin hearings pushed soap operas off American television screens throughout the summer, the President became increasingly vexed by the activities of Mr. Cox, to whom he had promised his 'full support' in the spring. Mr. Cox and his team of young attorneys were prying into the milk fund and I.T.T. matters, the Ellsberg break-in, the President's finances and his use of the Internal Revenue Service to 'screw' political opponents. Mr. Richardson, who resigned as Attorney General rather than dismiss Cox in the tapes battle of October 1973, told the Judiciary Committee in a sworn affidavit that Mr. Nixon had long wanted to rid himself of the meddlesome prosecutor. After Vice-President Spiro Agnew resigned .and was convicted of tax evasion that same October, Mr. Richardson said the President remarked: 'Now that we have disposed of that matter we can go ahead and get rid of Cox.'

Mr. Doar placed all of this before the judiciary Committee and concluded that 'reasonable men acting reasonably' would recommend impeachment. Mr. James St. Clair, the trial lawyer Mr. Nixon had summoned from Boston to handle his Watergate defence, protested eloquently that the President had first to be found guilty of a major crime and that there was no evidence to support any such finding. Mr. St. Clair focused his case on the payment of hush money to Howard Hunt, claiming that Hunt was given money for 'humanitarian purposes' at Dean's instigation, without the President's knowledge or approval. He dismissed the grand jury's finding that Mr. Nixon was a co-conspirator in the cover-up case as an 'artfully contrived' distortion of the facts. White House wire-tapping was a justifiable response to serious security leaks, he argued, and there was no proof of Presidential corruption in the I.T.T. and milk money cases. If Presidential aides had tried to misuse the tax service they had not succeeded and no crime had been committed.

Mr. Leon Jaworski, who had replaced Mr. Cox as special prosecutor, approached a different showdown with the President in the courts. Mr. Jaworski had subpoenaed sixty-four White House tapes for use at the cover-up trial of Mitchell, Haldeman, Ehrlichman and three other former Nixon associates. Claiming that Mr. Jaworski already had all the evidence he needed, Mr. Nixon rejected the subpoena on the grounds that he was entitled to withhold evidence from the courts if he deemed disclosure to be against the public interest.

The historic case of the United States versus Richard M. Nixon reached the Supreme Court on 8 July 1974. Sixteen days later the eight judges ruled unanimously against the President's claim of executive privilege, asserting plainly that the President is not above the law. The court's ruling came only hours before the Judiciary Committee began its final debate on possible grounds for impeachment and did incalculable damage to the President's position. Three days later, on Saturday, 27 July, six of the panel's seventeen Republicans joined all twenty-one of its Democrats in voting 27–11 to recommend that the President be impeached for obstruction of justice. The following Monday brought a 26–10 vote for a second article of impeachment accusing President Nixon of misusing his powers to violate the constitutional rights of. American citizens. A third article, based on the President's refusal to comply with the panel's subpoenas for more tapes, passed 21– 17.

The President was in his swimming trunks on a California beach when he heard that the committee had recommended his impeachment and removal from office. On the same day that the committee passed its second article of impeachment, Mr. John Connally, one of President

Nixon's former Treasury Secretaries, was indicted on federal charges of bribery, conspiracy to obstruct, justice and perjury to do with allegations that he took $10,000 from dairymen for recommending an increase in milk price supports. John Dean was sentenced to at least one year for obstructing justice in the Watergate cover-up.

Mr. Nixon tried to win back defecting loyalists by admitting on 5 August that he had withheld information from the public and his lawyer. He released three more tapes. He admitted that his impeachment was 'virtually a foregone conclusion', but told congress that his 'mistakes' did not justify the 'extreme step' of removal from office. Surrounded by former advertising executives more used to handling accounts for Disneyland and toilet cleansers than upholding constitutional principles, Mr. Nixon consistently approached the Watergate scandal as a threat to his public image rather than to political ethics.

Historians may count this refusal to treat Watergate as anything more than a matter of partisan vindictiveness and public relations a prime reason for Mr. Nixon's fall. As Magruder told Robert Mardian, a Nixon campaign lawyer and former assistant Attorney General, the morning after the Watergate burglary: 'We have a slight P.R. problem.'

1 January 1973: The United Kingdom joins the Common Market
BRITAIN WELCOMED INTO EUROPE
SOAMES CALLS FOR SINGLE VOICE IN WORLD POLITICS
BETTER OPPORTUNITIES FOR EVERYONE, SAYS HEATH
By Walter Farr, Common Market Correspondent, in Brussels

The entry of Britain, Eire and Denmark into the nine-nation Common Market at midnight was welcomed in the Market capitals last night as a first step towards a political union of Europe. Mr. Heath, for whom entry is regarded as a persona] triumph, said last night that it was a 'tremendous moment'. It meant that there would be 'better jobs and a higher standard of living. People are going to have better opportunities of living'. Sir Christopher Soames, in his first public statement as a member of the Commission in Brussels, said Europe must increasingly be seen to be exercising its influence by speaking with one voice.

Mr. Godber, Minister of Agriculture, said yesterday that housewives would not be facing higher prices, at least for the first few months, and later increases should be offset by greater prosperity. Mr. Wilson said that he could not celebrate an event not supported by the British people and achieved on 'utterly crippling' terms.

Enlargement of the Market to nine States makes it the world's largest trading group. While Britain drops out of E.F.T.A. – the European Free Trade Association – six of its members are linking with the Market, and links are also being forged with fifteen Mediterranean countries and with African territories to bring in a total of over 300 million people.

Britain's entry into the Common Market at midnight last night was welcomed in Market capitals as the first step to a political union embracing the greater part of Western Europe. With a population of 253 million, the Market, officially known as the European Economic Community, is easily the world's largest trading group. As the Union Jack and the flags of the other eight members of the enlarged market were hoisted in front of the Brussels E.E.C. headquarters, a spokesman for its main decision-making body, the Council of Ministers, said:

'We hope that British entry, which is one of the most important events in the history of this part of the world, will give the community new political momentum. The Common Market itself, which will now be completed gradually in the next five years, is an important but dull side of European integration.

'Belgium, which takes over the presidency of the European communities for the next six months, has already been conferring with the British and other governments on giving full priority to plans agreed by the heads of government of the nine market countries at their Paris summit for forming a European political union capped by a reinforced European Parliament. These talks will be continued when

British ministers are formally received into the Council of Ministers in Brussels on 15 January.'

The spokesman said that the core of the political union would be a system for forging common foreign policies similar to the decision-making apparatus now used for common economic policies. 'As a first step the emphasis will be on agreeing on a common trading policy towards America and maintaining a common policy in the dealings of the Nine with Russia and other Communist countries. "British entry makes this possible, but there is an undercurrent of uncertainty about some British ministers and members of the Opposition who would prefer to slow down the process of integration, because of the strong opposition to entry in Britain.' Leaders of most of Britain's Market partners are confident that Sweden, Norway, Turkey, Spain, Portugal and, one day, Greece will become full members of the E.E.C.

Sir Christopher Soames and Mr. George Thomson, the two British members of the E.E.C. Commission, will move into their Brussels homes early this month. They will immediately begin work on the commission on outline proposals for substantial aid for Britain's development areas from Common Market central funds. In his first public statement since his appointment to the Commission was confirmed, Sir Christopher laid great stress on the need for European political union. Europe, he said, must increasingly be seen to be exercising its influence in the world by speaking with one voice. Mr. Thomson stressed the need for a stronger European Parliament to keep a close watch on Market decision-making. Proposals for strengthening the Parliament are due to be discussed informally when British Tory and Liberal MPs take their seats for the first time in Strasbourg on 15 January.

The Queen Victoria, a British-owned pub, opposite the Commission headquarters, remained open throughout the night and became the centre of the first celebrations of British entry. As Commission officials prepared to hoist the flags of the Nine members of the enlarged Market there were cheers from a party of Britons who had travelled from

London to join in the celebrations. At midnight Britons celebrated in Schuman Square in front of the Common Market headquarters by waving small paper Union Jacks and singing 'Roll Out the Barrel'. An attempt was made to sing 'Land of Hope and Glory', but it petered out. On the thirteenth floor of the headquarters members of the outgoing commission gave a Champagne party at which the staff practised their English on each other. Many have been taking crash courses since the autumn.

18 April 1975: The Khmer Rouge come to power in Cambodia
WELCOME OF WHITE FLAGS
By Kenneth Clarke in Bangkok

After five years ravaged by a civil war which left some 250,000 dead, Cambodia was under the control of the Communist Khmer Rouge forces last night. Phnom Penh, the capital, surrendered to them early yesterday, ending a siege of three and a half months. A sea of white flags greeted the insurgents as they entered the city at 1 a.m. London time. Five hours later, formal notice of surrender was signed by the Cambodian chief of operations, Brigadier-General Mey Sichan. The guns fell silent when the defending forces were ordered to stop fighting by their High Command. Within an hour, the black uniformed insurgents were taking control of the city.

Although Prince Norodom Sihanouk, ousted five years ago, is titular head of the Cambodian Government in exile in Peking, he was reported to have said yesterday that Khieu Samphan, his forty-five-year-old deputy premier and chief commander of the 'Armed Force of National Unity in Cambodia', would execute direct power in the country, with other Khmer Rouge leaders. Prince Sihanouk said he would continue to represent Cambodia abroad and would guarantee 'Cambodian policies of non-alignment'. He would return to Phnom Penh 'maybe in a couple of days, maybe in a couple of weeks'. The date was uncertain because his mother was dying.

As the Khmer Rouge troops entered Phnom Penh yesterday

after fighting their way to the edge of the city on Wednesday night, thousands of people lined the streets to wave to them.

Smiling soldiers from opposing armies embraced each other according to reports sent out before communications dried up. There was no indication of the bloodbath of revenge which some observers had feared. However, Phnom Penh radio, now in Communist hands, monitored at the Cambodian Embassy in Bangkok announced: 'We enter as conquerors and are not here to talk about peace with the traitors of the Phnom Penh clique.' The announcer said Phnom Penh's military commander, General Chim Guon. General Lon Don, brother of the exiled former President Lon Nol, and the Chief Monk of the city were among the first to give themselves up. Armoured cars, jeeps and Government military lorries toured the city displaying the white banners of surrender, ordered by the General Staff to prevent further bloodshed and destruction of the city. Gunboats sailed along the Mekong and Tonlé Sap rivers, also displaying white flags.

Colonel Oum Phin Lieou, Cambodian military attaché at the Embassy in Bangkok, said that before losing radio contact with his headquarters he had been told that Mr. Samphan had made a broadcast appealing for calm and advising senior Government officials to flee the country if they valued their lives.

The fall of Phnom Penh came, after a fierce insurgent assault across the Bassac river, just to the south of the city centre, and a heavy barrage of rocket fire and artillery. The decision to surrender was taken, according to radio monitoring, by General Mey Sichan in the absence of the newly formed ruling committee under General Sak Sutsakhan and Mr. Long Boret, the Prime Minister. The appeal was said to have been signed by General Sak Sutsakhan as head of the Supreme Ruling Committee. One agency report quoted Prince Sihanouk sources in Peking as saying: 'Sihanouk has rejected the offer of the quislings in Phnom Penh.' The proposals were said to be unacceptable and the Prince, ousted by the Lon Nol coup five years ago, warned the 'puppet

Supreme Committee' to leave Phnom Penh because they had earned the right only to be hanged.

Mr Long Boret returned there last week after seeing Marshal Lon Nol off to his exile, although he knows he is on the Khmer Rouge execution list. His announcement said that in view of appeals by religious leaders and in view of the absence of the Supreme Committee and the absence of the Government of the Khmer Republic, he had ordered the three armed services to stop shooting. Speaking as representative of the Cambodian national armed forces general staff, he invited the Khmer Rouge leadership to come to Phnom Penh and other provincial capitals. He said officials would make arrangements with organisations of brother Cambodians of the other side to maintain order and security.

1 May 1975: The end of the Vietnam War as Saigon falls to the Communists
HANOI'S MAY DAY TRIUMPH
JUBILANT TROOPS ROLL INTO SAIGON

As May Day dawned in Saigon today, the red-and-blue flag of the Viet Cong fluttered above the presidential palace, and the Communist invaders prepared to celebrate victory. The South Vietnamese capital, now renamed Ho Chi Minh City, surrendered almost without a struggle yesterday, twenty-one years all but one week after the French were finally defeated by Ho Chi Minh's Communist forces at Dien Bien Phu. After a day in which Viet Cong guerrillas and North Vietnamese regular troops were greeted by cheering crowds and a sea of white flags, communications with Saigon were cut off abruptly.

Before the black-out, Peter Gill, Our Staff Correspondent, who chose to remain in the city, managed to send this message:

North Vietnamese armour and lorry convoys carrying thousands of jubilant Communist troops poured into central Saigon yesterday afternoon as South Vietnam's new revolutionary Government prepared to celebrate 1 May as Victory Day. 'The city of Saigon has been completely liberated,' said Mr, Vũ Văn Mẫu, Prime Minister of the neutralist Government which took power two days ago. 'I ask all the people to be happy at the victory of the Provisional Revolutionary Government' (the Viet Cong).

The former Government's unconditional surrender to Communist forces already on the outskirts of the capital came at 10.20 a.m. (3.20 a.m. London time) in a short broadcast from General Duong Văn 'Big' Minh, South Vietnam's third President in ten days. National police were ordered to fly white flags from their posts throughout the city, and within less than two hours Russian-made tanks led the first Communist cavalcade into the centre of the city.

The message was then cut off. But it clear from earlier reports that the Communists met only isolated pockets of resistance.

Laughing guerrillas, some of them teenage girls, drove through the streets exchanging waves and banter with the Saigonese. The collapse came within hours of the final evacuation of Americans which was followed by the looting of the U.S. Embassy by an angry mob. Meanwhile at least 18,000 refugees have fled in an armada of small boats and rafts to the safety of American vessels in the South China Sea.

As scores of transport aircraft shuttle Vietnamese evacuees from Guam, Wake Island, and the Philippines to America at the rate of up to 5,000 a day, President Ford is still seeking Congressional approval for £136 million in humanitarian aid for South Vietnam. The money would be used to reimburse accounts from which he financed the evacuation, and to help care for refugees.

18 August 1977: The death of 'The King of Rock and Roll'
U.S. MOURNS PRESLEY THE LOST REBEL
By Ann Morrow in Memphis

The great gates of a house in the heart of blues country opened yesterday and women who were prettier twenty years ago went inside to see Elvis Presley lying in his coffin. Soon the burnt lawns, which looked neglected, were like a battlefield. . There were stretchers every-where as women were revived with bags of rice and in some cases oxygen. About ten thousand people were there and scuffles and fist-fights broke out. And in Washington even the White House was caught up in America's mourning for the 'King of Rock and Roll' whose death on Tuesday seemed a milestone in the progress of popular culture.

The White House switchboard had been flooded with calls demanding that President Carter declare a national day of mourning for Presley. A Californian couple sent a telegram chiding Mr. Carter for failing to issue a statement and saying: 'No death has moved the American people so much since the death of John Fitzgerald Kennedy.' And in due course the White House issued a statement quoting the President as saying: 'Elvis Presley's death deprived our country of a part of itself. He was unique and irreplaceable . . . his music and his personality, fusing the styles of White country and Black rhythm and blues, permanently changed the face of American popular culture. His following was immense and he was a symbol to people the world over of the vitality, rebelliousness and good humour of his country.'

In Memphis, Tennessee, where Presley died on Tuesday at the age of forty-two, women clutching flowers had waited all night at the gates of his house, Graceland. The gates were covered with tulle hearts. White satin crosses covered with plastic red roses, were among the other tributes. It was hard, in fact, to see any of the flowers which were not plastic. Everywhere, even on the doughnut cafes, flags flew at half-mast and motels quickly put up signs saying: 'Rest in peace, Elvis.'

Graceland, neo-Colonial, with green louvred shutters and grubby, grey net curtains, stands high on a hill. From a top window you can see the Mississippi river and fields of rice and soya beans. Against the warm stone of the house, rather like Cotswold stone, there were flowers – horseshoes, hearts and red roses galore with fulsome messages of love. In the hallway of the house, at the entrance to the music room, stood the coffin banked with red roses and red satin. Standing to attention nearby in black suits were the Presley entourage. For most of the crowd seeing the body so quickly was rather a shock. A great knuckleduster ring was on one of his fingers and he really looked very tranquil.

The early dumb shock which had subdued the crowds changed through the day to anger and hysteria. At first there were only hundreds, but by the after moon there were nearly 3,000. They hammered on the gates to be allowed in for the macabre viewing. When the news got out that the fans would be allowed to see their rock'n'roll hero, and singer of songs like 'Hound Dog', 'Heartbreak Hotel' and 'Blue Suede Shoes', there had been a mad rush to the gates of the house, which has a juke box by the pool. The sheriff of Shelby County, Mr. Gene Barksdale, told the crowds: 'Elvis is looking just beautiful. He is in a copper casket lined with grey silk. He is wearing a white suit, a blue tie and a blue shirt.'

All day showbusiness friends were being driven into the house. But somebody attached to the Presley entourage said: 'He was more or less alone when he died.' There was some bitterness about allegations that he had been heavily reliant on drugs. But his addiction seems to have been much more to peanut butter, banana sandwiches and soda water. After a preliminary examination of the body, both Presley's personal physician, Dr. George Nichopoulos, and the local medical examiner said there was no evidence of drug abuse. The medical examiner, Dr. Jerry Francisco, said the preliminary examination showed Presley had died of a cardiac arrhythmia, or abnormal heart beat, due to undetermined causes.

All day fans poured into Memphis from all over the country. On a flight from Washington the sobs of one of his most devoted fans, thirty-four-year-old Miss Faith Townsend rather upset the rest of the passengers including Miss Caroline Kennedy. Miss Kennedy was trying to get some sleep – before working on the Presley assignment from the *New York News* where she is working as a copy girl. 'I thought it was bad enough that he was thinking of getting married again but this is unbelievable,' said Miss Townsend between applications of a damp tissue to her already pink nose. 'I had been making him a beautiful blanket, embroidering it with the words "The King of Music". He kissed me once.'

26 July 1978: Little fanfare for the first test-tube baby
TEST-TUBE BABY IS 5lb GIRL
By a *Daily Telegraph* Reporter

The world's first test-tube baby – a 5lb 12oz girl – was born just after midnight today. She is believed to have been delivered by caesarean section. She was born at Oldham General Hospital. The mother, Mrs. Lesley Browns, thirty-two, wife of a Bristol railway worker, and the baby were reported to be 'doing well', early today. A doctor said her condition at birth was normal.

The baby is the first to be conceived by the technique of fertilisation outside the mother's body, pioneered by the hospital's gynaecologist, Mr. Patrick Steptoe, and the Cambridge physiologist, Dr. Robert Edwards. Mrs. Brown and her husband Gilbert, thirty-eight, of Hassell Drive, Bristol, went to see Mr. Steptoe after they had been told they could not have children.

Mr. Steptoe and Dr. Edwards have spent more than twelve years perfecting the technique of removing the egg from a woman, fertilising it with the husband's sperm in the laboratory and implanting it in the womb. This method by-passes obstruction in fallopian tubes which can prevent fertilisation. The technique has already been tried in scores of cases but until now pregnancy has failed to go the full term.

19 August 1978: The first crossing of the Atlantic by balloon
NOW ROUND THE WORLD, SAY BALLOONISTS
By Tony Allen-Mills in Paris

Fresh from their triumph as the world's first transatlantic balloon-ists, three American adventurers yesterday set their sights on a new target – a balloon trip around the world in thirty days. Less than twenty-four hours after arriving in France at the end of a six-day, 3,000-mile odyssey on board the helium-filled balloon *Double Eagle*

II, Ben Abruzzo, forty-eight, Maxie Anderson, forty-four, and Larry Newman, fifty-one, were full of plans for their next epic voyage. Their transatlantic journey shattered world balloonist distance and endurance records. It was the first to beat the Atlantic after seventeen previous attempts.

The three men, all from Albuquerque, New Mexico, had only redrimmed eyes and, in Anderson's case slightly shaking hands, to show for their 137 hours and six minutes' flight from Presque Isle, Maine, to a barley field outside a small village, near Évreux, fifty-five miles west of Paris. But Ben Abruzzo made it clear at a Press conference yesterday that he had no intention of resting on his laurels. 'When we landed last night I said I'd quit this ballooning for good,' he said. 'But I woke up in the middle of the night and thought of a new voyage which I know we have to try. With our experience and technical know-how I am sure we can build a craft that will take us around the world, not in eighty but in thirty days. A lot of work will need to be done, but this trip has shown us that we can do it.'

Having only thought of the round-the-world trip hours previously, Abruzzo could offer no details of the proposed journey. 'After we've got home and had a rest, then we'll start studying the charts to see how it can be done,' he said. One of the sponsors for the *Double Eagle* expedition, Ross McAllister, commented that the main problem would be staying aloft for such a length of time. 'I don't think it could be done with helium — maybe something like hydrogen would work — and they'd have to travel at a much higher altitude than this time,' he said.

The announcement clearly came as a surprise to Anderson, who seemed to be suffering more than the other two from fatigue and prolonged exposure to freezing high-altitude temperatures. But he nodded and smiled his agreement. Larry Newman, the youngest crewman, arrived an hour late at the Press conference, held in the American Embassy, having overslept after a late-night visit to Maxim's restaurant to celebrate his arrival. Hugging his wife, Sandra, he commented: 'If

Ben and Maxie want to go around the world in thirty days, then I'll be right along there beside them.' Asked if his late arrival was connected with the softness of a bed in the American Ambassador's residence which had been used by Charles Lindbergh after his transatlantic solo flight in 1927, Newman looked at his wife and smiled bashfully. The American Ambassador had offered the balloonists the use of the historic room and Newman won the right to sleep in it after tossing a coin with the others.

Congratulations flowed into Paris from all over the world, including an invitation to visit the White House from President Carter. But Abruzzo made it clear one of the most valued messages was a telephone call yesterday morning from British balloonist Major Christopher Davey, of the Royal Tank Regiment, who narrowly failed in his attempt to cross the Atlantic three weeks ago when his balloon *Zanussi*, co-piloted by Donald Cameron, sank into the sea 117 miles off the French coast. Abruzzo said: 'Chris Davey telephoned us with the following message – "We congratulate you with a stiff upper lip – although we're weakening fast".'

Talking to Davey about the flight, Abruzzo said there were two things which had 'brought the Englishman to tears'. Firstly, *Double Eagle* had drifted over South-Western England, where leading British balloonists had their headquarters. 'Then to add insult to injury, we passed directly over the barracks of Major Davey's Army regiment – I think that brought him to his knees with grief,' Abruzzo added with a grin. One the main items on their schedule for the next few days was a trip to England to have dinner with Davey and Cameron, he added.

Anderson said that the flight had been relatively trouble-free. 'The worst ordeal was probably about a day and a half off the Irish coast. Our hearts really came into our mouths when we hit a trough and suddenly sank from about 27,000 to 4,000 feet. We didn't want to use up our essential ballast to regain height because of the experience of our last attempt to cross the Atlantic, when we ended up in the water off Iceland. We hung on for a couple of hours, then the afternoon sun warmed the balloon and we regained altitude,' he said.

Shortly before crossing the Irish coast the three crew members, fearing that they might run short of helium to stay aloft, tossed all non-essential gear overboard, including an expensive and computerised navigational system. 'Everything except basic food supplies and the radio went. We knew at that stage we could do without the navigation and as it weighed 30lb, into the sea it went,' Abruzzo said. Among the items jettisoned was the hang-glider with which Larry Newman had hoped to land at the end of the journey.

The Americans said they had two priorities during the journey – to get exercise and to sleep as much as possible. 'It wasn't easy getting exercise in a space eight foot by six,' Anderson commented. 'But we would shift our gear from one side of the catamaran [designed to give the crew maximum protection in the event of a ditching] to the other, and then after a rest, move it all back again. We knew from the experience of Davey and Cameron that our main enemy was exhaustion, so we were determined to get some sleep. The main problem for the British was that after the third day they were so tired they couldn't think well. We would sleep in shifts for about four and a half hours at a time at night, then try and grab another hour and a half during the day.'

Abruzzo and Anderson were responsible for the piloting of the craft – coaxing it to different altitudes to take advantage of favourable winds, while Newman handled the radio and navigation systems. In more reflective mood, Anderson was asked what he felt he had achieved by floating from America to Europe. 'We haven't made history, we've only completed it,' he said. 'People have been trying to do it since 1873 and now we've closed the book. And there's something else. Travelling in that balloon, you are standing on a balcony in the clouds and watching the world go by. It's such a magnificent sight. All in complete silence, that it can't be compared to anything else.'

Abruzzo, a property dealer, has been flying aircraft since his teens and is a balloonist with hundreds of hours' experience. Newman, a former airline pilot, now runs a hang-gliding manufacturing company and Anderson runs a mining business.

The giant silver and black balloon, 115 feet high, was yesterday being folded ready for return to America, where it will be displayed in the Smithsonian Institute in Washington. 'We don't know what state it is in,' Anderson said. 'Last night some French sightseers were so anxious to get a piece as a souvenir that they were tearing at it with their teeth.' Not every Frenchman was anxious to fete the three Americans however. Normandy farmer Roger Coquerelle was yesterday planning an official complaint after his field of barley was crushed by the hordes of well-wishers in their rush to reach the balloon.

17 January 1979: Revolution in Iran causes the downfall of the Shah
IRANIANS DANCE AS WEEPING SHAH QUITS
By James Allan in Teheran

Jubilant Iranians danced on the rooftops and in the streets yesterday when news that the Shah had left the country was broadcast on the national radio. Car drivers flashed their headlights and blew their horns while people ran excitedly from their homes and kissed and hugged each other with delight. Teheran became an endless traffic jam of noisy cars plastered with photographs of the Ayatollah Khomeini, the seventy-eight-year-old Shi'ite Moslem leader, who lives in exile in Paris.

Soldiers waving flowers instead of rifles joined with the crowds in the celebrations. Men and women clambered over army lorries, tanks and armoured cars to embrace the smiling troops. And the soldiers did not intervene when statues of the Shah, and of his father, were toppled from their plinths and smashed. Military helicopters whirred overhead, but the buzz of their engines was drowned in the din of hooters and chanting from the streets below.

The Shah and Queen Farah had only been gone about forty-five minutes when the news of their departure was broadcast to a nation which had been eagerly expecting it for days. Arrangements for the departure broke down in the sort of chaos and maladministration which has bedevilled Iran in its attempts to capitalise on its oil income and launch grandiose but badly-thought-out development projects.

A palace spokesman, still insisting that the Shah would not leave yesterday, organised a Press conference and took about fifty reporters to the airport where they were told it had been postponed till today and that the King had no intention of leaving yesterday. While the journalists were on the way back to the city centre the Shah and the Queen flew in a helicopter to the airport to be met by officials of the court and senior army officers, who also arrived by a fleet of helicopters bearing the Royal crest. As the Shah said goodbye to his entourage in the Imperial Pavilion there were tears in his eyes. Back at the Niavaran Palace, many of his staff and servants wept, too.

His departure was delayed for thirty minutes because Dr. Shapour Bakhtiar, the new Prime Minister, had to wait tell the Lower House of Parliament had given his civilian government a vote of confidence by 142 to 43, with thirteen abstentions. Eventually the Shah and the Queen were ready to leave and they boarded a Boeing 707 in blue and white livery which the Shah piloted himself on its journey to Aswan where he was to meet President Sadat of Egypt and spend a week's holiday. The Shah's three younger children Princess Farahnaz, fifteen, Prince Alireza, twelve, and Princess Leila, eight, and the Queen's mother had already left Iran quietly the previous evening in a military jet. It was learned later that they had arrived in Lubbock, Texas, to stay with the eighteen-year-old Crown Prince Reza at his lavish home there.

Before he left Iran, the Shah said: 'As I said when this Government was formed, I am feeling tired and need a rest. I also stated that when I felt that things were going well and the Government was settled I would take a trip and that trip starts now. I hope that the Government will be able to make up for the past and also be able to lay the foundations for the future. To achieve this we will need for a period of time co-operation and patriotism in its highest sense. Our economy must start again, the people must re-start their lives and we must prepare a better plan for the future. I have nothing else to say except that I will fulfil my duties on the basis of patriotism.' Before he left Iran, the Shah wished the new government every success and said he hoped it could undo the mistakes of the past. Asked how long he would be away, the Shah replied softly: 'I don't know.'

But the countless thousands of people still dancing and cheering in the streets last night were in no doubt. 'The Shah went. He's not coming back,' they shouted at each other and to anyone else in the vicinity. For them and for the Shah yesterday was the end of a thirty-seven-year reign that began when his father was deposed by Britain and Russia in 1941. It may also be the end of his dynasty and of 2,500 years of monarchy in Persia. The country which has been wracked by death and destruction for more than a year with little respite may now be in for a brief honeymoon, but acutely serious problems remain.

Fears of a coup are still widespread despite assurances by the generals that they would not allow one to happen. But perhaps equally dangerous for Iran's future stability is the steadily increasing level of activity by terrorist groups who, though not of any considerable size, could provoke a military backlash. Their latest victim was a retired American Army colonel living in Kerman, who had his throat cut this week with a piece of glass taken from his own back door. Three policemen were killed by terrorists on Monday in the city of Tabriz near the Turkish border, while Communists in the country are becoming more vociferous in their advocacy of an armed struggle.

In the Shah's absence, the powers of the monarchy will be taken over by the nine-man Regency Council appointed last Saturday. It includes the Prime Minister together with the heads of both houses of Parliament, a general, and several former politicians. But because the council represents the monarchy, which the Ayatollah Khomeini regards as illegal, he sees the council as illegal, too.

6 May 1980: Drama in London caught on television as the SAS end siege of the Iranian Embassy
SAS SQUAD STORM SIEGE EMBASSY
TWO HOSTAGES WERE MURDERED – SO WE HAD TO MOVE IN, SAYS McNEE
THREE TERRORISTS KILLED IN RESCUE AT BLAZING BUILDING
By T.A. Sandrock, Brian Silk and Gerald Bartlett

The six-day siege of the Iranian Embassy in Knightsbridge ended last night in a joint police-Special Air Services Regiment operation which resulted in the nineteen remaining hostages being brought alive from the burning, bomb-blasted building, and the deaths of three of the five gunmen. Sir David McNee, Metropolitan Police Commissioner, said the Embassy was stormed after it was learned that two hostages inside the building had been killed. The terrorists had threatened to kill one hostage every half-hour unless their demands were met. 'There was no alternative but to send in the SAS to end the siege,' Sir David added. Mr. Whitelaw, Home Secretary, who was at the scene, said: 'This operation will show that we in Britain will not tolerate terrorism. The world must learn this.'

Among the hostages rescued were three Britons – PC Trevor Lock, Simeon Harris, a BBC sound recordist, and Mr. Ronald Morris, a clerk at the embassy. One of the terrorists who survived the storming of the embassy was in hospital. The other was in custody. Iran's consul-general, Dr. Saytollah Ehdaie said later that one of the hostages shot by the gunmen was Abbas Lavasani, twenty-eight, the embassy's Press attaché. Dr. Ehdaie said: 'He wanted to be a martyr for Islam. We do not mourn his death. We are happy his wish was granted.' A Scotland Yard spokesman said three men, all believed to be Iranians, were seriously ill at St. Stephen's Hospital, Fulham, with gunshot wounds. The spokesman added that fourteen men and five women hostages were taken to the hospital, but not detained. Last night the rescued hostages were staying at a secret London address recovering from their ordeal.

After being interviewed by police they were being reunited with relatives.

The gunmen seized the embassy and the hostages last Wednesday and demanded the release of ninety-one political prisoners held in Iran's Khuzestan Province, where the mainly Arab population is demanding autonomy. At his Press conference, Sir David McNee said two bombs had gone off in the embassy before it was stormed, two people had been reported killed and there was a real threat that a third hostage would be killed. He said it was a matter of deep regret for him that the siege had ended in violence after every possible means had been tried to bring it to a peaceful conclusion. The hostages had been through a grim ordeal, and PC Lock had conducted himself throughout with a heroism which had won the admiration of all.

Ninety minutes after the explosions tore the heart out of the embassy, Mr. Whitelaw went to the Press Conference in the Royal Geographical Society, 150 yards away, and paid glowing tribute to the conduct of the police. 'I would like on behalf of the Government and I believe the people of this country to pay a very considerable tribute to the way the police handled this action,' he said. Sir David McNee said the SAS had been brought into the operation with the approval of Mr. Whitelaw. After fifteen minutes, the Home Secretary cut the Press conference short, saying that crimes were involved and he himself had a statement to make to Parliament today. He did not feel that detailed questions were appropriate at this time.

When police were trying to 'clear up' after the dramatic end to the siege, supporters of the Ayatollah Khomeini at barriers outside the Royal Albert Hall continued their demonstration chanting 'The C.I.A., C.I.A.' Some tried to break through the cordon of police, but were restrained. At dusk, firemen were still fighting to contain the blaze at the embassy which followed the explosions. Flames were leaping several feet through the gutted roof and a pall of black smoke, pushed by the stiff breezes, spread outwards and downwards over the waiting policemen.

Deputy Assistant Commissioner, John Dellow, who had been in charge of the siege operations, declined to answer questions, saying the matter was *sub judice* because a crime had been committed. He also refused to give the source of the explosions. There had been speculation that the explosions occurred because the SAS moved in, and also speculation that they may have used some sort of 'thunderflash' grenade to start with as a distraction for their assault.

It was disclosed that Sir David McNee had written a personal letter to the gunmen seeking their co-operation for a successful and peaceful conclusion to the incident. It was delivered to the embassy at 6.30 p.m. Just before 7 p.m. the body of a hostage murdered inside the embassy was pushed out of the entrance and a police stretcher party carried it away. Police began to suspect the situation between their negotiators and the gunmen was changing when, during late morning, the gunmen appeared irritated in their conversations and also tired. It was about an hour later around 1.20 p.m. that three shots were heard and the first hostage was killed. It was after this that the threats to kill one hostage every half-an-hour was made. Sir David's appeal to the gunmen was delivered, but there was no response. Then police called on the services of an Imam to speak to the gunmen by the police landline used during the negotiations. The religious leader had just finished his conversations when three more shots were heard. It was these shots that led police to believe that a second hostage had been killed.

The end of the siege came at 7.24 p.m. when the first explosion ripped through the embassy followed in less than a second by a second blast. Black smoke billowed up over the rooftop, the sky was full of screeching birds and on the ground police officers were hugging walls, bushes, vehicles as they ran doubled up with revolvers drawn. At the Press enclosure 150 yards away, journalists ran in confusion sending camera tripods, collapsible chairs, steel barriers flying, and tripping over cables. A girl television reporter yelling at her team: 'Give me a mike', and then, in the same breath, 'Get down, get down.' As one burst of shots came from the embassy, police and reporters fell over themselves as they ran from an exposed corner to dive behind the television and radio vans.

While the shooting continued and the air was filled with the choking smell from the smoke, down the road at the Albert Memorial gangs of skinheads were yelling in chorus. After only five minutes flames appeared at a first-floor window of the embassy and shortly afterwards a white flag was waved from another window directly above, but still the shooting continued. Above the cloud of black smoke a police helicopter appeared and circled overhead. Round the corner in Exhibition Road, women were screaming as gunfire began within seconds of the second explosion. There was automatic fire and single shots, and on a balcony only two doors from the embassy two police marksmen stood out in the open their rifles trained on the upper windows where the terrorists were exchanging fire. Most of the action appeared to be at the rear of the building as policemen were seen in Queen's Gate running with stretchers.

Many ambulances were standing by, but they could not get close because of the gunfire. After twenty minutes the fire took hold and flames were leaping up from the front of the building. Police carrying gas masks were running close to the entrance as the black smoke whirled above them. Then a dozen police ran to the Press barrier and hurled the steel railings aside to make way for fire engines to get through. Immediately after the first explosion eight of the hostages came out from a side exit of the embassy. They were obviously badly shaken, but were walking with the aid of police. Three stretchers were later carried out of the same exit. When the police standby was ordered just before the explosion, men from the Special Air Services Regiment assembled on the roof of the embassy. Immediately after the first explosion, ropes were lowered down the back of the embassy and SAS men slid down them, kicking in windows as they travelled and all gained entrance that way.

*

The text of the letter sent by Sir David McNee to the terrorists was issued last night. It said:

> I think it is right that I should explain to you clearly and in writing the way in which my police officers are dealing with the taking of hostages in the Iranian Embassy.
>
> I am responsible for preserving the peace and enforcing the law in London and I do this independently of politicians and government. I and my officers deeply wish to work to a peaceful solution of what has occurred.
>
> We fully understand how both the hostages and those who hold them feel threatened and frightened. You are cut off from your families and friends.
>
> But you need not feel frightened or threatened by the police. It is not our way in Britain to resort to violence against those who are peaceful.
>
> You have nothing to fear from my officers provided you do not harm those in your care. I firmly hope we can now bring this incident to a close peacefully and calmly.

Sir David's letter was written in English and Farsi, the Iranian language.

Earlier yesterday there was little activity at the besieged embassy as the Foreign Office continued discussions with Arab ambassadors in an attempt to achieve a peaceful end to the affair. The only real flurry of activity came when Mr. Simeon Harris, the BBC sound recordist, appeared at an upstairs window. It was the first time he had been seen since being taken hostage when the siege began. Three times in about twenty minutes he appeared at the window, the last time for about four minutes and accompanied by PC Trevor Lock. Mr. Harris spoke to four people standing on the pavement and at times emphasised what he was saying by vigorously waving his arms. The details of his conversations were not disclosed.

The attitude of the gunmen has changed little, according to the police, most times being 'mild', but sometimes being 'not so mild'. Throughout the day, at irregular intervals, the police negotiators or the gunmen opened conversations varying its length from three minutes to twenty minutes, and all conducted by telephone. The gunmen were thought to be holding the hostages in two rooms and appeared to be taking turns in guarding the hostages, talking to the police, and resting. Only one hostage at a time was being allowed to go to the lavatory under guard. None was allowed out of the rooms when any of the hostages were appearing at the windows to speak to police outside. Anyone speaking from the window had an armed guard. Although food had been passed into the embassy only three times since the siege began last Wednesday, police believe there were still sufficient supplies inside and that some of the women hostages had been ordered to prepare meals.

Sir David McNee, who cut short his holiday last week because of the siege, cancelled a visit to an international police chiefs' conference in Vienna which started yesterday and visited the scene several times yesterday. He has been reporting directly to Mr. Whitelaw, Home Secretary.

Until last night it looked as though the police waiting game – learned in previous sieges – was working. The policy of patience had paid dividends in every previous case: four I.R.A. gunmen surrendered to the police after six days at the last big siege in London – in December 1975 – when they took hostages inside a Balcombe Street flat; two months earlier police waited five days before armed robbers finally gave in at the Spaghetti House Restaurant in Knightsbridge.

21 May 1980: Mount St. Helens erupts
NINE DIE AS BLAST LOPS 2,000 FEET OFF U.S. VOLCANO
By Ian Brodie in Portland, Oregon

Nine deaths were confirmed and many people unaccounted for yesterday following the tremendous eruption of America's volcanic Mount St. Helens. The eruption seared a fifteen-mile arc on the north flank, unleashed massive mud flows, blotted out the sun with a huge column of black ash, and lopped 2,000 feet off the peak.

Among the missing was Harry Truman, the stubborn, eighty-four-year-old Presidential namesake who spent his life on the mountain and became something of a celebrity by rejecting every plea to leave. Spirit Lake, the hamlet at 4,000 feet where he lived with his sixteen cats and eighteen racoons, was wiped out by the explosive force of the eruption and the mud-flows triggered by tons of ice and snow which thawed instantly in the tremendous heat. Eight of the dead were trapped in their cars by mud or heat while the ninth victim was a crop-dusting pilot, apparently blinded by ash, who flew into a power line one hundred miles away. Two loggers miraculously walked out of the devastated area with burns over more than a third of their bodies.

Dr. Bob Christiansen of the United States Geological Survey, who had predicted Sunday's eruption, said that now Mount St. Helens had blown her top the pressures which had been building up had been released and another major eruption was unlikely. More than 2,000 people fled or were rescued by helicopter from the rugged area, forty miles north-east of Portland and a popular spot for hunting, fishing and cross-country skiing. The column of sulphurous ash belched thirteen miles into the sky and winds carried it hundreds of miles. In Yakima in Washington State, the 'black snow' turned mid-day into midnight as it settled to a depth of two to three inches. Hospital reported that those with respiratory ailments were having difficulties and people were advised to stay indoors and to breathe through gauze masks.

Captain Fred Stovel, an Air Force helicopter pilot flying rescue missions, said: 'I saw a great swath of destruction. All the trees were lying parallel, like big spokes emanating from the centre of the mountain. I don't believe anyone could have survived in the area.' Authorities feared herds of deer and elk were wiped out, too, although some dazed and frightened survivors were observed from the air. Elsewhere the mud flows, oozing along at 35 m.p.h, tore out bridges, buried cabins and caused flash floods. Ten-foot walls of water hurtled down the Toutle River carrying homes, cars and hundreds of logs in their path.

Local radio stations and newspapers were besieged by calls about the fate of Mr. Truman, who ran a small lodge for overnight guests. He refused to leave when Mount St. Helens began her convulsions in March after lying dormant for 123 years. The crusty, weather-beaten old man, whose wife died three years ago, had said: 'If I was forced to leave it would kill me. I have enough whisky and food in the larder to last me eight weeks. I'm not afraid of the mountain and I know the mountain isn't going to get me.' Geologists believe the eruption may have matched one 3,500 years ago when Mount St. Helens laid down a two-foot layer of pumice ash as far as fifty miles away, and another 450 years ago.

27 September 1980: China's one-child policy barely attracts the *Telegraph*'s attention
ONE CHILD ONLY ORDER IN CHINA
By Graham Earnshaw in Peking

The Central Committee of the Chinese Communist party has directed all party members and the Communist Youth League to set an example to the country by having only one child. The directive, carried in the *People's Daily*, did not indicate whether punitive measures would be taken against parents who disobeyed the ruling. It said China had to limit the population growth or risk national economic problems.

10 December 1980: The murder of a Beatle
LENNON WAS STALKED FOR THREE DAYS
WEEPING BEATLES FANS GATHER ON SITE OF MANHATTAN SHOOTING
KILLER 'PLOTTED AND SAVED FOR MURDER'
By Ian Ball in New York

A twenty-five-old man who ambushed John Lennon and shot him dead at point-blank range outside his New York home had stalked the former Beatle for three days, police said yesterday. Later, when Texas-born Mark David Chapman was formally charged in Manhattan Criminal Court with second degree murder, Assistant District Attorney Kim Hogrefe indicated that he had flown five thousand miles to New York from Honolulu specifically to kill Lennon. 'He borrowed to come to New York City to do what he has done,' said Mr. Hogrefe who described the killing as 'the deliberate, premeditated execution of John Lennon'.

The prosecutor said Chapman, unemployed for some time, was carrying $2,000 (about £830) in cash when he was seized moments after Lennon was shot. Mr. Hogrefe also said Chapman had a police record dating back to 1972, including an arrest this year for armed robbery and abduction. But later the police said that Chapman – who was able to buy his .38 calibre revolver at a Honolulu gunshop six weeks ago without any trouble – had no record. He had been confused with a man with a similar name and date of birth.

His court-appointed lawyer, Mr. Herbert Alderberg, said Chapman had twice attempted suicide and had been placed in mental institutions. The lawyer left some confusion over Chapman's reason for stalking Lennon. In court, he called the shooting 'a motiveless crime'. But after the proceedings he told reporters that his client had told him why he shot Lennon. He declined to elaborate beyond saying that 'he's been a fan of John Lennon since he was ten years old', and that he 'liked all the Beatles'.

Chapman was remanded in custody for a psychiatric examination.

Under New York State law, a first degree murder charge is allowed only after the killing of a law-enforcement officer. Before the court hearing, Chapman was held under unusually heavy security in the Tombs Prison in Manhattan, where a detective lieutenant said the killing was being considered 'just as important as the assassination of John F. Kennedy'. As he spoke, an all-night vigil by Beatle fans at the scene of the shooting had grown into a crowd of more than a thousand, some playing Lennon's songs on tape recorders, others threading flowers through the nineteenth-century apartment building's wrought-iron gates. Some of the Beatle generation, men and women, wept publicly.

Chapman was seen over the weekend loitering outside the Dakota, a stately, chateau-type apartment building where Lennon had bought five flats in recent years and was creating a spacious private domain overlooking Central Park. Some six hours before Chapman fired five times at Lennon, hitting him in the chest, back and one arm, the Beatle had autographed a record album for him. The young man had accosted Lennon as he and his Japanese-American wife, Yoko Ono, were leaving the Dakota to go to a recording studio.

Chapman, according to the police account, was crouching by the entrance to the Dakota courtyard when the Lennons returned by limousine from the recording studio at about 11 p.m. (4 a.m. Tuesday, British time). Instead of driving into the courtyard as many of the public figures who live at the Dakota are in the habit of doing, the Lennons got out of their Cadillac in the street and were walking under the building's high arched entrance. Chapman, according to Chief of Detectives James Sullivan, approached the couple with the revolver aimed at them. 'Mr. Lennon?' he asked. Then, without waiting for a reply, Chapman took what Sullivan described as a 'combat stance' and emptied his revolver at the Beatle. Three bullets which struck Lennon's chest severed major arteries to the heart. 'I'm shot!' Lennon gasped as he staggered up six steps to an office area where he collapsed. Police said Chapman stood in the courtyard and dropped the empty revolver.

The message 'Man shot – 1 West 72nd Street' was soon crackling over the police radio. The crew of the first patrol car at the scene – the men who arrested Chapman – contained two officers who described themselves as Beatles fans in their youth. One of them, officer Tony Palma, lifted the dying man from a pool of blood and placed him in the back of another patrol car for a futile dash to Roosevelt Hospital, a few hundred yards away. Several people who heard the shots and saw Chapman before he was taken away said that he seemed to be pleased with what he had done. 'He was smirking when the police look him away,' said one witness.

A surprising number of Beatle-lovers were affected so intensely by Lennon's murder that they talk of revenge. 'The switchboard's been lighting up here all night with threats,' said one New York policeman. He indicated that this was one reason why extraordinary security precautions had been ordered. 'We did not want another Jack Ruby,' the police officer said, referring to the Texan who shot and killed Lee Harvey Oswald in police headquarters in Dallas before he could be brought to trial for the assassination of President Kennedy.

Lennon was close to death when he arrived at the hospital but desperate measures were used to try to resuscitate him. 'We opened his chest and massaged his heart,' said Dr. Stephen Lynn, Director of Emergency Services. 'They're working on him like crazy,' said a hospital worker. 'There's blood all over the place.' A second police car had taken Lennon's wife to the hospital. She was not injured in the shooting but was on the point of collapse and had to be helped by friends. 'Tell me it isn't true,' she sobbed repeatedly when doctors said her husband was dead. Later she called for a silent vigil in memory of her husband. She said: 'There is no funeral for John. Later in the week we will set the time for a silent vigil to pray for his soul.'

Lennon, the angriest and certainly the most mystical of the Beatles, had found what he considered 'a sense of security' living in New York and spending weekends and summers at a waterfront estate on Long Island, a retreat secluded enough to permit Lennon and his wife to swim and sunbathe nude with their young son, Sean. The income from record royalties and films assured a life of leisured ease. Death came to him just as his musical career seemed ready to take off again after a dormant period following the break-up of the Beatles. A long-playing album, *Double Fantasy*, which he recorded in August with Yoko Ono, is now in the American Top 20 chart. He was busy composing again and was about to plunge into a new recording programme.

Eerily, only hours before he was shot, Lennon had talked of death. In a radio interview on Monday, he said he hoped to die before his wife 'because if Yoko died, I wouldn't know how to survive, I couldn't carry on'. He also spoke optimistically about his future as he re-entered the musical world, describing his new album as a greeting to long-time fans. 'I hope the young kids like it as well, but I'm really talking to the people who grew up with me. 'I'm saying, "Here I am now. How are you? How's your relationship going? Did you get through it all? Wasn't the '70s a drag, you know? Well, here we are, Let's make the '80s great because it's up to us to make what we can of it . . ." You have to give thanks to God or whatever is up there (for) the fact that we all survived. We all survived Vietnam, or Watergate, the tremendous upheaval of the whole world. We were the hit ones of the '60s. But the world's not like the '60s. The whole world's changed. I am going into an unknown future, but I'm still all here, and while there's life there's hope.'

America's mourning for John Winston Lennon was impressive in its scope, and sincerity. Some radio stations dropped all advertising during the morning so they could comply with requests from listeners for Beatles favourites. Many radio stations recorded telephoned expressions of grief from listeners and played them in breaks between the Beatles records. Many fans asked where they could send flowers. In record shops across the country, there was a rush to buy Lennon's newest album and Beatles records. Even President-elect Reagan, in New York for a brief visit before moving on to Washington to continue the work of assembling his Cabinet, offered a tribute. He described the Beatle's death as 'a great tragedy', but said his opposition to tougher gun-control laws had not changed. President Carter said in Washington that he was 'saddened' by Lennon's death and 'distressed by the senseless manner of it'. He added that Lennon had 'helped create the music and mood of our time'. Ringo Starr, the Beatle who was perhaps closest to Lennon, broke off a holiday with his wife to fly to New York yesterday. They spent about half an hour with Lennon's widow.

The feelings of the crowd outside the Lennons' home could be gauged from their comments:

'For every momentous occasion in my life there was a Beatle song – for all my romances there was a different Beatle tune' . . . 'What he gave the world can't be comprehended' . . .

'They were a part of my life, whether I wanted them to be or not' . . . 'From the time I was seven, I breathed the Beatles' . . . 'His music got us through a whole decade' . . . 'I guess this truly is the end of the '60s' . . . 'They just shot a genius – he took us places where he had never been before.'

30 July 1981: Prince Charles marries Diana
FAIRY-TALE WEDDING
WORLD AUDIENCE SEES PALACE KISS SET THE SEAL ON DAY OF PAGEANTRY AND JOY
MILLIONS SHARE HAPPINESS OF SPARKLING COUPLE
By Tony Allen-Mills

On a rare and enchanting day of popular joy, the Prince of Wales was married yesterday to Lady Diana Spencer, an English beauty who, by broad and affectionate acclaim, makes a perfect Princess and future Queen. After months of hectic and sometimes turbulent preparation, the stillness and majesty of St. Paul's Cathedral provided a magnificent setting for an occasion that will sparkle long in the memories of the royal couple, and the millions around the world who were able to share in their happiness.

There was the simple exchange of the wedding vows (with diverting errors by both bride and groom); the rich pageantry of the carriage processions; and the excitement of the common crowds, delighted most when the Prince and Princess of Wales obliged with a kiss on the balcony of Buckingham Palace, All these things, relayed by television to 700 million people, made a magical spectacle which, in the words of the Archbishop of Canterbury, Dr. Runcie, was the 'stuff of which fairy tales are made'.

The day, which mercifully stayed warm and dry, was filled with glorious moments to remember. The highlight for some was the captivating first sight of the bride in her dress, a floating cloud of ivory silk; for others, it was the fun of the honeymoon departure in an open carriage festooned with balloons and a 'Just Married' sign. Many, too, will have found special pleasure in the moving smile of joy that creased the face of the Queen as her eldest son was joined by his bride inside St. Paul's.

But if yesterday was full of pleasure for all the world, it was above all a day for the couple themselves. When the pomp and ceremony had finally died away, the enduring image was of the Prince and his lovely bride plighting their troths beneath the soaring Cathedral dome. Prince Charles, resplendent in his uniform as a naval commander, answered 'I will' in soft but clearly audible tones. His bride, her face hidden by her veil, seemed equally composed, but a trace of nerves showed charmingly through when she was asked by Dr. Runcie to take Charles Philip Arthur George as her wedded husband. 'I, Diana Frances, take thee, Philip Charles . . .' she responded, to the amusement of the Prince. But the score was appropriately evened when the Prince himself slipped up, omitting the word 'worldly' from his pledge to share his goods with his new wife.

Those minor mishaps apart, the service passed off as a brilliant success. Prince Charles had confessed that he had always longed for a musical wedding, and the mixture of ancient texts and more modern music proved a triumph. Sir David Willcocks, the Director of the Royal College of Music, conducted his own inspired setting of the National Anthem, the New Zealand Maori soprano Kiri Te

Kanawa was in stirring voice, and trumpet fanfares provided dramatic punctuation for the events of the morning. The Address was given by Dr. Runcie, who saw the 'fairy-tale' wedding not as the end of a romance but 'the place where the adventure really begins'. Stressing the virtues of a good marriage, Dr. Runcie reflected: 'If we solved all our economic problems and failed to build loving families, it would profit us nothing.'

The mood of splendour inside the Cathedral was carried to the jubilant crowds outside and along the route by public address systems and transistor radios. When Prince Charles said 'I will', a great cheer rang through the centre of the capital. It was repeated for Lady Diana, and again when Dr. Runcie pronounced the couple man and wife, the Prince having slipped a thin band of Welsh gold on to his bride's finger. Many of the hundreds of thousands who had camped out all night to watch the processions had copies of the order of service. Patiently standing by bus-stops and street-signs, they joined in the singing relayed to them from St. Paul's. It was a heart-felt display of popular affection for the thirty-two-year-old Prince and his twenty-year-old Princess, and in all their public appearances on what for them was also an intensely private day, the couple responded with warmth and appreciation.

Appearing on the balcony of Buckingham Palace shortly after one o'clock, they held hands, hugged, and finally and briefly, kissed, as a joyous crowd cheered them. Three times they disappeared through the tall french windows behind the balcony, and three times the crowd, nearly half a million strong, was rewarded with their return. After the first two appearances the chant changed to 'We want the Queen', and the monarch duly emerged, a smiling, elegant figure in a light full-pleated aquamarine coat and matching hat. Then it was 'We want the Queen Mum', and she too stepped forward, showing no signs of the illness that kept her off her feet last week. A groan from the crowd signalled the closing of the balcony doors, and before the start of the wedding breakfast, the Prince and Princess had their first chance to relax away from the public gaze.

Posing for the official wed ding photographs, taken by the Queen's cousin, the Earl of Lichfield, Prince Charles pulled faces at his bride to make her laugh for the cameras. A little later, 120 royal guests and relatives sat down to lobster and lamb, brill and chicken, strawberries and cream – Cornish cream, of course. Vintage Champagne, 1959 claret and 1955 port provided the liquid refreshment, and the toast was, jointly proposed by the Prince's two supporters – Prince Andrew in his naval uniform, and Prince Edward in morning dress.

By the time the Royal couple emerged once more much of the crowd had drifted away, but there were still thousands left to cheer them on their way to Waterloo. The balloons attached to the open carriage – blue and silver with the Prince of Wales's crest – had been fixed into place by Prince Andrew whose hand was also responsible for the scrawled 'Just Married' sign fixed to the back. A brief stop at the station, an hour's ride to Romsey in Hampshire, a short drive to Broadlands, the home of Prince Charles's murdered great-uncle Lord Mountbatten and the Royal couple's honeymoon had begun.

It had been a long and exhausting day for the Royal pair, and as they disappeared into Broadlands for a candlelit dinner together, there was opportunity to reflect on many of the other facets that made an occasion of such memorable sparkle. In the morning there were the contrasting sights of an immaculate Mrs. Nancy Reagan, impeccably attired in shades of pink, and of Mr. Spike Milligan, also impeccably attired, although not in pink (not the visible bits anyway). They took their places in the cathedral alongside men like the King of Tonga, whose colossal bulk was ushered to an especially large and strong chair and those foreign royals, like ex-King Constantine, who have no throne at all. President Mitterrand of France wore a lounge suit, in deference to the new spirit of equality that is sweeping his country, and the most striking hat was that of Princess Anne – an exotic bonnet of bright yellow and orange.

Outside the cathedral the crowds who waited so patiently through-out the day and night were on their best behaviour; by tea-time police reported a solitary arrest – for pickpocketing. Only a handful of crimes were reported. The horses were also on their best behaviour – with the exception of one that ran away in Trafalgar Square – and a hard-working team of cleaner-uppers received genial cheers. By late evening, the last crowds were dispersing, many already tired of jokes about going home to watch *Match of the Day* highlights on television. The Prince and Princess of Wales have made an idyllic start to their married life and the good wishes of a nation accompanied them yesterday.

Earl Spencer, the bride's father, did not have much to say yesterday, but his few words to the Press as he left his home to collect the bride at Clarence House, were fittingly a mixture of both future and past. 'The Spencer family has through the centuries fought for King and Country. Diana will be vowing to help her country for the rest of her life,' he said. 'She will be following in the traditions of her ancestors, and she will have at her side the man she loves.'

15 June 1982: Victory for Britain in the Falklands
ARGENTINE FORCES SURRENDER
WHITE FLAGS FLYING, MRS. THATCHER TELLS CHEERING M.P.s

Mrs. Thatcher told cheering M.P.s last night that Argentine troops in Port Stanley were flying the white flag after British troops had stormed the Falklands capital. There was a ceasefire and talks were going on for the surrender by the Argentines of both East and West Falkland, which they invaded on 2 April. The Prime Minister told the Commons in an emergency statement shortly before 10.15 p.m.: 'After successful attacks last night, General Moore [commander of the British land forces] decided to press forward. The Argentines retreated. Our forces reached the outskirts of Port Stanley. Large numbers of Argentine soldiers threw down their weapons. Our troops have been ordered not to fire except in self-defence. Talks are now in progress between General Menendez [Argentine commander] and our deputy commander, Brigadier Waters, about the surrender of the Argentine forces on East and West Falkland.' As she received the acclaim of

M.P.s, Mrs. Thatcher allowed herself a slight smile – her first in the Commons since the Falklands crisis began.

The Defence Secretary, Mr. Nott, asked later if war in the Falklands was now over, said: 'It looks like it.' But he added that matters in the Falklands still had to be 'buttoned up'. A Defence Ministry spokesman said he believed British troops were now totally in control around Port Stanley. The troops would probably stand fast until the morning when 'things would be sorted out'.

Shortly before news of last night's dramatic latest developments became known, the 7,000-strong Argentine garrison in the Falklands capital was reported to be fleeing in disarray, with 6,000 British troops in hot pursuit. The British troops swept through the so-called Galtieri line of fortifications, over-running trenches and machine-gun posts and meeting little resistance. But a few hours earlier there had been fierce fighting at Mount Tumbledown and Wireless Ridge, the 350-foot ridge overlooking the former Royal Marines barracks at Moody-Brook, on the outskirts of Port Stanley. British casualties were said to be much lighter than expected.

Argentina's three-man ruling junta was meeting late last night and President Galtieri was expected to make a nationwide television and radio address. An Argentine military spokesman in Buenos Aires said General Menendez was flying from the Falklands to meet the junta, after which he would return to Port Stanley.

29 January 1986: A tragedy for NASA as a space shuttle explodes shortly after lift-off
SPACE SHUTTLE BLOWN APART
MILLIONS WATCH ON TV AS SEVEN CREW DIE
MID-AIR BLAST LIKE A-BOMB
By Ian Ball in New York

America's space shuttle *Challenger* exploded at 1,977 m.p.h. with the force of a small tactical nuclear bomb one minute and twelve seconds after launching yesterday, killing the five men and two women on board and dealing a devastating blow to the entire space programme. Long after the moment of tragedy – a horrifying scene viewed live by millions of television viewers – America's space agency, NASA, could offer no explanation of what went wrong with its £860 million spaceship.

The crew included Mrs. Christa McAuliffe, thirty-seven, a mother of two who was picked out of more than 11,000 applicants to be the first teacher to fly in the shuttle in NASA's citizen-in-space programme, and astronaut Judy Resnik, thirty-six, the second American woman to fly in space. They died instantly in an explosion of 526,000 gallons of liquid hydrogen and liquid oxygen in the shuttle's disposable fuel tank – an explosion that shattered the ninety-ton shuttle into thousands of small pieces at an altitude of ten miles.

The commander of the flight, Francis Scobee, forty-six, was making his second space shuttle mission. He had reported nothing wrong in his brief time aloft yesterday. The shuttle's pilot, Michael Smith, forty, a navy test pilot and Vietnam veteran selected as an astronaut in 1980, was on his first space mission. The other crew members were Ronald McNair, thirty-five, an astronaut and an expert on lasers, Lieutenant-Colonel Ellison Onizuka, thirty-nine, a pilot and aerospace engineer, and Gregory Jarvis, forty-one, a Hughes Aircraft Corp engineer.

This was the first in-the-air disaster in fifty-six American manned space missions, although three astronauts were killed in January 1967 when a launch-tower caught fire during the Apollo programme. NASA's cameras and the American television networks recorded the disaster in vivid detail. Long after the original fireball – a red-orange-white inferno that brought stunned, fearful expressions to the faces of space officials at Cape Canaveral, Florida, and Mission Control in Houston, Texas – smoking trails of debris were still etched across the bright blue sky.

The two solid-fuel booster rockets that flank the space shuttle had continued on crazy journeys of their own, their trails forming a pattern resembling cattle horns. So much debris was flung down on the area that the coast guard, the navy and the air force deemed it unsafe for almost an hour to send large search parties into the main area of impact, some eight miles off the coast of Florida. The chance of recovering any bodies or even human fragments was considered extremely remote. But frogmen dropped into the water at the scene and a small armada of navy ships and coast guard cutters were instructed to recover every scrap of metal and plastic from the shuttle to help engineers determine what went wrong.

A frame-by-frame study of a film of the explosion made by one of the NASA 'chase planes' that accompany shuttles on their climb towards orbit offered some clues as to what went wrong. An errant tongue of flame could be seen near the base of the port booster rocket as the shuttle was throttling up to full engine power. A fraction of a second later, another, slightly larger flame, was visible near the base of the external fuel tank. A halo of what seemed like burning fuel formed around the base of the tank. Then came an explosion that sent flames spurting towards the shuttle's cockpit, developing into a fireball.

It was a catastrophe NASA knew theoretically could happen. But it was the ultimate disaster NASA knew also could not realistically be taken into consideration in its emergency planning.

In the first moments after a space-shuttle launch, there are various 'escape modes' in case of mechanical failure. The crew can ride a chute to the ground if a situation arises where they have to leave the space shuttle hurriedly while it is still tethered to its launch tower. Shuttle pilots also practise emergency procedures for a safe landing or a return immediately to the runway at Cape Canaveral if there is any major loss of power after take-off. But as one space observer said yesterday: 'How do you plan emergency procedures against the total disintegration of your spacecraft?'

There are no ejection seats in the space shuttle's cockpit and main cabin. There were engineering problems involved, but even if such an ejection system had proved feasible, it was felt that a human being would have only the slimmest chance of surviving bring hurled from a space vehicle charging up to its orbital speed.

The omens were not entirely propitious as preparations got under way for the launch at Cape Canaveral. This twenty-fifth mission in the space shuttle programme – the tenth by the shuttle *Challenger* – had been postponed five times, three because of weather. Overnight the temperature fell to twenty-four degrees. Icicles dangled from the space shuttle. With their hands, members of the launch crew knocked some off a space vehicle that would soon be belching out thousands of degrees of heat and generating a million pounds of thrust.

Veteran observers at the spaceport felt that the *Challenger*'s take-off yesterday was unusually slow. But no one suspected anything was wrong until the giant fireball suddenly filled the viewfinder of every camera tracking the shuttle. The familiar, calm voice of Mission Control fell silent for almost a minute after television viewers saw the explosion. Then the NASA commentator spoke the words everyone knew must be coming: 'Vehicle has exploded . . . we are awaiting word from any recovery forces downrange.'

29 April 1986: An explosion at Chernobyl sends a radioactive cloud across Europe
SOVIET ATOM LEAK ALARM
'WORLD'S WORST' REACTOR ACCIDENT
FALL-OUT 1,000 MILES ACROSS EUROPE
By Robin Gedye, Diplomatic Staff

Radioactivity from deep in the Soviet Union was being borne by the wind over Scandinavia last night after what may turn out to be the world's most serious nuclear reactor accident. In an unprecedented admission, Tass the official Soviet news agency, said the accident happened eighty miles north of Kiev in the Ukraine. After radioactive particles had been monitored more than 1,000 miles from the scene of the accident, a power plant at Chernobyl, a spokesman for the Danish nuclear laboratories at Risø said: 'The event must have been very serious.'

Several people near the core of the 'affected' area had been treated for injuries, Tass said. The Soviet Government announced: 'Measures are being undertaken to eliminate the consequences of the accident.' A commission of inquiry had been set up. Tass reported that 'one of the reactors' at Chernobyl was damaged. According to Danish specialists there are four reactors at the plant. The spokesman at Risø said: 'It is difficult to say exactly what has happened, but it would seem that the event took place at the weekend – probably during the night between Saturday and Sunday. We are looking at something very close to a meltdown.'

During a meltdown, a reactor 'burns' its way through the floor of its housing, causing severe contamination.

The worst accident previously reported at an industrial nuclear station was at Three Mile Island, Pennsylvania, seven years ago, when radiation was measured up to twenty miles from a crippled reactor. A nuclear specialist in Stockholm said last eight that radioactivity was widespread, but 'within the limit allowed inside nuclear power stations', although well above limits permitted outside. 'We have registered radioactivity just about everywhere we have looked. Unusual concentrations have been found in Denmark, Norway, Finland and Sweden.'

At the Ringhals nuclear power plant in Sweden, one hundred times the normal amount of Caesium 137 was measured, while in central Sweden iodine counts of between 300 and 800 per square metre were reported. Finland's nuclear authorities announced that they had measured up to five times the normal amounts of radiation. 'The question is whether this is the beginning or the end of the pollution. Whether the accident has been contained or not,' said an official.

Yesterday's increase in radiation was reported after a worker at the Formark nuclear plant, about sixty miles north of Stockholm, set off an alarm while passing through a routine radiation check. Six hundred workers were immediately evacuated from the plant until tests showed there had been no leak there. Within hours reports of increased radiation were flooding in from monitoring stations throughout Scandinavia. Kiev, with a population of 1,500,000 is the nearest big city to the Chernobyl plant. Experts said that providing the incident was not 'overly serious', prevailing winds would have carried radiation away.

Birgitta Dahl, the Energy Minister, said in a television interview that Sweden was not satisfied with Soviet behaviour after the accident. 'They should have warned us immediately,' she said. Swedish inquiries to Soviet officials who said at first that they knew of no leak, may have led to Moscow's report of the accident, she added. The minister said there was no danger to people in Sweden, but added: 'We must demand higher safety standards in the Soviet Union.' A Swedish expert said: 'Many of the Russian reactors do not have domes to contain any escapes, unlike those in Western Europe. This means that in the case of a core meltdown radiation will be released more quickly into the atmosphere.'

The Soviet Union seldom reports national disasters, either natural or man-made, unless injuries or damage are widespread or if foreigners are involved. Western analysts and exiled Soviet scientists said that a serious nuclear accident in the Chelyabinsk area of the Urals in 1958 killed hundreds of people and contaminated a huge area which is still out of bounds to travellers. The Soviet Union has refused to confirm the disaster which was believed to have been caused when stockpiled nuclear waste erupted like a volcano.

Radiation released in the nuclear accident in Russia poses no threat to Britain, a spokesman for the National Radiological Protection Board said yesterday. The radioactive fail-out reaching Scandinavia was only twice the natural background level of radiation. This was so low that it should not cause any harm if it was carried to Britain and there was no need for special precautions to be taken in this country. However, the Energy Department has asked for special checks by the Ministry of Agriculture on the radioactivity detection apparatus it maintains to warn of possible contamination to farmlands and coastal fishing waters.

Officials said there were no immediate reports of abnormal readings, but added that effects might not be immediately apparent because prevailing winds were not from the East. The accident is likely to increase public concern as to the safety of the British nuclear programme after recent disclosures about leakage from Sellafield. The Meteorological Office said it was 'highly unlikely' that the cloud would drift into parts of Scotland from Scandinavia.

A spokesman for the Atomic Energy Research Establishment at Harwell said it seemed likely that nuclear fuel material was drifting at a high altitude. 'When this sort of thing happens it blows up into the fairly high atmosphere and drifts horizontally,' he said. 'Think of a sort of sausage gradually spreading out.' A spokesman for British Nuclear Fuels at Sellafield said its own monitoring equipment had not picked up any unusual increase in radiation levels.

22 December 1988: Terrorism hits Lockerbie
PAN AM JET CRASHES ON SCOTS TOWN
ALL 258 KILLED ON FLIGHT 103
HEAVY CASUALTIES ON GROUND AS JUMBO DESTROYS HOUSES
By Ben Fenton, Joanna Coles and Richard Savill

A Pan Am Boeing jumbo jet carrying 255 adults and three children crashed on Lockerbie, south west Scotland, last night, killing all on board and destroying part of the small market town in Britain's worst air disaster. Early this morning rescue workers said there were many casualties, including fatalities, among people on the ground. A spokesman for the rescue and co-ordination centre at R.A.F. Pitreavie said: 'Our information is that forty houses were demolished. We have not heard of any survivors from those houses. There will be a lot of digging needed.'

The south side of Lockerbie was said to have been 'wiped out' and a crater twenty feet deep and one hundred feet wide was torn in the ground near the A74 trunk road. Eye-witnesses spoke of a 300-feet-wide fireball and a rain of 'liquid fire' that fell on the town. They said the plane hit a hill and started to break up before crashing close to a petrol station and destroying at least eight houses. Drivers were trapped on the main road and covered in burning aviation fuel, according to firemen. An Army Gazelle helicopter equipped with powerful searchlights went to the scene to search for the dead and injured feared to be lying unseen in the carnage.

Wreckage and bodies were found over a huge area. Firemen's rescue efforts were hindered by the risk of further explosions several hours after the aircraft came down near the petrol station.

Flight PA103 had taken off from Heathrow for New York at 6.25 p.m. and disappeared from radar screens at 7.19 p.m. Aviation experts immediately said that sabotage was a strong possibility as a cause for the crash, mainly because of the Boeing 747's impressive record of reliability arid because it was flying at 31,000 feet when contact was suddenly lost and the plane vanished from radar screens. The pilot apparently had no time to send a distress call. A Civil Aviation Authority spokesman said Scottish air traffic controllers at Prestwick spoke to the pilot minutes before the crash and there was no indication of any problems. Radar records do not indicate other aircraft in the vicinity.

Some eye-witnesses described the jet trailing flames as it flew over the town, coming down on the Sherwood Park housing estate in Lockerbie, which has a population of about 3,000.

Wreckage blocked the A74 close to the town. Mr. Ian Fisher, a Border TV reporter, said: 'The south side of the town near the main road has been wiped out. Houses are gutted. A huge pall of smoke is in the sky.'

The town hall was set up as an emergency mortuary. Of the first five casualties at the Dumfries and Galloway Infirmary, all were thought to be from the town rather than the plane. The forward section of the plane was found ablaze three miles east of Lockerbie, suggesting that the aircraft may have blown up in mid-air. The cockpit was found four miles from the town and a cabin door was discovered eighteen miles away. An emergency helicopter found the bodies of at least two passengers near the cockpit. A further report said nine or ten bodies were recovered about two miles from the scene of the crash.

Anxious relatives of people living in Lockerbie jammed telephone lines to the town. The Queen was said to be 'shocked and appalled' last night by the tragedy. Mr, Rifkind, Scottish Secretary, and about a dozen accident investigators were flying to the scene last night. Mrs. Thatcher was being kept informed of developments. Mr. Charles Price, the American Ambassador to Britain, flew to the scene of the disaster. Mr. Channon, Transport Secretary, is due to make a full Commons statement on the tragedy this morning.

ITN viewers last night saw houses in Lockerbie blazing furiously as firemen fought to contain fires. Small pieces of aircraft wreckage were strewn in the streets. The local medical officer said there were unlikely to be many injured. Most of those hit on the ground as the plane crashed would have died, he said.

Flight PA103 originated in Frankfurt yesterday afternoon, but passengers transferred to the crashed 747 jumbo, called Clipper Maid of the Seas, at Heathrow. Some of the passengers were American servicemen going home for Christmas. Among the passengers was also Mr, Bernt Carlsson, the Swedish U.N. Commissioner for Namibia. Helicopter rescue teams from across Britain were scrambled to help with the rescue effort. Two Chinooks with R.A.F. medical teams on board flew from R.A.F. Odiham, near Basingstoke, Hampshire. Search and rescue helicopters from R.A.F. Boulmer, near Newcastle, R.A.F. Leconsfield, near Hull, and R.A.F. Valley, Anglesey, and R.A.F. mountain rescue teams from R.A.F. Leeming and R.A.F. Leuchars were also dispatched. Carlisle Airport was opened as a refuelling station for the fleet of helicopters and a special landing zone was organised by Lockerbie police.

Ambulance officers at the scene said there was little hope of finding survivors from the plane and said there were 'walking wounded' wandering about the town after debris from the plane hit them. Two van-loads of blood supplies were rushed from Glasgow to the Dumfries and Galloway Infirmary, Dumfries, where casualties were being taken. Some three hundred people turned up at the hospital volunteering to give blood. The Scottish Ambulance Service headquarters in Glasgow also broadcast an appeal for off-duty staff to report to help at the hospital. Doctors from Lockerbie and neighbouring towns set up a first-aid centre in the town hall. Medical experts, including burns specialists, from hospitals in Harrogate, Edinburgh and Manchester were flown to the scene by R.A.F. helicopters as part of the rescue operation, co- ordinated from R.A.F. Pitreavie.

The fire brigade said at least part of the plane crashed into the Townfoot petrol station in the centre of Lockerbie and a number of houses. A woman told how she ran for her life as the jet crashed beside the garage where she was filling her car with petrol. Mrs. Marian Peel told a radio reporter: 'I pulled into the garage and was getting petrol when I heard a rumble that sounded like thunder. It just got louder and louder and louder. There was a great big crash and a big burst of fire. Within seconds there was debris flying all over the place. I just left the car and ran like hell. I didn't see the plane hit the ground because the garage has a canopy and it was the other side of the canopy. There was a lot of fire about and a lot of debris and flames flying all over the place. The tarmac was on fire in different places. I ran from the car and there were flames all round the tyres.'

Mr. Mike Carnahan, who lives two miles south of Lockerbie, told B.B.C. news: 'The whole sky was lit up with flames. It was actually raining fire, liquid fire. You could see several houses on the skyline with the roofs totally off and all you could see were the framing timbers. I don't think there is any chance of survivors. The way it exploded was just beyond description. I found a piece of an aluminium rivet buried in my car. I was so shocked I just drove away and got myself back home. From what I could see there could be no survivors. All I could see was fire. A lot of rescue services were trying to get there but all the roads were blocked with sightseers.' Firefighters were struggling to put out the flames in a huge crater beside the A74 road with wreckage from the jumbo strewn over a wide area.

News of the tragedy was treated with shock and horror among airport staff in Heathrow's terminal three where the flight boarded. An airport security man said: 'None of us can believe it. The passengers all looked happy and glad to be getting away. Quite a few of them had Christmas presents.' A Pan Am spokesman, Mr. Jeff Kriendler, told a New York press conference that there was no sign the aircraft was brought down by an explosion, sabotage or bad weather.

Shocked residents described last night how they thought an earthquake had struck Lockerbie when the stricken plane crashed and sent flames shooting hundreds of feet into the air. One home owner in Sherwood Crescent, where a number of homes were destroyed, said: 'I just heard this thin screaming sound. The ground shook; it felt for all the world like an earthquake. I was watching television at the time with my family. We just got out of the house as quickly as possible. We had to climb out through a window as pieces of debris blocked both doors. There were pieces of the plane everywhere and the house next to us was completely gutted. I don't know if there was anyone inside at the time. It is difficult to describe how I feel. I just can't believe a thing like this has happened.'

A local minister, the Reverend Alan Neil, who was visiting a friend in Sherwood Crescent, said: 'We just ran outside. There were cars ablaze on the road and the houses were burning like an inferno.' Mr. Archie Smith, a retired policeman who lives in Sherwood Crescent, said debris from the plane smashed into his house which went up in flames. 'The sky lit up and we fell to the floor. I thought the house was coming down on top of us. We just got out.'

Debris rained on villagers as they fled their burning homes. A mortuary was set up immediately in the town hall. Policemen guarding the entrance refused to say how many bodies had been brought in by a fleet of ambulances. Shocked residents stood silently on the streets as the emergency services mounted a disaster operation. Many were still unsure whether friends and relatives had survived. One woman said: 'The only way I can describe it was it was like an earthquake. Nobody knows what is happening. It's horrific.' Another resident added: 'There was just a huge ball of fire.'

Hours after the crash the air in the centre of the village was still thick with smoke and the reek of aviation fuel. The evidence of the carnage was everywhere. All telephone lines were down. Cars still smoking were left on the main street. A helicopter hovered above the destruction, with its powerful spotlight lighting up the worst affected areas.

It is believed that a section of the plane hit the small village of Corrie on a hill just outside Lockerbie before it broke up across the town. The Townfoot Garage took the brunt of one large section of the plane. Late into the night bodies were still reported to be lying in the fields behind it. A crater about fifty yards long and twenty yards wide stretched from behind the garage, through the remains of houses in Sherwood Crescent to theA74 on the west side of the village. Police evacuated the area and closed it off, but witnesses reported that there was nothing but rubble left of homes that were destroyed. The houses were knocked down to their foundations, with at most two feet of brickwork left at their base, they said. It appeared that part of the plane came down behind the petrol station and then ploughed through the houses and on to the carriageway of the A74.

16 February 1989: The row over Salman Rushdie's *The Satanic Verses* takes a darker turn
$3 MILLION IRAN PRICE ON RUSHDIE'S HEAD
By Nigel Reynolds, Arts Correspondent

Iran yesterday offered a reward of $1 million to any non-Iranian who carries out the 'execution order' of the Ayatollah Khomeini against the Indian-born author of *The Satanic Verses*, Salman Rushdie. As several thousand demonstrators gathered outside the British embassy in Tehran shouting and throwing stones, Hojatoleslam Hassan Sanei, chief of the Fifth June Foundation national fund, said any Iranian assassin would be paid $3 million.

Last night Mr. Rushdie was in hiding and there was a police guard outside his London home. He called off a tour of America due to start this weekend. Iran's national news agency announced that all books by Rushdie's publishers, Viking Penguin, had been banned. The French publishers, Presses de la Cité, said that they had abandoned plans to bring out *The Satanic Verses*. France has three million Moslems.

In a move to defuse the row over what Moslems see as 'blasphemy' in *The Satanic Verses*, Viking Penguin in London issued a statement regretting the distress the book had caused Moslems. The Iranian embassy to the Vatican demanded that the Pope should join in the crusade against *The Satanic Verses*. But a senior Vatican official said later: 'I doubt very much whether the Holy Father will take any action. It's their problem, not ours. We have enough of our own.'

After reports that 'hit squads' may be in England, *The Daily Telegraph* was told that an American Moslem was in London last week trying to find Mr. Rushdie. 'He wanted Mr. Rushdie's telephone number and address. He said he was going to kill him,' said Dr. Hesham el-Hessawy, chairman of the Islamic Society for the Promotion of Religious Tolerance. Police in Bradford, West Yorkshire, said they were seeking advice from the Crown Prosecution Service about whether they should take action against Mr. Sayed Abdul Quddus, joint secretary of the Bradford Council of Mosques. After the Ayatollah's threat, Mr. Quddus was reported as saying that he agreed with it and that Mr. Rushdie would be 'signing his own death warrant' if he set foot in West Yorkshire. The Home Office said it had investigated whether Mr. Quddus and Mr. Bashir Ansari, vice-president of the UK Islamic Mission in Rochdale, who was reported to have made similar remarks, could be deported for inflaming hatred. But both men have British citizenship and any action would be a matter for the police.

The Anglican Bishop of Bradford called for an emergency meeting of leaders from all religions to try to defuse what was described as the potentially explosive mood of Moslems. A spokesman for the Right Reverend Robert Williamson said: 'The bishop feels very strongly that something needs to be done to defuse the situation. There are genuine fears that further protests in Bradford could have horrendous consequences.'

The playwright Harold Pinter led a delegation to 10 Downing Street yesterday afternoon and handed in a letter signed by leading literary figures calling on the Government to take action. 'It is an intolerable and barbaric state of affairs,' he said. The Government should confront Iran over the affair, and remind Moslems in Britain that incitement to murder was against the law.

5 June 1989: The Chinese Government sends the tanks into Tiananmen Square
PEKING MASSACRE FAILS TO END PROTESTS
FRESH BARRICADES GO UP AMID CALLS FOR REVENGE
By Graham Hutchings in Peking

Tanks, machine-guns blazing, patrolled the streets of central Peking early today. But they failed to dampen the spirit of resistance as residents and pro-democracy students erected fresh barricades and called for revenge for the bloody show of force which ended the student occupation of Tiananmen Square. Diplomatic sources say at least 1,000 people must have died in the action. Chen Xitong, Peking's mayor, claimed that more than 1,000 troops had been injured, but did not make clear whether there were fatalities.

Last night buses blocked nearly every important road junction within two miles of the eastern side of the square. Many had been set on fire to deter the expected advance of troops. On one of the buses was written in Chinese characters: 'Avenge 4 June Massacre'. A banner on another said: 'Deng Xiaoping and Li Peng are enemies of the people.' As dawn approached, many people drifted away from the barricades and there were far fewer bystanders than on previous nights. After the bloodshed of the previous twenty-four hours, most people appeared to have obeyed the Government's instructions to stay indoors. However, at about 4 a.m., a column of twenty-five military vehicles, including armoured personnel carriers, swept along the northern ring road. Their destination was not clear, but could have been the city's university quarter in the north-west.

It is still not clear how many people were killed during the army's assault on Tiananmen Square. An unknown number of those who died were either shot, beaten or stabbed during attempts to clear the student encampment around the People's Monument to Revolutionary Heroes, in the centre of the square. According to witnesses, the attack began at 4 a.m. when the lights went out. The students who decided to stay in the square began to sing 'The Internationale'. Shortly afterwards, soldiers rushed out of the Great Hall of the People and armoured personnel carriers moved in, crushing students still in their tents. I watched at 5.30 a.m. as six tanks smashed through the buses and other formidable-looking obstacles as if they were cardboard. As they approached, they indiscriminately sprayed machine-gun fire down side roads where thousands had gathered. For one terrifying moment it seemed as though one of the tanks would turn up the lane where I and others had taken shelter. As panic set in, we broke cover and ran. After a fifty-yard dash, we realised we were not being pursued.

The tanks were the spearhead of the one convoy to approach the square from the east. It had been held up two miles away by demonstrators. By the time it started to move, other army units had gained control of the square from the west and north and were laying into the 3,000 or so remaining protesters. The students' Statue to Democracy, which they erected last week, was flattened by a tank. But though late on the scene, the convoy from the east approached at devastating speed. Once the tanks started to roll, at least fifteen troop lorries drove through a gap between the smashed buses. The convoy swept noisily down towards the square, past the Peking Hotel, where scores of guests were watching the night's action from their balconies. It ploughed through any obstacle and, according to witnesses, crushed protesters who could not escape in time. By 6 a.m., the people's defence of East Chang'an Avenue was at an end.

A few hours later, scenes like that at Chang'an could be found at many road junctions in the city centre, littered with smashed buses and other vehicles. Stones and broken glass lay all over the road. In a number of places, palls of smoke rose from burned-out military vehicles. The mood in the capital was one of sullen shock at the army's ruthless attack. By 10 a.m., thousands of people approached the square from the north-east and stopped within two hundred yards of thousands of troops sitting in rows of ten across Chang'an (Eternal Peace) Avenue. Behind them were scores of tanks, barrels pointing menacingly at the students and beyond along East Chang'an Avenue.

The crowd of demonstrators jeered and taunted the soldiers, who, in mid-morning, suddenly opened fire with machine-guns. The crowd retreated, leaving behind thirty to forty bodies. Shortly after the bodies were recovered, wall slogans appeared, written in blood. One read in Chinese: 'Li Peng, you will never sleep in peace.' Another, in English, said: 'All of these things are to be answered for.' In the west of the city thousands of demonstrators set fire to a column of one hundred armoured personnel carriers. And in Peking's university area, students set ablaze seven military vehicles and, according to a Western resident, captured an armoured personnel carrier with a machine-gun. Tanks, firing machine-guns to deter resistance, moved east along the main road from Tiananmen Square to the embassy district. A Western diplomat said two military convoys travelled round the embassy district firing shots.

It is understood that the main attack on the square was carried out by the 27th Army normally based in Hubei Province, central China. It is well disciplined, experienced and thought to be loyal to President Yang Shangkun, third-ranking member of the party's powerful Central Military Commission. Yang, eighty-two, is a long-time associate of Deng Xiaoping, the senior leader. Deng, who has not appeared in public for days, is thought to be in charge of the military operation. However, Yang took a hard line against the student movement from the first and appears to have enhanced his authority now that his troops have reclaimed the square. This turn of events may encourage him to challenge Deng for overall supremacy.

Central Peking was a desolate scene yesterday. Thousands of people were milling around bemused and shocked by events during the hours of darkness. A Western correspondent was savagely beaten by plainclothes policemen after they had picked him up walking away from Tiananmen Square. Students in Peking appealed to the city's workforce to go on strike today in protest at the military's crushing of their movement. Peking's Mayor Chen said on the radio: 'Peking remains in crisis. In this critical situation we have no choice but to adopt special measures to smash the counter-revolutionary violence.'

The army newspaper described the night's activities as a great triumph over a serious 'counter-revolutionary riot'. However, for a brief moment, the state-controlled Radio Peking took a different line. In one broadcast an announcer said: 'Thousands of people have been killed in a barbarous suppression of the people.' Successive broadcasts reverted to the government line.

10 November 1989: The Berlin Wall crumbles
THE IRON CURTAIN IS SWEPT ASIDE
EAST GERMANY THROWS OPEN ALL ITS BORDERS
KRENZ GAMBLES ON FREE TRAVEL POLICY TO STOP THE EXODUS
By Daniel Johnson in East Berlin

In the most dramatic breach yet of the Iron Curtain which has divided Europe since the Second World War, East Germany last night announced that it is throwing open all its border points and will lift virtually all restrictions on its citizens' freedom to travel. The Berlin Wall, which has been the ultimate symbol of the division of Germany since 1961, thus becomes little more than a museum piece. It will remain standing for the present as a symbol of the division of Germany. Its demolition will be used by the Eastern Bloc as a bargaining counter in disarmament talks with Nato.

The raising of the Iron Curtain from Stettin to Trieste, which

Winston Churchill denounced at Fulton, Missouri, in 1946, is now almost complete. With the borders of Germany, Hungary and Yugoslavia open, only Czechoslovakia maintains restrictions on a limited scale. Last night West Germany said it was prepared to take everyone who floods across the border. 'No one will be turned back,' said an Interior Ministry official in Bonn. On hearing the news, M.P.s in Bonn's parliament launched into a rousing and emotional rendition of the national anthem.

West German Chancellor Helmut Kohl, who said he might have to curtail his official visit to Poland, called for face-to-face talks on East Germany's political crisis with Herr Egon Krenz, the Communist State's leader. In opening his borders, Herr Krenz is gambling on regaining his people's confidence. If the gamble fails, the scale of the exodus could sweep away Krenz and his Communist leadership. Opinion on both sides of the Wall was divided on whether the decision was the last desperate throw of the dice by a bankrupt regime or a shrewd tactical ploy to stabilise a situation fast spiralling out of control.

More than 225,000 East Germans have left for West Germany this year, via Hungary, Czechoslovakia and Poland, and Western observers estimate the total wanting to leave is nearly 1.4 million out of the country's sixteen million population. The travel concession was announced at a dramatic Press conference in East Berlin by Herr Günter Schabowski, party spokesman, two days before the seventy-first anniversary of the end of the First World War. The newly-elected Politburo's extraordinary decision ended twenty-eight years of border incidents in which hundreds of refugees have been killed or wounded while attempting to cross the Berlin Wall or the border between the two Germanys. Under the provisional ordinance, all citizens would be able to use any border crossing point, including those at the Berlin Wall, without providing any proof of family connections, financial resources or any of the other prerequisites which have previously hindered free travel and emigration.

Herr Schabowski's announcement came at the end of the second day of the crisis meeting of the Central Committee of the ruling Communist Socialist Unity party. But the debate over a new electoral law, allowing free elections and ushering in a 'pluralist society', was overshadowed by the opening of East Germany's borders for the first time in forty years. The decision is certain to provoke a political storm in West Germany, as major cities like Bremen and Hanover refuse to accept any more refugees. Herr Schabowski claimed last night that West Germany's capacity to absorb a further influx of refugees was exhausted and opposition leaders in East Germany are now appealing to would-be émigrés not to leave. But last night Herr Manfred Rommel, President of the Conference of German city Councils and the Mayor of Stuttgart, estimated that up to two million East Germans may cross over. West Germany was facing a 'national emergency' and must take emergency measures, he said. Those should include commandeering all empty flats in all towns and cities to accommodate the refugee influx.

Four young East Germans crossed into West Germany at a northern crossing point, the first since East Germany opened its frontier. Curious East Germans flocked to crossing points at the Berlin Wall and passed through simply by showing their identity cards, said West German television. 'There was no problem,' said one West Berliner who saw East Berliners coming over. One TV scene showed East Berliners in tears as they crossed, just to see if it was possible, before returning to the East. One of the earliest crossings was made at Helmstedt, one hundred miles east of Hanover, by a woman dentist from Magdeburg. She said she simply wanted to see if it was possible to travel to the West. She promptly turned around and headed back to East Germany. A West Berliner hugged and danced with an East Berlin couple who crossed the white line which divides the city. But there were no reports of masses of refugees pouring into the West across the ten border and seven rail crossings.

The end of travel restrictions was the most dramatic event so far in a week which has already seen the fall of the East German government, the resignation and replacement of the entire Politburo and promises of reforms which theoretically could threaten the leading role of the Communist party. The redundancy of the Berlin Wall and the 'normalisation' of the German frontier may lead to more calls for reunification, but the East German leadership evidently believes neither the West nor the Soviet Union is ready yet to contemplate such a transformation of the European political scene.

Clive Freeman in West Berlin writes: West Berlin's governing mayor, Walter Momper, appealed on television to West Berliners not to grumble if lots of people started coming through the city barrier 'even if they want to stay and, of course, some of them will. Be tolerant'.

Russia hinted yesterday that it would accept a non-Communist government in East Germany if it remained in the Warsaw Pact. Mr. Gennady Gerasimov, Soviet Foreign Ministry spokesman, said in Moscow that German reunification would only be a realistic topic for discussion if Nato and the Warsaw Pact were dissolved.

Ian Brodie in Washington writes: President Bush said he was elated by the East German news, calling it 'a dramatic happening'. Admitting that he had been taken by surprise at the announcement, President Bush added that the Berlin Wall now had 'very little relevance. I am very pleased.' As part of President Bush's offer to help Bonn cope with refugees, the Pentagon said American armed forces in West Germany will provide temporary emergency housing for about 980. Two stand-by hospitals in Zweibrücken and Donaueschingen, plus flats in Bitburg, will be made available.

East German border police at Checkpoint Charlie were surprised to learn yesterday that citizens could now travel to the West freely. 'People are going to read this and say, "There must be some mistake",' said a young guard, shaken out of his normally severe bearing. 'It's not good,' another said an hour after the decision was announced. 'We will lose our jobs.' Traffic was light at the famous crossing meant for foreign travellers through the Berlin Wall. Pointing towards West Berlin, one East German complained: 'I just wanted to see if I could go over there for a look. I intend to come back.'

Early today hundreds of West Berliners stormed Checkpoint Charlie at the Berlin Wall. They pushed across the white demarcation line dividing East from West Berlin shouting: 'We want in, we want in.' Dozens of people were sitting on top of the Berlin Wall as good-humoured East German border guards made to attempt to remove them. Jens Richter trembled with emotion as he said: 'I never thought I would ever touch West German soil.'

East German border guards tried to restrain the masses who streamed across the checkpoint at Invalidenstrasse. 'If it goes on like this, then I shall take off my uniform,' said an East German officer.

All over East Germany millions were celebrating last night. As the evening wore on, East Berliners appeared on the streets and strangers embraced each other. 'This is the most wonderful day in our lives,' said Nora van Riesen, a medical student. 'We've waited so long for this.' Steffi Schatz, a young dentist, said: 'We still can't quite believe it. It hasn't sunk in. A few weeks ago I might have thought of emigrating. Now I shall never do that.' Another young Berliner added: 'Maybe not, but they can't regain our trust overnight after forty years.' Helge, a young doctor from the Baltic coast, said: 'You wait. There will be another 200,000 emigrants at least. It'll be hard for those of us who stay behind.' East German television broke into programmes on African elephant hunting, women's fashion and cultural issues to read the statement on the new travel law.

A waitress at an East Berlin restaurant whooped for joy and said: 'We will storm KaDeWe!' KaDeWe, the Department Store of the West, is West Berlin's most fashionable and best-known department store. 'We're off to the Kudamm,' pedestrians shouted as they whooped and cheered their way towards the Bornholmer Strasse crossing point. Kurfürstendamm is the main boulevard in the centre of West Berlin. 'I'm just going over to have a look,' said one excited man.

27 December 1989: The collapse of communism in Eastern Europe leads to a high-profile victim
THE FINAL DEFIANCE OF A HATED DICTATOR
By Our Foreign Staff

Romanian television showed film last night of an unrepentant Nicolae Ceauşescu at the army tribunal on Christmas Day which led to the execution of him and his wife, Elena. Ceauşescu was seen arguing angrily and declaring in a loud voice: 'I do not recognise this court. Read the constitution.' 'We've read the constitution,' an off-screen voice answered. 'We know it better than you.' Ceauşescu, wearing a black coat, and his wife sat at a table in a sparsely furnished room. 'I will answer nothing. I will sign nothing. I will not recognise this court,' Ceauşescu said.

'Who ordered the shooting of the people?' the interrogator asked. 'I will not answer a single question,' Ceauşescu replied. 'Do not interpret my silence as answers.' He occasionally touched his wife's hands which were folded in her lap. Her face betrayed no emotion. She wore a winter coat with a fur collar. 'I will only answer to the working class,' said Ceauşescu, who often stared at the ceiling. 'I will tell the people. The people should fight to destroy this band which together with foreign powers wants to destroy the country and has carried out a coup,' Ceauşescu shouted, pointing frantically with his finger and waving his arm. Mrs. Ceauşescu occasionally smiled and mumbled.

'What possessed you to reduce the people to the state they are in?' the interrogator asked. 'Not even the peasants had enough wheat and had to come to Bucharest to buy bread. Why did the people have to starve?' 'This is a lie,' Ceauşescu said. 'Think carefully. It is a lie and proves the lack of patriotism currently in the country.' 'You destroyed the Romanian people and their economy,' the interrogator said. 'Such things are unheard of in the civilised world.' 'We do not intend to argue with you,' Ceauşescu said. 'The population had everything it needed.' At one point Mrs. Ceauşescu turned to her husband and said:

'How can you let them speak to you like that? Will you allow them to speak to an academician in such a way?' She seemed exhausted and was slumped against the wall in her chair most of the time. 'Let Elena Ceauşescu tell us about the costs of publishing her books abroad,' the off-screen voice said. 'I gave my entire life for my people,' she said angrily, making chopping motions with her hand. 'Our people.'

'On the basis of the actions of the members of the Ceauşescu family, we condemn the two of you to death,' the off-screen voice said. 'We confiscate all your property.' Then there was a freeze-frame and the accused pair's reaction was not visible. 'Please enter into the minutes that all the conditions exist to bring a verdict of guilty,' the voice said. The voice, in an angry and decisive tone, then listed the articles under which the two were found guilty. 'We tried to get you a lawyer,' the voice said. 'Your crimes were such that you merit the biggest penalty.' Ceauşescu tried to comfort his wife by touching her hand. She looked down and licked her lips.

'It is sad that you do not wish to confess the crimes you have committed against the Romanian people,' the voice said. 'We mean here, Timisoara and Bucharest. You have not only deprived the people of bread and heating, but you imprisoned the Romanian spirit which could not express itself in any way. You took oxygen from the wounded,' the voice continued. 'Your terrorists supplied themselves in the Underground and opposed the people. You have drained us. You went to the Ayatollah to make your final goodbyes [a reference to Ceauşescu's state visit to Iran last week]. You call on the people. How can you face this very people?' Mrs. Ceauşescu laughed. 'This laugh says all that needs to be, said about you,' the voice said.

'On the basis of your behaviour, you belong in a madhouse,' the voice went on. 'The two of you, if you beg my pardon, should listen to what I am saying.' Ceauşescu throughout the trial often turned his head back and forth like a trapped animal. 'You have nothing to say about the revolution? The blood spilled in Timisoara?' the voice said. Ceauşescu stood up. 'I can only be accused by the people's parliament.

You are putschists, the destroyers of Romania's independence. I was respected when I went to the factories ...' – but the voice interrupted him before he could finish.

When ordered to stand, Ceauşescu and his wife refused. 'It is unanimously decided that Ceauşescu Nicolae and Ceauşescu Elena be given the maximum sentence for genocide against the Romanian people and the destruction of the Romanian land,' the voice said. 'I refuse to recognise this court,' v declared. The film then stopped.

The place of the trial was not announced and the film of the proceedings was obviously the work of an amateur with a shaky hand-held camera. Some Romanians who wanted a public trial were disappointed by the swift judgment and executions. But plainly the military authorities believed that while he was alive he would be a source of trouble. The television report showed Ceauşescu in custody and a doctor examining him before the military court sat in judgment. The hearing was conducted in front of hundreds of soldiers. There was a call for volunteers to form a firing squad and every man raised his hand. Two soldiers and one officer were selected, apparently after lots were drawn, and the condemned couple were taken to the execution wall in a military zone.

It was 4 p.m. on Christmas Day when the Ceauşescu died – the gunfire echoing the shots which have killed many Romanians. Romanians thirsting for the Ceauşescu' blood were granted their promised wish of seeing the corpses of their former leaders. Television pictures showed the bullet-riddled wall and the two bodies slumped in front of it. A close-up of the dictator's face left Romanians in no doubt that he was dead at last. Blood was oozing from an apparent head wound.

'We want to die together, we do not want mercy,' Captain Mihai Lupoi, of the new ruling National Salvation Front, quoted Mrs. Ceauşescu as saying. Captain Lupoi said the trial of the Ceauşescu's and their executions took place in a secret military installation whose location would never be revealed for fear of sabotage by remnants of

Ceauşescu's dreaded Securitate secret police. As the couple went to their execution, Mrs. Ceauşescu said to the escorting soldiers: 'I was like a mother to you.' According to Captain Lupoi, one of the soldiers replied: 'What sort of a mother were you, who killed our mothers?'

In the mountains of Transylvania, László Tőkés, the turbulent priest who sparked Romania's revolt, waits in misty exile. The arrest, a week before Christmas of the thirty-seven-year-old pastor of the Calvinist Hungarian Reformed Church in Timisoara, provoked the demonstrations which brought disgrace, downfall and death to Ceauşescu. Visiting his retreat involved a trek along unmarked mountain tracks at midnight and checks by vigilantes of the Hungarian farming community, civil police and militia who, ten days ago, escorted the pastor as their prisoner, now protect him against threats of reprisal by remnants of Ceauşescu's security police.

'I am not the hero who began this movement,' he says in slow and clinically accurate English. 'But I would claim that I am a pastor who has taken a position against the illegal activities of the government.' László Tőkés has been the most vociferous critic of the abuse of human rights by the Ceauşescu regime against the two million strong Hungarian minority in Romania. In Hungary itself, he has become a celebrity for his campaign on television against Ceauşescu's destruction of the villages of northern Transylvania in the so-called 'agricultural systemisation' programme.

Only a few hours after the execution of the dictator and his wife, the pastor said: 'It was political wisdom to do this, but I cannot say that I hated the man, because he was a ridiculous and almost comic figure. Ceauşescu thought he could stop history, like preventing rain moving across the frontiers, or holding back a waterfall – which was the democracy movement in Europe.'

Pastor Tőkés hints at a personal sense of contest over the years between himself and Ceauşescu: if the dictator had not fallen, he believes that his regime would have framed his own destruction. The crisis of the conflict came two weekends ago: two bishops, puppets of the regime, had ordered the pastor to be evicted from his church and living in Timisoara for insulting the Romanian people, and this was enforced by a civil court order. 'I protested against the methods of these bishops and I wanted to expose the facts. In my way, I am a revolutionary, but not a romantic one; I only act in concrete forms of the causes I fight for.'

Ten days before Christmas, security police moved in to carry out the eviction order. The demonstrations outside the presbytery grew into the march and the massacre of the Opera Square in Timisoara, the Bucharest revolt and the downfall of the Ceauşescu dynasty. 'Seeing the first demonstrations, I felt in me a deep pain and crisis. At first I wanted them to go away as I did not know what might result,' he said.

At 3 a.m. on the morning of Sunday, 17 December, after the demonstrators had gone away, police broke down the doors of his house, office and then his church. 'They came in as I stood by the table of God; they tore off my cassock, threw it down on the bench (where it still lies) and led me away.' He, his pregnant wife and small son were then taken in an armed convoy to the Transylvanian mountain village where five days of interrogation began. He is convinced he was to be framed as a paid agent of Hungary and the West, as the prime mover of recent discord against the Ceauşescu regime. Just before the interrogation session, scheduled for last Friday, he and his wife heard on the radio that Ceauşescu had fallen: 'We were inexpressibly glad he had gone.' The session was cancelled and the security police quit the village.

He now faces difficult choices: 'I always have the call of my parish, and I now have the call of Bucharest where I believe I can do something for the Hungarians in Romania and the Romanians themselves.' 'Christmas,' he concluded, 'is when we give gifts. The biggest gift after forty years is the gift of liberty, though it has brought mourning and sacrifice by the many heroes among the dead. Romania is a gift, too; now, perhaps, a real gift to Europe.'

23 December 1990: Breakthrough under the English Channel for the Channel Tunnel workers
MINERS, MOËT AND MONTY PYTHON
EXCITEMENT IN SHORT SUPPLY AS PRINCIPAL PLAYERS MISS THE GREAT CHANNEL TUNNEL BREAKTHROUGH
By Maurice Weaver

On the grey weekend morning that they joined our island to the Continent, a woman phoned Radio Kent and said it was a tragic day for Britain. A reporter from the *New York Times* surveying attitudes to the Chunnel in Dover's shopping centre reported with awe that an average passer-by in Fifth Avenue would probably have shown more interest; while at the under-sea site of the breakthrough, toasts were drunk in Moët to what was termed the tunnellers' equivalent of landing on the moon.

With such mixed emotions did Great Britain become a land-spur off Calais. They had burrowed beneath the twenty-one-mile strait that had kept us special, or at least different, for 8,000 years, by-passed Churchill's 'tank trap' and brought us face to face, grimly or exuberantly, depending on your view, with our identity as New Europeans. As great moments of history go, the breakthrough – or *'Percement 1990'*, as the French would have it – was strangely anti-climactic. Perhaps this was because political bloodletting at Westminster – manoeuvres which were arguably of rather less long-term political significance than the tunnel link – had robbed the ceremony of its principal players. Mrs. Thatcher had planned enthusiastically to be there to shake hands with M. Mitterrand, a greeting that would have surely matched those of Stanley and Livingstone, Reagan and Gorbachev. But she is unseated, and he developed a diplomatic cold.

We saw on big-screen TV this claustrophobic tunnel with a grey rock face and a miner called Graham Fagg wearing a hard hat and an orange sweatshirt going at it like a demon with an air drill. Then a jagged man-sized hole appeared, as though we were watching a TV film about bank robbers breaking into a vault. When the hole got bigger, Mr. Fagg's bottom disappeared through it and he was pictured being hugged by a French miner called Philippe Cozette. The most memorable image of the tunnel breakthrough was surely not the stage-managed sight of the two miners shaking hands, but the solemn customs and immigration officers, from both sides of the Channel, who with great dignity set up their desks just outside the tunnel entrance to process those who emerged. Monty Python, one felt, would have approved. Or maybe it was the rank-and-file tunnellers, ex-miners almost to a man, who on seeing the television cameras broke spontaneously into a jolly chorus of: ''Ere we go, 'ere we go, 'ere we go.'

The temperature in the tunnel was so high V.I.P.s were urged to remove their trousers before donning boiler-suits. Many of them did so, travelled through to the other side, and, according to Eurotunnel director Colin Kirkland: 'We had the devil's own job to match them up again.'

17 January 1991: The First Gulf War commences
U.S. UNLEASHES OPERATION DESERT STORM ON BAGHDAD
By Stephen Robinson and Ian Brodie in Washington

Almost six months into an uneasy standoff, President Bush, commander in chief, broke the almost unbearable tension which has gripped the American people and unleashed the U.S. Air Force over Baghdad. Mr. Bush waited a mere nineteen hours after the U.N. deadline for Iraq's withdrawal before acting to reverse the invasion, something he promised to do days after Iraqi tanks rolled into Kuwait on 2 August. Shortly after 7 p.m. Washington time, the President's spokesman, Mr. Marlin Fitzwater, hurried out of the Oval Office in the White House, where he had consulted Mr. Bush, to announce that Operation Desert Shield had become Operation Desert Storm.

'The liberation of Kuwait has begun. In conjunction with the forces of our coalition partners, the United States has moved under the codename Operation Desert Storm to enforce the mandates of the United Nations Security Council,' he said. 'As of 7 p.m. Eastern Standard Time, Operation Desert Storm forces were engaging targets in Kuwait and Iraq,' Mr. Fitzwater said in a hushed White House press room. Modern satellite communications had allowed television networks to report the first telephoned eyewitness accounts of the attacks on Baghdad to millions of Americans glued to their television screens while eating dinner.

The forty-first President of the United States had staked his reputation and his political life on reversing Iraq's aggression, which he said, soon after the invasion, 'would not stand'. While saying since the beginning of the week that hostilities would begin 'sooner rather than later', the White House did nothing to dampen speculation that there would be at least a two-day lull before an attack on Iraq. Mr. Bush was due to deliver a speech at 2 a.m. British time that had taken him three to four weeks to write and had gone through several drafts. White House officials said that although the war had taken five and a half months to be declared, Mr. Bush had been prepared for the use of force from the first day that Kuwait was invaded, 2 August.

President Bush, his place in history at stake, said early today that the allied coalition had no choice but to drive President Saddam Hussein out of Kuwait by force and promised Americans: 'We will not fail.' Declaring in a television address that 'the battle has been joined', Mr. Bush said he was determined to knock out President Saddam's potential to build a nuclear bomb, to destroy his chemical weapons facilities and also much of his large arsenal of artillery and tanks. 'Our goal is not the conquest of Iraq, it is the liberation of Kuwait,' said Mr. Bush, who looked and sounded less strained than in recent days, as if it was a relief to have taken the decision to go to war.

In his opening words from the White House, he said: 'Just two hours ago Allied air forces began an attack on military targets in Iraq and Kuwait. These attacks continue as I speak,' said a solemn President Bush, who said the conflict started when Saddam invaded 'a small and helpless neighbour'. He reported that so far allied ground forces had not been engaged, but initial reports from General Norman Schwarzkopf, his commanding general in the Gulf, were that the aerial bombardment – widely predicted as the opening salvo of the war and likely to last up to a week or more – was going according to plan. 'Our objectives are clear: Saddam Hussein's forces will leave Kuwait, the legitimate government of Kuwait will be restored to its rightful place, and Kuwait will once again be free.'

'Why act now, why not wait?' said the President, were the questions on many lips. 'The answer is clear, the world could wait no longer,' he said. The sanctions, which he had supported so enthusiastically at the start, showed no signs of achieving their objective, he said. It is a point that American politicians, and historians, will long argue. Furthermore, said the President: 'Saddam Hussein met every overture of peace with contempt.' Sanctions had been tried for more than five months, in which time Saddam had 'systematically raped, pillaged and plundered' Kuwait, committing 'unspeakable atrocities'. While the world waited, Saddam was working to add to his chemical arsenal an infinitely more dangerous weapon, that of nuclear weapons.

The fear among Mr. Bush's senior advisers is that the war will be long and costly. He said he had urged his military commanders to prevail as quickly as possible with the greatest degree of protection for American and allied lives. 'This will not be another Vietnam,' he said. 'Our troops will have the best possible support in the entire world. They will not be asked to fight with one hand tied behind their backs.' Kuwait had been 'crushed' and 'brutalised' and military action had only been taken after months of 'constant and virtually endless' diplomatic activity. He cited the comments of a number of individual American servicemen and women on their role in the Gulf and said he had called on them and their 'courageous comrades in arms to do what must be done'.

He said: 'Tonight America and the world are deeply grateful to them and to their families, and let me say to everyone listening and watching tonight that when the troops we have sent in have finished their work, I am determined to bring them home as soon as possible.'

The Americans and their allies were in the fight for more than the price of a gallon of petrol: 'We're here to chart the future for the next one hundred years. We have before us the opportunity to forge for ourselves and future generations a new world order – one ruled by law and not the rule of the jungle. I am convinced that not only will we prevail but that out of the horror of conflict will come a recognition that no nation can strike against the world order; that no nation will be allowed to assault its neighbour.' The declaration of war came from a man who was lampooned as a 'wimp' during the 1988 election, an unfair label given his own record as a carrier pilot in the Second World War when he was shot down by the Japanese.

Some officials in the Bush administration had believed he would allow a grace period of as long as forty-eight hours to make an unambiguous break between the passing of the U.N. deadline and combat. For the time being, Mr. Bush has the support of two out of three Americans, but the numbers could evaporate swiftly if casualty figures soar. As the President spoke on television from the Oval Office, a crowd of two hundred anti-war protesters kept up a chant of 'No Blood for Oil' and thumped 'drums of peace' in the small park across Pennsylvania Avenue from the White House. Across the country, the peace movement is gaining strength, although still only a fraction of its Vietnam size. Organisers are hoping for large marches this weekend.

1 March 1991: A quick end to the war
THE GULF: CEASEFIRE GREETED WITH JOY AND RELIEF
By Robert Fox with the British 4th Armoured Brigade in Kuwait

The ceasefire came as abruptly as the Gulf crisis had erupted. Troops at the headquarters of 4th Brigade huddled round a cheap plastic radio to hear President Bush's announcement. For the occasion they had brought their tracked carriers to a halt above the ravine of the Wadi Al-Batin, one of the main lines of attack in the one hundred-hour land war. The Brigade was backing up its sister formation of 7th Brigade in the hot pursuit of Iraqi forces fleeing from Kuwait City and the Republican Guard being pressed southward by the American airborne forces along the Euphrates. The British 1st Division was moving towards Kuwait from Iraq where it had been in action since Monday.

The news of the temporary cessation of hostilities was received with quiet joy and relief – no shouting and no cheers, only a few handshakes and smiles. The soldiers seemed too exhausted for anything more exuberant. For three days they had been traversing the southern Iraqi desert with almost no time for rest. 'Yes, I really think it is peace,' said Corporal Harris, thirty-four, from Glasgow. 'Looking at the faces of those Iraqi prisoners I think it will hold. I must say a tear came to the eye when I heard it on the radio in the front of my wagon. The first thing I want to do is to get a message back to Herself. I'll take her on a trip on the Orient Express now. Most of all, I'm happy for the Kuwaitis – really it was like England taking over Scotland. A big nation taking over a smaller one. Right from the start I knew it was right.'

Meanwhile his commander, Major Carel Bouwers, was taking in donations of ten Saudi riyals a go for the sweepstake on the date when peace would break out. 'I don't know if I should declare the winner yet; it depends if it is to be temporary or permanent.' Taking no chances the Brigade Chief of Staff, Major Julian James, a paratrooper with a neat line in cooling desert camouflage, shouted: 'Keep vigilant, it's only a temporary ceasefire. That means keep your weapons ready, but fire only if you are fired upon. It could go wrong in two days and we may have to go in again.'

But few on the bluffs above the wadi believed that fighting would resume. The speed and violence of the coalition attack had robbed Saddam Hussein of more than forty divisions in just over four days. The allied onslaught launched from Saudi Arabia on Sunday had been based on speed, firepower and surprise. It was a modern form of the German blitzkrieg – striking in depth by land and air. Above all, General Schwarzkopf's plan owed its inspiration to Soviet tactics of concentrating firepower in layers or echelons, rather than a broad front, and concealing the principal line of attack, or point of main effort, to the last moment. The tactic in current American military theology is called 'AirLand 2000', a blueprint from which General Schwarzkopf's script has barely deviated. The attack is based on deception and surprise, a poker player's bluff.

The British 1st Armoured Division has played a crucial role in this. From its first deployment it was portrayed as operating in the east to support a direct assault on Kuwait City by the U.S. Marines. From the beginning of this month it began manoeuvring to the west, linking up with the massing VII Corps of American armoured and mechanised infantry divisions. To maintain the bluff, recordings of radio signal traffic from previous exercises were broadcast to suggest to the Iraqis that the British were still on the east coast of Saudi Arabia. The deception ploy put tight constraints on reporters accredited to the British division in the field. Whole exercises were deemed too sensitive to be reported on grounds of operations security. Once battle was joined individual allied and enemy units could not be named. Nor could mention be made that the British were fighting inside Iraq itself.

To the same end, the precise aim of Operation Desert Sabre was kept under wraps. The mission of the coalition forces was quaintly phrased in the official brief: 'The defence of Kuwait once freed and the destruction of the Republican Guard Forces.' In other words Saddam Hussein would be a shorn Samson once deprived of his elite forces. The plan was to attack in four main sectors across the Saudi borders with Iraq and Kuwait. The U.S. Marines would attack up the coast in the east while the Arab forces of the Northern Army Command moved into Kuwait from the south-west border with Saudi Arabia.

Further west the five American divisions of the U.S. VII Corps, with the British division attached, were to go into Iraq to take on the Republican Guard. At the same time air assault forces of the U.S. 101st and 82nd Airborne forces, flanked by the French 6th Division, were to move deep into the Iraqi desert to draw out the two toughest divisions of the Guard, the Hammurabi and the Madina, heavily dug-in in northern Kuwait and south of Basra. The Tawalkana Division, already badly hit by American air strikes, was to be demolished by American tank forces charging north to meet up with the airborne divisions. The air assault was to prove the master stroke. Thousands of troops were moved hundreds of miles into Iraq by a single flight of 460 helicopters, the biggest helicopter assault in military history. The soldiers then secured a disused airfield so transport planes could fly in heavy guns, ammunition and light tanks.

The Iraqis fell for the ploy and moved the Republican Guard out of deep hiding to escape to Baghdad. Once exposed they were open to air attack by helicopter and fighter bomber. 'The Apache helicopters queued like a taxi rank to attack as the Guards tried to flee from northern Kuwait along Route 8,' said a senior staff officer who said the helicopters had knocked out eighty T-72 tanks still on their road transporters. Once the Americans were convinced that the Hammurabi and Madina divisions had been crippled, President Bush called off the fighting.

Elsewhere the Soviet tactics of shock attack by armoured forces seemed hardly required. Many field commanders had lost their ability to communicate with Baghdad early on in the air war. More devastating than the air attacks for front-line troops in the trenches, however, were the new munitions of American and British artillery, shells and rockets releasing dozens of bomblets over a wide area. In the event, most of the forces encountered by the tanks and infantry had little stomach for a fight, returning fire only occasionally by machinegun or T-55 tank. And in the devastation of the battle many Iraqis had little chance to think about surrender.

In the last hours of the fighting British forces received a reminder of Saddam's former military might. Near Route 8 in Kuwait the Queen's Royal Irish Hussars discovered a mobile Scud launcher which had been concealed for weeks in a market garden and evidently had been fired often. From his tank, Brigadier Christopher Hammerbeck, 4th Armoured Brigade commander, spotted a chemical decontamination lorry. One of the biggest surprises of the campaign was that Saddam did not attempt to use his chemical arsenal. 'He was given a warning of the consequences if he did, I am quite sure,' commented Brigadier Hammerbeck bluntly. 'Here at least, the rules of the game were learned early on.'

21 May 1991: Another Gandhi falls victim to assassins
RAJIV GANDHI IS ASSASSINATED
BOMB SHATTERS HOPES OF NEHRU DYNASTY RETURNING TO POWER
By Alan Philps, Rahul Bedi and Balram Tandon

Rajiv Gandhi, the former Prime Minister of India, was assassinated at an election rally last night while campaigning to return his family's dynasty to power. Mr. Gandhi, forty-six, was killed instantly by a bomb hidden either in a bouquet or a ceremonial shawl handed to him on a floodlit stage before beginning his speech at a meeting in the southern town of Sriperumbudur, twenty-five miles from Madras. The bomb exploded at about 10.30 p.m. local time (5.30 p.m. G.M.T.) as Mr. Gandhi, leader of the Congress party, was moving towards the dais. Part of his face was blown off and his body was badly mutilated, reporters at the scene said. At least fourteen others in the crowd around him, including three women and two of Mr. Gandhi's black cat commando bodyguards, also died. It was not clear whether the assassin was among them.

Police in Madras said the bomb, which ripped apart the dais, was probably remote-controlled and suspected that Sri Lankan Tamil militants could have been among those who carried out the attack. Tamils were angered by Mr. Gandhi's decision as Prime Minister to send the Indian army to intervene in Sri Lanka's civil war and help the Colombo government control a Tamil revolt.

Mr. Gandhi, whose family has ruled India for most of the years since independence in 1947, was campaigning to regain power in elections in the southern state of Tamil Nadu. Prime Minister from 1984–89, he was the main contender for power. Shortly before the attack Mr. Gandhi had placed a garland on a statue of his mother, Indira, who was assassinated by her Sikh bodyguards in 1984. Security forces were immediately placed on alert for further violence as news of the assassination spread. In Madras early today scores of cars were reported to have been smashed by gangs on the outskirts of the city.

The elections, the tenth since independence, have been the bloodiest ever, with two hundred people killed since campaigning began last month. Authorities had spread voting in the campaign over three days so that police could concentrate to control violence. The Congress party had been tipped to emerge as the biggest party from the week-long election, though without an outright majority, and Mr. Gandhi could have returned to the premiership. His body was due to be flown back to New Delhi last night. No one immediately claimed responsibility for the murder.

His death is the latest blow to strike the family. His younger brother, Sanjay, died in an air crash in 1980 while performing aerobatics. After his mother's death in 1984, Rajiv Gandhi, an airline pilot and political novice, was forced to step in to fill the gap. Though he has a son and a daughter by his Italian-born widow, Sonia, there is no one left to carry the torch of the Nehru dynasty.

Political observers believe it is also the end of the Congress party which was built on the basis of peaceful co-existence between Hindus and Muslims, as there are no charismatic politicians in waiting. The expected decline of the centrist party appears to leave the field open to extremists, particularly the right-wing Hindu revivalist Bharatiya Janata party.

The United News of India (UNI) news agency said Mr. Gandhi was identified by a senior police officer, who turned the mutilated body over as it was lying in the dirt. Mr. Gandhi, once one of the most carefully guarded men on the Indian sub-continent, had cut down on his security for the election campaign. He piloted his own executive jet and drove his own car during the campaign and did without security guards. He had adopted an open-style of campaigning, going out to meet crowds and casually receiving bouquets which, much to their delight, he would often pass back.

He regarded the elections as a major challenge and was determined to return to power after two years in opposition. His party has always won the majority in the south in parliamentary elections. This time, however, he faced hostility from the lower orders of the Hindu caste system as well as Tamil refugees from Sri Lanka angered at his sending the Indian army to intervene in the island's civil strife. Mr. Gandhi had been on the target list of Sikh terrorists fighting for an independent nation in northern Punjab state, but the Sikhs have not been known to operate in Tamil Nadu. Previous attempts have been made on his life: in 1986 when a Sikh youth fired shots at a meeting he was attending in Delhi, and in 1987 when he was attacked by a Sri Lankan sailor as he reviewed a guard of honour.

Last weekend most polls indicated that the Congress party had a majority in the elections, but some pollsters said it would fall short of winning a majority. At least one poll said Mr. Gandhi would sweep to victory. Mr. Gandhi, a graduate of Trinity College, Cambridge, was one of India's most charismatic leaders and one of the youngest Prime Ministers on the sub-continent. The Press Trust said he was cheerful and confident about his party's chances in the General Election, and his prospects of once again becoming Prime Minister. The Chief Election Commissioner, Mr. T.N. Seshan, was quoted last night as saying that the remaining two phases of the general elections will be postponed until next month.

Shortly before the blast, Mr. Gandhi told reporters he had accurately predicted heavy violence during the campaign for parliamentary elections. 'I told you there would be plenty of violence during these elections. Already the number of persons killed is high,' he said.

Mr. Gandhi's grandfather, Jawaharlal Nehru, was Prime Minister from 1947 to 1964. Mrs. Sonia Gandhi, his Italian-born wife, and his two children were not at the meeting during yesterday's campaign. Mrs. Gandhi, who was campaigning in Amethi, her husband's constituency, flew to Madras last night. Rahul, his son, was on his way home from the United States where he is studying. Mr. Chandra Shekhar, the Indian Prime Minister, was flying to New Delhi from Orissa, where he had been campaigning, to hold emergency meetings. Today has been declared a day of national mourning in India.

8 February 1992: The Maastricht Treaty is signed
THE FINAL ACT REMAINS OPEN TO INTERPRETATION
Boris Johnson sees the rather confused signing of the
Maastricht Treaty on European Union

When the ceremony was over, the band had played, and the pleni-potentiaries of the twelve E.C. countries had filed past the table with their specially issued black fountain pens, there was only one question in the Maastricht Provinciehuis. What, exactly, had they signed?

Mr. Hurd later blushingly confessed he had no idea what the difference was between the two enormous tomes, one bigger than the other, which now bore his signature. 'I didn't read every page,' he said. 'Where are the experts?' asked Mr. Francis Maude, Financial Secretary to the Treasury, who joined Mr. Hurd for the occasion. British officials rushed to explain. 'It's perfectly clear,' said one Foreign Office spokesman. 'The big book was the integrated text of the Union Treaty and the other was . . . er.'

The Government was stoutly resisting suggestions last night that Mr. Hurd, after two years of furious objections, had inadvertently signed the E.C. Social Charter. Dutch officials later confirmed that the largest volume was the text of the revised E.C. treaty agreed at Maastricht, now called the Treaty on European Union, while the smaller one was the Maastricht Final Act, consisting of the various annexes and protocols agreed. Commenting on the negotiations, which climaxed last December in the same round chandeliered room in the concrete pill-box on an island in the River Maas, Mr. Hurd said: 'It is a room full of memories – in the end, happy memories.' Each statesman in the room was content to put his own interpretation on the texts. Mr. Hurd saw it as a 'success for British objectives'.

In a speech delivered in Cambridge earlier in the day, he expertly glossed over the massive transfers of sovereignty involved. 'Our proposals on defence, shared with the Italians and the Dutch, prevailed,' he said. That will come as something of a surprise in Paris and Bonn, where fresh moves are already under way since the Maastricht summit to create a full-scale European army, largely independent of Nato control. Mr. Hurd claimed that 'the pillar structure of the treaty was a significant check for the ambitions of the federalist'. That was starkly at variance with the jubilation of M. Jacques Delors, E.C. commission president, who congratulated participants on an achievement in building a federal Europe which would have been 'scarcely conceivable two years ago'.

Mr. Hurd was forced to admit that the Government was already preparing for the next treaty changes in 1996, when France and Germany are likely to push for yet more powers for the European parliament. Speaking in Paris, President Mitterrand hailed the Treaty on Union as more important than the Community's founding Treaty of Rome. Mr. Hurd demurred, saying it was less radical than the 1986 Single European Act, which created the frontier-free Europe of next year.

20 November 1992: The *annus horribilis* for Queen Elizabeth II gets worse
FIRE SWEEPS WINDSOR CASTLE
'ABSOLUTELY DEVASTATED' QUEEN JOINS IN FIGHT TO SAVE THREATENED ART TREASURES
By Michael Fleet and Sean O'Neill

Windsor Castle was severely damaged by a fire which was brought under control late last night. Hundreds of firemen had battled to save the fabric of the castle, which houses one of the world's greatest collections of art treasures. The Queen was said by the Duke of York to be 'absolutely devastated' at the damage, which could amount to tens of millions of pounds. She and the Duke helped in the rescue of treasures.

The blaze swept through State rooms in the north-east corner of the building. Although the Queen was not in residence yesterday – her forty-fifth wedding anniversary – the Duke of York was working in his private quarters when the fire broke out and joined a human chain to save many precious objects. Later, he said that six paintings had been destroyed. Looking back at the flames and smoke last night, the Duke said: 'It is where I was brought up and it's a terrible sadness to see it in this condition.'

The fire, which began in the private chapel within the castle's Chester Tower, spread rapidly. More than two hundred firefighters from London and the Home Counties tried to control the flames. Police said the blaze was not the work of terrorists. The Queen, who was at Buckingham Palace, went immediately to Windsor when told of the fire. She visited the scene for an hour, surveying the damage being caused to the biggest inhabited castle in the world. The Prince of Wales arrived at the castle last night to see flames still licking from the castellations some nine hours after the fire started.

Late last night Berkshire Fire Service said they were satisfied the fire was under control, but firemen would be remaining at the scene well into today damping down and dealing with any erupting 'hot spots'. However, towards midnight, winds fanned the fire and flames leapt into the sky. The fire, watched by hundreds of people, was visible for miles around. It started in the Queen's private chapel and was spotted in a curtain. Workers thought they might be able to tackle it with extinguishers. But the fire took hold quickly and burst through to St. George's Hall where parts of the timber ceiling of the 180-foot long room, which is used for state banquets, collapsed.

From there it swept through the State apartments, which are open to the public when the Queen is in residence. It reached the State Entrance, near where a famous Dolls' House built by Sir Edwin Lutyens for Queen Mary is housed, and took hold in Brunswick Tower. There was severe smoke damage to parts of the building not actually touched by the flames. The Waterloo Chamber, whose twelfth century walls are adorned with carvings by the sculptor Grinling Gibbons, is thought to have been badly affected.

Fire crews fought to prevent the blaze spreading to the Royal Family's private quarters which adjoin the Chester Tower. At the western end of St George's Hall a firebreak was created to prevent the flames spreading into the imposing State Entrance where the Queen receives visiting statesmen.

The Duke of York, who was at the castle when the fire started at around 11.40 a.m., joined workmen, castle staff and soldiers of the Lifeguards regiment in forming a human chain to rescue treasures. These were laid out on giant sheets of plastic on a lawn in front of the burning castle before being taken away in a convoy of lorries. Paintings, carpets, desks, coat stands and even suits of armour were spread across the plastic sheets together with a 150-foot long dining table removed in sections. Throughout the operation a Gurkha soldier guarding the entrance to the castle stood rigidly impassive as around him hundreds joined in the rescue of treasures.

Two giant hoists lifted firefighters above the castle's turrets to direct water on to the flames while a dozen ladders were rested against the walls as hoses were aimed through arched windows whose glass had been blown out by the heat. The Queen arrived from Buckingham Palace at 3 p.m. and spoke to firefighters before going to her private rooms where she oversaw the removal of all her furniture and works of art, helping herself by taking paintings from the walls and wrapping them in cloth.

The Duke said he had informed his mother of the fire soon after it began. 'Her Majesty is absolutely devastated by what has happened. She has been inside the castle helping to take things out as a precaution. Other members of the Royal Family have been informed and are very shocked,' the Duke said. Asked about the Queen's reaction, Mr. Dickie Arbiter, a Buckingham Palace press officer, said: 'Probably the same reaction as yours if you saw your home burning. She appeared very upset.'

The fire was first noticed by members of the Queen's picture surveyors at work in the private chapel. 'They were removing and wrapping up paintings at the time and noticed the fire in a curtain. We have no idea how it started but it was horrifying how it spread so quickly,' the Duke said. The castle is undergoing a major renovation and the rooms were being cleared as part of that process and to prepare some for rewiring. The Duke was in the castle's mews across a quadrangle from the scene of the fire when it started. 'It is an immense relief that this happened in daylight when there were a lot of people around. Had it happened at night I think we would have lost a great deal more,' he said.

He added: 'They are moving works of art and furniture from all the rooms that could possibly be at risk. Therefore the contents of the Queen's apartments are being taken out and secured elsewhere. There's nowhere for the Queen to stay tonight so she will be returning to Buckingham Palace. I will stay so long as I can be of some use.'

The damage to the castle fabric was described as more severe than that caused by the 1986 Hampton Court fire, but the Duke said that the vast majority of treasures inside had been rescued. Most were moved by lorry to safe parts of the castle, including a riding school in the grounds which was the only building long enough to take a carpet from the Waterloo Chamber, a banqueting hall which suffered smoke and water damage.

Buckingham Palace said last night it hoped that the damage might not be as widespread as at first feared. 'A lot of the Royal collection was moved out because of the renovation work, and indeed the Queen lent a lot of paintings to galleries around the country last year,' said a spokeswoman. 'There is a Salvage Corps based at all the royal palaces and they are called upon to clear important objects in the event of a fire or a flood; and of course because of the work a lot of the items have been moved around. At the end of the day we are hoping that only a handful of works of art may have been lost.'

But Sir Roy Strong, former director of both the National Portrait

Gallery and the Victoria and Albert Museum, said Windsor Castle still housed the greatest concentration of the Queen's private collection. 'The art treasures are just untold,' he said on Sky TV. 'I pray nothing has happened to it because otherwise it could be one of the great national heritage tragedies of this century.' As well as the magnificent paintings, 'fabulous' collections of armour, furniture and eighteenth-century French tapestries were also at risk. The interior of the area of the castle affected was 'a superb example' of Regency decoration 'on a spectacular scale'.

Mr. David Harper, Fire Incident Commander, said the blaze was contained within one section of the castle. 'It's such a complicated building. You have to rely an awful lot on the people who work in it. The structure is very weak in certain areas and parts of it are close to collapse. The fire is quite a healthy size. It has vented itself in the roof, but there's little chance of it moving horizontally to the main part of the building.' There were fears that walls in the castle could collapse under the intense heat, and scaffolders stood by awaiting a chance to prop them up.

The Duke said it was impossible to judge the full extent of the damage until the fire had been completely beaten. 'The problem is that there are many "dead spaces" throughout the castle where people neither live nor work but where the fire can spread, making it much more difficult to control. There is also a lot of wood which made it spread much more quickly. But everyone involved has co-operated magnificently. There was no panic, fuss or mourning. It is a pretty nasty mess inside but everything we could possibly take out has been.'

Eight people were injured during the fire-fighting operation. One was a workman who fell from a ladder and is believed to have broken several bones as he tried to erect a fire barrier. A member of the castle staff was taken to hospital after hyperventilating. The third injured man was Mr. Dean Lansdell, a twenty-one-year-old painter and decorator working at the castle, who entered the private chapel after hearing shouts of 'Fire' from people inside. He was treated for burns at a hospital in Slough and said afterwards that he had saved three paintings from the wall of the chapel but was burned when he returned to collect another. 'It was an inferno in there. The curtains were ablaze and the whole room was about to go up. I picked up another painting which was on the floor and immediately felt my hands burning from the heat of the frame,' said Mr. Lansdell, from Farnborough, Hants. Five firemen were also treated for smoke effects and hypothermia.

Mr. David Harper, Berkshire assistant fire chief, said that as the flames were shooting from the roof they were in effect making the task easier to prevent a sideways sweep of the fire. But he added: 'It is sending itself through the roof. It is hard to contain because of the nature of the building.'

11 May 1994: Nelson Mandela is elected President of post-apartheid South Africa
PRESIDENT MANDELA
NEVER, NEVER AGAIN SHALL THIS BEAUTIFUL LAND EXPERIENCE
THE OPPRESSION OF ONE BY ANOTHER
By Trevor Fishlock and Alec Russell in Pretoria

South Africa had never known such splendour. The world and his wife came to celebrate the inauguration of President Nelson Mandela. It was a coronation, a rebirth, the beginning of the second republic, an independence day, the joyful climax of an epic struggle. Strong security in Pretoria, with police concerned that white extremists might try to attack the new president, did not blight an occasion which was relaxed, happy and informal: a huge garden party set to music on a warm and brilliant autumn day.

Mr. Mandela placed upon the occasion the imprimatur of his dignity and modesty. Smiling contentedly, he was acclaimed by the applause, cheers and ululations of thousands. Watched by a worldwide television audience, he swore his oath to serve South Africa and declared his determination to work for reconciliation. He spoke of the 'human disaster' of apartheid. 'We saw our country tear itself apart in terrible conflict. It was outlawed by the peoples of the world.' But today, he said, 'we feel fulfilled . . . humanity has taken us back into its bosom. The time for the healing of wounds has come, the moment to bridge the chasms that divided us. We enter into a covenant that we shall build a society in which all South Africans, black and white, will be able to walk tall. Never, never again will this beautiful land experience the oppression of one by another and suffer the indignity of being the skunk of the world.'

The Union Buildings in Pretoria, an imperial sandstone pile built eighty-one years ago, and for so long the bastion of white power and engine room of apartheid, formed the amphitheatre for the inauguration. In the distance, high on a hill, stood the massive and brooding Voortrekker Monument, raised as an assertion of Afrikaner nationalism. Heads of state, royalty, prime ministers and other representatives of 145 countries took part in South Africa's extraordinary day. Prince Philip represented Britain, the first member of the Royal Family to visit South Africa since 1947. Mr. Yasser Arafat jauntily acknowledged cheers. Prime Minister Benazir Bhutto of Pakistan shimmered by, as if on the catwalk. Vice-President Al Gore, Mrs. Hillary Clinton and Mr. Jesse Jackson led the American team. President Castro, a worn figure with a grizzled beard, was greeted with chants of 'Castro! Castro!' Here was the man who fought a twelve-year war against South Africa in Angola, who once vowed that his Cuban troops would march to Cape Town.

After the parliamentary ceremonies of the day before, and Mr. Mandela's election to the presidency, the inauguration was a dazzling multi-racial pageant, bright robes, gorgeous frocks, gaudy headdresses and the frilly fashions of Afrikaner chic. Many women wore dresses in the colours of the new national flag: black, gold, green, white, red and blue. Choirs sang sweetly, rhythm groups had people swaying and chanting, a naval band played 'Land of Hope and Glory'. The day was also a celebration of South Africa's return to the international fold after decades of being outlawed. The point was underscored by Mr. Boutros Boutros Ghali, U.N. Secretary General: 'Today South Africa regains its rightful place in the family of nations.'

So large was the crowd, with guests moving slowly to their seats, that the inauguration started eighty minutes late. Mr. Mandela entered the amphitheatre to loud cheers. He was accompanied by his daughter Zenani, who wore a red outfit crowned by an outsize top hat. Her mother, Mrs. Winnie Mandela, was moved, at the last minute, from the stalls to the dais.

Deputy Presidents F.W. de Klerk and Thabo Mbeki were sworn in, then Mr. Mandela read the oath and signed it, to a roar of applause. He kissed his daughter and shook hands with Mr. de Klerk. Prayers were said by Hindu, Jewish, Muslim and Christian clerics. A poet spoke verses in praise of the new president.

Mr. Mandela rose to make his speech, with its theme of reconciliation and nation-building. He concluded: 'God bless South Africa' He was hugged by Mr. Walter Sisulu, his old friend and fellow graduate of the 'university' of Robben Island. Among Mr. Mandela's special guests was Mr. James Gregory, a former Robben Island warder who regards him with awe.

A twenty-one-gun salute boomed. Helicopters and jets flew in salute. Few needed reminding that not so long ago these aircraft were attacking African National Congress guerrilla camps. Then, from behind a bullet-proof glass screen, Mr. Mandela addressed an excited crowd outside the Union Buildings. He praised Mr. de Klerk as 'a great reformer, one of the great sons of our soil'. Twelve hundred V.I.P.s joined Mr. Mandela for a banquet in a vast marquee at the presidency building. Five thousand others were served an African lunch on the lawn. Because of a transport failure Prince Philip, with Mr. Douglas Hurd, the Foreign Secretary, did not reach the banquet on time and had the African lunch. It included springbok pate, smoked ostrich and crocodile.

15 July 1995: Horror in Bosnia as 'ethnic cleansing' leads to atrocities
SILENCE IN THE CITY 'CLEANSED' OF ALL ITS MEN
U.N. AND RED CROSS URGE SERBS TO DISCLOSE FATE OF SREBRENICA CAPTIVES
By Patrick Bishop

Bosnian Serb soldiers and a very few civilians are all that moves in the empty streets of Srebrenica. The Muslim population has been driven from the town, probably never to return. Yesterday the United Nations High Commissioner of Refugees and the Red Cross were urgently seeking information about the fate of the men of Srebrenica, separated from their families when the Serbs stormed the enclave, and taken off to unknown holding places. Ominously, the Bosnian Serb army said it planned to screen the men to sift out 'war criminals'.

A Bosnian government official in Tuzla, Semsudin Hasanbegovic, claimed yesterday that Serb soldiers had dragged men out of columns of refugees and 'executed them on the spot'. There was no confirmation of the allegation. Unconfirmed reports said some of the men were being held at a football stadium in the nearby town of Bratunac with others at different locations. The U.N.H.C.R. and Red Cross were negotiating with the Bosnian Serb military and civilian authorities in Pale for permission to visit them. At the same time Red Cross teams were questioning refugees arriving in the government-held towns of Tuzla and Kladanj to draw up lists of missing men. Some fighters managed to escape from the town before the Serbs moved in and there were reports of continuing fighting. U.N. officials were told that 'hundreds' had been killed in the north-east corner of the enclave. As for those taken prisoner, human rights organisations are counting on international attention to dissuade the Serbs from further bloodshed and brutality. Instead they hope the captives will be kept as bargaining chips for future prisoner exchanges, which have gone on throughout the war.

In the great 'ethnic cleansing' campaigns in the summer of 1992, the Bosnian Serbs killed some of their captives and herded the rest into brutally administered concentration camps. Later, after an international outcry, all sides signed an agreement to hand over their prisoners. Since then, soldiers captured in the continuing war have been held in a variety of conditions. One major cause for concern was the Bosnian Serb practice of using PoWs to dig trenches in front-line areas. The Red Cross says that up to the fall of Srebrenica there were 1,247 detainees held in thirty-four places of detention on all sides of battle lines in Bosnia.

24 February 1997: Dolly the sheep is a first for cloning
SHE LOOKS EXACTLY LIKE ANY OTHER SHEEP. BUT THE CLONING METHOD USED TO PRODUCE DOLLY MAY CHANGE OUR LIVES
By Roger Highfield, Science Editor

The possibility that an adult human can be cloned from a single blood or skin cell was raised yesterday with the announcement that scientists have produced the world's first clone of an adult animal.

The clone, a Finn Dorset sheep called Dolly, paves the way to unprecedented genetic manipulation of farmyard animals, more cheaply and more accurately than ever before.

A single cell could be taken from a prize bull, elite racehorse or award-winning pig, and hundreds of identical animals produced using the patented cloning technology developed at the Roslin Institute and PPL Therapeutics, near Edinburgh. Introduction or deletion of genes in the cloned cells also offers the means to make animals that produce drugs in their milk, grow faster for meat production, or are resistant to diseases such as scrapie and B.S.E. The first sheep altered using the method may be born later this year, though it will be several years before scientists will have developed the means to alter many genes simultaneously, which will be necessary to boost growth or make leaner beef.

But any other use of the technology, for instance to mass-produce human eggs for use in in-vitro fertilisation, is outlawed, said Dr. Ron James, managing director of PPL. Dr. James said he had advised relevant regulatory committees about the development and its implications, but added: 'An Act of Parliament specifically forbids even doing with human eggs what we have done with sheep eggs.' And he acknowledged that there are limitations to the use of the technology at the farm – herds of identical livestock are at greater risk of disease – in addition to the inevitable qualms about mass-producing identical animals or designing animals for human use.

In earlier work, the Roslin team unveiled Megan and Morag, sheep that had been cloned by taking a cell from an early embryo, mass-producing it in the laboratory, and using these cells to 're-programme' two emptied eggs. Until now it has been thought impossible to perform the same feat using cells from an adult animal. Unlike embryo cells, which have the potential to develop into a vast range of cell types, adult cells are differentiated, that is they have turned into a liver, brain or, in this case, a cell from the udder.

Dr. Ian Wilmut, Dr. Keith Campbell and Dr. Jim McWhir at Edinburgh's Roslin Institute, working with Angelica Schnieke and Dr. Alex Kind at PPL Therapeutics, will announce the feat this week in the journal *Nature*, cloning cells from the mammary gland and connective tissue. This breakthrough, the first time that any new-born mammal has been derived from adult cells, offers PPL the possibility of using the technique to alter genetically sheep much more easily than before.

Previously, scientists have used a hit-and-miss affair: injecting DNA into an embryo and hoping that it is taken up, which only happens in ten per cent of cases or less. Instead, genes can be introduced into large numbers of cloned cells. Then the cells where genetic engineering has been successful are selected and mass-produced, producing a herd of identical 'transgenic' animals. 'We are looking at things like introducing genes for blood-clotting proteins that haemophiliacs lack,' said Dr. James, adding that they focused on cloning mammary cells to make it easier to ensure that human proteins will be made in the animal's milk. Moreover, the technique also enables the team to knock out genes, raising the possibility of deleting the prion protein – one linked to B.S.E. – from cows so they are resistant to the disease.

'Cloning cattle should be possible, because the embryology is not too dissimilar to sheep,' he said, adding that pigs would also be studied.

Cloning from adult animals may be more useful to agriculture than cloning from embryos, as farmers will be able to pick particularly productive and disease-resistant adult animals to copy. In this case, the resulting lamb – Dolly – was genetically identical to the sheep from which the cell was taken. Dolly is now several months old and is showing every sign of normal development.

'Animal breeding companies are already showing interest in the use of this technology to multiply their best animals,' said Roslin team leader Dr. Ian Wilmut. 'Genetic modification of the donor cells in culture before they are used in nuclear transfer will also allow us to introduce very precise changes in their DNA and open up the possibilities for a range of new products for the treatment of, for example, cancers and inflammation. What this will mostly be used for is to produce more health care products. It will enable us to study genetic diseases for which there is presently no cure and track down the mechanisms that are involved. The next step is to use the cells in culture in the lab and target genetic changes into that culture.'

The Roslin Institute has agreed to grant PPL an exclusive licence for the use of the technology to make human protein drugs. Patents to protect the new technology have been applied for. Previous efforts to clone Megan and Morag from embryo cells ran into a problems. Six in every ten attempts made in the original experiments worked. Five clones were produced but three sisters died – two within minutes of birth and the third within ten days. Post-mortem examinations revealed kidney and cardiovascular abnormalities.

3 May 1997: Tony Blair sweeps to power in a Labour landslide
THE NEW FAMILY AT NUMBER 10
BLAIR PROMISES TO GOVERN FOR ALL WITH 179 MAJORITY
By George Jones, Political Editor

Tony Blair promised to govern in the interests of the whole nation yesterday after making a triumphant entrance to Downing Street. Standing outside Number 10 after inflicting a devastating defeat on the Conservatives, he said there would be no return to the past. 'I say to the people of this country – we ran for office as "new" Labour, we will govern as "new" Labour,' said Mr. Blair, his party's first Prime Minister in eighteen years.

Accompanied by his wife Cherie, he left his official car in Whitehall and walked into Downing Street in bright sunshine, shaking hands with a crowd of cheering, flag-waving party workers and well-wishers. The Blairs then posed with their three children, Euan, thirteen, Nicholas, eleven, and Kathryn, nine, on the doorstep of Number 10 before Mr. Blair addressed the crowds. Earlier, as he had been driven from his home in Islington, north London, to Buckingham Palace, people came out of their homes and offices to applaud him. The jubilant scenes were reminiscent of Harold Wilson's victory in 1964 and Margaret Thatcher's arrival in Downing Street in 1979, which were similarly seen as marking the end of an era.

Mr. Blair told colleagues he believed the warmth of his reception showed that 'new' Labour's stunning success had created a mood of hope and a desire for change in the country. His first Cabinet appointment was John Prescott, who will be Deputy Prime Minister in charge of a new 'super ministry' with responsibility for the environment, transport and the regions. Mr. Prescott arrived in Downing Street on board the election battlebus in which he had travelled 11,000 miles around the country, visiting ninety marginals. His new ministry will be one of the most powerful outside the Treasury and will involve him in many of the Government's most important economic decisions.

Mr. Blair – said to be tired after little sleep – announced seven

Cabinet posts. The remaining two-thirds are expected today and the rest of the Government over the next few days. Gordon Brown will become Chancellor of the Exchequer and will introduce his first Budget, including the 'windfall' tax on the privatised utilities and the cut in VAT on domestic fuel, next month. Robin Cook becomes Foreign Secretary, Jack Straw will be Home Secretary, David Blunkett – the first blind Cabinet minister – is to be Secretary for Education and Employment, and Margaret Beckett is President of the Board of Trade. Lord Irvine of Lairg, Q.C., who is one of Mr. Blair's close confidantes, becomes Lord Chancellor. Lord Irvine introduced Mr. Blair to his wife when they both became pupils in his legal chambers in the 1970s. Speculation that Clare Short, the Left-wing spokesman for overseas development, would not be in the Cabinet was discounted by government sources.

The Tory party was in a state of shock as it sought to come to terms with the earthquake that had reshaped the political map of Britain and set a clutch of records. The Conservatives have been reduced to an English rump – with no M.P.s in Scotland or Wales for the first time in the party's history.

It was Labour's biggest electoral triumph, giving Mr. Blair a huge Commons majority of 179. Some of his M.P.s will be unable to find seats on the Government side of the chamber.

On the morning of polling day, Mr. Blair believed Labour could win by only about thirty to forty seats. It was only on the aircraft bringing him back to London from his constituency of Sedgefield, County Durham, just before dawn that he began to appreciate the scale of the landslide. After he touched down, Mr. Blair took a congratulatory call from Bill Clinton, whose two successful presidential campaigns provided much of the inspiration for Labour. The Tory losses were increased by tactical voting by Labour and Liberal Democrat supporters. The Liberal Democrats almost doubled their number of M.P.s to forty-six – their biggest representation at Westminster since the 1920s.

Mr. Blair, at forty-three, is the youngest Prime Minister since 1812 and has no previous ministerial experience. Speaking in Downing Street, he joined Paddy Ashdown, the Liberal Democrat leader, in paying tribute to the 'dignity and courage' shown by John Major during his departure from Downing Street. Mr. Blair put achieving a 'world class' education system at the top of his objectives followed by modernisation of the welfare state. He promised to work in partnership with business to create the dynamic, competitive economy of the future.

'It shall be a government rooted in strong values, the values of justice and progress and community, the values that have guided me all my political life,' he said. 'For eighteen long years my party has been in opposition. It could only say, it could not do. Today we are charged with the deep responsibility of government. Today, enough of talking – it is time now to do.'

The new Cabinet will meet for the first time on Thursday to draw up the legislative programme to be announced in the Queen's Speech on 14 May. Mr. Blair is said to be keen to 'hit the ground running', with early legislation on the party's manifesto commitments, including Scottish and Welsh devolution.

Fortified by two hours' sleep and a couple of slices of toast, Tony and Cherie Blair left their north London home yesterday and headed triumphantly for Downing Street. For the first time Mrs. Blair was allowed inside the Prime Minister's residence – a four-bedroom flat converted from servants' quarters in the rafters above the official Government offices. Together with their children Euan, Nicholas and Kathryn, she was given a guided tour – and an opportunity to decide if indeed this would be home.

Labour sources said nothing to contradict the disclosure early this week that the Blairs had chosen to move their children there. They did stress, however, this was Mrs. Blair's first glimpse, and she would be examining all the 'realistic options' at her disposal. These include moving into another larger residence – the Government owns three flats in Admiralty Arch and a house, usually reserved for the Home Secretary, in South Eaton Place – or simply staying put.

Should she have been in need of advice there was plenty to hand. The Blair clan – his father Leo, her mother Gale and her sister Lyndsey with her own children – were all invited to a family lunch yesterday at Downing Street and a chance to conduct their own viewing of the historic property. The overriding deciding factor will probably be security. The Blairs are conscious of the risk to their children, who are excited about the prospect of moving. Mr. and Mrs. Blair had prepared the children for such a day as yesterday. They had talked to them constantly about what would happen should their father be elected Prime Minister. Mr. Blair is known to be extremely grateful that their privacy was respected and believes that has helped them adjust. Party sources said that Mr. Blair would not be spending his first night as Prime Minister in Number 10, but would return to Islington.

The day began early for the Blairs. They had arrived back at their four-storey terrace home in an Islington crescent shortly after 6.30 a.m. to find a gathering of twenty supporters, each carrying a single red rose. The house was full. Mr. Blair's brother Bill, who lives nearby, and an assortment of aunts and cousins, were already in residence looking after the children who had been allowed to watch the progress of their father's political ambitions on television. Pinned to an outside wall was a colourful poster, drawn by the children, which read: 'Sign here if you were here on the night of the ELECTION.' Mr. and Mrs. Blair laughed and joked as they signed their two names, before taking in the four pints of milk and carton of orange juice left by the milkman. Mr. Blair, who had just received a congratulatory call on his mobile phone from President Clinton, was beaming as he waved to supporters and retreated inside.

The couple managed only two hours' sleep before waking to the business of the day. Crowds of wellwishers began gathering from dawn at the end of the street, which was cordoned off and guarded by police. Some handed bouquets and basket arrangements to officers. The first sign of life was when flame-haired Kathryn, dressed casually in black jeans and a green stripey T-shirt, set off around 9 a.m. with an adult friend to buy all the morning's newspapers. The Blair children had all been given permission to skip school for the day. Shortly afterwards Jonathan Powell, chief of staff, and Alastair Campbell, Mr. Blair's press secretary, arrived – both looking extremely relaxed. Mr. Blair spent two hours with the two men and on the telephone in his drawing room discussing his future government. Details of his speech were finalised, to include the well-worn themes of unity and one nation, and also to praise John Major. Magnanimity was to be the key.

At 11.30 a.m., as news of Mr. Major's final journey to Buckingham Palace as Prime Minister swept through the assembled media representatives outside Mr. Blair's residence, the first palpable symbol of his new-found authority arrived when an official J-registered Daimler drew up. A net curtain twitched in the upstairs right-hand window and out bobbed the head of Kathryn, alongside her cousin Lucy. The girls giggled as they surveyed the media throng below them, and waved shyly for the cameras during a game of peek-a-boo with photographers.

Four armed officers from the special escort corps, assigned as outriders, sped into the road on their BMW motorbikes. They had accompanied Mr. Major to Buckingham Palace, then, with the brutality that characterises politics, had left to attend to the new leader. Mr. Major had personally thanked them warmly two days previously – an indication that he strongly suspected he would not be afforded their services in the near future.

Mrs. Blair's hairdresser left shortly before noon, as police helicopters droned overhead. Things were definitely moving. At 12.10 p.m. Mr. Campbell emerged, mobile phone clamped to his ear, and surveyed a map of the planned route that the Blairs would take. They were to travel along Admiralty Arch and along the Mall. It was 12.15 p.m. before Mr. Blair, in dark blue suit, and his wife dressed in a rust-coloured tailored suit, stepped on to the street to roars from the assembled crowd, now 300-strong.

Neighbours hung out of windows or crowded on to balconies,

straining to see. The couple shook hands with a small band of supporters who lived in the street, before getting into the Daimler. But they drove just a few yards before jumping out at the police cordon where the main crowd stood cheering in the sunshine. They were followed by four dark blue Jaguars, into which were squeezed relatives and close friends invited to share the special day. The Blairs were on their way. Fifteen minutes later he would be with the Queen.

31 August 1997: Britain is shocked to discover Princess Diana is dead
PRINCESS DIANA AND DODI ARE KILLED IN PARIS CAR CRASH
PAPARAZZI BLAMED AS MERCEDES SMASHES INTO WALL
By Greg Neale, Helen Johnstone, Tom Baldwin,
Catherine Elsworth and Julian Nundy

Diana, Princess of Wales, was killed together with her boyfriend Dodi Fayed early today, after their car crashed in Paris while being chased by paparazzi photographers. The couple's driver was also killed and a bodyguard injured in the crash, which happened in a road tunnel alongside the river Seine. The thirty-six-year-old Princess was taken to the intensive care ward of the nearby Pitié-Salpêtrière Hospital, where doctors battled to save her. Initial reports said she had been in a 'distressed state', but able to walk from the mangled wreckage of the Mercedes limousine.

First reports had indicated that she suffered head injuries, a broken arm and serious leg injuries. Her condition was first described as serious, then grave. Then, shortly after 4.30 a.m., the Foreign Office and French officials announced that the Princess had died. Shock at the accident was coupled with revulsion at the circumstances of the crash. Paris police arrested five photographers, and one was reportedly beaten up by angry passers-by amid the confusion.

The couple's Mercedes limousine reportedly hit a wall and turned over in the accident. Prince Charles, who with the couple's sons, Prince William and Prince Harry, was staying at Balmoral, was informed of the accident soon afterwards. Prince Charles and Princess Diana were divorced a year ago last Thursday. The crash happened near the Pont de l'Alma, a bridge over the river Seine to the west of the city soon after midnight. The high-speed pursuit ended in a crash in the tunnel trapping several people in the pile-up. Police said five photographers had been detained at the scene; another was attacked by eyewitnesses. Tony Blair was woken in Downing Street and told of the accident. The Prime Minister was 'shocked and saddened by what he sees as a devastating, appalling tragedy', a Downing Street spokesman said.

A spokesman for Buckingham Palace, said the crash was 'an accident waiting to happen'. Michael Gibbons said he had had no official news on the crash. But he repeated the palace's anger at the actions of photographers who pursue the Royal Family around the world. A palace spokeswoman said soon afterwards: 'We are aware of this awful accident but we are awaiting further details. The Prince of Wales has been informed at Balmoral but at this stage it is too early to say what his movements will be until we have more details.'

The Princess was being driven by a security officer from the Ritz Hotel, according to early reports. The Ritz is owned by Dodi's father Mohammed Fayed, who is the owner of Harrods. Officials said the Princess's bodyguard was pulled from the wrecked car and was seriously injured. Other people were still trapped inside vehicles in the tunnel under the Pont de l'Alma bridge. It is believed the couple were heading for Dodi Fayed's luxury residence in the plush 16th arrondissement in the western part of the capital, when the accident happened. Mr. Fayed, aged forty-one, was reportedly given heart massage by the roadside, to no avail. His father flew to Paris in his private helicopter soon after being informed.

French Interior Minister Jean-Pierre Chevènement, Paris police prefect Philippe Massoni and the British consulate-general went to see Princess Diana in hospital, the prefecture said. Sir Michael Jay, Britain's ambassador to France, rushed to the hospital to be with the Princess as soon as he received word from the French authorities. The Foreign Office confirmed early this morning that the French authorities had told them that photographers were involved in the accident. Police cars and vans with flashing lights filled the site outside the tunnel and officers blocked off the area.

American tourists Tom Richardson and Joanna Luz were one of the first eyewitnesses on the scene. They told the cable television network CNN that they were walking nearby when they heard the crash and ran into the tunnel. Mr, Richardson, from San Diego, said: 'There was smoke. I think the car hit a wall. A man started running towards us telling us to go.' Miss Luz said: 'The horn was sounding for about two minutes. I think it was the driver against the steering wheel. There was a photographer on the scene within five seconds of the crash happening. As we were running out of the tunnel police and others were running in, but it took around five or seven minute s for them to get there. People were running towards the crash site and steering traffic away not knowing who was in the car. We were twenty yards from the accident but we did not see anyone in the car. The car was in the right lane facing on-coming traffic. The air bag was on the passenger's side. We did not see anyone on the driver's side.'

Princess Diana and Dodi Fayed were rounding off their holiday with a stay in Paris. The couple, who had been cruising aboard a yacht belonging to Dodi's father, were first spotted in the French capital yesterday. They arrived there after a week-long cruise around the French Riviera and coast of Sardinia. They were last seen publicly helping crew to load their luggage into a powerboat which took them to shore. The couple's close friendship has commanded world attention after it was first revealed barely two months ago. It blossomed during the past five weeks, as the couple took a series of holidays together in the Mediterranean. Less than two weeks ago the Princess and Mr. Fayed flew to the French Mediterranean resort of St. Tropez for their third holiday in each other's company in five weeks. The Princess and the Harrods heir arrived in Paris yesterday afternoon to round off their latest holiday together.

Robin Cook, the Foreign Secretary, said in the Philippines, shortly after hearing the news: 'We are deeply shocked by the news. Our first thoughts at the present time are with the Princess and her family. Our ambassador is at the hospital, and will provide every possible assistance we can. I think it will be doubly tragic if it does emerge that this accident was in part caused by persistent hounding of the Princess and her privacy by photographers.'

President Clinton and his wife, Hillary, were said this morning to be 'very concerned' after hearing of the accident. Joe Lockhart, a White House spokesman, said the Clintons were told of the accident by a military aide while they were attending a party on Martha's Vineyard.

21 April 1999: Horror at Columbine
HIGH SCHOOL MASSACRE BY STUDENTS
TWENTY-FIVE FEARED DEAD AS TEENAGERS IN BLACK TRENCHCOATS
ATTACK PUPILS WITH GUNS AND BOMBS
By John Hiscock in Denver, Ben Fenton in Washington, and Kenneth Clarke

Up to twenty-five people were killed yesterday after two teenagers in black trenchcoats, armed with automatic weapons and pipe bombs, burst into their school and opened fire on fellow pupils. Police said it appeared that the two had gone on a suicide mission, mowing down students before turning their weapons on themselves. The dead gunmen were found in the library of the school in Littleton, Colorado. John Stone, the Jefferson County Sheriff, said: 'It is a pretty gruesome sight.'

The dead men were members of a school gang, known as the Trenchcoat Mafia, who dressed all in black and wore sunglasses, and may have been former, or expelled, pupils. They struck at 11.30 a.m. local time, at Columbine High School. Hurling bombs along the corridors they fired weapons into crowds of terrified students. As screaming pupils ran for cover, paramedics tried to treat the injured. Police and five teams of Swat marksmen then moved in to surround the school. By this time the gunmen had barricaded themselves in with a reported seventeen hostages.

One student had ripped a page from an exercise book and written: 'Help, I'm bleeding to death' before sticking it in a window. Another bloodied young man dangled from a second-floor window, his right arm limp. He was helped down by two Swat team members. His condition was not immediately known. Among the injured were a girl, who was hit in the chest by nine bullets, and a physics teacher. Nineteen people were injured in the hail of bullets and taken to hospital. Many had serious gunshot wounds.

One student, Nick Foss, eighteen, said as he and others were hiding he heard people 'praying for their husbands, their children, you name it'. He said the gunmen just wanted to kill. Sheriff Stone said no shots had been fired by his men. All gunfire had come from the suspects who had automatic weapons. 'It appears to be a suicide mission,' he said. The two dead youths were found in the library by Swat teams sweeping through the school. He added that another suspect could still be at large. Members of the Trenchcoat Mafia were said to bear a grudge against athletes and ethnic students. They had said they would take revenge for 'being made fun of'.

Last night police were searching for and finding explosives and weapons as they moved through the building. Sheriff Stone said evidence of bombs had been found in the school and students had reported hearing explosions during the afternoon. One teenager being treated at a nearby medical centre had shrapnel as well as gunshot wounds. Before the full extent of the rampage became known, three youths, believed to be friends of the attackers, were arrested in a field near the school.

Last night, President Clinton went on nationwide television and said that he and his wife had been 'profoundly shocked and saddened' by the tragedy. 'We don't know all of the hows or whys of this tragedy,' he said. 'Perhaps we may never fully understand it. We do know we must do more to reach out to children to teach them to express their anger and resolve their conflicts with words not weapons and to recognise the early warning signs.'

Yesterday's murders will re-open controversy about gun legislation. Sheriff Stone added: 'What are these parents doing when they are letting their kids have automatic weapons?' Asked about motive, he shrugged his shoulders and said: 'Craziness.'

4

The New Century: Terrorism, Natural Disasters and Farewells 2000–15

4

Introduction

What role remains for newspapers in the age of television and the internet? At the *Telegraph*, as at other publications, the question has dominated strategic thinking in the early twenty-first century. And it has had to show deft footwork to continue to provide first-rate news reporting in a fast-changing world.

After the major events of the new century – most notably the attack on the Twin Towers on 9/11 – the demand for authoritative newspaper reports has been as great as ever. The *Telegraph*'s simple banner headline on 12 September 2001, WAR ON AMERICA, is still remembered today for its concise eloquence. And its network of correspondents around the world – from Rome to Baghdad to Tunis – has continued to be the bedrock of its news coverage. Whenever readers have been hungry for more background detail than TV news reports could provide, the *Telegraph* has been perfectly placed to fill in the gaps.

Major international crises are, of their nature, complex. And the more you examine them, the more complex they become. Balanced reporting is crucial – which is where newspapers have an indispensable role to play. As the Ukraine crisis escalated in May 2014, there was no danger of *Telegraph* readers being fobbed off with a one-eyed view of events. They could read Roland Oliphant's dispatch from Sevastopol, compare it with David Blair's dispatch from Donetsk and reach their own conclusions. The NATO airstrikes in Libya in October 2011 could have been just a blur, a montage of dramatic images. But there is nothing to beat a first-hand eyewitness report. 'The *Telegraph* counted fourteen smouldering cars and pick-up trucks and at least twenty-five dead bodies.' The bare figures have a lapidary authority.

Elsewhere, what emerges in these pieces is the more conversational tone adopted by modern news reporters, compared with their immediate predecessors, schooled in a more correct, less slangy, idiom. 'The EU's finance ministers wanted to get on with the job, so they slashed the period to two months,' reports Toby Helm from Frankfurt on 1 January 2002, the day the euro was introduced. It could be a bloke talking to another bloke in a pub, and none the worse for that.

At a time of falling circulations, the challenges facing newspapers have been formidable. Reporting events that have already been extensively reported in other media can be a daunting task. You cannot just regurgitate information with which the reader is already familiar. You need to add colour, context, humour, the personal touch. Gordon Rayner's report on the Diamond Jubilee pageant along the Thames in June 2012 – an event marred by miserable weather – is a fine example of a reporter bending over backwards to draw the reader in, rather than simply reporting what happened when. 'Has there ever been a more robust, a more determined or a more downright stubborn display of support for the Queen?' he begins his dispatch, laying down the gauntlet.

If any newspaper in Britain has striven to retain the best of the past, while also adapting to change, it is the *Telegraph*. Connoisseurs of old-fashioned newspaper reporting – curious, inquisitive, factually scrupulous without being dry – will surely relish the report on the Countryside March through London in September 2002 by the late W.F. Deedes, a *Telegraph* legend. Deedes is not there with an axe to grind. He is not there to preach. He is there to *listen*, to talk to people like Mrs. Proudlock, from Morpeth in Northumberland, who runs a small family haulage business, and get them to tell their story, without editorial interference. And, simply by playing the interested by-stander, he captures the whole flavour of the occasion in all its rich humanity. The piece could have been written by J.B. Priestley, another masterly observer of men and manners, in the 1930s.

Accurate facts are the bedrock of good journalism, and never did *Telegraph* reporters lay more immaculately researched – or more jaw-dropping – facts before their readers than during the paper's reporting of the parliamentary expenses scandal in 2009. It was one of the *Telegraph*'s finest hours, envied across Fleet Street, as M.P. after M.P. was skewered, not by flights of rhetoric, but by hard, undeniable facts. To read in cold print that the duck-house which Sir Peter Viggers infamously tried to claim on expenses had been 'based on an eighteenth-century building in Sweden', or that the same M.P. had tried to recoup an electrician's bill for £213.95 for, *inter alia*, 'hanging lights on a Christmas tree', was to be reminded of the glory of print journalism at its best. No television programme could have caught the nuts and bolts of the expenses scandal so effectively.

So long as there are major stories to report – stories of which other media can capture the buzz, the shock, the excitement, but not the full background and not the human nuances – quality newspapers will always be in demand.

1 January 2000: It wasn't actually the end of the millennium, but everybody celebrated as if it was
FANFARE FOR A MILLENNIUM
MILLIONS THRONG THE STREETS AS THE QUEEN LEADS CELEBRATIONS
By Robert Hardman and Caroline Davies

With just one chime of Big Ben, the century of world war, aviation and Winston Churchill, the millennium of discovery, imperialism and Shakespeare was gone. A dazzling shaft of fire spliced the capital while pyrotechnics, prayers and beacons across the nation signalled the arrival of the new epoch of the unknown.

And it was at Greenwich, the 'home' of time, that the Queen led Britain across the threshold of 2000, hand-in-hand with Prince Philip and the Prime Minister. In the Millennium Dome, focal point of the country's celebrations, she joined the Prime Minister and a 10,000-strong cross-section of British life to see in the new century at a spectacular concert with a firm emphasis on modernity.

Two and a half million people had congregated in London and along the Thames to watch the largest firework display in British history, ignited by a 'river of fire', a wall of flame shooting east to west at the same pace as the Earth and time. In towns and cities all over Britain, similar scenes could be found on a smaller scale as the nation erupted into celebration. And, as midnight swept around the globe, fireworks began a twenty-four-hour peppering of the entire planet, starting in the tiny Pacific states of Tonga and Kiribati, followed by New Zealand and then all points west.

People poured into central London, forcing police to close roads to the congested Embankment where revellers crushed together to watch the river of fire and the thirty-nine tons of fireworks blasted from six-teen barges. Those denied access found whatever vantage points they could, sitting on railing and window sills of Whitehall's government buildings, straining for a view. Parliament Square was thronged, with some revellers climbing on to traffic lights to witness Big Ben and the midnight fireworks. By mid-evening queues at mainline railways sta-tions taking people into the centre were stretching out on to the streets. London Underground stations were swamped. Police urged people attempting to return home on mainline trains to be patient. Waterloo Tube station was closed at 1.20 a.m. as more than 10,000 people tried to gain access to the Underground.

Across the rest of Britain, the big party was up and running and mobile phone networks struggled to cope with the sheer number of calls, crashing at times as they overloaded. On Unst, the most northerly of the Shetland Islands, the first of a nationwide chain of beacons was lit as the sun set on the Twentieth Century. The last beacons were lit along the Meridian Line at the millennial midnight. Hundreds of thousands of people across Scotland gathered for the biggest Hogmanay party they had ever seen. The capital, Edinburgh, one of the most popular places in the world to celebrate New Year's Eve, saw the biggest party ever. Meanwhile, Birmingham lined up a party fit for Britain's second largest city, with a glittering cast headed by Sir Cliff Richard at the National Indoor Arena.

Inside the Dome, a cast of 1,100 provided the action amid a riot of colour and music. Religion, which had been fighting a losing battle against entertainment in the run-up to the occasion, had the last word. The last few minutes before midnight were devoted to a special work by the composer Sir John Tavener. He had written a stirring choral anthem based on the official Millennium Resolution, the seven-line exhortation drawn up by a committee of Britain's churches. Sir John, however, was perplexed at the omission of any reference to God or Jesus. He had insisted on altering the text to include the words 'O Lord' at the end of every other line. As his anthem drew to a close to make way for the chimes of Big Ben, the last words of the Twentieth Century were, therefore, 'O Lord' The first words of the Twenty-first were soon ringing out around the Dome and all over the country: 'Should auld acquaintance be forgot . . .' They were even holding hands in the royal box.

Such spectacle was in marked contrast to the way the evening had started for the two main guests. New Year's Eve had started with more sombre moments for both the monarch and her first minister. The Queen's first engagement of the day took her to a shelter for the homeless in Southwark. There, she met heroin addicts and discussed hip replacements with a fifty-five-year-old man called Mouse who insisted on clutching his can of Special Brew throughout. 'The Queen seemed to know my name and she knew I had broken my hip and said she hoped I got better,' he said afterwards. 'It has really made my day.'

Tony Blair's evening began at Westminster Abbey where he attended an ecumenical service with his family before opening the London Eye. There was no shortage of razzmatazz surrounding the problematic Ferris wheel, just an embarrassing lack of passengers; safety checks had ruled out any of those. For the prime ministerial party, there was then a House of Lords reception before a special Jubilee Line train was laid on to take them from Westminster to North Greenwich, the station for the Dome. Among the other V.I.P.s on the guest list were John Prescott, the Deputy Prime Minister – minus his car – and many members of the Cabinet, including Peter Mandelson, who had once been Minister for All This.

Accommodating religion into such shameless festivity had been the subject of long debate. The organisers had wanted to keep the mood upbeat and modern while the Church of England wanted to remind everyone why B.C. had become A.D. in the first place. Agreement was finally reached for two minutes and four seconds of prayer involving three eleven-year-old Barnardo's children and the Archbishop of Canterbury, Dr. George Carey. It was the start of an impeccably New Britain half an hour. 'Lord, so many people are suffering as a result of wars. Help politicians everywhere to find new ways of stopping the fighting,' said Howard Comrie of Leeds.

Eight Greenwich children had been chosen to join the Queen in her box. After a brief chat, the Queen opened a symbolic gate which released the children to run across to the stage. There, they pulled several ropes which brought the vast yellow shrouds hanging from the rafters tumbling down. The first chime of midnight were the cue for wild cheers and Champagne. The Queen turned to Prince Philip and kissed him on both cheeks as Mr. and Mrs. Blair hugged each other. Champagne suddenly arrived – the Queen and Mr. Blair clinked glasses immediately – and was then quickly set aside for hand-holding and Auld Lang Syne. Finally, the entire Big Event for the Big Night came to its conclusion with a specially arranged version of the National Anthem.

In the language of the first millennium, MDCCCCLXXXXVIIII had become a more manageable MM. In the language of the third, it really was Y2K.

8 October 2000: Robert Mugabe attacks white farmers in Zimbabwe
TERRORISED FARMERS GIVE IN TO MUGABE'S KNIFE GANGS
By Christina Lamb and David Blair

White farmers in Zimbabwe, who have lived through months of violent land occupations and years of political and economic uncertainty, are finally abandoning farms owned by their families for generations. Eight months of President Robert Mugabe's campaign of harassment have left more than 1,000 farms under occupation. With no foreign exchange or credit, the country is rapidly running out of food and fuel.

So many farmers are giving up hope and fleeing Zimbabwe that a fundraising committee has been set up in Britain to help those arriving. Derek Arlett-Johnson, a third generation Zimbabwean who was president of his local branch of the Commercial Farmers Union in the Zimbabwean Midlands, is among those who have fled. He had worked all his life to own the land he farmed, but left when he received death threats and was confronted by gangs waving pangas, a heavy East African knife.

Mr. Arlett-Johnson arrived in Britain with just £700 to support his family and has been working as a casual farm labourer in Norfolk, harvesting wheat while he looks for a full-time job. 'I feel very bitter,' he said. 'It's like I'm giving in to Mugabe. But I've got a seven-year-old child and I'd rather be a father with nothing than a dead person with a farm. We are being driven out by violence and financial ruin. Most farmers have heavy loans and it is impossible to pay them back under these circumstances.' Another farmer now living near Derby, who still has relatives in Zimbabwe and did not want to be named, described how he had walked into his bank and thrown the keys of his estate on the manager's desk. 'Mugabe won't give up till he has got all the white farmers out,' he said. 'No one can plant for next season under those conditions. It's an impossible situation.'

George Campbell-Johnston, one of the trustees of the newly-created

Zimbabwe Farmers Trust, spent this weekend with four white farmers at a holiday cottage in Cornwall which he had rented so that they could relax and discuss their experiences. They fled after their families were attacked. 'It's ghastly to see these big farmers now reduced to getting jobs as tractor drivers,' said Mr. Campbell-Johnston, 'but at least they are safe.'

Many of Zimbabwe's 4,500 white farmers do not have British passports or relatives overseas and so have to stay or move to neighbouring countries like Zambia or South Africa. Zimbabwe newspapers run advertisements from agencies arranging moves to Australia. The latest method of harassment by squatters determined to seize land promised by Mugabe, is to set fire to it to drive the owners out. According to a report by the Commercial Farmers Union, gangs of squatters are setting hundreds of acres of veld alight. 'This illustrates the extent of the breakdown of law and order,' said the report.

At Stow Farm, near Marondera, fifty miles south east of Harare, Cathy and Ian Buckle watched as a bush fire lit by squatters turned their orchards into a black scar, just days before the couple were due to abandon their property with their eight-year-old son, Richard. Mrs. Buckle said: 'They have burnt down over half of our gum trees. How on earth can we make a living here?' Stow Farm was first invaded by a drunken mob in February. Mrs. Buckle, forty-two, was threatened by a gunman. Since then the Buckles' cow and sheep breeding business has been systematically destroyed as the invaders barred the couple from the 'liberated' two-thirds of their 1,000 acres. Mr. Buckle, forty-six, said: 'You keep hoping that law and order will return, but we can't run our business.'

Barely two miles away is Mitengo Farm, where mobs of more than one hundred squatters frequently confronted Nigel Sligh and his family. 'We don't see a future here,' said Mr. Sligh, whose father began farming in the early 1950s, and who had hoped to pass the farm on to his three children. 'If someone can guarantee that I can pass on my farm to my children, then I'd stay. But I could get a letter tomorrow taking the farm away from me. I'd be crazy to invest any money in it.' They are leaving for Britain in January. The government has listed 2,109 farms for 'compulsory acquisition' and has set a target of seizing almost seventy-five per cent of all Zimbabwe's white farms.

The situation is particularly bad for farmworkers who lose their livelihoods when their employers flee. The *Zimbabwe Daily News* reported last week that only 318 out of 500,000 farmworkers have been resettled on government-acquired land because they were considered 'alien' and too allied with the white farmers for whom they worked.

12 September 2001: 9/11
WAR ON AMERICA
By Philip Delves Broughton, Ben Fenden and Tony Harnden in Washington

The United States was on a war footing last night after the most devastating terrorist attack in history. Two hijacked passenger airliners crashed into the twin towers of New York's World Trade Center. Both towers collapsed with the loss of thousands of lives, sending out great clouds of thick dust that covered buildings and people in the streets like volcanic ash. Lower Manhattan was evacuated and the New York skyline changed for ever.

Minutes later in Washington DC a third hijacked aircraft crashed into the Pentagon, the heart of America's military machine. A fourth, believed to be heading for the presidential retreat Camp David, crashed near Pittsburgh. The atrocity was meticulous in its co-ordination and horrifying in its effect. A global television audience watched in disbelief as live footage showed the second plane hitting the Trade Centre minutes after the first. Land borders were closed and airspace cleared of all but military aircraft as U.S. forces were put on 'high alert'.

Financial centres were paralysed when Wall Street closed and shares plunged across world markets. The departments of Justice, State, Treasury, Defence and the C.I.A. were all evacuated. President Bush was flown to a bunker in Nebraska before returning to the White

House. He pledged: 'Make no mistake, we will hunt down and punish those responsible for these cowardly acts.'

America suffered the worst terrorist attack in history yesterday, with thousands feared dead as hijacked planes crashed into the financial and military centres of the world's most powerful nation. Two airliners hit the twin towers of the World Trade Center, an unmistakable part of the most famous city skyline in the world, causing both to collapse in flames and dust.

Forty minutes later a third plane crashed into the Pentagon in Washington DC, destroying one side of the five-sided structure. A fourth airliner crashed outside Pittsburgh, killing everybody on board. It was apparently heading for Camp David, the presidential retreat eighty-five miles away in the Maryland Mountains. It is thought that the hijacked pilot may have brought it down rather than attack the planned target. A total of 266 people were killed in the planes.

Authorities were trying to evacuate the World Trade Center when its towers collapsed within minutes of each other. About 50,000 people work there and tens of thousands visit it every day. Surrounding buildings and thousands of people in the streets below were covered in a thick coating of dust thrown up by the collapsed towers. Later a third building at the centre collapsed. Among the many missing people were two hundred firemen. 'I would not want to say what the death toll could be,' Rudolph Giuliani, the mayor, said. 'It will be a horrible number. I saw people dropping out of windows.'

Senior officers and hundreds of soldiers were feared dead in the Pentagon attack, which was carried out with a Boeing 757 hijacked shortly after it took off from Washington's Dulles airport on its way to Los Angeles. The rest of the Pentagon was immediately evacuated, but firemen were unable to reach the crash area because of intense heat. The National Guard was mobilised in Washington and New York and forces in the American capital were put on Threat Level Delta, the equivalent of a war alert. In the skies above both cities, the only planes to be seen were F-16 and F-15 fighters scrambled for fear of yet more attacks. At Norfolk, Virginia, one of main naval bases, five warships put to sea to protect the Atlantic coast and two aircraft carriers headed for New York.

President Bush, who was flown to the safety of a bunker in Nebraska, called for calm and promised revenge on the perpetrators. After returning to the White House, Mr. Bush told the nation in a television address of the 'quiet, unyielding anger' felt by Americans who had experienced an evil in their midst that had taken the lives of 'thousands' of their fellow citizens. He vowed to make no distinction between the terrorists and 'those who harbour them', a clear indication that U.S. forces would be used against any state judged to be culpable for the devastating attacks. Reassuring Americans that evil would not triumph, Mr. Bush said that federal offices and the U.S. economy would be 'open for business' by the morning. 'These acts shattered steel, but they cannot dent the steel of American resolve,' he said. Mr. Bush, who was told of the attacks as he read to primary-school children in Florida, said: 'Freedom itself was attacked this morning by a faceless coward and freedom will be defended. Make no mistake, the United States will hunt down and punish those responsible for these cowardly acts.'

Dick Cheney, the Vice President, and General Colin Powell, the Secretary of State, were collected by the Secret Service and taken back to heavily guarded quarters in the capital. Suspicion for the atrocities immediately focused on Osama bin Laden, the multi-millionaire Islamic terrorist. He is thought to be the only person capable of mounting such a well-planned attack, the most audacious in the history of terrorism. The extreme Islamic Taliban movement in Afghanistan, which has provided a home to bin Laden, denied responsibility. Abdul Salam Zaeef, the Taliban ambassador to Pakistan, condemned the attacks and said he hoped that the perpetrators would quickly be brought to justice. 'Osama is only a person,' he said. 'He does not have the facilities to carry out such activities. We want to tell the American people that Afghanistan feels their pain.'

However, early this morning, Senator Orrin Hatch said American intelligence officers had already intercepted communications between known associates of Osama bin Laden in which they discussed the successful striking of two targets. Last night, tracer fire was heard over Kabul and explosions reverberated across the Afghan capital. Initially the attack was thought to be an American strike on the Taliban regime, which is harbouring bin Laden. Later the Afghan resistance claimed responsibility.

The attack on the World Trade Center caused jubilation in Iraq and among some radical groups in the Middle East, which saw it as revenge for America's support for Israel. Islamic Jihad, responsible for many of the recent suicide bombings in Israel, said: 'The United States has provided a cover for these Zionist crimes. We are happy to see America suffer the pain and bitterness that our people feel.'

The Queen, who is at Balmoral, sent a message of sympathy to President Bush. She said: 'It is with growing disbelief and total shock that I am learning of the terrorist outrages in New York and Washington today. On behalf of the British people, Mr. President, may I express my heartfelt sympathy to the very many bereaved and injured and our admiration for those who are now trying to cope with these unfolding tragedies. Our thoughts and prayers are with you all.' Tony Blair said that Britain stood 'shoulder to shoulder' with America. He announced a series of security measures, including a halt to all flights across central London.

1 January 2002: Enter the Euro
BEGINNING OF THE END FOR OLD CURRENCIES
By Toby Helm in Frankfurt

Crisp, colourful euro notes began popping out of their first holes in the wall at midnight, and unscratched, glittering euro coins, symbols of the new, united Europe, have arrived. But as this brash new money enters wallets and purses across 'euroland' today, what will happen to the trusted old currencies that have been supplanted, the battered marks, francs and pesetas that have served their nations so well? Is it too late to spend them or exchange them? Or are they already just valueless souvenirs, relics of the old order. For those who still hold old notes and coins there is no need to panic. Those who planned Europe's new money may be consigning twelve currencies to death, but they are doing so quite slowly. Last night's arrival of euro notes and coins is not quite the end for the national currencies of the euro-zone. It is just the beginning of the end.

From today, a period of 'dual circulation' lasting a maximum of two months – its precise length varies according to the participating country – will begin in 'euroland', during which people can still pay for goods in old currencies or in euros if they have them. The idea is that dual circulation – accompanied by dual pricing in shops – will allow people in the euro-zone to get used to the new currency and spend their old money, getting change back in euros.

Shopkeepers across the twelve-nation area have said they will give change in euros whenever possible to help speed the changeover. Since September millions of retailers have been stocking up with packs of euro coins – a process known as 'front-loading'. They also asked to be 'front-loaded' with the new notes, but the European Central Bank (E.C.B.) refused to do this until just before the launch because of fears that counterfeiters would get their hands on them ahead of time and learn too much about their security features.

The original idea, envisaged when the euro was launched as a non-cash currency in eleven nations on 1 January 1999 (Greece then joined at the start of 2000, making twelve), was that dual circulation would last six months. But this was thought to be unnecessarily long by the E.U.'s impatient finance ministers, who wanted to get on with the job. So they slashed the period to two months and declared that after that all old currencies would cease to be legal tender. The E.C.B. believes that everything will move very fast and that by 15 January most transactions will be in euros.

Even after the end of February, there is no need to fret if a few old mark notes are found in a drawer or some pesetas in a cupboard. Old money will still be convertible into euros. Commercial banks will exchange in the relevant country for varying periods, and national central banks will do so for at least ten years. Inevitably, progress in changing cash, ticket and slot machines to the euro has varied from country to country and company to company. In Germany, Belgium, Luxembourg, Austria and the Netherlands, the E.C.B. predicted that one hundred per cent of cash machines would have been converted to euros by midnight last night. In Finland, they have been slower off the mark, converting only twenty-five per cent. Obtaining euros could prove difficult for a few weeks up in Lapland. An estimated ninety per cent of machines were expected to be ready in Spain and Italy, eighty-five per cent in France, eighty per cent in Ireland, fifty per cent in Portugal and seventy-five per cent in Greece.

Five per cent of the old currency is expected never to be turned into euros, to stay for good in piggy banks, forgotten about or kept as souvenirs. In reality, attitudes to how to handle the euro changeover vary wildly within the euro area. Some companies, such as the Berlin bus company B.V.G., are making a bold attempt to move to a euro-only system within one week. But the company knows this is ambitious and if people have no euros it will be tolerant and give them a free ride. Indeed, for many the changeover will bring free rides and parking for a while. In many German states fines for parking in metered zones have been suspended while machines are adapted to the euro.

Changing slot machines is a vast operation. Coca-Cola alone has 288,000 machines to adapt.

As for pricing of goods, 'double pricing' – in euros and old currencies – will remain in the dual circulation period. After February the aim is to move to euro-only pricing, but goods can still be advertised in old currencies. So for the real diehards, the mark, the franc, the peseta and the other nine currencies could live on, at least on humble price labels.

13 January 2002: Guantanamo Bay opens its doors to prisoners taken in Afghanistan
RAZOR WIRE AND CAGES HOLD U.S. 'BATTLEFIELD DETAINEES'
By Olga Craig and Charles Laurence

As the United States has avoided declaring them prisoners of war, conditions under which the Taliban are held do not fall under the Geneva Convention. Blindfolded and manacled, their heads shaved, they spilled out of the belly of the specially converted American C-141 cargo aircraft into the suffocating humidity of Guantanamo Bay. As the twenty senior Taliban and al-Qaeda fighters – among them one Briton – were herded across the tarmac by sixty U.S. marines armed with machine-guns this weekend, several stumbled and fell to their knees, their arms stretched skywards in submission. Four, their legs bandaged and their faces swathed in the turquoise surgical masks of tuberculosis sufferers, lay spread-eagled and still. All appeared terrified.

Guantanamo Bay, the remote American naval base in Cuba, is one of the most God-forsaken places on earth. Surrounded by shark-infested waters, two electrified razor-wire fences and a minefield, its conditions are harsh, its regime brutal: the prisoners knew they could expect relentless interrogation and spartan conditions. The first of an expected 2,000 terrorist prisoners to be flown to the naval base, they have been denied the protection of the Geneva Convention because they have been decreed to be 'battlefield detainees' and 'unlawful combatants'. The American authorities made clear that while the men would not be given the usual prisoner-of-war status, they could expect 'humane but uncomfortable' conditions. 'They are detainees, illegal combatants,' insisted Steve Lucas, a U.S. military spokesman. 'They are combatants who were detained by U.S. or coalition forces in opposition forces. Their legal status is being determined at the highest level.'

Donald Rumsfeld, America's Defence Secretary, has emphasised that the first priority will be 'extracting information' and that any decisions on legal processes and military tribunals will come later. 'You don't hurry through this,' he said. 'When you are talking about defending against terrorist actions against this country and our friends and allies around the world, you take your time and try to do it right. So you know that after you have gone through that first interrogation, it is best to wait a bit and see what other kinds of information come up from other people. From computers, from various types of intelligence-gathering . . . You might arrest somebody with pocket litter that connects the person to one of the people you are interrogating. You must be patient.'

Once the interrogations are over, officials will decide whether to return a prisoner to his country of origin for punishment or put him on trial before a military tribunal. The five military officers acting as judges will require a unanimous verdict to impose the death penalty, although a two-thirds vote of the officers will be enough to find a defendant guilty. A separate three-member panel would review the decision in the event of an appeal. It would hear arguments from defence lawyers and then make a recommendation to Mr. Rumsfeld, with the final word given to President Bush.

The prisoners already there, and those who will arrive in the next few days, are among the most experienced and fanatical terrorists captured. 'We asked for the bad guys first,' said Brigadier General Michael Lehnert, the commander of Joint Task Force 160, which is overseeing the transfer of prisoners from Kandahar in Afghanistan to Guantanamo Bay. 'These represent the worst elements of the al-Qaeda and the Taliban.' Those who arrived on Friday were herded on to white buses and driven to specially constructed six feet by eight feet cages where they will be held in isolation.

Initially, the prisoners were to be held in the relatively relaxed existing communal buildings, but Mr. Rumsfeld – who responded to that idea by saying, 'You have got to be kidding' – ordered marines on the base to build high-security cages. 'The first arrivals are being held in temporary maximum-security facilities which were built in the past few days,' a U.S. spokesman said. 'Those facilities are essentially outdoor cages or outdoor cells.' The cages, constructed from chain-link fences topped with canvas roofs, are encircled by several yards of razor wire. Each of the compounds will be lit by halogen floodlights twenty-four hours a day to ensure that the prisoners are constantly monitored. Each prisoner will be given a mattress and two towels, one to be used as a prayer mat. They will be given three meals a day and have access to 'a few toiletries' – a flanncl, toothpaste, soap and shampoo. They will not be given blankets or repellent to ward off the swarms of mosquitoes that thrive in the tropical swamp that forms the bay.

In light of recent attempts by al-Qaeda prisoners to overthrow their captors, they will be guarded around the clock by armed marines and kept in shackles. 'It will be humane but you would not want to be here,' said one senior officer at the base. 'There will be no freedom of movement.' It was unclear, contrary to some reports, whether the prisoners' beards – symbols of religious devotion – were shaved off by their captors. The conditions in which the prisoners will be held and their definition as battlefield detainees have evoked criticism from human rights groups and M.P.s. Amnesty International, in a letter to Mr. Rumsfeld, said: 'Housing detainees in eight feet by six feet cages, partially open to the elements, falls below minimum standards for humane treatment.' The organisation pointed out that the prisoners would not be adequately sheltered from the elements and said that the American captors' use of blindfolds and hoods amounted to cruel and degrading treatment.

Lieutenant General Hamid Gul, the former head of the I.S.I. security service in Pakistan, said yesterday: 'I think it is very strange behaviour that one didn't expect from the Americans . . . They are setting new trends in state behaviour by coining new terms like "battlefield detainees". One can safely say they are violating all norms of behaviour and violating the Geneva Convention.' Yesterday Donald Anderson, the Labour M.P. and chairman of the Commons foreign affairs select committee, added his disquiet. 'Whatever the formal category, these prisoners still have legal rights and what we have heard already suggests that human rights are indeed being put in jeopardy,' he said. Mr. Rumsfeld denied the allegations, insisting: 'There is no violation of human rights.' He said that because the al-Qaeda fighters were not soldiers they were not entitled to the rights accorded to prisoners-of-war.

Visiting Kabul, Senator Joe Biden, the Democrat chairman of the Senate's foreign relations committee, said he had 'no problem' with the 'unlawful combatants' definition. 'If the defence department were to detain these prisoners in a way that offended the American people, it would not last long. I cannot imagine that happening,' he said. Last night the International Committee of the Red Cross said that it had seen no evidence of maltreatment when it saw the prisoners before their transfer to the Guantanamo Bay naval base, and accepted the need to use chains during the flight given al-Qaeda members' history of hijacking aircraft.

24 September 2002: The countryside comes to London to protest against the Government, and has the support of the *Telegraph*

It was to be a march to vent rural wrath. But W.F. Deedes found good humour and politeness along the way as he joined the countryside protestors.

It exceeded hopes, was well-organised, so good-humoured, dignified; but at times it conveyed a depth of feeling I found solemn. There were men and women on that march who were not carrying banners or blowing horns, small farmers and their wives from the hills, country craftsmen, blacksmiths and their kind who sense that a way of life is slipping away from them. It was the life of their fathers and their grandfathers, but it will not be the life of their children and grandchildren. They're for the towns, not for rural penury. A parting of ways is taking place, a severance of family ties, and if you studied some of the sad faces on that account you glimpsed despair.

'But,' I heard a BBC lady say rather accusingly to a sorrowful-looking man early on Sunday morning, 'this march is also about hunting foxes.' Yes, ma'am, no disputing that. You could say it was mainly about foxhunting. The ban on hunting, threatened mainly by those who know nothing about it, turned out to be the long fuse to Sunday's benign explosion. Don't tell me that 400,000 people would have marched through London to save hill farmers and little country traders. But the ban held over the heads of the foxhunters has been read as a signal. Countrymen, beware! So those who are fond of shooting, enjoy fishing and love horses joined the march in large numbers. As one of the march banners put it succinctly: 'Guns wound, hounds don't.' If hunting is stopped and people discover what happens to foxes left to the mercy of shot guns, all those who shoot will provoke outcry. They'll be next for the chop, and, as the march demonstrated, they seem to be well aware of it.

At one point on the march I took a small refreshment outside a pub close to Purdey House, home to gun and rifle manufacturers of renown. I raised my glass to the premises. 'Here's all the luck in the world,' I said, 'and the way things are going, you may need it!' For this depth of feeling I encountered at times on Sunday has deep roots. In scores of snatched conversations it was expressed in different ways which might be summed up something like this: Foxhunting is an integral part of country life and has been for many years. Okay, we may appear to urban man an eccentric lot, but it is so much part of our lives that if you politicians and your supporters cannot perceive this, then nothing, but nothing in our lives is safe anymore. So we choose the business of hunting as ground on which to stand and fight. We see it as symbolic of this great divide between urban man and countryman, between your majority and our minority. And, if after last year's disaster visited on us by foot and mouth disease (coming on top of B.S.E.), you are sufficiently insensitive to snatch away a traditional recreation – for those who follow hunts, as well as those who ride – then we have every reason to fear the worst. If hunting goes, who among us is safe? That is why some of us, a few from distant parts paying fares they can ill afford, have travelled through the night to make our feelings known. It is pointless for ministers to deny rural poverty. A quarter of those involved in rural employment work at below the Government's poverty line. Yet they are proud of what they do.

There was this man from Ayrshire. I asked him what he did. 'I put up fences,' he said impressively. So many like him depend on the small farmers' income. But maybe I have started at the wrong end. Early morning in London under a clear sky, and roads from the mainline railway stations were full of people you hardly expected to see there. Those from the far north may have endured an uncomfortable night, but showed small signs of it.

'Why have you come all the way down here?' I later asked Mrs. Proudlock, from Morpeth, in Northumberland. Hers is a small family haulage business. They transport farmers and their beasts to market. The price of diesel has soared. 'But I cannot put prices up, because the poorer farmers could not afford it.' Mrs. Proudlock speaks for small rural business, smothered in regulations, paying through the nose for fuel, almost wholly dependent on an industry going downhill. So, I suggest to her, more and more who are living precariously will gravitate towards the towns. She nods, then adds: 'And there's plenty from the towns who are happy to take their places over; but they don't always see things our way.'

A good many townsfolk in this transmigration, I reflect, will naturally feel unfriendly to foxhunting. It has played no part in their lives. That is why the so-called foxhunting issue is all of a bigger piece and why it arouses such emotion. Knowing my wife, who has hunted much of her life, knowing my youngest daughter, a redundant joint Master of Foxhounds in Scotland, I get shirty with people who tell me that those who hunt enjoy inflicting cruelty on animals. That feeling was one of the inaudible battle cries of Sunday's march. How dare they tell us how to behave towards animals! We live with them. It is those who reside in cities who have lost their touch with the elementary; who, cut off from natural life and death, have been desensitised.

It was touching, by the way, to see how many people up from the country welcomed each other. I was warmly embraced by one or two women I cannot remember meeting – perhaps because I was wearing an old Barbour and carried a walking stick. But there's a serious point here. When you walk down the village street, you do greet people you don't know very well. It goes to the heart of this sense of the community about which Labour in abstract is so enthusiastic. You even dare at my age to smile at other people's small children, which is on the border of becoming an urban offence. Urban man tends to be altogether more reserved. His is a more cellular existence. At any rate, it was a joy to stand at the foot of St. James's Street as they poured through and witness uppermost this instinct to greet your fellow men gladly.

The welcoming instinct seemed to be infectious. We took a look at London Bridge, which never appears to be the most welcoming of London's railway stations. There were hard-pressed officials there fingering lists of trains that were bringing in the marchers. 'I didn't know this number of people lived in this country,' one official exclaimed to his colleague as they streamed off three platforms. None of that crowd looked to me the sort of toff which the Labour party supporter, determined to end foxhunting, treasures in his mind's eye. There were many more children than I recall seeing on the 1998 Countryside March. The schools were there in great force. Well, who wouldn't leave the confines of a boarding school on Sunday for an adventure in London? But not since the great Vietnam demonstration in Grosvenor Square in July 1968 have I seen so many young people looking so involved.

'What brings you and your three children here?' I asked a woman from Norfolk. She didn't say, as she might well have done, 'I can't very well leave three young children at home', she said, 'they're all seeing a bit of history.' Before I could properly interpret that, a man who told me he lived nearby in Mayfair, introduced himself and shook his head. 'You think this will make a difference?' he said, lip curling a little. 'I'm a reporter,' I explained, 'listening to what other people think.' He shook his head again and looked maddeningly wise. 'Look,' he said, 'Labour has an overwhelming majority on which today's event will make no impact at all. They will vote solidly for a ban and the Labour Government will back them to the hilt.'

'A valuable corrective to my enthusiasm,' I replied coolly, and in order not to look cross fastened my eye on a Jack Russell that was passing by. Such a jolly little chap. The dogs who joined the march, I must say, were a joy to behold – patient and plucky. Imagine being a very small pug and being required to walk all the way from Hyde Park to Victoria Street. But then, as a perfect stranger in St. James's observed to me and to the world at large: 'Look at them. None of them overweight . . .' There was truth there. Nearly all the marchers, some of them never to see seventy again, looked enviably fit and slim. And when around tea time a few spots of rain fell, there was little shuffling of umbrellas. They simply marched on. The weather, it has to be said, took the foxhunters' side. 'Red sky at night, shepherd's delight,' I recalled as my train rolled into London on Saturday evening under a sky flushed red. So it turned out to be.

There was another feeling, buried deep in some of the marchers which came to light when they talked. It was recently well-expressed by the Bishop of London, Richard Chartres. There were, he said, many things he found 'morally repugnant' but which he accepted could not be turned into a criminal offence. That line of thought ran strongly through some of the marchers. Mr. John Smithson, who runs a small business in Warwickshire and is a hunt supporter, said to me: 'Why single me and my sport out for punishment, when there's so much wrong going on in towns?' Edward Hall from Newbury was there with his three children, Rupert, Phoebe and Eliza. We met on a corner of Hyde Park just before the march got going. 'What do you want out of today?' I ask him. 'Less interference in my life,' he says simply. He came close to the heart of all this. But before enlarging on it, I think it well to admit that this march had far stronger political undertones than the 1998 affair.

There were some home-made banners addressed to Mr. Blair that we did not see on the march four years ago. 'Hedge-layers say billhooks to Blair' was one of the milder offerings. You may interpret this as saying that the Conservative Opposition seems not to be hurting Labour severely enough. That cockpit of the nation, the House of Commons chamber, is not a cockpit any more. They run office hours. Again, you may see it as declaring that politics have become too anaemic by half and more robust attitudes would be welcome. Or you may conclude that this Government does interfere a damn sight too much in other people's lives and this lay at the root of the protest. I fancy that last point comes closest to the mark, though it is not necessarily in the best interests of foxhunting.

It leaves it open for stalwart Labour supporters to say, as they enter the Aye lobby for a ban: 'This protest was really a broad-based attack on our party and our Leader and we'll have none of it.' Yes, it was in part a political protest. Edward Hall from Newbury got it in five words, but this takes us into another realm of thought. Public feeling for politics is at low ebb. If anyone doubts it, let them ponder the turn-out at the last general election and contemplate the way in which the BBC and other networks are striving to shrug off politics. Yet in the biggest demonstration ever staged in London, hundreds of thousands of people travelled uncomfortably to make a political point. The march teemed with young people who, we are assured, think politics a pain in the neck. So does the march mean that people, despairing of the democratic process, are moving towards direct action? I think not. This was not simply a well organised event. It was thoroughly good-tempered and orderly. The policemen on duty looked relaxed, not tense. In Parliament Square a degree of provocation was offered by those opposed to hunting – and was virtually ignored.

As one who has reported most of the big marches in London, from the Great Depression that set the unemployed marching on Westminster, through Mosley's affrays, the poll tax riots and the miners, I marvelled at the calm. A demonstration on that scale, throughout which people observed the courtesies, made it an epic. Some blew plastic horns loudly, some carried rather vulgar home-made posters, but it was never an ill-tempered show. Certainly, a lot of people on the march were thoroughly enjoying the experience and their faces proclaimed it. Plainly many of those who marched make a habit of keeping their homes and gardens tidy. Given the numbers and the need to fuel the human frame while on the hoof, the relative absence of litter was astonishing.

The fact remains that the idea behind this march drew the sort of crowd – only far larger – which in the nineteenth and twentieth centuries might have flocked to hear Gladstone, Disraeli and, later, David Lloyd George. We haven't many politicians today that can attract a hundred to the local market square. Yet this turned out to be of huge public appeal. 'If Labour chooses to ignore it, what then?' said the cynic from Mayfair. Then, I replied, in what I hoped were measured tones, it will cost them something politically. If they choose to snap their fingers at this, then a lot of people who don't give a rap about hunting will draw certain conclusions and that will do Labour lasting harm. At that, I received a very superior smile and returned one every bit as superior.

Such an event has this in common with foxhunting: it gives rise to false scents which divert the hounds from their quarry. This, above all, was a march on which you could hear the bell tolling for a way of life. This, as a good many of the marchers informed me in their different ways, has been going on for a long time. I spoke with farmers who do not have many thousands a year to live off, given the price of milk and meat, but whose land can still fetch £3,000-4,000 an acre, because so many people would like to develop it. We're not exempt in this country from a movement I have witnessed elsewhere in the world. A big exodus from the land goes on in Africa, India and other continents. Towns swell and, sadly, the squalid shanty towns on their fringes swell even faster. The process here could be reversed or at least slowed down, but this is unlikely under a government so out of touch with the earth, so unconcerned with rural needs, so beholden to urban man and woman for their votes. That is what drew them down on coaches running through the night. That is why some of them stood for hours in the corridors of trains.

Before coming to the march, I turned up Oliver Goldsmith's lines on the doomed village of Auburn:

> Princes and lords may flourish,
> or may fade.
> A breath can make them,
> as a breath has made.
> But a bold peasantry,
> their country's pride,
> When once destroy'd
> can never be supplied.

So it has happened before. And two and a half centuries on, it is happening again. Urban England rolls on over the green fields. That is what quickened their step, why some of their faces looked so dark.

16 February 2003: Opposition to the incipient Iraq war
ONE MILLION MARCH AGAINST WAR IN IRAQ IN LARGEST PROTEST EVER
STARK MESSAGE DELIVERED TO TONY BLAIR
By Rajeev Syal, Andrew Alderson and Catherine Milner

Britain witnessed its largest demonstration yesterday when an estimated one million protesters took to the streets of London to oppose the looming war against Iraq. The centre of the capital was paralysed by noisy but peaceful people from many political backgrounds. Former members of the Armed Forces, clergymen and young children all joined the march to Hyde Park. On a bright but chilly day, thousands of demonstrators carried banners with messages such as 'No War On Iraq' and 'Make Tea, Not War'. The crowds at the two starting points on the Embankment and Gower Street were so large that the police began the march early for safety reasons. When the two strands finally met in Piccadilly Circus, there were deafening cheers from the thousands who had gathered around the statue of Eros. Others sounded their horns and banged drums.

Large peace protests were also held all over the country and around the world. Up to 60,000 protesters gathered in Glasgow and up to 90,000 in Dublin, while Italy had the biggest protest, with an estimated two million peace campaigners on the streets of Rome. Those taking part in the London protest included the Reverend Jesse Jackson, the black former presidential hopeful, Ken Livingstone, the Mayor of London, and leading names from the world of showbusiness, including Harold Pinter, the playwright, and Harry Enfield, the comedian.

Some organisers from the Stop the War Coalition claimed that two million people had taken part in the protest – nearly five times the 400,000-plus crowd that took part in the Countryside March last September. Officially, the police said that there were at least 750,000 demonstrators, but this did not include those who had gone direct to Hyde Park. Officers privately said that the total appeared certain to have reached at least one million. As the march reached its peak, there were three arrests – two men were arrested for public order offences and another man for possession of an offensive weapon. More than 4,500 police were on duty in London and all leave was cancelled.

Charles Kennedy, the Liberal Democrat leader, was among the protesters. He called on the Prime Minister to recall the House of Commons when it is in recess next week. 'This is the riskiest moment for Britain since Suez,' he said. At Hyde Park Corner, Mo Mowlam, the former Labour minister, attacked her former colleagues. 'Things can only get better if we stick together. Keep it peaceful. Because being peaceful, people will have no excuse not to listen. Tony Blair and the Government have [boxed] themselves into a right corner,' she said.

The Reverend Jackson said he had come on the march to show President Bush and Mr. Blair that there was unity among people across the world against the war. 'I am here to show support for the British people, most of whom recognise that war is not the way to relieve the Iraqi people of their suffering,' he said. Bill Morris, the Unison trade union leader, warned that the anti-war movement could galvanise public opinion against the Prime Minister. 'The anti-war movement could be significant. We all know what happened with the Vietnam War in the U.S. Blair needs to be careful,' he said.

Outside the Ministry of Defence in Whitehall, a group of Gulf War veterans joined the march. Brian Matthews, forty, a former sergeant in the Parachute Regiment, said he believed the last Gulf War had been justified because Saddam had invaded Kuwait. This time, however, he said he could see no reason for declaring war other than a quest for oil. 'We chose not to finish the job last time when we had a chance. This time we are going in there to save the world economy, not the people of Iraq,' he said.

Many 'hard-Left' groups dominated the front of the march: most of the stewards surrounding the Reverend Jackson admitted to being members of the Socialist Workers Party. There were, however, tens of thousands of 'moderate' protesters. Jonathan Callow, fifty-seven, a businessman from Chelsea, west London, said he has been on only one other demonstration, when he marched with the Countryside Alliance last year. He decided to demonstrate against Mr. Blair's plans for a war because of his belief that President Bush was misguided and dangerous. 'We are being rushed into a war. The British people are being dictated to by a small minority that support Bush in middle America. We are our own people and should choose for ourselves,' Mr. Callow said.

Mary Chillingford, forty-eight, a housewife from Guildford, Surrey, said that she had also been on the Countryside March last year. She carried a banner declaring 'Hands Off Iraq' and said that she was demonstrating because she did not believe this was a just enough war for her son, a serving soldier, to die in. 'Saddam is not threatening us. The Government should spend the money on British jobs, hospitals and the rural economy,' she said. 'Britain is falling apart, and what do we do? We send troops to kill a man on the other side of the world. It's madness.'

A number of well-known musicians, including Ms. Dynamite, joined the march. Damon Albarn, the lead singer of Blur, said that the march had brought together people from all walks of life. 'Everyone is here: members of the Labour Party, the Tory Party and quite a few Liberals. None of us can see a reason to start a war and the rest of the world thinks it's stupidity,' he said.

Some marchers were chanting 'Tony Blair: murderer. George Bush: murderer.' Others shouted: 'One, two, three, four, we don't want your bloody war.' Dozens of Islamic demonstrators waved Palestinian flags. They chanted: 'Destroy Israel', much to the embarrassment of Mr. Livingstone, who was standing next to them. A group of twenty actors and writers gathered outside the Duke of York Theatre in St. Martin's Lane before joining the march. Emma Thompson, who was accompanied by her actor boyfriend Greg Wise, described the war as 'dishonest and senseless'.

In contrast to the peace march, just one man mounted a lone protest outside the Iraqi section of the Jordanian embassy in central London, holding a placard proclaiming his support of military action to bring down Saddam Hussein. Jacques More, forty-four, a writer from Croydon, south London, said: 'War is a last resort and it's a necessary resort when evil dictators rule and murder their own people.'

21 March 2003: The Iraq War begins
MARINES STORM INTO IRAQ TO LAUNCH THE BATTLE FOR BASRA
WE ALL HAVE GREAT PRIDE IN OUR TROOPS, SAYS BLAIR
WARPLANES TARGET SADDAM'S HOUSE IN BLITZ ON BAGHDAD
By Michael Smith, Defence Correspondent

The allied invasion of Iraq began last night. American and British forces launched a two-pronged assault on the strategic southern city of Basra. Huge explosions lit the night sky around the city and the sound of heavy bombers could be heard. 'We saw about thirty fireballs on the horizon towards Basra,' David Fox, a Reuters correspondent, said early today. Explosions were also heard in the northern city of Mosul shortly before 2 a.m., the Al-Jazeera television station reported.

Aircraft bombed targets in Baghdad, including one of Saddam

Hussein's houses, and Royal Marines commandos and U.S. marines stormed ashore on Al-Faw peninsula. Unconfirmed reports said they had captured the country's main port of Umm Qasr. The assault was preceded by a landing by U.S. navy Seal special forces, members of the S.B.S. and the Royal Marines brigade reconnaissance force which probed the Iraqi forces. In the second prong, U.S. marines supported by the tanks of 7th Armoured Brigade headed for Basra. They were expected to wait outside the city until early today to give the garrison time to surrender. Special forces, including the S.A.S. and S.B.S., were believed to be already in Basra negotiating a deal with local commanders. The attack on Baghdad came from cruise missiles, many fired from Royal Navy submarines. They hit presidential palaces and buildings housing the Special Republican Guard, leaving a guards' barracks in flames.

Donald Rumsfeld, the American Defence Secretary, said the city's four million inhabitants were about to see a sustained air attack, the expected 'shock and awe' campaign. It would be 'of a force and scope and scale that is beyond what has been seen before'. Pentagon officials said later that the shock and awe element was 'on hold' while they assessed whether the Iraqi leadership remained in place.

Helicopters taking troops from the 82nd Airborne Division and 16 Air Assault Brigade flew towards southern oilfields. As a red glow lit the horizon, there were reports that the Iraqis had set fire to three or four oil wells, adding urgency to the troops' mission to the rest. The only Iraqi response was ten missiles launched at Kuwait, two believed to be Scud-Bs, which Saddam has denied having. Signalling the depleted state of his arsenal, two others were Silkworm-type anti-ship missiles fired at ground forces. At least three missiles were shot down by U.S. Patriot missile batteries without injury or damage. Tests by Britain's joint nuclear, biological and chemical regiment showed no traces of chemical or biological agents in the warheads. Iraq claimed to have shot down two helicopters, but the U.S. said they crash-landed and that no one was hurt.

The allied attacks, codenamed Operation Iraqi Freedom, followed a surprise departure from the original battle plan when cruise missiles and F-117 Nighthawk stealth bombers attacked a building in southern Baghdad early yesterday after intelligence showed that Saddam and his two sons, Uday and Qusay, were there. Intelligence sources said that despite reports that the attack had failed to kill the Iraqi leader, it was 'still not clear' if he was alive.

As the cruise missiles fired by American ships and Royal Navy submarines sped towards Baghdad, RAF Tornado GR4s took off from Kuwait to join waves of attacks that included U.S. air force F-15 Strike Eagle and U.S. navy F/A-18 Hornet aircraft. Artillery including the 32 AS-90 155milimetre self-propelled guns of the 3rd Regiment Royal Horse Artillery blasted Iraqi front-line positions, softening them up before the invasion. The artillery attacks were co-ordinated by special forces, including the S.A.S. and S.B.S., whose presence inside Iraq was confirmed in the Commons by Geoff Hoon, the Defence Secretary. He warned M.P.s that the war might not be as short as some expected and that it would be risky.

The Queen sent a message to British troops, saying: 'May your mission be swift and decisive, your courage steady and true and your conduct in the highest traditions of your service both in waging war and bringing peace.' Tony Blair, in a television address, urged the country to unite behind the Armed Forces. 'They are the finest in the world and their families and all of Britain can have great pride in them,' he said.

15 April 2003: The human genome is decoded
HUMAN CODE IS SPELLED OUT IN THREE BILLION D.N.A. 'LETTERS'
By Roger Highfield, Science Editor

Scientists have finished reading the 'book of life', the three billion letters of D.N.A. that spell out the recipe of a person. Half a century after researchers in Cambridge first unveiled D.N.A.'s double helix molecular structure, an international team yesterday unveiled an accurate D.N.A. recipe – genome – of a human being.

The completion of the Human Genome Project, ahead of schedule and under budget, was announced yesterday by the International Human Genome Sequencing Consortium. The largest contributor was the Wellcome Trust Sanger Institute, at Hinxton near Cambridge, which carried out nearly a third of the work at a cost of £150 million. The effort was welcomed for providing 'the fundamental platform for understanding ourselves' and 'a healthier future' said the Prime Minister and the heads of government of the consortium's six member countries.

Scientists also unveiled their vision for the future of genome research in *Nature*, the journal that published the landmark paper by James Watson and Francis Crick in April 1953, when they described the double helix structure of deoxyribonucleic acid (D.N.A.), which contains instructions – as a series of chemical 'letters' – needed to build and operate every organism. The Human Genome Project is considered one of the most ambitious scientific undertakings, likened to splitting the atom or going to the Moon. But when it was launched in 1990, many were sceptical – not least because it was then thought it would cost about £2 billion and take until 2005. In fact, the project has cost around £1.7 billion and published its first draft in June 2000, which covered ninety per cent of the gene-containing part – at an error rate of one in 1,000 'letters' – with more than 150,000 gaps.

Yesterday's 'finished' sequence contains fewer than 400 gaps and ninety-nine per cent of it has an accuracy rate of less than one error every 10,000 letters. 'Never would I have dreamed in 1953 that my scientific life would encompass the path from D.N.A.'s double helix to the three billion steps of the human genome,' said Dr. James Watson, president of Cold Spring Harbor Laboratory and first leader of the Human Genome Project. 'When the opportunity arose to sequence the human genome, I knew it was something that could be done – and that must be done. The completion of the Human Genome Project is a truly momentous occasion for every human.'

When the project began, scientists had discovered fewer than one hundred human disease genes. Today, more than 1,400 disease genes have been identified. Professor Allan Bradley, a director of Sanger Institute, said: 'The health benefits could be phenomenal.' The U.S. National Human Genome Research Institute in Bethesda, Maryland, has set out a series of 'Grand Challenges' to energise the field, such as to understand the relationship between genomics, race and ethnicity. Another aim is to find new technologies that can read the entire genome of any person for less than £650, a challenge already being taken up by the company Solexa, which has come out of Cambridge University. 'We will begin to gain valuable new insights into human evolution, as well as human health and disease,' said Dr. Richard Gibbs, director of Baylor College of Medicine's Human Genome Sequencing Centre.

15 December 2003: Saddam Hussein is captured
'WE GOT HIM'
SADDAM CAPTURED HIDING IN EIGHT-FOOT HOLE UNDER HUT
FUGITIVE HELD BY U.S. TROOPS WITHOUT SHOT FIRED
BUSH HAILS SEIZURE AS IRAQIS CELEBRATE
DICTATOR FACES TRIAL IN SPECIAL BADHDAD COURT
By Alec Russell in Washington and Jack Fairweather in Baghdad

Saddam Hussein was in custody in Iraq last night after American forces unearthed him from a cramped hideaway in an eight-foot-deep hole under the floor of a mud hut on the outskirts of his home town, Tikrit. He is expected to be the first to be tried in an Iraqi court for war crimes set up last week and could face the death penalty. His trial is likely to be held after the coalition hands back sovereignty to Iraq in June. As the former dictator's capture was welcomed across the world, President George W. Bush said he would face 'the justice that he denied millions'. But he cautioned that the violence in Iraq and the fight against 'terrorists' were not over.

Saddam looked bewildered, wore dirty clothes and had a straggly beard when he was arrested. His appearance was a far cry from the swaggering poses of his twenty years in power. American troops discovered him under the hut in a small-walled compound on Saturday evening. 'He was caught like a rat,' said Major General Raymond Odierno, the commander of 4th Infantry Division. Although Saddam had a pistol, no shots were fired. Two other people were captured as the troops moved into the compound. In the hut, a suitcase with $750,000 in cash was found. A U.S. military source told *Newsweek* that Saddam's first words were: 'Don't shoot, I am Saddam Hussein, the president of the Republic of Iraq.' A family close to Saddam was reported to have tipped off the Americans. It was not clear if it would receive the $25 million offered by Washington for his arrest.

Paul Bremer, the United States proconsul in Iraq, confirmed the news of the arrest at a press conference in Baghdad with members of the American-appointed Iraqi governing council. 'Ladies and gentlemen . . . we got him,' he said, prompting an outburst of applause and cheers from Iraqi journalists. Adnan Pachachi, one of three members of the governing council who was taken to identify sixty-six-year-old Saddam, said the former president was 'unrepentant and defiant' and showed 'no remorse'. Lieutenant General Ricardo Sanchez, the head of American forces in Iraq, said that Saddam was co-operating at an undisclosed location, thought to be Baghdad airport, the most secure site in the country, where President Bush dropped in for a Thanksgiving dinner last month. Saddam, who had been on the run since the fall of Baghdad in April, appeared 'a tired man and also I think a man resigned to his fate', the general said.

In a brief televised address from the White House, Mr. Bush said: 'In the history of Iraq, a dark and painful era is over. A hopeful day has arrived. All Iraqis can now come together and reject violence and build a new Iraq. The capture of Saddam Hussein does not mean the end of violence in Iraq. We still face terrorists who would rather go on killing the innocent than accept the rise of liberty in the heart of the Middle East. Such men are a direct threat to the American people and they will be defeated.' The intention to try Saddam in the Iraqi war crimes court was announced by Dara Nuredin, a member of the governing council and the chairman of its legal committee. He said: 'If the case against him is completed with all the necessary proofs, he will be the first to appear before this court.'

Gunfire crackled in celebration as many Iraqis finally dared to believe at last that Saddam's Ba'athist regime was no more. A key element in the rejoicing was the release of an American military video showing the former dictator being given a medical examination. D.N.A. tests were taken as final confirmation of his identity. His meek submission was in stark contrast to the end of his sons, Uday and Qusay, who died in a gun battle in July. Since then he has issued a series of taped appeals to his followers. But the humbleness of his hideaway added to speculation that he has not played a major role in the insurgency.

The capture of Saddam is the greatest success for the American-led coalition since it invaded Iraq in March. It is also a major fillip for Mr. Bush as he prepares for next year's presidential election. But Pentagon officials underlined his warning that the bloody insurgency, which has claimed hundreds of lives in the past six months, was not over. A car bomb killed at least sixteen policemen and two civilians, including a seven-year-old girl, at a police station in the town of Ramadi, west of Baghdad, yesterday, indicating that there is much fighting ahead.

Mr. Bush telephoned Tony Blair, America's staunchest ally, to give him the news of the arrest after it was confirmed at dawn, Washington time. The Prime Minister, speaking in Downing Street, said the arrest 'removes the shadow that has been hanging over [the Iraqi people] for too long of the nightmare of a return to the Saddam regime'. Like Mr. Bush, he struck a sober note. 'Let this be more than a moment for simply rejoicing,' he said. 'Let it be a moment to reach out and reconcile.'

With hopes rising in Washington that this could be the start of a new period of international co-operation over Iraq, the main anti-war nations, France, Germany and Russia, also hailed the breakthrough, if a little less enthusiastically than America's allies. President Jacques

Chirac, of France, said through a spokesman that the capture was a 'major event which should strongly contribute to the democratisation and stabilisation of Iraq'. Dominique de Villepin, France's foreign minister, stood ready to participate in rebuilding the country. Igor Ivanov, the Russian foreign minister, said he expected that Saddam's arrest would help restore security in Iraq and enable a political resolution to the situation there 'under the authority of the United Nations'. Chancellor Gerhard Schroder, of Germany, sent a message of congratulations to Mr. Bush. 'It is with great joy that I learned of the capture of Saddam Hussein,' he wrote.

12 March 2004: Terrorism in Madrid
MASSACRE IN THE RUSH-HOUR
192 DIE AS BOMBS HIT COMMUTER TRAINS IN MADRID
ETA OR AL-QA'EDA? KORANIC TAPE IS FOUND IN VAN
By Isambard Wilkinson in Madrid

A series of simultaneous bomb explosions tore through four packed Spanish commuter trains at the height of the morning rush-hour yesterday, leaving at least 192 people dead and 1,400 injured in one of Europe's worst terrorist atrocities. The Spanish government immediately accused the Basque terrorist group Eta, but last night a claim of responsibility was made in the name of al-Qa'eda. Police found detonators and an Arabic-language tape with Koranic verses in a stolen van in the Madrid suburb where it was believed the bombs had been planted. Al-Qa'eda has repeatedly threatened members of the U.S.-led coalition in Iraq, including Spain which has 1,300 troops there.

Thirteen bombs were placed in trains heading into Atocha station, Madrid's busiest terminal. Ten of the 60lb devices, each hidden in a backpack, exploded. Several Britons were among the injured. The terrorists' methods, including carefully synchronised explosions and a determination to kill the maximum number of civilians, suggested Islamist involvement. A London-based Arabic newspaper, *Al-Quds Al-Arabi*, said it had received a letter purporting to come from al-Qa'eda claiming responsibility for the attacks on the 'crusaders' and warning that another strike against America was imminent. Ángel Acebes, the interior minister, said the discovery of the van opened 'all kinds of lines of investigation'. He added: 'I have just given instructions to the security forces not to rule out any line of investigation.'

The authorities said the death count would rise and almost certainly exceed the 202 killed in the Bali bombing of October 2002. That would make it the worst terrorist incident since September 11. 'This is mass murder,' José María Aznar, the prime minister, told Spaniards in a televised address following an emergency cabinet meeting. 'No negotiation is possible or desirable with these assassins, who so many times have sown death across Spain.'

As security forces defused the three bombs that did not go off, survivors spoke of terrible carnage. 'It looked like a platform of death,' said one witness who described a body on the station roof. Ana Maria Mayor, another passenger, said: 'I saw a baby torn to bits.' As scores of bloodied passengers staggered from stations and trains, the dead and dying were piled amid the wreckage. Cries of pain emanated from the smoke. Another witness, Mariano, twenty-eight, said: 'I had a girl in my arms and I lost her. She died in my arms.'

The scale and audacity of the attacks appeared to have been influenced by the September 11 attacks in America and subsequent Islamist attacks around the world. But Spanish officials said the explosives were the same as those used by Eta in the past and noted that the attacks came three days before the general election, a period normally marked by Eta blasts. Eta's political wing, the banned radical party Batasuna, said it 'absolutely rejected' the attacks and was convinced Eta was not responsible. It blamed 'Arab resisters'.

Some Spanish commentators have suggested a link between Eta and Islamist extremists, but this has never been proved. Eta often warns of its planned attacks but this time there was no call. The bombs started exploding at 7.39 a.m. in a commuter train heading for the bustling Atocha station. Blasts then hit trains and platforms at two suburban stations, El Pozo and Santa Eugenia. Both trains were heading to Atocha. Worst hit was a double-decker train at El Pozo, where two bombs killed seventy people. Security officials said the attacks had been timed so that bombs went off as all four trains arrived at Atocha, but the plan misfired because they were running two minutes late.

As campaigning for Sunday's election was halted, thousands of people gathered in towns across Spain, expressing outrage at the atrocity. Larger protests are planned tonight. The Queen sent a message to King Carlos of Spain. It said: 'These attacks of terrorism have struck without discrimination and have horrified the people of the United Kingdom.' Tony Blair said: 'This terrible attack underlines the threat that we all continue to face from terrorism in many countries.' President George W. Bush called the bombings a 'vicious act of terrorism'.

27 December 2004: An earthquake under the Indian Ocean unleashes a devastating tsunami
WAVE OF DEVASTATION
UNDERSEA EARTHQUAKE IS MOST POWERFUL IN FORTY YEARS
TSUNAMI LEAVES THOUSANDS DEAD, MILLIONS HOMELESS
By Peter Foster, South Asia Correspondent, Jonathan Petre and Richard Alleyne

More than 12,000 people were swept to their deaths in southern Asia yesterday when a giant wall of water caused by the most powerful earthquake for forty years devastated the region. A series of tsunami up to thirty feet high raced across the Indian Ocean and crashed into the coasts of Sri Lanka, southern India, Indonesia, Thailand and Malaysia, carrying away people, houses, hotels, fishing boats and cars. The waves, which can reach 500 m.p.h., even reached east Africa, smashing fishing boats and flooding low-lying areas 3,700 miles west of the epicentre of the earthquake, sixty miles off the Indonesian island of Sumatra. Experts said the underwater tremor, which measured 9.0 on the Richter scale, may have had such a widespread impact because it occurred relatively close to the ocean surface.

The Association of British Travel Agents said that about 10,000 Britons were likely to be in the disaster area. At least one British tourist died – in the Maldives – and thousands were stranded. Last night the Foreign Office switchboard was jammed as people sought information about friends and relatives. The helpline was described as busier than after the September 11 terrorist attacks on the United States.

The huge waves pitched boats into trees, washed away villages and resorts and carried off lorries and buses. As an international relief operation began, officials braced themselves for mounting casualty figures. Accurate counts were impossible, but preliminary estimates put the number of dead at more than 4,500 in Sri Lanka, 4,400 in Indonesia, 3,000 in India, 400 in Thailand, forty-two in Malaysia, fifteen in Somalia and thirty-two in the Maldives. In Sri Lanka entire fishing villages, built from wood and palm fronds were erased from the map, leaving a million people homeless as they fled before the advancing waves.

Katie Razzall, thirty-one, who was on honeymoon in Tangalla, a Sri Lankan resort, said: 'It was terrifying. The water behind us was ripping through the trees as we ran up a hill to safety. A few minutes later all the villagers were out again, picking up the debris on the beach and trying to tidy up when another even bigger series of waves hit us. There were houses with lorries smashed into them and the harbour wall was pushed 150 yards up the coast.' Miss Razzall said that hundreds of bodies had been laid out in the hospitals for relatives to identify.

The affected area across the Indian Ocean and Andaman Sea includes many of the world's most idyllic holiday destinations, including the Maldives and the Thai diving centre of Phuket – a favourite with Britons at this time of year. In southern India more than 2,000 mostly poor fishermen and their families were killed, leaving the beaches littered with bodies as the waters receded.

The Pope led appeals for a swift international effort, with the European Commission giving more than £2 million to meet 'initial needs'. The Queen sent a message of condolence. Witnesses from India to Indonesia said the waves struck without warning. Many described how the sea appeared suddenly to 'seethe and boil' as it engulfed thousands of miles of coast. 'It came out of nowhere,' said John Hyde, an Australian politician on holiday in Phuket. 'Suddenly the streets were awash and people were screaming as they ran from the beach.'

Many of the worst-affected areas, such as Sumatra, are in inaccessible and politically unstable regions. In Sri Lanka at least ten Britons were reported to have been admitted to hospital and an official Tamil website said that a Roman Catholic priest and 170 children at an orphanage had been killed. Soldiers were brought on to the streets of Galle, one of Sri Lanka's most picturesque holiday destinations, after looters began plundering buildings. In Aceh province, Sumatra, which has been racked by separatist violence for many years, there were reports of bodies wedged in trees and a hotel being washed away.

The tsunami destroyed a bridge in the town of Kawthaung, in southern Burma, close to the Thai border, killing ten people. Several trawlers were missing at sea. State television in the secretive, military-ruled country confirmed that the earthquake and several aftershocks had been felt but gave no details of damage or injuries. Phuket, where three-wheel tuk-tuk taxis floated through the streets, was among the worst hit resorts in Thailand, with reports of divers and sunbathers being swept out to sea. It is not known how many people were on the island when the waves struck, but David Fall, the British ambassador, said it could be thousands. British embassy teams were heading for the resort. On Phi Phi Island, Thailand, where hundreds of holiday bungalows were destroyed, the resort owner, Chan Marongtaechar, said he feared that many of his staff and scores of holidaymakers had drowned. About 4,000 foreign and Thai tourists were stranded on Phi Phi, the tiny island that was made famous by the 2000 film *The Beach*, starring Leonardo DiCaprio.

Among the many scenes of suffering there were also dramatic stories of survival, as in Thailand where eighty divers were rescued from the renowned Emerald Cave. All had been assumed dead after being swept into the cave.

8 July 2005: 7/7 in London
AL-QA'EDA BRINGS TERROR TO THE HEART OF LONDON
BOMBERS TARGET RUSH-HOUR CROWDS ON BUS AND TUBE
AT LEAST THIRTY-SEVEN DEAD AND 300 INJURED AFTER
FOUR EXPLOSIONS SHAKE CAPITAL

Three terrorist bombs ripped through London Underground trains during the morning rush-hour yesterday and a fourth destroyed a double-decker bus, killing at least thirty-seven people and wounding more than three hundred others. The Tube was shut down and bus services in the centre of the city halted, causing widespread travel disruption. Mainline stations were also closed for much of the day. Last night Jack Straw, the Foreign Secretary, said the explosions 'bore all the hallmarks' of al-Qa'eda.

The co-ordinated attacks were being compared to the train bombings in Madrid last year which killed 190 people. There were fears that the bus explosion, which left two people dead in Tavistock Square, was the work of a suicide bomber. If so, it would be the first such incident in Britain and Europe, indicating that vigilance by transport staff and passengers could be no defence against outrages.

The attacks were the worst terrorist attack on British soil since the bombing of Flight 103 over Lockerbie in 1989, which killed 270 people. The Queen, 'deeply shocked', sent a message to victims and relatives and Tony Blair urged defiance of the bombers who were trying to 'cow' the nation. Looking shaken by the extent of the carnage, the Prime Minister said: 'The purpose of terrorism is just that; it is to terrorise people – and we will not be terrorised. This is a very sad day for the British people, but we will hold true to the British way of life.'

He said 'this most terrible and tragic atrocity' had cost many innocent lives. Mr. Blair promised 'the most intense police and security service action to make sure that we bring those responsible to justice'. He added: 'When they try to intimidate us, we will not be intimidated. When they seek to change our country or our way of life by these methods, we will not be changed.' The Prime Minister had flown back to London from Gleneagles where he had been hosting the meeting of G8 leaders and brought with him promises of resolute support from countries as varied as America, Mexico, Russia and China, all of which have their own experiences of terrorism. President George W. Bush said: 'It's a war on terror for us all.'

The first bomb exploded at 8.51 a.m. in a train on the Circle Line as it travelled from Aldgate station, in east London, to Liverpool Street. The train was more than usually packed because of earlier disruption caused by signalling problems. Seven people were killed and dozens hurt. Underground staff had just registered the emergency calls flooding along their internal communication lines when, five minutes later, another bomb went off. This time it was on a Piccadilly Line train travelling west from King's Cross to Russell Square. The carriages were crammed with commuters and twenty-one were killed. Within minutes, ambulances and police began to arrive in force, following a detailed emergency plan that service leaders had developed in case of such an attack.

Survivors and the walking wounded were being led to safety 300 yards back down the track to King's Cross and ambulance personnel and fire crews were hurrying past them towards the dead and the maimed when radio circuits gave news of still further carnage at 9.17 a.m. This time a bomb shattered a westbound Circle Line train as it was leaving Edgware Road station towards Paddington. The blast tore through a wall and caused damage to two other trains. Seven people were killed and dozens of others injured. Staff from a hotel helped medical teams from St. Mary's Hospital, Paddington, to care for the walking wounded.

The fourth bomb, in a red double-decker passing the headquarters of the British Medical Association, went off at 9.47 a.m. The blast ripped off its roof. The bus, a number 30 from Hackney Wick to Marble Arch, had been re-routed because of the disruption caused by the attacks on the Underground. The injured were tended by passers-by, including Stephanie Riak Akuei, an American who had taken a first aid course.

She helped bandage and comfort those trapped on the bus. She said: 'I was on the corner and heard the noise. I went over and there were at least seven people who were obviously dead. There was a lot of body parts and human debris. There were people dead, people alive, trapped on the bus.' She was joined by doctors from the B.M.A. building and later by paramedics.

Rudolph Giuliani, the former mayor of New York, was close to Liverpool Street station when the first bomb went off. Mr. Giuliani, who galvanised his city after the September 11 attack on the World Trade Center that killed 3,000 people, said the London bombings brought those days back to him. 'They are a very eerie reminder of September 11,' he said. 'I was right near Liverpool Street when the first bombing took place, so I could hear the sirens and then kept hearing reports of different bombing, in different parts of the city. As we were walking through and driving through the streets of the city, it was remarkable how the people of London responded calmly and bravely.'

The capital, which a day earlier had been celebrating its unexpected victory in the race for the 2012 Olympics, was given a warning by police that the explosions could be part of a campaign of terrorism. They said that thousands of officers would be deployed across the transport network today. Andy Trotter, the deputy chief constable of British Transport Police, said: 'We don't know whether this is over.' No warning of the blasts was given and the intelligence services said that they had no indication from any sources that an attack was imminent. MI5 and Scotland Yard's anti-terrorist branch have consistently said that an attack on London, or anywhere else in the country, was inevitable and that the only question was when it would happen. Police said that at one stage they were receiving 42,000 calls an hour from anxious relatives and were asking members of the public to try to make direct contact with relatives and friends first.

With mainline stations closed for much of the day and the Underground for all of it, people who had managed to reach work were faced with a difficult journey home. Today many firms were arranging shuttle buses and taxis to get people to their offices. At King's Cross, Keith Hill, thirty-six, a manager at the Football Association heading home to Royston, Herts, said: 'It might sound like a cliché, but this could be the safest time to take a train.' As some railway stations reopened, thousands of people leaving the city for suburban homes began to wonder if their commuter mornings would ever be the same again.

The Queen ordered the Union Flag over Buckingham Palace to fly at half-mast and flags over all Government buildings will also be lowered. In a statement from the Palace, the Queen said: 'The dreadful events in London this morning have deeply shocked us all. I know I speak for the whole nation in expressing my sympathy to all those affected and the relatives of the killed and injured. I have nothing but admiration for the emergency services as they go about their work.'

Michael Howard, the Conservative leader, said that it was a 'dreadful day for London and for our country'. 'I entirely support what the Prime Minister has said about our determination to protect and defend our way of life. It is important that everyone should know that this country is completely united in our determination to defeat terrorism and to deal with those who are responsible for the appalling acts which we have seen today.' The Archbishop of Canterbury, Dr. Rowan Williams, said: 'The appalling events in London this morning have shocked us all. I want first and foremost to extend my personal sympathy and condolences to everyone who is suffering and grieving at this time.'

Cobra, the Cabinet Office emergency committee responsible for coping with domestic disasters, sat at various stages throughout the day. At around lunchtime, Charles Clarke, the Home Secretary, left the meeting to tell the House of Commons of the four blasts. As he spoke, Scotland Yard had already embarked on the largest manhunt since the height of the I.R.A.'s campaign thirty years ago. Sir Ian Blair, the Metropolitan Police commissioner, had given a warning that the G8 summit was a prime terrorist target. Anti-terrorist officers were studying a claim of responsibility on the internet from a group claiming links to Osama bin Laden's group, although by last night they had received no direct claims.

Senior officers hope that survivors' recollections, closed circuit television footage at stations and possibly from trains, as well as debris from the Underground and the bus, will provide key clues. Police sources said that, whether or not one or more of the attacks were carried out by suicide bombers, the terrorists would have a support network. The police have been giving private warnings for some time that, despite speculation about 'dirty bomb' attacks or other weapons of mass destruction, the most likely threat would come from a more conventional bombing assault such as that in Madrid during the Spanish elections in March last year. The Madrid gang, mainly North African terrorists, planted devices on crowded commuter trains and tried to blow up a high-speed passenger train. Several key members of the cell blew themselves up when they were cornered by police a month later.

The Pope sent a message of support to Britain in which he said he was deeply saddened by the bombings. 'Upon the people of Great Britain he invites the consolation that only God can give in such circumstances,' the message from the Vatican added.

5 September 2005: Hurricane Katrina hits the U.S.
WHITE HOUSE DEFENDS BUSH FROM POLITICAL BATTERING OVER KATRINA
By Francis Harris in Washington

The White House launched a huge operation yesterday to prevent the political damage wrought by Hurricane Katrina from engulfing President George W. Bush. With public shock at the scenes of death and destruction turning to anger, senior politicians were told to cancel plans for Labour Day today and report for duty. As many as 150 Britons were still unaccounted for after the hurricane, the foreign minister Lord Triesman said last night. Some may have been unable to contact relatives, he said. Police shot at eight people carrying guns in New Orleans yesterday, killing at least five. Deputy Police Chief W.J.

Riley said the shootings were on the Danziger Bridge, which connects Lake Pontchartrain and the Mississippi River.

Mr. Bush is to travel to the disaster zone in the Deep South for a second time today and has cancelled a critically important trip to Washington by China's president Hu Jintao tomorrow. The administration came under early criticism from Aaron Broussard, the council leader of Jefferson Parish, south of New Orleans. 'It's not just Katrina that caused all these deaths. Bureaucracy has committed murder here in the greater New Orleans area, and bureaucracy has to stand trial before Congress.'

Many commentators are blaming Mr. Bush. The flooded city was yesterday described in a headline as 'Baghdad on the Bayou'. Many have focused on the emergency management head Michael Brown, who previously managed a horse breeding association. Senior cabinet members, such as Condoleezza Rice, were sent South yesterday to confront criticisms from black leaders that the poor of New Orleans had been left to their fate because of their colour. There was some cheering news for the White House. A survey in *The Washington Post* showed forty-six per cent approved of the president's handling, while forty-seven per cent did not. Reporters say that behind the scenes, officials in Louisiana are saying up to 10,000 people may be dead. One mentioned 15,000.

The appalled reaction of a U.S. Army veteran of the war in Afghanistan said it all. 'This is a shell-shocker,' said Warren Ezell as he surveyed the evacuation of the last refugees from New Orleans. 'I never saw anything like this in Afghanistan. I can't believe this is America. It's a jagged pill to swallow. It's like walking into your house and it's upside down and turned round.'

He was standing in his desert fatigues outside the city's giant convention centre as the evacuation of tens of thousands of refugees finally hit top gear. All around him hundreds of elderly and disabled people, white and black, were slumped in the blazing sun surrounded by mounds of stinking refuse. In wheelchairs and shopping trolleys, on makeshift stretchers, they were awaiting their turn. By yesterday morning, the last of them had been driven away or flown out in the biggest emergency airlift in U.S. history. Smelling of corpses, excrement and rotting food, the convention centre, just a week ago a shining symbol of corporate achievement, was finally empty.

But the repercussions have barely begun. In a rare display of unanimity, soldiers, policemen and refugees agreed that the evacuation, hugely impressive as it was in its closing stages on Saturday, would not go down as one of America's finer hours. In particular, all spoke of a lack of direction, and a failure by the authorities to co-ordinate their response. Federal, state and city relief workers, police and troops have been pouring in, but often in an *ad hoc* response. One Texan marshal sporting a white Stetson and black bullet proof vest said he had driven in with his colleagues and stood guard on a key crossing. Asked who was in command, he shrugged. 'There is no one in charge.'

Particularly striking has been the apparent failure of anyone to take the initiative. Karen Alcorn, thirty-seven, a nurse, said: 'You talk to the National Guard and they say they have no orders. There were guards here since last Monday. Why could they not use their trucks to help get us out?' Tao Tran, sixty-one, knows something about being evacuated. He was brought out of Vietnam in the Saigon airlift and was staggered that he was going through the same experience thirty years later. 'There have been too many cooks in the kitchen,' he said. 'We don't know where we're going. No one has told us anything. We thought we'd be here a day or two, but after the second day nothing happened.'

It was probably only to be expected that even as the last of the refugees were finally being prepared for embarkation a fleet of yellow buses started arriving laden with – now unwanted – supplies. But the swamping of the city with aid and relief workers has come too late to change the minds of the refugees, black and white, that this has been anything but a shameful muddle on the part of everyone from the city's mayor to the nation's commander-in-chief.

Wayne Compton, fifty-nine, a Vietnam vet who is now a wheelchair-bound diabetic, finally broke down on Saturday afternoon as he sat in the blazing sun. 'I surrender,' he said. 'I fought in Vietnam and all week I have been hollering and shouting. But this morning I put out the white flag.' He was abandoned in his nursing home last week when the staff fled. Then after being rescued by neighbours, for four days he sat at the convention centre relying on the charity of fellow refugees. And now his wheelchair motor had broken down.

'We have been treated like animals,' he said. 'They can send boats to help people after the tsunami but they can't help their own. God bless them in Asia but I was always taught that first you take care of your own.' Then, in a final insult, a paramedic started shouting at him that he could stay in his wheelchair if he wished, but to stay would be to die. 'I am not an animal,' replied Mr. Cummings, in tears. 'Don't yell at me. I can't leave my chair.'

'I've never seen anything like this in Honduras, Guantanamo and Belize,' said a member of the Louisiana National Guard gazing over the debris. 'To think, this is home.'

29 May 2008: The Nepalese monarchy falls
NEPAL ABOLISHES ITS MONARCHY AFTER 239 YEARS
HOLIDAY AIR AS REPUBLIC IS DECLARED AND KING GIVEN FIFTEEN DAYS TO LEAVE PALACE
By Thomas Bell in Kathmandu

Nepal swept away more than two centuries of history last night when the monarchy was abolished with barely a whimper from the palace. King Gyanendra, whose seven-year reign began in tragedy, floundered in authoritarianism and ended in meek surrender, was given fifteen days to leave his palace. After that, according to the new government, it will be turned into a museum.

An overwhelming majority of an elected assembly, charged with drawing up a new constitution, backed the creation of a republic in the Himalayan nation, which endured ten years of war against

Maoist rebels, who are now the dominant partners in the new political landscape. The resolution, passed by 560 votes with only four against, says that Nepal will become 'an independent, indivisible, sovereign, secular and an inclusive democratic republic nation'. It adds: 'All the privileges enjoyed by the king and royal family will automatically come to an end.'

King Gyanendra, who inherited the throne after ten members of the royal family were massacred by Crown Prince Dipendra in 2001, was a victim of his own incompetence and historical forces beyond his control. The royal bureaucracy was stuffed with elderly functionaries incapable of accepting change. As a Maoist insurgency gripped the country, especially after 2001, the establishment fell back on what it knew best – authoritarianism practised by a tiny elite. The poor and the young flocked to the Maoist's republican cause, while King Gyanendra's high-handed response helped to spread republicanism to the political mainstream. When street demonstrations forced the king to end direct rule in 2006, he had few friends left. The Maoists won elections last month for the constitutional assembly.

The day the Nepalese monarchy fell had the air of a holiday from the start, as celebrating crowds gathered in streets that – for once – were free of chaotic traffic. Many marched beneath the hammer and sickle flag of the Maoist party. Om Prasad Risal, a thirty-four-year-old teacher, waited more than ten hours outside the assembly building for the vote to take place. 'I'm not bored,' he said. 'It's very exciting. The monarchy is the root cause of underdevelopment and that's why we want to root it out. The monarchy never did anything for the people. Morally or legally the king has no right to lead the country. But he has a right to live as a private citizen.' After leaving the palace Gyanendra is expected to retreat to the Kathmandu mansion where he lived before acceding to the throne. But there have been demands for him to go into exile, sealing the fall of the House of Shah after 239 years.

Overturning a centuries-old hierarchy is no small matter, and even as the vote was cast there was no agreement on what would replace the monarchy. For now, the leaders have agreed to disagree. It was almost midnight when the result came. As the crowds milled about outside the assembly, two small bombs exploded, causing brief moments of terror. There have been five bombings in Kathmandu in the past three days, blamed on Hindu fundamentalists who regard the king as an incarnation of the god Vishnu. But no one was hurt, and the crowds, who are accustomed to the threat of violence, quickly calmed.

The political wrangling points to the many problems ahead. A new constitution must now be drafted and the Maoists need the support of other parties to implement their plans. Big issues include the integration of former Maoist fighters into the politically conservative national army.

10 October 2008: A banking crisis hits Iceland, with effects felt in Britain
GIVE US OUR MONEY BACK
BROWN THREATENS ICELAND OVER RETURN OF
£20 BILLION TIED UP IN COLLAPSED BANKS
By James Kirkup, Christopher Hope and Jon Swaine

Gordon Brown has issued a public threat to Iceland, demanding the return of up to £20 billion belonging to British savers, companies and local councils. The Prime Minister said Britain would seize the assets of Icelandic companies and take 'further action against the authorities' over the collapse of the island's banks.

The diplomatic row, which has echoes of the Cod Wars of the 1970s, erupted after it emerged that more than one hundred local authorities have deposits in Iceland. They stand to lose a total of more than £1 billion. British companies are said to have as much as £12 billion in the failed banks and individual savers more than £6 billion. Unless the Icelandic government agrees to return the cash, British taxpayers will have to foot the bill to bail out local councils and other public bodies. This would come through increases in council tax or Treasury funds. It would mean the Government spending more public money because of the financial crisis after staking £500 billion in an attempt to rescue

British banks. Yesterday there were few signs that Mr. Brown's bail-out gamble was paying off. Bank shares rose but the FTSE-100 closed 1.2 per cent down. There was little evidence that banks were more prepared to lend to each other and no British bank has requested any of the £50 billion available.

Mr. Brown said the behaviour of the Icelandic government in failing to guarantee the return of British money was 'unacceptable'. He vowed to go beyond the action already taken against Landsbanki, one of the Icelandic banks which had its U.K. assets seized on Wednesday under anti-terrorism laws meant to stop extremist groups laundering money. Mr. Brown told the BBC: 'We are freezing the assets of Icelandic companies in the U.K. where we can. We will take further action against the Icelandic authorities wherever that is necessary to recover the money.' He has also called on the rest of the world to follow Britain's 'ground-breaking' move to save the banking system. Mr. Brown urged other governments to put money into struggling banks and offer similar guarantees to persuade them to resume lending to each other.

Icelandic investment companies own several high street chains including Debenhams, Whistles and Oasis as well as the Premier League football club West Ham United. A war of words started as Geir Haarde, the prime minister of Iceland, used a press conference to denounce the seizure of Landsbanki assets. The use of anti-terrorism legislation was 'not pleasant', he said.

The Treasury has guaranteed the deposits of the estimated 300,000 private British investors in the collapsed banks Landsbanki, Glitnir and Kaupthing, which have been put in government administration. But ministers say they cannot give the same assurance to wholesale investors, including councils and companies. *The Daily Telegraph* has established that at least 111 public bodies have £944.07 million deposited in Icelandic banks. That includes fifteen police authorities, which invested £95.72 million, and transport authorities including Transport for London, which deposited £40 million alone. The remaining bodies were local councils. Kent county council was the biggest investor, with £50 million – £59.76 per taxpayer in the county – at stake. The London borough of Haringey deposited £37 million, equal to £324.14 per taxpayer.

The Local Government Association insisted that the sums remained a small proportion of councils' total funds and said no front-line services would be cut. Ministers promised emergency help for councils 'facing severe short-term difficulties'. A team of Treasury officials may go to Reykjavik as soon as today to discuss an agreement with Iceland.

6 November 2008: Barack Obama creates history in America
THE DREAM COMES TRUE
AMERICA'S FIRST BLACK PRESIDENT COMPLETES AN EPIC JOURNEY BEGUN BY MARTIN LUTHER KING
By Anne Applebaum

The maps on the television screens started turning blue as soon as the polls had closed on the East Coast; by midnight, John McCain had conceded the presidency to Barack Obama. But I had known the election result many hours before. I did not have special access to internal campaign data, or an early glimpse of the exit polls. I simply had one conversation, and one email exchange, which together told me everything I needed to know.

The conversation was with my sister, who lives in Florida, a bitterly contested battleground state. Florida was split down the middle in 2000, went for George W. Bush in 2004, and was considered a possible McCain state this year. But as election day dawned, my sister told me that even though a huge percentage of Floridians had taken advantage of early voting, there were still queues – everywhere – and many of those standing in them were black. Clearly, those waiting, sometimes for hours, were not waiting to vote for Mr. McCain.

The subsequent email exchange was with an old friend, a staunch Republican who is married to an even stauncher Republican – a rather famous one, too. Despite this family circumstance she had, she confessed, just voted for Mr. Obama. Though she had had her doubts, she suddenly found, on election day, that the decision was easy. More than easy: uplifting. When she emerged from the polling booth, she had a spring in her step, because she had just voted for the first black president. 'And that's no small thing,' she wrote. 'Maybe even worth some higher taxes.'

And that was how, by about 10 a.m., East Coast time, before the polls had opened in much of the country, I knew two extremely important pieces of information. Number one: black Americans were, for the first time in recent history, already voting in high numbers. Really high numbers. If the image of the 2000 election was that of lawyers flocking to Florida to dispute the result, 2008 will be remembered for those first-time voters, patiently waiting their turn to mark a ballot or pull a lever. The Obama campaign had identified and steadily lobbied some 600,000 Florida blacks who registered to vote but did not show up in the past. Their efforts paid off, in Florida and everywhere else.

Number two: not just Democrats, not just independents, not just 'swing voters' but actual, hard-core Republicans were so moved by the prospect of a black president – and so disgusted by the Bush administration – that they switched sides and voted for Mr. Obama. This happened despite accusations that Mr. Obama was a socialist, a Marxist, a secret Muslim, a radical. None of those epithets really stuck. In the end his inclusive, centrist, bipartisan rhetoric proved more powerful than even the hard evidence of his solid, Left-liberal voting record.

He repeated some of it again in his acceptance speech, after quoting Abraham Lincoln, who was a Republican: 'I may not have won your vote tonight,' he told Mr. McCain's electorate, 'but I hear your voices, I want your help and I will be your president, too.' As a rule, I dislike the word 'historic' when used to describe elections: all elections are 'historic', after all. Despite the rhetoric, this election is not 'historic' in the sense that it presented the American people with some kind of monumental choice between presidents who would have had vastly different policies. Let us be clear: whoever walks into the White House on inauguration day has limited choices, narrow possibilities, and almost no room for manoeuvre. Left, Right, Democratic or Republican, it does not matter: the new president still has to make sure that banks continue to lend money, the housing market continues to function, Afghanistan and Iraq do not deteriorate into chaos. I have no doubt that President McCain would have made many of the same decisions as will President Obama.

Nevertheless, this was a completely different election and it has produced a kind of euphoria that I have never seen in American politics before. 'Change' did not seem like much of a slogan, when Obama supporters held it up on signs during rallies. 'Yes, We Can' did not seem like much of a clarion call. But when the first black President-elect took the podium, with the black First Lady in waiting beside him, it was impossible not to feel that something profound really had just changed. If nothing else, the worst chapter of the American story – a chapter that began more than three centuries ago, when the first slave ships docked in Britain's North American colonies – had just come to an end.

Early yesterday, black Americans were sending a text message to one another: 'Rosa sat so Martin could walk. Martin walked so Barack could run. Barack is running so our children can fly.' Rosa was Rosa Parks, who refused to give up her seat to a white man on an Alabama bus. Martin was Martin Luther King, who marched on Washington and quoted the Declaration of Independence back at Americans: 'We hold these truths to be self-evident, that all men are created equal.' Mr. Obama is their inheritor – and he knew it. 'If there is anyone out there who still doubts that America is a place where all things are possible,' he told a cheering, weeping Chicago crowd; and if anyone 'still wonders if the dream of our founders is alive in our time – tonight is your answer'.

Mr. McCain knew it, too. In a gracious concession speech, he praised Mr. Obama for 'inspiring the hopes of so many millions of Americans who had once wrongly believed that they had little at stake or little influence in the election of an American president'. A century ago, he reminded his audience, President Theodore Roosevelt, was condemned for inviting the black educator Booker T. Washington to dinner at the White House. 'America today is a world away from the cruel and frightful bigotry of that time. There is no better evidence of this than the election of an African American to the presidency of the United States.'

I am convinced it was not, in the end, a disadvantage for Mr. Obama to be black. His race was an enormous attraction for many white Americans, even – or perhaps especially – some white Republicans. Here is something that may be hard for foreigners to understand: Americans desperately want to believe their country stands for fairness, for equality, for democracy. After the mistakes made in Iraq and Guantanamo, the terrible financial crisis, the embarrassment of Hurricane Katrina, a vote for Mr. Obama allowed Americans to believe, once again, that the United States is still a virtuous nation. It is not just about being liked abroad, though being liked is nice: it is about being certain that we still are, as we have often told ourselves, an example to other nations, a 'city on a hill'. Americans stood in line for that certainty, they crossed party lines to vote for it, they donated record amounts of money to the Obama campaign in search of it. In, the end, it comes down to this: all Americans are told, as children, that 'anyone can grow up to be president of the United States'. And now, once again, we know that it is true.

8 May 2009: The *Telegraph* exposes the scandal of what M.P.s claim on expenses
THE TRUTH ABOUT THE CABINET'S EXPENSES

More than half the Cabinet are facing allegations over their use of Parliamentary expenses after details of their claims were obtained by *The Daily Telegraph*. They include Gordon Brown, who paid his brother for 'cleaning services' at his private flat in Westminster. Jack

Straw, the Justice Secretary, admitted yesterday that he had over-claimed for both his council tax and mortgage bills. The disclosures show the scale of ministers' claims and the extent to which politicians have exploited the expenses system to subsidise their lifestyles.

The Prime Minister is among thirteen members of the Cabinet facing questions over their use of Parliamentary expenses. Yesterday, after being approached by *The Daily Telegraph*, Mr. Brown repaid a plumbing bill he had claimed for twice during 2006. Receipts submitted by the Prime Minister to the Parliamentary authorities disclosed that between 2004 and 2006, he paid Andrew Brown for cleaning at his flat. Andrew Brown, a senior executive at E.D.F. Energy, received £6,577 over twenty-six months. Last night, the Prime Minister's office said he shared a cleaner with his brother. In a statement, Number 10 said Mr. Brown 'reimbursed him [the brother] for his share of the cost'.

The statement is likely to give rise to questions as to why the Prime Minister did not simply lodge receipts directly from the cleaner. He has directly employed other cleaners. However, the payments to Andrew Brown would not have been disclosed under controversial laws allowing the personal information to be blacked out from the publicly-released documents.

The disclosure of the expenses of the Cabinet raises questions about the parliamentary expenses system, coming within weeks of disclosures over questionable claims made by Jacqui Smith, the Home Secretary. This summer, M.P.s are due to publish a detailed breakdown of claims. However, *The Daily Telegraph* begins a series of articles today that detail the scandal of members' expenses across all parties. Many of the claims go beyond what members of the public would find acceptable. The disclosures underline the need for urgent reform of the system amid fears that the spending of taxpayers' money was not being appropriately monitored.

It can be disclosed that: Jack Straw, the Justice Secretary, received a fifty per cent discount on his council tax from his local authority but claimed the full amount. He discovered the 'mistake' last summer within weeks of the High Court ordering that M.P.s release details of their expenses. He has repaid the money. Lord Mandelson, the Business Secretary, claimed thousands of pounds to improve his constituency home after he had announced his resignation as an M.P. He sold the property for a profit of £136,000. Hazel Blears, the Communities Secretary, claimed for three different properties in a single year. She spent almost £5,000 on furniture in three months after buying the third flat in an upmarket area of London.

David Miliband, the Foreign Secretary, spent hundreds of pounds on gardening at his constituency home – leading his gardener to question whether it was necessary to spend the money on pot plants 'given [the] relatively short time you'll be here'. Alistair Darling, the Chancellor, changed his official 'second home' designation four times in four years. Geoff Hoon, the Transport Secretary, also switched his second home, which allowed him to extensively improve his family home in Derbyshire before buying a London town house also funded by the taxpayer. Andy Burnham, the Culture Secretary, Caroline Flint, the Minister for Europe, and Paul Murphy, the Welsh Secretary, also bought flats – or the freehold on a property they already owned – and claimed stamp duty and other moving costs. Mr. Burnham warned the parliamentary authorities that his wife might divorce him if expenses were not paid promptly.

In a statement issued last night, Downing Street defended Mr. Brown's claims. The statement said: 'At all times the Prime Minister has acted with the full approval of the parliamentary authorities. In relation to the cleaning services, Mr. Gordon Brown and Mr. Andrew Brown employed one cleaner who worked for both of them, the majority of time for Gordon Brown. Payment was made directly to her by Mr. Andrew Brown for the work in both flats. Mr. Gordon Brown reimbursed him for his share of the cost. Of course, Mr. Andrew Brown did not receive any financial benefit.'

Several senior ministers were repeatedly warned by the

parliamentary authorities and had claims rejected or withheld. This newspaper uncovered evidence suggesting that the second homes allowance, which allows annual claims of up to £24,222, has been exploited by dozens of M.P.s and is in need of immediate reform. In many cases, the House of Commons fees office uncovered serious wrongdoing but the M.P.s implicated were not independently investigated. The rules governing the Parliamentary expenses system are notoriously lax and difficult to interpret. The main principle is that the second home must be 'wholly, exclusively and necessarily incurred from the purpose of performing your Parliamentary duties'. Some Cabinet ministers appear to have far more straightforward claims than those highlighted today.

Ed Miliband, the Energy and Climate Secretary, claimed only £6,300 a year in rent for a modest home in his constituency. He also claimed utility and council tax bills. Alan Johnson, the Health Secretary, claimed for only his constituency home over the past four years. He also rented a modest property, but claimed for food and some furniture. Hilary Benn, the Environment Secretary, claimed only £147.78 in food.

21 May 2009: The most infamous expenses claim
THE PHANTOM MORTGAGE, THE INSURANCE MYSTERY AND A £1,600 DUCK HOUSE CAMERON FORCED TO ACT OVER £30,000 CLAIM
By Robert Winnett, Martin Beckford and Nick Allen

A Conservative whip can today be uncovered as the most senior M.P. to have claimed interest payments for a property which had no mortgage. Bill Wiggin, a contemporary of David Cameron at Eton, received more than £11,000 in parliamentary expenses to cover interest payments after declaring that his Herefordshire property was his 'second home'. Last night, another senior Tory, Sir Peter Viggers, was forced to announce his retirement at the next election, after claiming tens of thousands of pounds for gardening. He is expected to repay more than £10,000.

Mr. Wiggin, who has been a whip since January, joins two Labour

M.P.s, Elliot Morley and David Chaytor, who could face a police investigation into 'phantom mortgage' expenses. Lawyers believe such claims may be a criminal offence under the 2007 Fraud Act and the 1968 Theft Act. Last night, Mr. Wiggin said that the claims had been in error and he had meant them to relate to his London property, which he had previously designated as his second home. The sums matched those paid for the London house. However, he completed and signed twenty-three statements for parliamentary officials declaring that his second home was in Herefordshire. In 2007, he switched his claim back to the London property. Mr. Wiggin insisted he has not profited. 'It was purely an administrative error, and it was of absolutely no financial advantage to me,' he said.

The disclosures come on the fourteenth day of *The Daily Telegraph*'s investigation into the M.P.s' expenses system. This newspaper has now exposed claims made by more than 170 M.P.s from the main parties in England, Scotland and Northern Ireland. Although Gordon Brown has announced new rules to overhaul the system, there is still pressure on the Prime Minister and Mr. Cameron to act against individual M.P.s found to have abused expenses.

Anthony Steen, the Tory M.P., announced last night that he would stand down at the next election, after disclosures that he claimed £80,000 for his second home, including tree work. A Labour official said that up to fifty of the party's M.P.s could be deselected as a result of the expenses scandal. However, many constituency associations are fighting to protect their M.P.s, frustrating voters' attempts to discover details of their representative's expense claims.

As the *Telegraph* continues to release information on M.P.s' expenses, some of the questionable claims made by both Conservative and Labour M.P.s are disclosed today:

Sir Peter Viggers claimed for a £1,645 floating 'duck island' in the garden pond at his Hampshire home. In a statement, the Conservative Party said: 'Sir Peter Viggers has confirmed that he will retire as M.P. for Gosport at the next election. He will do so at the direct request of

David Cameron'; Ruth Kelly, the former Cabinet minister, claimed thousands of pounds of taxpayers' money for flood damage to her second home, although she had a building insurance policy at the time; Natascha Engel, a back-bench Labour M.P., claimed thousands of pounds for furniture, Champagne flutes and other household items, including a £2,000 sofa. She disclosed her own claims after deciding that some constituents would find them unacceptable and has organised a series of meetings for her constituents to judge whether she should stand down.

The latest disclosures come after Mr. Cameron challenged Mr. Brown to call a general election and the Prime Minister conceded for the first time that he feared the Conservatives could win. All the political parties have now agreed immediate restrictions on what can be claimed on expenses, banning furniture, household items and food, and capping mortgage interest or rent at £1,250 per month.

SIR PETER VIGGERS
By Nick Allen

A Tory grandee included with his expense claims the £1,645 cost of a floating duck island in the garden pond at his Hampshire home. Sir Peter Viggers, the M.P. for Gosport, submitted an invoice for a 'Stockholm' duck house to the Commons fees office. The floating structure, which is almost five feet high and is designed to provide protection for the birds, is based on an eighteenth-century building in Sweden. The receipt, from a firm specialising in bird pavilions, said: 'Price includes three anchor blocks, duck house and island.' It was announced last night that following *The Daily Telegraph*'s disclosures, Sir Peter will retire at the next election.

Sir Peter, a qualified jet pilot, lawyer and banker, has been an M.P. for twenty-five years and is a member of the Treasury select committee. He lists his recreations in *Who's Who* as opera, travel and trees. His expenses files reveal that he was paid more than £30,000 of taxpayers' money for 'gardening' over three years, including nearly

£500 for twenty-eight tons of manure. He had a similar arrangement with the fees office to Douglas Hogg, submitting an annual list of the costs of maintaining his second home and then dividing them across the year for monthly payments. Mr Hogg, who has said he will stand down at the next election, included with his expenses the cost of having a moat cleared.

Sir Peter included his duck island. His handwritten list of spending for the financial year 2006–07 amounted to £33,747.19 and included 'pond feature £1,645'. In March 2007 he submitted a single claim of £18,522.59 for the final seven months of the financial year, noting that he understood it would be 'limited by the annual maximum'. The fees office reduced the claim to £10,769.94 accordingly. It was unclear whether he received money specifically for the duck island. A fees officer scrawled 'not allowable' next to it. Sir Peter also submitted a £213.95 electrician's bill including fixing lights on a 'fountain' and 'hanging lights on Christmas tree'. The year before, the annual costs Sir Peter had submitted came to £24,164.96. He asked for part of that to be paid under a separate office costs allowance. They included £6,960 on gardening, £1,800 on grass cutting and estate management, £533.23 on garden design, £460 on pest control, and £250 on irrigation. He submitted 'sample invoices' of £782.50 and £750.

In February 2007 officials wrote to Sir Peter asking him to submit claims based on 'actual costs' per month. In 2007–08, the costs of maintaining his second home rose to £36,158.93 including £19,000 on gardening and £3,275 for roof and chimney repairs. He reached the maximum allowed by December 2007.

Sir Peter was educated at Cambridge and served as an industry minister under Margaret Thatcher. He owns a flat in central London and sold his second home last year for £800,000. In a statement before his retirement was announced, Sir Peter said: 'The claims I made were in accordance with the rules, and were all approved by the fees office. Since then the situation has changed and we must all take account of that. My expenses are being examined by David Cameron's scrutiny panel and I await any recommendations they may make.' Mr. Cameron has made clear that any 'excessive' amounts claimed by M.P.s will have to be paid back.

26 June 2009: Death of the 'King of Pop'
MICHAEL JACKSON DIES, AGED FIFTY
By Matthew Moore

Michael Jackson, the singer, died last night after suffering a suspected heart attack. He was fifty. The Los Angeles coroner, Fred Corral, said that Jackson was pronounced dead after arriving at U.C.L.A. Medical Centre in full cardiac arrest. A post-mortem examination is likely to take place today. Paramedics who responded to an emergency call to the singer's home in Los Angeles said that he had stopped breathing by the time they arrived. Sources at the U.C.L.A. Medical Centre said that the self-styled 'King of Pop' did not come out of a coma and died.

Jackson's mother Katherine and sister La Toya had rushed to the singer's bedside at the hospital, while hundreds of tearful fans gathered outside. Earlier, the singer's father Joe said that he had been told his son was 'in a bad way'. Jackson is widely credited with revolutionising pop music with albums including *Thriller*, *Bad* and *Dangerous*, but his career was tainted with allegations of child abuse. He was due to perform a highly anticipated fifty-date 'farewell' residency at the O2 Arena in London, starting next month. Fears for his health emerged after he postponed the earliest dates, and his aides were forced to deny that he was fighting skin cancer.

Jackson lived as a virtual recluse following his 2005 acquittal on charges including child molestation and kidnap. While lauded by fans and critics for his infectious pop songs, pioneering dance moves and innovative videos, his increasingly eccentric behaviour earned him the nickname 'Wacko Jacko'. He repeatedly denied undergoing cosmetic surgery, despite very visible changes to his face and skin tone, and was criticised for forcing his three children to wear veils whenever they were in public.

Last night leading figures in the entertainment industry expressed their shock at news of his sudden death, which was broken on the U.S. celebrity website T.M.Z. Quincy Jones, the music producer who worked with Jackson on *Thriller*, said: 'I am absolutely devastated at this tragic and unexpected news.' Paying tribute to the singer's 'talent, grace, professionalism and dedication', he added: 'I've lost my little brother today, and part of my soul has gone with him.' Jackson's friend, the illusionist Uri Geller, said there had been no indication that the singer was in a frail condition. 'I really have no words. He was a young and terribly fit man and he was getting ready for performances in England. He was just fine, the last I heard.' The Reverend Al Sharpton, the civil rights campaigner, described Jackson as a 'historic figure'. He said: 'Michael Jackson made culture accept a person of colour way before Tiger Woods, way before Oprah Winfrey, way before Barack Obama.'

There was speculation that the pressure of his upcoming London dates may have been too much for him. Jackson last toured twelve years ago. A.E.G. Live, which organised the O2 concerts, said Jackson had passed a lengthy physical exam in early 2009. But Max Clifford, the publicist and friend of Jackson, said: 'You wonder if the strain of getting fit for this major tour proved too much. In recent pictures he looked anything but healthy. He was always someone who seemed to find it difficult to cope with fame.'

Born in 1958, Jackson made his musical debut with four of his older brothers in the Jackson Five before embarking on a solo career. His 1982 album *Thriller* is still the best-selling album of all time, with more than twenty-six million copies sold. His lifetime sales tally is estimated at 750 million. In 1994, he married Lisa Marie Presley, the daughter of Elvis Presley. The couple separated two years later and Jackson later married Debbie Rowe, a nurse he met in 1997. They had two children, Prince Michael and Paris Michael Katherine, before divorcing in 1999. Jackson had custody of the two children and of a third, Prince Michael II, whose mother's name has never been made public.

16 January 2010: Haiti is the latest country to fall victim
to a devastating earthquake
A MOMENT OF JOY AMID THE DESPAIR
By Tom Leonard in Haiti

He was covered in dirt, half naked and had been buried in the rubble of his collapsed home for two and a half days. But two-year-old Redjeson Hausteen Claude could still manage a smile as he was reunited with his mother. Sadly, his delight and that of Daphnee Plaisin as she took her son from his Spanish rescuer, was a rare moment of joy in this benighted city. Yesterday, three days after an earthquake devastated the Haitian capital, killing at least 30,000 and probably many more, Port-au-Prince resembled a medieval city gripped by the plague. The bodies lay piled up in their thousands in alleys and side streets, while many survivors slept out in squares and parks under a sea of blue and white tarpaulins.

Haitians, famously forbearing despite their country's crushing poverty and history of natural disasters, were losing patience with the perceived indifference of the world. The armed gangs menacing supply convoys at the city's woefully undersized airport and the unknown protesters who had moved dead bodies into major streets so they could not be hidden from view might have represented a minority. But in the city's central Champs de Mars park, there was no missing the tension and frustration among a population that had seen next to nothing of the largesse promised by America and the rest of the world.

Locals confirmed with a weary wave out to sea that there were no American ships in the harbour, no marines in the streets and the local airport was even turning back foreign search-and-rescue teams. As a thousand-strong crowd gathered expectantly but in vain around three Red Cross vehicles parked outside the shattered presidential palace, there was no shortage of angry voices. 'It's a big scandal, we feel abandoned,' said Jean-Claude Hillaire, thirty-four, his voice rising passionately as dozens of countrymen crowded around him to hear his words. 'We haven't seen any water or food. It's been four days now and nobody has come yet – you know that. Now we want to know why.' He felt particularly let down by Barack Obama. 'I'm very angry with him. We were the first black people who put a mark on liberty,' he said, referring to Haiti's successful revolt against slavery. 'We now need help from the first black U.S. president.'

Across the road was one of the tent cities in which, he said, 'people are lying on the ground screaming for help'. In fact, many of the injured seemed too weak even to do that. The smell of excrement and uncollected rubbish is a constant presence in the city but was almost overpowering around the tents. Nicolas Cayo and his twenty-strong extended family had been living under two tarpaulins since the earthquake and were using up what little money they had buying water from street sellers. 'There's no food. I heard Obama was sending a lot of things but we haven't seen them yet. Maybe they're on the way,' he said. One of the bandaged little girls – three-year-old Marie – had been rescued from the rubble of her home only the previous day. Her mother, Souvenir, had not been so lucky and had been too big to be pulled out. 'We recovered the mother's body and took it to a cemetery,' Mr. Cayo explained, simply. 'We got a coffin and buried it ourselves.' Most corpses have not been afforded that honour and provided the most poignant – and damning – illustration of the city's desperate plight.

In poorer areas there had been no attempt to conceal the victims' bodies and they lay, tightly wrapped like Christmas presents or hidden only by a folded piece of corrugated paper, in the main streets where they died. In wealthier quarters, there appeared to have been no deaths until a sudden glance up an alleyway revealed dozens, neatly laid out in rows and covered only in their own clothes, their limbs distorted by rigor mortis.

The United Nations personnel, criticised by some aid agency workers on the ground for failing to offer adequate protection to their staff, were out in force. In the expensive suburb of Pétionville, they were swarming like blue-helmeted ants yesterday around the Montana Hotel, Port-au-Prince's finest. French and U.S. rescue teams were working in the midday heat to get seven known survivors – seven American and one Haitian – from beneath the concrete layer cake of the completely collapsed building. Two were still alive inside, another had died, said a French fireman. In the street outside, half a dozen Haitians hurried along bearing an injured woman on a makeshift stretcher made from planks nailed together. Given that only a handful of hospitals were open, they may have had a long journey.

31 March 2010: Success at last for the Large Hadron Collider
COLLIDER HERALDS A 'NEW ERA OF SCIENCE'
By Richard Alleyne, Science Correspondent

The Large Hadron Collider fired mankind into a 'new era of science' yesterday as it finally produced the world's first high-energy particle collision. After years of setbacks, the £4.4 billion machine smashed together protons using three times the speed and energy of previous experiments. The achievement, at 12.06 p.m. British time, meant the world's biggest experiment was finally up and running and scientists could start attempting to unravel the secrets of the universe.

Even though particle collisions have been achieved before, yesterday marked the first time one had involved enough power to produce meaningful scientific results. The first two protons hit each other with a total energy of seven trillion electron volts, sending sub-particles flying in every direction. Four detectors positioned along the seventeen-mile underground track picked up these collision 'events', providing readings which could rewrite the rules of physics once they have been analysed. The successful collision also dispelled fears that the machine could endanger the Earth by creating black holes that were so strong they could suck in planets and stars.

Dr. Lyn Evans, a Welsh scientist who is the L.H.C. project leader, said: 'It is quite emotional. We had a few problems but we have resolved them and the beams came into collision beautifully. Today is the end of a very long road. There have been some bumps but it is fantastic to see this today. It is a new era of science.' The experiment at the European Centre for Nuclear Research (C.E.R.N.), 300 feet below the Franco-Swiss border, aims to recreate the conditions present just after the Big Bang at the beginning of the universe, 13.7 billion years ago. This will allow researchers to examine the origin of stars and planets. 'We're within a billionth of a second of the Big Bang,' said James Gillies, a C.E.R.N. spokesman.

Scientists at a control room near Geneva broke into applause and popped Champagne corks when the first high energy collisions were recorded. The collider has been described as a seventeen-mile racetrack around which two streams of protons run in opposite directions before smashing into one another and breaking up into their smaller components. Reaching 99.99 per cent of the speed of light, each beam packs as much energy as a Eurostar train travelling at 90 m.p.h. Shooting the particle beams at each other over such a distance is the equivalent of firing needles at each other from either side of the Atlantic. Some of the theories the L.H.C. research could address include the existence of dark matter and the so-called 'God Particle', the Higgs boson, a hypothetical particle that scientists believe gives mass to other particles and thus to all matter in the universe.

The L.H.C. was launched with great fanfare in September 2008, but it was sidetracked just nine days later when a badly-soldered part overheated, causing extensive damage to the large magnets in the collider. It cost £30 million to repair and improve the machine before it was started again at the end of November last year. Since then, the collider has performed almost flawlessly, giving scientists valuable data in the month before Christmas, though it is still only running at about half power. Professor Rolf-Dieter Heuer, the director-general of C.E.R.N., said it was likely to take months for any scientific discoveries to be made as computers sort through the extensive data produced by the collisions.

15 January 2011: The Jasmine Revolution in Tunisia kicks off the Arab Spring
PEOPLE POWER TOPPLES TUNISIAN STRONGMAN AFTER DAYS OF VIOLENCE
By Richard Spencer, Middle East Correspondent

President Zine al-Abidine Ben Ali, the pro-American leader of Tunisia, fell to a wave of student protest last night, fleeing into exile from a country that had descended into bloodsoaked chaos. Mohamed Ghannouchi, the prime minister, announced he was taking over as acting president as the army moved in to seize control of the main airport in the capital Tunis. The collapse of the twenty-three-year dictatorship, the first collapse of an Arab leader to a 'people power' uprising, was met nervously by Tunisia's allies. The ousted leader was reportedly refused permission to enter French territory by President Nicolas Sarkozy. Last night a plane carrying Mr. Ben Ali was reported to have landed in Jeddah in Saudi Arabia.

The White House will be monitoring the stability of Tunisia's Arab neighbours. Like Tunisia, many have been led for decades by repressive regimes that depend on the support of America and fear the discontent of young, underemployed populations. While the protests in Tunisia were led by an educated, young population eager to expand their freedoms, in its neighbours much of the opposition is demanding the replacement of pro-Western regimes with Islamic rule.

The final moments of Mr. Ben Ali's dominance will be remembered for the drama on the streets as protests that have raged across the country for weeks finally reached the capital.

Demonstrators ignored a curfew, and took no notice of a promise by Mr. Ben Ali not to seek a sixth term of office in 2014. Instead of returning home, they took to the streets and the rooftops, even of government buildings and the interior ministry, hurling stones at symbols of authority. The police struck back. One report said another thirteen people were shot dead, bringing the total killed to almost eighty and occasional bursts of gunfire were heard in the capital throughout the night. Television pictures showed plain clothes police firing rounds, and hauling individual students to the ground, where they would be kicked and beaten by riot squads.

Thousands of Western tourists were told to stay indoors. Some described mobs breaking windows along the street outside their hotels. 'I was scared I was going to get hurt and I felt sorry for the people,' said Cynthia Rigby, fifty-five, from Liverpool. 'It is horrible out there.' The initial trigger for the riots was unemployment. They started after a young graduate, Mohamed Bouazizi, set himself alight on 17 December in protest at having the vegetable barrow that was his only means of earning a living taken from him for not having a licence. He died on 5 January.

Students also objected to the heavy censorship of information, including the internet, and to the corruption in the president's family. A U.S. diplomatic cable released by WikiLeaks described its ally as a 'police state'. On Thursday night Mr. Ben Ali admitted that he had failed to listen to the people. But this only served to encourage the protesters. He tried a final act of conciliation yesterday afternoon, sacking his government and saying he would call fresh elections. Soon after, state television said an 'important announcement' was imminent, and Mr. Ghannouchi called on Tunisians 'of all political persuasions and from all regions to demonstrate patriotism and unity'.

Earlier, a government statement had imposed a state of emergency. 'The police and the army are authorised to fire on any suspect person who has not obeyed orders or fled without the possibility of being stopped,' it said. One opposition leader, Najib Chebbi, said change had to be permanent. 'This is a crucial moment. There is a change of regime under way. Now it's the succession,' he told French television.

3 May 2011: Osama bin Laden meets his end
HE DIED COWERING BEHIND HIS WIFE
AL-QAEDA CHIEF KILLED BY U.S. SPECIAL FORCES IN $1 MILLION HIDEOUT
By Steven Swinford, Gordon Rayner and Duncan Gardham

Osama bin Laden used his wife as a human shield in a last desperate attempt to save his own life before he was gunned down by U.S. special forces in his hideout in Pakistan. Armed with an automatic weapon, the al–Qaeda leader's last act was to force his young bride to sacrifice her life as he tried to fire back at the U.S. Navy Seals storming the compound. Bin Laden was killed with a single shot to the head after being tracked down to a million-dollar compound just thirty-five miles from the Pakistani capital, Islamabad, where he is thought to have been living for six years.

The details of his last stand were disclosed by the White House after the thirteen-year hunt for the world's most wanted man reached a bloody conclusion. President Barack Obama, watching live footage of the raid in the White House, turned to his advisers after the most significant moment in the war on terror, and said: 'We got him.' Far from living in a cave or a tunnel, the terrorist mastermind had been 'hiding in plain view' less than a mile from Pakistan's main military academy in Abbottabad. The fifty-four year old, whose body was identified using D.N.A. and facial recognition techniques, was buried at sea to avoid any danger of his grave becoming a shrine.

News of bin Laden's death, conveyed on live television by Mr. Obama at 4.30 a.m. British time yesterday, prompted scenes of wild celebration on the streets of New York, the city where al-Qaeda's worst atrocity took place, and throughout America. The families of British victims of al-Qaeda also expressed their relief at his death. Also killed in the raid, alongside bin Laden's wife, understood to be his youngest spouse, Amal al-Sadah, twenty-seven, were the terrorist leader's son Khalid, twenty-two, and two brothers who acted as his 'couriers'. Bin Laden had been shot several times.

In other key developments: Pakistan was facing growing questions over whether it knew anything about bin Laden's whereabouts; Britain and the U.S. were put on heightened terrorist alert amid fears of a 'lone wolf' revenge attack; the White House was under pressure to release a photograph of bin Laden's body to head off conspiracy theorists.

There were angry scenes in the Muslim world at the news of bin Laden's burial at sea. A video of the burial may be released by U.S. authorities. It emerged that the raid was authorised by Mr. Obama, despite the fact he was not certain bin Laden was at the compound. An adviser described the decision as the 'gutsiest' by a U.S. president in recent times. The death of bin Laden meant the world was 'a safer place', President Obama said last night. Earlier, the White House described it as a 'defining moment in the war against al-Qaeda'. In a rare occasion where it 'welcomes' the death of any person, the U.N. Security Council last night issued a statement praising the assassination, which it called a 'critical development' in the fight against terrorism.

U.S. intelligence officials believe the architect of the September 11 attacks made a propaganda recording shortly before his death and expect that tape to surface soon. Intelligence indicated that the recording is already working its way through al-Qaeda's media pipeline, a U.S. official said. U.S. security services are sifting through a treasure trove of intelligence gathered at the compound, although officials refused to say what they had found. Counter–terrorism officials said that up to twelve senior al-Qaeda officials are believed to be based in Pakistan. The country was only informed of the U.S. operation after it scrambled jets in response to the attack at the compound.

John Brennan, the chief U.S. counter-terrorism adviser, said: 'It is inconceivable that bin Laden did not have a support system in the country that allowed him to stay there for such an extended period of time. People are referring to it [the compound] as hiding in plain sight. We are looking at how he was able to hide there for so long. I'm sure that a number of people have questions about whether there was some kind of support provided by the Pakistani government.' He added: 'If we had the opportunity to take bin Laden alive, the individuals were able and prepared to do that.'

Last night David Cameron, who said bin Laden's death would 'bring great relief around the world', chaired a meeting of the Cobra emergency committee to discuss the implications of the incident. There were warnings of reprisals by al-Qaeda. Leon Panetta, the director of the C.I.A., said al-Qaeda would 'almost certainly' try to avenge the killing. 'Though bin Laden is dead, al-Qaeda is not,' he said. 'The terrorists almost certainly will attempt to avenge him.' Since the U.S. identified the compound in August last year, Navy Seals have been conducting practice raids at a replica version of the compound. U.S. officials expressed incredulity that the Pakistani security services had failed to ask questions about the one-acre compound, which was eight times the size of any other building nearby and had walls up to eighteen-feet high topped with barbed wire. Mr. Brennan said: 'It clearly was very different from any other house out there. It had the appearance of a fortress. We have had some indication that the family that was there tried to remain anonymous.'

Mr. Brennan said that before the attack there was only 'circumstantial evidence' that bin Laden was present and several of the president's advisers had urged him not to go ahead. Referring to the moment the raid was watched in real time, Mr. Brennan said: 'It was one of the most anxiety-filled periods of time in the lives of any of the people assembled here yesterday. The minutes felt like days and the president was very concerned about the security of his personnel. It was clearly very tense.'

Speaking of bin Laden's wife, who was 'positioned' as a human shield, Mr. Brennan said: 'She fought back when there was an opportunity to get bin Laden. Living in this million-dollar-plus compound, in an area that is far away from the front, hiding behind a woman: it really speaks to just how false his narrative has been over the years.' Mr. Brennan said that al-Qaeda was a 'mortally wounded tiger', but warned it 'still has some life in it'. The U.S. is considering whether to release photographs of bin Laden. Mr. Brennan said: 'We are going to do everything we can to make sure that nobody has any basis to try to deny that we got Osama bin Laden.'

21 October 2011: Colonel Gaddafi meets his end
NO MERCY FOR A MERCILESS TYRANT
GADDAFI TRIES TO FLEE SIRTE AFTER TWO MONTHS IN HIDING
LIBYAN DICTATOR'S CONVOY IS HIT BY NATO AIR STRIKE
HE IS HUNTED DOWN BY REBELS AND SHOT IN THE HEAD
By Ben Farmer

He had often referred to his enemies as 'vermin' as he vowed to hunt them down alley by alley or die trying. But in the end it was Colonel Muammar Gaddafi who was hiding like 'a rat' when he was finally cornered in a drain, a gold-plated pistol to hand and pleading in vain for his life. After forty-two years as Libya's despotic leader, Gaddafi's past caught up with him in a field two miles west of his birthplace, after he had taken shelter in a culvert from rebel fighters and Nato bombs.

His final refuge could not have been more different from the palaces and villas where he had squandered his nation's oil wealth. The concrete drain pipe was seventy feet long and no more than three feet across, running under a dual carriageway on the outskirts of Sirte. Sand, rocks and discarded water bottles lined the interior. Three bodies of his companions lay outside. They did not look like elite bodyguards or members of an inner circle as they began to gather flies in the afternoon heat.

But then mobile phone footage of Gaddafi's capture showed that in the end the sixty-nine year old no longer bore any resemblance to a self-styled 'king of kings' with visions of a United States of Africa. The shaky images show him bloodied and unkempt and surrounded by jubilant rebels holding weapons to his head. His trademark mop of frizzy black hair was matted and thin and his robes were stained red from a wound to his head or neck. More than anything the footage showed him weak and confused.

'When we had him and we surrounded him he was talking like an idiot,' said twenty-year-old Mohammad Elhweje, who was one of ten fighters from Misurata who captured him. 'He was saying, "What's going on, what did I do?" No one could believe it.' Another, Mohammed Al Bibi, said Gaddafi had pleaded 'Don't shoot, don't shoot' as he tried to surrender. Precisely what happened next remains unclear, but at some point Gaddafi was shot in the head, giving rise to accusations that he had been executed, although they were denied last night. William Hague, the Foreign Secretary, conceded that videos and photographs posted online 'suggested' he had been assassinated, adding that Britain 'does not approve of extra-judicial killings'.

Gaddafi's death brought to an end the bloody eight-month battle to free Libya from his iron grip. Mahmoud Jibril, the prime minister of the interim National Transitional Council (N.T.C.), said: 'We have been waiting for this moment for a long time. Muammar Gaddafi has been killed. All the evils have vanished from this beloved country. It's time to start a new Libya, a united Libya, one people, one future.'

Between seventeen and twenty of Gaddafi's most senior supporters were killed or captured alongside him. The leader of his armed forces, Abu Bakr Younis, and Gaddafi's son Mutassim were killed, while Ahmed Ibrahim, a cousin and adviser, and Moussa Ibrahim, his official spokesman, were captured. There was confusion over the whereabouts of Saif al-Islam, the son Gaddafi wanted to succeed him. Early reports said he had been captured, but the N.T.C. later said it had no information on whether he had been killed or captured. It was thought he might still be at large. Nonetheless, Gaddafi and almost his entire inner circle had been wiped out.

David Cameron said he was proud of Britain's part in liberating the country and that it was a time to remember all Gaddafi's victims in Libya and in Britain, through the Lockerbie bombing, the shooting of

WPc Yvonne Fletcher and the victims of Libyan-aided I.R.A. terror-ism. President Barack Obama said the 'dark shadow of tyranny' had been lifted.

Gaddafi's final hours began with a dramatic attempt to break out of the city which had been pounded by rebel fighters for two weeks. Loyalists had staunchly defended District 2, an area of around 1,000 yards by 500 yards in the northwest of the city, feeding speculation that high-ranking members of the regime were hiding. As the circle closed, they tried a desperate dash for freedom soon after dawn yesterday. Fighters who witnessed it said that at 8.30 local time a column of fifteen to twenty cars tried to punch out into the western suburb of Zafran. The break caused confusion among rebels who were preparing an offensive into District 2 from the same direction. *The Daily Telegraph* witnessed an intense fight as rebel positions found themselves unexpectedly under fire. The convoy managed to evade the front line and drive about two miles west and then parked close to an electricity sub-station. 'Gaddafi and some of his inner circle tried to run away,' explained Ali Gadi, a twenty-one-year-old member of the unit which found him. In the confusion, the convoy had been followed by some rebel fighters from the western front, but they were lightly armed and understrength. 'They stopped out here. It wasn't clear who was with them and what sort of firepower they had,' said Mr. Gadi. 'We held back for a while to see what they would do.'

Unknown to the rebels, the convoy had not escaped the surveillance of Nato. Just as the rebel brigades were deciding what to do, it was hit by at least one bomb in a Nato air strike, causing devastation among the tightly-packed vehicles. The *Telegraph* counted fourteen smouldering cars and pick-up trucks and at least twenty-five dead bodies. Somehow Gaddafi escaped, but his situation was hopeless. He and a handful of others fled north around two hundred yards down the main road and sheltered in the drain.

As members of the al Watan brigade from Misurata approached the smouldering cars, they had no suspicion their hated former leader was close by. 'We thought Mutassim [Gaddafi's son] might have tried to escape,' said Mr. Elhweje. 'Then Gaddafi came out. One of our guys grabbed him in a bear hug.' Running on foot and with his baggage smouldering in the destroyed vehicles, Gaddafi was found with few possessions, but they were displayed among the fighters as spoils. One held a gold-plated automatic pistol which he said he had taken from the deposed leader. Another held a dainty-looking man's black leather boot which he said had been stripped from Gaddafi's foot.

Rebels marked the spot by spray-painting above the drain the words: 'This is the place where the rat Gaddafi was hiding.' Fighters swarmed from nearby to see the captive with their own eyes. The prisoner was then bundled into the back of a pick-up. Rebels and mobile phone footage confirm that at the time he was alive, though wounded. One clip showed him staggering on his feet and apparently talking. Gaddafi was driven to a dressing station and field hospital on the main road towards Misurata, on the west side of the city, but the vehicles just pulled up on the side of the road, then proceeded to Misurata in a swelling convoy. Pictures released later showed that at some point he had been shot – executed, perhaps – with a bullet to his left temple.

Mr. Jibril said last night that Gaddafi had been shot in the head 'in crossfire' between his supporters and new regime fighters. Forensic examinations confirmed he was killed by a shot to the head, but it was unclear if he was killed by rebels or his own forces. In Tripoli, as the first reports came through, crowds gathered in the streets, chanting: 'God is great, God is great, Gaddafi has been captured.' Their jubilant shouts were accompanied by the inevitable celebratory gunfire.

By 1.10 p.m. U.K. time, a presenter draped in the flag of the liberated Libya made the official announcement of Gaddafi's capture on N.T.C.-controlled state television. 'Gaddafi is in the hands of the rebels,' he said. 'We have captured Gaddafi. Libya is joyous, Libya is celebrating, Libya has given a lesson to all those who want to learn.' The N.T.C. spokesman Abdel Majid announced that Gaddafi had been 'wounded in both legs'. But even as the first questions were being asked about where Gaddafi would go on trial, the N.T.C. made another announcement, saying Gaddafi was dead. 'He was also hit in the head,' said Mr. Majid. 'There was a lot of firing against his group and he died.'

Incredibly, the Gaddafi-supporting television channel Al-Libiya remained defiant, saying the reports of his death were 'baseless'. The world would not have to wait long for evidence to prove otherwise. By 1.45 p.m. a picture of a blood-drenched Gaddafi, apparently still alive, had been posted online after being filmed by a rebel fighter on a mobile phone. It was followed by footage on Al-Jazeera television of Gaddafi being rolled over on the ground by jubilant rebel fighters who pulled off his shirt and appeared to kick him. Within hours his corpse was in Misurata, the city that suffered more than any other in the eight-month struggle to overthrow him, where it was placed in a mosque to be given a Muslim funeral. That of his son Mutassim was laid out on blankets on the floor in a private house in the city. The upper half of his body showed bullet wounds to the chest and neck.

In Sirte, meanwhile, it had become clear that resistance had finished and the besieging forces swept in. Everywhere there were signs of devastation. The streets were littered with masonry, spent bullet casings and burnt cars. It was difficult to find a building not riddled with bullet or shell-holes. Unexploded mortar rounds stood half buried in the asphalt. N.T.C. fighters hoisted the red, black and green national flag above a large utilities building in the centre of the district that had held out the longest. At the Libyan Embassy in London, Mahmoud al-Naku, the N.T.C.'s diplomatic envoy, said: 'A black era has come to an end forever. The Libyan people are looking forward to a promising future where they finally start building their free democratic state.'

Outside Libya, the families of the 270 victims of the Lockerbie bombing and of WPc Yvonne Fletcher fear the truth of what happened to their loved ones might have died with him. Dr. Jim Swire, who lost his daughter Flora in the Lockerbie bombing, said the apparent 'revenge' killing of Gaddafi had denied the world the opportunity to send him to the International Criminal Court to be tried. 'Gaddafi could have been a useful source of information about Lockerbie,' he said. 'I think he would have known that the attack was going to be done and how it was going to be done.'

The Prime Minister said Gaddafi's death meant the Libyan people now had 'an even greater chance' of building a better country. He said: 'I think today is a day to remember all of Colonel Gaddafi's victims, from those who died in connection with the Pan Am flight over Lockerbie, to Yvonne Fletcher in a London street, and obviously all the victims of I.R.A. terrorism who died through their use of Libyan Semtex. We should also remember the many, many Libyans who died at the hands of this brutal dictator and his regime.' He said that Britain would 'help' the new Libyan government.

Mr. Obama warned that there would be 'difficult days ahead' on the road to full democracy. He said: 'For four decades the Gaddafi regime ruled the Libyan people with an iron fist . . . today we can definitively say that the Gaddafi regime has come to an end.' Gaddafi's death paves the way for British and other Nato forces to end their six-month campaign in the north African country within weeks. Mr. Hague said: 'It brings much closer the end of the Nato mission.' However, he added that before leaving the country, 'I think we will want to be sure there aren't any other pockets of pro-Gaddafi forces'.

9 November 2011: The volume of scandals finally brings down Silvio Berlusconi
END IN SIGHT FOR BERLUSCONI, THE GREAT SURVIVOR
FINANCIAL CRISIS COULD FINALLY END RULE OF 'MODERN-DAY NERO'
By Nick Squires in Rome

He was labelled the great survivor, riding out sex scandals and corruption accusations which would have brought any other democratically elected leader to their knees. But last night it looked as though Silvio

Berlusconi, one of the world's most charismatic and controversial politicians, was finally throwing in the towel after dominating Italy's politics for seventeen years. In the end it was not the bunga bunga parties or the whiff of corruption that brought him down, but the financial mess that Italy finds itself in, for which the prime minister must shoulder a large part of the blame.

Despite enjoying a convincing parliamentary majority during much of his political career, he failed to enact the sort of structural reforms that Italy so desperately needed. With his hair implants, built-up heels and permanent sun tan, he became a gift for cartoonists and satirists. He earned global notoriety for his penchant for glamorous young starlets and showgirls, who were photographed lounging in the sun and taking topless showers at his villa on Sardinia's Costa Smeralda. His gaffes and schoolboy pranks earned him the ire of global leaders, including Angela Merkel, the German chancellor, and President Barack Obama, whom Mr. Berlusconi infamously called 'sun-tanned'.

He was inevitably portrayed as a dissolute emperor surrounded by dancing girls and fawning lackeys, a modern-day Nero who fiddled while all around him Italy burned. Or as one Italian commentator put in at the height of the sex scandals, 'a cross between Hugh Hefner and the Emperor Tiberius'. For much of his time in office he was mired in a web of scandal and corruption allegations, with charges ranging from tax fraud, bribery and false accounting to paying for sex with a seventeen-year-old nightclub dancer. And yet he still managed to get elected as prime minister three times.

Born and raised in Milan, he worked as a nightclub singer on cruise ships before building up a multi-billion pound empire based on construction, publishing and television channels, amid rumours – none of them ever proven – that his career was given a kick-start by the Mafia. He burst on to the political scene in the 1990s after the Christian Democrats imploded in a corruption scandal. Italians were dazzled by Mr. Berlusconi's slick salesman's patter, his portrayal of himself as an outsider untainted by cronyism and his promises to initiate a

Thatcher-esque revolution of economic reform. He created a new party from scratch and demonstrated his knack for connecting with ordinary Italians by calling it *Forza Italia* – Go Italy – which echoed a chant sung by fans of the national football team.

He won his first election in 1994, but his government lasted just a few months after it was brought down by Umberto Bossi, the mercurial leader of the devolutionist Northern League. Mr. Berlusconi bounced back in 2001, running an aggressive and lavishly-funded media campaign. Incredibly for a country where governments came and went with alarming frequency, he managed to stay in office until 2006, the longest prime ministerial term since the end of the Second World War. He was replaced by a lacklustre and uninspiring centre-Left government which he managed to oust in 2008.

Things began to go wrong during his latest stint as prime minister when Veronica Lario, his wife of twenty years, announced that she wanted a divorce. She accused him of 'consorting with minors' after he dropped into the eighteenth birthday party of an underwear model Noemi Letizia, who said she called him 'Papi' or Daddy. He was also the victim of a bizarre attack in which he suffered facial injuries after being hit with a model cathedral. Then came allegations from an escort, Patrizia D'Addario, that she had slept with him in a double bed given to the prime minister by Vladimir Putin. Dozens of other women came forward to say that they too had been paid to attend 'bunga bunga' sex parties.

The sleaze reached a crescendo when a seventeen-year-old, exotic dancer called Karima El Mahroug, who went by the stage name of Ruby the Heart Stealer, said she had also attended parties at which women performed stripteases. Prosecutors charged Mr. Berlusconi with paying for sex with an under-age prostitute and abuse of office. He is currently on trial and could face more than a decade in jail if the allegations are proven. 'His legacy in terms of Italy's national culture is a disaster,' said Roberto D'Alimonte, a professor of politics at LUISS university in Rome. 'You could fill books with all the negativity.'

Mr. Berlusconi also faces two corruption trials, one of them centring on allegations that he bribed his British tax lawyer, David Mills, the estranged husband of the former Cabinet minister Tessa Jowell. Many Italians were unmoved by the accusations, believing Mr. Berlusconi when he said he was the victim of a politically motivated witch hunt. Incredibly, Mr. Berlusconi may be down, but he might not be out. Shortly after he was seen writing a note in parliament that discussed his resignation, he said Italy's president would 'open consultations and decide on the future' of the country. 'I can see only the prospect of new elections,' he said. For a man who has shown himself unable to resist temptation, the prospect of offering himself up as a candidate once again may just prove too hard to resist.

4 June 2012: Queen Elizabeth's Diamond Jubilee is celebrated in spectacular fashion on the Thames
HAPPY AND GLORIOUS: THE RIVER QUEEN
A SPECTACLE TO ECHO DOWN THE AGES SETS THE SEAL ON A JOYOUS DAY
By Gordon Rayner, Chief Reporter

Has there ever been a more robust, a more determined or a more down-right stubborn display of support for the Queen? On a day when the weather could not have been more cruel, more than a million people turned out regardless to line the Thames and give the Sovereign the biggest, albeit the soggiest, party of her sixty-year reign. To repay them for their loyalty, the Queen smiled on through the cold and wet, resisting the joint temptations of an indoor berth and a hot cup of tea to wave non-stop from the windswept deck of the royal barge from start to finish of the Thames Diamond Jubilee Pageant.

Try explaining to the rest of the world why dozens camped overnight in pouring rain and bone-chilling cold for a passing glimpse of a tiny eighty-six-year-old woman in the distance and it may be difficult finding where to start. But no one knows better than the Queen that, for people who stood twenty deep in places on the river bank, the chance to say they saw her on her Diamond Jubilee weekend was what the day was all about. 'It was absolutely worth waiting for,' said a shivering Joanne Revitt, forty-eight, who watched the procession from the Embankment near the tower of Big Ben (or the Queen Elizabeth Tower, as M.P.s want to rename it). 'The Queen looked stunning and I am quite convinced she waved at me as she went past,' she added.

Countless thousands of others no doubt went home with the same belief, and they would have gone home happy as a result. It was, the Duke of Cambridge told one guest, a 'very emotional' day for his grandmother and at times it showed as she seemed slightly overwhelmed by the scale of the public's response. An estimated 1.2 million people, a bigger turnout than for last year's royal wedding, lined fourteen miles of riverbank, turning it into an unbroken chain of red, white and blue.

For the artists on the Millennium Bridge who had been invited to paint the twenty-first century's 'Canaletto Moment', however, the colour palette was overwhelmingly grey. No one would have blamed the Queen if she had turned out in oilskins, but instead she wowed the crowds in an ivory coloured bouclé dress and coat, braided with silk ribbon and with a silk organza frill, which included a clever nod to her three big jubilees. Made by the Queen's dresser Angela Kelly, it was embroidered with gold and silver spots and embellished with crystals to represent diamonds. Was it coincidence that it seemed to borrow from the Ditchley portrait of Elizabeth I wearing a similarly opulent spotted dress? For a woman who once said 'I have to be seen to be believed', chance seemed unlikely to have played a part in the Queen's choice of attire.

The day had begun with six million people around the country attending 10,000 street parties from Devon to Dumfriesshire, almost all of which had gone ahead despite the weather. The one notable exception was Downing Street, where David and Samantha Cameron decided to move their party indoors to escape a drenching. The motto of the Queen's first Prime Minister, Sir Winston Churchill, 'keep buggering on', seemed to have been lost on them.

At 2.10 p.m., as the trifles and chocolate fingers were being polished off around the country (triggering a mass retreat to the comfort of a dry sofa and a television set), the Queen and the Duke of Edinburgh made their entrance. Waiting for them at Chelsea Pier were the Prince of Wales and Duchess of Cornwall, together with an honour guard of twenty-two Chelsea Pensioners. Over her wrist, the Queen had brought what at first glance appeared to be a small towel (which would have been sensible enough) but later proved to be a shawl – her only concession to the drizzle – which she reluctantly deployed an hour later when even her stoicism began to be tested.

The tender from the Royal Yacht Britannia took her downstream to the royal barge, *Spirit of Chartwell*, a Thames pleasure cruiser that had been transformed into a handsome ship of state with gilded carvings, Royal Watermen in scarlet ceremonial dress and a royal coat of arms made from half a million gold buttons. Already on board were the Duke and Duchess of Cambridge and Prince Harry, the only other members of the Royal family given the honour of travelling with the Queen, who wants her Jubilee to focus on the direct line of succession. 'Spectacular!' the Queen told the Duke of Edinburgh as she surveyed the scene. 'So nice, so impressive.

The Duchess of Cambridge, the hardiest soul aboard, needed no protection from the elements other than a vermilion knee-length dress by Alexander McQueen and a hat from James Lock designed by Sylvia Fletcher, accessorised with a brooch of two silver dolphins, a gift from the Royal Navy Submarine Service. She had also brought with her a scarf in the new Strathearn tartan, created after the Royal wedding, when the Duke and Duchess were also given the titles of Earl and Countess of Strathearn. As they greeted crowds waiting at the waterside, the Duke said the support was 'fantastic' and 'wonderful', adding: 'Lots of people turned out today!'

The organisers of the 1,000-boat flotilla had insisted it would be 'the biggest single live event in the history of the world', and while historians may squabble over that, no one who was on the banks of the

Thames yesterday is likely to live to see anything quite like it again. Under the glass canopy of the royal barge (where she refused to sit on a purpose-built 'throne', perhaps fearing hypothermia would set in if she stayed still), the Queen beamed with delight as she greeted the cheering crowds and watched the biggest event staged on the Thames for 350 years. 'Just look at this!' the Duchess of Cornwall said to the Queen. 'Incredible!' 'So exciting!' the Duchess of Cambridge said to her husband.

The scale of the event's ambition was signalled by the first vessel in the flotilla: a 180-foot floating belfry weighing twelve tons whose eight specially cast bells pealed non-stop for the hour and a half it took to reach Tower Bridge, echoed by returning peals from every church and cathedral it passed. Immediately behind was the newest boat in the Pageant: the gilded and magnificent royal rowbarge, *Gloriana*, which gave spectators a flavour of a previous Elizabethan age as its eighteen oarsmen, led by the multiple Olympic gold medal winner Sir Steve Redgrave, powered the ninety-four-foot vessel downstream. It was the first time the Queen had seen her Jubilee gift in action. The £1 million *Gloriana*, one of the true stars of the show, had been specially commissioned for the event and was presented to the sovereign earlier in the year.

As they approached the royal barge, Garrison Sergeant Major (WO1) Bill Mott, who is reputed to possess the most powerful voice in the British Army, called *Gloriana* to order by barking at its crew to 'toss oars' in salute to Her Majesty, before leading three cheers for the Queen. Once all 260 man-powered boats had gone by, it was finally time for the Queen to join the procession, as *Spirit of Chartwell* slipped her moorings and fell in at the head of the powered vessels.

The Queen's cousin, Margaret Rhodes, had claimed the monarch 'slightly dreaded' the flotilla, perhaps following a bumpy trip upriver during her Silver Jubilee, and sick bags were reportedly on board just in case. But eight miles downstream, the organisers had deployed their secret weapon. At 9.30 in the morning they had closed the Thames

Flood Barrier for the entire day to slow the river from its usual 5 m.p.h. current to just a tenth of that speed and calm the tidal surge that normally makes the Thames rise by twenty-one feet every six hours. With the river tamed and 'locked' at high tide to make the boats easier to see, the Queen could cruise calmly at the head of the Royal Squadron, following a shrill whistle from the *Princess Elizabeth* steam locomotive on Battersea Rail Bridge above.

Behind her in the Royal Squadron were the rest of the Royal family and, of course, the Middletons, including a rather conservatively dressed Pippa. Then came the Dunkirk 'Little Ships', the lifeboats and the fireboats, representing service and duty, the twin touchstones of the Queen's sixty-year reign. Above all, though, this was a day for fun. Among the ten music barges carrying floating bands and orchestras down river, the London Philharmonic Orchestra, the last boat in the flotilla, cheekily conjured up the James Bond theme music as it passed MI6 headquarters at Vauxhall Cross and gave the sodden crowds an impromptu rendition of 'Singin' in the Rain'.

Everywhere along the seven-mile route, there were individual tributes to the Queen. These ranged from the full-sized horse puppet Joey, from the hit West End play *War Horse*, rearing up in salute on the roof of the National Theatre, to a troupe of dancers atop the Royal Festival Hall using semaphore to spell out Happy Diamond Jubilee. 'Just wonderful,' the Queen said to the Duke of Edinburgh as they saw the Joey puppet. 'Marvellous,' he replied. After two and a half years of planning, the only thing the pageant organisers could not control was the weather, which only worsened as the day wore on and forced the cancellation of a planned flypast of nine Navy helicopters.

Nothing summed up the day better than the sight of the London Philharmonic's choir, pausing opposite the Queen, belting out 'Land of Hope and Glory' as rain plastered their hair to their faces. Not since the band kept playing on the *Titanic* has there been a more indomitable musical rendition in the face of so much water. If you could have bottled the droplets dripping from the choir's chins, it could have been distilled and sold as Essence of Britishness.

The person who would have been the least surprised by the conditions was the Queen herself. Her Coronation Day, on 2 June 1953, was also hit by rain, as some of those in the crowd recalled. Twins June Palmer and Patricia Roper, seventy-nine, attended George VI's funeral, when it snowed, and the Coronation, when the rain was, if anything, even worse than yesterday. Despite the deluge and her advancing years Mrs. Roper said: 'I wouldn't have missed it for the world.'

Margarette Soulsby, from Dorset, who is the same age as the Queen, slept overnight in the tent that had been set up near Tower Bridge to reunite lost children with their parents, so determined was she to bag a prime spot. Having notched up the Silver Jubilee of George V in 1935, two Coronations, six royal weddings and four funerals, her only explanation for such doggedness was that: 'It is a wonderful celebration,' and 'I am very proud to be British.' Others had come from as far away as China, the United States and New Zealand to join the party. 'It's a once in a lifetime event,' said Michelle Butzbach, fourteen, who flew over from Germany for the weekend with two friends. 'We love the Queen and the Royal family and we'll never get the chance to see anything like this again.' Yesterday's pageant set a new record for a flotilla, beating the previous best of a measly 327 vessels set in Bremerhaven, Germany, last year. It also taught us new words, such as 'bascules', which is the proper name for Tower Bridge's pivoting roadway.

Adrian Evans, the Pageant Master, said the Queen had been 'thrilled' with the event and the Royal family had enjoyed it thoroughly. 'They had the most extraordinary day, there was so much exuberance,' he said. 'The Queen stood throughout the whole of it which was extraordinary and we did not expect that. I think it is testament to the commitment to all the people who turned out.' Mr. Evans said that apart from the gloomy weather, everything had gone 'pretty much to clockwork'. The Pageant Master added that the huge crowds and participants who turned out despite the weather were 'testament to the British bulldog spirit'. Not since 1662, when Charles II introduced his Queen, Catherine of Braganza, to the nation with a spectacular river pageant, have so many boats processed down the Thames with such unashamed patriotism. The event may have been a test of endurance, but it was also happy, and quite glorious.

9 April 2013: Margaret Thatcher dies
IRON LADY PROVED THAT BRITAIN WAS GREAT, SAYS CAMERON
By Steven Swinford and James Kirkup

Baroness Thatcher, Britain's greatest post-war Prime Minister, was a 'lion-hearted' leader who served the British people 'with all she had', David Cameron said yesterday. Lady Thatcher died at around 11 a.m. yesterday after suffering a stroke in her suite at The Ritz hotel. She passed away peacefully aged eighty-seven, after battling poor health for more than a decade.

Mr. Cameron yesterday delivered his tribute from the steps of Number 10, lauding her 'remarkable' legacy and said she was a 'patriot prime minister' who had 'saved our country'. He said that more than thirty years after she became Prime Minister, she would be remembered for taking on the unions, privatising state-run industry, winning the Falklands War and helping the Cold War to end in triumph. 'Margaret Thatcher took a country that was on its knees and made Britain stand tall again,' he said. 'It is a truly sad day for our country. We have lost a great leader, a great prime minister and a great Briton. She didn't just lead our country, she saved our country. We can't deny that Lady Thatcher divided opinion. For many of us, she was and is an inspiration. For others she was a force to be defined against. But if there is one thing that cuts through all of this – one thing that runs through everything she did – it was her lionhearted love for this country. She was the patriot prime minister and she fought for Britain's interests every single step of the way.'

Mr. Cameron said that Parliament will be recalled from Easter recess tomorrow so that Westminster can pay tribute to Lady Thatcher. She will be honoured next week with a ceremonial funeral with military honours, similar to those held for Queen Elizabeth, the Queen Mother, and Diana, Princess of Wales. At Lady Thatcher's request, there will be no lying in state and no military flypast. The Chelsea Pensioners, veterans who live at the Royal Hospital Chelsea, will play a central role in the ceremony and greet the coffin on arrival at St. Paul's Cathedral. Members of the Armed Forces are due to line the route of her funeral procession from the Palace of Westminster to St. Paul's. At the Church of St. Clement Danes on the Strand, her coffin will be transferred to a gun carriage drawn by the King's Troop Royal Horse Artillery. Some Conservatives said that she should have had a full state funeral, but accepted that the former Prime Minister had not wanted such an event.

The Daily Telegraph understands that Lady Thatcher had asked for her ashes to rest alongside those of her late husband, Sir Denis, who was buried in the cemetery at the Royal Hospital. Her family has asked that instead of flowers, well-wishers donate money to the hospital's charity appeal.

Lady Thatcher became Britain's first female prime minister in May 1979. Her radical brand of Conservatism saw her transform Britain's economy and set an international precedent which other nations strove to replicate. She made an even bigger impact on the international stage, where she was regarded alongside Ronald Reagan as one of the architects of the West's victory in the Cold War.

Mr. Cameron added: 'It is over thirty years since she first stood here in Downing Street as Prime Minister, and yet her impact here and abroad is still remarkable. When you negotiate in Brussels, it is still her rebate you're defending. When you stand in Budapest, Warsaw or Prague, you're standing in nations whose liberty she always defended. When people said that Britain could not be great again, she proved them wrong. Margaret Thatcher loved this country and she served it with all she had. For that, she has her well-earned place in history and the enduring respect and gratitude of the British people.'

Mikhail Gorbachev, the former president of the Soviet Union, said Lady Thatcher had been a 'politician whose word had considerable weight'. President Barack Obama described her as a 'true friend' to America. She died after a decade of deteriorating health following a series of small strokes. In 2008, her daughter Carol disclosed that Lady Thatcher had been diagnosed with dementia. Her doctor and carer were at her bedside when she died at The Ritz, where she had lived since December.

1 May 2013: Queen Beatrix becomes the third Queen in a row to abdicate from the Netherlands' throne
THE CROWN COUPLE AND A GENERATION IN WAITING
By Bruno Waterfield in Amsterdam

Heirs to twelve thrones gathered in Amsterdam yesterday to mark the abdication of Queen Beatrix and the crowning of Willem-Alexander, the first Dutch king for 123 years. Among the 2,000 guests attending the retirement of the queen and the investiture of the king were the Prince of Wales and the Duchess of Cornwall. They joined a who's who of monarchs-in-waiting including Prince Felipe of Spain, Japan's Princess Masako and the heirs to the monarchies of Belgium, Bahrain, Brunei, Denmark, Liechtenstein, Luxembourg, Norway, Thailand and Sweden.

In contrast to their distinguished guests, the Dutch royal family is the only one to have a policy of passing on the crown by abdication. Queen Beatrix, a perfectly healthy seventy-five year old, became the third consecutive queen to stand down in favour of a younger successor, a modern tradition the Dutch regard as having renewed the monarchy. Margaret Bosgrah, fifty-seven, who watched the ceremonies among crowds totalling 800,000 people, said: 'We are very proud about how we do it. It is an example for other kingdoms.'

As Amsterdam became a sea of orange, the celebrations were tinged with concern that the Dutch monarchy, and society as a whole, faces an uncertain future. The new king, at forty-six the youngest monarch in Europe, referred to a sense of unease during his investiture speech which was dominated by emotional tributes to Beatrix and Queen Maxima, forty-one, his Argentine-born wife. 'I follow in your footsteps. No one knows what the future may hold. But wherever my path leads, and however long it may be, I will always carry with me your warmth and your wisdom,' he said of his mother. 'I succeed to the throne at a time when many in the kingdom feel vulnerable and uncertain. It now seems less self-evident that the next generation will be better off than the last.'

The ceremonies began at 10 a.m. under blue skies on the capital's Dam Square in front of the Palace of the House of Orange. Giant television screens showed the scene inside. Just before signing the legal act of abdication, Queen Beatrix smiled, winked and took her son's hand, giving it a gentle squeeze clearly meant for his reassurance as the burden of monarchy descended on to his shoulders. 'Today I make way for a new generation,' she said, prompting the crowd to burst into applause. Shouts of 'thank you, Bea' rang out and many were in tears. As queen for thirty-three years, Beatrix became an institutional rock for the Dutch through recessions, social unrest and national tragedy. Jade Corston, nineteen, said the Queen had epitomised 'Dutchness' for her generation. 'I'm really going to miss her,' she added. 'She really was the spirit of the Netherlands and I feel she was always there for all my life. I love her. I think with Willem-Alexander we might end up with a president.'

The new king sometimes seemed nervous and overshadowed by the women in his family. Perhaps sensing the Dutch need for a queen, he highlighted the central role that Maxima will play, her popularity in the Netherlands undiminished by her father's role in Argentina's dictatorship during the 1970s.

6 December 2013: Nelson Mandela dies

SOUTH AFRICA'S GREATEST SON, A BEACON OF FREEDOM AROUND THE WORLD

NELSON MANDELA DIES AT HOME SURROUNDED BY HIS FAMILY, AGED NINETY-FIVE

By Aislinn Laing, Southern African Correspondent, in Johannesburg

Nelson Mandela, South Africa's first black president and its 'greatest son', who led his country out of apartheid and became a hero to millions around the world, died peacefully at his home in Johannesburg last night at the age of ninety-five. Mr. Mandela passed away with family members around him at his home in the suburb of Houghton just before 9 p.m., after more than a year of ill health caused by a lung infection. The announcement of Mr. Mandela's death came in a televised address to the nation by President Jacob Zuma at 11.30 p.m. in South Africa, or 9.30 p.m. in Britain. It followed several hours of speculation prompted by reports that his family and his friends had been flocking to his bedside.

'He is now resting,' Mr. Zuma said. 'He is now at peace. Our nation has lost its greatest son. Our people have lost a father. Although we knew that this day would come, nothing can diminish our sense of a profound and enduring loss.' Mr. Zuma announced a period of national mourning and said South African flags would fly at half-mast around the world until Mr. Mandela's state funeral was held in the coming weeks. His body is expected to be taken to the capital Pretoria, where he will lie in state.

'Nelson Mandela brought us together, and it is together that we will bid him farewell,' Mr. Zuma added. 'Let us express, each in our own way, the deep gratitude we feel for a life spent in service of the people of this country and in the cause of humanity.' It is not known which of Mr. Mandela's family members were with him when he died. He has been married three times and has three surviving children and seventeen grandchildren.

Mr. Mandela's death came five months before the twentieth anniversary of his inauguration as South Africa's first black, democratic president, a day for which he endured twenty-seven years' imprisonment at the hands of the apartheid government. The announcement of Mr. Mandela's death sent many South Africans on to the streets. Some made their way to his home in Houghton, where they lit candles and sang the struggle anthem 'Shosholoza'. Broadcasters began showing the coverage that they had prepared for so long, and television screens were filled with images of Mr. Mandela's well-known salt and pepper hair, his smile-crinkled eyes and bright shirts, beaming broadly as he clutched the hands of nearly every world leader and celebrity of his generation.

Tributes were made from around the world. David Cameron described Mr. Mandela as 'a hero of our time', while Barack Obama said he 'gave me a sense of what human beings can do when they are guided by their hopes and not by their fears'. The African National Congress, the party to which he gave his life, said he would remain for them 'our nearest and brightest star to guide us on our way'. The party said in a statement: 'Our nation has lost a colossus, an epitome of humility, equality, justice, peace and the hope of millions; here and abroad. The large African Baobab, who loved Africa as much as he loved South Africa, has fallen. Its trunk and seeds will nourish the earth for decades to come.'

Archbishop Emeritus Desmond Tutu, who together with Mr. Mandela and South Africa's last white president, F.W. de Klerk, earned a Nobel Peace Prize for reconciling his fractured nation, invited its citizens to pray 'as a family prays'. He said: 'We offer a prayer of thanksgiving. We give thanks to God that saintliness is not a perfection beyond our reach, but that saintliness is embodied by real human beings with all their flaws and foibles.'

Mr. Mandela's death coincided with the London premiere of the long-awaited adaptation of his memoir, *Long Walk to Freedom*, which was attended by his daughter Zindzi and the Duke and Duchess of Cambridge. In Johannesburg, members of Mr. Mandela's large family joined his wife, Graça, and former wife, Winnie, at his bedside as it became apparent that his long battle with ill health was being lost. One family friend who went to the house told the *Telegraph* just hours before his death was confirmed: 'I think it's beyond everyone now. It's what everyone knew for months but it's still hard.' In recent years, Mr. Mandela had suffered from a series of respiratory illness that most recently saw him spend several months in hospital in Pretoria. His release back to his home in September was greeted with none of the jubilation of his previous rallies back to health. This time, South Africans were under no illusion that the end was near.

Nelson Rolihlahla (meaning 'troublemaker') Mandela began as a fiery young lawyer who battled South Africa's apartheid, first by organising mass acts of defiance and later through armed resistance. When he was jailed in 1962, following a tip-off by the U.S. Central Intelligence Agency, he was seen as a terrorist in South Africa and abroad. By the time he was released twenty-seven years later, his name had become synonymous around the world with the struggle for justice against tyranny and oppression. Mr. Mandela's inauguration in 1994 as South Africa's first black president was attended by an estimated 100,000 people of all races, who formed a sea of supporters extending outwards from the lawns of the Union Buildings into Pretoria's streets. The crowds which will gather this week to bid farewell to Mr. Mandela are expected to be larger than at any event during his life. A memorial service is expected to be attended by tens of thousands of people including foreign heads of state. Many more will travel to the capital's City Hall where Mr. Mandela's body is expected to lie in state for up to a week.

28 April 2014: A remarkable event in St. Peter's Square
THE DAY OF FOUR POPES, AND TWO NEW SAINTS
By Nick Squires in Vatican City

Pope John Paul II's blood was once shed in St. Peter's Square during a failed assassination attempt. Yesterday a vial of that same blood formed the centrepiece of a ceremony in which the Polish pontiff was made a saint along with a predecessor, Pope John XXIII. An ampoule of it, taken from John Paul II after he survived the 1981 assassination attempt by a Turkish gunman, was reverently kissed by Pope Francis at the climax of an outdoor ceremony in St. Peter's Square watched by an estimated 800,000 people in the Vatican and on giant screens in the surrounding streets of Rome. Millions more tuned in around the world.

Catholic pilgrims from dozens of nations, many of whom had camped out on the streets and in piazzas overnight, flooded into St. Peter's Square at dawn to witness an event with no precedent in the history of the Roman Catholic Church – the canonisation of two former popes by two of their living successors, Francis and Benedict XVI, the eighty-seven-year-old Pope Emeritus. Wearing white papal vestments, Benedict, who looked frail thirteen months after his historic resignation from the Seat of St. Peter, was embraced by a smiling Francis at the beginning of the service. The Polish pope's blood, contained in an ornate reliquary decorated with silver olive branches, was presented to Francis by Floribeth Mora, a Costa Rican woman whose sudden recovery from an inoperable brain aneurysm in 2011 was declared the second miracle that was required for John Paul to be made a saint.

It was placed on a table near the high altar and stood alongside a relic from John XXIII – a piece of skin, encased in a similar reliquary, that was taken from his exhumed body when he was beatified in 2000, the first step towards being made a saint. 'Some people may be turned off by the concept of reliquaries, but it's a very beautiful part of our faith tradition,' said Father Thomas Rosica, a Vatican spokesman. 'It's a sign that the saints are still with us, that they don't fade away.'

John Paul II declared more saints – 482 – than all of his predecessors combined. Benedict canonised far fewer, just forty-four, but the pace has picked up again under Francis in just over a year. In May last year he canonised in one go more than 800 Italian martyrs from the fifteenth century who were massacred by the Ottomans for refusing to convert to Islam. Asked why the Catholic Church continued to make saints, a process regarded by some as arcane, if not medieval, Father Rosica said: 'Because they are heroes and the world needs heroes. They are role models for the rest of us as we try to live a holy life.'

While the crowds waved national flags and cheered wildly when Francis swept by in his white Mercedes Popemobile, some Catholics question the whole concept of canonising popes, saying it is too political. 'Modern popes bring with them a certain amount of political baggage. If you canonise a pope, it can be seen as a way of one faction protecting their favourite and enshrining his legacy,' said John Thavis, a Vatican analyst and the author of *The Vatican Diaries*, a best-selling book about dysfunction inside the Holy See. Victims of sex abuse by paedophile priests were also staunchly opposed to John Paul's canonisation, arguing that he turned a blind eye to reports of abusive clergy from dioceses around the world. John Paul has also been sharply criticised for his support for Marcial Maciel, a Mexican priest who founded the Legionaries of Christ movement, and who was revealed to have fathered several children and to have sexually abused them as well as other minors.

Francis has been careful to show no trace of favouritism towards either John XXIII, a progressive who initiated key reforms to the Church under the Second Vatican Council of the 1960s, or John Paul II, a conservative who tried to roll back some of those changes. 'We declare and define as saints the blessed John XXIII and John Paul II,' Francis said in a Latin prayer from the altar in front of St. Peter's Basilica. The former pontiffs were 'two men of courage', he told the crowds. 'They were priests, bishops and popes of the twentieth century. They lived through the tragic events of that century, but they were not overwhelmed by them. For them, God was more powerful, faith was more powerful.'

Many pilgrims were from John Paul II's homeland, Poland. 'It's very exciting,' said Lidia Pelic, fifty-four. 'To have four popes in one ceremony is a once in a lifetime event.' Among the royalty and heads of state at the ceremony, was Robert Mugabe, president of Zimbabwe. He is barred from the European Union but not from the Vatican City State.

10 May 2014: Conflict in Ukraine
TRIUMPHANT PUTIN TAKES CRIMEA'S SALUTE AS BLOODSHED GOES ON
By Roland Oliphant in Sevastopol and David Blair in Donetsk

Vladimir Putin made a triumphant first visit to Crimea yesterday, as one of the bloodiest days of the conflict in eastern Ukraine pushed the country further towards civil war. Ukraine's security forces claimed to have killed more than twenty pro-Russian insurgents in the eastern city of Mariupol in a gun battle that appeared to break out after a Victory Day parade to mark the end of the Second World War.

Mariupol, a city of 500,000 on the coast of the Donetsk region, has been one of the flashpoints of a pro-Russian insurgency that has tried to seize control of large parts of eastern Ukraine. Separatist rebels in the region are preparing for a referendum on independence similar to that which preceded Russia's annexation of Crimea in March. Mr. Putin was met by jubilant crowds when he flew into Sevastopol after reviewing the annual victory parade on Red Square in Moscow. In a display of Russian military might, he sailed on a cutter to review flag-bedecked Russian warships anchored in the bay, greeting the sailors of Russia's Black Sea fleet with a 'hello, comrades'.

After the review, thousands thronged the shore to watch a fly-past of seventy military aircraft, including helicopters, MiG fighters, and Bear nuclear bombers, to mark seventy years since the city was liberated from German forces in May 1944. Crowds shouted 'Russia!' and 'Thank you!' as Mr. Putin took to a stage to make a speech in which he praised Crimeans for 'fidelity to historic justice'. As Mr. Putin was speaking, fighting in Mariupol appears to have broken out after rebels seized control of the local police headquarters following the city's parade. Interior ministry troops surrounded the building and opened fire with heavy machineguns mounted on BMP armoured combat vehicles. As gunfire echoed over the city centre, the police station caught fire.

Arsen Avakov, the interior minister, said twenty 'terrorists' had been 'annihilated' and another four captured. 'Most of those who

attacked the building have left their weapons and hidden in the city,'
he added. But medical authorities said that three people had been
killed and twenty-five wounded. Local people disputed the interior
minister's version of events. They said the security forces also fired at
unarmed civilians in the streets of Mariupol. One man, who declined
to be named, said that police officers had sided with the pro-Russian
insurgents and helped them to take over the headquarters. 'Some of
the police were on the side of the people,' he said. Uniformed police
officers fought against interior ministry troops when the latter tried to
seize back the building, added the witness.

The bloodshed was in stark contrast to the scenes in Sevastopol,
where thousands had lined the streets to watch a parade of troops,
veterans and military vehicles. The traditional celebrations doubled as a
victory march for the soldiers and civilian irregulars who helped Russia
to seize and then annex the peninsula. Usually, Russian and Ukrainian
forces march side by side on 9 May in Sevastopol, both armies the
successors of regiments who fought in the desperate defence of the city
against the Nazi onslaught in 1941. 'We got on fine with them,' said
Sasha, a former Russian marine who settled in the city after finishing his
service. 'It's the politicians who put up those divisions between people.'

Instead, veterans of the Second World War and the Soviet war in
Afghanistan were joined by those who took part in the near-bloodless
seizure and annexation of Crimea in March. Besides serving members
of Russia's Black Sea Fleet, the march included civilian members of
the 'Self Defence of Sevastopol' and members of the Night Wolves
biker gang, which manned road blocks and helped Russian forces lay
siege to Ukrainian military bases during the crisis. Many of the soldiers
and irregular marchers sported newly minted medals with a yellow
and white coloured ribbon – the campaign medal for the 'liberation of
Crimea'. Especially loud cheers were reserved for a squad of veterans
of the Berkut, a special police unit blamed in Kiev for the deaths of
dozens of protesters, but lionised in Crimea and eastern Ukraine as
servicemen who defended the country from a coup.

The Ukrainian foreign ministry issued a formal protest against what it called an 'unauthorised visit' to Crimea by the Russian head of state. 'This provocation once again confirms that Russia deliberately seeks further escalation of tensions,' the ministry said, calling the visit a 'flagrant violation of Ukraine's sovereignty'. While Victory Day has been a major public holiday in the region since 1945, this year's celebration has become loaded with political meaning since Russian officials have explicitly likened the current conflict in Ukraine to the war against fascism. Rebels in eastern Ukraine frequently describe their movement as fighting against a 'fascist junta' in Kiev, and have appropriated the black and orange St. George's Ribbon, the symbol of the 1945 victory, as their badge.

Tensions are growing in eastern Ukraine after separatist leaders rejected a proposal by Mr. Putin to delay a referendum on independence. The poll on the autonomy of the self-proclaimed Donetsk People's Republic is scheduled to take place tomorrow. It is widely expected that the rebel authorities will proclaim a majority 'yes' vote, before declaring independence from Ukraine, in a re-run of the events leading up to the annexation of Crimea. While many fear Russia may use the vote as a pretext for a second, Crimean-style annexation, Mr. Putin has sent mixed signals about rebel insurgency, suggesting earlier that planned presidential elections in Ukraine on 25 May may be a 'step in the right direction'.

9 August 2014: Ebola sweeps Africa
DEATH AND DENIAL, THE CURSE OF EBOLA
HEALTH WORKERS FACE STRUGGLE AGAINST HOSTILITY AND IGNORANCE AS DEADLY DISEASE SPREADS IN THE FETID SLUMS OF MONROVIA
By Colin Freeman in New Kru Town, Liberia

If ever there was a likely spot for an outbreak of the deadly Ebola virus, New Kru Town in Liberia is it. A sprawling slum of the country's war-ravaged capital, Monrovia, it is home to 50,000 people and has next to no functioning lavatories, sinks or bathrooms. Sewage runs openly through its maze of corrugated shacks, and in Liberia's wet season – at its height now – tropical torrents turn it into one vast, warm, moist breeding pool for germs.

It hardly feels surprising then, in the wake of several locals dying from Ebola, to see health teams daubing blue crosses on a number of shacks around town. The crosses are not to identify those who have caught the disease, but to mark the relatively few New Kru Towners who have been visited by the teams and accepted their advice on how to avoid getting it. So far, only around five hundred houses have been marked – and with health workers themselves accused of spreading the disease, some parts of New Kru Town remain decidedly hostile.

'This is a very poor neighbourhood where sanitation is lacking and people are not well educated in the principles of hygiene,' said Tamba Bundor, the leader of a team of volunteers from the local health charity Community Development Services, a Unicef partner, as he drove his car through wet, sandy back lanes. 'It is where the first victims of Ebola died in Monrovia, and most people who have been affected became so because they did not adhere to the messages of prevention.'

Nearly 1,000 people have now died of the disease across West Africa. While the outbreak started in remote forested inland areas – possibly via fruit bats – New Kru Town is an example of the ease and unpredictability with which it has spread to urban capitals along the coastline, catching health officials off-guard. When some initial cases first appeared in Liberia's northern Lofa County in March, health officials initially thought they had it under control. But in June, a resident of a district of New Kru Town known as Carpet Street died, as did several others. According to Dr. Bernice Dahn, Liberia's chief medical officer, three of the victims died while being sheltered in a local church – a sign of how some people believe the disease is a curse that can be cured by prayer or witchcraft. 'We must stop keeping people suspected of Ebola in our churches on the grounds that we can heal them,' she warned at the time. 'The churches are not hospitals.'

Liberian hospitals, however, do not always inspire the kind of faith that people have in Liberian churches. A fortnight ago, one of the main local health facilities, Redemption Hospital, was stoned by a mob after a woman died in there from suspected Ebola, following nationwide rumours that health workers were passing on the disease. Today, the squat, single-storey building offers redemption no more, having been shut down temporarily, its staff afraid for their own safety. Safety is a concern, too, for Mr. Bundor and his colleagues, who were attacked as they tried to visit the house of the bereaved family on Carpet Street. The victim's relations were insisting that their loved one had died as a result of a family curse – a cause of death that, in New Kru Town anyway, carries less social stigma than dying of an infectious disease. 'The family of the victim were angry, saying it was a curse, not Ebola,' said Anthony Worpor, another of Mr. Bundor's health team, who was clad in a T-shirt that said: 'Save lives, wash your hands before you eat.' He said: 'A crowd gathered, and some accused us health workers of spreading the disease. They even began touching a local journalist we had brought with us, saying, "If you think it is us spreading it, then here you are, we will infect you".'

New Kru Town was originally named after the Kru, a powerful ethnic group. They were traditionally known for a certain independence of mind, and European slave traders used to complain that they were particularly resistant to capture, to the point where their price as slaves was considerably lower. They proved equally hostile to the freed American slaves who founded Liberia in the nineteenth century, when the latter tried to muscle in on their trading empires. Today, New Kru Town is home to a wider ethnic mix, but even so, suspicion of outside influences persists. While Mr. Bundor's education programme has already enjoyed some success, he estimates that forty per cent of New Kru Town's residents are still 'in denial' about Ebola's risks and the necessary health measures to avoid it.

Indeed, some residents seem to treat Mr. Bundor rather like a Christian door-to-door preacher, listening politely to his warnings but not heeding them. For example, at Alan's Bar, a dingy shebeen, a poster warning of the dangers of Ebola was fixed to the front door. Yet official health advice is to avoid bars and other public gathering places altogether now, a message that the groups of drinkers inside, listening to blaring African disco music, have chosen to ignore. The owner of the bar, Alan Tokba, told *The Daily Telegraph* that 'no dancing was allowed' inside, and that visitors were being asked to wash their hands as they went in.

Mr. Bundor admitted that it was 'not satisfactory'. Nor was he entirely happy with the efforts of Tina Teeh, twenty-six, a mother of three. Her house already bore the blue cross of one of New Kru Town's hygiene converts, but the bucket of chlorinated water she had for her children to wash their hands did not have a separate container to drip the fluid on to their hands first. 'I can't afford it,' she told the disapproving Mr. Bundor. 'But what if you end up ill?' he asked her. 'Then you will have to afford hospital fees.'

Another mother who claimed to have seen the light was Julie Life, thirty, who admitted having been sceptical that Ebola even existed when Mr. Bundor first visited her home a few days ago. She said her main reason for changing her mind was watching a deadly virus at work in the Tom Cruise film *Mission Impossible II*. As Mr. Bundor and his colleagues trudged off to root out New Kru Town's remaining Ebola 'deniers', it seemed an apt description of their task.

28 May 2015: America acts against corruption in Fifa
FIFA CHIEF BLATTER FACES QUESTIONING OVER 'DEEP-ROOTED CORRUPTION'
'KICKBACKS AND SLEAZE BECAME A WAY OF DOING BUSINESS AT FIFA'
By Claire Newell Edward Malnick and Luke Heighton

Sepp Blatter, the head of Fifa, could be interviewed 'within weeks' as part of a corruption investigation that engulfed football's governing body last night. Fourteen officials and executives were arrested at the request of the F.B.I. yesterday, some in Zurich, over bribes totalling $150 million. Fifa was accused of 'rampant, systemic and deep-rooted' corruption. Mr. Blatter, the Fifa president, was warned he could be questioned by the office of the Swiss attorney general. It is conducting its own inquiry into alleged vote-rigging over the Qatar World Cup bid. The escalation of that inquiry came as the F.B.I. claimed it had uncovered twenty-four years of 'brazen corruption . . . undisclosed illegal payments, kickbacks and bribes' by Fifa officials. The American inquiry alleges that votes for the award of the 2010 World Cup – ultimately given to South Africa – were bought with bribes.

In what was labelled the darkest day in the body's history: Fifa was accused of running a 'World Cup of fraud' by the head of the I.R.S. Criminal Investigation division; the F.B.I. said that the 'beautiful game' had been 'hijacked' by corruption; Swiss authorities announced that they had opened a criminal inquiry into the 2018 and 2022 World Cup decisions; U.S. authorities claimed that 'bribes and kickbacks' were paid in the awarding of the 2010 World Cup and the 2011 presidential election which was won by Mr. Blatter; Jack Warner, the former Fifa vice-president who stepped down in 2011 following corruption allegations, was accused of receiving $10 million in bribes.

The revelations came days before votes are due to be cast in the 2015 Fifa presidential election and will bolster calls for the organisation to be reformed and for the 2018 and 2022 votes, won by Russia and Qatar, to be re-run. Last night, Uefa called for the presidential election to be postponed. Damian Collins, the Conservative M.P. for Folkestone and Hythe who has campaigned against corruption in Fifa, said that there was 'no question' that the 2018 and 2022 decisions should be re-run. 'It's staggering that Fifa is ignoring calls for the votes to be re-run', said Mr. Collins. 'Several of the individuals involved in making the decision have resigned because of corruption charges and the words from the Department of Justice could not be more damning. One former executive committee member has pleaded guilty to criminal offences. Did Fifa know what was happening?'

Fifa has faced many corruption allegations in recent years, including over the decision to award the 2022 competition to Qatar. But the events this week will add to pressure on the president of world football's governing body. There are currently two criminal investigations into Fifa. Yesterday, Swiss police arrested several of its officials at the five-star Baur au Lac hotel in Zurich where they had gathered in preparation for Friday's vote. The men arrested there included Jeffrey Webb, the head of the Confederation of North, Central America and Caribbean Association Football (Concacaf) and Fifa vice-president and Costa Rica's national football chief Eduardo Li, who was expected to join Fifa's executive committee (Exco) on Friday. Eugenio Figueredo, of Uruguay, the president of South American football's governing body, Conmebol, was also held by Swiss police, as was Rafael Esquivel, the president of the Venezuelan Football Federation. They were joined by Exco member José Maria Marin, from Brazil, Fifa development officer Julio Rocha of Nicaragua, and the U.K.'s Costas Takkas, an attaché to the president of Concacaf.

Mr. Warner gave himself up to police in Trinidad last night and was expected to face an extradition hearing. The indictment claims that Mr. Warner, who was vice-president of Fifa until 2011, accepted $10 million from the government of South Africa to secure his vote. His two sons have pleaded guilty to charges of wire fraud conspiracy and structuring of financial transactions. It is understood that at least one of the sons was helping the F.B.I. with their investigation.

During a press conference, Kelly Currie, acting U.S. attorney for the eastern district of New York, where the charges were brought yesterday, said that they were 'issuing Fifa a red card'. He said: 'Today's announcement should send a message that enough is enough. After decades of what the indictment alleges to be brazen corruption, organised international soccer needs a new start – a new chance for its governing institutions to provide honest oversight and support of a sport that is beloved across the world, increasingly so here in the United States.' James Comey, the director of the F.B.I., added: 'Undisclosed and illegal payments, kickbacks and bribes became a way of doing business at Fifa.' Loretta Lynch, the U.S. attorney general, said that the corruption 'spans at least two generations of soccer officials who . . . have abused their positions of trust to acquire millions of dollars in bribes and kickbacks'.

A spokesman for the office of the Swiss attorney general said that Fifa's president 'could be questioned in the coming weeks' and that every person who had participated in World Cup votes could be interviewed as part of their inquiry. In a statement, Mr. Blatter said: 'Today's action by the Swiss office of the attorney general was set in motion when we submitted a dossier to the Swiss authorities late last year. Let me be clear: such misconduct has no place in football and we will ensure that those who engage in it are put out of the game.' He added: 'We welcome the actions and the investigations by the U.S. and Swiss authorities and believe that it will help to reinforce measures that Fifa has already taken to root out any wrongdoing in football.'